THE POEMS OF
SAMUEL TAYLOR COLERIDGE

Oxford University Press, Amen House, London E.C.4
GLASGOW NEW YORK TORONTO MELBOURNE WELLINGTON
BOMBAY CALCUTTA MADRAS KARACHI KUALA LUMPUR
CAPE TOWN IBADAN NAIROBI ACCRA

THE POEMS OF
SAMUEL TAYLOR COLERIDGE

INCLUDING POEMS AND VERSIONS OF
POEMS HEREIN PUBLISHED FOR THE
FIRST TIME, EDITED WITH TEXTUAL
AND BIBLIOGRAPHICAL NOTES

BY

ERNEST HARTLEY COLERIDGE

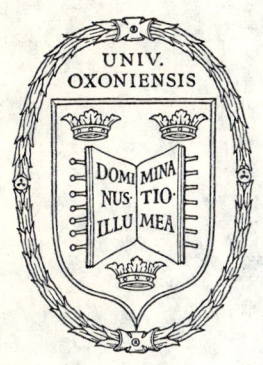

LONDON
OXFORD UNIVERSITY PRESS
NEW YORK TORONTO

SAMUEL TAYLOR COLERIDGE

Born, Ottery St. Mary . 21 October 1772
Died, Highgate . . 25 July 1834

This edition of The Poems of Samuel Taylor Coleridge *was first published in 1912 and reprinted in 1917, 1921, 1924, 1927, 1931, 1935, 1940, 1945, 1949, 1951, 1954, 1957, and 1960 (twice).*

PRINTED IN GREAT BRITAIN
O.S.A.

PREFACE

THE aim and purport of this edition of the Poems of Samuel Taylor Coleridge is to provide the general reader with an authoritative list of the poems hitherto published, and at the same time to furnish the student with an exhaustive summary of various readings derived from published and unpublished sources, viz. (1) the successive editions issued by the author, (2) holograph MSS., or (3) contemporary transcriptions. Occasion has been taken to include in the Text and Appendices a considerable number of poems, fragments, metrical experiments and first drafts of poems now published for the first time from MSS. in the British Museum, from Coleridge's Notebooks, and from MSS. in the possession of private collectors.

The text of the poems follows that of the last edition of the *Poetical Works* published in the author's lifetime—the three-volume edition issued by Pickering in the spring and summer of 1834.

I have adopted the text of 1834 in preference to that of 1829, which was selected by James Dykes Campbell for his monumental edition of 1893. I should have deferred to his authority but for the existence of conclusive proof that, here and there, Coleridge altered and emended the text of 1829, with a view to the forthcoming edition of 1834. In the Preface to the 'new edition' of 1852, the editors maintain that the three-volume edition of 1828 (a mistake for 1829) was the last upon which Coleridge was 'able to bestow personal care and attention', while that of 1834 was 'arranged mainly if not entirely at the discretion of his latest editor, H. N. Coleridge'. This, no doubt, was perfectly true with regard to the choice and arrangement of the poems, and the labour of seeing the three volumes through the press; but the fact remains that the text of 1829 differs from that of 1834, and that Coleridge himself, and not his 'latest editor', was responsible for that difference.

I have in my possession the proof of the first page of the 'Destiny of Nations' as it appeared in 1828 and 1829. Line 5 ran thus: 'The Will, the Word, the Breath, the Living God.' This line is erased and line 5 of 1834 substituted: 'To the Will Absolute, the One, the Good' and line 6, 'The I AM, the Word, the Life, the Living God,' is added, and, in 1834, appeared for the first time. Moreover, in the 'Songs of the Pixies', lines 9, 11, 12, 15, 16, as printed in 1834, differ from the readings of 1829 and all previous editions. Again, in 'Christabel' lines 6, 7 as printed in 1834 differ from the versions of 1828, 1829, and revert to the original reading of the MSS. and the First Edition. It is inconceivable that in Coleridge's lifetime and while his pen was still busy, his nephew should have meddled with, or remodelled, the master's handiwork.

The poems have been printed, as far as possible, in chronological order, but when no MS. is extant, or when the MS. authority is a first draft embodied in a notebook, the exact date can only be arrived at by a balance of probabilities. Some of the fragments (*vide post*, p. 493, n. 1) I have since discovered are not original compositions, but were selected passages from elder poets—amongst them Cartwright's lines, entitled 'The Second Birth', which are printed on p. 362 of the text; but for their insertion in the edition of 1893, for a few misreadings of the MSS., and for their approximate date, I was mainly responsible.

In preparing the textual and bibliographical notes which are now printed as footnotes to the poems I was constantly indebted for information and suggestions to the Notes to the Poems (pp. 561–654) in the edition of 1893. I have taken nothing for granted, but I have followed, for the most part, where Dykes Campbell led, and if I differ from his conclusions or have been able to supply fresh information, it is because fresh information based on fresh material was at my disposal.

No apology is needed for publishing a collation of the text of Coleridge's Poems with that of earlier editions or with the MSS. of first drafts and alternative versions. The first to attempt anything of the kind was Richard Herne Shepherd, the learned and accurate editor of the *Poetical Works* in four volumes, issued by Basil Montagu Pickering in 1877. Important variants are recorded by Mr. Campbell in his Notes to the edition of 1893; and in a posthumous volume, edited by Mr. Hale White in 1899 (*Coleridge's Poems*, &c.), the corrected parts of 'Religious Musings', the MSS. of 'Lewti', the 'Introduction to the Dark Ladié', and other poems are reproduced in facsimile. Few poets have altered the text of their poems so often, and so often for the better, as Coleridge. He has been blamed for 'writing so little', for deserting poetry for metaphysics and theology; he has been upbraided for winning only to lose the 'prize of his high calling'. Sir Walter Scott, one of his kindlier censors, rebukes him for 'the caprice and indolence with which he has thrown from him, as if in mere wantonness, those unfinished scraps of poetry, which like the Torso of antiquity defy the skill of his poetical brethren to complete them'. But whatever may be said for or against Coleridge as an 'inventor of harmonies', neither the fineness of his self-criticism nor the laborious diligence which he expended on perfecting his inventions can be gainsaid. His erasures and emendations are not only a lesson in the art of poetry, not only a record of poetical growth and development, but they discover and reveal the hidden springs, the thoughts and passions of the artificer.

But if this be true of a stanza, a line, a word here or there, inserted as an afterthought, is there use or sense in printing a number of trifling or, apparently, accidental variants? Might not a choice have been made, and the jots and tittles ignored or suppressed?

My plea is that it is difficult if not impossible to draw a line above which a variant is important and below which it is negligible; that, to use a word of the poet's own coining, his emendations are rarely if ever 'lightheartednesses'; and that if a collation of the printed text with MSS. is worth studying at all the one must be as decipherable as the other. Facsimiles are rare and costly productions, and an exhaustive table of variants is the nearest approach to a substitute. Many, I know, are the shortcomings, too many, I fear, are the errors in the footnotes to this volume, but now, for the first time, the MSS. of Coleridge's poems which are known to be extant are in a manner reproduced and made available for study and research.

Six poems of some length are now printed and included in the text of the poems for the first time.

The first, 'Easter Holidays' (p. 1), is unquestionably a 'School-boy Poem', and was written some months before the author had completed his fifteenth year. It tends to throw doubt on the alleged date of 'Time, Real and Imaginary'.

The second, 'An Inscription for a Seat,' &c. (p. 349), was first published in the *Morning Post*, on October 21, 1800, Coleridge's twenty-eighth birthday. It remains an open question whether it was written by Coleridge or by Wordsworth. Both were contributors to the *Morning Post*. Both wrote 'Inscriptions'. Both had a hand in making the 'seat'. Neither claimed or republished the poem. It favours or, rather, parodies the style and sentiments now of one and now of the other.

The third, 'The Rash Conjurer' (p. 399), must have been read by H. N. Coleridge, who included the last seven lines, the 'Epilogue', in the first volume of *Literary Remains*, published in 1836. I presume that, even as a fantasia, the subject was regarded as too extravagant, and, it may be, too coarsely worded for publication. It was no doubt in the first instance a 'metrical experiment', but it is to be interpreted allegorically. The 'Rash Conjurer', the *âme damnée*, is the adept in the black magic of metaphysics. But for that he might have been like his brothers, a 'Devonshire Christian'.

The fourth, 'The Madman and the Lethargist' (p. 414), is an expansion of an epigram in the Greek Anthology. It is possible that it was written in Germany in 1799, and is contemporary with the epigrams published in the *Morning Post* in 1802, for the Greek original is quoted by Lessing in a critical excursus on the nature of an epigram.

The fifth, 'Faith, Hope, and Charity' (p. 427), was translated from the Italian of Guarini at Calne, in 1815.

Of the sixth, 'The Delinquent Travellers' (p. 443), I know

nothing save that the MS., a first copy, is in Coleridge's handwriting. It was probably written for and may have been published in a newspaper or periodical. It was certainly written at Highgate.

Of the first drafts and alternative versions of well-known poems thirteen are now printed for the first time. Two versions of 'The Eolian Harp', preserved in the Library of Rugby School, and the dramatic fragment entitled 'The Triumph of Loyalty', are of especial interest and importance.

An exact reproduction of the text of the 'Ancyent Marinere' as printed in an early copy of the *Lyrical Ballads* of 1798 which belonged to S. T. Coleridge, and a collation of the text of the 'Introduction to the Tale of the Dark Ladié', as published in the *Morning Post*, Dec. 21, 1799, with two MSS. preserved in the British Museum, are included in Appendix No. I.

The text of the 'Allegoric Vision' has been collated with the original MS. and with the texts of 1817 and 1829.

A section has been devoted to 'Metrical Experiments'; eleven out of thirteen are now published for the first time. A few critical notes by Professor Saintsbury are, with his kind permission, appended to the text.

The bibliographical record of the successive editions of poems and dramas published by Coleridge himself and of the principal collected and selected editions which have been published since 1834 is long and intricate, but the history of the gradual accretions may be summed up in a few sentences. 'The Fall of Robespierre' was published in 1795. A first edition, entitled 'Poems on Various Subjects', was published in 1796. Second and third editions, with additions and subtractions, followed in 1797 and 1803. Two poems, 'The Rime of the Ancyent Marinere' and 'The Nightingale, a Conversation Poem', and two extracts from an unpublished drama ('Osorio') were included in the *Lyrical Ballads* of 1798. A quarto pamphlet containing three poems, 'Fears in Solitude,' 'France: An Ode,' 'Frost at Midnight,' was issued in the same year. 'Love' was first published in the second edition of the *Lyrical Ballads*, 1800. 'The Three Graves,' 'A Hymn before Sunrise, &c.,' and 'Idoloclastes Satyrane', were included in the *Friend* (Sept.–Nov., 1809). 'Christabel,' 'Kubla Khan,' and 'The Pains of Sleep' were published by themselves in 1816. *Sibylline Leaves*, which appeared in 1817 and was described as 'A Collection of Poems', included the contents of the editions of 1797 and 1803, the poems published in the *Lyrical Ballads* of 1798, 1800, and the quarto pamphlet of 1798, but excluded the contents of the first edition (except the 'Eolian Harp'), 'Christabel', 'Kubla Khan', and 'The Pains of Sleep'. The first collected edition of the *Poetical Works* (which included a selection of the poems published in the three first editions, a reissue of *Sibylline Leaves*, the 'Wanderings of Cain', a few poems recently contributed to periodicals, and the following dramas—the translation of Schiller's 'Piccolomini', published in 1800, 'Remorse'—a revised version of 'Osorio'—published in 1813, and 'Zapolya', published in 1817) was issued in three volumes in 1828. A second collected edition in three volumes, a reissue of 1828, with an amended text and the addition of 'The Improvisatore' and 'The Garden of Boccaccio', followed in 1829.

Finally, in 1834, there was a reissue in three volumes of the contents of 1829 with numerous additional poems then published or collected for the first time. The first volume contained twenty-six juvenilia printed from letters and MS. copybooks which had been preserved by the poet's family, and the second volume some forty 'Miscellaneous Poems', extracted from the Notebooks or reprinted from newspapers. The most important additions were 'Alice du Clos', then first published from MS., 'The Knight's Tomb' and the 'Epitaph'. 'Love, Hope, and Patience in Education', which had appeared in the *Keepsake* of 1830, was printed on the last page of the third volume.

After Coleridge's death the first attempt to gather up the fragments of his poetry was made by his 'latest editor' H. N. Coleridge in 1836. The first volume of *Literary Remains* contains the first reprint of 'The Fall of Robespierre', some thirty-six poems collected from the *Watchman*, the *Morning Post*, &c., and a selection of fragments then first printed from a MS. Notebook, now known as 'the Gutch Memorandum Book'.

PREFACE

H. N. Coleridge died in 1843, and in 1844 his widow prepared a one-volume edition of the Poems, which was published by Pickering. Eleven juvenilia which had first appeared in 1834 were omitted and the poems first collected in *Literary Remains* were for the first time included in the text. In 1850 Mrs. H. N. Coleridge included in the third volume of the *Essays on His Own Times* six poems and numerous epigrams and *jeux d'esprit* which had appeared in the *Morning Post* and *Courier*. This was the first reprint of the Epigrams as a whole. A 'new edition' of the Poems which she had prepared in the last year of her life was published immediately after her death (May, 1852) by Edward Moxon. It was based on the one-volume edition of 1844, with unimportant omissions and additions; only one poem, 'The Hymn', was published for the first time from MS.

In the same year (1852) the Dramatic Works (not including 'The Fall of Robespierre'), edited by Derwent Coleridge, were published in a separate volume.

In 1863 and 1870 the 'new edition' of 1852 was reissued by Derwent Coleridge with an appendix containing thirteen poems collected for the first time in 1863. The reissue of 1870 contained a reprint of the first edition of the 'Ancient Mariner'.

The first edition of the *Poetical Works*, based on all previous editions, and including the contents of *Literary Remains* (vol. i) and of *Essays on His Own Times* (vol. iii), was issued by Basil Montagu Pickering in four volumes in 1877. Many poems (including 'Remorse') were collated for the first time with the text of previous editions and newspaper versions by the editor, Richard Herne Shepherd. The four volumes (with a Supplement to vol. ii) were reissued by Messrs. Macmillan in 1880.

Finally, in the one-volume edition of the *Poetical Works* issued by Messrs. Macmillan in 1893, J. D. Campbell included in the text some twenty poems and in the Appendix a large number of poetical fragments and first drafts then printed for the first time from MS., by kind permission of the copyright owner, Mr. William Heinemann.

PREFACE

I desire to express my thanks to my kinsman Lord Coleridge for opportunity kindly afforded me of collating the text of the fragments first published in 1893 with the original MSS. in his possession, and of making further extracts; to Mr. Gordon Wordsworth for permitting me to print a first draft of the poem addressed to his ancestor on the 'Growth of an Individual Mind'; and to Miss Arnold of Fox How for a copy of the first draft of the lines 'On Revisiting the Sea-shore'.

I have also to acknowledge the kindness and courtesy of the Authorities of Rugby School, who permitted me to publish first drafts of 'The Eolian Harp' and other poems which had formerly belonged to Joseph Cottle and were presented by Mr. Shadworth Hodgson to the School Library.

I am indebted to my friend Mr. Thomas Hutchinson for valuable information with regard to the authorship of some of the fragments, and for advice and assistance in settling the text of the 'Metrical Experiments' and other points of difficulty.

Lastly, I wish to thank Mr. H. S. Milford for the invaluable assistance which he afforded me in revising my collation of the 'Songs of the Pixies' and the 'Introduction to the Tale of the Dark Ladié', and some of the earlier poems, and the Reader of the Oxford University Press for numerous hints and suggestions, and for the infinite care which he has bestowed on the correction of slips of my own or errors of the press.

ERNEST HARTLEY COLERIDGE.

1912

CONTENTS

	PAGE
PREFACE	v

1787

Easter Holidays. [MS. *Letter*, May 12, 1787.]	1
Dura Navis. [B.M. Add. MSS. 34,225]	2
Nil Pejus est Caelibe Vitâ. [Boyer's *Liber Aureus*.]	4

1788

| Sonnet: To the Autumnal Moon | 5 |

1789

Anthem for the Children of Christ's Hospital. [MS. O.]	5
Julia. [Boyer's *Liber Aureus*.]	6
Quae Nocent Docent. [Boyer's *Liber Aureus*.]	7
The Nose. [MS. O.]	8
To the Muse. [MS. O.]	9
Destruction of the Bastile. [MS. O.]	10
Life. [MS. O.]	11

1790

Progress of Vice. [MS. O.: Boyer's *Liber Aureus*.]	12
Monody on the Death of Chatterton. (First version.) [MS. O.: Boyer's *Liber Aureus*.]	13
An Invocation. [J. D. C.]	16
Anna and Harland. [MS. J. D. C.]	16
To the Evening Star. [MS. O.]	16
Pain. [MS. O.]	17
On a Lady Weeping. [MS. O. (c).]	17
Monody on a Tea-kettle. [MSS. O., S. T. C.]	18
Genevieve. [MSS. O., E.]	19

1791

On receiving an Account that his Only Sister's Death was Inevitable. [MS. O.]	20
On seeing a Youth Affectionately Welcomed by a Sister	21
A Mathematical Problem. [MS. *Letter*, March 31, 1791: MS. O. (c).]	21
Honour. [MS. O.]	24
On Imitation. [MS. O.]	26
Inside the Coach. [MS. O.]	26
Devonshire Roads. [MS. O.]	27
Music. [MS. O.]	28
Sonnet: On quitting School for College. [MS. O.]	29
Absence. A Farewell Ode on quitting School for Jesus College, Cambridge. [MS. E.]	29
Happiness. [MS. *Letter*, June 22, 1791: MS. O. (c).]	30

CONTENTS

1792

	PAGE
A Wish. Written in Jesus Wood, Feb. 10, 1792. [MS. *Letter*, Feb. 13, [1792].]	33
An Ode in the Manner of Anacreon. [MS. *Letter*, Feb. 13, [1792].]	33
To Disappointment. [MS. *Letter*, Feb. 13, [1792].]	34
A Fragment found in a Lecture-room. [MS. *Letter*, April [1792], MS. E.]	35
Ode. ('Ye Gales,' &c.) [MS. E.]	35
A Lover's Complaint to his Mistress. [MS. *Letter*, Feb. 13, [1792].]	36
With Fielding's 'Amelia.' [MS. O.]	37
Written after a Walk before Supper. [MS. *Letter*, Aug. 9, [1792].]	37

1793

Imitated from Ossian. [MS. E.]	38
The Complaint of Ninathóma. [MS. *Letter*, Feb. 7, 1793.]	39
Songs of the Pixies. [MS. 4°: MS. E.]	40
The Rose. [MS. *Letter*, July 28, 1793: MS. (*pencil*) in Langhorne's *Collins*: MS. E.]	45
Kisses. [MS. *Letter*, Aug. 5, 1793: MS. (*pencil*) in Langhorne's *Collins*: MS. E.]	46
The Gentle Look. [MS. *Letter*, Dec. 11, 1794: MS. E.]	47
Sonnet: To the River Otter	48
An Effusion at Evening. Written in August 1792. (First Draft.) [MS. E.]	49
Lines: On an Autumnal Evening	51
To Fortune	54

1794

Perspiration. A Travelling Eclogue. [MS. *Letter*, July 6, 1794.]	56
[Ave, atque Vale!] ('Vivit sed mihi,' &c.) [MS. *Letter*, July 13, [1794].]	56
On Bala Hill. [Morrison MSS.]	56
Lines: Written at the King's Arms, Ross, formerly the House of the 'Man of Ross'. [MS. *Letter*, July 13, 1794: MS. E: Morrison MSS: MS. 4°.]	57
Imitated from the Welsh. [MS. *Letter*, Dec. 11, 1794 MS. E.]	58
Lines: To a Beautiful Spring in a Village. [MS. E.]	58
Imitations: Ad Lyram. (Casimir, Book II, Ode 3.) [MS. E.]	59
To Lesbia. [Add. MSS. 27,702]	60
The Death of the Starling. [*ibid.*]	61
Moriens Superstiti. [*ibid.*]	61
Morienti Superstes. [*ibid.*]	62
The Sigh. [MS. *Letter*, Nov. 1794: Morrison MSS: MS. E.]	62
The Kiss. [MS. 4°: MS. E.]	63
To a Young Lady with a Poem on the French Revolution. [MS. *Letter*, Oct. 21, 1794: MS. 4°: MS. E.]	64
Translation of Wrangham's 'Hendecasyllabi ad Bruntonam e Granta Exituram' [Kal. Oct. MDCCXC]	66
To Miss Brunton with the preceding Translation	67
Epitaph on an Infant. ('Ere Sin could blight.') [MS. E.]	68
Pantisocracy. [MSS. *Letters*, Sept. 18, Oct. 19, 1794: MS. E.]	68
On the Prospect of establishing a Pantisocracy in America	69
Elegy: Imitated from one of Akenside's Blank-verse Inscriptions. [(No.) III.]	69
The Faded Flower	70

CONTENTS

	PAGE
The Outcast	71
Domestic Peace. (From 'The Fall of Robespierre,' Act I, l. 210.)	71
On a Discovery made too late. [MS. *Letter*, Oct. 21, 1794.]	72
To the Author of 'The Robbers'	72
Melancholy. A Fragment. [MS. *Letter*, Aug. 26, 1802.]	73
To a Young Ass: Its Mother being tethered near it. [MS. Oct. 24, 1794: MS. *Letter*, Dec. 17, 1794.]	74
Lines on a Friend who Died of a Frenzy Fever induced by Calumnious Reports. [MS. *Letter*, Nov. 6, 1794: MS. 4°: MS. E.]	76
To a Friend [Charles Lamb] together with an Unfinished Poem. [MS. *Letter*, Dec. 1794]	78
Sonnets on Eminent Characters: Contributed to the *Morning Chronicle*, in Dec. 1794 and Jan. 1795:—	
I. To the Honourable Mr. Erskine	79
II. Burke. [MS. *Letter*, Dec. 11, 1794.]	80
III. Priestley. [MS. *Letter*, Dec. 17, 1794.]	81
IV. La Fayette	82
V. Koskiusko. [MS. *Letter*, Dec. 17, 1794)	82
VI. Pitt	83
VII. To the Rev. W. L. Bowles. (First Version, printed in *Morning Chronicle*, Dec. 26, 1794.) [MS. *Letter*, Dec. 11, 1794.]	84
(Second Version.)	85
VIII. Mrs. Siddons	85

1795.

IX. To William Godwin, Author of 'Political Justice.' [Lines 9–14, MS. *Letter*, Dec. 17, 1794.]	86
X. To Robert Southey of Baliol College, Oxford, Author of the 'Retrospect' and other Poems. [MS. *Letter*, Dec. 17, 1794.]	87
XI. To Richard Brinsley Sheridan, Esq. [MS. *Letter*, Dec. 9, 1794: MS. E.]	87
XII. To Lord Stanhope on reading his Late Protest in the House of Lords. [*Morning Chronicle*, Jan. 31, 1795.]	89
To Earl Stanhope	89
Lines: To a Friend in Answer to a Melancholy Letter	90
To an Infant. [MS. E.]	91
To the Rev. W. J. Hort while teaching a Young Lady some Song-tunes on his Flute	92
Pity. [MS. E.]	93
To the Nightingale	93
Lines: Composed while climbing the Left Ascent of Brockley Coomb, Somersetshire, May 1795	94
Lines in the Manner of Spenser	94
The Hour when we shall meet again. (*Composed during Illness and in Absence.*)	96
Lines written at Shurton Bars, near Bridgewater, September 1795, in Answer to a Letter from Bristol	96
The Eolian Harp. Composed at Clevedon, Somersetshire. [MS. R.]	100
To the Author of Poems [Joseph Cottle] published anonymously at Bristol in September 1795	102
The Silver Thimble. The Production of a Young Lady, addressed to the Author of the Poems alluded to in the preceding Epistle. [MS. R.]	104
Reflections on having left a Place of Retirement	106

CONTENTS

	PAGE
Religious Musings. [1794–1796.]	108
Monody on the Death of Chatterton. [1790–1834.]	125

1796

The Destiny of Nations. A Vision	131
Ver Perpetuum. Fragment from an Unpublished Poem	148
On observing a Blossom on the First of February 1796	148
To a Primrose. The First seen in the Season	149
Verses: Addressed to J. Horne Tooke and the Company who met on June 28, 1796, to celebrate his Poll at the Westminster Election	150
On a Late Connubial Rupture in High Life [Prince and Princess of Wales]. [MS Letter, July 4, 1796]	152
Sonnet: On receiving a Letter informing me of the Birth of a Son. [MS. Letter, Nov. 1, 1796.]	152
Sonnet: Composed on a Journey Homeward; the Author having received Intelligence of the Birth of a Son, Sept. 20, 1796. [MS. Letter, Nov. 1, 1796.]	153
Sonnet: To a Friend who asked how I felt when the Nurse first presented my Infant to me. [MS. Letter, Nov. 1, 1796]	154
Sonnet: [To Charles Lloyd]	155
To a Young Friend on his proposing to domesticate with the Author. Composed in 1796	155
Addressed to a Young Man of Fortune [C. Lloyd]	157
To a Friend [Charles Lamb] who had declared his intention of writing no more Poetry	158
Ode to the Departing Year	160

1797

The Raven. [MS. S. T. C.]	169
To an Unfortunate Woman at the Theatre	171
To an Unfortunate Woman whom the Author had known in the days of her Innocence	172
To the Rev. George Coleridge	173
On the Christening of a Friend's Child	176
Translation of a Latin Inscription by the Rev. W. L. Bowles in Nether-Stowey Church	177
This Lime-tree Bower my Prison	178
The Foster-mother's Tale	182
The Dungeon	185
The Rime of the Ancient Mariner	186
Sonnets attempted in the Manner of Contemporary Writers	209
Parliamentary Oscillators	211
Christabel. [For MSS. vide p. 214]	213
Lines to W. L. while he sang a Song to Purcell's Music	236

1798

Fire, Famine, and Slaughter	237
Frost at Midnight	240
France: An Ode	243
The Old Man of the Alps	248
To a Young Lady on her Recovery from a Fever	252
Lewti, or the Circassian Love-chaunt. [For MSS. vide pp. 1049–52]	253
Fears in Solitude. [MS. W.]	256
The Nightingale. A Conversation Poem	264

CONTENTS

	PAGE
The Three Graves. [Parts I, II. MS. S. T. C.]	267
The Wanderings of Cain. [MS. S. T. C.]	285
To ——	292
The Ballad of the Dark Ladié	293
Kubla Khan	295
Recantation: Illustrated in the Story of the Mad Ox	299

1799

Hexameters. ('William my teacher,' &c.)	304
Translation of a Passage in Ottfried's Metrical Paraphrase of the Gospel	306
Catullian Hendecasyllables	307
The Homeric Hexameter described and exemplified	307
The Ovidian Elegiac Metre described and exemplified	308
On a Cataract. [MS. S. T. C.]	308
Tell's Birth-Place	309
The Visit of the Gods	310
From the German. ('Know'st thou the land,' &c.)	311
Water Ballad. [From the French.]	311
On an Infant which died before Baptism. ('Be rather,' &c.) [MS. Letter, Apr. 8, 1799]	312
Something Childish, but very Natural. Written in Germany. [MS. Letter, April 23, 1799.]	313
Home-Sick. Written in Germany. [MS. Letter, May 6, 1799.]	314
Lines written in the Album at Elbingerode in the Hartz Forest. [MS. Letter, May 17, 1799.]	315
The British Stripling's War-Song. [Add. MSS. 27,902]	317
Names. [From Lessing.]	318
The Devil's Thoughts. [MS. copy by Derwent Coleridge.]	319
Lines composed in a Concert-room	324
Westphalian Song	326
Hexameters. Paraphrase of Psalm xlvi. [MS. Letter, Sept. 29, 1799.]	326
Hymn to the Earth. [Imitated from Stolberg's *Hymne an die Erde.*] Hexameters	327
Mahomet	329
Love. [British Museum Add. MSS. No. 27,902: Wordsworth and Coleridge MSS.]	330
Ode to Georgiana, Duchess of Devonshire, on the Twenty-fourth Stanza in her 'Passage over Mount Gothard'	335
A Christmas Carol	338

1800

Talleyrand to Lord Grenville. A Metrical Epistle	340
Apologia pro Vita sua. ('The poet in his lone,' &c.) [MS. Notebook.]	345
The Keepsake	345
A Thought suggested by a View of Saddleback in Cumberland. [MS. Notebook.]	347
The Mad Monk	347
Inscription for a Seat by the Road Side half-way up a Steep Hill facing South	349
A Stranger Minstrel	350
Alcaeus to Sappho. [MS. Letter, Oct. 7, 1800.]	353

CONTENTS

	PAGE
The Two Round Spaces on the Tombstone. [MS. *Letter*, Oct. 9, 1800: Add. MSS. 28,322]	353
The Snow-drop. [MS. S. T. C.]	356

1801

On Revisiting the Sea-shore. [MS. *Letter*, Aug. 15, 1801: MS. A.]	359
Ode to Tranquillity	360
To Asra. [MS. (of *Christabel*) S. T. C. (c).]	361
Love's Sanctuary. [MS. Notebook.]	362

1802

Dejection: An Ode. [Written April 4, 1802.] [MS. *Letter*, July 19, 1802: Coleorton MSS.]	362
The Picture, or the Lover's Resolution	369
To Matilda Betham from a Stranger	374
Hymn before Sun-rise, in the Vale of Chamouni. [MS. A. (1803): MS. B. (1809): MS. C. (1815).]	376
The Good, Great Man	381
Inscription for a Fountain on a Heath	381
An Ode to the Rain	382
A Day-dream. ('My eyes make pictures,' &c.)	385
Answer to a Child's Question	386
The Day-dream. From an Emigrant to his Absent Wife	386
The Happy Husband. A Fragment	388

1803

| The Pains of Sleep. [MS. *Letters*, Sept. 11, Oct 3, 1803.] | 389 |

1804

| The Exchange | 391 |

1805

Ad Vilmum Axiologum. [To William Wordsworth.] [MS. Notebook.]	391
An Exile. [MS. Notebook]	392
Sonnet. [Translated from Marini.] [MS. Notebook.]	392
Phantom. [MS. Notebook.]	393
A Sunset. [MS. Notebook.]	393
What is Life? [MS. Notebook.]	394
The Blossoming of the Solitary Date-tree	395
Separation. [MS. Notebook.]	397
The Rash Conjurer. [MS. Notebook.]	399

1806

A Child's Evening Prayer. [MS. Mrs. S. T. C.]	401
Metrical Feet. Lesson for a Boy. [Lines 1–7, MS. Notebook.]	401
Farewell to Love	402
To William Wordsworth. [Coleorton MS: MS. W.]	403
An Angel Visitant. [? 1801.] [MS. Notebook.]	409

1807

| Recollections of Love. [MS. Notebook.] | 409 |
| To Two Sisters [Mary Morgan and Charlotte Brent] | 410 |

CONTENTS

1808
	PAGE
Psyche. [MS. S. T. C.]	412

1809
A Tombless Epitaph	413
For a Market-clock. (Impromptu.) [MS. *Letter*, Oct. 9, 1809 : MS. Notebook.]	414
The Madman and the Lethargist. [MS. Notebook.]	414

1810
The Visionary Hope	416

1811
Epitaph on an Infant. ('Its balmy lips,' &c.)	417
The Virgin's Cradle-hymn	417
To a Lady offended by a Sportive Observation that Women have no Souls	418
Reason for Love's Blindness	418
The Suicide's Argument. [MS. Notebook.]	419

1812
Time, Real and Imaginary	419
An Invocation. From *Remorse* [Act III, Scene 1, ll. 69-82]	420

1813
The Night-scene. [Add. MSS. 34,225]	421

1814
A Hymn	423
To a Lady, with Falconer's *Shipwreck*	424

1815
Human Life. On the Denial of Immortality	425
Song. From *Zapolya* (Act II, Sc. i, ll. 65-80)	426
Hunting Song. From *Zapolya* (Act IV, Sc. ii, ll. 56-71)	427
Faith, Hope, and Charity. From the Italian of Guarini	427
To Nature [? 1820]	429

1817
Limbo. [MS. Notebook : MS. S. T. C.]	429
Ne Plus Ultra [? 1826]. [MS. Notebook.]	431
The Knight's Tomb	432
On Donne's Poetry [? 1818]	433
Israel's Lament	433
Fancy in Nubibus, or the Poet in the Clouds. [MS. S. T. C.]	435

1820
The Tears of a Grateful People	436

1823
Youth and Age. [MS. S. T. C : MSS. (1, 2) Notebook.]	439
The Reproof and Reply	441

CONTENTS

1824

First Advent of Love. [MS. Notebook.]	443
The Delinquent Travellers	443

1825

Work without Hope. Lines composed 21st February, 1825	447
Sancti Dominici Pallium. A Dialogue between Poet and Friend. [MS. S. T. C.]	448
Song. ('Though veiled,' &c.) [MS. Notebook.]	450
A Character. [Add. MSS. 34,225]	451
The Two Founts. [MS. S. T. C.]	454
Constancy to an Ideal Object	455
The Pang more Sharp than All. An Allegory	457

1826

Duty surviving Self-love. The only sure Friend of declining Life.	459
Homeless	460
Lines suggested by the last Words of Berengarius; ob. Anno Dom. 1088	460
Epitaphium Testamentarium	462
Ἔρως ἀεὶ λάλη θρος ἑταῖρος	462

1827

The Improvisatore; or, 'John Anderson, My Jo, John'	462
To Mary Pridham [afterwards Mrs. Derwent Coleridge]. [MS. S. T. C.]	468

1828

Alice du Clos; or, The Forked Tongue. A Ballad. [MS. S. T. C.]	469
Love's Burial-place	475
Lines: To a Comic Author, on an Abusive Review [? 1825]. [Add. MSS. 34,225]	476
Cologne	477
On my Joyful Departure from the same City	477
The Garden of Boccaccio	478

1829

Love, Hope, and Patience in Education. [MS. *Letter*, July 1, 1829: MS. S. T. C.]	481
To Miss A. T.	482
Lines written in Commonplace Book of Miss Barbour, Daughter of the Minister of the U. S. A. to England	483

1830

Song, *ex improviso*, on hearing a Song in praise of a Lady's Beauty	483
Love and Friendship Opposite	484
Not at Home	484
Phantom or Fact. A Dialogue in Verse	484
Desire. [MS. S. T. C.]	485
Charity in Thought	486
Humility the Mother of Charity	486
[Coeli Enarrant.] [MS. S. T. C.]	486
Reason	487

CONTENTS

1832

	PAGE
Self-knowledge	487
Forbearance	488

1833

Love's Apparition and Evanishment	488
To the Young Artist Kayser of Kaserwerth	490
My Baptismal Birth-day	490
Epitaph. [For six MS. versions vide Note, p. 491.]	491

END OF THE POEMS

FRAGMENTS. (*For unnamed Fragments see* Index of First Lines.)	493
Over my Cottage	494
[The Night-Mare Death in Life]	495
A Beck in Winter	495
[Not a Critic—But a Judge]	497
[De Profundis Clamavi]	498
Fragment of an Ode on Napoleon	500
Epigram on Kepler	501
[Ars Poetica]	503
Translation of the First Strophe of Pindar's Second Olympic	503
Translation of a Fragment of Heraclitus	504
Imitated from Aristophanes	505
To Edward Irving	505
[Luther—De Dæmonibus]	506
The Netherlands	506
Elisa: Translated from Claudian	506
Profuse Kindness	507
Napoleon	507
The Three Sorts of Friends	509
Bo-Peep and I Spy—	509
A Simile	510
Baron Guelph of Adelstan. A Fragment	510
METRICAL EXPERIMENTS	511
An Experiment for a Metre ('I heard a Voice,' &c.)	511
Trochaics	512
The Proper Unmodified Dochmius	512
Iambics	512
Nonsense ('Sing, impassionate Soul,' &c.)	513
A Plaintive Movement	513
Nonsense Verses ('Ye fowls of ill presage')	514
Nonsense ('I wish on earth to sing')	514
'There in some darksome shade'	515
'Once again, sweet Willow, wave thee'	515
'Songs of Shepherds, and rustical Roundelays'	515
A Metrical Accident	516
Notes by George Saintsbury	516

CONTENTS

APPENDIX I

First Drafts, Early Versions, etc.

	PAGE
A. Effusion 35, August 20th, 1795. (First Draft.) [MS. R.]	519
Effusion, p. 96 [1797]. (Second Draft.) [MS. R.]	519
B. Recollection	521
C. The Destiny of Nations. (Draft I.) [Add. MSS. 34,225]	522
,, ,, ,, (Draft II.) [*ibid.*]	524
,, ,, ,, (Draft III.) [*ibid.*]	525
D. Passages in Southey's *Joan of Arc* (First Edition, 1796) contributed by S. T. Coleridge	525
E. The Rime of the Ancyent Marinere [1798]	528
F. The Raven. [*M. P.* March 10, 1798.]	546
G. Lewti; or, The Circassian's Love-Chant. (1.) [B. M. Add. MSS. 27,902.]	547
The Circassian's Love-Chaunt. (2.) [Add. MSS. 35,343.]	548
Lewti; or, The Circassian's Love-Chant. (3.) [Add. MSS. 35,343.]	549
H. Introduction to the Tale of the Dark Ladie. [*M. P.* Dec. 21, 1799.]	550
I. The Triumph of Loyalty. An Historic Drama. [Add. MSS. 34,225.]	558
J. Chamouny; The Hour before Sunrise. A Hymn. [*M. P.* Sept. 11, 1802.]	572
K. Dejection: An Ode. [*M. P.* Oct. 4, 1802.]	574
L. To W. Wordsworth. January 1807	579
M. Youth and Age. (MS. I, Sept. 10, 1823.)	582
,, ,, (MS. II. 1.)	583
,, ,, (MS. II. 2.)	584
N. Love's Apparition and Evanishment. (First Draft.)	585
O. Two Versions of the Epitaph. ('Stop, Christian,' &c.)	586
P. [Habent sua Fata—Poetae.] ('The Fox, and Statesman,' &c.)	587
Q. To John Thelwall	588
R. [Lines to T. Poole.] [1807.]	588

APPENDIX II

Allegoric Vision 589

APPENDIX III

Apologetic Preface to 'Fire, Famine, and Slaughter' . . 595

INDEX OF FIRST LINES 607

ABBREVIATIONS

MS. B. M. = MS. preserved in the British Museum.
MS. O. = MS. Ottery: i.e. a collection of juvenile poems in the handwriting of S. T. Coleridge (*circ.* 1793).
MS. O. (c.) = MS. Ottery, No. 3: a transcript (*circ.* 1823) of a collection of juvenile poems by S. T. Coleridge.
MS. S. T. C. = A single MS. poem in the handwriting of S. T. Coleridge.
MS. E. = MS. Estlin: i.e. a collection of juvenile poems in the handwriting of S. T. Coleridge presented to Mrs. Estlin of Bristol *circ.* 1795.
MS. 4° = A collection of early poems in the handwriting of S. T. Coleridge (*circ.* 1796).
MS. W. = An MS. in the handwriting of S. T. Coleridge, now in the possession of Mr. Gordon Wordsworth.
MS. R. = MS. Rugby: i.e. in the possession of the Governors of Rugby School.
C. I. = *Cambridge Intelligencer.*
M. C. = *Morning Chronicle.*
M. P. = *Morning Post.*
M. M. = *Monthly Magazine.*
An. Anth. = *Annual Anthology* of 1800.
P. R. = *Poetical Register*, 1802.
S. L. = *Sibylline Leaves* (1817).
F. F. = *Felix Farley's Bristol Journal*, 1818.
F. O. = *Friendship's Offering*, 1834.

B. L. = *Biographia Literaria.*
E. M. = *English Minstrelsy.*
L. A. = *Liber Aureus.*
L. B. = *Lyrical Ballads.*
L. R. = *Literary Remains.*
P. & D. W. = *Poetical and Dramatic Works.*
P. W. = *Poetical Works*
S. S. = *Selection of Sonnets.*

POEMS

EASTER HOLIDAYS[1]

Verse 1st

Hail! festal Easter that dost bring
Approach of sweetly-smiling spring,
 When Nature's clad in green:
When feather'd songsters through the grove
With beasts confess the power of love   5
 And brighten all the scene.

Verse 2nd

Now youths the breaking stages load
That swiftly rattling o'er the road
 To Greenwich haste away:
While some with sounding oars divide   10
Of smoothly-flowing Thames the tide
 All sing the festive lay.

Verse 3rd

With mirthful dance they beat the ground,
Their shouts of joy the hills resound
 And catch the jocund noise: 15
Without a tear, without a sigh
Their moments all in transports fly
 Till evening ends their joys.

Verse 4th

But little think their joyous hearts
Of dire Misfortune's varied smarts   20
 Which youthful years conceal:
Thoughtless of bitter-smiling Woe
Which all mankind are born to know
 And they themselves must feel.

---

[1] From a hitherto unpublished MS. The lines were sent in a letter to Luke Coleridge, dated May 12 1787.

Verse 5th

Yet he who Wisdom's paths shall keep 25
And Virtue firm that scorns to weep
   At ills in Fortune's power,
Through this life's variegated scene
In raging storms or calm serene
   Shall cheerful spend the hour. 30

Verse 6th

While steady Virtue guides his mind
Heav'n-born Content he still shall find
   That never sheds a tear:
Without respect to any tide
His hours away in bliss shall glide 35
   Like Easter all the year.

1787.

DURA NAVIS[1]

To tempt the dangerous deep, too venturous youth,
Why does thy breast with fondest wishes glow?
No tender parent there thy cares shall sooth,
No much-lov'd Friend shall share thy every woe.
Why does thy mind with hopes delusive burn? 5
Vain are thy Schemes by heated Fancy plann'd:
Thy promis'd joy thou'lt see to Sorrow turn
Exil'd from Bliss, and from thy native land.

Hast thou foreseen the Storm's impending rage,
When to the Clouds the Waves ambitious rise, 10
And seem with Heaven a doubtful war to wage,
Whilst total darkness overspreads the skies;
Save when the lightnings darting wingéd Fate
Quick bursting from the pitchy clouds between
In forkéd Terror, and destructive state[2] 15
Shall shew with double gloom the horrid scene?

---

[1] First published in 1893. The autograph MS. is in the British Museum.
[2] *State*, Grandeur [1792]. This school exercise, written in the 15th year of my age, does not contain a line that any clever schoolboy might not have written, and like most school poetry is a *Putting of Thought into Verse*; for such Verses as *strivings* of mind and struggles after the Intense and Vivid are a fair Promise of better things.—S. T. C. *aetat. suae* 51. [1823.]

DURA NAVIS

Shalt thou be at this hour from danger free?
Perhaps with fearful force some falling Wave
Shall wash thee in the wild tempestuous Sea,
And in some monster's belly fix thy grave;
Or (woful hap!) against some wave-worn rock
Which long a Terror to each Bark had stood
Shall dash thy mangled limbs with furious shock
And stain its craggy sides with human blood.

Yet not the Tempest, or the Whirlwind's roar
Equal the horrors of a Naval Fight,
When thundering Cannons spread a sea of Gore
And varied deaths now fire and now affright:
The impatient shout, that longs for closer war,
Reaches from either side the distant shores;
Whilst frighten'd at His streams ensanguin'd far
Loud on his troubled bed huge Ocean roars.[1]

What dreadful scenes appear before my eyes!
Ah! see how each with frequent slaughter red,
Regardless of his dying fellows' cries
O'er their fresh wounds with impious order tread!
From the dread place does soft Compassion fly!
The Furies fell each alter'd breast command;
Whilst Vengeance drunk with human blood stands by
And smiling fires each heart and arms each hand.

Should'st thou escape the fury of that day
A fate more cruel still, unhappy, view.
Opposing winds may stop thy luckless way,
And spread fell famine through the suffering crew,
Canst thou endure th' extreme of raging Thirst
Which soon may scorch thy throat, ah! thoughtless Youth!
Or ravening hunger canst thou bear which erst
On its own flesh hath fix'd the deadly tooth?

---

[1] I well remember old Jemmy Bowyer, the plagose Orbilius of Christ's Hospital, but an admirable educer no less than Educator of the Intellect, bade me leave out as many epithets as would turn the whole into eight-syllable lines, and then ask myself if the exercise would not be greatly improved. How often have I thought of the proposal since then, and how many thousand bloated and puffing lines have I read, that, by this process, would have tripped over the tongue excellently. Likewise, I remember that he told me on the same occasion—'Coleridge! the connections of a Declamation are not the transitions of Poetry—bad, however, as they are, they are better than "Apostrophes" and "O thou's", for at the worst they are something like common sense. The others are the grimaces of Lunacy.'—S. T. COLERIDGE.

Dubious and fluttering 'twixt hope and fear
With trembling hands the lot I see thee draw, 50
Which shall, or sentence thee a victim drear,
To that ghaunt Plague which savage knows no law:
Or, deep thy dagger in the friendly heart,
Whilst each strong passion agitates thy breast,
Though oft with Horror back I see thee start, 55
Lo! Hunger *drives* thee to th' inhuman feast.

These are the ills, that may the course attend—
Then with the joys of home contented rest—
Here, meek-eyed Peace with humble Plenty lend
Their aid united still, to make thee blest. 60
To ease each pain, and to increase each joy—
Here mutual Love shall fix thy tender wife,
Whose offspring shall thy youthful care employ
And gild with brightest rays the evening of thy Life.
1787.

NIL PEJUS EST CAELIBE VITÂ[1]

[IN CHRIST'S HOSPITAL BOOK]

I

What pleasures shall he ever find?
What joys shall ever glad his heart?
Or who shall heal his wounded mind,
If tortur'd by Misfortune's smart?
Who Hymeneal bliss will never prove, 5
That more than friendship, friendship mix'd with love.

II

Then without child or tender wife,
To drive away each care, each sigh,
Lonely he treads the paths of life
A stranger to Affection's tye: 10
And when from Death he meets his final doom
No mourning wife with tears of love shall wet his tomb.

[1] First published in 1893.

III

Tho' Fortune, Riches, Honours, Pow'r,
  Had giv'n with every other toy,
Those gilded trifles of the hour,
  Those painted nothings sure to cloy:
He dies forgot, his name no son shall bear
To shew the man so blest once breath'd the vital air.
1787.

SONNET [1]

TO THE AUTUMNAL MOON

MILD Splendour of the various-vested Night!
  Mother of wildly-working visions! hail!
I watch thy gliding, while with watery light
  Thy weak eye glimmers through a fleecy veil;
And when thou lovest thy pale orb to shroud
  Behind the gather'd blackness lost on high;
And when thou dartest from the wind-rent cloud
  Thy placid lightning o'er the awaken'd sky.

Ah such is Hope! as changeful and as fair!
  Now dimly peering on the wistful sight;
Now hid behind the dragon-wing'd Despair:
  But soon emerging in her radiant might
  She o'er the sorrow-clouded breast of Care
    Sails, like a meteor kindling in its flight.
1788.

ANTHEM [2]

FOR THE CHILDREN OF CHRIST'S HOSPITAL

SERAPHS! around th' Eternal's seat who throng
  With tuneful ecstasies of praise:
O! teach our feeble tongues like yours the song
  Of fervent gratitude to raise—

---

[1] First published in 1796: included in 1803, 1829, 1834. No changes were made in the text.
[2] First published in 1834.

Sonnet—Title] Effusion xviii, To the, &c. : Sonnet xviii, To the, &c., *1803*.
Anthem. For the Children, &c.] This Anthem was written as if intended to have been sung by the Children of Christ's Hospital. *MS. O.*
3 yours] you *MS. O.*

Like you, inspired with holy flame
To dwell on that Almighty name
Who bade the child of Woe no longer sigh,
And Joy in tears o'erspread the widow's eye.

  Th' all-gracious Parent hears the wretch's prayer;
    The meek tear strongly pleads on high;
  Wan Resignation struggling with despair
    The Lord beholds with pitying eye;
  Sees cheerless Want unpitied pine,
  Disease on earth its head recline,
And bids Compassion seek the realms of woe
To heal the wounded, and to raise the low.

  She comes! she comes! the meek-eyed Power I see
    With liberal hand that loves to bless;
  The clouds of Sorrow at her presence flee;
    Rejoice! rejoice! ye Children of Distress!
  The beams that play around her head
  Thro' Want's dark vale their radiance spread:
The young uncultur'd mind imbibes the ray,
And Vice reluctant quits th' expected prey.

  Cease, thou lorn mother! cease thy wailings drear;
    Ye babes! the unconscious sob forego;
  Or let full Gratitude now prompt the tear
    Which erst did Sorrow force to flow.
  Unkindly cold and tempest shrill
  In Life's morn oft the traveller chill,
But soon his path the sun of Love shall warm;
And each glad scene look brighter for the storm!
1789.

JULIA [1]

[IN CHRIST'S HOSPITAL BOOK]

Medio de fonte leporum
Surgit amari aliquid.

JULIA was blest with beauty, wit, and grace:
Small poets lov'd to sing her blooming face.
Before her altars, lo! a numerous train
Preferr'd their vows; yet all preferr'd in vain,

---

[1] First published in the *History of . . . Christ's Hospital*. By the Rev. W. Trollope, 1834, p. 192. Included in *Literary Remains*, 1836, i. 33, 34. First collected *P. and D. W.*, 1877-80.

---

14 its head on earth *MS. O.*
Julia. Medio, &c.] De medio fonte leporum. *Trollope.*

Till charming Florio, born to conquer, came
And touch'd the fair one with an equal flame.
The flame she felt, and ill could she conceal
What every look and action would reveal.
With boldness then, which seldom fails to move,
He pleads the cause of Marriage and of Love:
The course of Hymeneal joys he rounds,
The fair one's eyes danc'd pleasure at the sounds.
Nought now remain'd but 'Noes'—how little meant!
And the sweet coyness that endears consent.
The youth upon his knees enraptur'd fell:
The strange misfortune, oh! what words can tell?
Tell! ye neglected sylphs! who lap-dogs guard,
Why snatch'd ye not away your precious ward?
Why suffer'd ye the lover's weight to fall
On the ill-fated neck of much-lov'd Ball?
The favourite on his mistress casts his eyes,
Gives a short melancholy howl, and—dies.
Sacred his ashes lie, and long his rest!
Anger and grief divide poor Julia's breast.
Her eyes she fixt on guilty Florio first:
On him the storm of angry grief must burst.
That storm he fled: he wooes a kinder fair,
Whose fond affections no dear puppies share.
'Twere vain to tell, how Julia pin'd away:
Unhappy Fair! that in one luckless day—
From future Almanacks the day be crost!—
At once her Lover and her Lap-dog lost.
1789.

QUAE NOCENT DOCENT[1]

[IN CHRIST'S HOSPITAL BOOK]

O! mihi praeteritos referat si Jupiter annos!

OH! might my ill-past hours return again!
No more, as then, should Sloth around me throw
   Her soul-enslaving, leaden chain!
No more the precious time would I employ
In giddy revels, or in thoughtless joy,
A present joy producing future woe.

[1] First published in 1893.

---

12 danc'd] dance T. *Lit. Rem.*

8 QUAE NOCENT DOCENT

But o'er the midnight Lamp I'd love to pore,
I'd seek with care fair Learning's depths to sound,
   And gather scientific Lore:
Or to mature the embryo thoughts inclin'd,   10
That half-conceiv'd lay struggling in my mind,
The cloisters' solitary gloom I'd round.

'Tis vain to wish, for Time has ta'en his flight—
For follies past be ceas'd the fruitless tears:
   Let follies past to future care incite.   15
Averse maturer judgements to obey
Youth owns, with pleasure owns, the Passions' sway,
But sage Experience only comes with years.
1789.

THE NOSE[1]

Ye souls unus'd to lofty verse
   Who sweep the earth with lowly wing,
Like sand before the blast disperse—
   A Nose! a mighty Nose I sing!
As erst Prometheus stole from heaven the fire   5
   To animate the wonder of his hand;
Thus with unhallow'd hands, O Muse, aspire,
   And from my subject snatch a burning brand!
So like the Nose I sing—my verse shall glow—
Like Phlegethon my verse in waves of fire shall flow!   10

Light of this once all darksome spot
   Where now their glad course mortals run,
First-born of Sirius begot
   Upon the focus of the Sun—
I'll call thee —— ! for such thy earthly name—   15
   What name so high, but what too low must be?
Comets, when most they drink the solar flame
   Are but faint types and images of thee!

---

[1] First published in 1834. The third stanza was published in the *Morning Post*, Jan. 2, 1798, entitled 'To the Lord Mayor's Nose'. William Gill (see ll. 15, 20) was Lord Mayor in 1788.

The Nose—Title] Rhapsody *MS. O*: The Nose.—An Odaic Rhapsody *MS. O (c)*.
5 As erst from Heaven Prometheus stole the fire *MS. O (c)*.   7 hands] hand *MS. O (c)*.   10 waves of fire] fiery waves *MS. O (c)*.   15 I'll call thee Gill *MS. O*.   G—ll *MS. O (c)*.   16 high] great *MS. O (c)*.

> From thee, dear Muse! the gayer part,
> To laugh with pity at the crowds that press
> Where Fashion flaunts her robes by Folly spun,
> Whose hues gay-varying wanton in the sun.

1789.

DESTRUCTION OF THE BASTILE[1]

I

Heard'st thou yon universal cry,
  And dost thou linger still on Gallia's shore?
Go, Tyranny! beneath some barbarous sky
  Thy terrors lost and ruin'd power deplore!
    What tho' through many a groaning age
    Was felt thy keen suspicious rage,
    Yet Freedom rous'd by fierce Disdain
    Has wildly broke thy triple chain,
And like the storm which Earth's deep entrails hide,
At length has burst its way and spread the ruins wide.

* * * * * * *

IV

In sighs their sickly breath was spent; each gleam
  Of Hope had ceas'd the long long day to cheer;
Or if delusive, in some flitting dream,
  It gave them to their friends and children dear—
    Awaked by lordly Insult's sound
    To all the doubled horrors round,
    Oft shrunk they from Oppression's band
    While Anguish rais'd the desperate hand
For silent death; or lost the mind's controll,
Thro' every burning vein would tides of Frenzy roll.

---

[1] First published in 1834. *Note.* The Bastile was destroyed July 14, 1789.

Destruction of the Bastile—Title] An ode on the Destruction of the Bastile MS. *O*.

11 In MS. *O* stanza iv follows stanza i, part of the leaf being torn out. In another MS. copy in place of the asterisks the following note is inserted: 'Stanzas second and third are lost. We may gather from the context that they alluded to the Bastile and its inhabitants.' 12 long long] livelong MS. *O*.

THE NOSE

Burn madly, Fire! o'er earth in ravage run,
Then blush for shame more red by fiercer —— outdone!

    I saw when from the turtle feast
      The thick dark smoke in volumes rose!
    I saw the darkness of the mist
      Encircle thee, O Nose!
Shorn of thy rays thou shott'st a fearful gleam   25
  (The turtle quiver'd with prophetic fright)
Gloomy and sullen thro' the night of steam:—
  So Satan's Nose when Dunstan urg'd to flight,
Glowing from gripe of red-hot pincers dread
Athwart the smokes of Hell disastrous twilight shed!   30

    The Furies to madness my brain devote—
      In robes of ice my body wrap!
    On billowy flames of fire I float,
      Hear ye my entrails how they snap?
Some power unseen forbids my lungs to breathe!   35
  What fire-clad meteors round me whizzing fly!
I vitrify thy torrid zone beneath,
  Proboscis fierce! I am calcined! I die!
Thus, like great Pliny, in Vesuvius' fire,
I perish in the blaze while I the blaze admire.   40
  1789.

TO THE MUSE[1]

    Tho' no bold flights to thee belong;
    And tho' thy lays with conscious fear,
    Shrink from Judgement's eye severe,
    Yet much I thank thee, Spirit of my song!
    For, lovely Muse! thy sweet employ   5
    Exalts my soul, refines my breast,
    Gives each pure pleasure keener zest,
    And softens sorrow into pensive Joy.
    From thee I learn'd the wish to bless,
    From thee to commune with my heart;   10

[1] First published in 1834.

---

20 by fiercer Gill outdone *MS. O.*: more red for shame by fiercer G—ll *MS. O (c).*   22 dark] dank *MS. O, MS. O (c).*   25 rays] beams *MS. O (c).*   30 *MS. O (c)* ends with the third stanza.
To the Muse—Title] Sonnet I. To my Muse *MS. O.*

DESTRUCTION OF THE BASTILE

V

But cease, ye pitying bosoms, cease to bleed!
  Such scenes no more demand the tear humane;
I see, I see! glad Liberty succeed
  With every patriot virtue in her train!
    And mark yon peasant's raptur'd eyes;   25
    Secure he views his harvests rise;
    No fetter vile the mind shall know,
    And Eloquence shall fearless glow.
Yes! Liberty the soul of Life shall reign,
Shall throb in every pulse, shall flow thro' every vein!   30

VI

Shall France alone a Despot spurn?
  Shall she alone, O Freedom, boast thy care?
Lo, round thy standard Belgia's heroes burn,
  Tho' Power's blood-stain'd streamers fire the air,
    And wider yet thy influence spread,   35
    Nor e'er recline thy weary head,
    Till every land from pole to pole
    Shall boast one independent soul!
And still, as erst, let favour'd Britain be
First ever of the first and freest of the free!   40
  ? 1789.

LIFE[1]

As late I journey'd o'er the extensive plain
  Where native Otter sports his scanty stream,
Musing in torpid woe a Sister's pain,
  The glorious prospect woke me from the dream.

At every step it widen'd to my sight—   5
  Wood, Meadow, verdant Hill, and dreary Steep,
Following in quick succession of delight,—
  Till all—at once—did my eye ravish'd sweep!

[1] First published in 1834.

---

32 Shall She, O Freedom, all thy blessings share *MS. O erased.*
  Life—Title] Sonnet II. Written September, 1789 *MS. O*: Sonnet written just after the writer left the Country in Sept. 1789, *aetat.* 15 *MS. O (c).*
  6 dreary] barren *MS. O, MS. O (c).*   8 my ravish'd eye did sweep. *MS. O, MS. O (c).*

May this (I cried) my course through Life portray!
New scenes of Wisdom may each step display,   10
  And Knowledge open as my days advance!
Till what time Death shall pour the undarken'd ray,
  My eye shall dart thro' infinite expanse,
And thought suspended lie in Rapture's blissful trance.
  1789.

PROGRESS OF VICE[1]

[Nemo repente turpissimus]

Deep in the gulph of Vice and Woe
Leaps Man at once with headlong throw?
Him inborn Truth and Virtue guide,
Whose guards are Shame and conscious Pride.
In some gay hour Vice steals into the breast;   5
Perchance she wears some softer Virtue's vest.
By unperceiv'd degrees she tempts to stray,
Till far from Virtue's path she leads the feet away.

Then swift the soul to disenthrall
Will Memory the past recall,   10
  And Fear before the Victim's eyes
  Bid future ills and dangers rise.
But hark! the Voice, the Lyre, their charms combine—
Gay sparkles in the cup the generous Wine—
Th' inebriate dance, the fair frail Nymph inspires,   15
And Virtue vanquish'd—scorn'd—with hasty flight retires.

But soon to tempt the Pleasures cease;
Yet Shame forbids return to peace,
  And stern Necessity will force
  Still to urge on the desperate course.   20

---

[1] First published in 1834, from MS. O.

---

12 Till when death pours at length MS. O (c).
14 While thought suspended lies MS. O: While thought suspended lies in Transport's blissful trance MS. O (c).
Progress of Vice—Title] Progress of Vice. An Ode MS. O. The motto first appears in Boyer's *Liber Aureus*.
1 Vice] Guilt L. A.   3 inborn] innate L. A.   9 Yet still the heart to disenthrall L. A.   12 Bid] Bids MS. O.   ills] woes L. A.
13 But hark! their charms the voice L. A.   15 The mazy dance and frail young Beauty fires L. A.   20 Still on to urge MS. O.

The drear black paths of Vice the wretch must try,
Where Conscience flashes horror on each eye,
Where Hate—where Murder scowl—where starts Affright!
Ah! close the scene—ah! close—for dreadful is the sight.
1790.

MONODY ON THE DEATH OF CHATTERTON[1]

[FIRST VERSION, IN CHRIST'S HOSPITAL BOOK—1790]

> Cold penury repress'd his noble rage,
> And froze the genial current of his soul.

Now prompts the Muse poetic lays,
And high my bosom beats with love of Praise!
But, Chatterton! methinks I hear thy name,
For cold my Fancy grows, and dead each Hope of Fame.

When Want and cold Neglect had chill'd thy soul, 5
Athirst for Death I see thee drench the bowl!
    Thy corpse of many a livid hue
    On the bare ground I view,
Whilst various passions all my mind engage;
    Now is my breast distended with a sigh, 10
    And now a flash of Rage
Darts through the tear, that glistens in my eye.

    Is this the land of liberal Hearts!
    Is this the land, where Genius ne'er in vain
Pour'd forth her soul-enchanting strain? 15
    Ah me! yet Butler 'gainst the bigot foe
    Well-skill'd to aim keen Humour's dart,
    Yet Butler felt Want's poignant sting;
    And Otway, Master of the Tragic art,
    Whom Pity's self had taught to sing, 20

---

[1] First published in 1893. The version in the Ottery Copy-book (*MS. O*) was first published in *P. and D. W.*, 1880, ii. 355*-8*. Three MSS. of the *Monody*, &c. are extant: (1) the Ottery Copy-book [*MS. O*]; (2) Boyer's *Liber Aureus* = the text as printed; (3) the transcription of S. T. C.'s early poems made in 1823 [*MS. O (c)*]. Variants in 1 and 3 are given below.

24 Ah! close the scene, for dreadful *MS. O*.
Monody—Title] A Monody on Chatterton, who poisoned himself at the age of eighteen—written by the author at the age of sixteen. *MS. O (c)*.
Motto] *The motto does not appear in MS. O, but a note is prefixed*: 'This poem has since appeared in print, much altered, whether for the better I doubt. This was, I believe, written before the Author went to College' (J. T. C.).
6 drench] drain *MS. O, MS. O (c)*.   7 corpse] corse *MS. O, MS. O (c)*.
13 Hearts] Heart *MS. O, MS. O (c)*.   20 taught] bade *MS. O, MS. O (c)*.

14 MONODY ON THE DEATH OF CHATTERTON

   Sank beneath a load of Woe;
  This ever can the generous Briton hear,
And starts not in his eye th' indignant Tear?

   Elate of Heart and confident of Fame,
From vales where Avon sports, the Minstrel came,   25
    Gay as the Poet hastes along
    He meditates the future song,
How Ælla battled with his country's foes,
   And whilst Fancy in the air
   Paints him many a vision fair   30
His eyes dance rapture and his bosom glows.
With generous joy he views th' ideal gold:
   He listens to many a Widow's prayers,
   And many an Orphan's thanks he hears;
    He soothes to peace the care-worn breast,   35
    He bids the Debtor's eyes know rest,
   And Liberty and Bliss behold:
And now he punishes the heart of steel,
And her own iron rod he makes Oppression feel.

Fated to heave sad Disappointment's sigh,   40
To feel the Hope now rais'd, and now deprest,
To feel the burnings of an injur'd breast,
   From all thy Fate's deep sorrow keen
   In vain, O Youth, I turn th' affrighted eye;
   For powerful Fancy evernigh   45
The hateful picture forces on my sight.
   There, Death of every dear delight,
   Frowns Poverty of Giant mien!
In vain I seek the charms of youthful grace,
Thy sunken eye, thy haggard cheeks it shews,   50
The quick emotions struggling in the Face
   Faint index of thy mental Throes,
When each strong Passion spurn'd controll,
And not a Friend was nigh to calm thy stormy soul.

Such was the sad and gloomy hour   55
When anguish'd Care of sullen brow
Prepared the Poison's death-cold power.
Already to thy lips was rais'd the bowl,
When filial Pity stood thee by,

---

21 Sank] Sunk *MS. O, MS. O (c)*.   22 This ever] Which can the . . . ever hear *MS. O, MS. O (c)*.   29 whilst] while *MS. O*.   32 ideal] rising *MS. O*.   36 eyes] too *MS. O (c)*.   42 To feel] With all *MS. O*.   43 Lo! from thy dark Fate's sorrow keen *MS. O*.   45 powerful] busy *MS. O*.   50 cheeks it] cheek she *MS. O*: looks she *MS. O (c)*.   51 the] thy *MS. O*.

MONODY ON THE DEATH OF CHATTERTON 15

Thy fixéd eyes she bade thee roll 60
On scenes that well might melt thy soul—
Thy native cot she held to view,
Thy native cot, where Peace ere long
Had listen'd to thy evening song;
Thy sister's shrieks she bade thee hear, 65
And mark thy mother's thrilling tear,
She made thee feel her deep-drawn sigh,
And all her silent agony of Woe.

And from *thy* Fate shall such distress ensue?
Ah! dash the poison'd chalice from thy hand! 70
And thou had'st dash'd it at her soft command;
But that Despair and Indignation rose,
And told again the story of thy Woes,
Told the keen insult of th' unfeeling Heart,
The dread dependence on the low-born mind, 75
Told every Woe, for which thy breast might smart,
Neglect and grinning scorn and Want combin'd—
  Recoiling back, thou sent'st the friend of Pain
To roll a tide of Death thro' every freezing vein.

  O Spirit blest! 80
Whether th' eternal Throne around,
Amidst the blaze of Cherubim,
Thou pourest forth the grateful hymn,
Or, soaring through the blest Domain,
Enraptur'st Angels with thy strain,— 85
Grant me, like thee, the lyre to sound,
Like thee, with fire divine to glow—
But ah! when rage the Waves of Woe,
  Grant me with firmer breast t'oppose their hate,
And soar beyond the storms with upright eye elate![1] 90
1790.

60 eyes] eye *MS. O.*   61 On scenes which *MS. O.*   On] To *MS. O (c).*
64 evening] Evening's *MS. O (c).*   66 thrilling] frequent *MS. O (c).*
67 made] bade *MS. O, MS. O (c).*   78 sent'st] badest *MS. O.*   79
To] Quick.   freezing] icening *MS. O, MS. O (c).*   81 eternal] Eternal's
MS. O: endless *MS. O (c).*   82 Cherubim] Seraphim *MS. O.*   88 But
ah!] Like thee *MS. O, MS. O (c).*
89 To leave behind Contempt, and Want, and State, *MS. O.*
  To leave behind Contempt and Want and Hate *MS. O (c).*
  And seek in other worlds an happier Fate *MS. O, MS. O (c).*

---

[1] [Note to ll. 88–90.] 'Altho' this latter reflection savours of suicide, it will easily meet with the indulgence of the considerate reader when he reflects that the Author's imagination was at that time inflam'd with the idea of his beloved Poet, and perhaps uttered a sentiment which in his cooler moments he would have abhor'd the thought of.' [Signed] J. M. *MS. O (c).*

AN INVOCATION[1]

Sweet Muse! companion of my every hour!
Voice of my Joy! Sure soother of the sigh!
Now plume thy pinions, now exert each power,
And fly to him who owns the candid eye.

And if a smile of Praise thy labour hail   5
(Well shall thy labours then my mind employ)
Fly fleetly back, sweet Muse! and with the tale
O'erspread my Features with a flush of Joy!
1790.

ANNA AND HARLAND[2]

Within these wilds was Anna wont to rove
  While Harland told his love in many a sigh,
But stern on Harland roll'd her brother's eye,
They fought, they fell—her brother and her love!

To Death's dark house did grief-worn Anna haste,   5
  Yet here her pensive ghost delights to stay;
Oft pouring on the winds the broken lay—
And hark, I hear her—'twas the passing blast.

I love to sit upon her tomb's dark grass,
  Then Memory backward rolls Time's shadowy tide;   10
  The tales of other days before me glide:
With eager thought I seize them as they pass;
For fair, tho' faint, the forms of Memory gleam,
Like Heaven's bright beauteous bow reflected in the stream.
  ?1790.

TO THE EVENING STAR[3]

O meek attendant of Sol's setting blaze,
  I hail, sweet star, thy chaste effulgent glow;
On thee full oft with fixéd eye I gaze
  Till I, methinks, all spirit seem to grow.

---

[1] First published in 1893, from an autograph MS.
[2] First printed in the *Cambridge Intelligencer*, Oct. 25, 1794. First collected *P. and D. W.*, 1880, *Supplement*, ii. 359. The text is that of 1880 and 1893, which follow a MS. version.
[3] First published in *P. and D. W.*, 1880, *Supplement*, ii. 359, from *MS. O.*

Anna and Harland—Title] Anna and Henry *C. I.*
1 Along this glade *C. I.*   2 Henry *C. I.*   3 stern] dark *C. I.*   Harland] Henry *C. I.*   5 To her cold grave did woe-worn *C. I.*   6 stay] stray *C. I.*   7 the] a *C. I.*   9 dark] dank *C. I.*   10 Then] There *C. I.*   11 tales] forms *C. I.*   14 Like Heaven's bright bow reflected on the stream. *C. I.*

TO THE EVENING STAR

O first and fairest of the starry choir,
  O loveliest 'mid the daughters of the night,
Must not the maid I love like thee inspire
  Pure joy and *calm* Delight?

Must she not be, as is thy placid sphere
  Serenely brilliant? Whilst to gaze a while
Be all my wish 'mid Fancy's high career
  E'en till she quit this scene of earthly toil;
Then Hope perchance might fondly sigh to join
Her spirit in thy kindred orb, O Star benign!
  ? 1790.

PAIN[1]

Once could the Morn's first beams, the healthful breeze,
All Nature charm, and gay was every hour:—
But ah! not Music's self, nor fragrant bower
Can glad the trembling sense of wan Disease.
Now that the frequent pangs my frame assail,
Now that my sleepless eyes are sunk and dim,
And seas of Pain seem waving through each limb—
Ah what can all Life's gilded scenes avail?
I view the crowd, whom Youth and Health inspire,
Hear the loud laugh, and catch the sportive lay,
Then sigh and think—I too could laugh and play
And gaily sport it on the Muse's lyre,
Ere Tyrant Pain had chas'd away delight,
Ere the wild pulse throbb'd anguish thro' the night!
  ? 1790.

ON A LADY WEEPING[2]

IMITATION FROM THE LATIN OF NICOLAUS ARCHIUS

Lovely gems of radiance meek
Trembling down my Laura's cheek,
As the streamlets silent glide
Thro' the Mead's enamell'd pride,
Pledges sweet of pious woe,
Tears which Friendship taught to flow,

---

[1] First published in 1834. [2] First published in 1893. From *MS. O (c)*.

Pain—Title] Pain, a Sonnet *MS. O*: Sonnet Composed in Sickness *MS*.
3 But ah! nor splendid feasts *MS. O (c)*.   12 Muse's] festive *MS. O, MS. O (c)*.

Sparkling in yon humid light
Love embathes his pinions bright:
There amid the glitt'ring show'r
Smiling sits th' insidious Power;　　　　　　　　10
As some wingéd Warbler oft
When Spring-clouds shed their treasures soft
Joyous tricks his plumes anew,
And flutters in the fost'ring dew.

?1790.

MONODY ON A TEA-KETTLE[1]

O MUSE who sangest late another's pain,
To griefs domestic turn thy coal-black steed!
With slowest steps thy funeral steed must go,
Nodding his head in all the pomp of woe:
Wide scatter round each dark and deadly weed,　　　5
And let the melancholy dirge complain,
(Whilst Bats shall shriek and Dogs shall howling run)
The tea-kettle is spoilt and Coleridge is undone!

Your cheerful songs, ye unseen crickets, cease!
Let songs of grief your alter'd minds engage!　　　　10
For he who sang responsive to your lay,
What time the joyous bubbles 'gan to play,
The *sooty swain* has felt the fire's fierce rage;—
Yes, he is gone, and all my woes increase;
I heard the water issuing from the wound—　　　　15
No more the Tea shall pour its fragrant steams around!

O Goddess best belov'd! Delightful Tea!
With thee compar'd what yields the madd'ning Vine?
Sweet power! who know'st to spread the calm delight,
And the pure joy prolong to midmost night!　　　　20
Ah! must I all thy varied sweets resign?
Enfolded close in grief thy form I see;
No more wilt thou extend thy willing arms,
Receive the *fervent Jove*, and yield him all thy charms!

[1] First published in 1834, from *MS. O*. The text of 1893 follows an autograph MS. in the Editor's possession.

Monody] 1 Muse that late sang another's poignant pain *MS. S. T. C.*
3 In slowest steps the funeral steeds shall go *MS. S. T. C.*　　　4 Nodding their heads *MS. S. T. C.*　　　5 each deadly weed *MS. S. T. C.*　　　8 The] His *MS. S. T. C.*　　　9 songs] song *MS. S. T. C.*　　　15 issuing] hissing *MS. S. T. C.*　　　16 pour] throw *MS. S. T. C.*　　　steams] steam *MS. S. T. C.*
18 thee] whom *MS. S. T. C.*　　　Vine] Wine *MS. S. T. C.*　　　19 who] that *MS. S. T. C.*　　　21 various charms *MS. S. T. C.*　　　23 extend] expand *MS. S. T. C.*

MONODY ON A TEA-KETTLE

How sink the mighty low by Fate opprest!— 25
Perhaps, O Kettle! thou by scornful toe
Rude urg'd t' ignoble place with plaintive din,
May'st rust obscure midst heaps of vulgar tin;—
As if no joy had ever seiz'd my breast
When from thy spout the streams did arching fly,— 30
As if, infus'd, thou ne'er hadst known t' inspire
All the warm raptures of poetic fire!

But hark! or do I fancy the glad voice—
'What tho' the swain did wondrous charms disclose—
(Not such did Memnon's sister sable drest) 35
Take these bright arms with royal face imprest,
A better Kettle shall thy soul rejoice,
And with Oblivion's wings o'erspread thy woes!'
Thus Fairy Hope can soothe distress and toil;
On empty Trivets she bids fancied Kettles boil! 40

1790.

GENEVIEVE[1]

MAID of my Love, sweet Genevieve!
In Beauty's light you glide along:

---

[1] First published in the *Cambridge Intelligencer* for Nov. 1, 1794: included in the editions of 1796, 1803, 1828, 1829, and 1834. Three MSS. are extant; (1) an autograph in a copy-book made for the family [*MS. O*]; (2) an autograph in a copy-book presented to Mrs. Estlin [*MS. E*]; and (3) a transcript included in a copy-book presented to Sara Coleridge in 1823 [*MS. O (c)*]. In an unpublished letter dated Dec. 18, 1807, Coleridge invokes the aid of Richard ['Conservation'] Sharp on behalf of a 'Mrs. Brewman, who was elected a nurse to one of the wards of Christ's Hospital at the time that I was a boy there'. He says elsewhere that he spent full half the time from seventeen to eighteen in the sick ward of Christ's Hospital. It is doubtless to this period, 1789–90, that *Pain* and *Genevieve*, which, according to a Christ's Hospital tradition, were inspired by his 'Nurse's Daughter', must be assigned.

'This little poem was written when the Author was a boy'—*Note 1796, 1803*.

---

25 How low the mighty sink *MS. S. T. C.*   29 seiz'd] chear'd *MS. S. T. C.*
30–1   When from thy spout the stream did arching flow
    As if, inspir'd *MS. S. T. C.*
33 the glad] *Georgian MS. S. T. C.*   34 the swain] its form *MS. S. T. C.*
35 *Note.* A parenthetical reflection of the Author's. *MS. O.*   38 wings] wing *MS. S. T. C.*

Genevieve—Title] Sonnet iii. *MS. O*: Ode *MS. E*: A Sonnet *MS. O (c)*: Effusion xvii. *1796.*   The heading, *Genevieve*, first appears in 1803.

2 Thou glid'st along [so, too, in ll. 3, 4, 5, 7, 8, 13, 14] *MS. O, MS. E, MS. O (c), C. I.*

Your eye is like the Star of Eve,
And sweet your voice, as Seraph's song.
Yet not your heavenly beauty gives 5
This heart with Passion soft to glow:
Within your soul a voice there lives!
It bids you hear the tale of Woe.
When sinking low the sufferer wan
Beholds no hand outstretch'd to save, 10
Fair, as the bosom of the Swan
That rises graceful o'er the wave,
I've seen your breast with pity heave,
And *therefore* love I you, sweet Genevieve!
1789–90.

ON RECEIVING AN ACCOUNT THAT HIS ONLY SISTER'S DEATH WAS INEVITABLE[1]

THE tear which mourn'd a brother's fate scarce dry—
Pain after pain, and woe succeeding woe—
Is my heart destin'd for another blow?
O my sweet sister! and must thou too die?
Ah! how has Disappointment pour'd the tear 5
O'er infant Hope destroy'd by early frost!
How are ye gone, whom most my soul held dear!
Scarce had I lov'd you ere I mourn'd you lost;
Say, is this hollow eye, this heartless pain,
Fated to rove thro' Life's wide cheerless plain— 10
Nor father, brother, sister meet its ken—
My woes, my joys unshared! Ah! long ere then
On me thy icy dart, stern Death, be prov'd;—
Better to die, than live and not be lov'd!
1791.

[1] First published in 1834. The 'brother' (line 1) was Luke Herman Coleridge who died at Thorverton in 1790. Anne Coleridge, the poet's sister (the only daughter of his father's second marriage), died in March 1791.

4 Thy voice is lovely as the *MS. E*: Thy voice is soft, &c. *MS. O (c)*, *C. I.* 8 It bids thee hear the tearful plaint of woe *MS. E.* 10 no... save] no friendly hand that saves *MS. E.* outstretch'd] stretcht out *MS. O, MS. O (c), C. I.* 12 the wave] quick-rolling waves *MS. E.*
On receiving, &c.—Title] Sonnet v. *MS. O.*
1 tear] tears *MS. O.* 4 O my sweet sister must *thou* die *MS. O.* 7 gone] flown *MS. O.* 10 Fated] Destin'd *MS. O.* 11 father] Mother *MS. O.*

ON SEEING A YOUTH AFFECTIONATELY WELCOMED BY A SISTER[1]

I too a sister had! too cruel Death!
  How sad Remembrance bids my bosom heave!
Tranquil her soul, as sleeping Infant's breath;
  Meek were her manners as a vernal Eve.
Knowledge, that frequent lifts the bloated mind,   5
  Gave her the treasure of a lowly breast,
And Wit to venom'd Malice oft assign'd,
  Dwelt in her bosom in a Turtle's nest.
Cease, busy Memory! cease to urge the dart;
  Nor on my soul her love to me impress!   10
For oh I mourn in anguish—and my heart
  Feels the keen pang, th' unutterable distress.
Yet wherefore grieve I that her sorrows cease,
For Life was misery, and the Grave is Peace!
1791.

A MATHEMATICAL PROBLEM[2]

If Pegasus will let *thee* only ride him,
Spurning my clumsy efforts to o'erstride him,
Some fresh expedient the Muse will try,
And walk on stilts, although she cannot fly.

To the Rev. George Coleridge

Dear Brother,

I have often been surprised that Mathematics, the quintessence of Truth, should have found admirers so few and so languid. Frequent consideration and minute scrutiny have at length unravelled the cause; viz. that though Reason is feasted, Imagination is starved; whilst Reason is luxuriating in its proper Paradise, Imagination is wearily travelling on a dreary desert. To assist Reason by the stimulus of Imagination is the design of the following production. In the execution of it much may be objectionable. The verse (particularly in the introduction of the ode) may be accused of unwarrantable liberties, but they are liberties equally homogeneal with the

---

[1] First published in 1834.
[2] First published in 1834 without a title, but tabulated as 'Mathematical Problem' in 'Contents' 1 [p. xi].

A Mathematical Problem—Title] Prospectus and Specimen of a Translation of Euclid in a series of Pindaric Odes, communicated in a letter of the author to his Brother Rev. G. Coleridge [March 17, 1791]. *MS. O* (*c*).

exactness of Mathematical disquisition, and the boldness of Pindaric daring. I have three strong champions to defend me against the attacks of Criticism: the Novelty, the Difficulty, and the Utility of the work. I may justly plume myself that I first have drawn the nymph Mathesis from the visionary caves of abstracted idea, and caused her to unite with Harmony. The first-born of this Union I now present to you; with interested motives indeed—as I expect to receive in return the more valuable offspring of your Muse.

Thine ever,
S. T. C.

[CHRIST'S HOSPITAL], *March* 31, 1791.

This is now—this was erst,
Proposition the first—and Problem the first.

I

On a given finite line
Which must no way incline;
To describe an equi—
—lateral Tri—
—A, N, G, L, E.[1]
Now let A. B.
Be the given line
Which must no way incline;
The great Mathematician
Makes this Requisition,
That we describe an Equi—
—lateral Tri—
—angle on it:
Aid us, Reason—aid us, Wit!

II

From the centre A. at the distance A. B.
Describe the circle B. C. D.
At the distance B. A. from B. the centre
The round A. C. E. to describe boldly venture.[2]
(Third postulate see.)
And from the point C.
In which the circles make a pother
Cutting and slashing one another,
Bid the straight lines a journeying go.

---

[1] *Poetice* for Angle. *Letter*, 1791.   [2] Delendus 'fere'. *Letter*, 1791.

5 A E N G E E E L E. *Letter*, 1791.

A MATHEMATICAL PROBLEM

C. A. C. B. those lines will show.
    To the points, which by A. B. are reckon'd,
And postulate the second
For Authority ye know.
    A. B. C.
    Triumphant shall be
    An Equilateral Triangle,
Not Peter Pindar carp, nor Zoilus can wrangle.

III

Because the point A. is the centre
    Of the circular B. C. D.
And because the point B. is the centre
    Of the circular A. C. E.
A. C. to A. B. and B. C. to B. A.
Harmoniously equal for ever must stay;
    Then C. A. and B. C.
    Both extend the kind hand
    To the basis, A. B.
Unambitiously join'd in Equality's Band.
But to the same powers, when two powers are equal,
    My mind forbodes the sequel;
My mind does some celestial impulse teach,
    And equalises each to each.
Thus C. A. with B. C. strikes the same sure alliance,
That C. A. and B. C. had with A. B. before;
    And in mutual affiance
    None attempting to soar
    Above another,
    The unanimous three
C. A. and B. C. and A. B.
All are equal, each to his brother,
Preserving the balance of power so true:
Ah! the like would the proud Autocratrix[1] do!
At taxes impending not Britain would tremble,
Nor Prussia struggle her fear to dissemble;
    Nor the Mah'met-sprung Wight
    The great Mussulman
    Would stain his Divan
With Urine the soft-flowing daughter of Fright.

---

[1] Empress of Russia.

36 A C to C B and C B to C A. *Letter, 1791, MS. O (c).*   48 affiance] alliance *Letter, 1791.*   55 Autocratrix] Autocratorix *MS. O (c).*

IV

But rein your stallion in, too daring Nine!
Should Empires bloat the scientific line?
Or with dishevell'd hair all madly do ye run
For transport that your task is done?   65
  For done it is—the cause is tried!
  And Proposition, gentle Maid,
Who soothly ask'd stern Demonstration's aid,
  Has proved her right, and A. B. C.
    Of Angles three   70
  Is shown to be of equal side;
And now our weary steed to rest in fine,
'Tis rais'd upon A. B. the straight, the given line.

1791.

HONOUR[1]

O, curas hominum! O, quantum est in rebus inane!

The fervid Sun had more than halv'd the day,
When gloomy on his couch Philedon lay;
His feeble frame consumptive as his purse,
His aching head did wine and women curse;
His fortune ruin'd and his wealth decay'd,   5
Clamorous his duns, his gaming debts unpaid,
The youth indignant seiz'd his tailor's bill,
And on its back thus wrote with moral quill:
'Various as colours in the rainbow shown,
Or similar in emptiness alone,   10
How false, how vain are Man's pursuits below!
Wealth, Honour, Pleasure—what can ye bestow?
Yet see, how high and low, and young and old
Pursue the all-delusive power of Gold.
Fond man! should all Peru thy empire own,   15
For thee tho' all Golconda's jewels shone,
What greater bliss could all this wealth supply?
What, but to eat and drink and sleep and die?
Go, tempt the stormy sea, the burning soil—
Go, waste the night in thought, the day in toil,   20

---

[1] First published in 1834: included in *P. and D. W.*, 1877-80, and in 1893.

Honour] No title, but motto as above *MS. O.*: Philedon, *Eds. 1877, 1893*.

HONOUR

Dark frowns the rock, and fierce the tempests rave—
Thy ingots go the unconscious deep to pave!
Or thunder at thy door the midnight train,
Or Death shall knock that never knocks in vain.
Next Honour's sons come bustling on amain; 25
I laugh with pity at the idle train.
Infirm of soul! who think'st to lift thy name
Upon the waxen wings of human fame,—
Who for a sound, articulated breath—
Gazest undaunted in the face of death! 30
What art thou but a Meteor's glaring light—
Blazing a moment and then sunk in night?
Caprice which rais'd thee high shall hurl thee low,
Or Envy blast the laurels on thy brow.
To such poor joys could ancient Honour lead 35
When empty fame was toiling Merit's meed;
To Modern Honour other lays belong;
Profuse of joy and Lord of right and wrong,
Honour can game, drink, riot in the stew,
Cut a friend's throat;—what cannot Honour do? 40
Ah me!—the storm within can Honour still
For Julio's death, whom Honour made me kill?
Or will this lordly Honour tell the way
To pay those debts, which Honour makes me pay?
Or if with pistol and terrific threats 45
I make some traveller pay my Honour's debts,
A medicine for this wound can Honour give?
Ah, no! my Honour dies to make my Honour live.
But see! young Pleasure, and her train advance,
And joy and laughter wake the inebriate dance; 50
Around my neck she throws her fair white arms,
I meet her loves, and madden at her charms.
For the gay grape can joys celestial move,
And what so sweet below as Woman's love?
With such high transport every moment flies, 55
I curse Experience that he makes me wise;
For at his frown the dear deliriums flew,
And the changed scene now wears a gloomy hue.
A hideous hag th' Enchantress Pleasure seems,
And all her joys appear but feverous dreams. 60

34 Or] And *MS. O.*
43-4 Or will my Honour kindly tell the way
   To pay the debts *MS. O.*
60 feverous] feverish *MS. O.*

The vain resolve still broken and still made,
Disease and loathing and remorse invade;
The charm is vanish'd and the bubble's broke,—
A slave to pleasure is a slave to smoke!'
   Such lays repentant did the Muse supply; 65
When as the Sun was hastening down the sky,
In glittering state twice fifty guineas come,—
His Mother's plate antique had rais'd the sum.
Forth leap'd Philedon of new life possest:— 69
'Twas Brookes's all till two,—'twas Hackett's all the rest!
  1791.

ON IMITATION[1]

All are not born to soar—and ah! how few
In tracks where Wisdom leads their paths pursue!
Contagious when to wit or wealth allied,
Folly and Vice diffuse their venom wide.
On Folly every fool his talent tries; 5
It asks some toil to imitate the wise;
Tho' few like Fox can speak—like Pitt can think—
Yet all like Fox can game—like Pitt can drink.
?1791.

INSIDE THE COACH[2]

'Tis hard on Bagshot Heath to try
Unclos'd to keep the weary eye;
But ah! Oblivion's nod to get
In rattling coach is harder yet.
Slumbrous God of half-shut eye! 5
Who lovest with limbs supine to lie;
Soother sweet of toil and care
Listen, listen to my prayer;
And to thy votary dispense
Thy soporific influence! 10

---

[1] First published in 1834. In MS. O lines 3, 4 follow lines 7, 8 of the text.   [2] First published in 1834.

70 Brookes's, a famous gaming-house in Fleet Street. Hackett's, a brothel under the Covent Garden Piazza. *Note MS. O.*

Inside the Coach—Title] Ode to sleep. Travelling in the Exeter Coach with three other passengers over Bagshot Heath, after some vain endeavours to compose myself I composed this Ode—August 17, 1791. *MS. O.*

What tho' around thy drowsy head
The seven-fold cap of night be spread,
Yet lift that drowsy head awhile
And yawn propitiously a smile;
In drizzly rains poppean dews 15
O'er the tired inmates of the Coach diffuse;
And when thou'st charm'd our eyes to rest,
Pillowing the chin upon the breast,
Bid many a dream from thy dominions
Wave its various-painted pinions, 20
Till ere the splendid visions close
We snore quartettes in ecstasy of nose.
While thus we urge our airy course,
O may no jolt's electric force
Our fancies from their steeds unhorse, 25
And call us from thy fairy reign
To dreary Bagshot Heath again!

1791.

DEVONSHIRE ROADS[1]

The indignant Bard composed this furious ode,
As tired he dragg'd his way thro' Plimtree road![2]
    Crusted with filth and stuck in mire
    Dull sounds the Bard's bemudded lyre;
Nathless Revenge and Ire the Poet goad 5
To pour his imprecations on the road.

Curst road! whose execrable way
Was darkly shadow'd out in Milton's lay,
When the sad fiends thro' Hell's sulphureous roads
Took the first survey of their new abodes; 10
Or when the fall'n Archangel fierce
Dar'd through the realms of Night to pierce,
What time the Bloodhound lur'd by Human scent
Thro' all Confusion's quagmires floundering went.

Nor cheering pipe, nor Bird's shrill note 15
Around thy dreary paths shall float;
Their boding songs shall scritch-owls pour
To fright the guilty shepherds sore,

---

[1] First published in 1834.
[2] Plymtree Road, August 18, 1791. *Note, MS. O.* [Plimtree is about 3 miles N. of Ottery St. Mary. S. T. C. must have left the mail coach at Cullompton to make his way home on foot.]

---

12 Vulgo yclept night-cap *MS. O.*   13 that] thy *MS. O.*
Devonshire Roads] No title *MS. O.*

28 DEVONSHIRE ROADS

  Led by the wandering fires astray
  Thro' the dank horrors of thy way! 20
  While they their mud-lost sandals hunt
  May all the curses, which they grunt
   In raging moan like goaded hog,
   Alight upon thee, damnéd Bog!
1791.

MUSIC[1]

Hence, soul-dissolving Harmony
 That lead'st th' oblivious soul astray—
  Though thou sphere-descended be—
   Hence away!—
Thou mightier Goddess, thou demand'st my lay, 5
 Born when earth was seiz'd with cholic;
Or as more sapient sages say,
 What time the Legion diabolic
  Compell'd their beings to enshrine
  In bodies vile of herded swine, 10
  Precipitate adown the steep
  With hideous rout were plunging in the deep,
And hog and devil mingling grunt and yell
 Seiz'd on the ear with horrible obtrusion;—
Then if aright old legendaries tell, 15
 Wert thou begot by Discord on Confusion!

What though no name's sonorous power
Was given thee at thy natal hour!—
Yet oft I feel thy sacred might,
While concords wing their distant flight. 20
 Such Power inspires thy holy son
  Sable clerk of Tiverton!
And oft where Otter sports his stream,
I hear thy banded offspring scream.
Thou Goddess! thou inspir'st each throat; 25
'Tis thou who pour'st the scritch-owl note!
Transported hear'st thy children all
Scrape and blow and squeak and squall;
 And while old Otter's steeple rings,
 Clappest hoarse thy raven wings! 30
1791.

---

[1] First published in 1834.

Music—Title] Ode on the Ottery and Tiverton Church Music *MS. O.*

SONNET[1]

ON QUITTING SCHOOL FOR COLLEGE

FAREWELL parental scenes! a sad farewell!
To you my grateful heart still fondly clings,
Tho' fluttering round on Fancy's burnish'd wings
Her tales of future Joy Hope loves to tell.
Adieu, adieu! ye much-lov'd cloisters pale! 5
Ah! would those happy days return again,
When 'neath your arches, free from every stain,
I heard of guilt and wonder'd at the tale!
Dear haunts! where oft my simple lays I sang,
Listening meanwhile the echoings of my feet, 10
Lingering I quit you, with as great a pang,
As when erewhile, my weeping childhood, torn
By early sorrow from my native seat,
Mingled its tears with hers—my widow'd Parent lorn.
1791.

ABSENCE[2]

A FAREWELL ODE ON QUITTING SCHOOL FOR JESUS COLLEGE, CAMBRIDGE

WHERE graced with many a classic spoil
CAM rolls his reverend stream along,
I haste to urge the learnéd toil
That sternly chides my love-lorn song:
Ah me! too mindful of the days 5
Illumed by Passion's orient rays,
When Peace, and Cheerfulness and Health
Enriched me with the best of wealth.
Ah fair Delights! that o'er my soul
On Memory's wing, like shadows fly! 10
Ah Flowers! which Joy from Eden stole
While Innocence stood smiling by!—
But cease, fond Heart! this bootless moan:
Those Hours on rapid Pinions flown
Shall yet return, by Absence crown'd, 15
And scatter livelier roses round.

---

[1] First published in 1834.
[2] First published in *Cambridge Intelligencer*, October 11, 1794: included in 1796, 1803, 1828, 1829, and 1834.

Sonnet—Title] Sonnet on the Same (i. e. 'Absence, A Farewell Ode,' &c.) *1834.*
Sonnet—Title] Sonnet on Quitting Christ's Hospital *MS. O.* Absence, A Farewell Ode *1796, 1803.*

ABSENCE

The Sun who ne'er remits his fires
On heedless eyes may pour the day:
The Moon, that oft from Heaven retires,
Endears her renovated ray.   20
What though she leave the sky unblest
To mourn awhile in murky vest?
When she relumes her lovely light,
We bless the Wanderer of the Night.

1791.

HAPPINESS[1]

On wide or narrow scale shall Man
Most happily describe Life's plan?
Say shall he bloom and wither there,
Where first his infant buds appear;
Or upwards dart with soaring force,   5
And tempt some more ambitious course?
  Obedient now to Hope's command
I bid each humble wish expand,
And fair and bright Life's prospects seem,
While Hope displays her cheering beam,   10
And Fancy's vivid colourings stream,
While Emulation stands me nigh
The Goddess of the eager eye.
  With foot advanc'd and anxious heart
Now for the fancied goal I start:—   15
Ah! why will Reason intervene
Me and my promis'd joys between!
She stops my course, she chains my speed,
While thus her forceful words proceed:—
'Ah! listen, Youth, ere yet too late,   20
What evils on thy course may wait!
To bow the head, to bend the knee,
A minion of Servility,
At low Pride's frequent frowns to sigh,

---

[1] First published in 1834. The poem was sent to George Coleridge in a letter dated June 22, 1791. An adapted version of ll. 80-105 was sent to Southey, July 13, 1794.

Happiness—Title] Upon the Author's leaving school and entering into Life. *MS. O (c)*.
6 tempt] dare *MS. O, MS. O (c)*.   10 While] When *MS. O, MS. O (c)*. *Between* 11–13 How pants my breast before my eyes
          While Honour waves her radiant prize.
                And Emulation, &c. *MS. O, MS. O (c)*.
22 To bend the head, to bow *MS. O (c)*.   24 frowns] frown *MS. O, MS. O (c)*.

HAPPINESS

And watch the glance in Folly's eye; 25
To toil intense, yet toil in vain,
And feel with what a hollow pain
Pale Disappointment hangs her head
O'er darling Expectation dead!
  'The scene is changed and Fortune's gale 30
Shall belly out each prosperous sail.
Yet sudden wealth full well I know
Did never happiness bestow.
That wealth to which we were not born
Dooms us to sorrow or to scorn. 35
Behold yon flock which long had trod
O'er the short grass of Devon's sod,
To Lincoln's rank rich meads transferr'd,
And in their fate thy own be fear'd;
Through every limb contagions fly, 40
Deform'd and choked they burst and die.
  'When Luxury opens wide her arms,
And smiling wooes thee to those charms,
Whose fascination thousands own,
Shall thy brows wear the stoic frown? 45
And when her goblet she extends
Which maddening myriads press around,
What power divine thy soul befriends
That thou should'st dash it to the ground?—
No, thou shalt drink, and thou shalt know 50
Her transient bliss, her lasting woe,
Her maniac joys, that know no measure,
And Riot rude and painted Pleasure;—
Till (sad reverse!) the Enchantress vile
To frowns converts her magic smile; 55
Her train impatient to destroy,
Observe her frown with gloomy joy;
On thee with harpy fangs they seize
The hideous offspring of Disease,
Swoln Dropsy ignorant of Rest, 60
And Fever garb'd in scarlet vest,
Consumption driving the quick hearse,
And Gout that howls the frequent curse,
With Apoplex of heavy head
That surely aims his dart of lead. 65

---

25 in] of *MS. O (c)*.   41 Deformed, choaked *MS. O, MS. O (c)*.   45 brows] brow *MS. O, MS. O (c)*.   55 magic] wonted *MS. O, MS. O (c)*.   57 her frown] the fiend *MS. O, MS. O (c)*.

HAPPINESS

'But say Life's joys unmix'd were given
To thee some favourite of Heaven:
Within, without, tho' all were health—
Yet what e'en thus are Fame, Power, Wealth,
But sounds that variously express,   70
What's thine already—Happiness!
'Tis thine the converse deep to hold
With all the famous sons of old;
And thine the happy waking dream
While Hope pursues some favourite theme,   75
As oft when Night o'er Heaven is spread,
Round this maternal seat you tread,
Where far from splendour, far from riot,
In silence wrapt sleeps careless Quiet.
'Tis thine with Fancy oft to talk,   80
And thine the peaceful evening walk;
And what to thee the sweetest are—
The setting sun, the Evening Star—
The tints, which live along the sky,
And Moon that meets thy raptur'd eye,   85
Where oft the tear shall grateful start,
Dear silent pleasures of the Heart!
Ah! Being blest, for Heaven shall lend
To share thy simple joys a friend!
Ah! doubly blest, if Love supply   90
His influence to complete thy joy,
If chance some lovely maid thou find
To read thy visage in thy mind.

---

68 Without, within *MS. O, MS. O (c).*   76 is] has *MS. O, MS. O (c).*
77 *Note*—Christ's Hospital *MS. O*: Ottery S. Mary in Devonshire *MS. O (c).*
80-1   'Tis thine with faery forms to talk
        And thine the philosophic walk. *Letter to Southey, 1794.*
84 which] that *MS. O, MS. O (c), Letter, 1794.*   85 And] The *Letter, 1794.*
86 Where grateful oft the big drops start. *Letter, 1794.* shall] does
MS. O (c).
90-3   Ah! doubly blest, if Love supply
        Lustre to this now heavy eye,
        And with unwonted Spirit grace
        That fat* vacuity of face.
        Or if e'en Love, the mighty Love
        Shall find this change his power above;
        Some lovely maid perchance thou'lt find
        To read thy visage in thy mind. *MS. O, MS. O (c).*

---

* The Author was at this time, *aetat.* 17, remarkable for a plump face. *MS. O (c).*

HAPPINESS

  'One blessing more demands thy care:—
Once more to Heaven address the prayer: 95
For humble independence pray
The guardian genius of thy way;
Whom (sages say) in days of yore
Meek Competence to Wisdom bore,
 So shall thy little vessel glide   100
With a fair breeze adown the tide,
And Hope, if e'er thou 'ginst to sorrow,
Remind thee of some fair to-morrow,
Till Death shall close thy tranquil eye
 While Faith proclaims "Thou shalt not die!"'   105
1791.

A WISH[1]

WRITTEN IN JESUS WOOD, FEB. 10, 1792

Lo! through the dusky silence of the groves,
Thro' vales irriguous, and thro' green retreats,
With languid murmur creeps the placid stream
 And works its secret way.

Awhile meand'ring round its native fields   5
It rolls the playful wave and winds its flight:
Then downward flowing with awaken'd speed
 Embosoms in the Deep!

Thus thro' its silent tenor may my Life
Smooth its meek stream by sordid wealth unclogg'd,   10
Alike unconscious of forensic storms,
 And Glory's blood-stain'd palm!

And when dark Age shall close Life's little day,
Satiate of sport, and weary of its toils,
E'en thus may slumbrous Death my decent limbs   15
 Compose with icy hand!
1792.

AN ODE IN THE MANNER OF ANACREON[2]

 As late, in wreaths, gay flowers I bound,
 Beneath some roses Love I found:
 And by his little frolic pinion
 As quick as thought I seiz'd the minion,

---

[1] First published in 1893, from *MS. Letter to Mary Evans*, Feb. 13 [1792].
[2] First published in 1893, from *MS. Letter*, Feb. 13 [1792].

96-7   But if thou pour one votive lay
    For humble, &c. *Letter, 1794.*   96 *Not in Letter.*
101 adown Life's tide *MS. O, MS. O (c).*   102-3 *Not in Letter, 1794.*

Then in my cup the prisoner threw,   5
And drank him in its sparkling dew:
And sure I feel my angry guest
Fluttering *his wings* within my breast!
1792.

TO DISAPPOINTMENT[1]

Hence! thou fiend of gloomy sway,
That lov'st on withering blast to ride
O'er fond Illusion's air-built pride.
   Sullen Spirit! Hence! Away!

Where Avarice lurks in sordid cell,   5
Or mad Ambition builds the dream,
Or Pleasure plots th' unholy scheme
   There with Guilt and Folly dwell!

But oh! when Hope on Wisdom's wing
Prophetic whispers pure delight,   10
Be distant far thy cank'rous blight,
   Demon of envenom'd sting.

Then haste thee, Nymph of balmy gales!
Thy poet's prayer, sweet May! attend!
Oh! place my parent and my friend   15
   'Mid her lovely native vales.

Peace, that lists the woodlark's strains,
Health, that breathes divinest treasures,
Laughing Hours, and Social Pleasures
   Wait my friend in Cambria's plains.   20

Affection there with mingled ray
Shall pour at once the raptures high
Of filial and maternal Joy;
   Haste thee then, delightful May!

And oh! may Spring's fair flowerets fade,   25
May Summer cease her limbs to lave
In cooling stream, may Autumn grave
   Yellow o'er the corn-cloath'd glade;

Ere, from sweet retirement torn,
She seek again the crowded mart: 30
Nor thou, my selfish, selfish heart
   Dare her slow return to mourn!
1792.

---

[1] First published in *Letters of Samuel Taylor Coleridge*, 1895, i. 28, 29. The lines were included in a letter to Mrs. Evans, dated February 13, 1792.

A FRAGMENT FOUND IN A LECTURE-ROOM [1]

Where deep in mud Cam rolls his slumbrous stream,
And bog and desolation reign supreme;
Where all Boeotia clouds the misty brain,
The owl Mathesis pipes her loathsome strain.
Far, far aloof the frighted Muses fly,   5
Indignant Genius scowls and passes by:
The frolic Pleasures start amid their dance,
And Wit congeal'd stands fix'd in wintry trance.
But to the sounds with duteous haste repair
Cold Industry, and wary-footed Care;   10
And Dulness, dosing on a couch of lead,
Pleas'd with the song uplifts her heavy head,
The sympathetic numbers lists awhile,
Then yawns propitiously a frosty smile. . . .
[Caetera desunt.]

1792.

ODE [2]

Ye Gales, that of the Lark's repose
The impatient Silence break,
To yon poor Pilgrim's wearying Woes
Your gentle Comfort speak!
He heard the midnight whirlwind die,   5
He saw the sun-awaken'd Sky
Resume its slowly-purpling Blue:
And ah! he sigh'd—that I might find
The cloudless Azure of the Mind
And Fortune's brightning Hue!   10

Where'er in waving Foliage hid
The Bird's gay Charm ascends,
Or by the fretful current chid
Some giant Rock impends—
There let the lonely Cares respire   15
As small airs thrill the mourning Lyre

---

[1] First published in *Letters of Samuel Taylor Coleridge*, 1895, i. 44. The lines were sent in a letter to the Rev. G. Coleridge, dated April [1792].

[2] These lines, first published in the *Watchman* (No. IV, March 25, 1796, signed G. A. U. N. T.), were included in the volume of MS. Poems presented to Mrs. Estlin in April, 1795. They were never claimed by Coleridge or assigned to him, and are now collected for the first time.

Fragment. 1 slumbrous] reverend *MS. E.*   5 frighted] affrighted *MS. E.*   9 to] at *MS. E.*   12 Sooth'd with the song uprears *MS. E.*   13 The] Its *MS. E.*

Ode—Title] A Morning Effusion *Watchman.*   4 Comfort] solace *W.*   13 fretful] fretting *MS. E*   16 mourning] lonely *W.*

And teach the Soul her native Calm;
While Passion with a languid Eye
Hangs o'er the fall of Harmony
And drinks the sacred Balm.

Slow as the fragrant whisper creeps
   Along the lilied Vale,
The alter'd Eye of Conquest weeps,
   And ruthless War grows pale
Relenting that his Heart forsook
Soft Concord of auspicious Look,
And Love, and social Poverty;
The Family of tender Fears,
The Sigh, that saddens and endears,
   And Cares, that sweeten Joy.

Then cease, thy frantic Tumults cease,
   Ambition, Sire of War!
Nor o'er the mangled Corse of Peace
   Urge on thy scythéd Car.
And oh! that Reason's voice might swell
With whisper'd Airs and holy Spell
   To rouse thy gentler Sense,
As bending o'er the chilly bloom
The Morning wakes its soft Perfume
   With breezy Influence.

1792.

A LOVER'S COMPLAINT TO HIS MISTRESS[1]

WHO DESERTED HIM IN QUEST OF A MORE WEALTHY HUSBAND IN THE EAST INDIES

The dubious light sad glimmers o'er the sky:
'Tis silence all. By lonely anguish torn,
With wandering feet to gloomy groves I fly,
And wakeful Love still tracks my course forlorn.

And will you, cruel Julia! will you go?
And trust you to the Ocean's dark dismay?
Shall the wide wat'ry world between us flow?
And winds unpitying snatch my Hopes away?

---

[1] First published in 1893, from *MS. Letter*, Feb. 13 [1792].

17 her] its *W*.   18 languid] waning *W*.   19 Hangs] Bends *W*.
21–2   As slow the whisper'd measure creeps
        Along the steaming Vale. *W*.
24 grows] turns *W*.   31 Tumults] outrage *W*.   32 Thou scepter'd Demon, War *W*.   35 oh] ah *W*.   38 chilly] flowrets' *W*.

A LOVER'S COMPLAINT TO HIS MISTRESS 37

Thus could you sport with my too easy heart?
Yet tremble, lest not unaveng'd I grieve! 10
The winds may learn your own delusive art,
And faithless Ocean smile—but to deceive!
1792.

WITH FIELDING'S 'AMELIA'[1]

VIRTUES and Woes alike too great for man
  In the soft tale oft claim the useless sigh;
For vain the attempt to realise the plan,
  On Folly's wings must Imitation fly.
With other aim has Fielding here display'd 5
  Each social duty and each social care;
With just yet vivid colouring portray'd
  What every wife should be, what many are.
And sure the Parent[2] of a race so sweet
  With double pleasure on the page shall dwell, 10
Each scene with sympathizing breast shall meet,
  While Reason still with smiles delights to tell
Maternal hope, that her loved progeny
In all but sorrows shall Amelias be!
? 1792.

WRITTEN AFTER A WALK BEFORE SUPPER[3]

Tho' much averse, dear Jack, to flicker,
To find a likeness for friend V—ker,
I've made thro' Earth, and Air, and Sea,
A Voyage of Discovery!
And let me add (to ward off strife) 5
For V—ker and for V—ker's Wife—
She large and round beyond belief,
A superfluity of beef!

---

[1] First published in 1834.
[2] It is probable that the recipient of the *Amelia* was the mother of Coleridge's first love, Mary Evans.
[3] First published in 1796, and secondly in *P. and D. W.*, 1877-80. These lines, described as 'A Simile', were sent in a letter to the Rev. George Coleridge, dated August 9 [1792]. The Rev. Fulwood Smerdon, the 'Vicar' of the original MS., succeeded the Rev. John Coleridge as vicar of Ottery St. Mary in 1781. He was the 'Edmund' of 'Lines to a Friend', &c., *vide post*, pp. 74, 75.

With Fielding's 'Amelia'—Title] Sent to Mrs. —— with an *Amelia. MS. O.*
10 double] doubled *MS. O.*
Written after, &c.—Title] Epistle iii. Written, &c., *1796.*
  1 dear Jack] at folk *Letter, 1792.*   2 A simile for Vicar *Letter, 1792.*
6 For Vicar and for Vicar's wife *Letter, 1792.*   7 large] gross *Letter, 1792.*

  Her mind and body of a piece,
  And both composed of kitchen-grease.   10
  In short, Dame Truth might safely dub her
  Vulgarity enshrin'd in blubber!
  He, meagre bit of littleness,
  All snuff, and musk, and politesse;
  So thin, that strip him of his clothing,   15
  He'd totter on the edge of Nothing!
  In case of foe, he well might hide
  Snug in the collops of her side.

  Ah then, what simile will suit?
  Spindle-leg in great jack-boot?   20
  Pismire crawling in a rut?
  Or a spigot in a butt?
  Thus I humm'd and ha'd awhile,
  When Madam Memory with a smile
  Thus twitch'd my ear—'Why sure, I ween, 25
  In London streets thou oft hast seen
  The very image of this pair:
  A little Ape with huge She-Bear
  Link'd by hapless chain together:
  An unlick'd mass the one—the other   30
  An antic small with nimble crupper——'
  But stop, my Muse! for here comes supper.
1792.

IMITATED FROM OSSIAN[1]

The stream with languid murmur creeps,
 In Lumin's *flowery* vale:
Beneath the dew the Lily weeps
 Slow-waving to the gale.

---

[1] First published in 1796: included in 1803, 1828, 1829, and 1834. The following note was attached in 1796 and 1803:—The flower hangs its [heavy] head waving at times to the gale. 'Why dost thou awake me, O Gale?' it seems to say, 'I am covered with the drops of Heaven. The time of my fading is near, the blast that shall scatter my leaves. Tomorrow shall the traveller come; he that saw me in my beauty shall come. His eyes will search the field, [but] they will not find me. So shall they search in vain for the voice of Cona, after it has failed in the field.'—Berrathon, see Ossian's *Poems*, vol. ii. [ed. 1819, p. 481].

---

12 enshrin'd] enclos'd 19 will] can *Letter*, 1792. 23 I ha'd and hem'd *Letter*, 1792. 24 Madam] Mrs. *Letter*, 1792. 28 huge] large *Letter*, 1792. 29 Link'd] Tied *Letter*, 1792. 31 small] lean *Letter*, 1792: huge 1796, 1877, 1888, 1893. For Antic huge read *antic small* ' Errata ', 1796 p. [189].
Imitated, &c.—Title] Ode *MS. E.*

IMITATED FROM OSSIAN

'Cease, restless gale!' it seems to say,
  'Nor wake me with thy sighing!
The honours of my vernal day
  On rapid wing are flying.

'To-morrow shall the Traveller come
  Who late beheld me blooming:
His searching eye shall vainly roam
  The *dreary* vale of Lumin.'

With eager gaze and wetted cheek
  My wonted haunts along,
Thus, faithful Maiden! *thou* shalt seek
  The Youth of simplest song.

But I along the breeze shall roll
  The voice of feeble power;
And dwell, the Moon-beam of thy soul,
  In Slumber's nightly hour.

1793.

THE COMPLAINT OF NINATHÓMA[1]

FROM THE SAME

How long will ye round me be swelling,
  O ye blue-tumbling waves of the sea?
Not always in caves was my dwelling,
  Nor beneath the cold blast of the tree.
Through the high-sounding halls of Cathlóma
  In the steps of my beauty I strayed;
The warriors beheld Ninathóma,
  And they blesséd the white-bosom'd Maid!

A Ghost! by my cavern it darted!
  In moon-beams the Spirit was drest—

[1] First published in 1796: included in 1803, 1828, 1829, and 1834. These lines were included in a letter from Coleridge to Mary Evans, dated Feb. 7, 1793. In 1796 and 1803 the following note was attached:— 'How long will ye roll around me, blue-tumbling waters of Ocean. My dwelling is not always in caves; nor beneath the whistling tree. My [The] feast is spread in Torthoma's Hall. [My father delighted in my voice.] The youths beheld me in [the steps of] my loveliness. They blessed the dark-haired Nina-thomà.'—Berrathon [Ossian's *Poems*, 1819, ii. 484].

10 That erst, &c. *MS. E.*   15 faithful] lovely *MS. E.*   16 simplest] gentle *MS. E.*
The Complaint, &c.—Title] Effusion xxx. The Complaint, &c., *1796*.
5 halls] Hall *Letter, 1793*.   8 white-bosom'd] dark-tressed *Letter, 1793*.
Between 8-9 By my friends, by my Lovers discarded,
  Like the flower of the Rock now I waste
  That lifts her fair head unregarded,
  And scatters its leaves on the blast. *Letter, 1793*.

40 THE COMPLAINT OF NINATHÓMA

> For lovely appear the Departed
> When they visit the dreams of my rest!
> But disturb'd by the tempest's commotion
> Fleet the shadowy forms of delight—
> Ah cease, thou shrill blast of the Ocean!   15
> To howl through my cavern by night.

1793.

SONGS OF THE PIXIES[1]

The Pixies, in the superstition of Devonshire, are a race of beings invisibly small, and harmless or friendly to man. At a small distance from a village in that county, half-way up a wood-covered hill, is an excavation called the Pixies' Parlour. The roots of old trees form its ceiling; and on its sides are innumerable cyphers, among which the author discovered his own cypher and those of his brothers, cut by the hand of their childhood. At the foot of the hill flows the river Otter.

To this place the Author, during the summer months of the year 1793, conducted a party of young ladies; one of whom, of stature elegantly small, and of complexion colourless yet clear, was proclaimed the Faery Queen. On which occasion the following Irregular Ode was written.

I

> Whom the untaught Shepherds call
> Pixies in their madrigal,
> Fancy's children, here we dwell:
> Welcome, Ladies! to our cell.
> Here the wren of softest note   5
> Builds its nest and warbles well;
> Here the blackbird strains his throat;
> Welcome, Ladies! to our cell.

---

[1] First published in 1796: included in 1797, 1803, 1828, 1829, and 1834. *The Songs of the Pixies* forms part of the volume of MS. Poems presented to Mrs. Estlin, and of a quarto MS. volume which the poet retained for his own use.

---

13 disturb'd] dispers'd *Letter, 1793*.

Songs of the Pixies] This preface appears in all editions. Previous to 1834 the second paragraph read:—To this place the Author conducted a party of young Ladies, during the Summer months of the year 1793, &c.

The Songs of the Pixies, an irregular Ode. The lower orders of the people in Devonshire have a superstition concerning the existence of 'Pixies', a race of beings supposed to be invisibly small, and harmless or friendly to man. At a small village in the county, half-way up a Hill, is a large excavation called the 'Pixies'' Parlour. The roots of the trees growing above it form the ceiling—and on its sides are engraved innumerable cyphers, among which the author descried his own and those of his Brothers, cut by the rude hand of their childhood. At the foot of the Hill flows the River Otter. To this place the Author had the Honour of conducting a party of Young Ladies during the Summer months, on which occasion the following Poem was written. *MS. E.*

SONGS OF THE PIXIES

II

When fades the moon to shadowy-pale,
And scuds the cloud before the gale,　　　　　　　　10
Ere the Morn all gem-bedight
Hath streak'd the East with rosy light,
We sip the furze-flower's fragrant dews
Clad in robes of rainbow hues;
Or sport amid the shooting gleams　　　　　　　　15
To the tune of distant-tinkling teams,
While lusty Labour scouting sorrow
Bids the Dame a glad good-morrow,
Who jogs the accustom'd road along,
And paces cheery to her cheering song.　　　　　　20

III

But not our filmy pinion
We scorch amid the blaze of day,
When Noontide's fiery-tresséd minion
Flashes the fervid ray.
Aye from the sultry heat　　　　　　　　　　　　25
We to the cave retreat
O'ercanopied by huge roots intertwin'd
With wildest texture, blacken'd o'er with age:
Round them their mantle green the ivies bind,
Beneath whose foliage pale　　　　　　　　　　　30
Fann'd by the unfrequent gale
We shield us from the Tyrant's mid-day rage.

Note. The emendations in ll. 9, 11, 12, 15, 16 are peculiar to the edition of 1834, and are, certainly, Coleridge's own handiwork.

9 to] all *MS. 4°, MS. E, 1796, 1797, 1803, 1828, 1829.*　　　11 Ere Morn with living gems bedight *MS. 4°, MS. E, 1796, 1797, 1803, 1828, 1829.* 12 Hath streak'd] Purples *MS. 4°, MS. E, 1796, 1828, 1829* : Streaks *1797, 1803.* rosy] streaky *MS. E, 1796, 1828, 1829* : purple *1797, 1803. After l. 14 the following lines appear in MS. 4°, MS. E, 1796, 1797, 1803, 1828* :

　　Richer than the deepen'd bloom
　　That glows on Summer's lily-scented (scented *1797, 1803*) plume.

15 shooting] rosy *MS. 4°, MS. E, 1796, 1797, 1803, 1828, 1829.*　　15-16 gleam . . . team *MS. 4°, MS. E, 1796, 1797, 1803, 1828, 1829.*　　16 To the tune of] Sooth'd by the *MS. 4°, MS. E, 1796, 1797, 1803, 1828, 1829.*　　20 Timing to Dobbin's foot her cheery song. *MS. E, MS. 4° erased.*　　21 our] the *MS. E.*

IV

Thither, while the murmuring throng
Of wild-bees hum their drowsy song,
By Indolence and Fancy brought,   35
A youthful Bard, 'unknown to Fame,'
Wooes the Queen of Solemn Thought,
And heaves the gentle misery of a sigh
    Gazing with tearful eye,
As round our sandy grot appear   40
Many a rudely-sculptur'd name
    To pensive Memory dear!
Weaving gay dreams of sunny-tinctur'd hue,
    We glance before his view:
O'er his hush'd soul our soothing witcheries shed   45
And twine the future garland round his head.

V

When Evening's dusky car
    Crown'd with her dewy star
Steals o'er the fading sky in shadowy flight;
    On leaves of aspen trees   50
    We tremble to the breeze
Veil'd from the grosser ken of mortal sight.
    Or, haply, at the visionary hour,
Along our wildly-bower'd sequester'd walk,
We listen to the enamour'd rustic's talk;   55
Heave with the heavings of the maiden's breast,
Where young-eyed Loves have hid their turtle nest;
    Or guide of soul-subduing power
    The glance that from the half-confessing eye
Darts the fond question or the soft reply.   60

---

35 By rapture-beaming Fancy brought *MS. E*, *MS. 4°* erased.   37 Oft wooes *MS. E*: our faery garlands *MS. 4°*, *MS. E*, *1796, 1797, 1803, 1828, 1829*.

53–5   Or at the silent visionary hour
      Along our rude sequester'd walk
      We list th' enamour'd Shepherd's talk. *MS. E.*

    Or at the silent *MS. 4°* erased.

54 wildly-bower'd] wild *1797, 1803*.   57 hid] built *MS. 4°, MS. E, 1796, 1797, 1803, 1828, 1829*.   58 of] with *MS. E.*
59 The Electric Flash that from the melting eye.
                    MS. 4°, MS. E, 1796, 1797, 1803, 1828, 1829.
60 or] and *MS. E, 1796, 1797, 1803, 1828, 1829*.

SONGS OF THE PIXIES

VI

    Or through the mystic ringlets of the vale
    We flash our faery feet in gamesome prank;
    Or, silent-sandal'd, pay our defter court,
    Circling the Spirit of the Western Gale,
    Where wearied with his flower-caressing sport,   65
    Supine he slumbers on a violet bank;
Then with quaint music hymn the parting gleam
By lonely Otter's sleep-persuading stream;
Or where his wave with loud unquiet song
Dash'd o'er the rocky channel froths along;   70
Or where, his silver waters smooth'd to rest,
The tall tree's shadow sleeps upon his breast.

VII

        Hence thou lingerer, Light!
        Eve saddens into Night.
Mother of wildly-working dreams! we view   75
    The sombre hours, that round thee stand
    With down-cast eyes (a duteous band!)
Their dark robes dripping with the heavy dew.
        Sorceress of the ebon throne!
        Thy power the Pixies own,   80
        When round thy raven brow
        Heaven's lucent roses glow,

61-5   Or haply in the flower-embroider'd vale
        We ply our faery feet in gamesome prank;
        Or pay our wonted court
        Circling the Spirits of the Western Gale,
        Where tir'd with vernal sport *MS. E.*

63   Or in deft homage pay our silent court *MS. 4º erased.*

68-70   By lonely Otter's 'peace-persuading' stream
        Or where his frothing wave with merry song
        'Dash'd o'er the rough rock lightly leaps along' *MS. E.*

68   peace-persuading stream *MS. 4º erased.*

69-70   Or where his waves with loud unquiet song
        Dash'd o'er the rocky channel froth along
           MS. 4º, 1796 ('froths' *in text,* 'froth' *errata*).

70   froths] froth *1828, 1829.*

75-7   Mother of wild'ring dreams thy course pursue.
        With downcast eyes around thee stand
        The sombre Hours, a duteous band. *MS. E.*

And clouds in watery colours drest
Float in light drapery o'er thy sable vest:
What time the pale moon sheds a softer day 85
Mellowing the woods beneath its pensive beam:
For mid the quivering light 'tis ours to play,
Aye dancing to the cadence of the stream.

VIII

Welcome, Ladies! to the cell
Where the blameless Pixies dwell: 90
But thou, Sweet Nymph! proclaim'd our Faery Queen,
With what obeisance meet
Thy presence shall we greet?
For lo! attendant on thy steps are seen
Graceful Ease in artless stole, 95
And white-robed Purity of soul,
With Honour's softer mien;
Mirth of the loosely-flowing hair,
And meek-eyed Pity eloquently fair,
Whose tearful cheeks are lovely to the view, 100
As snow-drop wet with dew.

IX

Unboastful Maid! though now the Lily pale
Transparent grace thy beauties meek;
Yet ere again along the impurpling vale,
The purpling vale and elfin-haunted grove, 105
Young Zephyr his fresh flowers profusely throws,
We'll tinge with livelier hues thy cheek;
And, haply, from the nectar-breathing Rose
Extract a Blush for Love!
1793.

92 obedience *MS. 4º, 1796: Correction made in Errata.* 94 For lo!
around thy *MS. E.* 97 softer] gentler *MS. E.* 99 meek-eyed]
meekest *MS. E.* 100 cheeks are] cheek is *MS. E.*

104-5 Yet ere again the impurpled vale
And elfin-haunted grove *MS. 4º.*

104-6 Yet ere again the purpling vale
And elfin-haunted Grove
Young Zephyr with fresh flowrets strews. *MS. 4º, MS. E.*

108 nectar-breathing] nectar-dropping *MS. E.* 109 for] of *MS. E.*

THE ROSE[1]

As late each flower that sweetest blows
I pluck'd, the Garden's pride!
Within the petals of a Rose
A sleeping Love I spied.

Around his brows a beamy wreath 5
Of many a lucent hue;
All purple glow'd his cheek, beneath,
Inebriate with dew.

I softly seiz'd the unguarded Power,
Nor scared his balmy rest: 10
And placed him, caged within the flower,
On spotless Sara's breast.

But when unweeting of the guile
Awoke the prisoner sweet,
He struggled to escape awhile 15
And stamp'd his faery feet.

Ah! soon the soul-entrancing sight
Subdued the impatient boy!
He gazed! he thrill'd with deep delight!
Then clapp'd his wings for joy. 20

[1] First published in 1796, included in 1797, 1803, 1828, 1829, and 1834. A copy of this poem is written in pencil on the blank page of Langhorne's *Collins*; a note adds, 'This "Effusion" and "Kisses" were addressed to a Miss F. Nesbitt at Plymouth, whither the author accompanied his eldest brother, to whom he was paying a visit, when he was twenty-one years of age.' In a letter to his brother George, dated July 28, 1793, Coleridge writes, 'presented a moss rose to a lady. Dick Hart [George Coleridge's brother-in-law] asked if she was not afraid to put it in her bosom, as, perhaps, there might be love in it. I immediately wrote the following little ode or song or what you please to call it. [The Rose.] It is of the namby-pamby genus.' *Letters of S. T. C.*, 1895, i. 54.

The Rose—Title] On presenting a moss rose to Miss F. Nesbitt. *MS. (pencil)*. Effusion xxvi. *1796*.

5 beamy] lucent *MS. E*: lucid *Letter, 1793*.   6 lucent] changing *MS. E*: mingled *Letter, 1793*.

12   On lovely Nesbitt's breast. *MS. (pencil)*.
           On Angelina's breast. *Letter, 1793*.
           On spotless Anna's breast. *MS. E*.
[Probably Anna Buclé, afterwards Mrs. Cruikshank.]

13 But when all reckless *Letter, 1793*.   14 prisoner] slumberer *Letter, 1793*.   16 faery] angry *Letter, 1793*.

'And O!' he cried—'Of magic kind
What charms this Throne endear!
Some other Love let Venus find—
I'll fix *my* empire *here.*'[1]

1793.

KISSES[2]

Cupid, if storying Legends tell aright,
Once fram'd a rich Elixir of Delight.
A Chalice o'er love-kindled flames he fix'd,
And in it Nectar and Ambrosia mix'd:
With these the magic dews which Evening brings, 5
Brush'd from the Idalian star by faery wings:
Each tender pledge of sacred Faith he join'd,
Each gentler Pleasure of th' unspotted mind—

---

[1] *Letters of S. T. C.*, 1895, i. p. 55.
[2] First published in 1796: included in 1797 (*Supplement*), 1803, and 1844. Three MSS. are extant, (1) as included in a letter to George Coleridge, Aug. 5, 1793; (2) as written in pencil in a copy of Langhorne's *Collins* in 1793; (3) *MS. E.*   *Poems*, 1796 (Note 7, p. 181), and footnotes in 1797 and 1803, supply the original Latin:

> Effinxit quondam blandum meditata laborem
>   Basia lascivâ Cypria Diva manu.
> Ambrosiae succos occultâ temperat arte,
>   Fragransque infuso nectare tingit opus.
> Sufficit et partem mellis, quod subdolus olim
>   Non impune favis surripuisset Amor.
> Decussos violae foliis admiscet odores
>   Et spolia aestivis plurima rapta rosis.
> Addit et illecebras et mille et mille lepores,
>   Et quot Acidalius gaudia Cestus habet.
> Ex his composuit Dea basia; et omnia libens
>   Invenias nitidae sparsa per ora Cloës.
>   Carm[ina] Quad[ragesimalia], vol. ii.

21-2   'And, O', he cried, 'What charms refined
            This magic throne endear *Letter, 1793, MS. E.*
23 Another Love may *Letter, 1793*.

Kisses—Title] Cupid turn'd Chymist *Letter, 1793, Pencil*.   The Compound *MS. E*: Effusion xxvi. *1796*: The Composition of a Kiss *1797*: Kisses *1803, 1844, 1852*.

1 storying] ancient *Pencil*.   3 Chalice] cauldron *Letter, 1793*.   8
gentler] gentle *Pencil*.

Day-dreams, whose tints with sportive brightness glow,
And Hope, the blameless parasite of Woe.   10
The eyeless Chemist heard the process rise,
The steamy Chalice bubbled up in sighs;
Sweet sounds transpired, as when the enamour'd Dove
Pours the soft murmuring of responsive Love.
The finish'd work might Envy vainly blame,   15
And 'Kisses' was the precious Compound's name.
With half the God his Cyprian Mother blest,
And breath'd on Sara's lovelier lips the rest.
1793.

THE GENTLE LOOK[1]

THOU gentle Look, that didst my soul beguile,
  Why hast thou left me? Still in some fond dream
Revisit my sad heart, auspicious Smile!
  As falls on closing flowers the lunar beam:
What time, in sickly mood, at parting day   5
  I lay me down and think of happier years;

[1] First published in 1796: included in 1797, 1803, 1828, 1829, and 1834. The 'four *last* lines' of the Sonnet as sent to Southey, on Dec. 11, 1794, were written by Lamb. *Letters of S. T. C.*, 1895, i. 111, 112.

9	Gay Dreams whose tints with beamy brightness glow. *Letter, 1793, MS. E.*
9–10	And { Hopes the blameless parasites of Woe / Fond *Bristol MS.*
	And Dreams whose tints with beamy brightness glow. *Pencil, Bristol MS.*
11–12	With joy he view'd his chymic process rise, The steaming cauldron bubbled up in sighs. *Letter, 1793.*
11–12	the chymic process rise, The steaming chalice *Pencil, MS. E.*
11–12	the chymic process rise, The charming cauldron *Bristol MS.*
14	Murmuring] murmurs *Letter, 1793.* Cooes the soft murmurs *Pencil.*
15	not Envy's self could blame *Letter, 1793, Pencil.* might blame. *MS. E.*
17	With part *Letter, 1793, MS. E.*
18	on Nesbitt's lovely lips the rest. *Letter, 1793, Pencil.* on Mary's lovelier lips the rest. *MS. E.* on lovely Nesbitt's lovely lips the rest. *Bristol MS.*

The Gentle Look—Title] Irregular Sonnet *MS. E*: Effusion xiv. *1796*: Sonnet III. *1797, 1803*: Sonnet viii. *1828, 1829, 1834*: The Smile *P. W. 1885*: The Gentle Look *P. W. 1893.*

1 Thou] O *Letter, 1794.*

Of joys, that glimmer'd in Hope's twilight ray,
  Then left me darkling in a vale of tears.
O pleasant days of Hope—for ever gone!
  Could I recall you!—But that thought is vain.   10
Availeth not Persuasion's sweetest tone
  To lure the fleet-wing'd Travellers back again:
Yet fair, though faint, their images shall gleam
Like the bright Rainbow on a willowy stream.[1]
?1793.

SONNET[2]

TO THE RIVER OTTER

DEAR native Brook! wild Streamlet of the West!
  How many various-fated years have past,
What happy and what mournful hours, since last
I skimm'd the smooth thin stone along thy breast,
Numbering its light leaps! yet so deep imprest   5
Sink the sweet scenes of childhood, that mine eyes
  I never shut amid the sunny ray,
But straight with all their tints thy waters rise,
  Thy crossing plank, thy marge with willows grey,
And bedded sand that vein'd with various dyes   10
Gleam'd through thy bright transparence! On my way,
  Visions of Childhood! oft have ye beguil'd
Lone manhood's cares, yet waking fondest sighs:
  Ah! that once more I were a careless Child!
?1793.

---

[1] Compare ll. 13, 14 with ll. 13, 14 of *Anna and Harland* and ll. 17, 18 of *Recollection*. *Vide* Appendix.

[2] Lines 2-11 were first published in the *Watchman*, No. V, April 2, 1796, as lines 17-26 of *Recollection*. First published, as a whole, in *Selection of Sonnets*, 1796, included in 1797, 1803, *Sibylline Leaves*, 1828, 1829, and 1834.

---

9 gone] flown *MS. E.*   10 you] one *Letter, 1794.*
13-14   Anon they haste to everlasting Night,
      Nor can a Giant's arm arrest them in their flight *Letter, 1794.*
    On on, &c., *MS. E.*

Sonnet—Title] Sonnet No. IV. To the, &c., *1797, 1803.*

3 What blissful and what anguish'd hours *Watchman, S. S., 1797, 1803.*
7 ray] blaze *Watchman, S. S., 1797, 1803.*   8 thy] their *S. L. Corrected in Errata,* p. [xii].

9   The crossing plank, and margin's willowy maze *Watchman.*
    Thy crossing plank, thy margin's willowy maze
                                    S. S., 1797, 1803.

11 On my way] to the gaze *Watchman, S. S., 1797, 1803.*   14 Ah! that I were once more, &c. *S. L. Corrected in Errata,* p. [xii].

First Draft

AN EFFUSION AT EVENING

WRITTEN IN AUGUST, 1792

IMAGINATION, Mistress of my Love!
Where shall mine Eye thy elfin haunt explore?
Dost thou on yon rich Cloud thy pinions bright
Embathe in amber-glowing Floods of Light?
Or, wild of speed, pursue the track of Day 5
In other worlds to hail the morning Ray?
'Tis time to bid the faded shadowy Pleasures move
On shadowy Memory's wings across the Soul of Love;
And thine o'er *Winter's* icy plains to fling
Each flower, that binds the breathing Locks of *Spring*, 10
When blushing, like a bride, from primrose Bower
She starts, awaken'd by the pattering Shower!

Now sheds the setting Sun a purple gleam,
Aid, lovely Sorc'ress! aid the Poet's dream.
With faery wand O bid my Love arise, 15
The dewy brilliance dancing in her Eyes;
As erst she woke with soul-entrancing Mien
The thrill of Joy extatic yet serene,
When link'd with Peace I bounded o'er the Plain
And Hope itself was all I knew of Pain! 20

Propitious Fancy hears the votive sigh—
The absent Maiden flashes on mine Eye!
When first the matin Bird with startling Song
Salutes the Sun his veiling Clouds among,
I trace her footsteps on the {accustom'd / steaming} Lawn, 25
I view her glancing in the gleams of Dawn!
When the bent Flower beneath the night-dew weeps
And on the Lake the silver Lustre sleeps,
Amid the paly Radiance soft and sad
She meets my lonely path in moonbeams clad. 30
With *her* along the streamlet's brink I rove;
With *her* I list the warblings of the Grove;
And seems in each low wind *her* voice to float,
Lone-whispering Pity in each soothing Note!

As oft in climes beyond the western Main
Where boundless spreads the wildly-silent Plain,
The savage Hunter, who his drowsy frame
Had bask'd beneath the Sun's unclouded Flame,
Awakes amid the tempest-troubled air,
The Thunder's Peal and Lightning's lurid glare—
Aghast he hears the rushing Whirlwind's Sweep,
And sad recalls the sunny hour of Sleep!
So lost by storms along Life's wild'ring Way
Mine Eye reverted views that cloudless Day,
When,——! on thy banks I joy'd to rove
While Hope with kisses nurs'd the infant Love!

Sweet ——! where Pleasure's streamlet glides
Fann'd by soft winds to curl in mimic tides;
Where Mirth and Peace beguile the blameless Day;
And where Friendship's fixt star beams a mellow'd Ray;
Where Love a crown of thornless Roses wears;
Where soften'd Sorrow smiles within her tears;
And Memory, with a Vestal's meek employ,
Unceasing feeds the lambent flame of Joy!
No more thy Sky Larks less'ning from my sight
Shall thrill th' attunéd Heartstring with delight;
No more shall deck thy pensive Pleasures sweet
With wreaths of sober hue my evening seat!
Yet dear to [My] Fancy's Eye thy varied scene
Of Wood, Hill, Dale and sparkling Brook between:
Yet sweet to [My] Fancy's Ear the warbled song,
That soars on Morning's wing thy fields among!

Scenes of my Hope! the aching Eye ye leave,
Like those rich Hues that paint the clouds of Eve!
Tearful and saddening with the sadden'd Blaze
Mine Eye the gleam pursues with wistful Gaze—
Sees Shades on Shades with deeper tint impend,
Till chill and damp the moonless Night descend!

1792.

LINES[1]

ON AN AUTUMNAL EVENING

O THOU wild Fancy, check thy wing! No more
Those thin white flakes, those purple clouds explore!
Nor there with happy spirits speed thy flight
Bath'd in rich amber-glowing floods of light;
Nor in yon gleam, where slow descends the day,   5
With western peasants hail the morning ray!
Ah! rather bid the perish'd pleasures move,
A shadowy train, across the soul of Love!
O'er Disappointment's wintry desert fling
Each flower that wreath'd the dewy locks of Spring,   10
When blushing, like a bride, from Hope's trim bower
She leapt, awaken'd by the pattering shower.

Now sheds the sinking Sun a deeper gleam,
Aid, lovely Sorceress! aid thy Poet's dream!
With faery wand O bid the Maid arise,   15
Chaste Joyance dancing in her bright-blue eyes;
As erst when from the Muses' calm abode
I came, with Learning's meed not unbestowed;
When as she twin'd a laurel round my brow,
And met my kiss, and half return'd my vow,   20
O'er all my frame shot rapid my thrill'd heart,
And every nerve confess'd the electric dart.

O dear Deceit! I see the Maiden rise,
Chaste Joyance dancing in her bright-blue eyes!
When first the lark high-soaring swells his throat,   25
Mocks the tir'd eye, and scatters the loud note,
I trace her footsteps on the accustom'd lawn,
I mark her glancing mid the gleam of dawn.

---

[1] First published in 1796: included in 1797, 1803, 1828, 1829 and 1834. In *Social Life at the English Universities*, by Christopher Wordsworth, M.A., 1874, it is recorded that this poem was read by Coleridge to a party of college friends on November 7, 1793.

Title] Effusion xxxvi. Written in Early Youth, The Time, An Autumnal Evening *1796*: Written in etc. *1803*: An Effusion on an Autumnal Evening. Written in Early Youth *1797* (*Supplement*).

A first draft, headed 'An Effusion at Evening, Written in August, 1792' is included in the MS. volume presented to Mrs. Estlin in April, 1795 (*vide ante*, pp. 49, 50).

28 gleam] gleams *1796, 1797, 1803, 1893*.

When the bent flower beneath the night-dew weeps
And on the lake the silver lustre sleeps, 30
Amid the paly radiance soft and sad,
She meets my lonely path in moon-beams clad.
With her along the streamlet's brink I rove;
With her I list the warblings of the grove;
And seems in each low wind her voice to float 35
Lone-whispering Pity in each soothing note!

Spirits of Love! ye heard her name! Obey
The powerful spell, and to my haunt repair.
Whether on clust'ring pinions ye are there,
Where rich snows blossom on the Myrtle-trees, 40
Or with fond languishment around my fair
Sigh in the loose luxuriance of her hair;
O heed the spell, and hither wing your way,
Like far-off music, voyaging the breeze!

Spirits! to you the infant Maid was given 45
Form'd by the wond'rous Alchemy of Heaven!
No fairer Maid does Love's wide empire know,
No fairer Maid e'er heav'd the bosom's snow.
A thousand Loves around her forehead fly;
A thousand Loves sit melting in her eye; 50
Love lights her smile—in Joy's red nectar dips
His myrtle flower, and plants it on her lips.
She speaks! and hark that passion-warbled song—
Still, Fancy! still that voice, those notes prolong.
As sweet as when that voice with rapturous falls
Shall wake the soften'd echoes of Heaven's Halls! 55

[1] O (have I sigh'd) were mine the wizard's rod,
Or mine the power of Proteus, changeful God!

---

[1] Note to line 57. Poems, 1796, pp. 183-5:—I entreat the Public's pardon for having carelessly suffered to be printed such intolerable stuff as this and the thirteen following lines. They have not the merit even of originality: as every thought is to be found in the Greek Epigrams. The lines in this poem from the 27th to the 36th, I have been told are

---

51-3 in Joy's bright nectar dips
 The flamy rose, and plants it on her lips!
 Tender, serene, and all devoid of guile,
 Soft is her soul, as sleeping infants' smile
 She speaks, &c. *1796, 1803.*

54 still those mazy notes *1796, 1803.*

55-6 Sweet as th' angelic harps, whose rapturous falls
 Awake the soften'd echoes of Heaven's Halls. *1796, 1803.*

A flower-entangled Arbour I would seem
To shield my Love from Noontide's sultry beam: 60
Or bloom a Myrtle, from whose od'rous boughs
My Love might weave gay garlands for her brows.
When Twilight stole across the fading vale,
To fan my Love I'd be the Evening Gale;
Mourn in the soft folds of her swelling vest, 65
And flutter my faint pinions on her breast!
On Seraph wing I'd float a Dream by night,
To soothe my Love with shadows of delight:—
Or soar aloft to be the Spangled Skies,
And gaze upon her with a thousand eyes! 70

As when the Savage, who his drowsy frame
Had bask'd beneath the Sun's unclouded flame,
Awakes amid the troubles of the air,
The skiey deluge, and white lightning's glare—
Aghast he scours before the tempest's sweep, 75
And sad recalls the sunny hour of sleep:—
So tossed by storms along Life's wild'ring way,
Mine eye reverted views that cloudless day,

a palpable imitation of the passage from the 355th to the 370th line of the Pleasures of Memory Part 3. I do not perceive so striking a similarity between the two passages; at all events I had written the Effusion several years before I had seen Mr Rogers' Poem.—It may be proper to remark that the tale of Florio in the 'Pleasures of Memory' is to be found in Lochleven, a poem of great merit by Michael Bruce.—In Mr Rogers' Poem* the names are Florio and Julia; in the Lochleven Lomond and Levina—and this is all the difference. We seize the opportunity of transcribing from the Lochleven of Bruce the following exquisite passage, expressing the effects of a fine day on the human heart.

> Fat on the plain, and mountain's sunny side
> Large droves of oxen and the fleecy flocks
> Feed undisturb'd; and fill the echoing air
> With Music grateful to their [the] Master's ear.
> The Traveller stops and gazes round and round
> O'er all the plains [scenes] that animate his heart
> With mirth and music. Even the mendicant
> Bow-bent with age, that on the old gray stone
> Sole-sitting suns him in the public way,
> Feels his heart leap, and to himself he sings.
> [*Poems* by Michael Bruce, 1796, p. 94.]

---

* For Coleridge's retractation of the charge of plagiarism and apology to Rogers see 'Advertisement to Supplement of 1797', pp. 244, 245.

54 LINES

When by my native brook I wont to rove,
While Hope with kisses nurs'd the Infant Love. 80

Dear native brook! like Peace, so placidly
Smoothing through fertile fields thy current meek!
Dear native brook! where first young Poesy
Stared wildly-eager in her noontide dream!
Where blameless pleasures dimple Quiet's cheek, 85
As water-lilies ripple thy slow stream!
Dear native haunts! where Virtue still is gay,
Where Friendship's fix'd star sheds a mellow'd ray,
Where Love a crown of thornless Roses wears,
Where soften'd Sorrow smiles within her tears; 90
And Memory, with a Vestal's chaste employ,
Unceasing feeds the lambent flame of joy!
No more your sky-larks melting from the sight
Shall thrill the attunéd heart-string with delight—
No more shall deck your pensive Pleasures sweet 95
With wreaths of sober hue my evening seat.
Yet dear to Fancy's eye your varied scene
Of wood, hill, dale, and sparkling brook between!
Yet sweet to Fancy's ear the warbled song,
That soars on Morning's wing your vales among. 100

Scenes of my Hope! the aching eye ye leave
Like yon bright hues that paint the clouds of eve!
Tearful and saddening with the sadden'd blaze
Mine eye the gleam pursues with wistful gaze:
Sees shades on shades with deeper tint impend, 105
Till chill and damp the moonless night descend.

1793.

TO FORTUNE[1]

To the Editor of the 'Morning Chronicle'

SIR,—The following poem you may perhaps deem admissible into your journal—if not, you will commit it εἰς ἱερὸν μένος Ἡφαίστοιο.—I am, with more respect and gratitude than I ordinarily feel for Editors of Papers, your obliged, &c.,

CANTAB.—S. T. C.

[1] First published, *Morning Chronicle*, Nov. 7, 1793. First collected 1893.

86 thy] a *1796, 1803*.

To Fortune

On buying a Ticket in the Irish Lottery

Composed during a walk to and from the Queen's Head, Gray's Inn Lane, Holborn, and Hornsby's and Co., Cornhill.

PROMPTRESS of unnumber'd sighs,
O snatch that circling bandage from thine eyes!
O look, and smile! No common prayer
Solicits, Fortune! thy propitious care!
For, not a silken son of dress,   5
I clink the gilded chains of *politesse*,
Nor ask thy boon what time I scheme
Unholy Pleasure's frail and feverish dream;
Nor yet my view life's *dazzle* blinds—
Pomp!—Grandeur! Power!—I give you to the winds!   10
Let the little bosom cold
Melt only at the sunbeam ray of gold—
My pale cheeks glow—the big drops start—
The rebel *Feeling* riots at my heart!
And if in lonely durance pent,   15
Thy poor mite mourn a brief imprisonment—
That mite at Sorrow's faintest sound
Leaps from its scrip with an elastic bound!
But oh! if ever song thine ear
Might soothe, O haste with fost'ring hand to rear   20
One Flower of Hope! At Love's behest,
Trembling, I plac'd it in my secret breast:
And thrice I've view'd the vernal gleam,
Since oft mine eye, with Joy's electric beam,
Illum'd it—and its sadder hue   25
Oft moisten'd with the Tear's ambrosial dew!
Poor wither'd floweret! on its head
Has dark Despair his sickly mildew shed!
But thou, O Fortune! canst relume
Its deaden'd tints—and thou with hardier bloom   30
May'st haply tinge its beauties pale,
And yield the unsunn'd stranger to the western gale!

1793.

PERSPIRATION. A TRAVELLING ECLOGUE[1]

The dust flies smothering, as on clatt'ring wheel
Loath'd Aristocracy careers along;
The distant track quick vibrates to the eye,
And white and dazzling undulates with heat,
Where scorching to the unwary traveller's touch,   5
The stone fence flings its narrow slip of shade;
Or, where the worn sides of the chalky road
Yield their scant excavations (sultry grots!),
Emblem of languid patience, we behold
The fleecy files faint-ruminating lie.   10
1794.

[AVE, ATQUE VALE!][2]

Vivit sed mihi non vivit—nova forte marita,
  Ah dolor! alterius carâ a cervice pependit.
Vos, malefida valete accensae insomnia mentis,
  Littora amata valete! Vale, ah! formosa Maria!
1794.

ON BALA HILL[3]

With many a weary step at length I gain
Thy summit, Bala! and the cool breeze plays
Cheerily round my brow—as hence the gaze
Returns to dwell upon the journey'd plain.

'Twas a long way and tedious!—to the eye   5
Tho' fair th' extended Vale, and fair to view
The falling leaves of many a faded hue
That eddy in the wild gust moaning by!

Ev'n so it far'd with Life! in discontent
Restless thro' Fortune's mingled scenes I went,   10

---

[1] First published, *Letters of Samuel Taylor Coleridge*, 1895, i. 73, 74. The lines were sent in a letter to Southey, dated July 6, 1794.

[2] First published, *Biog. Lit.* 1847, Biog. Supplement, ii. 340. This Latin quatrain was sent in a letter to Southey, dated July 13, 1794.

[3] First published (as Coleridge's) in 1893, from an unsigned autograph MS. found among the Evans Papers. The lines are all but identical with Southey's Sonnet to Lansdown Hill (Sonnet viii), dated 1794, and first published in 1797, and were, probably, his composition. See *Athenaeum*, January 11, 1896.

On Bala Hill. 2 Bala] Lansdown *Poems, 1797.*
3 Cheerily] Gratefully *Poems, 1797.*

Yet wept to think they would return no more!
O cease fond heart! in such sad thoughts to roam,
For surely thou ere long shalt reach thy home,
And pleasant is the way that lies before.
1794.

LINES[1]

WRITTEN AT THE KING'S ARMS, ROSS, FORMERLY THE HOUSE OF THE 'MAN OF ROSS'

RICHER than Miser o'er his countless hoards,
Nobler than Kings, or king-polluted Lords,
Here dwelt the MAN OF ROSS! O Traveller, hear!
Departed Merit claims a reverent tear.
Friend to the friendless, to the sick man health,   5
With generous joy he view'd his modest wealth;
He heard the widow's heaven-breath'd prayer of praise,
He mark'd the shelter'd orphan's tearful gaze,
Or where the sorrow-shrivell'd captive lay,
Pour'd the bright blaze of Freedom's noon-tide ray.   10

---

[1] First published in the *Cambridge Intelligencer*, September 27, 1794: included in *A Pedestrian Tour through North Wales*. By J. Hucks, 1795, p. 15: 1796, 1797, 1803, 1828, 1829, and 1834.

In a letter to Southey dated July 13, 1794, Coleridge writes:—'At Ross . . . we took up our quarters at the King's Arms, once the house of Kyrle, the Man of Ross. I gave the window-shutter the following effusion —"Richer than Misers" etc.' J. Hucks, in his *Tour*, 1795, p. 15, writes to the same effect. There are but slight variations in the text as printed in the *Cambridge Intelligencer* and in Hucks' *Tour*. In 1796 lines 5–10 of the text, which were included in *A Monody on the Death of Chatterton* (1796), are omitted, and the poem numbered only fourteen lines. In 1797 lines 5–10 were restored to the *Man of Ross* and omitted from the *Monody*. The poem numbered twenty lines. In 1803 lines 5–10 were again omitted from the *Man of Ross*, but not included in the *Monody*. The poem numbered fourteen lines. The text of 1828, 1829 is almost identical with that of 1834.

Four MS. versions are extant, (1) the Letter to Southey, July 13, 1794: (2) the Estlin Copy-book: (3) the Morrison MSS.: (4) the MS. 4° Copy-book.

---

12 O] But *Poems, 1797*.

Lines—Title] Written . . . Mr. Kyrle, 'the Man of Ross'. *MS. E.*

1 Misers o'er their *Letter, 1794, J. H., MS. E, 1803*.   4 the glistening tear *Letter, 1794*: a] the *J. H., MS. E. Lines 5–10 are not in MS. 4°, 1796, 1803: in 1797 they follow l. 14 of the text.*   5 to the poor man wealth, *Morrison MSS.*   7 heard] hears *1797, 1828, 1829.*   8 mark'd] marks *1797, 1828.*   9 And o'er the dowried maiden's glowing cheek, *Letter, 1794, Morrison MSS.*: virgin's snowy cheek, *J. H., MS. E.*   10 Bade bridal love suffuse its blushes meek. *Letter, 1794, MS. E, Morrison MSS.* Pour'd] Pours *1797, 1828, 1829*.

Beneath this roof if thy cheer'd moments pass,
Fill to the good man's name one grateful glass:
To higher zest shall Memory wake thy soul,
And Virtue mingle in the ennobled bowl.
But if, like me, through Life's distressful scene   15
Lonely and sad thy pilgrimage hath been;
And if thy breast with heart-sick anguish fraught,
Thou journeyest onward tempest-tossed in thought;
Here cheat thy cares! in generous visions melt,
And *dream* of Goodness, thou hast never felt!   20
    1794.

IMITATED FROM THE WELSH[1]

If while my passion I impart,
  You deem my words untrue,
O place your hand upon my heart—
  Feel how it throbs for *you*!

Ah no! reject the thoughtless claim   5
  In pity to your Lover!
That thrilling touch would aid the flame
  It wishes to discover.
  ?1794.

LINES[2]

TO A BEAUTIFUL SPRING IN A VILLAGE

Once more! sweet Stream! with slow foot wandering near,
I bless thy milky waters cold and clear.
Escap'd the flashing of the noontide hours,
With one fresh garland of Pierian flowers
(Ere from thy zephyr-haunted brink I turn)   5
My languid hand shall wreath thy mossy urn.
For not through pathless grove with murmur rude
Thou soothest the sad wood-nymph, Solitude;
Nor thine unseen in cavern depths to well,
The Hermit-fountain of some dripping cell!   10

---

[1] First published in 1796: included in 1803, 1828, 1829, and 1834.
[2] First published in 1796: included in *Annual Register*, 1796: 1797, 1803, 1828, 1829, and 1834.

---

11 If 'neath this roof thy wine cheer'd moments pass *Letter, J. H., MS. E, MS. 4º, 1803*. 14 ennobled] sparkling *Letter, 1794*. 15 me] mine *1803*.
Imitated, &c.—Title] Song *MS. E*: Effusion xxxi. Imitated &c., *1796*.
Lines—Title] Lines addressed to a Spring in Village of Kirkhampton near Bath *MS. E*.
7 groves in murmurs *MS. E*.

Pride of the Vale! thy useful streams supply
The scatter'd cots and peaceful hamlet nigh.
The elfin tribe around thy friendly banks
With infant uproar and soul-soothing pranks,
Releas'd from school, their little hearts at rest,   15
Launch paper navies on thy waveless breast.
The rustic here at eve with pensive look
Whistling lorn ditties leans upon his crook,
Or, starting, pauses with hope-mingled dread
To list the much-lov'd maid's accustom'd tread: 20
She, vainly mindful of her dame's command,
Loiters, the long-fill'd pitcher in her hand.

Unboastful Stream! thy fount with pebbled falls
The faded form of past delight recalls,
What time the morning sun of Hope arose,   25
And all was joy; save when another's woes
A transient gloom upon my soul imprest,
Like passing clouds impictur'd on thy breast.
Life's current then ran sparkling to the noon,
Or silvery stole beneath the pensive Moon: 30
Ah! now it works rude brakes and thorns among,
Or o'er the rough rock bursts and foams along!
   1794.

IMITATIONS

AD LYRAM[1]

(CASIMIR, BOOK II. ODE 3)

The solemn-breathing air is ended—
  Cease, O Lyre! thy kindred lay!
From the poplar-branch suspended
  Glitter to the eye of Day!

---

[1] First published in the *Watchman*, No. II, March 9, 1796: included in *Literary Remains*, 1836, I. 41–3. First collected in 1844.

21-2   And now essays his simple Faith to prove
        By all the soft solicitudes of Love. *MS. E.*

30 Or silver'd its smooth course beneath the Moon. *MS. 4º.*   31
rude] the thorny *MS. 4º erased.*

For ll. 29–32 But ah! too brief in Youths' enchanting reign,
     Ere Manhood wakes th' unweeting heart to pain,
     Silent and soft thy silver waters glide:
     So glided Life, a smooth and equal Tide.
     Sad Change! for now by choking Cares withstood
     It hardly bursts its way, a turbid, boist'rous Flood! *MS. E.*

Ad Lyram—Title] Song. [*Note.* Imitated from Casimir.] *MS. E.*

IMITATIONS

On thy wires hov'ring, dying, 5
  Softly sighs the summer wind:
I will slumber, careless lying,
  By yon waterfall reclin'd.

In the forest hollow-roaring
  Hark! I hear a deep'ning sound— 10
Clouds rise thick with heavy low'ring!
  See! th' horizon blackens round!

Parent of the soothing measure,
  Let me seize thy wetted string!
Swiftly flies the flatterer, Pleasure, 15
  Headlong, ever on the wing.[1]

1794.

TO LESBIA[2]

Vivamus, mea Lesbia, atque amemus.
CATULLUS.

My Lesbia, let us love and live,
And to the winds, my Lesbia, give

---

[1] If we except Lucretius and Statius, I know not of any Latin poet, ancient or modern, who has equalled Casimir in boldness of conception, opulence of fancy, or beauty of versification. The Odes of this illustrious Jesuit were translated into English about 150 years ago, by a Thomas Hill, I think. [—by G. H. [G. Hils.] London, 1646. 12mo. *Ed. L. R.* 1836.] I never saw the translation. A few of the Odes have been translated in a very animated manner by Watts. I have subjoined the third ode of the second book, which, with the exception of the first line, is an effusion of exquisite elegance. In the imitation attempted, I am sensible that I have destroyed the *effect of suddenness*, by translating into two stanzas what is one in the original.

AD LYRAM.

Sonori buxi Filia sutilis,
Pendebis alta, Barbite, populo,
  Dum ridet aer, et supinas
    Solicitat levis aura frondes:
Te sibilantis lenior halitus
Perflabit Euri: me iuvet interim
  Collum reclinasse, et virenti
    Sic temere iacuisse ripa.
Eheu! serenum quae nebulae tegunt
Repente caelum! quis sonus imbrium!
  Surgamus—heu semper fugaci
    Gaudia praeteritura passu!

'Advertisement' to *Ad Lyram*, in *Watchman*, II, March 9, 1796.

[2] First published in the *Morning Post*, April 11, 1798: included in *Literary Remains*, 1836, i. 274. First collected in *P. W.*, 1893.

To Lesbia—Title] Lines imitated from Catullus. *M. P.*

IMITATIONS

  Each cold restraint, each boding fear
  Of age and all her saws severe.
  Yon sun now posting to the main   5
  Will set,—but 'tis to rise again;—
  But we, when once our mortal light
  Is set, must sleep in endless night.
  Then come, with whom alone I'll live,
  A thousand kisses take and give!   10
  Another thousand!—to the store
  Add hundreds—then a thousand more!
  And when they to a million mount,
  Let confusion take the account,—
  That you, the number never knowing,   15
  May continue still bestowing—
  That I for joys may never pine,
  Which never can again be mine!

? 1794.

THE DEATH OF THE STARLING[1]

Lugete, O Veneres, Cupidinesque.—CATULLUS.

  PITY! mourn in plaintive tone
  The lovely starling dead and gone!
   Pity mourns in plaintive tone
   The lovely starling dead and gone.
  Weep, ye Loves! and Venus! weep   5
  The lovely starling fall'n asleep!
  Venus sees with tearful eyes—
  In her lap the starling lies!
  While the Loves all in a ring
  Softly stroke the stiffen'd wing.   10

? 1794.

MORIENS SUPERSTITI[2]

  THE hour-bell sounds, and I must go;
  Death waits—again I hear him calling;—
  No cowardly desires have I,
  Nor will I shun his face appalling.

---

[1] First published, *Literary Remains*, 1836, i. 274. First collected, *P. W.*, 1893. The titles 'Lesbia' and 'The Death of the Starling' first appear in 1893.

[2] First published in the *Morning Post*, May 10, 1798, with a prefatory note :—'The two following verses from the French, never before published, were written by a French Prisoner as he was preparing to go to the Guillotine': included in *Literary Remains*, 1836, i. 275. First collected *P. W.*, 1893.

To Lesbia 4 her] its *L. R.*   7 mortal] little *L. R.*   1**8** *signed* Mortimer *M. P.*
 The Death &c. 7 sees] see *L. R.*

I die in faith and honour rich—
But ah! I leave behind my treasure
In widowhood and lonely pain;—
To live were surely then a pleasure!

My lifeless eyes upon thy face
Shall never open more to-morrow;
To-morrow shall thy beauteous eyes
Be closed to Love, and drown'd in Sorrow;
To-morrow Death shall freeze this hand,
And on thy breast, my wedded treasure,
I never, never more shall live;—
Alas! I quit a life of pleasure.

MORIENTI SUPERSTES

YET art thou happier far than she
Who feels the widow's love for thee!
For while her days are days of weeping,
Thou, in peace, in silence sleeping,
In some still world, unknown, remote,
The mighty parent's care hast found,
Without whose tender guardian thought
No sparrow falleth to the ground.

? 1794.

THE SIGH[1]

WHEN Youth his faery reign began
Ere Sorrow had proclaim'd me man;
While Peace the present hour beguil'd,
And all the lovely Prospect smil'd;
Then Mary! 'mid my lightsome glee
I heav'd the painless Sigh for thee.

And when, along the waves of woe,
My harass'd Heart was doom'd to know
The frantic burst of Outrage keen,
And the slow Pang that gnaws unseen;

---

[1] First published in 1796: included in 1797, 1803, 1828, 1829. Coleridge dated the poem, June 1794, but the verses as sent to Southey, in a letter dated November, 1794 (*Letters of S. T. C.*, 1895, i. 100, 101), could not have taken shape before the August of that year, after the inception of Pantisocracy and his engagement to Sarah Fricker.

The Sigh—Title] Ode *MS. E*: Song *Letter, Nov. 1794, Morrison MSS.*: Effusion xxxii: The Sigh *1796*.

7 along th'] as tossed on *1803*.   waves] wilds *Letter, 1794, MS. E*.
9 of] the *1803*.

THE SIGH

Then shipwreck'd on Life's stormy sea
I heaved an anguish'd Sigh for thee!

But soon Reflection's power imprest
A stiller sadness on my breast;
And sickly Hope with waning eye
Was well content to droop and die:
I yielded to the stern decree,
Yet heav'd a languid Sigh for thee!

And though in distant climes to roam,
A wanderer from my native home,
I fain would soothe the sense of Care,
And lull to sleep the Joys that were!
Thy Image may not banish'd be—
Still, Mary! still I sigh for thee.

1794.

THE KISS[1]

ONE kiss, dear Maid! I said and sigh'd—
Your scorn the little boon denied.
Ah why refuse the blameless bliss?
Can danger lurk within a kiss?

Yon viewless wanderer of the vale,
The Spirit of the Western Gale,
At Morning's break, at Evening's close
Inhales the sweetness of the Rose,
And hovers o'er the uninjur'd bloom
Sighing back the soft perfume.
Vigour to the Zephyr's wing
Her nectar-breathing kisses fling;

---

[1] First published in 1796: included in 1797, 1803, 1828, 1829, and 1834.

---

13 power] hand *Letter, Nov. 1794, MS. E.*   18 a] the *Letter, 1794.*
21-2   I fain would woo a gentle Fair
       To soothe the aching sense of Care *Letter, Nov. 1794.*
21 sense of] aching *MS. E.*   *Below l.* 24 June 1794 *Poems, 1796.*

The Kiss—Title] Ode *MS. E* : Effusion xxviii *1796*: The Kiss *1797, 1828, 1829, 1834* : To Sara *1803. MSS. of* The Kiss *are included in the Estlin volume and in S. T. C.'s quarto copy-book.*

11-15   Vigor to his languid wing
        The Rose's fragrant kisses bring,
        And He o'er all her brighten'd hue
        Flings the glitter of the dew.
        See she bends her bashful head. *MS. E.*

And He the glitter of the Dew
Scatters on the Rose's hue.
Bashful lo! she bends her head,
And darts a blush of deeper Red! 15

Too well those lovely lips disclose
The triumphs of the opening Rose;
O fair! O graceful! bid them prove
As passive to the breath of Love. 20
In tender accents, faint and low,
Well-pleas'd I hear the whisper'd 'No!'
The whispered 'No'—how little meant!
Sweet Falsehood that endears Consent!
For on those lovely lips the while 25
Dawns the soft relenting smile,
And tempts with feign'd dissuasion coy
The gentle violence of Joy.

? 1794.

TO A YOUNG LADY[1]

WITH A POEM ON THE FRENCH REVOLUTION

MUCH on my early youth I love to dwell,
Ere yet I bade that friendly dome farewell,
Where first, beneath the echoing cloisters pale,
I heard of guilt and wonder'd at the tale!
Yet though the hours flew by on careless wing, 5
Full heavily of Sorrow would I sing.
Aye as the Star of Evening flung its beam
In broken radiance on the wavy stream,
My soul amid the pensive twilight gloom
Mourn'd with the breeze, O Lee Boo![2] o'er thy tomb. 10

---

[1] First published in *The Watchman*, No. I, March 1, 1796: included in 1796, 1797, 1803, 1828, 1829, and 1834. Three MSS. are extant: (1) the poem as sent to Southey in a letter dated Oct. 21, 1794 (see *Letters of S. T. C.*, 1855, i. 94, 95); (2) the Estlin volume; (3) the MS. 4° copy-book.

[2] Lee Boo, the son of Abba Thule, Prince of the Pelew Islands, came over to England with Captain Wilson, died of the small-pox, and is

---

13-14 And He o'er all her brighten'd hue
       Sheds the glitter of the dew. *MS. 4° erased.*

18 The fragrant triumphs of the Rose. *MS. E.* 26 Dawns]
Dawn'd *MS. E.*   27 And] That *MS. E.*

To a Young Lady—Title] Verses addressed to a Lady with a poem relative to a recent event in the French Revolution *MS. E.*

2 friendly] guardian *MS. Letter, 1794, MS. E.*   3 cloisters]
cloister *MS. E.*   5 careless] rosy *MS. E.*   9 My pensive soul amid the twilight gloom *MS. Letter, 1794.*   10 Boo] Bo *MS. E.*

TO A YOUNG LADY

Where'er I wander'd, Pity still was near,
Breath'd from the heart and glisten'd in the tear:
No knell that toll'd but fill'd my anxious eye,
And suffering Nature wept that *one* should die![1]

Thus to sad sympathies I sooth'd my breast, 15
Calm, as the rainbow in the weeping West:
When slumbering Freedom roused by high Disdain
With giant Fury burst her triple chain!
Fierce on her front the blasting Dog-star glow'd;
Her banners, like a midnight meteor, flow'd; 20
Amid the yelling of the storm-rent skies!
She came, and scatter'd battles from her eyes!
Then Exultation waked the patriot fire
And swept with wild hand the Tyrtaean lyre:
Red from the Tyrant's wound I shook the lance, 25
And strode in joy the reeking plains of France!

Fallen is the Oppressor, friendless, ghastly, low,
And my heart aches, though Mercy struck the blow.
With wearied thought once more I seek the shade,
Where peaceful Virtue weaves the Myrtle braid. 30
And O! if Eyes whose holy glances roll,
Swift messengers, and eloquent of soul;

---

buried in Greenwich churchyard. See Keate's *Account of the Pelew Islands*. 1788.

[1] And suffering Nature, &c. Southey's *Retrospect*.

  'When eager patriots fly the news to spread
   Of glorious conquest, and of thousands dead;
   All feel the mighty glow of victor joy—
   *   *   *   *   *   *   *   *
   But if extended on the gory plain,
   And, snatch'd in conquest, some lov'd friend be slain,
   Affection's tears will dim the sorrowing eye,
   And suffering Nature grieve that one should die.'

From the *Retrospect* by Robert Southey, published by Dilly [1795, pp. 9, 10]. *MS. 4º.*

---

12 glisten'd] glitter'd *MS. Letter, 1794*.   13 anxious] anguish'd *MS. Letter, 1794*.   16 Calm] Bright *MS. E*.   17 by] with *1829*.   23 waked] woke *MS. Letter, 1794, MS. E.*   24 with wilder hand th' empassion'd lyre *MS. Letter, 1794*: with wilder hand th' Alcaean lyre *MS. 4º, MS. E, Watchman, 1796, 1797, 1803, 1828, 1829.*   25 wound] wounds *MS. Letter, 1794*.   27 In ghastly horror lie th' Oppressors low *MS. Letter, 1794, MS. E, MS. 4º, 1796, Watchman*.   29 With sad and wearied thought I seek the shade *MS. E*: With wearied thought I seek the amaranth shade *MS. Letter, 1794*.   30 the] her *MS. Letter, 1794, MS. E*.   32 The eloquent messengers of the pure soul *MS. Letter, 1794, MS. E, MS. 4º, Watchman, 1796*.

TO A YOUNG LADY

If Smiles more winning, and a gentler Mien
Than the love-wilder'd Maniac's brain hath seen
Shaping celestial forms in vacant air, 35
If these demand the empassion'd Poet's care—
If Mirth and soften'd Sense and Wit refined,
The blameless features of a lovely mind;
Then haply shall my trembling hand assign
No fading wreath to Beauty's saintly shrine. 40
Nor, Sara! thou these early flowers refuse—
Ne'er lurk'd the snake beneath their simple hues;
No purple bloom the Child of Nature brings
From Flattery's night-shade: as he feels he sings.

September 1794.

TRANSLATION[1]

OF WRANGHAM'S 'HENDECASYLLABI AD BRUNTONAM E GRANTA EXITURAM' [KAL. OCT. MDCCXC]

MAID of unboastful charms! whom white-robed Truth
Right onward guiding through the maze of youth,
Forbade the Circe Praise to witch thy soul,
And dash'd to earth th' intoxicating bowl:
Thee meek-eyed Pity, eloquently fair, 5
Clasp'd to her bosom with a mother's care;
And, as she lov'd thy kindred form to trace,
The slow smile wander'd o'er her pallid face.

For never yet did mortal voice impart
Tones more congenial to the sadden'd heart: 10
Whether, to rouse the sympathetic glow,

---

[1] First published in *Poems*, by Francis Wrangham, London, 1795, pp. 79-83. First collected in *P. and D. W.*, 1880, ii. 360* (*Supplement*).

33 winning] cunning *MS. Letter, 1794*. 36 empassion'd] wond'ring *MS. Letter, 1794*. 40 wreath] flowers *MS. Letter, 1794, MS. E.*

41-4   Nor, Brunton! thou the blushing wreath refuse,
    Though harsh her notes, yet guileless is my Muse.
    Unwont at Flattery's Voice to plume her wings,
    A Child of Nature, as she feels she sings. *MS. Letter, 1794.*

    Nor——! thou the blushing wreath refuse
    Tho' harsh her song, yet guileless is the Muse.
    Unwont &c. *MS. E.*

42-4   No Serpent lurks beneath their simple hues.
    No purple blooms from Flattery's nightshade brings,
    The Child of Nature—as he feels he sings. *MS. 4° erased.*

43-4   Nature's pure Child from Flatt'ry's night-shade brings
    No blooms rich-purpling: as he feels he sings. *MS. 4°.*

Below l. 44 September, 1794 *1797, 1803*: September 1792 *1828, 1829, 1834*.

Thou pourest lone Monimia's tale of woe;
Or haply clothest with funereal vest
The bridal loves that wept in Juliet's breast.
O'er our chill limbs the thrilling Terrors creep, 15
Th' entrancéd Passions their still vigil keep;
While the deep sighs, responsive to the song,
Sound through the silence of the trembling throng.

But purer raptures lighten'd from thy face,
And spread o'er all thy form an holier grace, 20
When from the daughter's breasts the father drew
The life he gave, and mix'd the big tear's dew.
Nor was it thine th' heroic strain to roll
With mimic feelings foreign from the soul:
Bright in thy parent's eye we mark'd the tear; 25
Methought he said, 'Thou art no Actress here!
A semblance of thyself the *Grecian* dame,
And Brunton and Euphrasia still the same!'

O soon to seek the city's busier scene,
Pause thee awhile, thou chaste-eyed maid serene, 30
Till Granta's sons from all her sacred bowers
With grateful hand shall weave Pierian flowers
To twine a fragrant chaplet round thy brow,
Enchanting ministress of virtuous woe!
1794.

TO MISS BRUNTON[1]

WITH THE PRECEDING TRANSLATION

THAT darling of the Tragic Muse,
   When Wrangham sung her praise,
Thalia lost her rosy hues,
   And sicken'd at her lays:

But transient was th' unwonted sigh; 5
   For soon the Goddess spied
A sister-form of mirthful eye,
   And danc'd for joy and cried:

'Meek Pity's sweetest child, proud dame,
   The fates have given to you! 10
Still bid your Poet boast her name;
   I have *my* Brunton too.'
1794.

---

[1] First published in *Poems*, by Francis Wrangham, 1795, p. 83. First collected in *P. and D. W.*, 1880, ii. 362* (*Supplement*).

EPITAPH ON AN INFANT[1]

Ere Sin could blight or Sorrow fade,
  Death came with friendly care:
The opening Bud to Heaven convey'd,
  And bade it blossom *there*.

1794.

PANTISOCRACY[2]

No more my visionary soul shall dwell
On joys that were; no more endure to weigh
The shame and anguish of the evil day,
Wisely forgetful! O'er the ocean swell

---

[1] First published in the *Morning Chronicle*, September 23, 1794: included in *The Watchman*, No. IX, May 5, 1796, *Poems* 1796, 1797, 1803, 1828, 1829, and 1834. These well-known lines, which vexed the soul of Charles Lamb, were probably adapted from 'An Epitaph on an Infant' in the churchyard of Birchington, Kent (*A Collection of Epitaphs*, 1806, i. 219):—

> Ah! why so soon, just as the bloom appears,
> Drops the fair blossom in the vale of tears?
> Death view'd the treasure in the desart given
> And claim'd the right of planting it in Heav'n.

In *MS. E* a Greek version (possibly a rejected prize epigram) is prefixed with the accompanying footnote.

> Ηλυθες εἰς αιδην, καὶ δή τυ ποθεῦσι τοκηες·
> Ηλυθες αδυ βρεφος! τοι βραχυ δυνε φαος.
> Ομμα μεν εις σεο σημα Πατηρ πικρον ποτιβαλλει
> Ευσεβεης δε Θεῳ δωρα διδωσιν ἑα!*

* Translation of the Greek Epitaph. 'Thou art gone down into the Grave, and heavily do thy Parents feel the Loss. Thou art gone down into the Grave, sweet Baby! Thy short Light is set! Thy Father casts an Eye of Anguish towards thy Tomb—yet with uncomplaining Piety resigns to God his own Gift!'

Equal or Greater simplicity marks all the writings of the Greek Poets.—The above [i.e. the Greek] Epitaph was written in Imitation of them. [S. T. C.]

[2] First published in the *Life and Correspondence of R. Southey*, 1849, i. 224. First collected 1852 (Notes). Southey includes the sonnet in a letter to his brother Thomas dated Oct. 19, 1794, and attributes the authorship to Coleridge's friend S. Favell, with whom he had been in correspondence. He had already received the sonnet in a letter from Coleridge (dated Sept. 18, 1794), who claims it for his own and apologizes for the badness of the poetry. The octave was included (ll. 129-36) in the second version of the *Monody on the Death of Chatterton*, first printed in Lancelot Sharpe's edition of the *Poems* of Chatterton published at Cambridge in 1794. Mrs. H. N. Coleridge (*Poems*, 1852, p. 382) prints the sonnet and apologizes for the alleged plagiarism. It is difficult to believe that either the first eight or last six lines of the sonnet were not written by Coleridge. It is included in the MS. volume of Poems which Coleridge presented to Mrs. Estlin in 1795. The text is that of *Letter Sept. 18, 1794*.

Pantisocracy—Title] Sonnet *MS. E.*   1 my] the *MS. E.*

Sublime of Hope, I seek the cottag'd dell
Where Virtue calm with careless step may stray,
And dancing to the moonlight roundelay,
The wizard Passions weave an holy spell.
Eyes that have ach'd with Sorrow! Ye shall weep
Tears of doubt-mingled joy, like theirs who start
From Precipices of distemper'd sleep,
On which the fierce-eyed Fiends their revels keep,
And see the rising Sun, and feel it dart
New rays of pleasance trembling to the heart.
1794.

ON THE PROSPECT OF ESTABLISHING A PANTISOCRACY IN AMERICA [1]

Whilst pale Anxiety, corrosive Care,
The tear of Woe, the gloom of sad Despair,
  And deepen'd Anguish generous bosoms rend;—
Whilst patriot souls their country's fate lament;
Whilst mad with rage demoniac, foul intent,
  Embattled legions Despots vainly send
To arrest the immortal mind's expanding ray
  Of everlasting Truth;—I other climes
Where dawns, with hope serene, a brighter day
Than e'er saw Albion in her happiest times,
  With mental eye exulting now explore,
  And soon with kindred minds shall haste to enjoy
(Free from the ills which here our peace destroy)
Content and Bliss on Transatlantic shore.
1794.

ELEGY [2]

IMITATED FROM ONE OF AKENSIDE'S BLANK-VERSE INSCRIPTIONS [(No.) III.]

Near the lone pile with ivy overspread,
  Fast by the rivulet's sleep-persuading sound,

---

[1] First published in the *Co-operative Magazine and Monthly Herald*, March 6, 1826, and reprinted in the *Athenæum*, Nov. 5, 1904. First collected in 1907. It has been conjectured, but proof is wanting, that the sonnet was written by Coleridge.

[2] First published in the *Morning Chronicle*, September 23, 1794: included in *The Watchman*, No. III, March 17, 1794: in *Sibylline Leaves*, 1817: 1828, 1829, and 1834, but omitted in 1852 as of doubtful origin.

Pantisocracy. 8 Passions weave] Passion wears *Letter, Oct. 19 1794, 1852.* 9 Sorrow] anguish *Letter, Oct. 19 1794, 1852.* 10 like theirs] as those *Letter, Oct. 19 1794, 1852*: as they, *MS. E.* 13 feel] find *Letter, Oct. 19 1794, 1852.* 14 pleasance] pleasure *Letter, Oct. 19 1794, 1852.*

Elegy—Title] An Elegy *Morning Chronicle, Watchman.* 1 the] yon *M. C.*

Where 'sleeps the moonlight' on yon verdant bed—
  O humbly press that consecrated ground!

For there does Edmund rest, the learnéd swain!   5
  And there his spirit most delights to rove:
Young Edmund! fam'd for each harmonious strain,
  And the sore wounds of ill-requited Love.

Like some tall tree that spreads its branches wide,
  And loads the West-wind with its soft perfume,   10
His manhood blossom'd; till the faithless pride
  Of fair Matilda sank him to the tomb.

But soon did righteous Heaven her Guilt pursue!
  Where'er with wilder'd step she wander'd pale,
Still Edmund's image rose to blast her view,   15
  Still Edmund's voice accus'd her in each gale.

With keen regret, and conscious Guilt's alarms,
  Amid the pomp of Affluence she pined;
Nor all that lur'd her faith from Edmund's arms
  Could lull the wakeful horror of her mind.   20

Go, Traveller! tell the tale with sorrow fraught:
  Some tearful Maid perchance, or blooming Youth,
May hold it in remembrance; and be taught
  That Riches cannot pay for Love or Truth.
?1794.

THE FADED FLOWER[1]

UNGRATEFUL he, who pluck'd thee from thy stalk,
Poor faded flow'ret! on his careless way;
Inhal'd awhile thy odours on his walk,
Then onward pass'd and left thee to decay.
Ah! melancholy emblem! had I seen   5
Thy modest beauties dew'd with Evening's gem,
I had not rudely cropp'd thy parent stem,
But left thee, blushing, 'mid the enliven'd green.
And now I bend me o'er thy wither'd bloom,

The elegy as printed in the *Morning Chronicle* is unsigned. In *The Watchman* it is signed T.

[1] First published in the *Monthly Magazine*, August, 1836. First collected in *P. W.*, 1893.

---

6 And there his pale-eyed phantom loves to rove *M. C.*   10 West-wind] Zephyr *M. C.*   11 till] ere *M. C.*   12 Lucinda sunk *M. C.*   13 Guilt] crime *M. C.*   14 step] steps *M. C.*   17 remorse and tortur'd Guilt's *M. C.*   20 Could soothe the conscious horrors of her mind *M. C.*   horror] horrors *The Watchman*.   22 tearful] lovely *M. C.*

And drop the tear—as Fancy, at my side,   10
Deep-sighing, points the fair frail Abra's tomb—
'Like thine, sad Flower, was that poor wanderer's pride!
Oh! lost to Love and Truth, whose selfish joy
Tasted her vernal sweets, but tasted to destroy!'
1794.

THE OUTCAST[1]

PALE Roamer through the night! thou poor Forlorn!
Remorse that man on his death-bed possess,
Who in the credulous hour of tenderness
Betrayed, then cast thee forth to Want and Scorn!
The world is pitiless: the chaste one's pride   5
Mimic of Virtue scowls on thy distress:
Thy Loves and they that envied thee deride:
And Vice alone will shelter Wretchedness!
O! I could weep to think that there should be
Cold-bosom'd lewd ones, who endure to place   10
Foul offerings on the shrine of Misery,
And force from Famine the caress of Love;
May He shed healing on the sore disgrace,
He, the great Comforter that rules above!
?1794.

DOMESTIC PEACE[2]

[FROM 'THE FALL OF ROBESPIERRE', ACT I, L. 210]

   TELL me, on what holy ground
   May Domestic Peace be found?
   Halcyon daughter of the skies,
   Far on fearful wings she flies,
   From the pomp of Sceptered State,   5
   From the Rebel's noisy hate.

   In a cottag'd vale She dwells,
   Listening to the Sabbath bells!

---

[1] First published in 1796: included in 1797, 1803, 1828, 1829, and 1834. 'The first half of Effusion xv was written by the Author of "Joan of Arc", an Epic Poem.' Preface to *Poems*, 1796, p. xi.

[2] First published in the *Fall of Robespierre*, 1795: included (as 'Song', p. 13) in 1796, 1797, 1803, 1828, 1829, and 1834.

The Outcast—Title] Effusion xv. *1796*: Sonnet vii. *1797*: Sonnet vi. *1803*: Sonnet ix. *1828, 1829, and 1834*: An Unfortunate *1893*.

7 Thy kindred, when they see thee, turn aside *1803*.   9 O I am sad *1796, 1797, 1803, 1828, 1829*.   10 Men, born of woman *1803*.

13-14 Man has no feeling for thy sore Disgrace:
   Keen blows the Blast upon the moulting Dove. *1803*.

13 the] thy *1796, 1797, 1828*.

Domestic Peace—Title] Effusion xxv. *1796*.

72 DOMESTIC PEACE

  Still around her steps are seen
  Spotless Honour's meeker mien,   10
  Love, the sire of pleasing fears,
  Sorrow smiling through her tears,
  And conscious of the past employ
  Memory, bosom-spring of joy.
1794.

ON A DISCOVERY MADE TOO LATE[1]

THOU bleedest, my poor Heart! and thy distress
Reasoning I ponder with a scornful smile
And probe thy sore wound sternly, though the while
Swoln be mine eye and dim with heaviness.
Why didst thou listen to Hope's whisper bland? 5
Or, listening, why forget the healing tale,
When Jealousy with feverous fancies pale
Jarr'd thy fine fibres with a maniac's hand?
Faint was that Hope, and rayless!—Yet 'twas fair
And sooth'd with many a dream the hour of rest: 10
Thou should'st have lov'd it most, when most opprest,
And nurs'd it with an agony of care,
Even as a mother her sweet infant heir
That wan and sickly droops upon her breast!
 1794.

TO THE AUTHOR OF 'THE ROBBERS'[2]

SCHILLER! that hour I would have wish'd to die.
If thro' the shuddering midnight I had sent
From the dark dungeon of the Tower time-rent
That fearful voice, a famish'd Father's cry—

---

[1] First published in 1796: *Selection of Sonnets, Poems* 1796: in 1797, 1803, 1828, 1829, and 1834. It was sent in a letter to Southey, dated October 21, 1794. (*Letters of S. T. C.*, 1895, i. 92.)

[2] First published in 1796: included in *Selection of Sonnets*, 1796: in 1797, 1803, 1828, 1829, and 1834. The following 'Note' (Note 6, pp. 180, 181) was printed in 1796, and appears again in 1797 as a footnote, p. 83:—' One night in Winter, on leaving a College-friend's room, with

---

On a Discovery—Title] Effusion xix. *1796* (in 'Contents' *To my Heart*): Sonnet II. On a Discovery made too late *1797, 1803, and again in P. and D. W., 1877-80*: Sonnet xi. *1828, 1829, 1834*.

 2-4 Doth Reason ponder with an anguish'd smile
   Probing thy sore wound sternly, tho' the while
   Her eye be swollen and dim with heaviness. *Letter, 1794.*

6 the] its *Letter, 1794.*   7 feverous] feverish *1796, 1797, 1803, 1828, 1829.*
14 wan] pale *Letter, 1794.*

To the Author of 'The Robbers'—Title] Effusion xx. To the Author, &c.

TO THE AUTHOR OF 'THE ROBBERS'

Lest in some after moment aught more mean 5
Might stamp me mortal! A triumphant shout
Black Horror scream'd, and all her *goblin* rout
Diminish'd shrunk from the more withering scene!
Ah! Bard tremendous in sublimity!
Could I behold thee in thy loftier mood 10
Wandering at eve with finely-frenzied eye
Beneath some vast old tempest-swinging wood!
Awhile with mute awe gazing I would brood:
Then weep aloud in a wild ecstasy!
? 1794.

MELANCHOLY [1]

A FRAGMENT

STRETCH'D on a moulder'd Abbey's broadest wall,
   Where ruining ivies propp'd the ruins steep—
Her folded arms wrapping her tatter'd pall,
  [2] Had Melancholy mus'd herself to sleep.

whom I had supped, I carelessly took away with me "The Robbers", a drama, the very name of which I had never before heard of:— A Winter midnight—the wind high—and "The Robbers" for the first time!—The readers of Schiller will conceive what I felt. Schiller introduces no supernatural beings; yet his human beings agitate and astonish more than all the *goblin* rout—even of Shakespeare.' See for another account of the midnight reading of 'The Robbers', Letter to Southey, November [6], 1794, *Letters of S. T. C.*, 1895, i. 96, 97.

In the *Selection of Sonnets*, 1796, this note was reduced to one sentence. 'Schiller introduces no Supernatural Beings.' In 1803 the note is omitted, but a footnote to line 4 is appended: 'The Father of Moor in the Play of the Robbers.'

[1] First published in the *Morning Post*, December 12, 1797 (not, as Coleridge says, the *Morning Chronicle*); included in *Sibylline Leaves*, 1817 (with an addition), and, again, in *P. and D. W.*, 1877-80, and (in its first shape) in 1828, 1829, 1834, 1852, and 1893. Sent in Letter to Sotheby, Aug. 26, 1802.

[2] Bowles borrowed these lines unconsciously, I doubt not. I had repeated the poem on my first visit [Sept. 1797]. *MS. Note, S. T. C.* See, too, *Letter*, Aug. 26, 1802. [Here Melancholy on the pale crags laid, Might muse herself to sleep—*Coomb Ellen*, written September, 1798.]

[To 'Schiller', *Contents*] 1796: Sonnet viii. To the Author of 'The Robbers' 1797: Sonnet xv. 1803: Sonnet xii. To the Author of the Robbers 1828, 1829, 1834.

Lines 1-4 are printed in the reverse order (4, 3, 2, 1). *Selections.*

5-6   That in no after moment aught less vast
       Might stamp me human! *Selections.*

       That in no after moment aught less vast
       Might stamp me mortal! *1797, 1803.*

8 From the more with'ring scene diminish'd past. *Selections, 1797, 1803.*

Melancholy. 1 Upon a mouldering *Letter, Aug. 26, 1802.* 2 Where ruining] Whose running *M. P.* propp'd] prop *Letter, Aug. 26, 1802.*

74   MELANCHOLY

The fern was press'd beneath her hair,   5
The dark green Adder's Tongue¹ was there;
And still as pass'd the flagging sea-gale weak,
The long lank leaf bow'd fluttering o'er her cheek.

That pallid cheek was flush'd: her eager look
Beam'd eloquent in slumber! Inly wrought,   10
Imperfect sounds her moving lips forsook,
And her bent forehead work'd with troubled thought.
Strange was the dream——
? 1794.

TO A YOUNG ASS²

ITS MOTHER BEING TETHERED NEAR IT

Poor little Foal of an oppressèd race!
I love the languid patience of thy face:
And oft with gentle hand I give thee bread,
And clap thy ragged coat, and pat thy head.
But what thy dulled spirits hath dismay'd,   5
That never thou dost sport along the glade?

¹ A Plant found on old walls and in wells and mois[t] [h]edges.—It is often called the Hart's Tongue. *M. C. Asplenium Scolopendrium*, more commonly called Hart's Tongue. *Letter*, 1802. A botanical mistake. The plant I meant is called the Hart's Tongue, but this would unluckily spoil the poetical effect. *Cedat ergo Botanice. Sibylline Leaves*, 1817. A botanical mistake. The plant which the poet here describes is called the Hart's Tongue, *1828, 1829, 1852*.
² First published in the *Morning Chronicle*, December 30, 1794: included in 1796, 1797, 1803, 1828, 1829, and 1834. A MS. version, dated October 24, 1794 (see *P. W.*, 1893, pp. 477, 488), was presented by Coleridge to Professor William Smyth, Professor of Modern History at Cambridge, 1807–49; a second version was included in a letter to Southey, dated December 17, 1794 (*Letters of S. T. C.*, 1895, i. 119, 120).

---

7 pass'd] came *Letter, 1802.*   sea-gale] sea-gales *M. C., Letter, 1802.*
8 The] Her *Letter, 1802.*   9 That] Her *Letter, 1802.*   13 *Not in Letter 1802.*

13   Strange was the dream that fill'd her soul,
            Nor did not whisp'ring spirits roll
        A mystic tumult, and a fateful rhyme,
        Mix'd with wild shapings of the unborn time!
                                    M. C., Sibylline Leaves, 1817.

To a Young Ass—Title] Monologue to a Young Jack Ass in Jesus Piece. Its mother near it chained to a log *MS. Oct. 24, 1794*: Address to a Young Jack-Ass and its Tether'd mother *MS. Dec. 17, 1794*: Address, &c. In familiar verse *Morning Chronicle, Dec. 30, 1794*: Effusion xxxiii. To a Young Ass, &c. *1796*.
3 gentle] friendly *MS. Dec. 1794, M. C.*   4 pat] scratch *MS. Oct. 1794, M. C.*
5 spirits] spirit *MSS. Oct. Dec. 1794, M. C.*   6 along] upon *MS. Dec. 1794, M. C.*

TO A YOUNG ASS

And (most unlike the nature of things young)
That earthward still thy moveless head is hung?
Do thy prophetic fears anticipate,
Meek Child of Misery! thy future fate?   10
The starving meal, and all the thousand aches
'Which patient Merit of the Unworthy takes'?
Or is thy sad heart thrill'd with filial pain
To see thy wretched mother's shorten'd chain?
And truly, very piteous is *her* lot—   15
Chain'd to a log within a narrow spot,
Where the close-eaten grass is scarcely seen,
While sweet around her waves the tempting green!

Poor Ass! thy master should have learnt to show
Pity—best taught by fellowship of Woe!   20
For much I fear me that *He* lives like thee,
Half famish'd in a land of Luxury!
How *askingly* its footsteps hither bend?
It seems to say, 'And have I then *one* friend?'
Innocent foal! thou poor despis'd forlorn!   25
I hail thee *Brother*—spite of the fool's scorn!
And fain would take thee with me, in the Dell
Of Peace and mild Equality to dwell,
Where Toil shall call the charmer Health his bride,
And Laughter tickle Plenty's ribless side!   30

---

8 That still to earth thy moping head is hung MSS. *Oct. Dec. 1794, M. C.*
9 Doth thy prophetic soul MS. *Oct. 1794.*   12 Which] That MSS.
Oct. Dec. 1794.   14 shorten'd] lengthen'd MS. *Dec. 1794, M. C.*
16 within] upon MSS. *Oct. Dec. 1794, M. C.*   19 thy] her 1796.   21
For much I fear, that He lives e'en as she, *1796.*   23 footsteps hither
bend] steps toward me tend MS. *Oct. 1794* : steps towards me bend MS. *Dec.
1794, M. C.*: footsteps t'ward me bend *1796.*   25 despised and forlorn MS.
Oct. 1794.   27 would] I'd MSS. *Oct. Dec. 1794.*   in] to MS. *Oct. 1794.*
28 Of high-soul'd Pantisocracy to dwell MS. *Dec. 1794, M. C.*

28 foll.   Where high-soul'd Pantisocracy shall dwell!
Where Mirth shall tickle Plenty's ribless side,*
And smiles from Beauty's Lip on sunbeams glide,
Where Toil shall wed young Health that charming Lass!
And use his sleek cows for a looking-glass—
Where Rats shall mess with Terriers hand-in-glove
And Mice with Pussy's Whiskers sport in Love MS. *Oct. 1794.*

* This is a truly poetical line of which the author has assured us that
he did not *mean* it to have any *meaning. Note by Ed. of MS. Oct. 1794.*

How thou wouldst toss thy heels in gamesome play,
And frisk about, as lamb or kitten gay!
Yea! and more musically sweet to me
Thy dissonant harsh bray of joy would be,
Than warbled melodies that soothe to rest   35
The aching of pale Fashion's vacant breast!
    1794.

LINES ON A FRIEND[1]

WHO DIED OF A FRENZY FEVER INDUCED BY CALUMNIOUS REPORTS

EDMUND! thy grave with aching eye I scan,
And inly groan for Heaven's poor outcast—Man!
'Tis tempest all or gloom : in early youth
If gifted with th' Ithuriel lance of Truth
We force to start amid her feign'd caress   5
Vice, siren-hag! in native ugliness;
A Brother's fate will haply rouse the tear,
And on we go in heaviness and fear!
But if our fond hearts call to Pleasure's bower
Some pigmy Folly in a careless hour,   10
The faithless guest shall stamp the enchanted ground,
And mingled forms of Misery rise around :
Heart-fretting Fear, with pallid look aghast,
That courts the future woe to hide the past;
Remorse, the poison'd arrow in his side,   15
And loud lewd Mirth, to Anguish close allied:

---

[1] First published in 1796 : included in 1797, 1803, 1828, 1829, and 1834. Four MS. versions are extant, (1) in Letter to Southey, Nov. [6], 1794 (*Letters of S. T. C.*, 1895, i. 98, 99) : (2) in letter to George Coleridge, Nov. 6, 1794 : (3) in the Estlin copy-book : (4) in the MS. 4°. The Friend was the Rev. Fulwood Smerdon, vicar of Ottery St. Mary, who died in August 1794.

35-6   Than Handel's softest airs that soothe to rest
        The tumult of a scoundrel Monarch's Breast. *MS. Oct. 1794.*
        Than *Banti's* warbled airs that sooth to rest
        The tumult &c. *MS. Dec. 1794.*

36   The tumult of some SCOUNDREL Monarch's breast. *M. C. 1796.*

Lines on a Friend—Title] On the Death of a Friend who died of a Frenzy Fever brought on by anxiety *MS. E.*

1 —! thy grave *MS. Letter to R. S.* : Smerdon! thy grave *MS. Letter to G. C.*   3 early] earliest *MS. Letters to R. S. and G. C.*, *MS. E.*   5 We] He *MS. Letters to R. S. and G. C.*, *MS. E*, *MS. 4°*, *1796.*   7 will] shall *MS. Letters to R. S. and G. C.*, *MS. E.*   8 And on he goes *MS. Letters to R. S. and G. C.*, *MS. E*, *1796*: Onward we move *1803.*   9 his fond heart *MS. Letters to R. S. and G. C.*, *MS. E*, *1796.*   11 quick stamps *MS. Letters to R. S. and G. C.*, *MS. E*, *MS. 4°.*   12 threaten round *MS. Letters to R. S. and G. C.*

LINES ON A FRIEND

Till Frenzy, fierce-eyed child of moping Pain,
Darts her hot lightning-flash athwart the brain.

Rest, injur'd shade! Shall Slander squatting near
Spit her cold venom in a dead man's ear? 20
'Twas thine to feel the sympathetic glow
In Merit's joy, and Poverty's meek woe ;
Thine all, that cheer the moment as it flies,
The zoneless Cares, and smiling Courtesies.
Nurs'd in thy heart the firmer Virtues grew, 25
And in thy heart they wither'd! Such chill dew
Wan Indolence on each young blossom shed ;
And Vanity her filmy net-work spread,
With eye that roll'd around in asking gaze,
And tongue that traffick'd in the trade of praise. 30
Thy follies such! the hard world mark'd them well!
Were they more wise, the Proud who never fell?
Rest, injur'd shade! the poor man's grateful prayer
On heaven-ward wing thy wounded soul shall bear.

As oft at twilight gloom thy grave I pass, 35
And sit me down upon its recent grass,
With introverted eye I contemplate
Similitude of soul, perhaps of—Fate!
To me hath Heaven with bounteous hand assign'd
Energic Reason and a shaping mind, 40
The daring ken of Truth, the Patriot's part,
And Pity's sigh, that breathes the gentle heart—
Sloth-jaundic'd all! and from my graspless hand
Drop Friendship's precious pearls, like hour-glass sand.
I weep, yet stoop not! the faint anguish flows, 45
A dreamy pang in Morning's feverous doze.

Is this piled earth our Being's passless mound?
Tell me, cold grave! is Death with poppies crown'd?

17 fierce-eyed] frantic *MS. Letters to R. S. and G. C., MS. E erased* [See *Lamb's Letter to Coleridge*, June 10, 1796].   19 squatting] couching *MS. Letter to G. C., MS. E* [See *Lamb's Letter*, June 10, 1796].   23 cheer] cheers *MS. E.*   25 firmer] generous *MS. Letters to R. S. and G. C.* : manly *MS. E.*   29 roll'd] prowl'd *MS. Letters to R. S. and G. C., MS. E.*

33–4   the poor man's prayer of praise
     On heavenward wing thy wounded soul shall raise. *1796.*

35 As oft in Fancy's thought *MS. Letters to R. S. and G. C.*   39 bounteous] liberal *MS. Letters to R. S. and G. C., MS. E.*   41 ken] soul *MS. Letter to R. S.*   46 feverous] feverish *all MSS. and Eds.* 1796–1829.   47 this] that *MS. Letters to R. S. and G. C., MS. E.*   passless] hapless *Letter to G. C.*

Tired Sentinel! mid fitful starts I nod,
And fain would sleep, though pillowed on a clod! 50
1794.

TO A FRIEND[1]
[CHARLES LAMB]
TOGETHER WITH AN UNFINISHED POEM

THUS far my scanty brain hath built the rhyme
Elaborate and swelling: yet the heart
Not owns it. From thy spirit-breathing powers
I ask not now, my friend! the aiding verse,
Tedious to thee, and from thy anxious thought 5
Of dissonant mood. In fancy (well I know)
From business wandering far and local cares,
Thou creepest round a dear-lov'd Sister's bed
With noiseless step, and watchest the faint look,
Soothing each pang with fond solicitude, 10
And tenderest tones medicinal of love.
I too a Sister *had*, an only Sister—
She lov'd me dearly, and I doted on her!
To her I pour'd forth all my puny sorrows
(As a sick Patient in a Nurse's arms) 15
And of the heart those hidden maladies
That e'en from Friendship's eye will shrink asham'd.

[1] First published in 1796; included in 1797, 1803, and, again, in 1844. Lines 12-19 ('I too a sister . . . Because she was not') are published in 1834 (i. 35) under the heading 'The Same', i. e. the same as the preceding poem, 'On seeing a Youth affectionately welcomed by a Sister.' The date, December 1794, affixed in 1797 and 1803, is correct. The poem was sent in a letter from Coleridge to Southey, dated December 1794. (*Letters of S. T. C.*, 1895, i. 128.) The 'Unfinished Poem' was, certainly, *Religious Musings*, begun on Christmas Eve, 1794. The text is that of 1844.

---

49 Sentinel] Centinel *all MSS. and Eds. 1796-1829*. mid] with *Letters to R. S. and G. C.* Below l. 50 *the date* (November 1794) *is affixed in 1796, 1797, and 1803*.

To a Friend—Title] To C. Lamb *MS. Letter, Dec. 1794*: Effusion xxii. To a Friend, &c. *1796*: To Charles Lamb with an unfinished Poem *1844*.

1-3 Thus far my sterile brain hath fram'd the song
Elaborate and swelling: but the heart
Not owns it. From thy spirit-breathing power
MS. Letter, Dec. 1794.

7 *Not in MS. Letter, Dec. 1794*.
Between 13 *and* 14 On her soft bosom I reposed my cares
And gain'd for every wound a healing tear.
MS. Letter, 1794.

15 a] his *MS. Letter, 1794, 1796, 1797, 1803*. 17 That shrink asham'd from even Friendship's eye. *MS. Letter, 1794, 1796, 1797*.

O! I have wak'd at midnight, and have wept,
Because she was not!—Cheerily, dear Charles!
Thou thy best friend shalt cherish many a year: 20
Such warm presages feel I of high Hope.
For not uninterested the dear Maid
I've view'd—her soul affectionate yet wise,
Her polish'd wit as mild as lambent glories
That play around a sainted infant's head. 25
He knows (the Spirit that in secret sees,
Of whose omniscient and all-spreading Love
Aught to *implore*[1] were impotence of mind)
That my mute thoughts are sad before his throne,
Prepar'd, when he his healing ray vouchsafes, 30
Thanksgiving to pour forth with lifted heart,
And praise Him Gracious with a Brother's Joy!
1794.

SONNETS ON EMINENT CHARACTERS

CONTRIBUTED TO THE 'MORNING CHRONICLE' IN DECEMBER 1794
AND JANUARY 1795

[The Sonnets were introduced by the following letter:—

'MR. EDITOR—If, Sir, the following Poems will not disgrace your poetical department, I will transmit you a series of *Sonnets* (as it is the fashion to call them) addressed like these to eminent Contemporaries.

'JESUS COLLEGE, CAMBRIDGE.' S. T. C.]

I[2]

TO THE HONOURABLE MR. ERSKINE

WHEN British Freedom for an happier land
  Spread her broad wings, that flutter'd with affright,
ERSKINE! thy voice she heard, and paus'd her flight
Sublime of hope, for dreadless thou didst stand

---

[1] I utterly recant the sentiment contained in the lines—
'Of whose omniscient and all-spreading Love
Aught to *implore* were impotence of mind,'
it being written in Scripture, '*Ask*, and it shall be given you,' and my human reason being moreover convinced of the propriety of offering *petitions* as well as thanksgivings to Deity. [Note of S. T. C., in *Poems*, 1797 and 1803.]

[2] First published in the *Morning Chronicle*, Dec. 1, 1794: included in 1796, 1803, 1828, 1829, and 1834.

---

18 wak'd] woke *MS. Letter, 1794, 1796, 1797, 1803*.   21 warm] high: high] warm *MS. Letter, 1794*.   presages] presagings *1803*.   25 sainted] holy *MS. Letter, 1794*.   26 that] who *MS. Letter, 1794*.   31 To pour forth thanksgiving *MS. Letter, 1794, 1796, 1797, 1803*.

To the Honourable Mr. Erskine—Title] Effusion v. *1796*: Sonnet x. *1803*: Sonnet iv. *1828, 1829, 1834*.

4 for dreadless] where fearless *M. C. Dec. 1, 1794*.

80   SONNETS ON EMINENT CHARACTERS

   (Thy censer glowing with the hallow'd flame)   5
   A hireless Priest before the insulted shrine,
   And at her altar pour the stream divine
Of unmatch'd eloquence. Therefore thy name

Her sons shall venerate, and cheer thy breast
   With blessings heaven-ward breath'd. And when the doom
   Of Nature bids thee die, beyond the tomb   11
Thy light shall shine: as sunk beneath the West

Though the great Summer Sun eludes our gaze,
Still burns wide Heaven with his distended blaze. *⁎*
   December 1, 1794.

   ⁎ 'Our elegant correspondent will highly gratify every reader of taste by the continuance of his exquisitely beautiful productions. No. II. shall appear on an early day.'

II [1]

BURKE

As late I lay in Slumber's shadowy vale,
   With wetted cheek and in a mourner's guise,
   I saw the sainted form of FREEDOM rise:
She spake! not sadder moans the autumnal gale—

'Great Son of Genius! sweet to me thy name,   5
   Ere in an evil hour with alter'd voice
   Thou bad'st Oppression's hireling crew rejoice
Blasting with wizard spell my laurell'd fame.

'Yet never, BURKE! thou drank'st Corruption's bowl![2]
   Thee stormy Pity and the cherish'd lure   10

---

[1] First published in the *Morning Chronicle*, Dec. 9, 1794: included in 1796, 1803, 1828, 1829, and 1834. This Sonnet was sent in a letter to Southey, dated December 11, 1794. *Letters of S. T. C.*, 1895, i. 118.

[2] *Yet never*, BURKE! *thou drank'st Corruption's bowl!*
When I composed this line, I had not read the following paragraph in the *Cambridge Intelligencer* (of Saturday, November 21, 1795):—

'*When Mr. Burke first crossed over the House of Commons from the Opposition to the Ministry, he received a pension of £1200 a year charged on the Kings Privy Purse. When he had completed his labours, it was then a question what recom-*

---

  6 A] An *M. C.*, *1796–1803, 1828, 1829*.   the insulted] her injur'd *M. C.*
  7 pour] pour'dst *M. C.*, *1796, 1803*.   8 unmatch'd] matchless *M. C.*
  10 With heav'n-breath'd blessings; and, when late the doom *M. C.*   11 die] rise *1803*.

    13–14   Though the great Sun not meets our wistful gaze
           Still glows wide Heaven *M. C.*
  Below l. 14 Jesus College Cambridge *M. C.*

  Burke—Title] Effusion ii. *1796*: Sonnet vii. *1803*: Sonnet ii. *1828, 1829, 1834*.

  1 As late I roam'd through Fancy's shadowy vale *MS. Letter, Dec. 11, 1794*.
  4 She] *lie MS. Letter, 1794*.

Of Pomp, and proud Precipitance of soul
Wilder'd with meteor fires. Ah Spirit pure!

'That Error's mist had left thy purgéd eye:
So might I clasp thee with a Mother's joy!'
December 9, 1794.

III[1]

PRIESTLEY

Though rous'd by that dark Vizir Riot rude
  Have driven our Priestley o'er the Ocean swell;
  Though Superstition and her wolfish brood
Bay his mild radiance, impotent and fell;

Calm in his halls of brightness he shall dwell!   5
  For lo! Religion at his strong behest
  Starts with mild anger from the Papal spell,
And flings to Earth her tinsel-glittering vest,

Her mitred State and cumbrous Pomp unholy;
  And Justice wakes to bid th' Oppressor wail   10
  Insulting aye the wrongs of patient Folly;
And from her dark retreat by Wisdom won

pense his service deserved. Mr. Burke wanting a present supply of money, it was thought that a pension of £2000 *per annum* for *forty years certain*, would sell for eighteen years' purchase, and bring him of course £36,000. But this pension must, by the very unfortunate act, of which Mr. Burke was himself the author, have come before Parliament. Instead of this Mr. Pitt suggested the idea of a pension of £2000 a year for *three lives*, to be charged on the King's Revenue of the West India 4½ per cents. This was tried at the market, but it was found that it would not produce the £36,000 which were wanted. In consequence of this a pension of £2500 per annum, *for three lives* on the 4½ West India Fund, the lives to be nominated by Mr. Burke, that he may accommodate the purchasers is *finally* granted to this disinterested patriot. He has thus retir'd from the trade of politics, with pensions to the amount of £3700 a year.' 1796, Note, pp. 177–9.

[1] First published in the *Morning Chronicle*, December 11, 1794: included in 1796, 1803, 1828, 1829, and 1834. In all editions prior to 1852, 'Priestley' is spelled 'Priestly'. The Sonnet was sent to Southey in a letter dated December 17, 1794.

---

12 Urg'd on with wild'ring fires *MS. Letter, Dec. 17, 1794, M. C.*   Below
l. 14 Jesus College *M. C.*

Priestley—Title] Effusion iv. *1796* : Sonnet ix. *1803* : Sonnet iii. *1828, 1829, 1834.*

1-2 Tho' king-bred rage with lawless uproar rude
    Hath driv'n *M. C.*
Tho' king-bred rage with lawless tumult rude
    Have driv'n *MS. Letter, Dec. 17, 1794.*

7 Disdainful rouses from the Papal spell, *M. C., MS. Letter, 1794.*   11
That ground th' ensnared soul of patient Folly. *M. C., MS. Letter, 1794.*

82 SONNETS ON EMINENT CHARACTERS

Meek NATURE slowly lifts her matron veil
To smile with fondness on her gazing Son!

December 11, 1794.

IV[1]

LA FAYETTE

As when far off the warbled strains are heard
    That soar on Morning's wing the vales among;
    Within his cage the imprison'd Matin Bird
Swells the full chorus with a generous song:

He bathes no pinion in the dewy light, 5
    No Father's joy, no Lover's bliss he shares,
    Yet still the rising radiance cheers his sight—
His fellows' Freedom soothes the Captive's cares!

Thou, FAYETTE! who didst wake with startling voice
    Life's better Sun from that long wintry night, 10
    Thus in thy Country's triumphs shalt rejoice
And mock with raptures high the Dungeon's might:

For lo! the Morning struggles into Day,
And Slavery's spectres shriek and vanish from the ray!

*** The above beautiful sonnet was written antecedently to the joyful account of the Patriot's escape from the Tyrant's Dungeon. [Note in *M. C.*]

December 15, 1794.

V[2]

KOSKIUSKO

O WHAT a loud and fearful shriek was there,
    As though a thousand souls one death-groan pour'd!
    Ah me! they saw beneath a Hireling's sword
Their KOSKIUSKO fall! Through the swart air

---

[1] First published in the *Morning Chronicle*, December 15, 1794: included in 1796, 1828, 1829, and 1834.

[2] First published in the *Morning Chronicle*, December 16, 1794: included in 1796, 1828, 1829, 1834. The Sonnet was sent to Southey in a letter dated December 17, 1794. *Letters of S. T. C.*, 1895, i. 117.

La Fayette—Title] Effusion ix. *1796*: Sonnet xiii. *1803*: Sonnet vii. *1828, 1829, 1834.*

Koskiusko—Title] Effusion viii. *1796* : Sonnet vi. *1828, 1829, 1834.*

3-4 Great *Kosciusko* 'neath an hireling's sword
    The warriors view'd! Hark! through the list'ning air
                            MS. Letter, Dec. 17, 1794.
Great KOSCIUSKO 'neath an Hireling's sword
His country view'd. Hark through the list'ning air *M. C.*
Ah me! they view'd beneath an hireling's sword
Fall'n Kosciusko! Thro' the burthened air *1796, 1828, 1829.*

SONNETS ON EMINENT CHARACTERS

(As pauses the tir'd Cossac's barbarous yell 5
  Of Triumph) on the chill and midnight gale
  Rises with frantic burst or sadder swell
The dirge of murder'd Hope! while Freedom pale
Bends in such anguish o'er her destin'd bier,
  As if from eldest time some Spirit meek 10
  Had gather'd in a mystic urn each tear
That ever on a Patriot's furrow'd cheek

Fit channel found; and she had drain'd the bowl
In the mere wilfulness, and sick despair of soul!

December 16, 1794.

VI[1]

PITT

Not always should the Tear's ambrosial dew
  Roll its soft anguish down thy furrow'd cheek!
  Not always heaven-breath'd tones of Suppliance meek
Beseem thee, Mercy! Yon dark Scowler view,
Who with proud words of dear-lov'd Freedom came— 5
  More blasting than the mildew from the South!
  And kiss'd his country with Iscariot mouth
(Ah! foul apostate from his Father's fame!)[2]
Then fix'd her on the Cross of deep distress,
  And at safe distance marks the thirsty Lance 10
  Pierce her big side! But O! if some strange trance
The eye-lids of thy stern-brow'd Sister[3] press,

---

[1] First published in the *Morning Chronicle*, December 23, 1794, and, secondly, in *The Watchman*, No. V, April 2, 1796; included in 1796, 1803, and in 1852, with the following note:—'This Sonnet, and the ninth, to Stanhope, were among the pieces withdrawn from the second edition of 1797. They reappeared in the edition of 1803, and were again withdrawn in 1828, solely, it may be presumed, on account of their political vehemence. They will excite no angry feelings, and lead to no misapprehensions now, and as they are fully equal to their companions in poetical merit, the Editors have not scrupled to reproduce them. These Sonnets were originally entitled "Effusions".'

[2] Earl of Chatham.   [3] Justice.

---

5 As] When *M. C., MS. Letter, Dec. 17, 1794*.   8 The 'dirge of Murder'd Hope' *MS. Letter, Dec. 17, 1794*.   12 That ever furrow'd a sad Patriot's cheek *MS. Letter, 1794, M. C., 1796*.

13-14 And she had drench'd the sorrows of the bowl
    E'en till she reel'd intoxicate of soul *MS. Letter, 1794, M. C.*
    And she had drain'd the sorrows of the bowl
    E'en till she reel'd, &c. *1796*.

Pitt—Title] Effusion iii. *1796*: To Mercy *Watchman*: Sonnet viii. *1803*: Sonnet iii. *1852*.

8 Staining most foul a Godlike Father's name *M. C., Watchman*.

Seize, Mercy! thou more terrible the brand,   13
And hurl her thunderbolts with fiercer hand!

December 23, 1794.

VII[1]

TO THE REV. W. L. BOWLES[2]

[FIRST VERSION, PRINTED IN 'MORNING CHRONICLE',
DECEMBER 26, 1794]

My heart has thank'd thee, BOWLES! for those soft strains,
   That, on the still air floating, tremblingly
   Wak'd in me Fancy, Love, and Sympathy!
For hence, not callous to a Brother's pains

Thro' Youth's gay prime and thornless paths I went;   5
   And, when the *darker* day of life began,
   And I did roam, a thought-bewilder'd man!
Thy kindred Lays an healing solace lent,

Each lonely pang with dreamy joys combin'd,
   And stole from vain REGRET her scorpion stings;   10
   While shadowy PLEASURE, with mysterious wings,
Brooded the wavy and tumultuous mind,

Like that great Spirit, who with plastic sweep
Mov'd on the darkness of the formless Deep!

---

[1] First published in the *Morning Chronicle*, December 26, 1794. First collected, *P. and D. W.*, 1877, i. 138. The sonnet was sent in a letter to Southey, dated December 11, 1794. *Letters of S. T. C.*, 1895, i. 111.

[2] Author of *Sonnets and other Poems*, published by Dilly. To Mr. Bowles's poetry I have always thought the following remarks from Maximus Tyrius peculiarly applicable:—'I am not now treating of that poetry which is estimated by the pleasure it affords to the ear—the ear having been corrupted, and the judgment-seat of the perceptions; but of that which proceeds from the intellectual Helicon, that which is *dignified*, and appertaining to *human* feelings, and entering into the soul.'—The 13th Sonnet for exquisite delicacy of painting; the 19th for tender simplicity; and the 25th for manly pathos, are compositions of, perhaps, unrivalled merit. Yet while I am selecting these, I almost accuse myself of causeless partiality; for surely never was a writer so equal in excellence!— S. T. C. [In this note as it first appeared in the *Morning Chronicle* a Greek sentence preceded the supposed English translation. It is not to be found in the *Dissertations* of Maximus Tyrius, but the following passage which, for verbal similitudes, may be compared with others (e. g. 20, 8, p. 243 : 21, 3, p. 247 ; 28, 3, p. 336) is to be found in Davies and Markland's edition (Lips. 1725), vol. ii, p. 203 :—Οὔ τί τοι λέγω τὴν δι' αὐλῶν καὶ ᾠδῶν καὶ χορῶν καὶ ψαλμάτων, ἄνευ λόγου ἐπὶ τῇ ψυχῇ ἰοῦσαν, τῷ τερπνῷ τῆς ἀκοῆς τιμηθεῖσαν . . . τὴν ἀληθῆ καὶ ἐκ τοῦ Ἑλικῶνος μοῦσαν, . . .]

---

13 Seize thou more terrible th' avenging brand *M. C.*
To the Rev. W. L. Bowles—3 Wak'd] Woke *MS. Letter, Dec. 11, 1794.*

[SECOND VERSION][1]

My heart has thank'd thee, Bowles! for those soft strains
  Whose sadness soothes me, like the murmuring
  Of wild-bees in the sunny showers of spring!
For hence not callous to the mourner's pains

Through Youth's gay prime and thornless paths I went: 5
  And when the mightier Throes of mind began,
  And drove me forth, a thought-bewilder'd man,
Their mild and manliest melancholy lent

A mingled charm, such as the pang consign'd
  To slumber, though the big tear it renew'd;   10
  Bidding a strange mysterious Pleasure brood
Over the wavy and tumultuous mind,

As the great Spirit erst with plastic sweep
Mov'd on the darkness of the unform'd deep.

VIII[2]

MRS. SIDDONS

As when a child on some long Winter's night
  Affrighted clinging to its Grandam's knees
  With eager wond'ring and perturb'd delight
Listens strange tales of fearful dark decrees

---

[1] First published in 1796: included in 1797, 1803, 1828, 1829, and 1834.
[2] First published in the *Morning Chronicle*, December 29, 1794, under the signature, S. T. C.: included in 1796 (as C. L.'s) and in 1797 as Charles Lamb's, but reassigned to Coleridge in 1803. First collected, *P. and D. W.*, 1877, i. 140, 141. This sonnet may have been altered by Coleridge, but was no doubt written by Lamb and given by him to Coleridge to make up his tale of sonnets for the *Morning Chronicle*. In 1796 and 1797 Coleridge acknowledged the sonnet to be Lamb's; but in 1803, Lamb, who was seeing that volume through the press, once more handed it over to Coleridge.

To the Rev. W. L. Bowles (Second Version)—Title] Effusion i. *1796*: Sonnet i. *1797, 1803, 1828, 1829, 1834*.
6-7 And when the darker day of life began
    And I did roam, &c. *1796, 1797, 1803*.
9 such as] which oft *1797, 1803*.   11 a] such *1797, 1803*.
13-14 As made the soul enamour'd of her woe:
    No common praise, dear Bard! to thee I owe. *1797, 1803*.

Mrs. Siddons—Title] Effusion vii. *1796*: Sonnet viii. *1797, p. 224*: Sonnet xii. *1803*.
4 dark tales of fearful strange decrees *M. C.*

Mutter'd to wretch by necromantic spell;
  Or of those hags, who at the witching time
  Of murky Midnight ride the air sublime,
And mingle foul embrace with fiends of Hell:

Cold Horror drinks its blood! Anon the tear
  More gentle starts, to hear the Beldame tell
  Of pretty Babes, that lov'd each other dear,
Murder'd by cruel Uncle's mandate fell:

Even such the shiv'ring joys thy tones impart,
Even so thou, SIDDONS! meltest my sad heart!
December 29, 1794.

IX

TO WILLIAM GODWIN[1]

AUTHOR OF 'POLITICAL JUSTICE'

O FORM'D t' illume a sunless world forlorn,
  As o'er the chill and dusky brow of Night,
  In Finland's wintry skies the Mimic Morn[2]
Electric pours a stream of rosy light,

Pleas'd I have mark'd OPPRESSION, terror-pale,
  Since, thro' the windings of her dark machine,
  Thy steady eye has shot its glances keen—
And bade th' All-lovely 'scenes at distance hail'.

Nor will I not thy holy guidance bless,
  And hymn thee, GODWIN! with an ardent lay;
  For that thy voice, in Passion's stormy day,
When wild I roam'd the bleak Heath of Distress,

Bade the bright form of Justice meet my way—
And told me that her name was HAPPINESS.
January 10, 1795.

---

[1] First published in the *Morning Chronicle*, January 10, 1795. First collected, *P. and D. W.*, 1877, i. 143. The last six lines were sent in a letter to Southey, dated December 17, 1794. *Letters of S. T. C.*, 1895, i. 117.
[2] Aurora Borealis.

Mrs. *Siddons*—6 Of Warlock Hags that *M. C.*

SONNETS ON EMINENT CHARACTERS

X[1]

TO ROBERT SOUTHEY

OF BALIOL COLLEGE, OXFORD, AUTHOR OF THE 'RETROSPECT', AND OTHER POEMS

SOUTHEY! thy melodies steal o'er mine ear
Like far-off joyance, or the murmuring
Of wild bees in the sunny showers of Spring—
Sounds of such mingled import as may cheer

The lonely breast, yet rouse a mindful tear: 5
  Wak'd by the Song doth Hope-born FANCY fling
Rich showers of dewy fragrance from her wing,
Till sickly PASSION'S drooping Myrtles sear

Blossom anew! But O! more thrill'd, I prize
  Thy sadder strains, that bid in MEMORY'S Dream   10
The faded forms of past Delight arise;
  Then soft, on Love's pale cheek, the tearful gleam

Of Pleasure smiles—as faint yet beauteous lies
The imag'd Rainbow on a willowy stream.
January 14, 1795.

XI[2]

TO RICHARD BRINSLEY SHERIDAN, ESQ.

IT was some Spirit, SHERIDAN! that breath'd
O'er thy young mind such wildly-various power!

---

[1] First published in the *Morning Chronicle*, January 14, 1795. First collected, *P. and D. W.*, 1877, i. 142. This sonnet was sent in a letter to Southey, dated December 17, 1794. *Letters of S. T. C.*, 1895, i. 120.

[2] First published in the *Morning Chronicle*, January 29, 1795: included in 1796, 1803, 1828, 1829, and 1834. Two MS. versions are extant; one in a letter to Southey, dated December 9, 1794 (*Letters of S. T. C.*, 1895,

---

To R. B. Sheridan—Title] To Sheridan *MS. E*: Effusion vi. *1796*: Sonnet xi. *1803*: Sonnet v. *1828, 1829, 1834.*

1-5   Some winged Genius, Sheridan! imbreath'd
      His *various* influence on thy natal hour:
      My fancy bodies forth the Guardian power,
      His temples with Hymettian flowrets wreath'd
      And sweet his voice *MS. Letter, Dec.* 9, 1794.

1-2   Was it some Spirit, SHERIDAN! that breath'd
      His *various* &c. *M. C.*

1-3   Some winged Genius, Sheridan! imbreath'd
      O'er thy young Soul a wildly-various power!
      My Fancy meets thee in her shaping hour *MS. E.*

My soul hath mark'd thee in her shaping hour,
Thy temples with Hymettian[1] flow'rets wreath'd:

And sweet thy voice, as when o'er LAURA's bier
   Sad Music trembled thro' Vauclusa's glade
   Sweet, as at dawn the love-lorn Serenade
That wafts soft dreams to SLUMBER's listening ear.

Now patriot Rage and Indignation high
   Swell the full tones! And now thine eye-beams dance
   Meanings of Scorn and Wit's quaint revelry!
Writhes inly from the bosom-probing glance

The Apostate by the brainless rout ador'd,
As erst that elder Fiend beneath great Michael's sword.
January 29, 1795.

i. 118), and a second in the Estlin copy-book. In 1796 a note to line 4 was included in Notes, p. 179, and in 1797 and 1803 affixed as a footnote, p. 95:—'Hymettian Flowrets. Hymettus, a mountain near Athens, celebrated for its honey. This alludes to Mr. Sheridan's classical attainments, and the following four lines to the exquisite sweetness and almost *Italian* delicacy of his poetry. In Shakespeare's *Lover's Complaint* there is a fine stanza almost prophetically characteristic of Mr. Sheridan.

    So on the tip of his subduing tongue
    All kind of argument and question deep,
    All replication prompt and reason strong
    For his advantage still did wake and sleep,
    To make the weeper laugh, the laugher weep:
    He had the dialect and different skill
    Catching all passions in his craft of will;
    That he did in the general bosom reign
    Of young and old.'

[1] Hymettus, a mountain of Attica famous for honey. *M. C.*

---

8 wafts] bears *MS. Letter, 1794, M. C., MS. E.*   9 Rage] Zeal *MS. Letter, 1794, MS. E, M. C.*   10 thine] his *Letter, 1794, M. C.*

12   While inly writhes from the Soul-probing glance *M. C.*

12–14 Th' Apostate by the brainless rout ador'd
      Writhes inly from the bosom-probing glance
      As erst that nobler Fiend *MS. Letter, 1794, MS. E.*

14 elder] other *M. C.*

TO LORD STANHOPE

ON READING HIS LATE PROTEST IN THE HOUSE OF LORDS

['MORNING CHRONICLE,' JAN. 31, 1795]

Stanhope! I hail, with ardent Hymn, thy name!
Thou shalt be bless'd and lov'd, when in the dust
Thy corse shall moulder—Patriot pure and just!
And o'er thy tomb the grateful hand of Fame

Shall grave:—'Here sleeps the Friend of Humankind!' 5
For thou, untainted by Corruption's bowl,
Or foul Ambition, with undaunted soul
Hast spoke the language of a Free-born mind

Pleading the cause of Nature! Still pursue
Thy path of Honour!—To thy Country true, 10

Still watch th' expiring flame of Liberty!
O Patriot! still pursue thy virtuous way,
As holds his course the splendid Orb of Day,
Or thro' the stormy or the tranquil sky!

One of the People.

1795.

TO EARL STANHOPE

Not, Stanhope! with the Patriot's doubtful name
I mock thy worth—Friend of the Human Race!
Since scorning Faction's low and partial aim
Aloof thou wendest in thy stately pace,

Thyself redeeming from that leprous stain, 5
Nobility: and aye unterrify'd
Pourest thine Abdiel warnings on the train
That sit complotting with rebellious pride

---

[1] First collected in 1893. Mr. Campbell assigned the authorship of the Sonnet to Coleridge, taking it to be 'the original of the one to Stanhope printed in the *Poems* of 1796 and 1803'. For 'Corruption's bowl' (l. 6) see *Sonnet to Burke*, line 9 (*ante*, p. 80).

[2] First published in 1796: included in 1803, in Cottle's *Early Rec.* i. 203, and in *Rem.* 1848, p. 111. First collected in 1852.

To Earl Stanhope—Title] Effusion x. *1796* (To Earl Stanhope *Contents*): Sonnet xvi. *1803*: Sonnet ix. *1852*.

'Gainst *Her*[1] who from the Almighty's bosom leapt
  With whirlwind arm, fierce Minister of Love!
  Wherefore, ere Virtue o'er thy tomb hath wept,
Angels shall lead thee to the Throne above:

And thou from forth its clouds shalt hear the voice,
Champion of Freedom and her God! rejoice!
  1795.

LINES[2]

TO A FRIEND IN ANSWER TO A MELANCHOLY LETTER

Away, those cloudy looks, that labouring sigh,
The peevish offspring of a sickly hour!
Nor meanly thus complain of Fortune's power,
When the blind Gamester throws a luckless die.

Yon setting Sun flashes a mournful gleam
Behind those broken clouds, his stormy train:
To-morrow shall the many-colour'd main
In brightness roll beneath his orient beam!

Wild, as the autumnal gust, the hand of Time
Flies o'er his mystic lyre: in shadowy dance
The alternate groups of Joy and Grief advance
Responsive to his varying strains sublime!

Bears on its wing each hour a load of Fate;
The swain, who, lull'd by Seine's mild murmurs, led
His weary oxen to their nightly shed,
To-day may rule a tempest-troubled State.

Nor shall not Fortune with a vengeful smile
Survey the sanguinary Despot's might,
And haply hurl the Pageant from his height
Unwept to wander in some savage isle.

There shiv'ring sad beneath the tempest's frown
Round his tir'd limbs to wrap the purple vest;
And mix'd with nails and beads, an equal jest!
Barter for food, the jewels of his crown.
  ? 1795.

[1] Gallic Liberty.
[2] First published in 1796: included in 1803, 1828, 1829, and 1834.

Lines, &c.—Title] Epistle II. To a Friend, &c. *1796*: To a Friend, &c. *1803*.

TO AN INFANT[1]

Ah! cease thy tears and sobs, my little Life!
I did but snatch away the unclasp'd knife:
Some safer toy will soon arrest thine eye,
And to quick laughter change this peevish cry!
Poor stumbler on the rocky coast of Woe,   5
Tutor'd by Pain each source of pain to know!
Alike the foodful fruit and scorching fire
Awake thy eager grasp and young desire;
Alike the Good, the Ill offend thy sight,
And rouse the stormy sense of shrill Affright!   10
Untaught, yet wise! mid all thy brief alarms
Thou closely clingest to thy Mother's arms,
Nestling thy little face in that fond breast
Whose anxious heavings lull thee to thy rest!
Man's breathing Miniature! thou mak'st me sigh—   15
A Babe art thou—and such a Thing am I!
To anger rapid and as soon appeas'd,
For trifles mourning and by trifles pleas'd,
Break Friendship's mirror with a tetchy blow,
Yet snatch what coals of fire on Pleasure's altar glow!   20

O thou that rearest with celestial aim
The future Seraph in my mortal frame,

[1] First published in 1796: included in 1797 (*Supplement*), 1803, 1828, 1829, and 1834. A MS. version numbering 16 lines is included in the Estlin volume.

To an Infant—Title] Effusion xxxiv. To an Infant *1796*.

1-10   How yon sweet Child my Bosom's grief beguiles
         With soul-subduing Eloquence of smiles!
         Ah lovely Babe! in thee myself I scan—
         Thou weepest! sure those Tears proclaim thee Man!
         And now some glitt'ring Toy arrests thine eye,
         And to quick laughter turns the peevish cry.
         Poor Stumbler on the rocky coast of Woe,
         Tutor'd by Pain the source of Pain to know!
         Alike the foodful Fruit and scorching Fire
         Awake thy eager grasp and young desire;
         Alike the Good, the Ill thy aching sight
         Scare with the keen Emotions of Affright! *MS. E.*

8-11   Or rouse thy screams, or wake thy young desire:
         Yet art thou wise, for mid thy brief alarms *1797*.

9-10 *om. 1797*.   14 Whose kindly Heavings lull thy cares to Rest *MS. E.*   19 tetchy] fretful *1797*.

Thrice holy Faith! whatever thorns I meet
As on I totter with unpractis'd feet,
Still let me stretch my arms and cling to thee,
Meek nurse of souls through their long Infancy!
1795.

TO THE REV. W. J. HORT[1]

WHILE TEACHING A YOUNG LADY SOME SONG-TUNES ON HIS FLUTE

I

Hush! ye clamorous Cares! be mute!
  Again, dear Harmonist! again
Thro' the hollow of thy flute
  Breathe that passion-warbled strain:
Till Memory each form shall bring
  The loveliest of her shadowy throng;
And Hope, that soars on sky-lark wing,
  Carol wild her gladdest song!

II

O skill'd with magic spell to roll
The thrilling tones, that concentrate the soul!
Breathe thro' thy flute those tender notes again,
While near thee sits the chaste-eyed Maiden mild;
And bid her raise the Poet's kindred strain
In soft impassion'd voice, correctly wild.

III

  In Freedom's UNDIVIDED dell,
Where *Toil* and *Health* with mellow'd *Love* shall dwell,
  Far from folly, far from men,
  In the rude romantic glen,
  Up the cliff, and thro' the glade,
  Wandering with the dear-lov'd maid,
  I shall listen to the lay,
  And ponder on thee far away
Still, as she bids those thrilling notes aspire
('Making my fond attunéd heart her lyre'),
Thy honour'd form, my Friend! shall reappear
And I will thank thee with a raptur'd tear.
1795.

[1] First published in 1796, and again in 1863.

To the Rev. W. J. Hort—Title] To the Rev. W. J. H. while Teaching, &c. *1796, 1863.*
24 her] his *1863.*

PITY [1]

Sweet Mercy! how my very heart has bled
 To see thee, poor Old Man! and thy grey hairs
 Hoar with the snowy blast: while no one cares
To clothe thy shrivell'd limbs and palsied head.
My Father! throw away this tatter'd vest   5
 That mocks thy shivering! take my garment—use
 A young man's arm! I'll melt these frozen dews
That hang from thy white beard and numb thy breast.
My Sara too shall tend thee, like a child:
 And thou shalt talk, in our fireside's recess,   10
 Of purple Pride, that scowls on Wretchedness.—
He did not so, the Galilaean mild,
 Who met the Lazars turn'd from rich men's doors
 And call'd them Friends, and heal'd their noisome sores!
?1795.

TO THE NIGHTINGALE [2]

Sister of love-lorn Poets, Philomel!
How many Bards in city garret pent,
While at their window they with downward eye
Mark the faint lamp-beam on the kennell'd mud,
And listen to the drowsy cry of Watchmen   5
(Those hoarse unfeather'd Nightingales of Time!),
How many wretched Bards address *thy* name,
And hers, the full-orb'd Queen that shines above.
But I *do* hear thee, and the high bough mark,
Within whose mild moon-mellow'd foliage hid   10
Thou warblest sad thy pity-pleading strains.
O! I have listen'd, till my working soul,
Waked by those strains to thousand phantasies,
Absorb'd hath ceas'd to listen! Therefore oft,
I hymn thy name: and with a proud delight   15

[1] First published in 1796: included in *Selection of Sonnets, Poems* 1796, in 1797, 1803, 1828, 1829, and 1834.
[2] First published in 1796: included in 1803 and in *Lit. Rem.*, i. 38 First collected in 1844. Lines 18-20 exist in a *MS. fragment*.

Pity—Title] Effusion xvi. *1796* (*Contents*—To an Old Man): Sonnet vi. *1797*: Sonnet v. *1803*: Sonnet x. *1828, 1829, 1834*: Charity *1893*.
7 arm] arms *1796, 1828*.
12-14   He did not scowl, the Galilaean mild,
   Who met the Lazar turn'd from rich man's doors,
      And call'd him Friend, and wept upon his sores. *1797, 1803*.
13 men's] man's *1796, Selection of Sonnets, 1797, 1803, 1828, 1829*.
To the Nightingale—Title] Effusion xxiii. To the, &c. *1796*.
12 O have I *1796*.

TO THE NIGHTINGALE

Oft will I tell thee, Minstrel of the Moon!
'Most musical, most melancholy' Bird!
That all thy soft diversities of tone,
Tho' sweeter far than the delicious airs
That vibrate from a white-arm'd Lady's harp,   20
What time the languishment of lonely love
Melts in her eye, and heaves her breast of snow,
Are not so sweet as is the voice of her,
My Sara—best beloved of human kind!
When breathing the pure soul of tenderness,   25
She thrills me with the Husband's promis'd name!
1795.

LINES[1]

COMPOSED WHILE CLIMBING THE LEFT ASCENT OF BROCKLEY COOMB, SOMERSETSHIRE, MAY 1795

WITH many a pause and oft reverted eye
I climb the Coomb's ascent: sweet songsters near
Warble in shade their wild-wood melody:
Far off the unvarying Cuckoo soothes my ear.
Up scour the startling stragglers of the flock   5
That on green plots o'er precipices browze:
From the deep fissures of the naked rock
The Yew-tree bursts! Beneath its dark green boughs
(Mid which the May-thorn blends its blossoms white)
Where broad smooth stones jut out in mossy seats,   10
I rest:—and now have gain'd the topmost site.
Ah! what a luxury of landscape meets
My gaze! Proud towers, and Cots more dear to me,
Elm-shadow'd Fields, and prospect-bounding Sea!
Deep sighs my lonely heart: I drop the tear: 15
Enchanting spot! O were my Sara here!

LINES IN THE MANNER OF SPENSER[2]

O PEACE, that on a lilied bank dost love
To rest thine head beneath an Olive-Tree,
I would that from the pinions of thy Dove

---

[1] First published in 1796: included in 1797 (*Supplement*), 1803, 1828, 1829, and 1834.
[2] First published in 1796: included in 1797, 1803, 1828, 1829, and 1834.

18 diversities] Distinguishments *MS. fragment*.
Lines composed, &c.—Title] Effusion xxi. Composed while climbing the Left Ascent of Brockley Coomb, in the County of Somerset, May 1795 *1796*: Sonnet v. Composed, &c. *1797*: Sonnet xiv. Composed, &c. *1803*.
7 deep] forc'd *1796, 1797, 1803, 1828, 1829*.
Lines in the Manner, &c.—Title] Effusion xxiv. In the, &c. *1796*: In the, &c. *1797*.

LINES IN THE MANNER OF SPENSER

One quill withouten pain ypluck'd might be!
For O! I wish my Sara's frowns to flee,
And fain to her some soothing song would write,
Lest she resent my rude discourtesy,
Who vow'd to meet her ere the morning light,
But broke my plighted word—ah! false and recreant wight!

Last night as I my weary head did pillow
With thoughts of my dissever'd Fair engross'd,
Chill Fancy droop'd wreathing herself with willow,
As though my breast entomb'd a pining ghost.
'From some blest couch, young Rapture's bridal boast,
Rejected Slumber! hither wing thy way;
But leave me with the matin hour, at most!
As night-clos'd floweret to the orient ray,
My sad heart will expand, when I the Maid survey.'

But Love, who heard the silence of my thought,
Contriv'd a too successful wile, I ween:
And whisper'd to himself, with malice fraught—
'Too long our Slave the Damsel's *smiles* hath seen:
To-morrow shall he ken her alter'd mien!'
He spake, and ambush'd lay, till on my bed
The morning shot her dewy glances keen,
When as I 'gan to lift my drowsy head—
'Now, Bard! I'll work thee woe!' the laughing Elfin said.

Sleep, softly-breathing God! his downy wing
Was fluttering now, as quickly to depart;
When twang'd an arrow from Love's mystic string,
With pathless wound it pierc'd him to the heart.
Was there some magic in the Elfin's dart?
Or did he strike my couch with wizard lance?
For straight so fair a Form did upwards start
(No fairer deck'd the bowers of old Romance)
That Sleep enamour'd grew, nor mov'd from his sweet trance!

My Sara came, with gentlest look divine;
Bright shone her eye, yet tender was its beam:
I felt the pressure of her lip to mine!
Whispering we went, and Love was all our theme—
Love pure and spotless, as at first, I deem,
He sprang from Heaven! Such joys with Sleep did 'bide,
That I the living Image of my Dream

17 Like snowdrop opening to the solar ray, *1796.*   19 'heard the silence of my thought' *1797, 1803.*   26 to lift] uplift *1797, 1803.*

Fondly forgot. Too late I woke, and sigh'd—
'O! how shall I behold my Love at eventide!' 45
1795.

THE HOUR WHEN WE SHALL MEET AGAIN [1]

(Composed during Illness, and in Absence.)

Dim Hour! that sleep'st on pillowing clouds afar,
O rise and yoke the Turtles to thy car!
Bend o'er the traces, blame each lingering Dove,
And give me to the bosom of my Love!
My gentle Love, caressing and carest, 5
With heaving heart shall cradle me to rest!
Shed the warm tear-drop from her smiling eyes,
Lull with fond woe, and medicine me with sighs!
While finely-flushing float her kisses meek,
Like melted rubies, o'er my pallid cheek. 10
Chill'd by the night, the drooping Rose of May
Mourns the long absence of the lovely Day;
Young Day returning at her promis'd hour
Weeps o'er the sorrows of her favourite Flower;
Weeps the soft dew, the balmy gale she sighs, 15
And darts a trembling lustre from her eyes.
New life and joy th' expanding flow'ret feels:
His pitying Mistress mourns, and mourning heals!
? 1795.

LINES [2]

WRITTEN AT SHURTON BARS, NEAR BRIDGEWATER, SEPTEMBER
1795, IN ANSWER TO A LETTER FROM BRISTOL

Good verse *most* good, and bad verse then seems better
Receiv'd from absent friend by way of Letter.
For what so sweet can labour'd lays impart
As one rude rhyme warm from a friendly heart?—ANON.

---

[1] First published in *The Watchman*, No. III, March 17, 1796 (*signed* C.):
included in 1797, 1803, 1844, and 1852. It was first reprinted, after 1803,
in *Table Talk*, 1835, ii. 358-9, under 'the sportive title "Darwiniana"',
on the supposition that it was written' in half-mockery of Darwin's style
with its *dulcia vitia*. (See 1852, *Notes*, p. 885.)

[2] First published in 1796: included in 1797, 1803, 1828, 1829, and 1834.

Below l. 45 July 1795 *1797, 1803.*
The Hour, &c.—Title] Darwiniana. The Hour, &c. *L. R., 1844*: Composed
during illness and absence *1852.*
9-10 *om. 1803.*   14 her] the *Lit. Rem., 1844, 1852.*   17 New] Now
Watchman.
Lines written, &c.—Title] Epistle I. Lines written, &c. The motto is
printed on the reverse of the half-title 'Poetical Epistles' [pp. 109, 110],

LINES AT SHURTON BARS

Nor travels my meandering eye
The starry wilderness on high;
 Nor now with curious sight
I mark the glow-worm, as I pass,
Move with 'green radiance'[1] through the grass, 5
 An emerald of light.

O ever present to my view!
My wafted spirit is with you,
 And soothes your boding fears:
I see you all oppressed with gloom 10
Sit lonely in that cheerless room—
 Ah me! You are in tears!

Belovéd Woman! did you fly
Chill'd Friendship's dark disliking eye,
 Or Mirth's untimely din? 15
With cruel weight these trifles press
A temper sore with tenderness,
 When aches the void within.

But why with sable wand unblessed
Should Fancy rouse within my breast 20
 Dim-visag'd shapes of Dread?
Untenanting its beauteous clay
My Sara's soul has wing'd its way,
 And hovers round my head!

---

[1] The expression 'green radiance' is borrowed from Mr. Wordsworth, a Poet whose versification is occasionally harsh and his diction too frequently obscure; but whom I deem unrivalled among the writers of the present day in manly sentiment, novel imagery, and vivid colouring. Note, 1796, p. 185 : Footnote, 1797, p. 88.
[The phrase 'green radiance' occurs in *An Evening Walk*, ll. 264-8, first published in 1793, and reprinted in 1820. In 1836 the lines were omitted.

 Oft has she taught them on her lap to play
 Delighted with the glow-worm's harmless ray,
 Toss'd light from hand to hand; while on the ground
 Small circles of green radiance gleam around.]

1796: Ode to Sara, written at Shurton Bars, &c. *1797, 1803*. The motto is omitted in *1797, 1803*: The motto is prefixed to the poem in *1828, 1829*, and *1834*. In *1797* and *1803* a note is appended to the title :—Note. *The first stanza alludes to a Passage in the Letter.* [The allusions to a 'Passage in the Letter' must surely be contained not in the first but in the second and third stanzas. The reference is, no doubt, to the alienation from Southey, which must have led to a difference of feeling between the two sisters Sarah and Edith Fricker.]

I felt it prompt the tender Dream,
When slowly sank the day's last gleam;
   You rous'd each gentler sense,
As sighing o'er the Blossom's bloom
Meek Evening wakes its soft perfume
   With viewless influence.

And hark, my Love! The sea-breeze moans
Through yon reft house! O'er rolling stones
   In bold ambitious sweep
The onward-surging tides supply
The silence of the cloudless sky
   With mimic thunders deep.

Dark reddening from the channell'd Isle[1]
(Where stands one solitary pile
   Unslated by the blast)
The Watchfire, like a sullen star
Twinkles to many a dozing Tar
   Rude cradled on the mast.

Even there—beneath that light-house tower—
In the tumultuous evil hour
   Ere Peace with Sara came,
Time was, I should have thought it sweet
To count the echoings of my feet,
   And watch the storm-vex'd flame.

And there in black soul-jaundic'd fit
A sad gloom-pamper'd Man to sit,
   And listen to the roar:
When mountain surges bellowing deep
With an uncouth monster-leap
   Plung'd foaming on the shore.

Then by the lightning's blaze to mark
Some toiling tempest-shatter'd bark;
   Her vain distress-guns hear;
And when a second sheet of light
Flash'd o'er the blackness of the night—
   To see *no* vessel there!

But Fancy now more gaily sings;
Or if awhile she droop her wings,
   As skylarks 'mid the corn,

---

[1] The Holmes, in the Bristol Channel.

26 sank] sunk *1796–1829.*   33 With broad impetuous *1797, 1803.*
34 fast-encroaching *1797, 1803.*   48 storm-vex'd] troubled *1797, 1803.*
49 black and jaundic'd fit *1797.*

LINES AT SHURTON BARS

On summer fields she grounds her breast:
The oblivious poppy o'er her nest 65
 Nods, till returning morn.

O mark those smiling tears, that swell
The open'd rose! From heaven they fell,
 And with the sun-beam blend.
Blest visitations from above, 70
Such are the tender woes of Love
 Fostering the heart they bend!

When stormy Midnight howling round
Beats on our roof with clattering sound,
 To me your arms you'll stretch: 75
Great God! you'll say—To us so kind,
O shelter from this loud bleak wind
 The houseless, friendless wretch!

The tears that tremble down your cheek,
Shall bathe my kisses chaste and meek 80
 In Pity's dew divine;
And from your heart the sighs that steal
Shall make your rising bosom feel
 The answering swell of mine!

How oft, my Love! with shapings sweet 85
I paint the moment, we shall meet!
 With eager speed I dart—
I seize you in the vacant air,
And fancy, with a husband's care
 I press you to my heart! 90

'Tis said, in Summer's evening hour
Flashes the golden-colour'd flower
 A fair electric flame:[1]

---

[1] LIGHT *from plants*. In Sweden a very curious phenomenon has been observed on certain flowers, by M. Haggern, lecturer in natural history. One evening he perceived a faint flash of light repeatedly dart from a marigold. Surprised at such an uncommon appearance, he resolved to examine it with attention; and, to be assured it was no deception of the eye, he placed a man near him, with orders to make a signal at the moment when he observed the light. They both saw it constantly at the same moment.

The light was most brilliant on marigolds of an orange or flame colour; but scarcely visible on pale ones. The flash was frequently seen on the same flower two or three times in quick succession; but more commonly at intervals of several minutes; and when several flowers in the same

100   LINES AT SHURTON BARS

And so shall flash my love-charg'd eye
When all the heart's big ecstasy   95
 Shoots rapid through the frame!
1795.

THE EOLIAN HARP[1]
COMPOSED AT CLEVEDON, SOMERSETSHIRE

MY pensive Sara! thy soft cheek reclined
Thus on mine arm, most soothing sweet it is
To sit beside our Cot, our Cot o'ergrown
With white-flower'd Jasmin, and the broad-leav'd Myrtle,
(Meet emblems they of Innocence and Love!)   5
And watch the clouds, that late were rich with light,
Slow saddening round, and mark the star of eve
Serenely brilliant (such should Wisdom be)
Shine opposite! How exquisite the scents
Snatch'd from yon bean-field! and the world *so* hush'd!   10
The stilly murmur of the distant Sea
Tells us of silence.

     And that simplest Lute,
Placed length-ways in the clasping casement, hark!

place emitted their light together, it could be observed at a considerable distance.

This phenomenon was remarked in the months of July and August at sun-set, and for half an hour when the atmosphere was clear; but after a rainy day, or when the air was loaded with vapours nothing of it was seen.

The following flowers emitted flashes, more or less vivid, in this order:—

1. The marigold, *galendula* [*sic*] *officinalis*.
2. Monk's-hood, *tropaelum* [*sic*] *majus*.
3. The orange-lily, *lilium bulbiferum*.
4. The Indian pink, *tagetes patula et erecta*.

From the rapidity of the flash, and other circumstances, it may be conjectured that there is something of electricity in this phenomenon. Notes to *Poems*, 1796. Note 13, pp. 186, 188.

In 1797 the above was printed as a footnote on pp. 93, 94. In 1803 the last stanza, lines 91–96, was omitted, and, of course, the note disappeared. In 1828, 1829, and 1834 the last stanza was replaced but the note was not reprinted.

[1] First published in 1796: included in 1797, 1803, *Sibylline Leaves*, 1817, 1828, 1829, and 1834.

The Eolian Harp—Title] Effusion xxxv. Composed August 20th, 1795, At Clevedon, Somersetshire *1796*: Composed at Clevedon Somersetshire *1797, 1803*: The Eolian Harp. Composed, &c. *S. L. 1817, 1828, 1829, 1834*.
 5 *om. 1803*. 8 *om. 1803*. 11 Hark! the still murmur *1803*. 12
And th' Eolian Lute, *1803*. 13 *om. 1803*.

THE EOLIAN HARP

How by the desultory breeze caress'd,
Like some coy maid half yielding to her lover,   15
It pours such sweet upbraiding, as must needs
Tempt to repeat the wrong! And now, its strings
Boldlier swept, the long sequacious notes
Over delicious surges sink and rise,
Such a soft floating witchery of sound   20
As twilight Elfins make, when they at eve
Voyage on gentle gales from Fairy-Land,
Where Melodies round honey-dropping flowers,
Footless and wild, like birds of Paradise,
Nor pause, nor perch, hovering on untam'd wing!   25
O! the one Life within us and abroad,
Which meets all motion and becomes its soul,
A light in sound, a sound-like power in light,
Rhythm in all thought, and joyance every where—
Methinks, it should have been impossible   30
Not to love all things in a world so fill'd;
Where the breeze warbles, and the mute still air
Is Music slumbering on her instrument.

And thus, my Love! as on the midway slope
Of yonder hill I stretch my limbs at noon,   35
Whilst through my half-clos'd eye-lids I behold
The sunbeams dance, like diamonds, on the main,
And tranquil muse upon tranquillity;
Full many a thought uncall'd and undetain'd,
And many idle flitting phantasies,   40

16 upbraiding] upbraidings *1796, 1797, 1803, Sibylline Leaves, 1817*. Lines 21-33 are om. in *1803*, and the text reads:

> Such a soft floating witchery of sound—
> Methinks, it should have been impossible
> Not to love all things in a World like this,
> Where e'en the Breezes of the simple Air
> Possess the power and Spirit of Melody!
> *And thus, my Love*, &c.

26-33 are not in *1796, 1797*. In *Sibylline Leaves*, for lines 26-33 of the text, four lines are inserted:

> Methinks it should have been impossible
> Not to love all things in a world like this,
> Where even the breezes, and the common air,
> Contain the power and spirit of Harmony.

Lines 26-33 were first included in the text in *1828*, and reappeared in *1829* and *1834*. They are supplied in the *Errata*, pp. [xi, xii], of *Sibylline Leaves*, with a single variant (l. 33): Is Music slumbering on *its* instrument.

102   THE EOLIAN HARP

Traverse my indolent and passive brain,
As wild and various as the random gales
That swell and flutter on this subject Lute!
  And what if all of animated nature
Be but organic Harps diversely fram'd,   45
That tremble into thought, as o'er them sweeps
Plastic and vast, one intellectual breeze,
At once the Soul of each, and God of all?
  But thy more serious eye a mild reproof
Darts, O belovéd Woman! nor such thoughts   50
Dim and unhallow'd dost thou not reject,
And biddest me walk humbly with my God.
Meek Daughter in the family of Christ!
Well hast thou said and holily disprais'd
These shapings of the unregenerate mind;   55
Bubbles that glitter as they rise and break
On vain Philosophy's aye-babbling spring.
For never guiltless may I speak of him,
The Incomprehensible! save when with awe
I praise him, and with Faith that inly *feels*;[1]   60
Who with his saving mercies healéd me,
A sinful and most miserable man,
Wilder'd and dark, and gave me to possess
Peace, and this Cot, and thee, heart-honour'd Maid!
  1795.

TO THE AUTHOR OF POEMS[2]
[JOSEPH COTTLE]
PUBLISHED ANONYMOUSLY AT BRISTOL IN SEPTEMBER 1795

UNBOASTFUL BARD! whose verse concise yet clear
Tunes to smooth melody unconquer'd sense,

[1] L'athée n'est point à mes yeux un faux esprit; je puis vivre avec lui aussi bien et mieux qu'avec le dévot, car il raisonne davantage, mais il lui manque un sens, et mon ame ne se fond point entièrement avec la sienne : il est froid au spectacle le plus ravissant, et il cherche un syllogisme lorsque je rends une [un *1797, 1803*] action de grace. 'Appel a l'impartiale postérité', par la Citoyenne Roland, troisième partie, p. 67. Notes to *Poems*. Note 10, 1796, p. 183. The above was printed as a footnote to p. 99, 1797, and to p. 132, 1803.

[2] First published in 1796: included in 1797 (*Supplement*), 1803, and 1852.

---

44 And] Or *1796, 1797, 1803*.   64 dear honoured Maid *1893*.
To the Author of Poems—Title] Epistle iv. To the Author, &c. *1796*: Lines to Joseph Cottle *1797*: To the Author, &c., *with footnote*, 'Mr. Joseph Cottle' *1803*.
1 Unboastful Bard] My honor'd friend *1797*.

TO THE AUTHOR OF POEMS

May your fame fadeless live, as 'never-sere'
The Ivy wreathes yon Oak, whose broad defence
Embowers me from Noon's sultry influence!
For, like that nameless Rivulet stealing by,
Your modest verse to musing Quiet dear
Is rich with tints heaven-borrow'd: the charm'd eye
Shall gaze undazzled there, and love the soften'd sky.

Circling the base of the Poetic mount
A stream there is, which rolls in lazy flow
Its coal-black waters from Oblivion's fount:
The vapour-poison'd Birds, that fly too low,
Fall with dead swoop, and to the bottom go.
Escaped that heavy stream on pinion fleet
Beneath the Mountain's lofty-frowning brow,
Ere aught of perilous ascent you meet,
A mead of mildest charm delays th' unlabouring feet.

Not there the cloud-climb'd rock, sublime and vast,
That like some giant king, o'er-glooms the hill;
Nor there the Pine-grove to the midnight blast
Makes solemn music! But th' unceasing rill
To the soft Wren or Lark's descending trill
Murmurs sweet undersong 'mid jasmin bowers.
In this same pleasant meadow, at your will
I ween, you wander'd—there collecting flowers
Of sober tint, and herbs of med'cinable powers!

There for the monarch-murder'd Soldier's tomb
You wove th' unfinish'd[1] wreath of saddest hues;
And to that holier[2] chaplet added bloom
Besprinkling it with Jordan's cleansing dews.
But lo your Henderson[3] awakes the Muse——
His Spirit beckon'd from the mountain's height!
You left the plain and soar'd mid richer views!

'The first in order of the verses which I have thus endeavoured to reprieve from immediate oblivion was originally addressed "To the Author of Poems published anonymously at Bristol". A second edition of these poems has lately appeared with the Author's name prefixed: and I could not refuse myself the gratification of seeing the name of that man among my poems without whose kindness they would probably have remained unpublished; and to whom I know myself greatly and variously obliged, as a Poet, a man, and a Christian.' 'Advertisement' to *Supplement*, 1797, pp. 243, 244.

[1] 'War,' a Fragment. [2] 'John Baptist,' a poem.
[3] 'Monody on John Henderson.'

So Nature mourn'd when sunk the First Day's light, 35
With stars, unseen before, spangling her robe of night!

Still soar, my Friend, those richer views among,
Strong, rapid, fervent, flashing Fancy's beam!
Virtue and Truth shall love your gentler song;
But Poesy demands th' impassion'd theme: 40
Waked by Heaven's silent dews at Eve's mild gleam
What balmy sweets Pomona breathes around!
But if the vext air rush a stormy stream
Or Autumn's shrill gust moan in plaintive sound,
With fruits and flowers she loads the tempest-honor'd ground.

1795.

THE SILVER THIMBLE[1]

THE PRODUCTION OF A YOUNG LADY, ADDRESSED TO THE
AUTHOR OF THE POEMS ALLUDED TO IN THE PRECEDING EPISTLE

*She had lost her Silver Thimble, and her complaint being
accidentally overheard by him, her Friend, he immediately sent
her four others to take her choice of.*

As oft mine eye with careless glance
Has gallop'd thro' some old romance,
Of speaking Birds and Steeds with wings,
Giants and Dwarfs, and Fiends and Kings;
Beyond the rest with more attentive care 5
I've lov'd to read of elfin-favour'd Fair——
How if she long'd for aught beneath the sky
And suffer'd to escape one votive sigh,
Wafted along on viewless pinions aery
It laid itself obsequious at her feet: 10
Such things, I thought, one might not hope to meet
Save in the dear delicious land of Faery!
But now (by proof I know it well)
There's still some peril in free wishing——
Politeness is a licensed *spell*, 15
And *you*, dear Sir! the Arch-magician.

[1] First published in 1796: included for the first time in Appendix to
1863. Mrs. Coleridge told her daughter (*Biog. Lit.*, 1847, ii. 411) that she
wrote but little of these verses.

---

35 sunk] sank *1797*.
The Silver Thimble—Title] Epistle v. The Production of a Young Lady, &c.
1796 : From a Young Lady *Appendix*, *1863*.

THE SILVER THIMBLE

You much perplex'd me by the various set:
They were indeed an elegant quartette!
My mind went to and fro, and waver'd long;
At length I've chosen (Samuel thinks me wrong)
That, around whose azure rim
Silver figures seem to swim,
Like fleece-white clouds, that on the skiey Blue,
Waked by no breeze, the self-same shapes retain;
Or ocean-Nymphs with limbs of snowy hue
Slow-floating o'er the calm cerulean plain.

Just such a one, *mon cher ami*,
(The finger shield of industry)
Th' inventive Gods, I deem, to Pallas gave
What time the vain Arachne, madly brave,
Challeng'd the blue-eyed Virgin of the sky
A duel in embroider'd work to try.
And hence the thimbled Finger of grave Pallas
To th' erring Needle's point was more than callous.
But ah the poor Arachne! She unarm'd
Blundering thro' hasty eagerness, alarm'd
With all a *Rival's* hopes, a *Mortal's* fears,
Still miss'd the stitch, and stain'd the web with tears.
Unnumber'd punctures small yet sore
Full fretfully the maiden bore,
Till she her lily finger found
Crimson'd with many a tiny wound;
And to her eyes, suffus'd with watery woe,
Her flower-embroider'd web danc'd dim, I wist,
Like blossom'd shrubs in a quick-moving mist:
Till vanquish'd the despairing Maid sunk low.

O Bard! whom sure no common Muse inspires,
I heard your Verse that glows with vestal fires!
And I from unwatch'd needle's erring point
Had surely suffer'd on each finger-joint
Those wounds, which erst did poor Arachne meet;
While he, the much-lov'd Object of my choice
(My bosom thrilling with enthusiast heat),
Pour'd on mine ear with deep impressive voice,
How the great Prophet of the Desart stood
And preach'd of Penitence by Jordan's Flood;
On War; or else the legendary lays
In simplest measures hymn'd to Alla's praise;

Or what the Bard from his heart's inmost stores
O'er his *Friend's* grave in loftier numbers pours: 60
Yes, Bard polite! you but obey'd the laws
Of Justice, when the thimble you had sent;
What wounds your thought-bewildering Muse might cause
'Tis well your finger-shielding gifts prevent.   SARA.
1795.

REFLECTIONS ON HAVING LEFT A PLACE OF RETIREMENT[1]

Sermoni propriora.—HOR.

Low was our pretty Cot: our tallest Rose
Peep'd at the chamber-window. We could hear
At silent noon, and eve, and early morn,
The Sea's faint murmur. In the open air
Our Myrtles blossom'd; and across the porch 5
Thick Jasmins twined: the little landscape round
Was green and woody, and refresh'd the eye.
It was a spot which you might aptly call
The Valley of Seclusion! Once I saw
(Hallowing his Sabbath-day by quietness) 10
A wealthy son of Commerce saunter by,
Bristowa's citizen: methought, it calm'd
His thirst of idle gold, and made him muse
With wiser feelings: for he paus'd, and look'd
With a pleas'd sadness, and gaz'd all around, 15
Then eyed our Cottage, and gaz'd round again,
And sigh'd, and said, it was a Blessèd Place.
And we *were* bless'd. Oft with patient ear
Long-listening to the viewless sky-lark's note
(Viewless, or haply for a moment seen 20
Gleaming on sunny wings) in whisper'd tones

[1] First published in the *Monthly Magazine*, October, 1796, vol. ii, p. 712: included in 1797, 1803, *Sibylline Leaves*, 1817, 1828, 1829, and 1834.

Reflections, &c.—Title] Reflections on entering into active life. A Poem which affects not to be Poetry *M. Mag*. *The motto was prefixed in 1797.*

12-17   Bristowa's citizen—he paus'd and look'd
         With a pleased sadness and gaz'd all around,
         Then eye'd our cottage and gaz'd round again,
         And said it was a *blessed little place*. *Monthly Magazine.*

17   And sigh'd, and said, *it was a blessed place*. *1797, 1803.*

21 wings] wing *M. M., 1797, 1803, S. L.*

21-3   Gleaming on sunny wing,) 'And such,' I said,
         'The inobtrusive song *1803.*

ON HAVING LEFT A PLACE OF RETIREMENT 107

I've said to my Belovéd, 'Such, sweet Girl!
The inobtrusive song of Happiness,
Unearthly minstrelsy! then only heard
When the Soul seeks to hear; when all is hush'd,   25
And the Heart listens!'

                             But the time, when first
From that low Dell, steep up the stony Mount
I climb'd with perilous toil and reach'd the top,
Oh! what a goodly scene! *Here* the bleak mount,
The bare bleak mountain speckled thin with sheep;   30
Grey clouds, that shadowing spot the sunny fields;
And river, now with bushy rocks o'er-brow'd,
Now winding bright and full, with naked banks;
And seats, and lawns, the Abbey and the wood,
And cots, and hamlets, and faint city-spire;   35
The Channel *there*, the Islands and white sails,
Dim coasts, and cloud-like hills, and shoreless Ocean—
It seem'd like Omnipresence! God, methought,
Had built him there a Temple: the whole World
Seem'd *imag'd* in its vast circumference: 40
No *wish* profan'd my overwhelméd heart.
Blest hour! It was a luxury,—to be!

   Ah! quiet Dell! dear Cot, and Mount sublime!
I was constrain'd to quit you. Was it right,
While my unnumber'd brethren toil'd and bled,   45
That I should dream away the entrusted hours
On rose-leaf beds, pampering the coward heart
With feelings all too delicate for use?
Sweet is the tear that from some Howard's eye
Drops on the cheek of one he lifts from earth: 50
And he that works me good with unmov'd face,
Does it but half: he chills me while he aids,
My benefactor, not my brother man!
Yet even this, this cold beneficence
Praise, praise it, O my Soul! oft as thou scann'st   55
The sluggard Pity's vision-weaving tribe!
Who sigh for Wretchedness, yet shun the Wretched,
Nursing in some delicious solitude
Their slothful loves and dainty sympathies!

---

40 Was imag'd *M. M.*   46 entrusted] trusted *M. M.*, 1797.   55
Seizes my Praise, when I reflect on those *1797, 1803, Sibylline Leaves, 1817*
(line as in text supplied in *Errata*).

108 ON HAVING LEFT A PLACE OF RETIREMENT

I therefore go, and join head, heart, and hand, 60
Active and firm, to fight the bloodless fight
Of Science, Freedom, and the Truth in Christ.

Yet oft when after honourable toil
Rests the tir'd mind, and waking loves to dream,
My spirit shall revisit thee, dear Cot! 65
Thy Jasmin and thy window-peeping Rose,
And Myrtles fearless of the mild sea-air.
And I shall sigh fond wishes—sweet Abode!
Ah!—had none greater! And that all had such!
It might be so—but the time is not yet. 70
Speed it, O Father! Let thy Kingdom come!
1795.

RELIGIOUS MUSINGS[1]

A DESULTORY POEM, WRITTEN ON THE CHRISTMAS EVE OF 1794

This is the time, when most divine to hear,
The voice of Adoration rouses me,

[1] First published in 1796: included in 1797, 1803, 1828, 1829, and 1834. Lines 260-357 were published in *The Watchman*, No. II, March 9, 1796, entitled 'The Present State of Society'. In the editions of 1796, 1797, and 1803 the following lines, an adaptation of a passage in the First Book of Akenside's *Pleasures of the Imagination*, were prefixed as a motto:—

> What tho' first,
> In years unseason'd, I attun'd the lay
> To idle Passion and unreal Woe?
> Yet serious Truth her empire o'er my song
> Hath now asserted; Falsehood's evil brood,
> Vice and deceitful Pleasure, she at once
> Excluded, and my Fancy's careless toil
> Drew to the better cause!

An 'Argument' followed on a separate page:—

Introduction. Person of Christ. His prayer on the Cross. The process of his Doctrines on the mind of the Individual. Character of the Elect. Superstition. Digression to the present War. Origin and Uses of Government and Property. The present State of Society. The French Revolution. Millenium. Universal Redemption. Conclusion.

69 none] *none M. M.* all] *all M. M.* 70-1 om. *1803.*
Religious Musings—Title] —— on Christmas Eve. In the year of Our Lord, 1794.

1-23 This is the time, when most divine to hear,
As with a Cherub's 'loud uplifted' trump
The voice of Adoration my thrill'd heart
Rouses! And with the rushing noise of wings

RELIGIOUS MUSINGS

As with a Cherub's trump: and high upborne,
Yea, mingling with the Choir, I seem to view
The vision of the heavenly multitude,
Who hymned the song of Peace o'er Bethlehem's fields!
Yet thou more bright than all the Angel-blaze,
That harbingered thy birth, Thou Man of Woes!
Despiséd Galilaean! For the Great
Invisible (by symbols only seen)
With a peculiar and surpassing light
Shines from the visage of the oppressed good man,
When heedless of himself the scourgéd saint
Mourns for the oppressor. Fair the vernal mead,
Fair the high grove, the sea, the sun, the stars;
True impress each of their creating Sire!
Yet nor high grove, nor many-colour'd mead,
Nor the green ocean with his thousand isles,

>   Transports my spirit to the favor'd fields
>   Of Bethlehem, there in shepherd's guise to sit
>   Sublime of extacy, and mark entranc'd
>   The glory-streaming VISION throng the night.*
>   Ah not more radiant, nor loud harmonies
>   Hymning more unimaginably sweet
>   With choral songs around th' ETERNAL MIND,
>   The constellated company of WORLDS
>   Danc'd jubilant: what time the startling East
>   Saw from her dark womb leap her flamy child!
>   Glory to God in the Highest! PEACE on Earth!
>   Yet thou more bright than all that Angel Blaze,
>   Despiséd GALILAEAN! Man of Woes!
>   For chiefly in the oppressed Good Man's face
>   The Great Invisible (by symbols seen)
>   Shines with peculiar and concentred light,
>   When all of Self regardless the scourg'd Saint
>   Mourns for th' oppressor. O thou meekest Man!
>   Meek Man and lowliest of the Sons of Men!
>   Who thee beheld thy imag'd Father saw.†
>   His Power and Wisdom from thy awful eye
>   Blended their beams, and loftier Love sat there
>   Musing on human weal, and that dread hour
>   *When thy insulted*, &c. 1796.

* And suddenly there was with the Angel a multitude of the heavenly Host, praising God and saying glory to God in the highest and on earth peace. Luke ii. 13 *1796*.

† Philip saith unto him, Lord! shew us the Father and it sufficeth us. Jesus saith unto him, Have I been so long time with you, and yet hast thou not known me, Philip? He that **hath seen** me hath seen the Father. John xiv. 9 *1796*.

7 Angel-blaze] Angel-Host *1803*.

Nor the starred azure, nor the sovran sun,
E'er with such majesty of portraiture
Imaged the supreme beauty uncreate,
As thou, meek Saviour! at the fearful hour
When thy insulted anguish winged the prayer
Harped by Archangels, when they sing of mercy!
Which when the Almighty heard from forth his throne
Diviner light filled Heaven with ecstasy!
Heaven's hymnings paused: and Hell her yawning mouth
Closed a brief moment.

                              Lovely was the death
Of Him whose life was Love! Holy with power
He on the thought-benighted Sceptic beamed
Manifest Godhead, melting into day
What floating mists of dark idolatry
Broke and misshaped the omnipresent Sire:[1]
And first by Fear uncharmed the drowsèd Soul.
Till of its nobler nature it 'gan feel
Dim recollections; and thence soared to Hope,
Strong to believe whate'er of mystic good
The Eternal dooms for His immortal sons.
From Hope and firmer Faith to perfect Love
Attracted and absorbed: and centered there
God only to behold, and know, and feel,
Till by exclusive consciousness of God
All self-annihilated it shall make[2]

---

[1] Τὸ Νοητὸν διῃρήκασιν εἰς πολλῶν Θεῶν ἰδιότητας. DAMAS. DE MYST. AEGYPT. *Footnote* to line 34, *1797, 1803, 1828, 1829*. [This note, which should be attached to l. 33, is a comment on the original line 'Split and mishap'd' &c., of 1796. The quotation as translated reads thus:—'Men have split up the Intelligible One into the peculiar attributes of Gods many'.]

[2] See this *demonstrated* by Hartley, vol. 1, p. 114, and vol. 2, p. 329. See it likewise proved, and freed from the charge of Mysticism, by Pistorius in his Notes and Additions to part second of Hartley on Man, Addition the 18th, the 653rd page of the third volume of Hartley, Octavo Edition. *Note* to line 44, *1797*. [David Hartley's *Observations on Man* were published in 1749. His son republished them in 1791, with Notes, &c., from the German of H. A. Pistorius, Pastor and Provost of the Synod at Poseritz in the Island of Rügen.]

26	Diviner light flash'd extacy o'er Heaven! *1796*.
32–4	What mists dim-floating of Idolatry Split and mishap'd the Omnipresent Sire: And first by Terror, Mercy's startling prelude, Uncharm'd the Spirit spell-bound with earthy lusts. *1796*.
39	From Hope and stronger Faith to perfect Love *1796*.

RELIGIOUS MUSINGS 111

God its Identity: God all in all!
We and our Father one!

                            And blest are they,   45
Who in this fleshly World, the elect of Heaven,
Their strong eye darting through the deeds of men,
Adore with steadfast unpresuming gaze
Him Nature's essence, mind, and energy!
And gazing, trembling, patiently ascend   50
Treading beneath their feet all visible things
As steps, that upward to their Father's throne
Lead gradual—else nor glorified nor loved.
They nor contempt embosom nor revenge:
For they dare know of what may seem deform   55
The Supreme Fair sole operant: in whose sight
All things are pure, his strong controlling love
Alike from all educing perfect good.
Their's too celestial courage, inly armed—
Dwarfing Earth's giant brood, what time they muse   60
On their great Father, great beyond compare!
And marching onwards view high o'er their heads
His waving banners of Omnipotence.

Who the Creator love, created Might
Dread not: within their tents no Terrors walk.   65
For they are holy things before the Lord
Aye unprofaned, though Earth should league with Hell;
God's altar grasping with an eager hand
Fear, the wild-visag'd, pale, eye-starting wretch,
Sure-refug'd hears his hot pursuing fiends   70

    54 embosom] imbosom *1796, 1797, 1803.*
    64–71   They cannot dread created might, who love
                God the Creator! fair and lofty thought!
                It lifts and swells my heart! and as I muse,
                Behold a VISION gathers in my soul,
                Voices and shadowy shapes! In human guise
                I seem to see the phantom, FEAR, pass by,
                Hotly-pursued, and pale! From rock to rock
                He bounds with bleeding feet, and thro' the swamp,
                The quicksand and the groaning wilderness,
                Struggles with feebler and yet feebler flight.
                But lo! an altar in the wilderness,
                And eagerly yet feebly lo! he grasps
                The altar of the living God! and there
                With wan reverted face the trembling wretch
                All wildly list'ning to his Hunter-fiends
                Stands, till the last faint echo of their yell
                Dies in the distance. *Soon refresh'd from Heaven* &c. *1803.*

Yell at vain distance. Soon refresh'd from Heaven
He calms the throb and tempest of his heart.
His countenance settles; a soft solemn bliss
Swims in his eye—his swimming eye uprais'd:
And Faith's whole armour glitters on his limbs!   75
And thus transfigured with a dreadless awe,
A solemn hush of soul, meek he beholds
All things of terrible seeming: yea, unmoved
Views e'en the immitigable ministers
That shower down vengeance on these latter days.   80
For kindling with intenser Deity
From the celestial Mercy-seat they come,
And at the renovating wells of Love
Have fill'd their vials with salutary wrath,[1]
To sickly Nature more medicinal   85
Than what soft balm the weeping good man pours
Into the lone despoiléd traveller's wounds!

Thus from the Elect, regenerate through faith,
Pass the dark Passions and what thirsty cares[2]

[1] And I heard a great voice out of the Temple saying to the seven Angels, pour out the vials of the wrath of God upon the earth.   Revelation, xvi. 1.   *Note* to line 91, *Notes*, 1796, p. 90.

[2] Our evil Passions, under the influence of Religion, become innocent, and may be made to animate our virtue—in the same manner as the thick mist melted by the Sun, increases the light which it had before excluded. In the preceding paragraph, agreeably to this truth, we had allegorically narrated the transfiguration of Fear into holy Awe.   *Footnote* to line 91, *1797*: to line 101, *1803*.

74-7   Swims in his eyes: his swimming eyes uprais'd:
        And Faith's whole armour girds his limbs! And thus
        Transfigur'd, with a meek and dreadless awe,
        A solemn hush of spirit *he beholds* 1803.

78-84   Yea, and there,
        Unshudder'd unaghasted, he shall view
        E'en the SEVEN SPIRITS, who in the latter day
        Will shower hot pestilence on the sons of men,
        For he shall know, his heart shall understand,
        That kindling with intenser Deity
        They from the MERCY-SEAT like rosy flames,
        From God's celestial MERCY-SEAT will flash,
        And at the wells of renovating LOVE
        Fill their Seven Vials *with salutary wrath.* 1796.

81-3   For even these on wings of healing come,
        Yea, kindling with intenser Deity
        From the Celestial MERCY SEAT they speed,
        And at the renovating &c. 1803.

86 soft] sweet *1803.*

Drink up the spirit, and the dim regards 90
Self-centre. Lo they vanish! or acquire
New names, new features—by supernal grace
Enrobed with Light, and naturalised in Heaven.
As when a shepherd on a vernal morn
Through some thick fog creeps timorous with slow foot, 95
Darkling he fixes on the immediate road
His downward eye: all else of fairest kind
Hid or deformed. But lo! the bursting Sun!
Touched by the enchantment of that sudden beam
Straight the black vapour melteth, and in globes 100
Of dewy glitter gems each plant and tree;
On every leaf, on every blade it hangs!
Dance glad the new-born intermingling rays,
And wide around the landscape streams with glory!

There is one Mind, one omnipresent Mind, 105
Omnific. His most holy name is Love.
Truth of subliming import! with the which
Who feeds and saturates his constant soul,
He from his small particular orbit flies
With blest outstarting! From himself he flies, 110
Stands in the sun, and with no partial gaze
Views all creation; and he loves it all,
And blesses it, and calls it very good!
This is indeed to dwell with the Most High!
Cherubs and rapture-trembling Seraphim 115
Can press no nearer to the Almighty's throne.
But that we roam unconscious, or with hearts
Unfeeling of our universal Sire,
And that in His vast family no Cain
Injures uninjured (in her best-aimed blow 120
Victorious Murder a blind Suicide)
Haply for this some younger Angel now
Looks down on Human Nature: and, behold!
A sea of blood bestrewed with wrecks, where mad
Embattling Interests on each other rush 125
With unhelmed rage!

'Tis the sublime of man,
Our noontide Majesty, to know ourselves

96–7   Darkling with earnest eyes he traces out
       Th' immediate road, all else of fairest kind *1803*.
98 the burning Sun *1803*   115 The Cherubs and the trembling
Seraphim *1803*.   119–21 *om. 1803*.

RELIGIOUS MUSINGS

Parts and proportions of one wondrous whole!
This fraternises man, this constitutes
Our charities and bearings. But 'tis God   130
Diffused through all, that doth make all one whole;
This the worst superstition, him except
Aught to desire, Supreme Reality![1]
The plenitude and permanence of bliss!
O Fiends of Superstition! not that oft   135
The erring Priest hath stained with brother's blood
Your grisly idols, not for this may wrath
Thunder against you from the Holy One!
But o'er some plain that steameth to the sun,
Peopled with Death; or where more hideous Trade   140
Loud-laughing packs his bales of human anguish;
I will raise up a mourning, O ye Fiends!
And curse your spells, that film the eye of Faith,
Hiding the present God; whose presence lost,
The moral world's cohesion, we become   145
An Anarchy of Spirits! Toy-bewitched,
Made blind by lusts, disherited of soul,
No common centre Man, no common sire
Knoweth! A sordid solitary thing,
Mid countless brethren with a lonely heart   150
Through courts and cities the smooth savage roams
Feeling himself, his own low self the whole;

---

[1] If to make aught but the Supreme Reality the object of final pursuit, be Superstition; if the attributing of sublime properties to things or persons, which those things or persons neither do or can possess, be Superstition; then Avarice and Ambition are Superstitions: and he who wishes to estimate the evils of Superstition, should transport himself, not to the temple of the Mexican Deities, but to the plains of Flanders, or the coast of Africa.—Such is the sentiment convey'd in this and the subsequent lines. *Footnote* to line 135, *1797* : to line 143, *1803*.

135-41   O Fiends of Superstition! not that oft
        Your pitiless rites have floated with man's blood
        The skull-pil'd Temple, not for this shall wrath
        Thunder against you from the Holy One!
        But (whether ye th' unclimbing Bigot mock
        With secondary Gods, or if more pleas'd
        Ye petrify th' imbrothell'd Atheist's heart,
        The Atheist your worst slave) I o'er some plain
        Peopled with Death, and to the silent Sun
        Steaming with tyrant-murder'd multitudes;
        Or where mid groans and shrieks loud-laughing Trade
        More hideous packs his bales of living anguish *1796*.

When he by sacred sympathy might make
The whole one Self! Self, that no alien knows!
Self, far diffused as Fancy's wing can travel! 155
Self, spreading still! Oblivious of its own,
Yet all of all possessing! This is Faith!
This the Messiah's destined victory!

But first offences needs must come! Even now[1]
(Black Hell laughs horrible—to hear the scoff!) 160
Thee to defend, meek Galilaean! Thee
And thy mild laws of Love unutterable,
Mistrust and Enmity have burst the bands
Of social peace: and listening Treachery lurks
With pious fraud to snare a brother's life; 165
And childless widows o'er the groaning land
Wail numberless; and orphans weep for bread!
Thee to defend, dear Saviour of Mankind!
Thee, Lamb of God! Thee, blameless Prince of Peace!
From all sides rush the thirsty brood of War!— 170
Austria, and that foul Woman of the North,
The lustful murderess of her wedded lord!
And he, connatural Mind![2] whom (in their songs
So bards of elder time had haply feigned)
Some Fury fondled in her hate to man, 175
Bidding her serpent hair in mazy surge
Lick his young face, and at his mouth imbreathe

---

[1] January 21st, 1794, in the debate on the Address to his Majesty, on the speech from the Throne, the Earl of Guildford (*sic*) moved an Amendment to the following effect:—'That the House hoped his Majesty would seize the earliest opportunity to conclude a peace with France,' &c. This motion was opposed by the Duke of Portland, who 'considered the war to be merely grounded on one principle—the preservation of the CHRISTIAN RELIGION'. May 30th, 1794, the Duke of Bedford moved a number of Resolutions, with a view to the Establishment of a Peace with France. He was opposed (among others) by Lord Abingdon in these remarkable words: 'The best road to Peace, my Lords, is WAR! and WAR carried on in the same manner in which we are taught to worship our CREATOR, namely, with all our souls, and with all our minds, and with all our hearts, and with all our strength.' [*Footnote* to line 159, *1797, 1803, 1828, 1829,* and *1834*.]

[2] That Despot who received the wages of an hireling that he might act the part of a swindler, and who skulked from his impotent attacks on the liberties of France to perpetrate more successful iniquity in the plains of *Poland. Note* to line 193. *Notes*, 1796, p. 170.

---

165 pious] *pious 1796–1829.*   176 mazy surge] tortuous folds *1796.*
177 imbreathe] inbreathe *1797, 1803, 1828, 1829.*

Horrible sympathy! And leagued with these
Each petty German princeling, nursed in gore!
Soul-hardened barterers of human blood![1] 180
Death's prime slave-merchants! Scorpion-whips of Fate!
Nor least in savagery of holy zeal,
Apt for the yoke, the race degenerate,
Whom Britain erst had blushed to call her sons!
Thee to defend the Moloch Priest prefers 185
The prayer of hate, and bellows to the herd,
That Deity, Accomplice Deity
In the fierce jealousy of wakened wrath
Will go forth with our armies and our fleets
To scatter the red ruin on their foes! 190
O blasphemy! to mingle fiendish deeds
With blessedness!

              Lord of unsleeping Love,[2]
From everlasting Thou! We shall not die.
These, even these, in mercy didst thou form,
Teachers of Good through Evil, by brief wrong 195
Making Truth lovely, and her future might
Magnetic o'er the fixed untrembling heart.

In the primeval age a dateless while
The vacant Shepherd wander'd with his flock,
Pitching his tent where'er the green grass waved. 200
But soon Imagination conjured up
An host of new desires: with busy aim,
Each for himself, Earth's eager children toiled.
So Property began, twy-streaming fount,

---

[1] The Father of the present Prince of Hesse Cassell supported himself and his strumpets at Paris by the vast sums which he received from the British Government during the American War for the flesh of his subjects. *Notes*, 1796, p. 176.

[2] Art thou not from everlasting, O Lord, mine Holy One? We shall not die. O Lord! thou hast ordained them for judgment, &c. Habakkuk i. 12. *Note* to line 212. *Notes*, 1796, p. 171. *Footnote, 1828, 1829, 1834.*

Art thou not, &c. In this paragraph the Author recalls himself from his indignation against the instruments of Evil, to contemplate the *uses* of these Evils in the great process of divine Benevolence. In the first age, Men were innocent from ignorance of Vice; they fell, that by the knowledge of consequences they might attain intellectual security, i. e. Virtue, which is a wise and strong-nerv'd Innocence. *Footnote* to line 196, 1797: to line 204, 1803.

202 An] A *1834.*

RELIGIOUS MUSINGS

Whence Vice and Virtue flow, honey and gall. 205
Hence the soft couch, and many-coloured robe,
The timbrel, and arched dome and costly feast,
With all the inventive arts, that nursed the soul
To forms of beauty, and by sensual wants
Unsensualised the mind, which in the means 210
Learnt to forget the grossness of the end,
Best pleasured with its own activity.
And hence Disease that withers manhood's arm,
The daggered Envy, spirit-quenching Want,
Warriors, and Lords, and Priests—all the sore ills[1] 215
That vex and desolate our mortal life.
Wide-wasting ills! yet each the immediate source
Of mightier good. Their keen necessities
To ceaseless action goading human thought
Have made Earth's reasoning animal her Lord; 220
And the pale-featured Sage's trembling hand
Strong as an host of arméd Deities,
Such as the blind Ionian fabled erst.

From Avarice thus, from Luxury and War
Sprang heavenly Science; and from Science Freedom. 225
O'er waken'd realms Philosophers and Bards
Spread in concentric circles: they whose souls,
Conscious of their high dignities from God,
Brook not Wealth's rivalry! and they, who long
Enamoured with the charms of order, hate 230
The unseemly disproportion: and whoe'er

---

[1] I deem that the teaching of the gospel for hire is wrong; because it gives the teacher an improper bias in favour of particular opinions on a subject where it is of the last importance that the mind should be perfectly unbiassed. Such is my private opinion; but I mean not to censure all hired teachers, many among whom I know, and venerate as the best and wisest of men—God forbid that I should think of these, when I use the word PRIEST, a name, after which any other term of abhorrence would appear an anti-climax. By a Priest I mean a man who holding the scourge of power in his right hand and a bible (translated by authority) in his left, doth necessarily cause the bible and the scourge to be associated ideas, and so produces that temper of mind which leads to Infidelity—Infidelity which judging of Revelation by the doctrines and practices of established Churches honors God by rejecting Christ. See 'Address to the People', p. 57, sold by Parsons, Paternoster Row. *Note* to line 235. *Notes*, 1796, pp. 171, 172.

---

222 an] a *1834*.   223 *om. 1796, 1803.*

Turn with mild sorrow from the Victor's car
And the low puppetry of thrones, to muse
On that blest triumph, when the Patriot Sage[1]
Called the red lightnings from the o'er-rushing cloud 235
And dashed the beauteous terrors on the earth
Smiling majestic. Such a phalanx ne'er
Measured firm paces to the calming sound
Of Spartan flute! These on the fated day,
When, stung to rage by Pity, eloquent men 240
Have roused with pealing voice the unnumbered tribes
That toil and groan and bleed, hungry and blind—
These, hush'd awhile with patient eye serene,
Shall watch the mad careering of the storm;
Then o'er the wild and wavy chaos rush 245
And tame the outrageous mass, with plastic might
Moulding Confusion to such perfect forms,
As erst were wont,—bright visions of the day!—
To float before them, when, the summer noon,
Beneath some arched romantic rock reclined 250
They felt the sea-breeze lift their youthful locks;
Or in the month of blossoms, at mild eve,
Wandering with desultory feet inhaled
The wafted perfumes, and the flocks and woods
And many-tinted streams and setting sun 255
With all his gorgeous company of clouds
Ecstatic gazed! then homeward as they strayed
Cast the sad eye to earth, and inly mused
Why there was misery in a world so fair.

Ah! far removed from all that glads the sense, 260
From all that softens or ennobles Man,
The wretched Many! Bent beneath their loads
They gape at pageant Power, nor recognise
Their cots' transmuted plunder! From the tree
Of Knowledge, ere the vernal sap had risen 265
Rudely disbranchéd! Blessed Society!
Fitliest depictured by some sun-scorched waste,
Where oft majestic through the tainted noon

---

[1] Dr. Franklin. *Note* to line 253. *Notes*, 1796, p. 172.

254-5 The wafted perfumes, gazing on the woods
    The many tinted streams *1803.*

257 In extacy! *1803.*   266 Blessed] O *Blest* 1796, *Watchman*: **evil** *1803*: *Blessed* 1797, 1828, 1829.

RELIGIOUS MUSINGS

The Simoom sails, before whose purple pomp [1]
Who falls not prostrate dies! And where by night,   270
Fast by each precious fountain on green herbs
The lion couches: or hyaena dips
Deep in the lucid stream his bloody jaws;
Or serpent plants his vast moon-glittering bulk,
Caught in whose monstrous twine Behemoth [2] yells,   275
His bones loud-crashing!

                O ye numberless,
Whom foul Oppression's ruffian gluttony
Drives from Life's plenteous feast! O thou poor Wretch
Who nursed in darkness and made wild by want,
Roamest for prey, yea thy unnatural hand   280
Dost lift to deeds of blood! O pale-eyed form,
The victim of seduction, doomed to know
Polluted nights and days of blasphemy;
Who in loathed orgies with lewd wassailers
Must gaily laugh, while thy remembered Home   285
Gnaws like a viper at thy secret heart!
O agéd Women! ye who weekly catch
The morsel tossed by law-forced charity,

---

[1] At eleven o'clock, while we contemplated with great pleasure the rugged top of Chiggre, to which we were fast approaching, and where we were to solace ourselves with plenty of good water, IDRIS cried out with a loud voice, 'Fall upon your faces, for here is the Simoom'. I saw from the S.E. an haze come on, in colour like the purple part of the rainbow, but not so compressed or thick. It did not occupy twenty yards in breadth, and was about twelve feet high from the ground.—We all lay flat on the ground, as if dead, till IDRIS told us it was blown over. The meteor, or purple haze, which I saw, was indeed passed; but the light air that still blew was of heat to threaten suffocation. Bruce's *Travels*, vol. 4, p. 557. *Note* to line 288. *Notes*, 1796, pp. 172, 173.

[2] Behemoth, in Hebrew, signifies wild beasts in general. Some believe it is the Elephant, some the Hippopotamus; some affirm it is the Wild Bull. Poetically, it designates any large Quadruped. [Footnote to l. 279, *1797*: to l. 286, *1803*. Reprinted in *1828*, *1829*, and *1834*. The note to l. 294 in *1796*, p. 173 ran thus: Used poetically for a very large quadruped, but in general it designates the elephant.]

---

270 by] at *Watchman*.   273 bloody] gore-stained *1803*.   274 plants] rolls *1796*.

277–8 Ye whom Oppression's ruffian gluttony
      Drives from the feast of life *1803*.

280–1 Dost roam for prey—yea thy unnatural hand
      Liftest to deeds of blood *1796*.

281 Dost] Dar'st *Watchman*.

283–4 Nights of pollution, days of blasphemy,
      Who in thy orgies with loath'd wassailers *1803*.

And die so slowly, that none call it murder!
O loathly suppliants! ye, that unreceived 290
Totter heart-broken from the closing gates
Of the full Lazar-house; or, gazing, stand,
Sick with despair! O ye to Glory's field
Forced or ensnared, who, as ye gasp in death,
Bleed with new wounds beneath the vulture's beak! 295
O thou poor widow, who in dreams dost view
Thy husband's mangled corse, and from short doze
Start'st with a shriek; or in thy half-thatched cot
Waked by the wintry night-storm, wet and cold
Cow'rst o'er thy screaming baby! Rest awhile 300
Children of Wretchedness! More groans must rise,
More blood must stream, or ere your wrongs be full.
Yet is the day of Retribution nigh:
The Lamb of God hath opened the fifth seal:[1]
And upward rush on swiftest wing of fire 305
The innumerable multitude of wrongs
By man on man inflicted! Rest awhile,
Children of Wretchedness! The hour is nigh

---

[1] See the sixth chapter of the Revelation of St. John the Divine.—And I looked and beheld a pale horse; and his name that sat on him was Death, and Hell followed with him. And power was given unto them over the FOURTH part of the Earth to kill with sword, and with hunger, and with pestilence, and with the beasts of the Earth.—And when he had opened the fifth seal, I saw under the altar the souls of them that were slain for the word of God, and for the testimony which they held; and white robes were given unto every one of them; and it was said unto them, that they should rest yet for a little season, until their fellow servants also, and their brethren that should be killed as they were should be fulfilled. And I beheld when he had opened the sixth seal, the stars of Heaven fell unto the Earth, even as a fig-tree casteth her untimely figs when she is shaken of a mighty wind: And the kings of the earth, and the great men, and the rich men, and the chief captains, &c. *Note* to line 324. *Notes*, 1796, pp. 174, 175.

---

290 O loathly-visag'd Suppliants! ye that oft *1796*: O loathly-visag'd supplicants! that oft *Watchman*.
291-2   Rack'd with disease, from the unopen'd gate
        Of the full Lazar-house, heart-broken crawl! *1796*, *Watchman*.
293-6   O ye to scepter'd Glory's gore-drench'd field
        Forc'd or ensnar'd, who swept by Slaughter's scythe
        Stern nurse of Vultures! steam in putrid heaps *1796*.

        O ye that steaming to the silent Noon,
        People with Death red-eyed Ambition's plains!
        O Wretched *Widow Watchman*.
300 Cow'rest *1796*.   302 stream] steam *1796, Watchman, 1797, 1803*.
305 And upward spring on swiftest plume of fire *Watchman*.

RELIGIOUS MUSINGS

And lo! the Great, the Rich, the Mighty Men,
The Kings and the Chief Captains of the World,   310
With all that fixed on high like stars of Heaven
Shot baleful influence, shall be cast to earth,
Vile and down-trodden, as the untimely fruit
Shook from the fig-tree by a sudden storm.
Even now the storm begins:[1] each gentle name.   315
Faith and meek Piety, with fearful joy
Tremble far-off—for lo! the Giant Frenzy
Uprooting empires with his whirlwind arm
Mocketh high Heaven; burst hideous from the cell
Where the old Hag, unconquerable, huge,   320
Creation's eyeless drudge, black Ruin, sits
Nursing the impatient earthquake.
                             O return!
Pure Faith! meek Piety! The abhorréd Form[2]
Whose scarlet robe was stiff with earthly pomp,
Who drank iniquity in cups of gold,   325
Whose names were many and all blasphemous,
Hath met the horrible judgment! Whence that cry?
The mighty army of foul Spirits shrieked
Disherited of earth! For she hath fallen
On whose black front was written Mystery;   330
She that reeled heavily, whose wine was blood;
She that worked whoredom with the Daemon Power,
And from the dark embrace all evil things
Brought forth and nurtured: mitred Atheism!
And patient Folly who on bended knee   335
Gives back the steel that stabbed him; and pale Fear
Haunted by ghastlier shapings than surround
Moon-blasted Madness when he yells at midnight!
Return pure Faith! return meek Piety!

[1] Alluding to the French Revolution *1834*: The French Revolution *1796*: This passage alludes to the French Revolution: and the subsequent paragraph to the downfall of Religious Establishments. I am convinced that the Babylon of the Apocalypse does not apply to Rome exclusively; but to the union of Religion with Power and Wealth, wherever it is found. *Footnote* to line 320, *1797*, to line 322, *1803*.

[2] And there came one of the seven Angels which had the seven vials, and talked with me, saying unto me, come hither! I will show unto thee the judgment of the great Whore, that sitteth upon many waters: with whom the kings of the earth have committed fornication, &c. Revelation of St. John the Divine, chapter the seventeenth. *Note* to l. 343. *Notes*, 1796, p. 175.

337 Hunted by ghastlier terrors *1796, Watchman*. Haunted] Hunted *1797, 1803, 1828, 1829*.

The kingdoms of the world are your's: each heart 340
Self-governed, the vast family of Love
Raised from the common earth by common toil
Enjoy the equal produce. Such delights
As float to earth, permitted visitants!
When in some hour of solemn jubilee 345
The massy gates of Paradise are thrown
Wide open, and forth come in fragments wild
Sweet echoes of unearthly melodies,
And odours snatched from beds of Amaranth,
And they, that from the crystal river of life 350
Spring up on freshened wing, ambrosial gales!
The favoured good man in his lonely walk
Perceives them, and his silent spirit drinks
Strange bliss which he shall recognise in heaven.
And such delights, such strange beatitudes 355
Seize on my young anticipating heart
When that blest future rushes on my view!
For in his own and in his Father's might
The Saviour comes! While as the Thousand Years[1]
Lead up their mystic dance, the Desert shouts! 360
Old Ocean claps his hands! The mighty Dead
Rise to new life, whoe'er from earliest time
With conscious zeal had urged Love's wondrous plan,
Coadjutors of God. To Milton's trump

[1] The Millenium:—in which I suppose, that Man will continue to enjoy the highest glory, of which his human nature is capable.—That all who in past ages have endeavoured to ameliorate the state of man will rise and enjoy the fruits and flowers, the imperceptible seeds of which they had sown in their former Life: and that the wicked will during the same period, be suffering the remedies adapted to their several bad habits. I suppose that this period will be followed by the passing away of this Earth and by our entering the state of pure intellect; when all Creation shall rest from its labours. *Footnote to line 365, 1797, to line 367, 1803.*

345-8   When on some solemn Jubilee of Saints
       The sapphire-blazing gates of Paradise
       Are thrown wide open, and thence voyage forth
       Detachments wild of seraph-warbled airs *1796, Watchman.*
355 beatitudes] beatitude *1796, Watchman, 1797, 1803, 1828, 1829.*
356 Seize on] Have seiz'd *Watchman.*
359-61   The SAVIOUR comes! While as to solemn strains,
       The THOUSAND YEARS lead up their mystic dance
       Old OCEAN claps his hands! the DESERT shouts!
       And soft gales wafted from the haunts of spring
       Melt the primaeval North! *The Mighty Dead 1796.*

RELIGIOUS MUSINGS

The high groves of the renovated Earth 365
Unbosom their glad echoes : inly hushed,
Adoring Newton his serener eye
Raises to heaven : and he of mortal kind
Wisest, he[1] first who marked the ideal tribes
Up the fine fibres through the sentient brain. 370
Lo! Priestley there, patriot, and saint, and sage,
Him, full of years, from his loved native land
Statesmen blood-stained and priests idolatrous
By dark lies maddening the blind multitude
Drove with vain hate. Calm, pitying he retired, 375
And mused expectant on these promised years.

O Years! the blest pre-eminence of Saints!
Ye sweep athwart my gaze, so heavenly bright,
The wings that veil the adoring Seraphs' eyes,
What time they bend before the Jasper Throne[2] 380
Reflect no lovelier hues! Yet ye depart,
And all beyond is darkness! Heights most strange,
Whence Fancy falls, fluttering her idle wing.
For who of woman born may paint the hour,
When seized in his mid course, the Sun shall wane 385

---

[1] David Hartley. [*Footnote* to line 392, *1796*, to line 375, *1797*, to line 380, *1803* : reprinted in *1828, 1829,* and *1834.*]

[2] Rev. chap. iv. v. 2 and 3.—And immediately I was in the Spirit : and behold, a Throne was set in Heaven and one sat on the Throne. And he that sat was to look upon like a jasper and a sardine stone, &c. [*Footnote* to line 386, *1797*, to line 389, *1803* : reprinted in *1828, 1829,* and *1834.*]

---

365 The odorous groves of Earth reparadis'd *1796*.
370-2 Down the fine fibres from the sentient brain
Roll subtly-surging. Pressing on his steps
Lo! PRIESTLEY there, Patriot, and Saint, and Sage
Whom that my fleshly eye hath never seen
A childish pang of impotent regret
Hath thrill'd my heart. Him from his *native land 1796.*
Up the fine fibres thro' the sentient brain
Pass in fine surges. Pressing on his steps
Lo! Priestley there 1803.
378-80 Sweeping before the rapt prophetic Gaze
Bright as what glories of the jasper throne
Stream from the gorgeous and face-veiling plumes
Of Spirits adoring! Ye blest years! must end *1796.*
380 they bend] he bends *1797, 1803, 1828, 1829.*

Making noon ghastly! Who of woman born
May image in the workings of his thought,
How the black-visaged, red-eyed Fiend outstretched[1]
Beneath the unsteady feet of Nature groans,
In feverous slumbers—destined then to wake,   390
When fiery whirlwinds thunder his dread name
And Angels shout, Destruction! How his arm
The last great Spirit lifting high in air
Shall swear by Him, the ever-living One,
Time is no more!

                    Believe thou, O my soul,[2]   395
Life is a vision shadowy of Truth;
And vice, and anguish, and the wormy grave,
Shapes of a dream! The veiling clouds retire,
And lo! the Throne of the redeeming God
Forth flashing unimaginable day   400
Wraps in one blaze earth, heaven, and deepest hell.

Contemplant Spirits! ye that hover o'er
With untired gaze the immeasurable fount
Ebullient with creative Deity!
And ye of plastic power, that interfused   405
Roll through the grosser and material mass
In organizing surge! Holies of God!
(And what if Monads of the infinite mind?)
I haply journeying my immortal course
Shall sometime join your mystic choir! Till then   410
I discipline my young and novice thought
In ministeries of heart-stirring song,
And aye on Meditation's heaven-ward wing
Soaring aloft I breathe the empyreal air
Of Love, omnific, omnipresent Love,   415

---

[1] The final Destruction impersonated. [*Footnote* to line 394, *1797*, to line 396, *1803*: reprinted in *1828, 1829*, and *1834*.]

[2] This paragraph is intelligible to those, who, like the Author, believe and feel the sublime system of Berkley (*sic*); and the doctrine of the final Happiness of all men. *Footnote* to line 402, *1797*, to line 405, *1803*.

---

387 May image in his wildly-working thought *1796*: May image, how the red-eyed Fiend outstretcht *1803*.   390 feverous] feverish *1796, 1797, 1803, 1828, 1829*.   *Between* 391, 392 Destruction! when the Sons of Morning shout, The Angels shout, Destruction *1803*.   393 The Mighty Spirit *1796*.   400 *om. 1803*.   401 blaze] Light *1803*.   411 and novice] noviciate *1796, 1797, 1803, 1828, 1829*.

Whose day-spring rises glorious in my soul
As the great Sun, when he his influence
Sheds on the frost-bound waters—The glad stream
Flows to the ray and warbles as it flows.

1794–1796.

MONODY ON THE DEATH OF CHATTERTON[1]

O what a wonder seems the fear of death,
Seeing how gladly we all sink to sleep,
Babes, Children, Youths, and Men,
Night following night for threescore years and ten!
But doubly strange, where life is but a breath   5
To sigh and pant with, up Want's rugged steep.

Away, Grim Phantom! Scorpion King, away!
Reserve thy terrors and thy stings display
For coward Wealth and Guilt in robes of State!
Lo! by the grave I stand of one, for whom   10
A prodigal Nature and a niggard Doom
(*That* all bestowing, *this* withholding all)
Made each chance knell from distant spire or dome
Sound like a seeking Mother's anxious call,
Return, poor Child! Home, weary Truant, home!   15

[1] The 'Monody', &c., dated in eds. 1796, 1797, 1803, 'October, 1794,' was first published at Cambridge in 1794, in *Poems*, By Thomas Rowley [i. e. Chatterton] and others edited by Lancelot Sharpe (pp. xxv–xxviii). An *Introductory Note* was prefixed :—'The Editor thinks himself happy in the permission of an ingenious friend to insert the following Monody.' The variants marked 1794 are derived from that work. The 'Monody' was not included in *Sibylline Leaves*, 1817. For MS. variants *vide ante*, 'Monody', &c., Christ's Hospital Version.

Coleridge told Cottle, May 27, 1814 that lines 1–4 were written when he was 'a mere boy' (*Reminiscences*, 1847, p. 348); and, again, April 22, 1819, he told William Worship that they were written 'in his thirteenth

---

1–15 When faint and sad o'er Sorrow's desart wild
Slow journeys onward, poor Misfortune's child;
When fades each lovely form by Fancy drest,
And inly pines the self-consuming breast;
(No scourge of scorpions in thy right arm dread,
No helmèd terrors nodding o'er thy head,)
Assume, O Death! the cherub wings of Peace,
And bid the heartsick Wanderer's Anguish cease.
1794, 1796, 1797, 1803, 1828.

[Lines 1–15 of the text were first printed in 1829.]

Thee, Chatterton! these unblest stones protect
From want, and the bleak freezings of neglect.
Too long before the vexing Storm-blast driven
Here hast thou found repose! beneath this sod!
Thou! O vain word! *thou* dwell'st not with the clod! 20
Amid the shining Host of the Forgiven
Thou at the throne of mercy and thy God
The triumph of redeeming Love dost hymn
(Believe it, O my Soul!) to harps of Seraphim.

Yet oft, perforce ('tis suffering Nature's call), 25
I weep that heaven-born Genius *so* should fall;
And oft, in Fancy's saddest hour, my soul
Averted shudders at the poison'd bowl.
Now groans my sickening heart, as still I view
    Thy corse of livid hue; 30
Now Indignation checks the feeble sigh,
Or flashes through the tear that glistens in mine eye!

Is this the land of song-ennobled line?
Is this the land, where Genius ne'er in vain
    Pour'd forth his lofty strain? 35
Ah me! yet Spenser, gentlest bard divine,
Beneath chill Disappointment's shade,
His weary limbs in lonely anguish lay'd.
    And o'er her darling dead
    Pity hopeless hung her head, 40
While 'mid the pelting of that merciless storm,'
Sunk to the cold earth Otway's famish'd form!

---

year as a school exercise'. The Monody numbered 107 lines in 1794, 143 in 1796, 135 in 1797, 119 in 1803, 143 in 1828, 154 in 1829, and 165 lines in 1834.

---

16 these] yon *1794, 1796, 1797, 1803, 1828.*
18-24 Escap'd the sore wounds of Affliction's rod
    Meek at the throne of Mercy and of God,
    Perchance, thou raisest high th' enraptur'd hymn
      Amid the blaze of Seraphim! *1794, 1796, 1797, 1803, 1828.*

25 Yet oft ('tis Nature's bosom-startling call) *1794, 1796, 1828*: Yet oft ('tis Nature's call) *1797, 1803.*   26 should] shall *1829.*   30 Thy] The *1794.*

31-32 And now a flash of Indignation high
    Darts through the tear that glistens in mine eye.
                            1794, 1796, 1797, 1803, 1828.

35 his] her *1794.*   37 Disappointment's deadly shade *1794.*
merciless] pitiless *1794.*

ON THE DEATH OF CHATTERTON

Sublime of thought, and confident of fame,
From vales where Avon[1] winds the Minstrel came.
    Light-hearted youth! aye, as he hastes along,   45
    He meditates the future song,
How dauntless Ælla fray'd the Dacyan foe;
    And while the numbers flowing strong
    In eddies whirl, in surges throng,
Exulting in the spirits' genial throe   50
In tides of power his life-blood seems to flow.

And now his cheeks with deeper ardors flame,
His eyes have glorious meanings, that declare
More than the light of outward day shines there,
A holier triumph and a sterner aim!   55
Wings grow within him; and he soars above
Or Bard's or Minstrel's lay of war or love.
Friend to the friendless, to the sufferer health,
He hears the widow's prayer, the good man's praise;
To scenes of bliss transmutes his fancied wealth,   60
And young and old shall now see happy days.
On many a waste he bids trim gardens rise,
Gives the blue sky to many a prisoner's eyes;
And now in wrath he grasps the patriot steel,
And her own iron rod he makes Oppression feel.   65
Sweet Flower of Hope! free Nature's genial child!
That didst so fair disclose thy early bloom,

---

[1] Avon, a river near Bristol, the birth-place of Chatterton.

---

45 aye, as] *om.* 1797, 1803.   46 He] And *1797, 1803.*
47-56 How dauntless Ælla fray'd the Dacyan foes;
    And, as floating high in air,
    Glitter the sunny Visions fair,
    His eyes dance rapture, and his bosom glows!
                           1794, 1796, 1797, 1803, 1828.
[*1794* reads 'Danish foes'; *1797, 1803* read 'See, as floating', &c.
Lines 48-56 were added in *1829.*]

58-71 Friend to the friendless, to the sick man Health,
    With generous Joy he views th' *ideal* wealth;
    He hears the Widow's heaven-breath'd prayer of Praise;
    He marks the shelter'd Orphan's tearful gaze;
    Or where the sorrow-shrivell'd Captive lay,   5
    Pours the bright Blaze of Freedom's noon-tide Ray:
    And now, indignant 'grasps the patriot steel'
    And her own iron rod he makes Oppression feel.

128 ON THE DEATH OF CHATTERTON

Filling the wide air with a rich perfume!
For thee in vain all heavenly aspects smil'd;
From the hard world brief respite could they win—
The frost nipp'd sharp without, the canker prey'd within! 70
Ah! where are fled the charms of vernal Grace,
And Joy's wild gleams that lighten'd o'er thy face?
Youth of tumultuous soul, and haggard eye!
Thy wasted form, thy hurried steps I view,
On thy wan forehead starts the lethal dew, 75
And oh! the anguish of that shuddering sigh!

 Such were the struggles of the gloomy hour,
  When Care, of wither'd brow,
 Prepar'd the poison's death-cold power: 80
Already to thy lips was rais'd the bowl,
  When near thee stood Affection meek
(Her bosom bare, and wildly pale her cheek)
Thy sullen gaze she bade thee roll
On scenes that well might melt thy soul; 85
Thy native cot she flash'd upon thy view.

  Clad in Nature's rich array,
  And bright in all her tender hues,
Sweet Tree of Hope! thou loveliest child of Spring! 10
How fair didst thou disclose thine early bloom,
 Loading the west winds with its soft perfume!
And Fancy, elfin form of gorgeous wing,
[And Fancy hovering round on shadowy wing, *1794.*]
On every blossom hung her fostering dews,
 That, changeful, wanton'd to the orient Day! 15
But soon upon thy poor unshelter'd Head
[Ah! soon, &c. *1794.*]
Did Penury her sickly mildew shed:
And soon the scathing Lightning bade thee stand
In frowning horror o'er the blighted Land *1794, 1796, 1828.*

[Lines 1–8 of the preceding variant were omitted in *1797.* Line 9 reads 'Yes! Clad,' &c., and line 12 reads 'Most fair,' &c. The entire variant, 'Friend . . . Land,' was omitted in *1803*, but reappears in *1828*. The quotation marks 'grasps the patriot steel' which appear in *1796*, but not in *1794*, were inserted in *1828*, but omitted in *1829, 1834*. Lines 1–6 were included in 'Lines written at the King's Arms, Ross', as first published in the *Cambridge Intelligencer*, Sept. 27, 1794, and in the editions of *1797, 1828, 1829,* and *1834*.]

72 Ah! where] Whither *1794, 1797.* 73 that lighten'd] light-flashing *1797, 1803.* 76 wan] cold *1794, 1796, 1797, 1803, 1828.* lethal] anguish'd *1794, 1796, 1797, 1828.* 77 And dreadful was that bosom-rending sigh *1794, 1796, 1797, 1803, 1828.* 78 the gloomy] that gloomy *1803.* 80 Prepar'd the poison's power *1797, 1803.*

ON THE DEATH OF CHATTERTON

Thy native cot, where still, at close of day,
Peace smiling sate, and listen'd to thy lay;
Thy Sister's shrieks she bade thee hear,
And mark thy Mother's thrilling tear;   90
    See, see her breast's convulsive throe,
    Her silent agony of woe!
Ah! dash the poison'd chalice from thy hand!

And thou hadst dashed it, at her soft command,
But that Despair and Indignation rose,   95
And told again the story of thy woes;
Told the keen insult of the unfeeling heart,
The dread dependence on the low-born mind;
Told every pang, with which thy soul must smart,
Neglect, and grinning Scorn, and Want combined!   100
Recoiling quick, thou badest the friend of pain
Roll the black tide of Death through every freezing vein!
                O spirit blest!
Whether the Eternal's throne around,
Amidst the blaze of Seraphim,   105
Thou pourest forth the grateful hymn,
Or soaring thro' the blest domain
Enrapturest Angels with thy strain,—
Grant me, like thee, the lyre to sound,
Like thee with fire divine to glow;—   110
But ah! when rage the waves of woe,
Grant me with firmer breast to meet their hate,
And soar beyond the storm with upright eye elate!

Ye woods! that wave o'er Avon's rocky steep,
To Fancy's ear sweet is your murmuring deep!   115
For here she loves the cypress wreath to weave;
Watching with wistful eye, the saddening tints of eve.
Here, far from men, amid this pathless grove,
In solemn thought the Minstrel wont to rove,
Like star-beam on the slow sequester'd tide   120
Lone-glittering, through the high tree branching wide.

---

90 And mark thy mother's tear *1797, 1803*.   98 low-born] low-bred *1794*.   99 with] at *1794*.   must] might *1794*.   102 black] dark *1794*. 103-13 These lines, which form the conclusion (ll. 80-90) of the Christ's Hospital Version, were printed for the first time in *1834*, with the following variants: l. 104 the Eternal's] th' Eternal; l. 105 Seraphim] Cherubim; l. 112 to meet] t'oppose; l. 113 storm] storms.   120 slow] rude *1794*.   121 Lone-glittering thro' the Forest' murksome pride *1794*.

And here, in Inspiration's eager hour,
When most the big soul feels the mastering power,
  These wilds, these caverns roaming o'er,
  Round which the screaming sea-gulls soar,   125
With wild unequal steps he pass'd along,
Oft pouring on the winds a broken song:
Anon, upon some rough rock's fearful brow
Would pause abrupt—and gaze upon the waves below.

Poor Chatterton! *he* sorrows for thy fate   130
Who would have prais'd and lov'd thee, ere too late.
Poor Chatterton! farewell! of darkest hues
This chaplet cast I on thy unshaped tomb;
But dare no longer on the sad theme muse,
Lest kindred woes persuade a kindred doom: 135
For oh! big gall-drops, shook from Folly's wing,
Have blacken'd the fair promise of my spring;
And the stern Fate transpierc'd with viewless dart
The last pale Hope that shiver'd at my heart!

Hence, gloomy thoughts! no more my soul shall dwell 140
On joys that were! no more endure to weigh
The shame and anguish of the evil day,
Wisely forgetful! O'er the ocean swell
Sublime of Hope I seek the cottag'd dell
Where Virtue calm with careless step may stray;   145
And, dancing to the moon-light roundelay,
The wizard Passions weave an holy spell!

O Chatterton! that thou wert yet alive!
Sure thou would'st spread the canvass to the gale,
And love with us the tinkling team to drive   150
O'er peaceful Freedom's undivided dale;
And we, at sober eve, would round thee throng,
Would hang, enraptur'd, on thy stately song,
And greet with smiles the young-eyed Poesy
All deftly mask'd as hoar Antiquity.   155

Alas, vain Phantasies! the fleeting brood
Of Woe self-solac'd in her dreamy mood!

---

123 mastering] mad'ning *1794, 1796, 1797, 1803, 1828.*   **129** Here the Monody ends *1794.*   130-65 First printed in *1796.*   **133** unshaped] shapeless *1803.*   136-9 *om. 1803.*   **147** an] a *1834.*
153 Would hang] Hanging *1796, 1797, 1803, 1828, 1829.*

Yet will I love to follow the sweet dream,
Where Susquehannah pours his untamed stream;
And on some hill, whose forest-frowning side   160
Waves o'er the murmurs of his calmer tide,
Will raise a solemn Cenotaph to thee,
Sweet Harper of time-shrouded Minstrelsy!
And there, sooth'd sadly by the dirgeful wind,
Muse on the sore ills I had left behind.   165

1790-1834.

THE DESTINY OF NATIONS[1]

A VISION

Auspicious Reverence! Hush all meaner song,
Ere we the deep preluding strain have poured
To the Great Father, only Rightful King,
Eternal Father! King Omnipotent!
To the Will Absolute, the One, the Good!   5
The I AM, the Word, the Life, the Living God!

---

[1] First published, in its entirety, in *Sibylline Leaves*, 1817: included in 1828, 1829, and 1834. Two hundred and fifty-five lines were included in Book II of *Joan of Arc, An Epic Poem*, by Robert Southey, Bristol and London, 1796, 4°. The greater part of the remaining 212 lines were written in 1796, and formed part of an unpublished poem entitled *The Progress of Liberty* or *The Vision of the Maid of Orleans*, or *Visions of the Maid of Orleans*, or *Visions of the Maid of Arc*, or *The Vision of the Patriot Maiden*. (See letter to Poole, Dec. 13, and letter to J. Thelwall, Dec. 17, 1796, *Letters of S. T. C.*, 1895, i. 192, 206. See, too, Cottle's *Early Recollections*, 1837, i. 230; and, for Lamb's criticism of a first draft of the poem, his letters to Coleridge, dated Jan. 5 and Feb. 12, 1797.) For a reprint of *Joan of Arc*, Book the Second (Preternatural Agency), see Cottle's *Early Recollections*, 1837, ii. 241-62.

The texts of 1828, 1829 (almost but not quite identical) vary slightly from that of the *Sibylline Leaves*, 1817, and, again, the text of 1834 varies from that of 1828 and 1829. These variants (on a proof-sheet of the edition of 1828) are in Coleridge's own handwriting, and afford convincing evidence that he did take some part in the preparation of the text of his poems for the last edition issued in his own lifetime.

---

1 No more of Usurpation's doom'd defeat *4°*.
5-6 Beneath whose shadowy banners wide unfurl'd
   Justice leads forth her tyrant-quelling hosts.
                                4°, Sibylline Leaves.
5 The Will, The Word, The Breath, The Living God *1828, 1829*.
6 *Added in 1834*.

THE DESTINY OF NATIONS

  Such symphony requires best instrument.
Seize, then, my soul! from Freedom's trophied dome
The Harp which hangeth high between the Shields
Of Brutus and Leonidas! With that
Strong music, that soliciting spell, force back
Man's free and stirring spirit that lies entranced.
  For what is Freedom, but the unfettered use
Of all the powers which God for use had given?
But chiefly this, him First, him Last to view
Through meaner powers and secondary things
Effulgent, as through clouds that veil his blaze.
For all that meets the bodily sense I deem
Symbolical, one mighty alphabet
For infant minds; and we in this low world
Placed with our backs to bright Reality,
That we may learn with young unwounded ken
The substance from its shadow. Infinite Love,
Whose latence is the plenitude of All,
Thou with retracted beams, and self-eclipse
Veiling, revealest thine eternal Sun.

  But some there are who deem themselves most free
When they within this gross and visible sphere
Chain down the wingéd thought, scoffing ascent,
Proud in their meanness: and themselves they cheat
With noisy emptiness of learnéd phrase,
Their subtle fluids, impacts, essences,
Self-working tools, uncaused effects, and all
Those blind Omniscients, those Almighty Slaves,
Untenanting creation of its God.

9-12 The Harp which hanging high between the shields
  Of Brutus and Leonidas oft gives
   A fitful music to the breezy touch
  Of patriot spirits that demand their fame. *4°.*

12 Man's] Earth's *Sibylline Leaves, 1828, 1829.*

15 But chiefly this with holiest habitude
  Of constant Faith, him First, him Last to view *4°.*

23-6 Things from their shadows. Know thyself my Soul!
  Confirm'd thy strength, thy pinions fledged for flight
  Bursting this shell and leaving next thy nest
  Soon upward soaring shalt thou fix intense
  Thine eaglet eye on Heaven's Eternal Sun! *4°.*

  The substance from its shadow—Earth's broad shade
  Revealing by Eclipse, the Eternal Sun. *Sibylline Leaves.*

[The text of lines 23-6 is given in the Errata p. [lxii].]

THE DESTINY OF NATIONS

But Properties are God: the naked mass
(If mass there be, fantastic guess or ghost)
Acts only by its inactivity.
Here we pause humbly. Others boldlier think
That as one body seems the aggregate
Of atoms numberless, each organized;
So by a strange and dim similitude
Infinite myriads of self-conscious minds
Are one all-conscious Spirit, which informs
With absolute ubiquity of thought
(His one eternal self-affirming act!)
All his involvéd Monads, that yet seem
With various province and apt agency
Each to pursue its own self-centering end.
Some nurse the infant diamond in the mine;
Some roll the genial juices through the oak;
Some drive the mutinous clouds to clash in air,
And rushing on the storm with whirlwind speed,
Yoke the red lightnings to their volleying car.
Thus these pursue their never-varying course,
No eddy in their stream. Others, more wild,
With complex interests weaving human fates,
Duteous or proud, alike obedient all,
Evolve the process of eternal good.

And what if some rebellious, o'er dark realms
Arrogate power? yet these train up to God,
And on the rude eye, unconfirmed for day,
Flash meteor-lights better than total gloom.
As ere from Lieule-Oaive's vapoury head
The Laplander beholds the far-off Sun
Dart his slant beam on unobeying snows,
While yet the stern and solitary Night
Brooks no alternate sway, the Boreal Morn
With mimic lustre substitutes its gleam,
Guiding his course or by Niemi lake
Or Balda Zhiok,[1] or the mossy stone
Of Solfar-kapper,[2] while the snowy blast

---

[1] Balda-Zhiok, i.e. mons altitudinis, the highest mountain in Lapland.
[2] Solfar-kapper: capitium Solfar, hic locus omnium, quotquot veterum

---

37 *om.* 4°.   40 seems] is 4°.   44 Form one all-conscious Spirit, who directs 4°.   46 *om.* 4°.   47 involvéd] component 4°.
54 lightnings] lightning 4°.   70 Niemi] Niemi's 4°.

Drifts arrowy by, or eddies round his sledge,
Making the poor babe at its mother's back [1]
Scream in its scanty cradle: he the while 75
Wins gentle solace as with upward eye
He marks the streamy banners of the North,
Thinking himself those happy spirits shall join
Who there in floating robes of rosy light
Dance sportively. For Fancy is the power 80
That first unsensualises the dark mind,
Giving it new delights; and bids it swell
With wild activity; and peopling air,
By obscure fears of Beings invisible,
Emancipates it from the grosser thrall 85
Of the present impulse, teaching Self-control,
Till Superstition with unconscious hand
Seat Reason on her throne. Wherefore not vain,
Nor yet without permitted power impressed,
I deem those legends terrible, with which 90
The polar ancient thrills his uncouth throng:
Whether of pitying Spirits that make their moan
O'er slaughter'd infants, or that Giant Bird
Vuokho, of whose rushing wings the noise
Is Tempest, when the unutterable Shape 95
Speeds from the mother of Death, and utters once [2]
That shriek, which never murderer heard, and lived.

Lapponum superstitio sacrificiisque religiosoque cultui dedicavit, celebratissimus erat, in parte sinus australis situs, semimilliaris spatio a mari distans. Ipse locus, quem curiositatis gratia aliquando me invisisse memini, duabus praealtis lapidibus, sibi invicem oppositis, quorum alter musco circumdatus erat, constabat.

[1] The Lapland women carry their infants at their backs in a piece of excavated wood which serves them for a cradle: opposite to the infant's mouth there is a hole for it to breathe through.

Mirandum prorsus est et vix credibile nisi cui vidisse contigit. Lappones hyeme iter facientes per vastos montes, perque horrida et invia tesqua, eo praesertim tempore quo omnia perpetuis nivibus obtecta sunt et nives ventis agitantur et in gyros aguntur, viam ad destinata loca absque errore invenire posse, lactantem autem infantem, si quem habeat, ipsa mater in dorso baiulat, in excavato ligno (Gieed'k ipsi vocant) quod pro cunis utuntur, in hoc infans pannis et pellibus convolutus colligatus iacet.—LEEMIUS DE LAPPONIBUS.

[2] Jaibme Aibmo.

---

90 deem] deemed *1829*.
96-7 Speeds from the mother of Death his destin'd way
To snatch the murderer from his secret cell. *4º*.

THE DESTINY OF NATIONS

Or if the Greenland Wizard in strange trance
Pierces the untravelled realms of Ocean's bed
Over the abyss, even to that uttermost cave   100
By mis-shaped prodigies beleaguered, such
As Earth ne'er bred, nor Air, nor the upper Sea:
Where dwells the Fury Form, whose unheard name
With eager eye, pale cheek, suspended breath,
And lips half-opening with the dread of sound,   105
Unsleeping Silence guards, worn out with fear
Lest haply 'scaping on some treacherous blast
The fateful word let slip the Elements
And frenzy Nature. Yet the wizard her,
Arm'd with Torngarsuck's power, the Spirit of Good,[1] 110
Forces to unchain the foodful progeny
Of the Ocean stream;—thence thro' the realm of Souls,
Where live the Innocent, as far from cares
As from the storms and overwhelming waves
That tumble on the surface of the Deep,   115
Returns with far-heard pant, hotly pursued
By the fierce Warders of the Sea, once more,
Ere by the frost foreclosed, to repossess
His fleshly mansion, that had staid the while
In the dark tent within a cow'ring group   120
Untenanted.—Wild phantasies! yet wise,
On the victorious goodness of high God
Teaching reliance, and medicinal hope,

---

[1] They call the Good Spirit, Torngarsuck. The other great but malignant spirit a nameless female; she dwells under the sea in a great house where she can detain in captivity all the animals of the ocean by her magic power. When a dearth befalls the Greenlanders, an Angekok or magician must undertake a journey thither: he passes through the kingdom of souls, over an horrible abyss into the palace of this phantom, and by his enchantments causes the captive creatures to ascend directly to the surface of the ocean. See Crantz, *History of Greenland*, vol. i. 206.

Between lines **99–100**
(Where live the innocent as far from cares
As from the storms and overwhelming waves
Dark tumbling on the surface of the deep.)
4°, Sibylline Leaves, 1828, 1829.
These lines form part of an addition (lines 111–21) which dates from *1834*.
103 Where] There *4°, Sibylline Leaves, 1828, 1829.*   **105** *om. 4°.*   **107** 'scaping] escaping *4°, Sibylline Leaves, 1828, 1829.*   **108** fateful word] fatal sound *4°.*   **112–21** thence thro' . . . Untenanted are not included in *4°, Sibylline Leaves, 1828,* or *1829*. For lines 113–15 vide *ante*, variant of line 99 of the text.   **112** Ocean] Ocean's *1828, 1829.*

136   THE DESTINY OF NATIONS

Till from Bethabra northward, heavenly Truth
With gradual steps, winning her difficult way,   125
Transfer their rude Faith perfected and pure.

If there be Beings of higher class than Man,
I deem no nobler province they possess,
Than by disposal of apt circumstance
To rear up kingdoms: and the deeds they prompt,   130
Distinguishing from mortal agency,
They choose their human ministers from such states
As still the Epic song half fears to name,
Repelled from all the minstrelsies that strike
The palace-roof and soothe the monarch's pride.   135
And such, perhaps, the Spirit, who (if words
Witnessed by answering deeds may claim our faith)

> 130 foll. To rear some realm with patient discipline,
> Aye bidding PAIN, dark ERROR's uncouth child,
> Blameless Parenticide! his snakey scourge   125
> Lift fierce against his Mother! Thus they make
> Of transient Evil ever-during Good
> Themselves probationary, and denied
> Confess'd to view by preternatural deed
> To o'erwhelm the will, save on some fated day   130
> Headstrong, or with petition'd might from God.
> And such perhaps the guardian Power whose ken
> Still dwelt on France. He from the invisible World
> Burst on the MAIDEN's eye, impregning Air
> With Voices and strange Shapes, illusions apt   135
> Shadowy of Truth. [And first a landscape rose
> More wild and waste and desolate, than where
> The white bear drifting on a field of ice
> Howls to her sunder'd cubs with piteous rage
> And savage agony.] Mid the drear scene   140
> A craggy mass uprear'd its misty brow,
> Untouch'd by breath of Spring, unwont to know
> Red Summer's influence, or the chearful face
> Of Autumn; yet its fragments many and huge
> Astounded ocean with the dreadful dance   145
> Of whirlpools numberless, absorbing oft
> The blameless fisher at his perilous toil. 4º.

Note—Lines 148–223 of the Second Book of *Joan of Arc* are by Southey. Coleridge's unpublished poem of 1796 (*The Visions of the Maid of Orleans*) begins at line 127 of the text, ending at line 277. The remaining portion of the *Destiny of Nations* is taken from lines contributed to the Second Book. Lines 136–40 of variant 130 foll. form the concluding fragment of the *Destiny of Nations*. Lines 141–3 of the variant are by Southey. (See his Preface to *Joan of Arc*, 1796, p. vi.) The remaining lines of the variant were never reprinted.

132 human] mortal *Sibylline Leaves* (correction made in Errata, p. [xii]).

THE DESTINY OF NATIONS

Held commune with that warrior-maid of France
Who scourged the Invader. From her infant days,
With Wisdom, mother of retired thoughts,   140
Her soul had dwelt; and she was quick to mark
The good and evil thing, in human lore
Undisciplined. For lowly was her birth,
And Heaven had doomed her early years to toil
That pure from Tyranny's least deed, herself   145
Unfeared by Fellow-natures, she might wait
On the poor labouring man with kindly looks,
And minister refreshment to the tired
Way-wanderer, when along the rough-hewn bench
The sweltry man had stretched him, and aloft   150
Vacantly watched the rudely-pictured board
Which on the Mulberry-bough with welcome creak
Swung to the pleasant breeze. Here, too, the Maid
Learnt more than Schools could teach: Man's shifting mind,
His vices and his sorrows! And full oft   155
At tales of cruel wrong and strange distress
Had wept and shivered. To the tottering Eld
Still as a daughter would she run: she placed
His cold limbs at the sunny door, and loved
To hear him story, in his garrulous sort,   160
Of his eventful years, all come and gone.

So twenty seasons past. The Virgin's form,
Active and tall, nor Sloth nor Luxury
Had shrunk or paled. Her front sublime and broad,
Her flexile eye-brows wildly haired and low,   165
And her full eye, now bright, now unillumed,
Spake more than Woman's thought; and all her face
Was moulded to such features as declared
That Pity there had oft and strongly worked,
And sometimes Indignation. Bold her mien,   170
And like an haughty huntress of the woods
She moved: yet sure she was a gentle maid!
And in each motion her most innocent soul
Beamed forth so brightly, that who saw would say
Guilt was a thing impossible in her!   175
Nor idly would have said—for she had lived
In this bad World, as in a place of Tombs,
And touched not the pollutions of the Dead.

171 an] a *1834*.

COLERIDGE

F

138   THE DESTINY OF NATIONS

'Twas the cold season when the Rustic's eye
From the drear desolate whiteness of his fields   180
Rolls for relief to watch the skiey tints
And clouds slow-varying their huge imagery;
When now, as she was wont, the healthful Maid
Had left her pallet ere one beam of day
Slanted the fog-smoke. She went forth alone   185
Urged by the indwelling angel-guide, that oft,
With dim inexplicable sympathies
Disquieting the heart, shapes out Man's course
To the predoomed adventure. Now the ascent
She climbs of that steep upland, on whose top   190
The Pilgrim-man, who long since eve had watched
The alien shine of unconcerning stars,
Shouts to himself, there first the Abbey-lights
Seen in Neufchâtel's vale; now slopes adown
The winding sheep-track vale-ward: when, behold   195
In the first entrance of the level road
An unattended team! The foremost horse
Lay with stretched limbs; the others, yet alive
But stiff and cold, stood motionless, their manes
Hoar with the frozen night-dews. Dismally   200
The dark-red dawn now glimmered; but its gleams
Disclosed no face of man. The maiden paused,
Then hailed who might be near. No voice replied.
From the thwart wain at length there reached her ear
A sound so feeble that it almost seemed   205
Distant: and feebly, with slow effort pushed,
A miserable man crept forth: his limbs
The silent frost had eat, scathing like fire.
Faint on the shafts he rested. She, meantime,
Saw crowded close beneath the coverture   210
A mother and her children—lifeless all,
Yet lovely! not a lineament was marred—
Death had put on so slumber-like a form!
It was a piteous sight; and one, a babe,
The crisp milk frozen on its innocent lips,   215
Lay on the woman's arm, its little hand
Stretched on her bosom.

                    Mutely questioning;
The Maid gazed wildly at the living wretch.

201 now] new *Sibylline Leaves*, 1828.

THE DESTINY OF NATIONS

He, his head feebly turning, on the group
Looked with a vacant stare, and his eye spoke 220
The drowsy calm that steals on worn-out anguish.
She shuddered; but, each vainer pang subdued,
Quick disentangling from the foremost horse
The rustic bands, with difficulty and toil
The stiff cramped team forced homeward. There arrived, 225
Anxiously tends him she with healing herbs,
And weeps and prays—but the numb power of Death
Spreads o'er his limbs; and ere the noon-tide hour,
The hovering spirits of his Wife and Babes
Hail him immortal! Yet amid his pangs, 230
With interruptions long from ghastly throes,
His voice had faltered out this simple tale.

The Village, where he dwelt an husbandman,
By sudden inroad had been seized and fired
Late on the yester-evening. With his wife 235
And little ones he hurried his escape.
They saw the neighbouring hamlets flame, they heard
Uproar and shrieks! and terror-struck drove on
Through unfrequented roads, a weary way!
But saw nor house nor cottage. All had quenched 240
Their evening hearth-fire: for the alarm had spread.
The air clipt keen, the night was fanged with frost,
And they provisionless! The weeping wife
Ill hushed her children's moans; and still they moaned,
Till Fright and Cold and Hunger drank their life. 245
They closed their eyes in sleep, nor knew 'twas Death.
He only, lashing his o'er-wearied team,
Gained a sad respite, till beside the base
Of the high hill his foremost horse dropped dead.
Then hopeless, strengthless, sick for lack of food, 250
He crept beneath the coverture, entranced,
Till wakened by the maiden.—Such his tale.

Ah! suffering to the height of what was suffered,
Stung with too keen a sympathy, the Maid
Brooded with moving lips, mute, startful, dark! 255
And now her flushed tumultuous features shot
Such strange vivacity, as fires the eye
Of Misery fancy-crazed! and now once more
Naked, and void, and fixed, and all within
The unquiet silence of confuséd thought 260

And shapeless feelings. For a mighty hand
Was strong upon her, till in the heat of soul
To the high hill-top tracing back her steps,
Aside the beacon, up whose smouldered stones
The tender ivy-trails crept thinly, there,   265
Unconscious of the driving element,
Yea, swallowed up in the ominous dream, she sate
Ghastly as broad-eyed Slumber! a dim anguish
Breathed from her look! and still with pant and sob,
Inly she toiled to flee, and still subdued,   270
Felt an inevitable Presence near.

Thus as she toiled in troublous ecstasy,
A horror of great darkness wrapt her round,
And a voice uttered forth unearthly tones,
Calming her soul,—'O Thou of the Most High   275
Chosen, whom all the perfected in Heaven
Behold expectant——'

[The following fragments were intended to form part of the poem when finished.]

[1] 'Maid beloved of Heaven!
(To her the tutelary Power exclaimed)
Of Chaos the adventurous progeny   280
Thou seest; foul missionaries of foul sire,
Fierce to regain the losses of that hour
When Love rose glittering, and his gorgeous wings
Over the abyss fluttered with such glad noise,
As what time after long and pestful calms,   285
With slimy shapes and miscreated life
Poisoning the vast Pacific, the fresh breeze
Wakens the merchant-sail uprising. Night
An heavy unimaginable moan
Sent forth, when she the Protoplast beheld   290
Stand beauteous on Confusion's charmèd wave.
Moaning she fled, and entered the Profound
That leads with downward windings to the Cave
Of Darkness palpable, Desert of Death
Sunk deep beneath Gehenna's massy roots.   295
There many a dateless age the Beldame lurked

[1] These are very fine Lines, tho' I say it, that should not: but, hang me, if I know or ever did know the meaning of them, tho' my own composition. *MS. Note by S. T. C.*

289 An] A *1834*.

THE DESTINY OF NATIONS

And trembled; till engendered by fierce Hate,
Fierce Hate and gloomy Hope, a Dream arose,
Shaped like a black cloud marked with streaks of fire.
It roused the Hell-Hag: she the dew-damp wiped   300
From off her brow, and through the uncouth maze
Retraced her steps; but ere she reached the mouth
Of that drear labyrinth, shuddering she paused,
Nor dared re-enter the diminished Gulph.
As through the dark vaults of some mouldered Tower   305
(Which, fearful to approach, the evening hind
Circles at distance in his homeward way)
The winds breathe hollow, deemed the plaining groan
Of prisoned spirits; with such fearful voice
Night murmured, and the sound through Chaos went.   310
Leaped at her call her hideous-fronted brood!
A dark behest they heard, and rushed on earth;
Since that sad hour, in Camps and Courts adored,
Rebels from God, and Tyrants o'er Mankind!'

            From his obscure haunt   315
Shrieked Fear, of Cruelty the ghastly Dam,
Feverous yet freezing, eager-paced yet slow,
As she that creeps from forth her swampy reeds,
Ague, the biform Hag! when early Spring
Beams on the marsh-bred vapours.   320

---

300 dew-damp] dew-damps 4°.   314 Tyrants] Monarchs 4°, *Sibylline Leaves, 1828, 1829.*

Between lines 314 and 315 of the text, the text of the original version (after line 259 of *Joan of Arc*, Book II) continues:—

> 'These are the fiends that o'er thy native land   260
> Spread Guilt and Horror. Maid belov'd of Heaven!
> Dar'st thou inspir'd by the holy flame of Love
> Encounter such fell shapes, nor fear to meet
> Their wrath, their wiles? O Maiden dar'st thou die?'
> 'Father of Heaven! I will not fear,' she said,   265
> 'My arm is weak, but mighty is thy sword.'
>
> She spake and as she spake the trump was heard
> That echoed ominous o'er the streets of Rome,
> When the first Caesar totter'd o'er the grave
> By Freedom delv'd: the Trump, whose chilling blast   270
> On Marathon and on Plataea's plain
> Scatter'd the Persian.—From his obscure haunt, &c.

[Lines 267-72, She spake ... the Persian, are claimed by Southey.]

316 Shriek'd Fear the ghastliest of Ambition's throng 4°.   317 Feverous] Fev'rish 4°, *Sibylline Leaves, 1817, 1828, 1829.*

142 THE DESTINY OF NATIONS

'Even so (the exulting Maiden said)
The sainted Heralds of Good Tidings fell,
And thus they witnessed God! But now the clouds
Treading, and storms beneath their feet, they soar
Higher, and higher soar, and soaring sing   325
Loud songs of triumph! O ye Spirits of God,
Hover around my mortal agonies!'
She spake, and instantly faint melody
Melts on her ear, soothing and sad, and slow,
Such measures, as at calmest midnight heard   330
By agéd Hermit in his holy dream,
Foretell and solace death; and now they rise
Louder, as when with harp and mingled voice
The white-robed multitude of slaughtered saints
At Heaven's wide-open'd portals gratulant   335
Receive some martyred patriot. The harmony[1]
Entranced the Maid, till each suspended sense
Brief slumber seized, and confused ecstasy.

---

[1] Rev. vi. 9, 11: And when he had opened the fifth seal, I saw under the altar the souls of them that were slain for the word of God and for the Testimony which they held. And white robes were given unto every one of them; and it was said unto them, that they should rest yet for a little Season, until their fellow-servants also, and their brethren that should be killed, as they were, should be fulfilled.

Between lines 320 and 321 of the text, the text of *Joan of Arc*, Book II, continues:—

'Lo she goes!
To Orleans lo! she goes—the mission'd Maid!
The Victor Hosts wither beneath her arm!
And what are Crecy, Poictiers, Azincour   280
But noisy echoes in the ear of Pride?'
Ambition heard and startled on his throne;
But strait a smile of savage joy illum'd
His grisly features, like the sheety Burst
Of Lightning o'er the awaken'd midnight clouds   285
Wide flash'd. [For lo! a flaming pile reflects
Its red light fierce and gloomy on the face
Of SUPERSTITION and her goblin Son
Loud-laughing CRUELTY, who to the stake
A female fix'd, of bold and beauteous mien,   290
Her snow-white Limbs by iron fetters bruis'd
Her breast expos'd.] JOAN saw, she saw and knew
Her perfect image. Nature thro' her frame
One pang shot shiv'ring; but, that frail pang soon
Dismiss'd, 'Even so, &c. *4º.*

[The passage included in brackets was claimed by Southey.]

330 calmest] calmy *4º.*

THE DESTINY OF NATIONS

At length awakening slow, she gazed around:
And through a mist, the relict of that trance   340
Still thinning as she gazed, an Isle appeared,
Its high, o'er-hanging, white, broad-breasted cliffs,
Glassed on the subject ocean. A vast plain
Stretched opposite, where ever and anon
The plough-man following sad his meagre team   345
Turned up fresh sculls unstartled, and the bones
Of fierce hate-breathing combatants, who there
All mingled lay beneath the common earth,
Death's gloomy reconcilement! O'er the fields
Stept a fair Form, repairing all she might,   350
Her temples olive-wreathed; and where she trod,
Fresh flowerets rose, and many a foodful herb.
But wan her cheek, her footsteps insecure,
And anxious pleasure beamed in her faint eye,
As she had newly left a couch of pain,   355
Pale Convalescent! (Yet some time to rule
With power exclusive o'er the willing world,
That blessed prophetic mandate then fulfilled—
Peace be on Earth!) An happy while, but brief,
She seemed to wander with assiduous feet,   360
And healed the recent harm of chill and blight,
And nursed each plant that fair and virtuous grew.

But soon a deep precursive sound moaned hollow:
Black rose the clouds, and now, (as in a dream)
Their reddening shapes, transformed to Warrior-hosts, 365
Coursed o'er the sky, and battled in mid-air.
Nor did not the large blood-drops fall from Heaven
Portentous! while aloft were seen to float,
Like hideous features looming on the mist,
Wan stains of ominous light! Resigned, yet sad,   370
The fair Form bowed her olive-crownéd brow,
Then o'er the plain with oft-reverted eye

> 339-40 But lo! no more was seen the ice-pil'd mount
> And meteor-lighted dome.—An Isle appear'd 4°.
> 342 white] rough 4°. 361 and] or 4°.
> 366-7 The Sea meantime his Billows darkest roll'd,
> And each stain'd wave dash'd on the shore a corse. 4°.
> 369-72 His hideous features blended with the mist,
> The long black locks of SLAUGHTER. PEACE beheld
> And o'er the plain 4°.
> 369 Like hideous features blended with the clouds *Sibylline Leaves, 1817*.
> (*Errata:* for '*blended*', &c., read '*looming on the mist*'. *S. L.*, p. [xii].)

Fled till a place of Tombs she reached, and there
Within a ruined Sepulchre obscure
Found hiding-place.
                The delegated Maid   375
Gazed through her tears, then in sad tones exclaimed;—
'Thou mild-eyed Form! wherefore, ah! wherefore fled?
The Power of Justice like a name all light,
Shone from thy brow; but all they, who unblamed
Dwelt in thy dwellings, call thee Happiness.   380
Ah! why, uninjured and unprofited,
Should multitudes against their brethren rush?
Why sow they guilt, still reaping misery?
Lenient of care, thy songs, O Peace! are sweet,[1]
As after showers the perfumed gale of eve,   385
That flings the cool drops on a feverous cheek;
And gay thy grassy altar piled with fruits.
But boasts the shrine of Dæmon War one charm,[2]
Save that with many an orgie strange and foul,[3]
Dancing around with interwoven arms,   390
The Maniac Suicide and Giant Murder
Exult in their fierce union! I am sad,
And know not why the simple peasants crowd
Beneath the Chieftains' standard!' Thus the Maid.

  To her the tutelary Spirit said: 395
'When Luxury and Lust's exhausted stores
No more can rouse the appetites of kings;
When the low flattery of their reptile lords
Falls flat and heavy on the accustomed ear;
When eunuchs sing, and fools buffoonery make,   400
And dancers writhe their harlot-limbs in vain;
Then War and all its dread vicissitudes
Pleasingly agitate their stagnant hearts;

---

[1] A grievous defect here in the rhyme recalling assonance of Pēace, swēet &ebreve;ve, chēek. Better thus:—

    Sweet are thy Songs, O Peace! lenient of care.
                                                                            S. T. C., 1828.

[2] 388-93 Southeyan. To be omitted. *S. T. C., 1828.*
[3] A vile line [*foul* is underlined]. *S. T. C., 1828.*

378-9   The name of JUSTICE written on thy brow
           Resplendent shone *4°, S. L. 1817.*
(The reading of the text is given as an emendation in the *Errata, Sibylline Leaves*, 1817, p. [xii].)

386 That plays around the sick man's throbbing temples *4°.*   394
Chieftains'] Chieftain's *4°.*   395 said] replied *4°, S. L., 1828.*

THE DESTINY OF NATIONS 145

Its hopes, its fears, its victories, its defeats,
Insipid Royalty's keen condiment!   405
Therefore uninjured and unprofited
(Victims at once and executioners),
The congregated Husbandmen lay waste
The vineyard and the harvest. As along
The Bothnic coast, or southward of the Line,   410
Though hushed the winds and cloudless the high noon,
Yet if Leviathan, weary of ease,
In sports unwieldy toss his island-bulk,
Ocean behind him billows, and before
A storm of waves breaks foamy on the strand.   415
And hence, for times and seasons bloody and dark,
Short Peace shall skin the wounds of causeless War,
And War, his strainéd sinews knit anew,
Still violate the unfinished works of Peace.
But yonder look! for more demands thy view!'   420
He said: and straightway from the opposite Isle
A vapour sailed, as when a cloud, exhaled
From Egypt's fields that steam hot pestilence,
Travels the sky for many a trackless league,
Till o'er some death-doomed land, distant in vain,   425
It broods incumbent. Forthwith from the plain,
Facing the Isle, a brighter cloud arose,
And steered its course which way the vapour went.

The Maiden paused, musing what this might mean.

Between lines 421 and 423 of the text, the text of *Joan of Arc,* Book II, inserts:—

> A Vapor rose, pierc'd by the MAIDEN's eye.
> Guiding its course OPPRESSION sate within,*
> With terror pale and rage, yet laugh'd at times
> Musing on Vengeance: trembled in his hand
> A Sceptre fiercely-grasp'd. O'er Ocean westward
> The Vapor sail'd *4º.*

* These images imageless, these *Small-Capitals* constituting themselves Personifications, I despised even at that time; but was forced to introduce them, to preserve the connection with the machinery of the Poem, previously adopted by Southey. S. T. C.

After 429 of the text, the text of *Joan of Arc* inserts:—

> ENVY sate guiding—ENVY, hag-abhorr'd!
> Like JUSTICE mask'd, and doom'd to aid the fight   410
> Victorious 'gainst oppression. Hush'd awhile *4º.*

[These lines were assigned by Coleridge to Southey.]

146   THE DESTINY OF NATIONS

But long time passed not, ere that brighter cloud 430
Returned more bright; along the plain it swept;
And soon from forth its bursting sides emerged
A dazzling form, broad-bosomed, bold of eye,
And wild her hair, save where with laurels bound.
Not more majestic stood the healing God,[1] 435
When from his bow the arrow sped that slew
Huge Python. Shriek'd Ambition's giant throng,
And with them hissed the locust-fiends that crawled
And glittered in Corruption's slimy track.
Great was their wrath, for short they knew their reign; 440
And such commotion made they, and uproar,
As when the mad Tornado bellows through
The guilty islands of the western main,
What time departing from their native shores.[2]
Eboe, or Koromantyn's plain of palms, 445
The infuriate spirits of the murdered make
Fierce merriment, and vengeance ask of Heaven.
Warmed with new influence, the unwholesome plain
Sent up its foulest fogs to meet the morn:
The Sun that rose on Freedom, rose in Blood! 450

'Maiden beloved, and Delegate of Heaven!
(To her the tutelary Spirit said)
Soon shall the Morning struggle into Day,
The stormy Morning into cloudless Noon.
Much hast thou seen, nor all canst understand— 455
But this be thy best omen—Save thy Country!'
Thus saying, from the answering Maid he passed,
And with him disappeared the heavenly Vision.

'Glory to Thee, Father of Earth and Heaven!
All-conscious Presence of the Universe! 460

---

[1] The Apollo Belvedere.
[2] The Slaves in the West-India Islands consider Death as a passport to their native country. The Sentiment is thus expressed in the Introduction to a Greek Prize Ode on the Slave-Trade, of which

---

434 with] by *4º*.
437–8   Shriek'd Ambition's ghastly throng
          And with them those the locust Fiends that crawl'd * *4º*.

* —if Locusts how could they *shriek*? I must have caught the contagion of *unthinkingness*. S. T. C. *4º*.

458 heavenly] goodly *4º*.

THE DESTINY OF NATIONS

Nature's vast ever-acting Energy! [1]
In will, in deed, Impulse of All to All!
Whether thy Love with unrefracted ray
Beam on the Prophet's purgéd eye, or if
Diseasing realms the Enthusiast, wild of thought,   465
Scatter new frenzies on the infected throng,
Thou both inspiring and predooming both,

the Ideas are better than the Language or Metre, in which they are conveyed :—

> Ὦ σκότου πύλας, Θάνατε, προλείπων
> Ἐς γένος σπεύδοις ὑποζευχθὲν Ἄτᾳ *·
> Οὐ ξενισθήσῃ γενύων σπαραγμοῖς
>   Οὐδ' ὀλολυγμῷ,
>
> Ἀλλὰ καὶ κύκλοισι χοροιτύποισι
> Κάσματων χαρᾷ· φοβερὸς μὲν ἐσσί,
> Ἀλλ' ὁμῶς Ἐλευθερίᾳ συνοικεῖς,
>   Στυγνὲ Τύραννε!
>
> Δασκίοις ἐπὶ πτερύγεσσι σῇσι
> Ἆ! θαλάσσιον καθορῶντες οἶδμα
> Αἰθεροπλάγκτοις ὑπὸ πόσσ' ἀνεῖσι
>   Πατρίδ' ἐπ' αἶαν,
>
> Ἔνθα μὰν Ἐρασταὶ Ἐρωμένῃσιν
> Ἀμφὶ πηγῇσιν κιτρίνων ὑπ' ἀλσῶν,
> Ὅσσ' ὑπὸ βροτοῖς ἔπαθον βροτοί, τὰ
>   Δεινὰ λέγοντι.

* o before ζ ought to have been made long; δοῖς ὑπὸζ is an Amphimacer not (as the metre here requires) a Dactyl. *S. T. C.*

LITERAL TRANSLATION.

Leaving the gates of Darkness, O Death! hasten thou to a Race yoked to Misery! Thou wilt not be received with lacerations of Cheeks, nor with funereal ululation, but with circling Dances and the joy of Songs. Thou art terrible indeed, yet thou dwellest with LIBERTY, stern GENIUS! Borne on thy dark pinions over the swelling of Ocean they return to their native country. There by the side of fountains beneath Citron groves, the Lovers tell to their Beloved, what horrors, being Men, they had endured from Men.

[1] Tho' these Lines may bear a sane sense, yet they are easily, and more naturally interpreted with a very false and dangerous one. But I was at that time one of the *Mongrels*, the Josephidites [Josephides = the Son of Joseph], a proper name of distinction from those who believe *in*, as well as believe Christ the only begotten Son of the Living God before all Time. *MS. Note by S. T. C.*

---

463 Love] Law 4°.

Fit instruments and best, of perfect end:
Glory to Thee, Father of Earth and Heaven!'

      And first a landscape rose   470
More wild and waste and desolate than where
The white bear, drifting on a field of ice,
Howls to her sundered cubs with piteous rage
And savage agony.
 1796.

VER PERPETUUM[1]

FRAGMENT

From an unpublished poem.

The early Year's fast-flying vapours stray
In shadowing trains across the orb of day:
And we, poor Insects of a few short hours,
 Deem it a world of Gloom.
Were it not better hope a nobler doom,   5
Proud to believe that with more active powers
 On rapid many-coloured wing
 We thro' one bright perpetual Spring
Shall hover round the fruits and flowers,
Screen'd by those clouds and cherish'd by those showers!   10
 1796.

ON OBSERVING A BLOSSOM ON THE FIRST OF FEBRUARY 1796[2]

Sweet flower! that peeping from thy russet stem
Unfoldest timidly, (for in strange sort
This dark, frieze-coated, hoarse, teeth-chattering month

---

[1] First published without title ('*From an unpublished poem*') in *The Watchman*, No. iv, March 25, 1796, and reprinted in *Literary Remains*, 1836, i. 44, with an extract from the Essay in the *Watchman* in which it was included:—'In my calmer moments I have the firmest faith that all things work together for good. But alas! it seems a long and dark process.' First collected with extract only in Appendix to 1863. First entitled 'Fragment from an Unpublished Poem' in 1893, and 'Ver Perpetuum' in 1907.

[2] First published in *The Watchman*, No. vi, April 11, 1796: included in 1797, 1803, *Sibylline Leaves*, 1817, 1828, 1829, and 1834.

For lines 470–74 vide *ante* var. of lines 130 foll.
On observing, &c.—Title] Lines on observing, &c., Written near Sheffield, *Watchman, 1797, 1803.*

Hath borrow'd Zephyr's voice, and gazed upon thee
With blue voluptuous eye) alas, poor Flower!   5
These are but flatteries of the faithless year.
Perchance, escaped its unknown polar cave,
Even now the keen North-East is on its way.
Flower that must perish! shall I liken thee
To some sweet girl of too too rapid growth   10
Nipp'd by consumption mid untimely charms?
Or to Bristowa's bard,[1] the wondrous boy!
An amaranth, which earth scarce seem'd to own,
Till disappointment came, and pelting wrong
Beat it to earth? or with indignant grief   15
Shall I compare thee to poor Poland's hope,
Bright flower of hope killed in the opening bud?
Farewell, sweet blossom! better fate be thine
And mock my boding! Dim similitudes
Weaving in moral strains, I've stolen one hour   20
From anxious Self, Life's cruel taskmaster!
And the warm wooings of this sunny day
Tremble along my frame and harmonize
The attempered organ, that even saddest thoughts
Mix with some sweet sensations, like harsh tunes   25
Played deftly on a soft-toned instrument.

1796.

TO A PRIMROSE [2]

THE FIRST SEEN IN THE SEASON

Nitens et roboris expers
Turget et insolida est: et spe delectat.
OVID, *Metam.* [xv. 203].

THY smiles I note, sweet early Flower,
That peeping from thy rustic bower
The festive news to earth dost bring,
A fragrant messenger of Spring.

---

[1] Chatterton.
[2] First published in *The Watchman*, No. viii, April 27, 1796: reprinted in *Literary Remains*, 1836, i. 47. First collected in Appendix to 1863.

---

5 With 'blue voluptuous eye' *1803*.   *Between* 13 *and* 14 Blooming mid Poverty's drear wintry waste *Watchman, 1797, 1803, S. L., 1817, 1828.*
16 hope] hopes, *Watchman*.

21 From black anxiety that gnaws my heart.
For her who droops far off on a sick bed. *Watchman, 1797, 1803*.

24 Th' attempered brain, that ev'n the saddest thoughts *Watchman, 1797, 1803*.

To a Primrose.—Motto: et] at *L. R., App. 1863*.

TO A PRIMROSE

But, tender blossom, why so pale? 5
Dost hear stern Winter in the gale?
And didst thou tempt the ungentle sky
To catch one vernal glance and die?

Such the wan lustre Sickness wears
When Health's first feeble beam appears; 10
So languid are the smiles that seek
To settle on the care-worn cheek,

When timorous Hope the head uprears,
Still drooping and still moist with tears,
If, through dispersing grief, be seen 15
Of Bliss the heavenly spark serene.

And sweeter far the early blow,
Fast following after storms of Woe,
Than (Comfort's riper season come)
Are full-blown joys and Pleasure's gaudy bloom. 20
1796.

VERSES[1]

ADDRESSED TO J. HORNE TOOKE AND THE COMPANY WHO MET ON
JUNE 28TH, 1796, TO CELEBRATE HIS POLL AT THE WEST-
MINSTER ELECTION

BRITONS! when last ye met, with distant streak
So faintly promis'd the pale Dawn to break;
So dim it stain'd the precincts of the Sky
E'en *Expectation* gaz'd with doubtful Eye.
But now such fair Varieties of Light 5
O'ertake the heavy sailing Clouds of Night;
Th' Horizon kindles with so rich a red,
That tho' the *Sun still hides* his glorious head
Th' impatient Matin-bird, *assur'd of Day*,
Leaves his low nest to meet its earliest ray; 10
Loud the sweet song of Gratulation sings,
And high in air claps his rejoicing wings!
Patriot and Sage! whose breeze-like Spirit first
The lazy mists of Pedantry dispers'd

---

[1] First printed in the *Transactions* of the Philobiblon Society. First published in *P. W.*, 1893. The verses (without the title) were sent by Coleridge in a letter to the Rev. J. P. Estlin, dated July 4, [1796].

17-20 *om. L. R., App. 1863.*

(Mists in which Superstition's *pigmy* band 15
Seem'd Giant Forms, the Genii of the Land!),
Thy struggles soon shall wak'ning Britain bless,
And Truth and Freedom hail thy wish'd success.
Yes *Tooke*! tho' foul Corruption's wolfish throng
Outmalice Calumny's imposthum'd Tongue, 20
Thy Country's noblest and *determin'd* Choice,
Soon shalt thou thrill the Senate with thy voice;
With gradual Dawn bid Error's phantoms flit,
Or wither with the lightning's flash of Wit;
Or with sublimer mien and tones more deep, 25
Charm sworded Justice from mysterious Sleep,
'By violated Freedom's loud Lament,
Her Lamps extinguish'd and her Temple rent;
By the forc'd tears her captive Martyrs shed;
By each pale Orphan's feeble cry for bread; 30
By ravag'd Belgium's corse-impeded Flood,
And Vendee steaming still with brothers' blood!'
And if amid the strong impassion'd Tale,
Thy Tongue should falter and thy Lips turn pale;
If transient Darkness film thy aweful Eye, 35
And thy tir'd Bosom struggle with a sigh:
Science and Freedom shall demand to hear
Who practis'd on a Life so doubly dear;
Infus'd the unwholesome anguish drop by drop,
Pois'ning the sacred stream they could not stop! 40
Shall bid thee with recover'd strength relate
How dark and deadly is a Coward's Hate:
What seeds of death by wan Confinement sown,
When Prison-echoes mock'd Disease's groan!
Shall bid th' indignant Father flash dismay, 45
And drag the unnatural Villain into Day
Who[1] to the sports of his flesh'd Ruffians left
Two lovely Mourners of their Sire bereft!
'Twas wrong, like this, which Rome's *first Consul* bore,
So by th' insulted Female's name *he* swore 50
Ruin (and rais'd her reeking dagger high)
Not to the *Tyrants* but the Tyranny!
1796.

---

[1] 'Dundas left thief-takers in Horne Tooke's House for three days, with his two Daughters *alone*; for Horne Tooke keeps no servant.'— S. T. C. to *Estlin*.

31, 32 These lines are borrowed from the first edition (4°) of the *Ode to the Departing Year*.

ON A LATE CONNUBIAL RUPTURE IN HIGH LIFE[1]

[PRINCE AND PRINCESS OF WALES]

I SIGH, fair injur'd stranger! for thy fate;
  But what shall sighs avail thee? thy poor heart,
'Mid all the 'pomp and circumstance' of state,
  Shivers in nakedness. Unbidden, start

Sad recollections of Hope's garish dream, 5
  That shaped a seraph form, and named it Love,
Its hues gay-varying, as the orient beam
  Varies the neck of Cytherea's dove.

To one soft accent of domestic joy
  Poor are the shouts that shake the high-arch'd dome; 10
Those plaudits that thy *public* path annoy,
  Alas! they tell thee—Thou'rt a wretch *at home!*

O then retire, and weep! *Their very woes
  Solace the guiltless.* Drop the pearly flood
On thy sweet infant, as the full-blown rose, 15
  Surcharg'd with dew, bends o'er its neighbouring bud.

And ah! that Truth some holy spell might lend
  To lure thy Wanderer from the Syren's power;
Then bid your souls inseparably blend
  Like two bright dew-drops meeting in a flower. 20
1796.

SONNET[2]

ON RECEIVING A LETTER INFORMING ME OF THE BIRTH OF A SON

WHEN they did greet me father, sudden awe
  Weigh'd down my spirit: I retired and knelt
Seeking the throne of grace, but inly felt

---

[1] First published in the *Monthly Magazine*, September 1796, vol. ii, p. 647, reprinted in *Felix Farley's Bristol Journal*, Saturday, Oct. 8, 1796, and in the *Poetical Register*, 1806–7 [1811, vol. vi, p. 365]. First collected in *P. and D. W.*, 1877, i. 187. The lines were sent in a letter to Estlin, dated July 4, 1796.

[2] First published in the 'Biographical Supplement' to the *Biographia Literaria*, 1847, ii. 379. First collected in *P. and D. W.*, 1877–80. This

---

On a Late, &c.—Title] To an Unfortunate Princess *MS. Letter, July 4, 1796.*
  17 might] could *MS. Letter, 1796.* 18 thy] the *Felix Farley's*, &c.
20 meeting] bosomed *MS. Letter, 1796.*

Sonnet on receiving, &c.—Title] Sonnet written on receiving letter informing me of the birth of a son, I being at Birmingham *MS. Letter, Nov. 1, 1796.*

No heavenly visitation upwards draw
My feeble mind, nor cheering ray impart. 5
 Ah me! before the Eternal Sire I brought
 Th' unquiet silence of confuséd thought
And shapeless feelings: my o'erwhelméd heart
Trembled, and vacant tears stream'd down my face.
And now once more, O Lord! to thee I bend, 10
 Lover of souls! and groan for future grace,
That ere my babe youth's perilous maze have trod,
 Thy overshadowing Spirit may descend,
 And he be born again, a child of God.

Sept. 20, 1796.

SONNET[1]

COMPOSED ON A JOURNEY HOMEWARD; THE AUTHOR HAVING RECEIVED INTELLIGENCE OF THE BIRTH OF A SON, SEPT. 20, 1796

OFT o'er my brain does that strange fancy roll
 Which makes the present (while the flash doth last)
 Seem a mere semblance of some unknown past,
Mixed with such feelings, as perplex the soul
Self-questioned in her sleep; and some have said[2] 5

and the two succeeding sonnets were enclosed in a letter to Poole, dated November 1, 1796. A note was affixed to the sonnet 'On Receiving', &c.: 'This sonnet puts in no claim to poetry (indeed as a composition I think so little of them that I neglected to repeat them to you) but it is a most faithful picture of my feelings on a very interesting event. When I was with you they were, indeed, excepting the first, in a rude and undrest shape.'

[1] First published in 1797: included in 1803, *Sibylline Leaves*, 1817, 1828, 1829, and 1834.

[2] Ἦν που ἡμῶν ἡ ψυχὴ πρὶν ἐν τῷδε τῷ ἀνθρωπίνῳ εἴδει γενέσθαι. Plat. *Phaedon.* Cap. xviii. 72 e.

---

8 shapeless] hopeless *B. L.*

Sonnet composed, &c.—Title] Sonnet composed on my journey home from Birmingham *MS. Letter, 1796*: Sonnet ix. To a Friend, &c. *1797*: Sonnet xvii. To a Friend, &c. *1803*.

1–11 Oft of some unknown Past such Fancies roll
 Swift o'er my brain as make the Present seem
 For a brief moment like a most strange dream
 When not unconscious that she dreamt, the soul
 Questions herself in sleep! and some have said
 We lived ere yet this fleshly robe we wore. *MS. Letter, 1796.*

We liv'd, ere yet this robe of flesh we wore.[1]
O my sweet baby! when I reach my door,
If heavy looks should tell me thou art dead,
(As sometimes, through excess of hope, I fear)
I think that I should struggle to believe   10
Thou wert a spirit, to this nether sphere
Sentenc'd for some more venial crime to grieve;
Did'st scream, then spring to meet Heaven's quick reprieve,
While we wept idly o'er thy little bier!

1796.

SONNET[2]

TO A FRIEND WHO ASKED, HOW I FELT WHEN THE NURSE FIRST PRESENTED MY INFANT TO ME

CHARLES! my slow heart was only sad, when first
I scann'd that face of feeble infancy:
For dimly on my thoughtful spirit burst
All I had been, and all my child might be!
But when I saw it on its mother's arm,   5
And hanging at her bosom (she the while
Bent o'er its features with a tearful smile)
Then I was thrill'd and melted, and most warm
Impress'd a father's kiss: and all beguil'd
Of dark remembrance and presageful fear,   10
I seem'd to see an angel-form appear—
'Twas even thine, belovéd woman mild!
So for the mother's sake the child was dear,
And dearer was the mother for the child.

1796.

---

[1] Almost all the followers of Fénelon believe that men are degraded Intelligences who had all once existed together in a paradisiacal or perhaps heavenly state. The first four lines express a feeling which I have often had—the present has appeared like a vivid dream or exact similitude of some past circumstances. *MS. Letter to Poole*, Nov. 1, 1796.

[2] First published in 1797: included in 1803, *Sibylline Leaves*, 1817, 1828, 1829, and 1834. The 'Friend' was, probably, Charles Lloyd.

---

6 robe of flesh] fleshy robe *1797, 1803*.   8 art] wert *MS. Letter, 1796, 1797, 1803*.

Sonnet, &c.—Title] To a Friend who wished to know, &c. *MS. Letter, Nov. 1, 1796*: Sonnet x. To a Friend *1797*: Sonnet xix. To a Friend, &c. *1803*.

4 child] babe *MS. Letter, 1796, 1797, 1803*.   5 saw] watch'd *MS. Letter, 1796*.   11 angel-form] Angel's form *MS. Letter, 1796, 1797, 1803*.

SONNET[1]

[TO CHARLES LLOYD]

The piteous sobs that choke the Virgin's breath
  For him, the fair betrothéd Youth, who lies
  Cold in the narrow dwelling, or the cries
With which a Mother wails her darling's death,
These from our nature's common impulse spring,   5
  Unblam'd, unprais'd; but o'er the piléd earth
  Which hides the sheeted corse of grey-hair'd Worth,
If droops the soaring Youth with slacken'd wing;
If he recall in saddest minstrelsy
  Each tenderness bestow'd, each truth imprest,   10
Such grief is Reason, Virtue, Piety!
And from the Almighty Father shall descend
  Comforts on his late evening, whose young breast
Mourns with no transient love the Agéd Friend.
1796.

TO A YOUNG FRIEND[2]

ON HIS PROPOSING TO DOMESTICATE WITH THE AUTHOR
Composed in 1796

A mount, not wearisome and bare and steep,
  But a green mountain variously up-piled,
Where o'er the jutting rocks soft mosses creep,
Or colour'd lichens with slow oozing weep;
  Where cypress and the darker yew start wild;   5
And, 'mid the summer torrent's gentle dash
Dance brighten'd the red clusters of the ash;
  Beneath whose boughs, by those still sounds beguil'd,
Calm Pensiveness might muse herself to sleep;
  Till haply startled by some fleecy dam,   10

---

[1] First published in *Poems on the Death of Priscilla Farmer*. By her Grandson, 1796, folio. It prefaced the same set of Lloyd's Sonnets included in the second edition of *Poems* by S. T. Coleridge, 1797. It was included in C. Lloyd's *Nugae Canorae*, 1819. First collected in *P. and D. W.*, 1877-80.

[2] First published in 1797: included in 1803, *Sibylline Leaves*, 1817, 1828 and 1834.

Sonnet] 13 Comforts on his late eve, whose youthful friend. MS. correction by S. T. C. in copy of *Nugae Canorae* in the British Museum.
To a Young Friend—Title] To C. Lloyd on his proposing to domesticate, &c. *1797* : To a Friend, &c. *1803*. 'Composed in 1796' was added in *S. L.*
8 those still] stilly *1797*: stillest *1803*.

That rustling on the bushy cliff above
With melancholy bleat of anxious love,
  Made meek enquiry for her wandering lamb:
  Such a green mountain 'twere most sweet to climb,
E'en while the bosom ach'd with loneliness—
How more than sweet, if some dear friend should bless
  The adventurous toil, and up the path sublime
Now lead, now follow: the glad landscape round,
Wide and more wide, increasing without bound!

  O then 'twere loveliest sympathy, to mark
The berries of the half-uprooted ash
Dripping and bright; and list the torrent's dash,—
  Beneath the cypress, or the yew more dark,
Seated at ease, on some smooth mossy rock;
In social silence now, and now to unlock
The treasur'd heart; arm linked in friendly arm,
Save if the one, his muse's witching charm
Muttering brow-bent, at unwatch'd distance lag;
  Till high o'er head his beckoning friend appears,
And from the forehead of the topmost crag
  Shouts eagerly: for haply *there* uprears
That shadowing Pine its old romantic limbs,
  Which latest shall detain the enamour'd sight
Seen from below, when eve the valley dims,
  Tinged yellow with the rich departing light;
And haply, bason'd in some unsunn'd cleft,
A beauteous spring, the rock's collected tears,
Sleeps shelter'd there, scarce wrinkled by the gale!
  Together thus, the world's vain turmoil left,
Stretch'd on the crag, and shadow'd by the pine,
  And bending o'er the clear delicious fount,
Ah! dearest youth! it were a lot divine
To cheat our noons in moralising mood,
While west-winds fann'd our temples toil-bedew'd:
  Then downwards slope, oft pausing, from the mount,
To some lone mansion, in some woody dale,
Where smiling with blue eye, Domestic Bliss
Gives *this* the Husband's, *that* the Brother's kiss!

  Thus rudely vers'd in allegoric lore,
The Hill of Knowledge I essayed to trace;

11 cliff] clift *S. L., 1828, 1829.*   16 How heavenly sweet *1797, 1803.*
42 youth] Lloyd *1797*: Charles *1803.*   46 lone] low *1797, 1803.*

That verdurous hill with many a resting-place,
And many a stream, whose warbling waters pour
  To glad, and fertilise the subject plains ;
That hill with secret springs, and nooks untrod,
And many a fancy-blest and holy sod 55
  Where Inspiration, his diviner strains
Low-murmuring, lay ; and starting from the rock's
Stiff evergreens, (whose spreading foliage mocks
Want's barren soil, and the bleak frosts of age,
And Bigotry's mad fire-invoking rage !) 60
O meek retiring spirit ! we will climb,
Cheering and cheered, this lovely hill sublime ;
  And from the stirring world up-lifted high
(Whose noises, faintly wafted on the wind,
To quiet musings shall attune the mind, 65
  And oft the melancholy *theme* supply),
  There, while the prospect through the gazing eye
Pours all its healthful greenness on the soul,
We'll smile at wealth, and learn to smile at fame,
Our hopes, our knowledge, and our joys the same, 70
  As neighbouring fountains image each the whole :
Then when the mind hath drunk its fill of truth
  We'll discipline the heart to pure delight,
Rekindling sober joy's domestic flame.
They whom I love shall love thee, honour'd youth ! 75
  Now may Heaven realise this vision bright !
  1796.

ADDRESSED TO A YOUNG MAN OF FORTUNE[1]
[C. LLOYD]

WHO ABANDONED HIMSELF TO AN INDOLENT AND CAUSELESS
MELANCHOLY

HENCE that fantastic wantonness of woe,
  O Youth to partial Fortune vainly dear !

[1] First published in the *Cambridge Intelligencer*, December 17, 1796 : included in the Quarto Edition of the *Ode on the Departing Year*, 1796, in

60 And mad oppression's thunder-clasping rage *1797, 1803*. 69
We'll laugh at wealth, and learn to laugh at fame *1797, 1803*. 71 In
1803 the poem ended with line 71. In the *Sibylline Leaves, 1829*, the last
five lines were replaced. 72 hath drunk] has drank *1797* : hath drank
S. L., 1828, 1829. 75 She whom I love, shall love thee. Honour'd youth
1797, S. L., 1817, 1828, 1829. The change of punctuation dates from 1834.

Addressed to, &c.—Title] Lines, &c., *C. I.* : To a Young Man who abandoned himself to a causeless and indolent melancholy *MS. Letter, 1796*.

TO A YOUNG MAN OF FORTUNE

To plunder'd Want's half-shelter'd hovel go,
   Go, and some hunger-bitten infant hear
   Moan haply in a dying mother's ear: 5
Or when the cold and dismal fog-damps brood
O'er the rank church-yard with sear elm-leaves strew'd,
Pace round some widow's grave, whose dearer part
   Was slaughter'd, where o'er his uncoffin'd limbs
The flocking flesh-birds scream'd! Then, while thy heart 10
   Groans, and thine eye a fiercer sorrow dims,
Know (and the truth shall kindle thy young mind)
What Nature makes thee mourn, she bids thee heal!
   O abject! if, to sickly dreams resign'd,
All effortless thou leave Life's commonweal 15
   A prey to Tyrants, Murderers of Mankind.
    1796.

TO A FRIEND[1]

[CHARLES LAMB]

WHO HAD DECLARED HIS INTENTION OF WRITING NO MORE POETRY

DEAR Charles! whilst yet thou wert a babe, I ween
That Genius plung'd thee in that wizard fount
Hight Castalie: and (sureties of thy faith)
That Pity and Simplicity stood by,
And promis'd for thee, that thou shouldst renounce 5
The world's low cares and lying vanities,
Steadfast and rooted in the heavenly Muse,
And wash'd and sanctified to Poesy.

Sibylline Leaves, 1828, 1829, and 1834. The lines were sent in a letter to John Thelwall, dated December 17, 1796 (*Letters of S. T. C.*, 1895, i. 207, 208).
[1] First published in a Bristol newspaper in aid of a subscription for the family of Robert Burns (the cutting is bound up with the copy of *Selection of Sonnets* (*S. S.*) in the Forster Library in the Victoria and Albert Museum): reprinted in the *Annual Anthology*, 1800: included in *Sibylline Leaves*, 1817, 1828, 1829, and 1834.

6-7 These lines were omitted in the *MS. Letter* and *4° 1796*, but were replaced in *Sibylline Leaves*, 1817.   8 Or seek some widow's *MS. Letter, Dec. 17, 1796.*   11 eye] eyes *MS. Letter, Dec. 9, 1796, C. I.*
15-16   earth's common weal
    A prey to the thron'd Murderess of Mankind. *MS. Letter, 1796.*
    All effortless thou leave Earth's commonweal
    A prey to the thron'd Murderers of Mankind. *C. I., 1796, 4°.*
1 whilst] while *An. Anth.*   3 of] for *S. S., An. Anth.*

TO A FRIEND

Yes—thou wert plung'd, but with forgetful hand
Held, as by Thetis erst her warrior son: 10
And with those recreant unbaptizéd heels
Thou'rt flying from thy bounden ministeries—
So sore it seems and burthensome a task
To weave unwithering flowers! But take thou heed:
For thou art vulnerable, wild-eyed boy,   15
And I have arrows[1] mystically dipped
Such as may stop thy speed. Is thy Burns dead?
And shall he die unwept, and sink to earth
'Without the meed of one melodious tear'?
Thy Burns, and Nature's own belovéd bard,   20
Who to the 'Illustrious[2] of his native Land
So properly did look for patronage.'
Ghost of Mæcenas! hide thy blushing face!
They snatch'd him from the sickle and the plough—
To gauge ale-firkins.

                    Oh! for shame return!   25
On a bleak rock, midway the Aonian mount,
There stands a lone and melancholy tree,
Whose agéd branches to the midnight blast
Make solemn music: pluck its darkest bough,
Ere yet the unwholesome night-dew be exhaled,   30
And weeping wreath it round thy Poet's tomb.
Then in the outskirts, where pollutions grow,
Pick the rank henbane and the dusky flowers
Of night-shade, or its red and tempting fruit,
These with stopped nostril and glove-guarded hand   35
Knit in nice intertexture, so to twine,
The illustrious brow of Scotch Nobility!
    1796.

---

[1]
[Πολλά μοι ὑπ' ἀγκῶνος ὠκέα βέλη
Ἔνδον ἐντὶ φαρέτρας
Φωνᾶντα συνετοῖσιν.]
            Pind. *Olymp.* ii. 149, κ. τ. λ.

[2] Verbatim from Burns's Dedication of his Poems to the Nobility and Gentry of the Caledonian Hunt.

---

25 gauge] guard *S. L., 1817* (For 'guard' read 'guage'. **Errata**, p. [xii]).
33 stinking hensbane *S. S., An. Anth.* : hensbane *S. L., 1817.*   35 Those with stopped nostrils *MS. correction in printed slip of the newspaper.* See *P. and D. W.,* 1877, ii. 379.   *After* 37 E S T E E S I *1796, An. Anth.*

ODE TO THE DEPARTING YEAR[1]

Ἰοὺ ἰού, ὦ ὦ κακά.
Ὕπ' αὖ με δεινὸς ὀρθομαντείας πόνος
Στροβεῖ, ταράσσων φροιμίοις δυσφροιμίοις.
. . . .
Τὸ μέλλον ἥξει. Καὶ σύ μ' ἐν τάχει παρὼν
Ἄγαν ἀληθόμαντιν οἰκτείρας ἐρεῖς.

Aeschyl. *Agam.* 1173-75; 1199-1200.

ARGUMENT

THE Ode[2] commences with an address to the Divine Providence that regulates into one vast harmony all the events of time, however calamitous some of them may appear to mortals. The second Strophe calls on men to suspend their private joys and sorrows, and devote them for a while to the cause of human nature in general. The first Epode speaks of the Empress of Russia, who died of an apoplexy on the 17th of November 1796; having just concluded a subsidiary treaty with the Kings combined against France. The first and second Antistrophe describe the Image of the Departing Year, etc., as in a vision. The second Epode prophesies, in anguish of spirit, the downfall of this country.

I

SPIRIT who sweepest the wild Harp of Time!
It is most hard, with an untroubled ear
Thy dark inwoven harmonies to hear!
Yet, mine eye fix'd on Heaven's unchanging clime
Long had I listen'd, free from mortal fear,   5
 With inward stillness, and a bowéd mind;
 When lo! its folds far waving on the wind,

---

[1] First published in the *Cambridge Intelligencer*, December 31, 1796, and at the same time issued in a quarto pamphlet (the Preface is dated December 26): included in 1797, 1803, *Sibylline Leaves*, 1817, 1828, 1829, and 1834. The Argument was first published in 1797. In 1803 the several sentences were printed as notes to the Strophes, Antistrophes, &c.

This Ode was written on the 24th, 25th, and 26th days of December, 1796; and published separately on the last day of the year. *Footnote*, *1797, 1803*: This Ode was composed and was first published on the last day of that year. *Footnote*, *S. L., 1817, 1828, 1829, 1834*.

[2] The Ode commences with an address to the great BEING, or Divine

---

Ode to the, &c.—Title] Ode for the last day of the Year 1796, *C. I.*: Ode on the Departing Year *4°, 1797, 1803, S. L., 1817, 1828, 1829*.

Motto] 3-5 All editions (*4°* to *1834*) read ἐφημίοις for δυσφροιμίοις, and Ἄγαν γ' for Ἄγαν ; and all before 1834 μην for μ' ἐν.

I] Strophe I *C. I., 4°, 1797, 1803.*   1 Spirit] Being *1803*.   4 unchanging] unchanged *4°*.   5 free] freed *4°*.   6 and a bowéd] and submitted *1803, S. L., 1817, 1828, 1829*.

 7 When lo! far onwards waving on the wind
   I saw the skirts of the DEPARTING YEAR. *C. I., 4°, 1797, 1803.*

ODE TO THE DEPARTING YEAR

I saw the train of the Departing Year!
  Starting from my silent sadness
  Then with no unholy madness,   10
Ere yet the enter'd cloud foreclos'd my sight,
I rais'd the impetuous song, and solemnis'd his flight.

II[1]

  Hither, from the recent tomb,
  From the prison's direr gloom,
  From Distemper's midnight anguish;   15
And thence, where Poverty doth waste and languish;
  Or where, his two bright torches blending,
    Love illumines Manhood's maze;
  Or where o'er cradled infants bending,
    Hope has fix'd her wishful gaze;   20
  Hither, in perplexéd dance,
  Ye Woes! ye young-eyed Joys! advance!
By Time's wild harp, and by the hand
  Whose indefatigable sweep
  Raises its fateful strings from sleep,   25
I bid you haste, a mix'd tumultuous band!
  From every private bower,
    And each domestic hearth,
  Haste for one solemn hour;
And with a loud and yet a louder voice,   30
O'er Nature struggling in portentous birth,
  Weep and rejoice!
Still echoes the dread Name that o'er the earth [2]

Providence, who regulates into one vast Harmony all the Events of Time, however Calamitous some of them appear to mortals. *1803.*

[1] The second Strophe calls on men to suspend their private Joys and Sorrows, and to devote their passions for a while to the cause of human Nature in general. *1803.*

[2] The Name of Liberty, which at the commencement of the French

---

11 Ere yet he pierc'd the cloud and mock'd my sight *C. I.*   foreclos'd] forebade *4°, 1797, 1803.*   II] Strophe II *C. I., 4°, 1797, 1803.*

15-16   From Poverty's heart-wasting languish
          From Distemper's midnight anguish *C. I., 4°, 1797, 1803.*

22 Ye Sorrows, and ye Joys advance *C. I.*   ye] and *4°, 1797, 1803.*
25 Forbids its fateful strings to sleep *C. I., 4°, 1797, 1803.*   31 O'er the sore travail of the common Earth *C. I., 4°.*

33-7   Seiz'd in sore travail and portentous birth
          (Her eyeballs flashing a pernicious glare)
          Sick Nature struggles! Hark! her pangs increase!
          Her groans are horrible! but O! most fair
          The promis'd Twins she bears—Equality and Peace! *C. I., 4°.*

Let slip the storm, and woke the brood of Hell:
  And now advance in saintly Jubilee   35
Justice and Truth! They too have heard thy spell,
  They too obey thy name, divinest Liberty!

III[1]

I mark'd Ambition in his war-array!
  I heard the mailéd Monarch's troublous cry—
'Ah! wherefore does the Northern Conqueress stay![2]   40
Groans not her chariot on its onward way?'
    Fly, mailéd Monarch, fly!
    Stunn'd by Death's twice mortal mace,
    No more on Murder's lurid face
The insatiate Hag shall gloat with drunken eye!   45
    Manes of the unnumber'd slain!
    Ye that gasp'd on Warsaw's plain!
    Ye that erst at Ismail's tower,
When human ruin choked the streams,
  Fell in Conquest's glutted hour,   50
Mid women's shrieks and infants' screams!
    Spirits of the uncoffin'd slain,

Revolution was both the occasion and the pretext of unnumbered crimes
and horrors. *1803.*

[1] The first Epode refers to the late Empress of Russia, who died of an
apoplexy on the 17th of November, 1796, having just concluded a subsidiary
treaty with the kings combined against France. *1803.* The Empress died
just as she had engaged to furnish more effectual aid to the powers
combined against France. *C. I.*

[2] A subsidiary Treaty had been just concluded; and Russia was to
have furnished more effectual aid than that of pious manifestoes to the
Powers combined against France. I rejoice—not over the deceased
Woman (I never dared figure the Russian Sovereign to my imagination
under the dear and venerable Character of WOMAN—WOMAN, that complex
term for Mother, Sister, Wife!) I rejoice, as at the disenshrining of a
Daemon! I rejoice, as at the extinction of the evil Principle impersonated!
This very day, six years ago, the massacre of Ismail was perpetrated.
THIRTY THOUSAND HUMAN BEINGS, MEN, WOMEN, AND CHILDREN, murdered
in cold blood, for no other crime than that their garrison had defended
the place with perseverance and bravery. Why should I recal the
poisoning of her husband, her iniquities in Poland, or her late un-

---

36 thy] the *1797, 1803.* III] Epode *C. I., 4°, 1797, 1803.* 40 Ah!
whither *C. I., 4°.* 41 on] o'er *C. I., 4°, 1797, 1803.* 43 'twice mortal'
mace *C. I., 4°, 1797, 1803.* 45 The insatiate] That tyrant *C. I.* drunken]
frenzied *C. I.*

Between 51 and 52
    Whose shrieks, whose screams were vain to stir
    Loud-laughing, red-eyed Massacre *C. I., 4°, 1797, 1803.*

ODE TO THE DEPARTING YEAR 163

    Sudden blasts of triumph swelling,
Oft, at night, in misty train,
    Rush around her narrow dwelling! 55
The exterminating Fiend is fled—
    (Foul her life, and dark her doom)
Mighty armies of the dead
    Dance, like death-fires, round her tomb!
Then with prophetic song relate, 60
Each some Tyrant-Murderer's fate!

motived attack on Persia, the desolating ambition of her public life, or the libidinous excesses of her private hours! I have no wish to qualify myself for the office of Historiographer to the King of Hell—! December, 23, 1796. *4°*.

---

58 armies] Army *C. I., 4°, 1797, 1803.*   61 Tyrant-Murderer's] scepter'd Murderer's *C. I., 4°, 1797, 1803.*

After 61 When shall sceptred SLAUGHTER cease?
    A while he crouch'd, O Victor France!
    Beneath the lightning of thy lance;
    With treacherous dalliance courting PEACE—*
    But soon upstarting from his coward trance
    The boastful bloody Son of Pride betray'd
    His ancient hatred of the dove-eyed Maid.
    A cloud, O Freedom! cross'd thy orb of Light,
    And sure he deem'd that orb was set in night:
    For still does MADNESS roam on GUILT's bleak dizzy height! *C. I.*

    When shall sceptred, &c.
    . . . .
    With treacherous dalliance wooing Peace.
    But soon up-springing from his dastard trance
    The boastful bloody Son of Pride betray'd
    His hatred of the blest and blessing Maid.
    One cloud, O Freedom! cross'd thy orb of Light,
    And sure he deem'd that orb was quench'd in night:
    For still, &c. *4°.*

* To juggle this easily-juggled people into better humour with the supplies (and themselves, perhaps, affrighted by the successes of the French) our Ministry sent an Ambassador to Paris to sue for Peace. The supplies are granted: and in the meantime the Archduke Charles turns the scale of victory on the Rhine, and Buonaparte is checked before Mantua. Straightways our courtly messenger is commanded to *uncurl* his lips, and propose to the lofty Republic to *restore* all *its* conquests, and to suffer England to *retain* all *hers* (at least all her *important* ones), as the only terms of Peace, and the ultimatum of the negotiation!

    Θρασύνει γὰρ αἰσχρόμητις
Τάλαινα ΠΑΡΑΚΟΠΑ πρωτοπήμων.—AESCHYL., *Ag.* 222-4.

The friends of Freedom in this country are idle. Some are timid; some are selfish; and many the torpedo torch of hopelessness has numbed into inactivity. We would fain hope that (if the above account be

IV[1]

Departing Year! 'twas on no earthly shore
  My soul beheld thy Vision![2] Where alone,
  Voiceless and stern, before the cloudy throne,
Aye Memory sits: thy robe inscrib'd with gore,   65
With many an unimaginable groan
  Thou storied'st thy sad hours! Silence ensued,
  Deep silence o'er the ethereal multitude,
Whose locks with wreaths, whose wreaths with glories shone.
    Then, his eye wild ardours glancing,   70
    From the choiréd gods advancing,
The Spirit of the Earth made reverence meet,
And stood up, beautiful, before the cloudy seat.

V

    Throughout the blissful throng,
    Hush'd were harp and song: 75
Till wheeling round the throne the Lampads seven,
    (The mystic Words of Heaven)
    Permissive signal make:
The fervent Spirit bow'd, then spread his wings and spake!

---

accurate—it is only the French account) this dreadful instance of infatuation in our Ministry will rouse them to one effort more; and that at one and the same time in our different great towns the people will be called on to think solemnly, and declare their thoughts fearlessly by every method which the *remnant* of the Constitution allows. *4°*.

[1] The first Antistrophe describes the Image of the Departing Year, as in a vision; and concludes with introducing the Planetary Angel of the Earth preparing to address the Supreme Being. *1803*.

[2] '*My soul beheld thy vision!*' i.e. Thy Image in a vision. *4°*.

IV] Antistrophe I. *C. I., 4°, 1797, 1803*.

62 no earthly] an awful *C. I.*   65 thy... gore] there garmented with gore *C. I., 4°, 1797*.

65-7   Aye Memory sits: thy vest profan'd with gore.
         Thou with an unimaginable groan
         Gav'st reck'ning of thy Hours! *1803*.

68 ethereal] choired *C. I.*   69 Whose purple locks with snow-white glories shone *C. I., 4°*: Whose wreathed locks with snow-white glories shone *1797, 1803*.   70 wild] strange *C. I.*

V] Antistrophe II. *C. I., 4°, 1797, 1803*.

74-9   On every Harp on every Tongue
         While the mute Enchantment hung:
         Like Midnight from a thunder-cloud
         Spake the sudden Spirit loud. *C. I., 4°, 1797, 1803*.
         The sudden Spirit cried aloud. *C. I.*
         Like Thunder from a Midnight Cloud
         Spake the sudden Spirit loud *1803*.

ODE TO THE DEPARTING YEAR

'Thou in stormy blackness throning 80
    Love and uncreated Light,
By the Earth's unsolaced groaning,
    Seize thy terrors, Arm of might!
By Peace with proffer'd insult scared,
    Masked Hate and envying Scorn! 85
    By years of Havoc yet unborn!
And Hunger's bosom to the frost-winds bared!
    But chief by Afric's wrongs,
    Strange, horrible, and foul!
    By what deep guilt belongs 90
To the deaf Synod, 'full of gifts and lies!'[1]
By Wealth's insensate laugh! by Torture's howl!
    Avenger, rise!
For ever shall the thankless Island scowl,
Her quiver full, and with unbroken bow? 95
Speak! from thy storm-black Heaven O speak aloud!
    And on the darkling foe
Open thine eye of fire from some uncertain cloud!
O dart the flash! O rise and deal the blow!
The Past to thee, to thee the Future cries! 100
    Hark! how wide Nature joins her groans below!
    Rise, God of Nature! rise.'

---

[1] Gifts used in Scripture for corruption. *C. I.*

83 Arm] God *C. I.*
Between 83 *and* 84
    By Belgium's corse-impeded flood,*
    By Vendee steaming [streaming *C. I.*] Brother's blood.
        C. I., 4°, 1797, 1803.
      * The Rhine. *C. I., 1797, 1803.*

85 And mask'd Hate *C. I.*   87 By Hunger's bosom to the bleak winds bar'd *C. I.*   89 Strange] Most *C. I.*   90 By] And *C. I.*
91 Synod] Senate *1797, 1803.*   102 *Here the Ode ends C. I.*

94-102 For ever shall the bloody island scowl?
    For ever shall her vast and iron bow
    Shoot Famine's evil arrows o'er the world,*
    Hark! how wide Nature joins her groans below;
    Rise, God of Mercy, rise! why sleep thy bolts unhurl'd? *C. I.*

    For ever shall the bloody Island scowl?
    For aye, unbroken shall her cruel Bow
    Shoot Famine's arrows o'er thy ravaged World?
    Hark! how wide Nature joins her groans below—
    Rise, God of Nature, rise, why sleep thy Bolts unhurl'd?
        4°, 1797, 1803.

    Rise God of Nature, rise! ah! why those bolts unhurl'd?
        1797, 1803.

* 'In Europe the smoking villages of Flanders and the putrified fields

VI[1]

The voice had ceas'd, the Vision fled;
Yet still I gasp'd and reel'd with dread.
And ever, when the dream of night   105
Renews the phantom to my sight,
Cold sweat-drops gather on my limbs;
  My ears throb hot; my eye-balls start;
My brain with horrid tumult swims;
  Wild is the tempest of my heart;   110
And my thick and struggling breath
Imitates the toil of death!
No stranger agony confounds
  The Soldier on the war-field spread,
When all foredone with toil and wounds,   115
  Death-like he dozes among heaps of dead!
(The strife is o'er, the day-light fled,
  And the night-wind clamours hoarse!
See! the starting wretch's head
  Lies pillow'd on a brother's corse!)   120

VII

Not yet enslaved, not wholly vile,
O Albion! O my mother Isle!
Thy valleys, fair as Eden's bowers
Glitter green with sunny showers;
Thy grassy uplands' gentle swells   125
  Echo to the bleat of flocks;
(Those grassy hills, those glittering dells
    Proudly ramparted with rocks)
And Ocean mid his uproar wild

---

[1] The poem concludes with prophecying in anguish of Spirit the Downfall of this Country. *1803*.

---

of La Vendée—from Africa the unnumbered victims of a detestable Slave-Trade. In Asia the desolated plains of Indostan, and the millions whom a rice-contracting Governor caused to perish. In America the recent enormities of the Scalp-merchants. The four quarters of the globe groan beneath the intolerable iniquity of the nation.' See 'Addresses to the People', p. 46. *C. I.*

VI] Epode II. *4º, 1797, 1803*.
  103 Vision] Phantoms *4º, 1797, 1803*.   106 phantom] vision *4º, 1797, 1803*.   107 sweat-drops] sweat-damps *4º, 1797, 1803*.   113 stranger] uglier *4º*.   119 starting] startful *4º, 1797, 1803*.   121 O doom'd to fall, enslav'd and vile *4º, 1797, 1803*.

ODE TO THE DEPARTING YEAR 167

  Speaks safety to his Island-child!   130
  Hence for many a fearless age
  Has social Quiet lov'd thy shore;
  Nor ever proud Invader's rage
Or sack'd thy towers, or stain'd thy fields with gore.

VIII

Abandon'd of Heaven![1] mad Avarice thy guide, 135
At cowardly distance, yet kindling with pride—
Mid thy herds and thy corn-fields secure thou hast stood,
And join'd the wild yelling of Famine and Blood!
The nations curse thee! They with eager wondering

---

[1] '*Disclaim'd of Heaven!*'—The Poet from having considered the peculiar advantages, which this country has enjoyed, passes in rapid transition to the uses, which we have made of these advantages. We have been preserved by our insular situation, from suffering the actual horrors of War ourselves, and we have shewn our gratitude to Providence for this immunity by our eagerness to spread those horrors over nations less happily situated. In the midst of plenty and safety we have raised or joined the yell for famine and blood. Of the one hundred and seven last years, fifty have been years of War. Such wickedness cannot pass unpunished. We have been proud and confident in our alliances and our fleets—but God has prepared the canker-worm, and will smite the *gourds* of our pride. 'Art thou better than populous No, that was situate among the rivers, that had the waters round about it, whose rampart was the Sea? Ethiopia and Egypt were her strength and it was infinite: Put and Lubim were her helpers. Yet she was carried away, she went into captivity: and they cast lots for her honourable men, and all her great men were bound in chains. Thou also shalt be drunken: all thy strongholds shall be like fig trees with the first ripe figs; if they be shaken, they shall even fall into the mouth of the eater. Thou hast multiplied thy merchants above the stars of heaven. Thy crowned are as the locusts; and thy captains as the great grasshoppers which camp in the hedges in the cool-day; but when the Sun ariseth they flee away, and their place is not known where they are. There is no healing of thy bruise; thy wound is grievous: all, that hear the report of thee, shall clap hands over thee: for upon whom hath not thy wickedness passed continually?' *Nahum*, chap. iii. *4°, 1797, 1803.*

---

133 proud Invader's] sworded Foeman's *4°, 1797*: sworded Warrior's *1803*.
135-9 Disclaim'd of Heaven! mad Avarice at thy side *4°, 1797*.
 At coward distance, yet with kindling pride—
 Safe 'mid thy herds and cornfields thou hast stood,
 And join'd the yell of Famine and of Blood.
 All nations curse thee: and with eager wond'ring *4°, 1797*.
135 O abandon'd *1803*.
137-8 Mid thy Corn-fields and Herds thou in plenty hast stood
 And join'd the loud yellings of Famine and Blood. *1803*.
139 They] and *1797, 1803, S. L. 1817*.

Shall hear Destruction, like a vulture, scream! 140
Strange-eyed Destruction! who with many a dream
Of central fires through nether seas up-thundering
Soothes her fierce solitude; yet as she lies
By livid fount, or red volcanic stream,
If ever to her lidless dragon-eyes, 145
O Albion! thy predestin'd ruins rise,
The fiend-hag on her perilous couch doth leap,
Muttering distemper'd triumph in her charmèd sleep.

IX

Away, my soul, away!
In vain, in vain the Birds of warning sing— 150
And hark! I hear the famish'd brood of prey
Flap their lank pennons on the groaning wind!
Away, my soul, away!
I unpartaking of the evil thing,
With daily prayer and daily toil 155
Soliciting for food my scanty soil,
Have wail'd my country with a loud Lament.
Now I recentre my immortal mind
In the deep Sabbath of meek self-content;
Cleans'd from the vaporous passions that bedim 160
God's Image, sister of the Seraphim.[1]
1796.

[1] 'Let it not be forgotten during the perusal of this Ode that it was written many years before the abolition of the Slave Trade by the British Legislature, likewise before the invasion of Switzerland by the French Republic, which occasioned the Ode that follows [*France: an Ode.* First published as *The Recantation: an Ode*], a kind of Palinodia.' *MS. Note by S. T. C.*

---

142 fires] flames *4°*.
144   Stretch'd on the marge of some fire-flashing fount
       In the black Chamber of a sulphur'd mount. *4°*.
144 By livid fount, or roar of blazing stream *1797*.   146 Visions of thy predestin'd ruins rise *1803*.   151 famish'd] famin'd *4°*.   156 Soliciting my scant and blameless soil *4°*.

159-60 In the long sabbath of high self-content.
       Cleans'd from the fleshly passions that bedim *4°*.
       In the deep sabbath of blest self-content
       Cleans'd from the fears and anguish that   dim *1797*.
       In the blest sabbath of high self-content
       Cleans'd from bedimming Fear, and Anguish weak and blind.
                                                           1803.
161 *om. 1803.*

THE RAVEN[1]

A CHRISTMAS TALE, TOLD BY A SCHOOL-BOY TO HIS LITTLE BROTHERS AND SISTERS

UNDERNEATH an old oak tree
There was of swine a huge company,
That grunted as they crunched the mast:
For that was ripe, and fell full fast.
Then they trotted away, for the wind grew high:　　5
One acorn they left, and no more might you spy.
Next came a Raven, that liked not such folly:
He belonged, they did say, to the witch Melancholy!
Blacker was he than blackest jet,
Flew low in the rain, and his feathers not wet.　　10

---

[1] First published in the *Morning Post*, March 10, 1798 (with an introductory letter, *vide infra*): included (with the letter, and except line 15 the same text) in the *Annual Anthology*, 1800, in *Sibylline Leaves*, 1817 (pp. vi-viii), 1828, 1829, and 1834.

[To the editor of the *Morning Post*.]

'Sir,—I am not absolutely certain that the following Poem was written by EDMUND SPENSER, and found by an Angler buried in a fishing-box :—

'Under the foot of Mole, that mountain hoar,
　Mid the green alders, by the Mulla's shore.'

But a learned Antiquarian of my acquaintance has given it as his opinion that it resembles SPENSER's minor Poems as nearly as Vortigern and Rowena the Tragedies of WILLIAM SHAKESPEARE.—The Poem must be read in *recitative*, in the same manner as the Aegloga Secunda of the Shepherd's Calendar.

CUDDY.'　　　　　　　　　　　　　　　　　　　　M. P., *An. Anth.*

The Raven—Title] 'A Christmas Tale,' &c., was first prefixed in *S. L. 1817*. The letter introduced the poem in the *Morning Post*. In the *Annual Anthology* the 'Letter' is headed 'The Raven'. Lamb in a letter to Coleridge, dated Feb. 5, 1797, alludes to this poem as 'Your *Dream*'.

1-8　　　Under the arms of a goodly oak-tree
　　　　There was of Swine a large company.
　　　　They were making a rude *repast*,
　　　　Grunting as they crunch'd the *mast*.
　　　　Then they trotted away: for the wind blew high—　　5
　　　　One acorn they left, ne more mote you spy.
　　　　Next came a Raven, who lik'd not such folly:
　　　　He belong'd, I believe, to the witch MELANCHOLY!
　　　　M.P., An. Anth., and (with variants given below) MS. S. T. C.

1 Beneath a goodly old oak tree *MS. S. T. C.* : an old] a huge *S. L. 1817, 1828, 1829.*　　6 ne more] and no more *MS. S. T. C.*　　7 Next] But soon *MS. S. T. C.*　　8 belonged it was said *S. L. 1817.*　　10 in the rain his feathers were wet *M. P., An. Anth., MS. S. T. C.*

He picked up the acorn and buried it straight
By the side of a river both deep and great.
  Where then did the Raven go?
  He went high and low,
Over hill, over dale, did the black Raven go.   15
  Many Autumns, many Springs
  Travelled[1] he with wandering wings:
  Many Summers, many Winters—
  I can't tell half his adventures.

At length he came back, and with him a She, 20
And the acorn was grown to a tall oak tree.
They built them a nest in the topmost bough,
And young ones they had, and were happy enow.
But soon came a Woodman in leathern guise,
His brow, like a pent-house, hung over his eyes. 25
He'd an axe in his hand, not a word he spoke,
But with many a hem! and a sturdy stroke,
At length he brought down the poor Raven's own oak.
His young ones were killed; for they could not depart,
And their mother did die of a broken heart. 30

The boughs from the trunk the Woodman did sever;
And they floated it down on the course of the river.
They sawed it in planks, and its bark they did strip,
And with this tree and others they made a good ship.
The ship, it was launched; but in sight of the land 35
Such a storm there did rise as no ship could withstand.
It bulged on a rock, and the waves rush'd in fast:
Round and round flew the raven, and cawed to the blast.

---

[1] Seventeen or eighteen years ago an artist of some celebrity was so pleased with this doggerel that he amused himself with the thought of making a Child's Picture Book of it ; but he could not hit on a picture for these four lines. I suggested a *Round-about* with four seats, and the four seasons, as Children, with Time for the shew-man. Footnote, *Sibylline Leaves*, 1817.

---

15 O'er hill, o'er dale *M. P.* 17 with] on *MS. S. T. C.* 20 came back] return'd *M. P., An. Anth., MS. S. T. C.* 21 to a tall] a large *M. P., An. Anth., MS. S. T. C.* 22 topmost] uppermost *MS. S. T. C.* 23 happy] jolly *M. P., An. Anth.* 26 and *he* nothing spoke *M. P., An. Anth., MS. S. T. C.* 28 At length] Wel-a-day *MS. S. T. C.* : At last *M. P., An. Anth.* 30 And his wife she did die *M. P., An. Anth., MS. S. T. C.* 31 The branches from off it *M.P., An. Anth.* : The branches from off this the *MS. S. T. C.* 32 And floated *MS. S. T. C.* 33 They saw'd it to planks, and its rind *M. P., An. Anth.* : They saw'd it to planks and its bark *MS. S. T. C.* 34 they built up a ship *M. P., An. Anth.* 36 Such ... ship] A tempest arose which no ship *M. P., An. Anth., MS. S. T. C.* 38 The auld raven flew round and round *M. P., An. Anth.* : The old raven flew round and round *MS. S. T. C., S. L. 1817, 1828, 1829.*

He heard the last shriek of the perishing souls—
See! see! o'er the topmast the mad water rolls! 40
Right glad was the Raven, and off he went fleet,
And Death riding home on a cloud he did meet,
And he thank'd him again and again for this treat:
They had taken his all, and REVENGE IT WAS SWEET!
1797.

TO AN UNFORTUNATE WOMAN AT THE THEATRE[1]

MAIDEN, that with sullen brow
  Sitt'st behind those virgins gay,
Like a scorch'd and mildew'd bough,
  Leafless 'mid the blooms of May!

Him who lur'd thee and forsook, 5
  Oft I watch'd with angry gaze,
Fearful saw his pleading look,
  Anxious heard his fervid phrase.

[1] First published in the *Morning Post*, December 7, 1797: included in the *Annual Anthology*, 1800, in *Sibylline Leaves*, 1828, 1829, and 1834. For MS. sent to Cottle, see *E. R.* 1834, i. 213, 214.

39 He heard the sea-shriek of their perishing souls *M. P., An. Anth., MS. S. T. C.*
40-4 They be sunk! O'er the topmast the mad water rolls
  The Raven was glad that such fate they did *meet*.
  They had taken his all and REVENGE WAS SWEET. *M. P., An. Anth.*
40 See she sinks *MS. S. T. C.*   41 Very glad was the Raven, this fate they did meet *MS. S. T. C.*   42-3 *om. MS. S. T. C.*   44 Revenge was sweet. *An. Anth., MS. S. T. C., S. L.* 1817, 1828, 1829.

After l. 44, *two lines were added in Sibylline Leaves,* 1817:—
  We must not think so; but forget and forgive,
  And what Heaven gives life to, we'll still let it live.*

* Added thro' cowardly fear of the Goody! What a Hollow, where the Heart of Faith ought to be, does it not betray? this alarm concerning Christian morality, that will not permit even a Raven to be a Raven, nor a Fox a Fox, but demands conventicular justice to be inflicted on their unchristian conduct, or at least an antidote to be annexed. *MS. Note by S.T.C.*

To an Unfortunate Woman at the Theatre—Title] To an Unfortunate Woman in the Back Seats of the Boxes at the Theatre *M. P.*: To an Unfortunate Young Woman whom I had known in the days of her Innocence *MS. sent to Cottle, E. R. i. 213*: To an Unfortunate Woman whom the Author knew in the days of her Innocence. Composed at the Theatre *An. Anth.* 1800.   1 Maiden] Sufferer *An. Anth.*

In place of 5-12 Inly gnawing, thy distresses
  Mock those starts of wanton glee;
  And thy inmost soul confesses
    Chaste Affection's [affliction's *An. Anth.*] majesty.
                MS. Cottle, An. Anth.

Soft the glances of the Youth,
  Soft his speech, and soft his sigh;　　　　　10
But no sound like simple Truth,
  But no *true* love in his eye.

Loathing thy polluted lot,
  Hie thee, Maiden, hie thee hence!
Seek thy weeping Mother's cot,　　　　　15
  With a wiser innocence.

Thou hast known deceit and folly,
  Thou hast *felt* that Vice is woe:
With a musing melancholy
  Inly arm'd, go, Maiden! go.　　　　　20

Mother sage of Self-dominion,
  Firm thy steps, O Melancholy!
The strongest plume in Wisdom's pinion
  Is the memory of past folly.

Mute the sky-lark and forlorn,　　　　　25
  While she moults the firstling plumes,
That had skimm'd the tender corn,
  Or the beanfield's odorous blooms.

Soon with renovated wing
  Shall she dare a loftier flight,　　　　　30
Upward to the Day-Star spring,
  And embathe in heavenly light.

1797.

TO AN UNFORTUNATE WOMAN[1]

WHOM THE AUTHOR HAD KNOWN IN THE DAYS OF HER INNOCENCE

MYRTLE-LEAF that, ill besped,
  Pinest in the gladsome ray,
Soil'd beneath the common tread
  Far from thy protecting spray!

[1] First published in 1797: included in 1803, *Sibylline Leaves*, 1828, 1829, and 1834.

---

14 Maiden] Sufferer *An. Anth.*　　　　22 Firm are thy steps *M. P.*
25 sky-lark] Lavrac *MS. Cottle, An. Anth.*　　　26 the] those *MS. Cottle,
M. P., An. Anth.*　　　27 Which late had *M. P.*　　　31 Upwards to the
day star sing *MS. Cottle, An. Anth.*

Stanzas ii, iii, v, vi are not in *MS. Cottle* nor in the *Annual Anthology*.

To an Unfortunate Woman whom, &c.—Title] Allegorical Lines on the Same Subject *MS. Cottle.*

TO AN UNFORTUNATE WOMAN

When the Partridge o'er the sheaf 5
   Whirr'd along the yellow vale,
Sad I saw thee, heedless leaf!
   Love the dalliance of the gale.

Lightly didst thou, foolish thing!
   Heave and flutter to his sighs, 10
While the flatterer, on his wing,
   Woo'd and whisper'd thee to rise.

Gaily from thy mother-stalk
   Wert thou danc'd and wafted high—
Soon on this unshelter'd walk 15
   Flung to fade, to rot and die.

1797.

TO THE REV. GEORGE COLERIDGE[1]

OF OTTERY ST. MARY, DEVON

With some Poems

Notus in fratres animi paterni.
      HOR. *Carm.* lib. II. 2.

A BLESSÉD lot hath he, who having passed
His youth and early manhood in the stir
And turmoil of the world, retreats at length,
With cares that move, not agitate the heart,
To the same dwelling where his father dwelt; 5

---

[1] First published as the Dedication to the *Poems* of 1797: included in 1803, *Sibylline Leaves*, 1817, 1828, 1829, and 1834. In a copy of the *Poems* of 1797, formerly in the possession of the late Mr. Frederick Locker-Lampson, Coleridge affixed the following note to the Dedication—'N.B. If this volume should ever be delivered according to its direction, *i.e.* to Posterity, let it be known that the Reverend George Coleridge was displeased and thought his character endangered by the Dedication.'— S. T. Coleridge. *Note to P. and D. W.*, 1877-80, i. 163.

---

5   When the scythes-man o'er his sheaf
      Caroll'd in the yellow vale *MS. Cottle.*
    When the rustic o'er his sheaf
      Caroll'd in, &c. *1797.*
[*Note.* The text of Stanza ii dates from 1803.]
9 foolish] poor fond *MS. Cottle.*   15 Soon upon this sheltered walk, *MS. Cottle, Second Version.*   16 to fade, and rot, *MS. Cottle.*
To the Rev. George Coleridge—Motto] lib. I. 2 *S. L. 1817, 1828, 1829, 1834.*

174 TO THE REV. GEORGE COLERIDGE

And haply views his tottering little ones
Embrace those agéd knees and climb that lap,
On which first kneeling his own infancy
Lisp'd its brief prayer. Such, O my earliest Friend!
Thy lot, and such thy brothers too enjoy. 10
At distance did ye climb Life's upland road,
Yet cheer'd and cheering: now fraternal love
Hath drawn you to one centre. Be your days
Holy, and blest and blessing may ye live!

To me the Eternal Wisdom hath dispens'd 15
A different fortune and more different mind—
Me from the spot where first I sprang to light
Too soon transplanted, ere my soul had fix'd
Its first domestic loves; and hence through life
Chasing chance-started friendships. A brief while 20
Some have preserv'd me from life's pelting ills;
But, like a tree with leaves of feeble stem,
If the clouds lasted, and a sudden breeze
Ruffled the boughs, they on my head at once
Dropped the collected shower; and some most false, 25
False and fair-foliag'd as the Manchineel,
Have tempted me to slumber in their shade
E'en mid the storm; then breathing subtlest damps,
Mix'd their own venom with the rain from Heaven,
That I woke poison'd! But, all praise to Him 30
Who gives us all things, more have yielded me
Permanent shelter; and beside one Friend,
Beneath the impervious covert of one oak,
I've rais'd a lowly shed, and know the names
Of Husband and of Father; not unhearing 35
Of that divine and nightly-whispering Voice,
Which from my childhood to maturer years
Spake to me of predestinated wreaths,
Bright with no fading colours!

Yet at times
My soul is sad, that I have roam'd through life 40
Still most a stranger, most with naked heart

10 Thine and thy Brothers' favourable lot. *1803.*   23 and] or *1797, 1803.*   30 That I woke prison'd! But (the praise be His *1803.*
33-4   I as beneath the covert of an oak
       Have rais'd *1803.*

35 not] nor *1797, 1803, S. L. 1817, 1828, 1829.*

TO THE REV. GEORGE COLERIDGE 175

At mine own home and birth-place: chiefly then,
When I remember thee, my earliest Friend!
Thee, who didst watch my boyhood and my youth;
Didst trace my wanderings with a father's eye; 45
And boding evil yet still hoping good,
Rebuk'd each fault, and over all my woes
Sorrow'd in silence! He who counts alone
The beatings of the solitary heart,
That Being knows, how I have lov'd thee ever, 50
Lov'd as a brother, as a son rever'd thee!
Oh! 'tis to me an ever new delight,
To talk of thee and thine: or when the blast
Of the shrill winter, rattling our rude sash,
Endears the cleanly hearth and social bowl; 55
Or when, as now, on some delicious eve,
We in our sweet sequester'd orchard-plot
Sit on the tree crook'd earth-ward; whose old boughs,
That hang above us in an arborous roof,
Stirr'd by the faint gale of departing May, 60
Send their loose blossoms slanting o'er our heads!

Nor dost not thou sometimes recall those hours,
When with the joy of hope thou gavest thine ear
To my wild firstling-lays. Since then my song
Hath sounded deeper notes, such as beseem 65
Or that sad wisdom folly leaves behind,
Or such as, tuned to these tumultuous times,
Cope with the tempest's swell!

These various strains,
Which I have fram'd in many a various mood,
Accept, my Brother! and (for some perchance 70
Will strike discordant on thy milder mind)
If aught of error or intemperate truth
Should meet thine ear, think thou that riper Age
Will calm it down, and let thy love forgive it!

NETHER-STOWEY, SOMERSET, *May* 26, 1797.

47-9 Rebuk'd each fault, and wept o'er all my woes.
  Who counts the beatings of the lonely heart *1797, 1803*.
Between 52-3 My eager eye glist'ning with memry's tear *1797*.   62
thou] *thou* all editions to *1834*.   *Between* 66-7 Or the high raptures of
prophetic Faith *1797, 1803*.   68 strains] songs *1797, 1803*.

ON THE CHRISTENING OF A FRIEND'S CHILD[1]

This day among the faithful plac'd
  And fed with fontal manna,
O with maternal title grac'd,
  Dear Anna's dearest Anna!

While others wish thee wise and fair, 5
  A maid of spotless fame,
I'll breathe this more compendious prayer—
  May'st thou deserve thy name!

Thy mother's name, a potent spell,
  That bids the Virtues hie 10
From mystic grove and living cell,
  Confess'd to Fancy's eye;

Meek Quietness without offence;
  Content in homespun kirtle;
True Love; and True Love's Innocence, 15
  White Blossom of the Myrtle!

Associates of thy name, sweet Child!
  These Virtues may'st thou win;
With face as eloquently mild
  To say, they lodge within. 20

So, when her tale of days all flown,
  Thy mother shall be miss'd here;
When Heaven at length shall claim its own
  And Angels snatch their Sister;

Some hoary-headed friend, perchance, 25
  May gaze with stifled breath;
And oft, in momentary trance,
  Forget the waste of death.

Even thus a lovely rose I've view'd
  In summer-swelling pride; 30
Nor mark'd the bud, that green and rude
  Peep'd at the rose's side.

---

[1] First published in the Supplement to *Poems*, 1797: reprinted in *Literary Remains*, 1836, i. 48, 49: included in 1844 and 1852. The lines were addressed to Anna Cruickshank, the wife of John Cruickshank, who was a neighbour of Coleridge at Nether-Stowey.

THE CHRISTENING OF A FRIEND'S CHILD

  It chanc'd I pass'd again that way
   In Autumn's latest hour,
  And wond'ring saw the selfsame spray   35
   Rich with the selfsame flower.

  Ah fond deceit! the rude green bud
   Alike in shape, place, name,
  Had bloom'd where bloom'd its parent stud,
   Another and the same!   40

1797.

TRANSLATION [1]

OF A LATIN INSCRIPTION BY THE REV. W. L. BOWLES IN NETHER-STOWEY CHURCH

  DEPART in joy from this world's noise and strife
  To the deep quiet of celestial life!
  Depart!—Affection's self reproves the tear
  Which falls, O honour'd Parent! on thy bier;—
  Yet Nature will be heard, the heart will swell, 5
  And the voice tremble with a last Farewell!

1797.

[*The Tablet is erected to the Memory of Richard Camplin, who died Jan.* 20, 1792.

  'Lætus abi! mundi strepitu curisque remotus;
   Lætus abi! cæli quà vocat alma Quies.
  Ipsa fides loquitur lacrymamque incusat inanem,
   Quæ cadit in vestros, care Pater, Cineres.
  Heu! tantum liceat meritos hos solvere Ritus, 5
   Naturæ et tremulâ dicere Voce, Vale!']

---

[1] First published in *Literary Remains*, 1836, i. 50. First collected in *P. and D. W.*, 1877, ii. 365.

---

6 Et longum tremulâ *L. R. 1836.*

THIS LIME-TREE BOWER MY PRISON[1]

[ADDRESSED TO CHARLES LAMB, OF THE
INDIA HOUSE, LONDON]

In the June of 1797 some long-expected friends paid a visit to the author's cottage; and on the morning of their arrival, he met with an accident, which disabled him from walking during the whole time of their stay. One evening, when they had left him for a few hours, he composed the following lines in the garden-bower.[2]

> WELL, they are gone, and here must I remain,
> This lime-tree bower my prison! I have lost
> Beauties and feelings, such as would have been

---

[1] First published in the *Annual Anthology*, 1800, reprinted in Mylius' *Poetical Classbook*, 1810: included in *Sibylline Leaves*, 1817, in 1828, 1829, and 1834. The poem was sent in a letter to Southey, July 9, 1797, and in a letter to C. Lloyd, [July, 1797]. See *Letters of S. T. C.*, 1895, i. 225-7 and *P. W.*, 1893, p. 591.

[2] 'Ch. and Mary Lamb—dear to my heart, yea, as it were my Heart.—S. T. C. Æt. 63; 1834—1797-1834 = 37 years!' (Marginal note written by S. T. Coleridge over against the introductory note to 'This Lime-Tree Bower my Prison', in a copy of the *Poetical Works*, 1834.)

This Lime-Tree, &c.—Title] This Lime-Tree Bower my Prison. A Poem Addressed, &c. *An. Anth.*: the words 'Addressed to', &c., are omitted in *Sibylline Leaves*, 1828, 1829, and 1834.

1-28
    Well, they are gone, and here must I remain,
    Lam'd by the scathe of fire, lonely and faint,
    This lime-tree bower my prison! They, meantime,
    My Friends, whom I may never meet again,
    On springy heath, along the hill-top edge   5
    Wander delighted, and look down, perchance,
    On that same rifted dell, where many an ash
    Twists its wild limbs beside the ferny rock
    Whose plumy* ferns forever nod and drip
    Spray'd by the waterfall. But chiefly thou   10
    My gentle-hearted *Charles!* thou who had pin'd
                              MS. Letter to Southey, July 17, 1797.

* The ferns that grow in moist places grow five or six together, and form a complete 'Prince of Wales's Feather'—that is plumy. *Letter to Southey.*

1-28
    Well they are gone, and here I must remain,
    This lime-tree, . . . hill-top edge
    Delighted wander, and look down, perchance,
    On that same rifted dell, where the wet ash
    Twists its wild limbs above, . . . who hast pin'd
                              MS. Letter to Lloyd [*July*, 1797].

3 Such beauties and such feelings, as had been *An. Anth., S. L.*

THIS LIME-TREE BOWER MY PRISON

Most sweet to my remembrance even when age
Had dimm'd mine eyes to blindness! They, meanwhile, 5
Friends, whom I never more may meet again,
On springy[1] heath, along the hill-top edge,
Wander in gladness, and wind down, perchance,
To that still roaring dell, of which I told;
The roaring dell, o'erwooded, narrow, deep, 10
And only speckled by the mid-day sun;
Where its slim trunk the ash from rock to rock
Flings arching like a bridge;—that branchless ash,
Unsunn'd and damp, whose few poor yellow leaves
Ne'er tremble in the gale, yet tremble still, 15
Fann'd by the water-fall! and there my friends
Behold the dark green file of long lank weeds,[2]
That all at once (a most fantastic sight!)
Still nod and drip beneath the dripping edge
Of the blue clay-stone.

                  Now, my friends emerge 20
Beneath the wide wide Heaven—and view again
The many-steepled tract magnificent
Of hilly fields and meadows, and the sea,
With some fair bark, perhaps, whose sails light up
The slip of smooth clear blue betwixt two Isles 25
Of purple shadow! Yes! they wander on
In gladness all; but thou, methinks, most glad,
My gentle-hearted Charles! for thou hast pined
And hunger'd after Nature, many a year,
In the great City pent, winning thy way 30
With sad yet patient soul, through evil and pain
And strange calamity! Ah! slowly sink
Behind the western ridge, thou glorious Sun!
Shine in the slant beams of the sinking orb,

---

[1] 'Elastic, I mean.' *MS. Letter to Southey.*
[2] The *Asplenium Scolopendrium*, called in some countries the Adder's Tongue, in others the Hart's Tongue, but Withering gives the Adder's Tongue as the trivial name of the *Ophioglossum* only.

---

4 my remembrance] to have remembered *An. Anth.*   6 My Friends, whom I may never meet again *An. Anth., S. L.*   20 blue] dim *An. Anth.* 22 tract] track *An. Anth., S. L.* 1828.   24 bark, perhaps, which lightly touches *An. Anth.*   28 hast] had'st *An. Anth.*   31 patient] bowed *MS. Letter to Southey.*   34 beams] heaven *MS. Letter to Southey.*

180 THIS LIME-TREE BOWER MY PRISON

Ye purple heath-flowers! richlier burn, ye clouds! 35
Live in the yellow light, ye distant groves!
And kindle, thou blue Ocean! So my friend
Struck with deep joy may stand, as I have stood,
Silent with swimming sense; yea, gazing round
On the wide landscape, gaze till all doth seem 40
Less gross than bodily; and of such hues
As veil the Almighty Spirit, when yet he makes
Spirits perceive his presence.

                              A delight
Comes sudden on my heart, and I am glad
As I myself were there! Nor in this bower, 45
This little lime-tree bower, have I not mark'd
Much that has sooth'd me. Pale beneath the blaze
Hung the transparent foliage; and I watch'd
Some broad and sunny leaf, and lov'd to see
The shadow of the leaf and stem above 50
Dappling its sunshine! And that walnut-tree
Was richly ting'd, and a deep radiance lay
Full on the ancient ivy, which usurps
Those fronting elms, and now, with blackest mass

---

38 foll. Struck with joy's deepest calm, and gazing round
            On the wide view* may gaze till all doth seem
            Less gross than bodily; a living thing
            That acts upon the mind, and with such hues
            As clothe th' Almighty Spirit, when he makes.
                                          MS. Letter to Southey.

      * You remember I am a *Berkleyan*. *Note to Letter.*

40 wide] wild *S. L.*

40 (for *wild* r. *wide*; and the two following lines thus:
            Less gross than bodily; and of such hues
            As veil the Almighty Spirit *Errata, S. L.*, p. [xii].)
            As veil the Almighty Spirit, when he makes *1828.*

41 foll. Less gross than bodily, a living thing
            Which acts upon the mind and with such hues
            As cloathe the Almighty Spirit, when he makes
                                            An. Anth., S. L.

45 foll. As I myself were there! Nor in the bower
            Want I sweet sounds or pleasing shapes. **I watch'd**
            The sunshine of each broad transparent leaf
            Broke by the shadows of the leaf or stem
            Which hung above it: and that walnut tree
                                          MS. Letter to Southey.

THIS LIME-TREE BOWER MY PRISON

Makes their dark branches gleam a lighter hue 55
Through the late twilight: and though now the bat
Wheels silent by, and not a swallow twitters,
Yet still the solitary humble-bee
Sings in the bean-flower! Henceforth I shall know
That Nature ne'er deserts the wise and pure; 60
No plot so narrow, be but Nature there,
No waste so vacant, but may well employ
Each faculty of sense, and keep the heart
Awake to Love and Beauty! and sometimes
'Tis well to be bereft of promis'd good, 65
That we may lift the soul, and contemplate
With lively joy the joys we cannot share.
My gentle-hearted Charles! when the last rook
Beat its straight path along the dusky air
Homewards, I blest it! deeming its black wing 70
(Now a dim speck, now vanishing in light)
Had cross'd the mighty Orb's dilated glory,
While thou stood'st gazing; or, when all was still,
Flew creeking o'er thy head, and had a charm [1]
For thee, my gentle-hearted Charles, to whom 75
No sound is dissonant which tells of Life.
    1797.

---

[1] Some months after I had written this line, it gave me pleasure to find [to observe *An. Anth., S. L. 1828*] that Bartram had observed the same circumstance of the Savanna Crane. 'When these Birds move their wings in flight, their strokes are slow, moderate and regular; and even when at a considerable distance or high above us, we plainly hear the quill-feathers: their shafts and webs upon one another creek as the joints or working of a vessel in a tempestuous sea.'

---

55 branches] foliage *MS. Letter to Southey.*   56 and though the rapid bat *MS. Letter to Southey.*   60-64 *om. in MS. Letter to Lloyd.*   61-2 No scene so narrow but may well employ *MS. Letter to Southey, An. Anth.*   68 My Sister and my Friends *MS. Letter to Southey*: My Sara and my Friends *MS. Letter to Lloyd.*   70 Homewards] Homeward *MS. Letter to Lloyd.*   71 *om. in MS. Letter to Lloyd.*   in the light *An. Anth., S. L.* (omit *the* before *light. Errata, S. L.*, [p xii]).   72 Cross'd like a speck the blaze of setting day *MS. Letter to Southey*: Had cross'd the mighty orb's dilated blase. *MS. Letter to Lloyd.*   73 While ye [you *MS. Letter to Lloyd*] stood *MS. Letter to Southey.*   74 thy head] your heads *MSS. Letters to Southey and Lloyd.*   75 For you my Sister and my Friends *MS. Letter to Southey*: For you my Sara and my Friends *MS. Letter to Lloyd.*

THE FOSTER-MOTHER'S TALE[1]

A DRAMATIC FRAGMENT

[From *Osorio*, Act IV. The title and text are here printed from *Lyrical Ballads*, 1798.]

Foster-Mother. I never saw the man whom you describe.
Maria. 'Tis strange! he spake of you familiarly
As mine and Albert's common Foster-mother.
Foster-Mother. Now blessings on the man, whoe'er he be,
That joined your names with mine! O my sweet lady, 5
As often as I think of those dear times
When you two little ones would stand at eve
On each side of my chair, and make me learn
All you had learnt in the day; and how to talk
In gentle phrase, then bid me sing to you— 10
'Tis more like heaven to come than what *has* been!
Maria. O my dear Mother! this strange man has left me
Troubled with wilder fancies, than the moon

---

[1] First published in the first edition of the *Lyrical Ballads*, 1798, and reprinted in the editions of 1800, 1802, and 1805. The 'dramatic fragment' was excluded from the acting version of *Remorse*, but was printed in an Appendix, p. 75, to the Second Edition of the Play, 1813. It is included in the body of the work in *Sibylline Leaves*, 1817, and again in 1852, and in the Appendix to *Remorse* in the editions of 1828, 1829, and 1834. It is omitted from 1844. 'The "Foster-Mother's Tale," (From Mr. C.'s own handwriting)' was published in Cottle's *Early Recollections*, i. 235.

'The following scene as unfit for the stage was taken from the Tragedy in 1797, and published in the *Lyrical Ballads*. But this work having been long out of print, and it having been determined, that this with my other poems in that collection (the *Nightingale, Love*, and the *Ancient Mariner*) should be omitted in any future edition, I have been advised to reprint it as a Note to the Second Scene of Act the Fourth, p. 55.' App. to *Remorse*, Ed. 2, 1813. [This note is reprinted in 1828 and 1829, but in 1834 only the first sentence is prefixed to the scene.]

The Foster-Mother's Tale—Title] Foster-Mother's Tale. (Scene—Spain) *Cottle*, 1837: The, &c. A Narration in Dramatic Blank Verse *L. B. 1800*. In *Remorse, App.*, 1813 and in 1828, 1829, 1834, the *dramatis personae* are respectively Teresa and Selma. The fragment opens thus:—*Enter Teresa and Selma.*

   Ter. 'Tis said, he spake of you familiarly
    As mine and Alvar's common foster-mother.
In Cottle's version, the scene begins at line 4.

1 man] Moor *Osorio, MS. I.*   12–16 O my dear Mother ... She gazes idly! *om.* 1813, 1828, 1829, 1834.   12 me] us *Cottle*, 1837. 13 the] yon *Osorio, MS. I.*

Breeds in the love-sick maid who gazes at it,
Till lost in inward vision, with wet eye 15
She gazes idly!—But that entrance, Mother!
Foster-Mother. Can no one hear? It is a perilous tale!
Maria. No one.
Foster-Mother. My husband's father told it me,
Poor old Leoni!—Angels rest his soul!
He was a woodman, and could fell and saw 20
With lusty arm. You know that huge round beam
Which props the hanging wall of the old Chapel?
Beneath that tree, while yet it was a tree,
He found a baby wrapt in mosses, lined
With thistle-beards, and such small locks of wool 25
As hang on brambles. Well, he brought him home,
And rear'd him at the then Lord Velez' cost.
And so the babe grew up a pretty boy,
A pretty boy, but most unteachable—
And never learnt a prayer, nor told a bead, 30
But knew the names of birds, and mock'd their notes,
And whistled, as he were a bird himself:
And all the autumn 'twas his only play
To get the seeds of wild flowers, and to plant them
With earth and water, on the stumps of trees. 35
A Friar, who gather'd simples in the wood,
A grey-haired man—he lov'd this little boy,
The boy lov'd him—and, when the Friar taught him,
He soon could write with the pen: and from that time,
Lived chiefly at the Convent or the Castle. 40
So he became a very learnéd youth.
But Oh! poor wretch!—he read, and read, and read,
Till his brain turn'd—and ere his twentieth year,
He had unlawful thoughts of many things:
And though he prayed, he never lov'd to pray 45
With holy men, nor in a holy place—
But yet his speech, it was so soft and sweet,
The late Lord Velez ne'er was wearied with him.

16 In *Lyrical Ballads*, 1800, the scene begins with the words: 'But that entrance'. But that entrance, Selma? *1813.* 19 Leoni] Sesina *1813, 1828, 1829, 1834.* 27 Velez'] Valdez' *1813, 1828, 1829, 1834*: Valez' *S. L. 1817.* 34 To gather seeds *1813, S. L. 1817, 1828, 1829, 1834.* 36 gather'd] oft culled *S. L. 1817.* 41 So he became a rare and learned youth *1813, 1828, 1829, 1834.*

41-2 So he became a very learned man.
    But O poor youth *Cottle, 1837.*

48 Velez] Valdez *1813, 1828, 1829, 1834*: Valez *S. L. 1817.*

And once, as by the north side of the Chapel
They stood together, chain'd in deep discourse, 50
The earth heav'd under them with such a groan,
That the wall totter'd, and had well-nigh fallen
Right on their heads. My Lord was sorely frighten'd;
A fever seiz'd him, and he made confession
Of all the heretical and lawless talk 55
Which brought this judgment: so the youth was seiz'd
And cast into that hole. My husband's father
Sobb'd like a child—it almost broke his heart:
And once as he was working in the cellar,
He heard a voice distinctly; 'twas the youth's, 60
Who sung a doleful song about green fields,
How sweet it were on lake or wild savannah,
To hunt for food, and be a naked man,
And wander up and down at liberty.
He always doted on the youth, and now 65
His love grew desperate; and defying death,
He made that cunning entrance I describ'd:
And the young man escap'd.
    Maria.   'Tis a sweet tale:
Such as would lull a listening child to sleep,
His rosy face besoil'd with unwiped tears.— 70
And what became of him?
    Foster-Mother.   He went on shipboard
With those bold voyagers, who made discovery
Of golden lands. Leoni's younger brother
Went likewise, and when he return'd to Spain,
He told Leoni, that the poor mad youth, 75
Soon after they arriv'd in that new world,
In spite of his dissuasion, seiz'd a boat,
And all alone, set sail by silent moonlight
Up a great river, great as any sea,
And ne'er was heard of more: but 'tis suppos'd, 80
He liv'd and died among the savage men.
  1797.

54 made a confession *Osorio*.   A fever seiz'd the youth and he made confession *Cottle, 1837*.   57 hole] cell *L. B. 1800*: den *1813*. [And fetter'd in that den. *MS. S. T. C.*].   59 in the cellar] near this dungeon *1813, 1828, 1829, 1834*.   62 wild] wide *1813, 1828, 1829, 1834*.   65 He always] Leoni *L. B. 1800*.   68-9 *om. L. B. 1800*.   73 Leoni's] Sesina's *1813, 1828, 1829, 1834*.   **younger**] youngest *S. L. 1817*.   75 Leoni] Sesina *1813, 1828, 1829, 1834*.

THE DUNGEON[1]

[From *Osorio*, Act V; and *Remorse*, Act V, Scene i. The title and text are here printed from *Lyrical Ballads*, 1798.]

AND this place our forefathers made for man!
This is the process of our love and wisdom,
To each poor brother who offends against us—
Most innocent, perhaps—and what if guilty?
Is this the only cure? Merciful God! 5
Each pore and natural outlet shrivell'd up
By Ignorance and parching Poverty,
His energies roll back upon his heart,
And stagnate and corrupt; till chang'd to poison,
They break out on him, like a loathsome plague-spot; 10
Then we call in our pamper'd mountebanks—
And this is their best cure! uncomforted
And friendless solitude, groaning and tears,
And savage faces, at the clanking hour,
Seen through the steams and vapour of his dungeon, 15
By the lamp's dismal twilight! So he lies
Circled with evil, till his very soul
Unmoulds its essence, hopelessly deform'd
By sights of ever more deformity!

With other ministrations thou, O Nature! 20
Healest thy wandering and distemper'd child:
Thou pourest on him thy soft influences,
Thy sunny hues, fair forms, and breathing sweets,
Thy melodies of woods, and winds, and waters,
Till he relent, and can no more endure 25
To be a jarring and a dissonant thing,
Amid this general dance and minstrelsy;
But, bursting into tears, wins back his way,
His angry spirit heal'd and harmoniz'd
By the benignant touch of Love and Beauty. 30
1797.

[1] First published in the *Lyrical Ballads*, 1798, and reprinted in the *Lyrical Ballads*, 1800. First collected (as a separate poem) in *Poems*, 1893, p. 85.

---

1 our] my *Osorio*, Act V, i. 107. *1813, 1828, 1829, 1834*.   man] men *Osorio*.   15 steams and vapour] steaming vapours *Osorio*, V, i. 121: steam and vapours *1813, 1828, 1829, 1834*.

THE RIME OF THE ANCIENT MARINER [1]

IN SEVEN PARTS

Facile credo, plures esse Naturas invisibiles quam visibiles in rerum universitate. Sed horum omnium familiam quis nobis enarrabit? et gradus et cognationes et discrimina et singulorum munera? Quid agunt? quae loca habitant? Harum rerum notitiam semper ambivit ingenium humanum, nunquam attigit. Juvat, interea, non diffiteor, quandoque in animo, tanquam in tabulâ, majoris et melioris mundi imaginem contemplari : ne mens assuefacta hodiernae vitae minutiis se contrahat nimis, et tota subsidat in pusillas cogitationes. Sed veritati interea invigilandum est, modusque servandus, ut certa ab incertis, diem a nocte, distinguamus.—T. BURNET, *Archaeol. Phil.* p. 68.[2]

ARGUMENT

How a Ship having passed the Line was driven by storms to the cold Country towards the South Pole; and how from thence she made her course to the tropical Latitude of the Great Pacific Ocean; and of the strange things that befell; and in what manner the Ancyent Marinere came back to his own Country. [*L. B.* 1798.] [3]

---

[1] The *Ancient Mariner* was first published in the *Lyrical Ballads*, 1798. It was reprinted in the succeeding editions of 1800, 1802, and 1805. It was first published under the Author's name in *Sibylline Leaves*, 1817, and included in 1828, 1829, and 1834. For the full text of the poem as published in 1798, vide Appendices. The marginal glosses were added in 1815–1816, when a collected edition of Coleridge's poems was being prepared for the press, and were first published in *Sibylline Leaves*, 1817, but it is possible that they were the work of a much earlier period. The text of the *Ancient Mariner* as reprinted in *Lyrical Ballads*, 1802, 1805 follows that of 1800.

[2] The text of the original passage is as follows : 'Facilè credo, plures esse naturas invisibiles quam visibiles, in rerum universitate : pluresque Angelorum ordines in cælo, quam sunt pisces in mari : Sed horum omnium familiam quis nobis enarrabit ? Et gradus, et cognationes, et discrimina, et singulorum munera ? Harum rerum notitiam semper ambivit ingenium humanum, nunquam attigit ... Juvat utique non etc. : *Archaeologiae Philosophicae sive Doctrina Antiqua De Rerum Originibus.* Libri Duo: Londini, MDCXCII, p. 68.'

[3] How a Ship, having first sailed to the Equator, was driven by Storms to the cold Country towards the South Pole; how the Ancient Mariner cruelly and in contempt of the laws of hospitality killed a Seabird and how he was followed by many and strange Judgements: and in what manner he came back to his own Country. [*L. B.* 1800.]

The Rime, &c.—Title] The Rime of the Ancyent Marinere. In Seven Parts *L.B. 1798* : The Ancient Mariner. A Poet's Reverie *L.B. 1800, 1802, 1805.*

[*Note.*—The 'Argument' was omitted in *L. B. 1802, 1805, Sibylline Leaves, 1817,* and in *1828, 1829,* and *1834.*]

Part 1

<small>An ancient Mariner meeteth three Gallants bidden to a wedding-feast, and detaineth one.</small>

It is an ancient Mariner,
And he stoppeth one of three.
'By thy long grey beard and glittering eye,
Now wherefore stopp'st thou me?

The Bridegroom's doors are opened wide,   5
And I am next of kin;
The guests are met, the feast is set:
May'st hear the merry din.'

He holds him with his skinny hand,
'There was a ship,' quoth he.   10
'Hold off! unhand me, grey-beard loon!'
Eftsoons his hand dropt he.

<small>The Wedding-Guest is spell-bound by the eye of the old seafaring man, and constrained to hear his tale.</small>

He holds him with his glittering eye—
The Wedding-Guest stood still,
And listens like a three years' child: 15
The Mariner hath his will.

The Wedding-Guest sat on a stone:
He cannot choose but hear;
And thus spake on that ancient man,
The bright-eyed Mariner.   20

'The ship was cheered, the harbour cleared,
Merrily did we drop

<small>The Mariner tells how the ship sailed southward with a good wind and fair weather, till it reached the line.</small>

Below the kirk, below the hill,
Below the lighthouse top.

The Sun came up upon the left,   25
Out of the sea came he!
And he shone bright, and on the right
Went down into the sea.

PART I] I *L. B. 1798, 1800*. The Rime of the Ancient Mariner. In Seven Parts. *S. L., 1828, 1829.*   1 It is an ancyent Marinere *L. B. 1798* [ancient is spelled 'ancyent' and Mariner 'Marinere' throughout *L.B. 1798*].   3 thy glittering eye *L. B. 1798, 1800.*   4 stopp'st thou] stoppest *L. B. 1798, 1800.*

Between 8 *and* 13
        But still he holds the wedding guest—
          There was a Ship, quoth he—
        'Nay, if thou'st got a laughsome tale,
          'Marinere, [Mariner! *1800*] come with me.'
        He holds him with his skinny hand—
          Quoth he, there was a Ship—
        Now get thee hence thou greybeard Loon!
          Or my Staff shall make thee skip.   *L. B. 1798, 1800.*

188 THE RIME OF THE ANCIENT MARINER

Higher and higher every day,
Till over the mast at noon—'   30
The Wedding-Guest here beat his breast,
For he heard the loud bassoon.

The Wedding-Guest heareth the bridal music; but the Mariner continueth his tale.

The bride hath paced into the hall,
Red as a rose is she;
Nodding their heads before her goes   35
The merry minstrelsy.

The Wedding-Guest he beat his breast,
Yet he cannot choose but hear;
And thus spake on that ancient man,
The bright-eyed Mariner.   40

The ship driven by a storm toward the south pole.

'And now the STORM-BLAST came, and he
Was tyrannous and strong:
He struck with his o'ertaking wings,
And chased us south along.

With sloping masts and dipping prow,   45
As who pursued with yell and blow
Still treads the shadow of his foe,
And forward bends his head,
The ship drove fast, loud roared the blast,
And southward aye we fled.   50

And now there came both mist and snow,
And it grew wondrous cold:
And ice, mast-high, came floating by,
As green as emerald.

Between 40 *and* 55

Listen, Stranger! Storm and Wind,
  A Wind and Tempest strong!
For days and weeks it play'd us freaks—
  Like chaff we drove along.

Listen Stranger! Mist and Snow,
  And it grew wondrous cauld;
And Ice mast-high came floating by
  As green as Emerauld.   *L. B. 1798.*

Between 40 *and* 51

But now the Northwind came more fierce,
  There came a Tempest strong!
And Southward still for days and weeks
  Like Chaff we drove along.   *L. B. 1800.*

Lines 41–50 of the text were added in *Sibylline Leaves*, 1817. [*Note.* The emendation in the marginal gloss, 'driven' for 'drawn' first appears in *1893.*]

The land of ice, and of fearful sounds where no living thing was to be seen.

And through the drifts the snowy clifts 55
Did send a dismal sheen:
Nor shapes of men nor beasts we ken—
The ice was all between.

The ice was here, the ice was there,
The ice was all around: 60
It cracked and growled, and roared and howled,
Like noises in a swound!

Till a great sea-bird, called the Albatross, came through the snow-fog, and was received with great joy and hospitality.

At length did cross an Albatross,
Thorough the fog it came;
As if it had been a Christian soul, 65
We hailed it in God's name.

It ate the food it ne'er had eat,
And round and round it flew.
The ice did split with a thunder-fit;
The helmsman steered us through! 70

And lo! the Albatross proveth a bird of good omen, and followeth the ship as it returned northward through fog and floating ice.

And a good south wind sprung up behind;
The Albatross did follow,
And every day, for food or play,
Came to the mariner's hollo!

In mist or cloud, on mast or shroud, 75
It perched for vespers nine;
Whiles all the night, through fog-smoke white,
Glimmered the white Moon-shine.'

The ancient Mariner inhospitably killeth the pious bird of good omen.

'God save thee, ancient Mariner!
From the fiends, that plague thee thus!— 80
Why look'st thou so?'—With my cross-bow
I shot the ALBATROSS.

PART II

The Sun now rose upon the right:
Out of the sea came he,
Still hid in mist, and on the left 85
Went down into the sea.

---

55 clifts] clift *S. L.* [probably a misprint. It is not corrected in the *Errata.*]   57 Nor ... nor] Ne ... ne *L. B. 1798.*   62 Like noises of a swound *L. B. 1798*: A wild and ceaseless sound *L. B. 1800.*   65 And an it were *L. B. 1798*: As if *MS. Corr. S. T. C.*   67 The Mariners gave it biscuit-worms *L. B. 1798, 1800.*   77 fog-smoke white] fog smoke-white *L. B. 1798 (corr. in Errata).*   PART II] II *L. B. 1798, 1800*: The Rime of the Ancient Mariner, Part the Second, *S. L. 1828, 1829.*   83 The Sun came up *L. B. 1798.*   85 And broad as a weft upon the left *L. B. 1798.*

190 THE RIME OF THE ANCIENT MARINER

  And the good south wind still blew behind,
  But no sweet bird did follow,
  Nor any day for food or play
  Came to the mariners' hollo!   90

His shipmates cry out against the ancient Mariner, for killing the bird of good luck.

  And I had done a hellish thing,
  And it would work 'em woe:
  For all averred, I had killed the bird
  That made the breeze to blow.
  Ah wretch! said they, the bird to slay,   95
  That made the breeze to blow!

But when the fog cleared off, they justify the same, and thus make themselves accomplices in the crime.

  Nor dim nor red, like God's own head,
  The glorious Sun uprist:
  Then all averred, I had killed the bird
  That brought the fog and mist.   100
  'Twas right, said they, such birds to slay,
  That bring the fog and mist.

The fair breeze continues; the ship enters the Pacific Ocean, and sails northward, even till it reaches the Line.

  The fair breeze blew, the white foam flew,
  The furrow followed free;
  We were the first that ever burst   105
  Into that silent sea.

The ship hath been suddenly becalmed.

  Down dropt the breeze, the sails dropt down,
  'Twas sad as sad could be;
  And we did speak only to break
  The silence of the sea!   110

  All in a hot and copper sky,
  The bloody Sun, at noon,
  Right up above the mast did stand,
  No bigger than the Moon.

  Day after day, day after day,   115
  We stuck, nor breath nor motion;

---

89 Nor] Ne *L. B. 1798*.   90 mariners'] Marinere's *L. B. 1798, 1800, S. L. 1817*: Mariner's *L. B. 1800*.   91 a] an *all editions to 1834*.   95–6 *om. L. B. 1798, 1800*: were added in *Sibylline Leaves*.   97 Nor...nor] ne...ne *L. B. 1798*.   like an Angel's head *L. B. 1800*.   103 The breezes blew *L. B. 1798, 1800*.   104 * The furrow stream'd off free *S. L. 1817*.   116 nor...nor] ne...ne *L. B. 1798*.

* In the former editions the line was,
   The furrow follow'd free:
But I had not been long on board a ship, before I perceived that this was the image as seen by a spectator from the shore, or from another vessel. From the ship itself, the *Wake* appears like a brook flowing off from the stern. *Note to S. L. 1817.*

THE RIME OF THE ANCIENT MARINER 191

As idle as a painted ship
Upon a painted ocean.

And the Albatross begins to be avenged.

Water, water, every where,
And all the boards did shrink; 120
Water, water, every where,
Nor any drop to drink.

The very deep did rot: O Christ!
That ever this should be!
Yea, slimy things did crawl with legs 125
Upon the slimy sea.

About, about, in reel and rout
The death-fires danced at night;
The water, like a witch's oils,
Burnt green, and blue and white. 130

A Spirit had followed them; one of the invisible inhabitants of this planet, neither departed souls nor angels; concerning whom the learned Jew, Josephus, and the Platonic Constantinopolitan, Michael Psellus, may be consulted. They are very numerous, and there is no climate or element without one or more.

And some in dreams assuréd were
Of the Spirit that plagued us so;
Nine fathom deep he had followed us
From the land of mist and snow.

And every tongue, through utter drought, 135
Was withered at the root;
We could not speak, no more than if
We had been choked with soot.

The shipmates, in their sore distress, would fain throw the whole guilt on the ancient Mariner: in sign whereof they hang the dead sea-bird round his neck.

Ah! well a-day! what evil looks
Had I from old and young! 140
Instead of the cross, the Albatross
About my neck was hung.

122 Nor] Ne *L. B. 1798.*   123 deep] deeps *L. B. 1798, 1800*
139 well a-day] wel-a-day *L.B. 1798, 1800.*

PART III

    There passed a weary time. Each throat
Was parched, and glazed each eye.
A weary time! a weary time!   145
How glazed each weary eye,
When looking westward, I beheld
A something in the sky.

The ancient Mariner beholdeth a sign in the element afar off.

    At first it seemed a little speck,
And then it seemed a mist;   150
It moved and moved, and took at last
A certain shape, I wist.

    A speck, a mist, a shape, I wist!
And still it neared and neared:
As if it dodged a water-sprite,   155
It plunged and tacked and veered.

At its nearer approach, it seemeth him to be a ship; and at a dear ransom he freeth his speech from the bonds of thirst.

    With throats unslaked, with black lips baked,
We could nor laugh nor wail;
Through utter drought all dumb we stood!
I bit my arm, I sucked the blood,   160
And cried, A sail! a sail!

    With throats unslaked, with black lips baked,
Agape they heard me call:

Between 143 *and* 149
        I saw a something in the sky
          No bigger than my fist;
        At first it seem'd, &c. *L. B. 1798.*

Between 143 *and* 147
         So past a weary time, each throat
           Was parch'd and glaz'd each eye,
        When looking westward, &c. *L. B. 1800.*

[Lines 143–8 of the text in their present shape were added in *Sibylline Leaves, 1817.*]

PART III] III *L. B. 1798, 1800*: The Rime of the Ancient Mariner, Part the Third, *S. L. 1828, 1829.*

154 And still it ner'd and ner'd. *L. B. 1798, 1800.*   155 And, an it dodg'd *L. B. 1798*: And, as if it dodg'd *L. B. 1800, S. L. 1817.*

157–60   With throat unslack'd with black lips baked
        Ne could we laugh, ne wail,
      Then while thro' drouth all dumb they stood
    I bit my arm, and suck'd the blood *L. B. 1798.*

157 With throat unslack'd, &c. *L. B. 1800, 1802, S. L. 1817.*   160 Till I bit my arm and suck'd the blood *L. B. 1800.*   162 With throat unslack'd, &c. *L. B. 1798, 1800, 1802, S. L. 1817.*

THE RIME OF THE ANCIENT MARINER 193

<small>A flash of joy;</small>

Gramercy! they for joy did grin,
And all at once their breath drew in,   165
As they were drinking all.

<small>And horror follows. For can it be a ship that comes onward without wind or tide?</small>

See! see! (I cried) she tacks no more!
Hither to work us weal;
Without a breeze, without a tide,
She steadies with upright keel!   170

The western wave was all a-flame.
The day was well nigh done!
Almost upon the western wave
Rested the broad bright Sun;
When that strange shape drove suddenly   175
Betwixt us and the Sun.

<small>It seemeth him but the skeleton of a ship.</small>

And straight the Sun was flecked with bars,
(Heaven's Mother send us grace!)
As if through a dungeon-grate he peered
With broad and burning face.   180

Alas! (thought I, and my heart beat loud)
How fast she nears and nears!
Are those *her* sails that glance in the Sun,
Like restless gossameres?

<small>And its ribs are seen as bars on the face of the setting Sun.</small>

<small>The Spectre-Woman and her Death-mate, and no other on board the skeleton ship.</small>

Are those *her* ribs through which the Sun   185
Did peer, as through a grate?
And is that Woman all her crew?
Is that a DEATH? and are there two?
Is DEATH that woman's mate?

167-70   She doth not tack from side to side—
       Hither to work us weal.
   Withouten wind, withouten tide
       She steddies with upright keel. *L. B. 1798.*

170 She steddies *L. B. 1800, S. L. 1817.*   177 straight] strait *L. B. 1798, 1800.*   182 neres and neres *L. B. 1798, 1800.*   183 *her*] her *1834, and also in* 185 *and* 190.

Between 184-90   Are those her naked ribs, which fleck'd
     The sun that did behind them peer?
  And are those two all, all the crew,*
     That woman and her fleshless Pheere?

  His bones were black with many a crack,
     All black and bare I ween;
  Jet-black and bare, save where with rust
  Of mouldy damps and charnel crust
     They're patch'd with purple and green. *L. B. 1798.*

     * those] these *Errata, L. B. 1798.*

Like vessel, like crew!

Death and Life-in-Death have diced for the ship's crew, and she (the latter) winneth the ancient Mariner.

Her lips were red, *her* looks were free,   190
Her locks were yellow as gold:
Her skin was as white as leprosy,
The Night-mare LIFE-IN-DEATH was she,
Who thicks man's blood with cold.

The naked hulk alongside came,   195
And the twain were casting dice;
'The game is done! I've won! I've won!'
Quoth she, and whistles thrice.

Are those *her* ribs which fleck'd the Sun
  Like the bars of a dungeon grate?
And are those two all, all the crew
  That woman and her mate?
                MS. Correction of S. T. C. in L. B. 1798.

Are those *her* Ribs, thro' which the Sun
  Did peer as thro' a grate?
And are those two all, all her crew,
  That Woman, and her Mate?
His bones were black with many a crack
.   .   .   .
They were patch'd with purple and green.   *L. B. 1800.*

This Ship it was a plankless thing,
—A bare Anatomy!
A plankless spectre—and it mov'd
Like a Being of the Sea!
The Woman and a fleshless Man
Therein sate merrily.

His bones were black, &c. (as in *1800*).

This stanza was found added in the handwriting of the Poet in the margin of a copy of the Bristol Edition [1798] of *Lyrical Ballads*. It is here printed for the first time. *Note P. and D. W.*, 1877–80, ii. 36.

190-4.   *Her* lips are red, *her* looks are free,
         Her locks are yellow as gold:
       Her skin is as white as leprosy,
       And she is far liker Death than he;
         Her flesh makes the still air cold.   *L. B. 1798.*

       Her lips were red, *her* looks were free,
         Her locks were as yellow as gold:
       Her skin was as white as leprosy,
       And she was far liker Death than he;
         Her flesh made the still air cold.   *L. B. 1800.*

196 casting] playing *L. B. 1798, 1800.*   197 The game is done, I've, I've won *S. L. 1817, 1828, 1829, 1834, 1844.* The restoration of the text of 1798 and 1800 dates from 1852.   198 whistles] whistled *L. B. 1798, 1800.*

THE RIME OF THE ANCIENT MARINER 195

<small>No twilight within the [1] courts of the Sun.</small>

The Sun's rim dips; the stars rush out:
At one stride comes the dark;   200
With far-heard whisper, o'er the sea,
Off shot the spectre-bark.

<small>At the rising of the Moon,</small>

We listened and looked sideways up!
Fear at my heart, as at a cup,
My life-blood seemed to sip!   205
The stars were dim, and thick the night,
The steersman's face by his lamp gleamed white;
From the sails the dew did drip—

[1] *Om.* in *Sibylline Leaves, 1817.*

Between 198–218 A gust of wind sterte up behind
  And whistled thro' his bones;
 Thro' the { holes of his eyes and the hole of his mouth
      hole *L. B. 1802, 1805*
 Half-whistles and half-groans.

With never a whisper in the Sea
 Off darts the Spectre-ship;
While clombe above the Eastern bar
The horned Moon with one bright Star
 Almost atween the tips.
 [Almost between the tips. *L. B. 1800.*]

One after one by the horned Moon
 (Listen, O Stranger! to me)
Each turn'd his face with a ghastly pang
 And curs'd me with his ee.

Four times fifty living men,
 With never a sigh or groan, *L. B. 1798, 1800.*

Between 198–9 A gust of wind ... half groans. *S. L.* (Page 15 erase the second stanza. *Errata, S. L.,* p. [xi].)

Between 201–12

With never a whisper on the main
 Off shot the spectre ship;
And stifled words and groans of pain
 Mix'd on each { murmuring } lip.
        trembling
And we look'd round, and we look'd up,
And fear at our hearts, as at a cup,
 The Life-blood seem'd to sip—

The sky was dull, and dark the night,
The helmsman's face by his lamp gleam'd bright,
 From the sails the dews did drip—
Till clomb above the Eastern Bar,
The horned Moon, with one bright star
 Within its nether tip.
    Undated MS. correction of S. T. C. (first published 1893).

208 dew] dews *S. L. 1817.*

                    Till clomb above the eastern bar
                    The hornéd Moon, with one bright star   210
                    Within the nether tip.

One after   One after one, by the star-dogged Moon,
another,   Too quick for groan or sigh,
                    Each turned his face with a ghastly pang,
                    And cursed me with his eye.   215

His shipmates   Four times fifty living men,
drop down   (And I heard nor sigh nor groan)
dead.   With heavy thump, a lifeless lump,
                    They dropped down one by one.

But Life-in-   The souls did from their bodies fly,—   220
Death begins   They fled to bliss or woe!
her work on   And every soul, it passed me by,
the ancient   Like the whizz of my cross-bow!
Mariner.

Part IV

The Wedding-   'I fear thee, ancient Mariner!
Guest feareth   I fear thy skinny hand!   225
that a Spirit   And thou art long, and lank, and brown,
is talking to   As is the ribbed sea-sand.[1]
him;

                    I fear thee and thy glittering eye,
                    And thy skinny hand, so brown.'—
But the   Fear not, fear not, thou Wedding-Guest!   230
ancient Ma-   This body dropt not down.
riner assureth
him of his
bodily life, and   Alone, alone, all, all alone,
proceedeth to   Alone on a wide wide sea!
relate his hor-   And never a saint took pity on
rible penance.   My soul in agony.   235

He despiseth   The many men, so beautiful!
the creatures   And they all dead did lie:
of the calm,

---

[1] For the last two lines of this stanza, I am indebted to Mr. WORDSWORTH. It was on a delightful walk from Nether Stowey to Dulverton, with him and his sister, in the Autumn of 1797, that this Poem was planned, and in part composed. [Note by S. T. C., first printed in *Sibylline Leaves*.]

---

209 clomb] clombe *S. L. 1817, 1828*.

PART IV] IV. *L. B. 1798, 1800*: The Rime of the Ancient Mariner, Part the Fourth *S. L. 1828, 1829*.

220 The] Their *L. B. 1798, 1800*.   224 ancyent Marinere *L. B. 1798*.

233-4   Alone on the wide wide sea;
            And Christ would take no pity on *L. B. 1798, 1800*.

THE RIME OF THE ANCIENT MARINER 197

    And a thousand thousand slimy things
    Lived on; and so did I.

<small>And envieth that *they* should live, and so many lie dead.</small>
    I looked upon the rotting sea,   240
    And drew my eyes away;
    I looked upon the rotting deck,
    And there the dead men lay.

    I looked to heaven, and tried to pray;
    But or ever a prayer had gusht,   245
    A wicked whisper came, and made
    My heart as dry as dust.

    I closed my lids, and kept them close,
    And the balls like pulses beat;
    For the sky and the sea, and the sea and the sky 250
    Lay like a load on my weary eye,
    And the dead were at my feet.

<small>But the curse liveth for him in the eye of the dead men.</small>
    The cold sweat melted from their limbs,
    Nor rot nor reek did they:
    The look with which they looked on me   255
    Had never passed away.

    An orphan's curse would drag to hell
    A spirit from on high;
    But oh! more horrible than that
    Is the curse in a dead man's eye!   260
    Seven days, seven nights, I saw that curse,
    And yet I could not die.

<small>In his loneliness and fixedness he yearneth towards the journeying Moon, and the stars that still sojourn, yet still move onward; and every where the blue sky belongs to</small>
    The moving Moon went up the sky,
    And no where did abide:
    Softly she was going up,   265
    And a star or two beside—

    Her beams bemocked the sultry main,
    Like April hoar-frost spread;
    But where the ship's huge shadow lay,
    The charmèd water burnt alway   270
    A still and awful red.

<small>them, and is their appointed rest, and their native country and their own natural homes, which they enter unannounced, as lords that are certainly expected and yet there is a silent joy at their arrival.</small>

<small>238 And a million, million slimy things *L. B. 1798, 1800.*   242 rotting] eldritch *L. B. 1798*: ghastly *L. B. 1800.*   249 And] Till *L. B. 1798, 1800.*   251 load] cloud *S. L.* (for *cloud* read *load. Errata, S. L.*, p. [xi]).   254 Ne rot, ne reek *L. B. 1798.*   260 the curse] a curse *1828, 1829.*   268 Like morning frosts yspread *L. B. 1798.*</small>

198 THE RIME OF THE ANCIENT MARINER

<small>By the light of the Moon he beholdeth God's creatures of the great calm.</small>

Beyond the shadow of the ship,
I watched the water-snakes:
They moved in tracks of shining white,
And when they reared, the elfish light   275
Fell off in hoary flakes.

Within the shadow of the ship
I watched their rich attire:
Blue, glossy green, and velvet black,
They coiled and swam; and every track   280
Was a flash of golden fire.

<small>Their beauty and their happiness.</small>

O happy living things! no tongue
Their beauty might declare:
A spring of love gushed from my heart,

<small>He blesseth them in his heart.</small>

And I blessed them unaware: 285
Sure my kind saint took pity on me,
And I blessed them unaware.

<small>The spell begins to break.</small>

The self-same moment I could pray;
And from my neck so free
The Albatross fell off, and sank   290
Like lead into the sea.

Part V

Oh sleep! it is a gentle thing,
Beloved from pole to pole!
To Mary Queen the praise be given!
She sent the gentle sleep from Heaven,   295
That slid into my soul.

<small>By grace of the holy Mother, the ancient Mariner is refreshed with rain.</small>

The silly buckets on the deck,
That had so long remained,
I dreamt that they were filled with dew;
And when I awoke, it rained.   300

My lips were wet, my throat was cold,
My garments all were dank;
Sure I had drunken in my dreams,
And still my body drank.

Part V] V. *L. B. 1798, 1800*: The Rime of the Ancient Mariner, Part the Fifth *S. L. 1828, 1829*.
  294 To Mary-queen *L. B. 1798, 1800*.   given] yeven *L. B. 1798*.   300 awoke] woke (*a pencilled correction in 1828, ? by S. T. C.*).

THE RIME OF THE ANCIENT MARINER 199

I moved, and could not feel my limbs: 305
I was so light—almost
I thought that I had died in sleep,
And was a blessèd ghost.

He heareth sounds and seeth strange sights and commotions in the sky and the element.

And soon I heard a roaring wind:
It did not come anear;   310
But with its sound it shook the sails,
That were so thin and sere.

The upper air burst into life!
And a hundred fire-flags sheen,
To and fro they were hurried about!   315
And to and fro, and in and out,
The wan stars danced between.

And the coming wind did roar more loud,
And the sails did sigh like sedge;
And the rain poured down from one black cloud;   320
The Moon was at its edge.

The thick black cloud was cleft, and still
The Moon was at its side:
Like waters shot from some high crag,
The lightning fell with never a jag,   325
A river steep and wide.

The bodies of the ship's crew are inspired [inspirited, S. L.] and the ship moves on;

The loud wind never reached the ship,
Yet now the ship moved on!
Beneath the lightning and the Moon
The dead men gave a groan.   330

They groaned, they stirred, they all uprose,
Nor spake, nor moved their eyes;

309 The roaring wind! it roar'd far off *L. B. 1798.*   313 burst] bursts *L. B. 1798.*   315 were] are *L. B. 1798.*   317 The stars dance on between. *L. B. 1798.*

317-24   The coming wind doth roar more loud;
       The sails do sigh, like sedge:
    The rain pours down from one black cloud
       And the Moon is at its edge.
    Hark! hark! the thick black cloud is cleft,
       And the Moon is at its side *L. B. 1798.*

325 fell] falls *L. B. 1798.*

327-8   The strong wind reach'd the ship: it roar'd
       And dropp'd down like a stone! *L. B. 1798.*

332 nor ... nor] ne ... ne *L. B. 1798.*

200 THE RIME OF THE ANCIENT MARINER

It had been strange, even in a dream,
To have seen those dead men rise.

The helmsman steered, the ship moved on; 335
Yet never a breeze up-blew;
The mariners all 'gan work the ropes,
Where they were wont to do;
They raised their limbs like lifeless tools—
We were a ghastly crew. 340

The body of my brother's son
Stood by me, knee to knee:
The body and I pulled at one rope,
But he said nought to me.

But not by the souls of the men, nor by dæmons of earth or middle air, but by a blessed troop of angelic spirits, sent down by the invocation of the guardian saint.

'I fear thee, ancient Mariner!' 345
Be calm, thou Wedding-Guest!
'Twas not those souls that fled in pain,
Which to their corses came again,
But a troop of spirits blest:

For when it dawned—they dropped their arms,
And clustered round the mast; 351
Sweet sounds rose slowly through their mouths,
And from their bodies passed.

Around, around, flew each sweet sound,
Then darted to the Sun; 355
Slowly the sounds came back again,
Now mixed, now one by one.

Sometimes a-dropping from the sky
I heard the sky-lark sing;
Sometimes all little birds that are, 360
How they seemed to fill the sea and air
With their sweet jargoning!

And now 'twas like all instruments,
Now like a lonely flute;
And now it is an angel's song, 365
That makes the heavens be mute.

Between 344–5
    And I quak'd to think of my own voice
      How frightful it would be! *L. B. 1798.*

345–9 *om. in L. B. 1798, added in L. B. 1800.*   350 The daylight dawn'd
L. B. 1798.   359 sky-lark] Lavrock *L. B. 1798*

It ceased; yet still the sails made on
A pleasant noise till noon,
A noise like of a hidden brook
In the leafy month of June,   370
That to the sleeping woods all night
Singeth a quiet tune.

Till noon we quietly sailed on,
Yet never a breeze did breathe:
Slowly and smoothly went the ship,   375
Moved onward from beneath.

The lonesome Spirit from the south-pole carries on the ship as far as the Line, in obedience to the angelic troop, but still requireth vengeance.

Under the keel nine fathom deep,
From the land of mist and snow,
The spirit slid: and it was he
That made the ship to go.   380
The sails at noon left off their tune,
And the ship stood still also.

The Sun, right up above the mast,
Had fixed her to the ocean:
But in a minute she 'gan stir,   385
With a short uneasy motion—
Backwards and forwards half her length
With a short uneasy motion.

Then like a pawing horse let go,
She made a sudden bound: 390

Between 372-3

  Listen, O listen, thou Wedding-guest!
  'Marinere! thou hast thy will:
'For that, which comes out of thine eye, doth make
  'My body and soul to be still.'

  Never sadder tale was told
    To a man of woman born:
  Sadder and wiser thou wedding-guest!
    Thou't rise to-morrow morn.

  Never sadder tale was heard
    By a man of woman born:
  The Marineres all return'd to work
    As silent as beforne.

  The Marineres all 'gan pull the ropes,
    But look at me they n'old;
  Thought I, I am as thin as air—
    They cannot me behold. *L. B.* 1798.

373 quietly] silently *L. B.* 1798, 1800.

It flung the blood into my head,
And I fell down in a swound.

<small>The Polar Spirit's fellow-dæmons, the invisible inhabitants of the element, take part in his wrong; and two of them relate, one to the other, that penance long and heavy for the ancient Mariner hath been accorded to the Polar Spirit, who returneth southward.</small>

How long in that same fit I lay,
I have not to declare;
But ere my living life returned, 395
I heard and in my soul discerned
Two voices in the air.

'Is it he?' quoth one, 'Is this the man?
By him who died on cross,
With his cruel bow he laid full low 400
The harmless Albatross.

The spirit who bideth by himself
In the land of mist and snow,
He loved the bird that loved the man
Who shot him with his bow.' 405

The other was a softer voice,
As soft as honey-dew:
Quoth he, 'The man hath penance done,
And penance more will do.'

PART VI

FIRST VOICE

'But tell me, tell me! speak again, 410
Thy soft response renewing—
What makes that ship drive on so fast?
What is the ocean doing?'

SECOND VOICE

'Still as a slave before his lord,
The ocean hath no blast; 415
His great bright eye most silently
Up to the Moon is cast—

If he may know which way to go;
For she guides him smooth or grim.
See, brother, see! how graciously 420
She looketh down on him.'

392 down in] into *L. B. 1798, 1800.*
PART VI] VI. *L. B. 1798, 1800*: The Rime of the Ancient Mariner. Part the Sixth *S. L. 1828, 1829.*

FIRST VOICE

<small>The Mariner hath been cast into a trance; for the angelic power causeth the vessel to drive northward faster than human life could endure.</small>

'But why drives on that ship so fast,
Without or wave or wind?'

SECOND VOICE

'The air is cut away before,
And closes from behind. 425

Fly, brother, fly! more high, more high!
Or we shall be belated:
For slow and slow that ship will go,
When the Mariner's trance is abated.'

<small>The supernatural motion is retarded; the Mariner awakes, and his penance begins anew.</small>

I woke, and we were sailing on 430
As in a gentle weather:
'Twas night, calm night, the moon was high;
The dead men stood together.

All stood together on the deck,
For a charnel-dungeon fitter: 435
All fixed on me their stony eyes,
That in the Moon did glitter.

The pang, the curse, with which they died,
Had never passed away:
I could not draw my eyes from theirs, 440
Nor turn them up to pray.

<small>The curse is finally expiated.</small>

And now this spell was snapt: once more
I viewed the ocean green,
And looked far forth, yet little saw
Of what had else been seen— 445

Like one, that on a lonesome road
Doth walk in fear and dread,
And having once turned round walks on,
And turns no more his head;
Because he knows, a frightful fiend 450
Doth close behind him tread.

---

423 Withouten wave *L. B. 1798*.   440-1 een from theirs; Ne turn *L. B. 1798*.
442-6   And in its time the spell was snapt,
    And I could move my een:
 I look'd far-forth, but little saw
    Of what might else be seen. *L. B. 1798*.
446 lonesome] lonely *L. B. 1798*.

But soon there breathed a wind on me,
Nor sound nor motion made:
Its path was not upon the sea,
In ripple or in shade. 455

It raised my hair, it fanned my cheek
Like a meadow-gale of spring—
It mingled strangely with my fears,
Yet it felt like a welcoming.

Swiftly, swiftly flew the ship, 460
Yet she sailed softly too:
Sweetly, sweetly blew the breeze—
On me alone it blew.

And the ancient Mariner beholdeth his native country.

Oh! dream of joy! is this indeed
The light-house top I see? 465
Is this the hill? is this the kirk?
Is this mine own countree?

We drifted o'er the harbour-bar,
And I with sobs did pray—
O let me be awake, my God! 470
Or let me sleep alway.

The harbour-bay was clear as glass,
So smoothly it was strewn!
And on the bay the moonlight lay,
And the shadow of the Moon. 475

453 Nor ... nor] Ne ... ne *L. B. 1798.*   464 O dream *L. B. 1798, 1800.*
Between 475-80

> The moonlight bay was white all o'er,
> Till rising from the same,
> Full many shapes, that shadows were,
> Like as of torches came.
>
> A little distance from the prow
> Those dark-red shadows were;
> But soon I saw that my own flesh
> Was red as in a glare.
>
> I turn'd my head in fear and dread,
> And by the holy rood,
> The bodies had advanc'd, and now
> Before the mast they stood.
>
> They lifted up their stiff right arms,
> They held them strait and tight;
> And each right-arm burnt like a torch,
> A torch that's borne upright.
> Their stony eye-balls glitter'd on
> In the red and smoky light.

THE RIME OF THE ANCIENT MARINER 205

    The rock shone bright, the kirk no less,
    That stands above the rock:
    The moonlight steeped in silentness
    The steady weathercock.

    And the bay was white with silent light,   480
    Till rising from the same,
The angelic spirits leave the dead bodies,   Full many shapes, that shadows were,
    In crimson colours came.

And appear in their own forms of light.   A little distance from the prow
    Those crimson shadows were: 485
    I turned my eyes upon the deck—
    Oh, Christ! what saw I there!

    Each corse lay flat, lifeless and flat,
    And, by the holy rood!
    A man all light, a seraph-man,   490
    On every corse there stood.

    This seraph-band, each waved his hand:
    It was a heavenly sight!
    They stood as signals to the land,
    Each one a lovely light;   495

    This seraph-band, each waved his hand,
    No voice did they impart—
    No voice; but oh! the silence sank
    Like music on my heart.

    But soon I heard the dash of oars,   500
    I heard the Pilot's cheer;
    My head was turned perforce away
    And I saw a boat appear.

  I pray'd and turn'd my head away
    Forth looking as before.
  There was no breeze upon the bay,
    No wave against the shore. *L. B. 1798.*

487 Oh, Christ!] O Christ *L. B. 1798, 1800.*   498 oh!] O *L. B. 1798, 1800.*   500 But soon] Eftsones *L. B. 1798.*
Between 503-4
    Then vanish'd all the lovely lights;*
     The bodies rose anew:
    With silent pace, each to his place,
     Came back the ghastly crew,
    The wind, that shade nor motion made,
     On me alone it blew. *L. B. 1798.*

 * Then vanish'd all the lovely lights,
   The spirits of the air,
 No souls of mortal men were they,
   But spirits bright and fair.
     MS. Correction by S. T. C. in a copy of L. B. 1798.

The Pilot and the Pilot's boy,
I heard them coming fast:
Dear Lord in Heaven! it was a joy   505
The dead men could not blast.

I saw a third—I heard his voice:
It is the Hermit good!
He singeth loud his godly hymns   510
That he makes in the wood.
He'll shrieve my soul, he'll wash away
The Albatross's blood.

Part VII

The Hermit of the Wood,

This Hermit good lives in that wood
Which slopes down to the sea.   515
How loudly his sweet voice he rears!
He loves to talk with marineres
That come from a far countree.

He kneels at morn, and noon, and eve—
He hath a cushion plump: 520
It is the moss that wholly hides
The rotted old oak-stump.

The skiff-boat neared: I heard them talk,
'Why, this is strange, I trow!
Where are those lights so many and fair, 525
That signal made but now?'

Approacheth the ship with wonder.

'Strange, by my faith!' the Hermit said—
'And they answered not our cheer!
The planks looked warped! and see those sails,
How thin they are and sere!   530
I never saw aught like to them,
Unless perchance it were

Brown skeletons of leaves that lag
My forest-brook along;

---

511 makes] maketh (*a pencilled correction in 1828, ? by S. T. C.*).
PART VII] VII. *L. B. 1798, 1800*: The Rime of the Ancient Mariner, Part the Seventh *S. L. 1829*: The Ancient Mariner. Part the Seventh *1828*.
517 marineres] mariners *L. B. 1800*.   518 That come from a far Contrée. *L. B. 1798*.   523 neared] ner'd *L. B. 1798, 1800*.   529 looked] look *L. B. 1798, 1800, S. L.*   533 Brown] The *L. R. 1798, 1800, S. L.* [for *The* read *Brown. Errata, S. L. 1817*, p. (xi)].

When the ivy-tod is heavy with snow, 535
And the owlet whoops to the wolf below,
That eats the she-wolf's young.'

'Dear Lord! it hath a fiendish look—
(The Pilot made reply)
I am a-feared'—'Push on, push on!' 540
Said the Hermit cheerily.

The boat came closer to the ship,
But I nor spake nor stirred;
The boat came close beneath the ship,
And straight a sound was heard. 545

The ship suddenly sinketh.

Under the water it rumbled on,
Still louder and more dread:
It reached the ship, it split the bay;
The ship went down like lead.

The ancient Mariner is saved in the Pilot's boat.

Stunned by that loud and dreadful sound, 550
Which sky and ocean smote,
Like one that hath been seven days drowned
My body lay afloat;
But swift as dreams, myself I found
Within the Pilot's boat. 555

Upon the whirl, where sank the ship,
The boat spun round and round;
And all was still, save that the hill
Was telling of the sound.

I moved my lips—the Pilot shrieked 560
And fell down in a fit;
The holy Hermit raised his eyes,
And prayed where he did sit.

I took the oars: the Pilot's boy,
Who now doth crazy go, 565
Laughed loud and long, and all the while
His eyes went to and fro.
'Ha! ha!' quoth he, 'full plain I see,
The Devil knows how to row.'

And now, all in my own countree, 570
I stood on the firm land!
The Hermit stepped forth from the boat,
And scarcely he could stand.

543 nor . . . nor] ne . . . ne *L. B.* 1798.

208 THE RIME OF THE ANCIENT MARINER

The ancient Mariner earnestly entreateth the Hermit to shrieve him; and the penance of life falls on him.

'O shrieve me, shrieve me, holy man!'
The Hermit crossed his brow. 575
'Say quick,' quoth he, 'I bid thee say—
What manner of man art thou?'

Forthwith this frame of mine was wrenched
With a woful agony,
Which forced me to begin my tale; 580
And then it left me free.

And ever and anon throughout his future life an agony constraineth him to travel from land to land;

Since then, at an uncertain hour,
That agony returns:
And till my ghastly tale is told,
This heart within me burns. 585

I pass, like night, from land to land;
I have strange power of speech;
That moment that his face I see,
I know the man that must hear me:
To him my tale I teach. 590

What loud uproar bursts from that door!
The wedding-guests are there:
But in the garden-bower the bride
And bride-maids singing are:
And hark the little vesper bell, 595
Which biddeth me to prayer!

O Wedding-Guest! this soul hath been
Alone on a wide wide sea:
So lonely 'twas, that God himself
Scarce seemed there to be. 600

O sweeter than the marriage-feast,
'Tis sweeter far to me,
To walk together to the kirk
With a goodly company!—

To walk together to the kirk, 605
And all together pray,
While each to his great Father bends,
Old men, and babes, and loving friends
And youths and maidens gay!

577 What manner man *L. B. 1798, 1800.*
582-5   Since then at an uncertain hour,
    Now ofttimes and now fewer,
That anguish comes and makes me tell
    My ghastly aventure. *L. B. 1798.*

583 agony] agency [*a misprint*] *L. B. 1800.*   588 That] The *L. B. 1798, 1800.*

And to teach, by his own example, love and reverence to all things that God made and loveth.

Farewell, farewell! but this I tell 610
To thee, thou Wedding-Guest!
He prayeth well, who loveth well
Both man and bird and beast.

He prayeth best, who loveth best
All things both great and small; 615
For the dear God who loveth us,
He made and loveth all.

The Mariner, whose eye is bright,
Whose beard with age is hoar,
Is gone: and now the Wedding-Guest 620
Turned from the bridegroom's door.

He went like one that hath been stunned,
And is of sense forlorn:
A sadder and a wiser man,
He rose the morrow morn. 625

1797–1798.

SONNETS ATTEMPTED IN THE MANNER OF CONTEMPORARY WRITERS[1]

[SIGNED 'NEHEMIAH HIGGINBOTTOM']

I

Pensive at eve on the *hard* world I mus'd,
And *my poor* heart was sad: so at the Moon

---

[1] First published in the *Monthly Magazine* for November, 1797. They were reprinted in the *Poetical Register* for 1803 (1805); by Coleridge in the *Biographia Literaria*, 1817, i. 26–8*; and by Cottle in *Early Recollections*, i. 290–2; and in *Reminiscences*, p. 160. They were first collected in *P. and D. W.*, 1877–80, i. 211–13.

* 'Under the name of Nehemiah Higginbottom I contributed three sonnets, the first of which had for its object to excite a good-natured laugh at the spirit of doleful egotism and at the recurrence of favourite phrases, with the double defect of being at once trite and licentious. The second was on low creeping language and thoughts under the pretence of *simplicity*. The third, the phrases of which were borrowed entirely from my own poems, on the indiscriminate use of elaborate and swelling language and imagery. . . . So general at the time and so decided was the opinion

---

610 Farewell, farewell]. *The comma to be omitted. Errata, L. B. 1798.* 618 The Marinere *L. B. 1798.*
Sonnets, &c.—Title] Sonnet I *M. M.*

I gaz'd—and sigh'd, and sigh'd!—for, ah! how soon
Eve darkens into night. Mine eye perus'd
With tearful vacancy the *dampy* grass
Which wept and glitter'd in the *paly* ray;
And *I did pause me* on my lonely way,
And *mused me* on those *wretched ones* who pass
O'er the black heath of Sorrow. But, alas!
Most of *Myself* I thought: when it befell
That the *sooth* Spirit of the breezy wood
Breath'd in mine ear—'All this is very well;
But much of *one* thing is for *no* thing good.'
Ah! my *poor heart's* INEXPLICABLE SWELL!

II

TO SIMPLICITY

O! I do love thee, meek *Simplicity*!
For of thy lays the lulling simpleness
Goes to my heart and soothes each small distress,
Distress though small, yet haply great to me!
'Tis true on Lady Fortune's gentlest pad
I amble on; yet, though I know not why,
So sad I am!—but should a friend and I
Grow cool and *miff*, O! I am *very* sad!

concerning the characteristic vices of my style that a celebrated physician (now alas! no more) speaking of me in other respects with his usual kindness to a gentleman who was about to meet me at a dinner-party could not, however, resist giving him a hint not to mention *The House that Jack Built* in my presence, for that I was as sore as a boil about that sonnet, he not knowing that I was myself the author of it.'

Coleridge's first account of these sonnets in a letter to Cottle [November, 1797] is much to the same effect :—' I sent to the *Monthly Magazine* (1797) three mock Sonnets in ridicule of my own Poems, and Charles Lloyd's and Lamb's, etc., etc., exposing that affectation of unaffectedness, of jumping and misplaced accent in common-place epithets, flat lines forced into poetry by italics (signifying how well and mouthishly the author would read them), puny pathos, etc., etc. The instances were almost all taken from myself and Lloyd and Lamb. I signed them " Nehemiah Higginbottom". I think they may do good to our young Bards.' [*E. R.*, i. 289 ; *Rem.* 160.]

Sonnets, &c.—1. 4 darkens] saddens *B. L.*, i. 27. 6 Which] That *B. L.*, i. 27. 8 those] the *B. L.*, i. 27. who] that *B. L.*, i. 27. 9 black] bleak *B. L.*, i. 27. 14 Ah!] Oh! *B. L.*, i. 27. 11] Sonnet II. To Simplicity *M. M.* : no title in *B. L.* 6 yet, though] and yet *B. L.*, i. 27. 8 Frown, pout and part then I am *very* sad *B. L.*, i. 27.

OF CONTEMPORARY WRITERS

And then with sonnets and with sympathy
My dreamy bosom's mystic woes I pall; 10
Now of my false friend plaining plaintively,
Now raving at mankind in general;
But, whether sad or fierce, 'tis simple all,
All very simple, meek Simplicity!

III

ON A RUINED HOUSE IN A ROMANTIC COUNTRY

AND this reft house is that the which he built,
Lamented Jack! And here his malt he pil'd,
Cautious in vain! These rats that squeak so wild,
Squeak, not unconscious of their father's guilt.
Did ye not see her gleaming thro' the glade? 5
Belike, 'twas she, the maiden all forlorn.
What though she milk no cow with crumpled horn,
Yet *aye* she haunts the dale where *erst* she stray'd;
And *aye* beside her stalks her amorous knight!
Still on his thighs their wonted brogues are worn, 10
And thro' those brogues, still tatter'd and betorn,
His hindward charms gleam an unearthly white;
As when thro' broken clouds at night's high noon
Peeps in fair fragments forth the full-orb'd harvest-moon!

1797.

PARLIAMENTARY OSCILLATORS[1]

ALMOST awake? Why, what is this, and whence,
  O ye right loyal men, all undefiléd?
Sure, 'tis not possible that Common-Sense
  Has hitch'd her pullies to each heavy eye-lid?

---

[1] First published in the *Cambridge Intelligencer*, January 6, 1798: included in *Sibylline Leaves*, 1817: *Essays on His own Times*, 1850, iii. 969-70. First collected in *P. and D. W.*, 1877-80. In *Sibylline Leaves* the poem is incorrectly dated 1794.

---

12 in gener-al *Cottle, E. R.*, i. 288.
III] Sonnet III. To, &c. *M. M.*   10 their] his *Cottle, E. R.*, i. 292.   13 As when] Ah! thus *B. L.*, i. 27.
Parliamentary Oscillators—Title] To Sir John Sinclair, S. Thornton, Alderman Lushington, and the whole Troop of Parliamentary Oscillators *C. I.*
2 right] tight *C. I.*   3 It's hardly possible *C. I.*

212 PARLIAMENTARY OSCILLATORS

Yet wherefore else that start, which discomposes 5
  The drowsy waters lingering in your eye?
  And are you *really* able to descry
That precipice three yards beyond your noses?

Yet flatter you I cannot, that your wit
  Is much improved by this long loyal dozing; 10
And I admire, no more than Mr. Pitt,
  Your jumps and starts of patriotic prosing—

Now cluttering to the Treasury Cluck, like chicken,
  Now with small beaks the ravenous *Bill* opposing;[1]
With serpent-tongue now stinging, and now licking, 15
  Now semi-sibilant, now smoothly glozing—

Now having faith implicit that he can't err,
  Hoping his hopes, alarm'd with his alarms;
And now believing him a sly inchanter,
  Yet still afraid to break his brittle charms, 20

Lest some mad Devil suddenly unhamp'ring,
  Slap-dash! the imp should fly off with the steeple,
On revolutionary broom-stick scampering.—
  O ye soft-headed and soft-hearted people,

If you can stay so long from slumber free, 25
  My muse shall make an effort to salute 'e:
For lo! a very dainty simile
  Flash'd sudden through my brain, and 'twill just suit 'e!

You know that water-fowl that cries, Quack! Quack!?
  Full often have I seen a waggish crew 30
Fasten the Bird of Wisdom on its back,
  The ivy-haunting bird, that cries, Tu-whoo!

Both plung'd together in the deep mill-stream,
  (Mill-stream, or farm-yard pond, or mountain-lake,)
Shrill, as a *Church and Constitution* scream, 35
  Tu-whoo! quoth Broad-face, and down dives the Drake!

---

[1] Pitt's 'treble assessment at seven millions' which formed part of the budget for 1798. The grant was carried in the House of Commons, Jan. 4, 1798.

---

9 But yet I cannot flatter you, your wit *C.I.*   14 the] his *C.I.*
24 O ye soft-hearted and soft-headed, &c. *C.I.*   26, 28 'e] ye *C.I.*
29 that cries] which cries *C.I.*   30 Full often] Ditch-full oft *C.I.*
31 Fasten] Fallen *C.I.*

The green-neck'd Drake once more pops up to view,
  Stares round, cries Quack! and makes an angry pother;
Then shriller screams the Bird with eye-lids blue,
  The broad-faced Bird! and deeper dives the other. 40
Ye *quacking* Statesmen! 'tis even so with you—
  One Peasecod is not liker to another.

Even so on Loyalty's Decoy-pond, each
  Pops up his head, as fir'd with British blood,
Hears once again the Ministerial screech, 45
  And once more seeks the bottom's blackest mud!
    1798.

(Signed: LABERIUS.)

CHRISTABEL [1]

PREFACE

The first part of the following poem was written in the year 1797, at Stowey, in the county of Somerset. The second part, after my return from Germany, in the year 1800, at Keswick, Cumberland. It is probable that if the

---

[1] First published, together with *Kubla Khan* and *The Pains of Sleep*, 1816: included in 1828, 1829, and 1834. Three MSS. of *Christabel* have passed through my hands. The earliest, which belonged to Wordsworth, is partly in Coleridge's handwriting and partly in that of Mary Hutchinson (Mrs. Wordsworth). The probable date of this MS., now in the possession of the poet's grandson, Mr. Gordon Wordsworth, is April–October, 1800. Later in the same year, or perhaps in 1801, Coleridge made a copy of the First Part (or Book), the Conclusion to the First Book, and the Second Book, and presented it to Mrs. Wordsworth's sister, Sarah Hutchinson. A facsimile of the MS., now in the possession of Miss Edith Coleridge, was issued in collotype in the edition of *Christabel* published in

---

Preface] Prefixed to the three issues of 1816, and to 1828, 1829, 1834.
  Christabel—Preface. 2 The year one thousand seven hundred and ninety seven *1816, 1828, 1829*. 3, 4 The year one thousand eight hundred *1816, 1828, 1829*. 4 *after* 'Cumberland'] Since the latter date, my poetic powers have been, till very lately, in a state of suspended animation. But as, in my very first conception of the tale, I had the whole present to my mind, with the wholeness, no less than the liveliness of a vision; I trust that I shall be able to embody in verse the three parts yet to come, in the course of the present year. *It is probable*, &c. *1816, 1828, 1829* : *om. 1834.*

poem had been finished at either of the former periods, or if even the first and second part had been published in the year 1800, the impression of its originality would have been much greater than I dare at present expect. But for this I have only my own indolence to blame. The dates are mentioned for the exclusive purpose of precluding charges of plagiarism or servile imitation from myself. For there is amongst us a set of critics, who seem to hold, that every possible thought and image is traditional; who have no notion that there are such things as fountains in the world, small as well as great; and who would therefore charitably derive every rill they behold flowing, from a perforation

1907, under the auspices of the Royal Society of Literature. In 1801, or at some subsequent period (possibly not till 1815), Miss Hutchinson transcribed Coleridge's MS. The water-mark of the paper is 1801. Her transcript, now in the possession of Mr. A. H. Hallam Murray, was sent to Lord Byron in October, 1815. It is possible that this transcription was the 'copy' for the First Edition published in 1816; but, if so, Coleridge altered the text whilst the poem was passing through the press.

The existence of two other MSS. rests on the authority of John Payne Collier (see *Seven Lectures on Shakespeare and Milton*. By S. T. Coleridge, 1856, pp. xxxix-xliii).

The first, which remained in his possession for many years, was a copy in the handwriting of Sarah Stoddart (afterwards Mrs. Hazlitt). J. P. Collier notes certain differences between this MS., which he calls the 'Salisbury Copy', and the text of the First Edition. He goes on to say that before *Christabel* was published Coleridge lent him an MS. in his own handwriting, and he gives two or three readings from the second MS. which differ from the text of the 'Salisbury Copy' and from the texts of those MSS. which have been placed in my hands.

The copy of the First Edition of *Christabel* presented to William Stewart Rose's valet, David Hinves, on November 11, 1816, which Coleridge had already corrected, is now in the possession of Mr. John Murray. The emendations and additions inscribed on the margin of this volume were included in the collected edition of Coleridge's *Poetical Works*, published by William Pickering in 1828. The editions of 1829 and 1834 closely followed the edition of 1828, but in 1834 there was in one particular instance (Part I, lines 6-10) a reversion to the text of the First Edition. The MS. of the 'Conclusion of Part II' forms part of a letter to Southey dated May 6, 1801. (*Letters of S. T. C.*, 1895, i. 355.) The following abbreviations have been employed to note the MSS. and transcriptions of *Christabel*:—

1. The Wordsworth MS., partly in Coleridge's (lines 1-295) and partly in Mary Hutchinson's (lines 295-655) handwriting = *MS. W.*
2. The Salisbury MS., copied by Sarah Stoddart = *S. T. C. (a).*
3. The MS. lent by Coleridge to Payne Collier = *S. T. C. (b).*
4. Autograph MS. in possession of Miss Edith Coleridge (reproduced in facsimile in 1907) = *S. T. C. (c).*
5. Transcription made by Sarah Hutchinson = *S. H.*
6. Corrections made by Coleridge in the Copy of the First Edition presented to David Hinves = *H. 1816.*

made in some other man's tank. I am confident, however, that as far as the present poem is concerned, the celebrated poets[1] whose writings I might be suspected of having imitated, either in particular passages, or in the tone and the spirit of the whole, would be among the first to vindicate me from the charge, and who, on any striking coincidence, would permit me to address them in this doggerel version of two monkish Latin hexameters.[2]

> 'Tis mine and it **is** likewise yours;
> But an if this will not do;
> Let it be mine, good friend! for I
> Am the poorer of the two.

I have only to add that the metre of Christabel is not, properly speaking, irregular, though it may seem so from its being founded on a new principle: namely, that of counting in each line the accents, not the syllables. Though the latter may vary from seven to twelve, yet in each line the accents will be found to be only four. Nevertheless, this occasional variation in number of syllables is not introduced wantonly, or for the mere ends of convenience, but in correspondence with some transition in the nature of the imagery or passion.

Part I

'Tis the middle of night by the castle clock,
And the owls have awakened the crowing cock;
Tu—whit!——Tu—whoo!
And hark, again! the crowing cock,
How drowsily it crew.

---

[1] Sir Walter Scott and Lord Byron.
[2] The 'Latin hexameters', 'in the lame and limping metre of a barbarous Latin poet', ran thus:
'Est meum et est tuum, amice! at si amborum nequit esse,
Sit meum, amice, precor: quia certe sum magi' pauper.'
It is interesting to note that Coleridge translated these lines in November, 1801, long before the 'celebrated poets' in question had made, or seemed to make, it desirable to 'preclude a charge of plagiarism'.

---

23 doggrel *1816, 1828, 1829*.
Part I] Book the First *MS. W., S. T. C. (c), S. H.*: Part the First *1828, 1829*.
3 Tu-u-whoo! Tu-u-whoo! *MS. W., S. T. C. (c), S. H.*

Sir Leoline, the Baron rich,
Hath a toothless mastiff bitch;
From her kennel beneath the rock
She maketh answer to the clock,
Four for the quarters, and twelve for the hour;   10
Ever and aye, by shine and shower,
Sixteen short howls, not over loud;
Some say, she sees my lady's shroud.

Is the night chilly and dark?
The night is chilly, but not dark.   15
The thin gray cloud is spread on high,
It covers but not hides the sky.
The moon is behind, and at the full;
And yet she looks both small and dull.
The night is chill, the cloud is gray: 20
'Tis a month before the month of May,
And the Spring comes slowly up this way.

The lovely lady, Christabel,
Whom her father loves so well,
What makes her in the wood so late,   25
A furlong from the castle gate?
She had dreams all yesternight
Of her own betrothéd knight;
And she in the midnight wood will pray
For the weal of her lover that's far away.   30

She stole along, she nothing spoke,
The sighs she heaved were soft and low,
And naught was green upon the oak
But moss and rarest misletoe:

6-7   Sir Leoline the Baron ~~bold~~
        Hath a toothless mastiff old *H. 1816*.
        Sir Leoline, the Baron rich,
        Hath a toothless mastiff which *H. 1816, 1828, 1829, 1893*.

9 She makes *MS. W., S. T. C. (c), S. H., First Edition*: Maketh *H. 1816, 1828, 1829*.   11 moonshine or shower *MS.W., S.T.C.(c), S.H., First Edition*: by shine or shower *H. 1816*.

Between 28-9   Dreams, that made her moan and leap,
                 As on her bed she lay in sleep.
                                First Edition: Erased *H. 1816*: Not in any *MS*.

32 The breezes they were whispering low *S. T. C. (a)*: The breezes they were still also *MS. W., S. T. C. (c), S. H., First Edition*.   34 But the moss and misletoe *MS. W., S. T. C. (c), S. H.*

She kneels beneath the huge oak tree, 35
And in silence prayeth she.

The lady sprang up suddenly,
The lovely lady, Christabel!
It moaned as near, as near can be,
But what it is she cannot tell.— 40
On the other side it seems to be,
Of the huge, broad-breasted, old oak tree.

The night is chill; the forest bare;
Is it the wind that moaneth bleak?
There is not wind enough in the air 45
To move away the ringlet curl
From the lovely lady's cheek—
There is not wind enough to twirl
The one red leaf, the last of its clan,
That dances as often as dance it can, 50
Hanging so light, and hanging so high,
On the topmost twig that looks up at the sky.

Hush, beating heart of Christabel!
Jesu, Maria, shield her well!
She folded her arms beneath her cloak, 55
And stole to the other side of the oak.
    What sees she there?

There she sees a damsel bright,
Drest in a silken robe of white,
That shadowy in the moonlight shone: 60
The neck that made that white robe wan,
Her stately neck, and arms were bare;
Her blue-veined feet unsandal'd were,
And wildly glittered here and there
The gems entangled in her hair. 65

35 kneels] knelt *MS. W.*, *S. T. C.* (c), *S. H.*   37 sprang] leaps *MS. W.*, *S. T. C.* (c), *S. H.*, *First Edition.*   39 can] could *H. 1816.*   45-7 *om. MS. W.*   52 up] out *MS. W.*, *S. H.*   54 Jesu Maria *MS. W.*, *S. T. C.* (c), *S. H.*

58-66   A damsel bright
        Clad in a silken robe of white,
        Her neck, her feet, her arms were bare,
        And the jewels were tumbled in her hair.
        I guess, &c. *MS. W*

60 *om. MS. S. T. C.*

61-6   Her neck, her feet, her arms were bare,
        And the jewels were tumbled in her hair.
        I guess, &c. *S. T. C.* (a), *S. T. C.* (c), *S. H.*

I guess, 'twas frightful there to see
A lady so richly clad as she—
Beautiful exceedingly!

Mary mother, save me now!
(Said Christabel,) And who art thou? 70

The lady strange made answer meet,
And her voice was faint and sweet:—
Have pity on my sore distress,
I scarce can speak for weariness:
Stretch forth thy hand, and have no fear! 75
Said Christabel, How camest thou here?
And the lady, whose voice was faint and sweet,
Did thus pursue her answer meet:—

My sire is of a noble line,
And my name is Geraldine: 80
Five warriors seized me yestermorn,
Me, even me, a maid forlorn:
They choked my cries with force and fright,
And tied me on a palfrey white.
The palfrey was as fleet as wind, 85
And they rode furiously behind.

 61–6 Her neck, her feet, her arms were bare,
    And the jewels disorder'd in her hair.
    I guess, &c. *First Edition.*

 65 And the jewels were tangled in her hair. *S. T. C.* (b).

[In the Hinves copy (Nov., 1816), ll. 60–5 are inserted in the margin and the two lines 'Her neck ... her hair' are erased. This addition was included in *1828, 1829, 1834*, &c.]

74 scarce can] cannot *H. 1816.* 76 Said Christabel] Alas! but say *H. 1816.*

 81–3 Five ruffians seized me yestermorn,
    Me, even me, a maid forlorn;
    They chok'd my cries with wicked might.
        MS. W., S. T. C. (a); *MS. S. T. C.* (c); *S. H.*
    Five warriors, &c. as in the text *S. T. C.* (b).

[Lines 82, 83, 84½ are erased in *H. 1816*. Lines 81–4, 89, 90, which Scott prefixed as a motto to Chapter XI of *The Black Dwarf* (1818), run thus:—

    Three ruffians seized me yestermorn,
    Alas! a maiden most forlorn;
    They choked my cries with wicked might,
    And bound me on a palfrey white:
    As sure as Heaven shall pity me,
    I cannot tell what men they be. *Christabel.*

The motto to Chapter XXIV of *The Betrothed* (1825) is slightly different:—
    Four Ruffians ... palfrey white.

CHRISTABEL

They spurred amain, their steeds were white:
And once we crossed the shade of night.
As sure as Heaven shall rescue me,
I have no thought what men they be;   90
Nor do I know how long it is
(For I have lain entranced I wis)
Since one, the tallest of the five,
Took me from the palfrey's back,
A weary woman, scarce alive.   95
Some muttered words his comrades spoke:
He placed me underneath this oak;
He swore they would return with haste;
Whither they went I cannot tell—
I thought I heard, some minutes past,   100
Sounds as of a castle bell.
Stretch forth thy hand (thus ended she),
And help a wretched maid to flee.

Then Christabel stretched forth her hand,
And comforted fair Geraldine: 105
O well, bright dame! may you command
The service of Sir Leoline;
And gladly our stout chivalry
Will he send forth and friends withal
To guide and guard you safe and free   110
Home to your noble father's hall.

She rose: and forth with steps they passed
That strove to be, and were not, fast.

88 once] twice *MS. W.*, *S. T. C.* (*c*), *S. H.*   92 For I have lain in fits, I wis *MS. W.*, *S. T. C.* (*a*), *S. T. C.* (*c*), *S. H.*, *First Edition*. [Text, which follows *S. T. C.* (*b*), *H. 1816*, was first adopted in *1828*.]   96 comrades] comrade *MS. W.*   98 He] They *MS. W.*

106-11   Saying that she should command
        The service of Sir Leoline;
        And straight be convoy'd, free from thrall,
        Back to her noble father's hall.
            MS. W., *S. T. C.* (*c*), *S. H.*, *First Edition*.
[Text, which follows *H. 1816*, was first adopted in *1828*.]

112-22   So up she rose and forth they pass'd
        With hurrying steps yet nothing fast.
        Her lucky stars the lady blest,
        And Christabel she sweetly said—
        All our household are at rest,
        Each one sleeping in his bed:

Her gracious stars the lady blest,
And thus spake on sweet Christabel: 115
All our household are at rest,
The hall as silent as the cell;
Sir Leoline is weak in health,
And may not well awakened be,
But we will move as if in stealth,   120
And I beseech your courtesy,
This night, to share your couch with me.

They crossed the moat, and Christabel
Took the key that fitted well;
A little door she opened straight,   125
All in the middle of the gate;
The gate that was ironed within and without,
Where an army in battle array had marched out.
The lady sank, belike through pain,
And Christabel with might and main   130
Lifted her up, a weary weight,
Over the threshold of the gate:
Then the lady rose again,
And moved, as she were not in pain.

So free from danger, free from fear,   135
They crossed the court: right glad they were.
And Christabel devoutly cried
To the lady by her side,
Praise we the Virgin all divine
Who hath rescued thee from thy distress!   140

> Sir Leoline is weak in health,
> And may not awakened be,
> So to my room we'll creep in stealth,
> And you to-night must sleep with me.
> *MS. W., S. T. C. (a), S. T. C. (c), S. H.*

[So, too, *First Edition*, with the sole variant, 'And may not well awakened be '.]

114-17 Her smiling stars the lady blest,
And thus bespake sweet Christabel:
All our household is at rest,
The hall as silent as a cell. *S. T. C. (b).*

[In *H. 1816* ll. 112-22 of the text are inserted in Coleridge's handwriting. Line 113 reads: 'yet were not fast'. Line 122 reads: 'share your bed with me'. In *1828*, ll. 117-22 were added to the text, and 'Her gracious stars' (l. 114) was substituted for 'Her lucky stars'.]

137 And Christabel she sweetly cried *MS. W., S. T. C. (c), S. H.*   139 Praise we] O praise *MS. W., S. T. C. (c), S. H.*

Alas, alas! said Geraldine,
I cannot speak for weariness.
So free from danger, free from fear,
They crossed the court: right glad they were.

Outside her kennel, the mastiff old 145
Lay fast asleep, in moonshine cold.
The mastiff old did not awake,
Yet she an angry moan did make!
And what can ail the mastiff bitch?
Never till now she uttered yell 150
Beneath the eye of Christabel.
Perhaps it is the owlet's scritch:
For what can ail the mastiff bitch?

They passed the hall, that echoes still,
Pass as lightly as you will! 155
The brands were flat, the brands were dying,
Amid their own white ashes lying;
But when the lady passed, there came
A tongue of light, a fit of flame;
And Christabel saw the lady's eye, 160
And nothing else saw she thereby,
Save the boss of the shield of Sir Leoline tall,
Which hung in a murky old niche in the wall.
O softly tread, said Christabel,
My father seldom sleepeth well. 165

Sweet Christabel her feet doth bare,
And jealous of the listening air
They steal their way from stair to stair,
Now in glimmer, and now in gloom,
And now they pass the Baron's room, 170
As still as death, with stifled breath!
And now have reached her chamber door;

---

145 Outside] Beside *MS. W.*, *S. T. C.* (c), *S. H.* 146 Lay fast] Was stretch'd *H. 1816*. [Not in S. T. C.'s handwriting.] 160 *om.* *S. T. C.* (a). 161 And nothing else she saw thereby *MS. W.*, *S. T. C.* (c), *S. H.* 163 niche] nitch *all MSS. and First Edition.*

166-9   Sweet Christabel her feet she bares,
        And they are creeping up the stairs,
        Now in glimmer, and now in gloom.
                MS. W., *S. T. C.* (c), *S. H., First Edition.*

167 *Added in 1828.* 171 With stifled breath, as still as death *H. 1816*. [Not in S. T. C.'s handwriting.]

And now doth Geraldine press down
The rushes of the chamber floor.

The moon shines dim in the open air, 175
And not a moonbeam enters here.
But they without its light can see
The chamber carved so curiously,
Carved with figures strange and sweet,
All made out of the carver's brain, 180
For a lady's chamber meet:
The lamp with twofold silver chain
Is fastened to an angel's feet.

The silver lamp burns dead and dim;
But Christabel the lamp will trim. 185
She trimmed the lamp, and made it bright,
And left it swinging to and fro,
While Geraldine, in wretched plight,
Sank down upon the floor below.

O weary lady, Geraldine, 190
I pray you, drink this cordial wine!
It is a wine of virtuous powers;
My mother made it of wild flowers.

And will your mother pity me,
Who am a maiden most forlorn? 195
Christabel answered—Woe is me!
She died the hour that I was born.
I have heard the grey-haired friar tell
How on her death-bed she did say,
That she should hear the castle-bell 200
Strike twelve upon my wedding-day.
O mother dear! that thou wert here!
I would, said Geraldine, she were!

173-4   And now they with their feet press down
      The rushes of her chamber floor.   *MS. W., S. T. C. (c), S. H.*
     And now with eager feet press down
      The rushes of her chamber floor.
              First Edition, H. 1816. [Not in S. T. C.'s handwriting.]
191 cordial] spicy *MS. W., S. T. C. (a), S. T. C. (c), S. H.*
Between 193-4
      Nay, drink it up, I pray you do,
      Believe me it will comfort you.
                    MS. W., S. T. C. (a), S. T. O. (c), S. H.
[The omission was made in the First Edition.]

CHRISTABEL

But soon with altered voice, said she—
'Off, wandering mother! Peak and pine!   205
I have power to bid thee flee.'
Alas! what ails poor Geraldine?
Why stares she with unsettled eye?
Can she the bodiless dead espy?
And why with hollow voice cries she,   210
'Off, woman, off! this hour is mine—
Though thou her guardian spirit be,
Off, woman, off! 'tis given to me.'

Then Christabel knelt by the lady's side,
And raised to heaven her eyes so blue—   215
Alas! said she, this ghastly ride—
Dear lady! it hath wildered you!
The lady wiped her moist cold brow,
And faintly said, ''tis over now!'

Again the wild-flower wine she drank: 220
Her fair large eyes 'gan glitter bright,
And from the floor whereon she sank,
The lofty lady stood upright:
She was most beautiful to see,
Like a lady of a far countrée.   225

And thus the lofty lady spake—
'All they who live in the upper sky,
Do love you, holy Christabel!
And you love them, and for their sake
And for the good which me befel,   230
Even I in my degree will try,
Fair maiden, to requite you well.
But now unrobe yourself; for I
Must pray, ere yet in bed I lie.'

Quoth Christabel, So let it be!   235
And as the lady bade, did she.
Her gentle limbs did she undress,
And lay down in her loveliness.

But through her brain of weal and woe
So many thoughts moved to and fro,   240
That vain it were her lids to close;
So half-way from the bed she rose,

205-10, 212 *om. MS. W.*   219 And faintly said I'm better now *MS. W., S. T. C.* (a): I am better now *S. T. C.* (c), *S. H.*   225 far] fair *MS. W.*

224   CHRISTABEL

And on her elbow did recline
To look at the lady Geraldine.

Beneath the lamp the lady bowed,   245
And slowly rolled her eyes around;
Then drawing in her breath aloud,
Like one that shuddered, she unbound
The cincture from beneath her breast:
Her silken robe, and inner vest,   250
Dropt to her feet, and full in view,
Behold! her bosom and half her side——
A sight to dream of, not to tell!
O shield her! shield sweet Christabel!

Yet Geraldine nor speaks nor stirs;   255
Ah! what a stricken look was hers!
Deep from within she seems half-way
To lift some weight with sick assay,
And eyes the maid and seeks delay;
Then suddenly, as one defied,   260
Collects herself in scorn and pride,
And lay down by the Maiden's side!—
And in her arms the maid she took,
        Ah wel-a-day!
And with low voice and doleful look   265
These words did say:
'In the touch of this bosom there worketh a spell,

Between 252-3 Are lean and old and foul of hue. *MS. W., S. T. C.* (c), *S. H.*   254 And she is to sleep with Christabel. *MS. W.*: And she is to sleep by Christabel. *S. T. C.* (c), *S. H., First Edition*: And must she sleep by Christabel. *H. 1816* [not in S. T. C.'s handwriting]: And she is alone with Christabel. *H. 1816 erased* [not in S. T. C.'s handwriting]: And must she sleep with Christabel. *H. 1816 erased* [not in S. T. C.'s handwriting].   255-61 *om. MS. W., S. T. C.* (c), *S. H., First Edition*: included in *H. 1816*. [Not in S. T. C.'s handwriting.] *First published in 1828.*

Between 254 *and* 263
        She took two paces and a stride,
        And lay down by the maiden's side,
                MS. W., S. T. C. (c), *S. H., First Edition.*

        She gaz'd upon the maid, she sigh'd
        She took two paces and a stride,
        Then
        And lay down by the Maiden's side.   *H. 1816 erased.*
265 low] sad *MS. W., S. T. C.* (c), *S. H.*   267 this] my *MS. W., S. T. C.* (c), *S. H.*

Which is lord of thy utterance, Christabel!
Thou knowest to-night, and wilt know to-morrow,
This mark of my shame, this seal of my sorrow; 270
    But vainly thou warrest,
      For this is alone in
    Thy power to declare,
      That in the dim forest
    Thou heard'st a low moaning, 275
And found'st a bright lady, surpassingly fair;
And didst bring her home with thee in love and in charity,
To shield her and shelter her from the damp air.'

The Conclusion to Part I

It was a lovely sight to see
The lady Christabel, when she 280
Was praying at the old oak tree.
    Amid the jaggéd shadows
    Of mossy leafless boughs,
    Kneeling in the moonlight,
      To make her gentle vows; 285
Her slender palms together prest,
Heaving sometimes on her breast;
Her face resigned to bliss or bale—
Her face, oh call it fair not pale,
And both blue eyes more bright than clear, 290
Each about to have a tear.

With open eyes (ah woe is me!)
Asleep, and dreaming fearfully,
Fearfully dreaming, yet, I wis,
Dreaming that alone, which is— 295
O sorrow and shame! Can this be she,
The lady, who knelt at the old oak tree?

---

270 The mark of my shame, the seal of my sorrow. *MS. W.*, *S. T. C. (c)*, *S. H.*   277 And didst bring her home with thee, with love and with charity. *MS. W.*, *S. T. C. (c)*, *S. H.*   278 To shield her, and shelter her, and shelter far from the damp air. *MS. W.*

The Conclusion to Part I] The Conclusion of Book the First *MS. W.*: The Conclusion to Book the First *S. T. C. (c)*, *S. H.*

294 *Here in MS. W. the handwriting changes.* 'Dreaming' *was written by S. T. C.*, 'yet' *by Mary Hutchinson.*   295 is] *is H. 1816.*   297 who] that *MS. W.*, *S. T. C. (c)*, *S. H.*, *H. 1816.*

And lo! the worker of these harms,
That holds the maiden in her arms,
Seems to slumber still and mild,   300
As a mother with her child.

A star hath set, a star hath risen,
O Geraldine! since arms of thine
Have been the lovely lady's prison.
O Geraldine! one hour was thine—   305
Thou'st had thy will! By tairn and rill,
The night-birds all that hour were still.
But now they are jubilant anew,
From cliff and tower, tu—whoo! tu—whoo!
Tu—whoo! tu—whoo! from wood and fell!   310

And see! the lady Christabel
Gathers herself from out her trance;
Her limbs relax, her countenance
Grows sad and soft; the smooth thin lids
Close o'er her eyes; and tears she sheds—   315
Large tears that leave the lashes bright!
And oft the while she seems to smile
As infants at a sudden light!

Yea, she doth smile, and she doth weep,
Like a youthful hermitess,   320
Beauteous in a wilderness,
Who, praying always, prays in sleep.
And, if she move unquietly,
Perchance, 'tis but the blood so free
Comes back and tingles in her feet.   325
No doubt, she hath a vision sweet.
What if her guardian spirit 'twere,
What if she knew her mother near?
But this she knows, in joys and woes,
That saints will aid if men will call: 330
For the blue sky bends over all!
1797.

---

306 Tairn or Tarn (derived by Lye from the Icelandic *Tiorn*, stagnum, palus) is rendered in our dictionaries as synonymous with Mere or Lake; but it is properly a large Pool or Reservoir in the Mountains, commonly the Feeder of some Mere in the valleys. Tarn Watling and Blellum Tarn, though on lower ground than other Tarns, are yet not exceptions, for both are on elevations, and Blellum Tarn feeds the Wynander Mere. *Note to S. T. C.* (c).   324 A query is attached to this line *H. 1816.*

Part II

Each matin bell, the Baron saith,
Knells us back to a world of death.
These words Sir Leoline first said,
When he rose and found his lady dead:　335
These words Sir Leoline will say
Many a morn to his dying day!

And hence the custom and law began
That still at dawn the sacristan,
Who duly pulls the heavy bell,　340
Five and forty beads must tell
Between each stroke—a warning knell,
Which not a soul can choose but hear
From Bratha Head to Wyndermere.

Saith Bracy the bard, So let it knell!　345
And let the drowsy sacristan
Still count as slowly as he can!
There is no lack of such, I ween,
As well fill up the space between.
In Langdale Pike and Witch's Lair,　350
And Dungeon-ghyll so foully rent,
With ropes of rock and bells of air
Three sinful sextons' ghosts are pent,
Who all give back, one after t'other,
The death-note to their living brother;　355
And oft too, by the knell offended,
Just as their one! two! three! is ended,
The devil mocks the doleful tale
With a merry peal from Borodale.

The air is still! through mist and cloud　360
That merry peal comes ringing loud;
And Geraldine shakes off her dread,
And rises lightly from the bed;
Puts on her silken vestments white,
And tricks her hair in lovely plight,　365

Part II] Book the Second *MS. W.*: Christabel Book the Second *S. T. C.* (*c*), *S. H.*
344 Wyndermere] Wyn'dermere *MS. W., S. T. C.* (*c*), *S. H., First Edition.*
353 sinful] simple *MS. W.*　354 A query is attached to this line *H. 1816.*
356 the] their *MS. W., S. T. C.* (*c*), *S. H.*　359 Borodale] Borrowdale *MS. W., S. H., First Edition, 1828, 1829* : Borrodale *S. T. C.* (*c*).　360 The air is still through many a cloud *MS. W., S. T. C.* (*c*), *S. H.*　363 the] her *MS. W., S. T. C.* (*c*), *S. H.*　364 silken] simple *MS. W.*

And nothing doubting of her spell
Awakens the lady Christabel.
'Sleep you, sweet lady Christabel?
I trust that you have rested well.'

And Christabel awoke and spied 370
The same who lay down by her side—
O rather say, the same whom she
Raised up beneath the old oak tree!
Nay, fairer yet! and yet more fair!
For she belike hath drunken deep 375
Of all the blessedness of sleep!
And while she spake, her looks, her air
Such gentle thankfulness declare,
That (so it seemed) her girded vests
Grew tight beneath her heaving breasts. 380
'Sure I have sinn'd!' said Christabel,
'Now heaven be praised if all be well!'
And in low faltering tones, yet sweet,
Did she the lofty lady greet
With such perplexity of mind 385
As dreams too lively leave behind.

So quickly she rose, and quickly arrayed
Her maiden limbs, and having prayed
That He, who on the cross did groan,
Might wash away her sins unknown, 390
She forthwith led fair Geraldine
To meet her sire, Sir Leoline.

The lovely maid and the lady tall
Are pacing both into the hall,
And pacing on through page and groom, 395
Enter the Baron's presence-room.

The Baron rose, and while he prest
His gentle daughter to his breast,
With cheerful wonder in his eyes
The lady Geraldine espies, 400
And gave such welcome to the same,
As might beseem so bright a dame!

But when he heard the lady's tale,
And when she told her father's name,
Why waxed Sir Leoline so pale, 405
Murmuring o'er the name again,
Lord Roland de Vaux of Tryermaine?

CHRISTABEL

Alas! they had been friends in youth;
But whispering tongues can poison truth;
And constancy lives in realms above; 410
And life is thorny; and youth is vain;
And to be wroth with one we love
Doth work like madness in the brain.
And thus it chanced, as I divine,
With Roland and Sir Leoline. 415
Each spake words of high disdain
And insult to his heart's best brother:
They parted—ne'er to meet again!
But never either found another
To free the hollow heart from paining— 420
They stood aloof, the scars remaining,
Like cliffs which had been rent asunder;
A dreary sea now flows between;—
But neither heat, nor frost, nor thunder,
Shall wholly do away, I ween, 425
The marks of that which once hath been.

Sir Leoline, a moment's space,
Stood gazing on the damsel's face:
And the youthful Lord of Tryermaine
Came back upon his heart again. 430

O then the Baron forgot his age,
His noble heart swelled high with rage;
He swore by the wounds in Jesu's side
He would proclaim it far and wide,
With trump and solemn heraldry, 435
That they, who thus had wronged the dame,
Were base as spotted infamy!
'And if they dare deny the same,
My herald shall appoint a week,
And let the recreant traitors seek 440
My tourney court—that there and then
I may dislodge their reptile souls
From the bodies and forms of men!'
He spake: his eye in lightning rolls!
For the lady was ruthlessly seized; and he kenned 445
In the beautiful lady the child of his friend!

---

414 thus] so *MS. Letter to Poole, Feb. 1813.* 418 They] And *MS. W.,
S. T. C. (c), S. H.* 419 But] And *MS. W.*
424–5 But neither frost nor heat nor thunder
Can wholly, &c., *MS. Letter to Poole, Feb. 1813.*
441 tourney] Tournay *MS. W., S. T. C. (c), First Edition.*

And now the tears were on his face,
And fondly in his arms he took
Fair Geraldine, who met the embrace,
Prolonging it with joyous look.   450
Which when she viewed, a vision fell
Upon the soul of Christabel,
The vision of fear, the touch and pain!
She shrunk and shuddered, and saw again—
(Ah, woe is me! Was it for thee,   455
Thou gentle maid! such sights to see?)

Again she saw that bosom old,
Again she felt that bosom cold,
And drew in her breath with a hissing sound:
Whereat the Knight turned wildly round,   460
And nothing saw, but his own sweet maid
With eyes upraised, as one that prayed.

The touch, the sight, had passed away,
And in its stead that vision blest,
Which comforted her after-rest   465
While in the lady's arms she lay,
Had put a rapture in her breast,
And on her lips and o'er her eyes
Spread smiles like light!
      With new surprise,
'What ails then my belovéd child?'   470
The Baron said—His daughter mild
Made answer, 'All will yet be well!'
I ween, she had no power to tell
Aught else: so mighty was the spell.

Yet he, who saw this Geraldine,   475
Had deemed her sure a thing divine:
Such sorrow with such grace she blended,
As if she feared she had offended
Sweet Christabel, that gentle maid!
And with such lowly tones she prayed   480
She might be sent without delay
Home to her father's mansion.
       'Nay!

453 The vision foul of fear and pain *MS. W.*, *S.T.C.* (a), *S.T.C.* (c), *S. H.*: The vision of fear, the touch of pain *S.T.C.* (b).   463 The pang, the sight was passed away *S.T.C.* (a): The pang, the sight, had passed away *MS. W.*, *S.T.C.* (c), *S. H.*

CHRISTABEL

Nay, by my soul!' said Leoline.
'Ho! Bracy the bard, the charge be thine!
Go thou, with music sweet and loud,   485
And take two steeds with trappings proud,
And take the youth whom thou lov'st best
To bear thy harp, and learn thy song,
And clothe you both in solemn vest,
And over the mountains haste along,   490
Lest wandering folk, that are abroad,
Detain you on the valley road.

'And when he has crossed the Irthing flood,
My merry bard! he hastes, he hastes
Up Knorren Moor, through Halegarth Wood,   495
And reaches soon that castle good
Which stands and threatens Scotland's wastes.

'Bard Bracy! bard Bracy! your horses are fleet,
Ye must ride up the hall, your music so sweet,
More loud than your horses' echoing feet!   500
And loud and loud to Lord Roland call,
Thy daughter is safe in Langdale hall!
Thy beautiful daughter is safe and free—
Sir Leoline greets thee thus through me!
He bids thee come without delay   505
With all thy numerous array
And take thy lovely daughter home:
And he will meet thee on the way
With all his numerous array
White with their panting palfreys' foam: 510
And, by mine honour! I will say,
That I repent me of the day
When I spake words of fierce disdain
To Roland de Vaux of Tryermaine!—
—For since that evil hour hath flown,   515
Many a summer's sun hath shone;
Yet ne'er found I a friend again
Like Roland de Vaux of Tryermaine.

The lady fell, and clasped his knees,
Her face upraised, her eyes o'erflowing;   520
And Bracy replied, with faltering voice,
His gracious Hail on all bestowing!—

---

490 om. MS. W.   503 beautiful] beauteous MS. W.   507 take] fetch MS. W., S. T. C. (c), S. H.   516 Many a summer's suns have shone MS. W., S. T. C. (c), S. H.

'Thy words, thou sire of Christabel,
Are sweeter than my harp can tell;
Yet might I gain a boon of thee, 525
This day my journey should not be,
So strange a dream hath come to me,
That I had vowed with music loud
To clear yon wood from thing unblest,
Warned by a vision in my rest! 530
For in my sleep I saw that dove,
That gentle bird, whom thou dost love,
And call'st by thy own daughter's name—
Sir Leoline! I saw the same
Fluttering, and uttering fearful moan, 535
Among the green herbs in the forest alone.
Which when I saw and when I heard,
I wonder'd what might ail the bird;
For nothing near it could I see,
Save the grass and green herbs underneath the old tree.

'And in my dream methought I went 541
To search out what might there be found;
And what the sweet bird's trouble meant,
That thus lay fluttering on the ground.
I went and peered, and could descry 545
No cause for her distressful cry;
But yet for her dear lady's sake
I stooped, methought, the dove to take,
When lo! I saw a bright green snake
Coiled around its wings and neck. 550
Green as the herbs on which it couched,
Close by the dove's its head it crouched;
And with the dove it heaves and stirs,
Swelling its neck as she swelled hers!
I woke; it was the midnight hour, 555
The clock was echoing in the tower;
But though my slumber was gone by,
This dream it would not pass away—
It seems to live upon my eye!
And thence I vowed this self-same day 560
With music strong and saintly song
To wander through the forest bare,
Lest aught unholy loiter there.'

---

559 seems] seem'd *MS. W., S. T. C.* (c).   560 vowed] swore *MS. W.*
563 loiter] wander *MS. W.*

CHRISTABEL

Thus Bracy said: the Baron, the while,
Half-listening heard him with a smile;
Then turned to Lady Geraldine,
His eyes made up of wonder and love;
And said in courtly accents fine,
'Sweet maid, Lord Roland's beauteous dove,
With arms more strong than harp or song,
Thy sire and I will crush the snake!'
He kissed her forehead as he spake,
And Geraldine in maiden wise
Casting down her large bright eyes,
With blushing cheek and courtesy fine
She turned her from Sir Leoline;
Softly gathering up her train,
That o'er her right arm fell again;
And folded her arms across her chest,
And couched her head upon her breast,
And looked askance at Christabel——
Jesu, Maria, shield her well!

A snake's small eye blinks dull and shy;
And the lady's eyes they shrunk in her head,
Each shrunk up to a serpent's eye,
And with somewhat of malice, and more of dread,
At Christabel she looked askance!—
One moment—and the sight was fled!
But Christabel in dizzy trance
Stumbling on the unsteady ground
Shuddered aloud, with a hissing sound;
And Geraldine again turned round,
And like a thing, that sought relief,
Full of wonder and full of grief,
She rolled her large bright eyes divine
Wildly on Sir Leoline.

The maid, alas! her thoughts are gone,
She nothing sees—no sight but one!
The maid, devoid of guile and sin,
I know not how, in fearful wise,
So deeply had she drunken in
That look, those shrunken serpent eyes,

---

582 Jesu, Maria] Jesu Maria *MS. W.*
hissing sound *MS. W.*, *S. T. C.* (c), *S. L.*

591 Shuddered aloud with
596 on] o'er *MS. W.*

That all her features were resigned
To this sole image in her mind:
And passively did imitate   605
That look of dull and treacherous hate!
And thus she stood, in dizzy trance,
Still picturing that look askance
With forced unconscious sympathy
Full before her father's view——   610
As far as such a look could be
In eyes so innocent and blue!

And when the trance was o'er, the maid
Paused awhile, and inly prayed:
Then falling at the Baron's feet,   615
'By my mother's soul do I entreat
That thou this woman send away!'
She said: and more she could not say:
For what she knew she could not tell,
O'er-mastered by the mighty spell.   620

Why is thy cheek so wan and wild,
Sir Leoline? Thy only child
Lies at thy feet, thy joy, thy pride,
So fair, so innocent, so mild;
The same, for whom thy lady died!   625
O by the pangs of her dear mother
Think thou no evil of thy child!
For her, and thee, and for no other,
She prayed the moment ere she died:
Prayed that the babe for whom she died,   630
Might prove her dear lord's joy and pride!
  That prayer her deadly pangs beguiled,
        Sir Leoline!
  And wouldst thou wrong thy only child,
        Her child and thine?   635

Within the Baron's heart and brain
If thoughts, like these, had any share,
They only swelled his rage and pain,
And did but work confusion there.
His heart was cleft with pain and rage,   640
His cheeks they quivered, his eyes were wild,

---

613 And] But *MS. W.*, *S. T. C.* (c), *S. H.*, *First Edition*. 615 her Father's Feet *MS. W.*, *S. T. C.* (c), *S. H.*, *First Edition, 1828*. 620 the] that *MS. W.* 639 but] not *MS. W.*

CHRISTABEL 235

Dishonoured thus in his old age;
Dishonoured by his only child,
And all his hospitality
To the wronged daughter of his friend   645
By more than woman's jealousy
Brought thus to a disgraceful end—
He rolled his eye with stern regard
Upon the gentle minstrel bard,
And said in tones abrupt, austere—   650
'Why, Bracy! dost thou loiter here?
I bade thee hence!' The bard obeyed;
And turning from his own sweet maid,
The agéd knight, Sir Leoline,
Led forth the lady Geraldine!   655
    1800.

The Conclusion to Part II

A little child, a limber elf,
Singing, dancing to itself,
A fairy thing with red round cheeks,
That always finds, and never seeks,
Makes such a vision to the sight   660
As fills a father's eyes with light;
And pleasures flow in so thick and fast
Upon his heart, that he at last
Must needs express his love's excess
With words of unmeant bitterness.   665
Perhaps 'tis pretty to force together
Thoughts so all unlike each other;
To mutter and mock a broken charm,
To dally with wrong that does no harm.
Perhaps 'tis tender too and pretty   670
At each wild word to feel within

---

645 wronged] insulted *MS. W.*, *S. T. C.* (c), *S. H.*, *First Edition*, *1828*, *1829*.
  The Conclusion to Part II] Not in any of the MSS. or in *S. H.* For the first manuscript version see *Letter to Southey, May 6, 1801.* (*Letters of S. T. C.*, 1895, i. 355.)

659 'finds' and 'seeks' are italicized in the letters.

660-1   Doth make a vision to the sight
        Which fills a father's eyes with light. *Letter, 1801.*

664 In *H. 1816* there is a direction (not in S. T. C.'s handwriting) to print line 664 as two lines.   665 In words of wrong and bitterness. *Letter, 1801.*

A sweet recoil of love and pity.
And what, if in a world of sin
(O sorrow and shame should this be true!)
Such giddiness of heart and brain 675
Comes seldom save from rage and pain,
So talks as it's most used to do.
1801.

LINES TO W. L.[1]

WHILE HE SANG A SONG TO PURCELL'S MUSIC

WHILE my young cheek retains its healthful hues,
  And I have many friends who hold me dear,
  L——[2]! methinks, I would not often hear
Such melodies as thine, lest I should lose
All memory of the wrongs and sore distress 5
  For which my miserable brethren weep!
  But should uncomforted misfortunes steep
My daily bread in tears and bitterness;
And if at Death's dread moment I should lie
  With no belovéd face at my bed-side, 10
  To fix the last glance of my closing eye,
Methinks such strains, breathed by my angel-guide,
Would make me pass the cup of anguish by,
  Mix with the blest, nor know that I had died!
1797.

---

[1] First published in the *Annual Anthology* for 1800: included in *Sibylline Leaves*, 1817, 1828, 1829, and 1834. A MS. is extant dated Sept. 14, 1797.

Lines to W. L.—Title] To Mr. William Linley *MS. 1797*: Sonnet XII, To W. L.——[2]! Esq., while he sung &c. *An. Anth.*: To W. L. Esq. &c. *S. L. 1828, 1829*: Lines to W. Linley, Esq. *1893*.
3 L——[2]!] Linley! *MS. 1893*. 10 at] by *An. Anth.* 12 Methinks] O God! *An. Anth.*

FIRE, FAMINE, AND SLAUGHTER[1]

A WAR ECLOGUE

The Scene a desolated Tract in La Vendée. FAMINE *is discovered lying on the ground; to her enter* FIRE *and* SLAUGHTER.

Fam. SISTERS! sisters! who sent you here?
Slau. [*to Fire*]. I will whisper it in her ear.
Fire. No! no! no!
Spirits hear what spirits tell:
'Twill make a holiday in Hell. 5
    No! no! no!
Myself, I named him once below,
And all the souls, that damnéd be,
Leaped up at once in anarchy,
Clapped their hands and danced for glee. 10
They no longer heeded me;
But laughed to hear Hell's burning rafters
Unwillingly re-echo laughters!
    No! no! no!
Spirits hear what spirits tell: 15
'Twill make a holiday in Hell!
  Fam. Whisper it, sister! so and so!
In a dark hint, soft and slow.
  Slau. Letters four do form his name—
And who sent you?
  Both.   The same! the same! 20

---

[1] First published in the *Morning Post*, January 8, 1798: included in *Annual Anthology*, 1800, and (with an Apologetic Preface, vide *Appendices*) in *Sibylline Leaves*, 1828, 1829, and 1834. The poem was probably written in 1796. See *Watchman, passim*.

Fire, Famine, &c.—Title] Scene: A depopulated Tract in La Vendée. Famine is discovered stretched on the ground; to her enter Slaughter and Fire *M. P., Jan. 8, 1798.*

2 SLAUGHTER. I will name him in your ear. *M. P.*   5 a] an *all editions to 1834.*   11 me] *me M. P.*

16 a] an *all editions to 1834.*

17-18 FAMINE. Then sound it not, yet let me know;
        Darkly hint it—soft and low! *M. P.*
        In a dark hint, soft and low. *An. Anth.*

19 Four letters form his name. *M. P.*   20 *Both*] FAMINE *MP.*

Slau. He came by stealth, and unlocked my den,
And I have drunk the blood since then
Of thrice three hundred thousand men.
   Both. Who bade you do't?
   Slau.   The same! the same!   25
Letters four do form his name.
He let me loose, and cried Halloo!
To him alone the praise is due.
   Fam. Thanks, sister, thanks! the men have bled,
Their wives and their children faint for bread.
I stood in a swampy field of battle;   30
With bones and skulls I made a rattle,
To frighten the wolf and carrion-crow
And the homeless dog—but they would not go.
So off I flew: for how could I bear
To see them gorge their dainty fare?   35
I heard a groan and a peevish squall,
And through the chink of a cottage-wall—
Can you guess what I saw there?
   Both. Whisper it, sister! in our ear.
   Fam. A baby beat its dying mother: 40
I had starved the one and was starving the other!
   Both. Who bade you do't?
   Fam.   The same! the same!
Letters four do form his name.
He let me loose, and cried, Halloo!
To him alone the praise is due.   45
   Fire. Sisters! I from Ireland came!
Hedge and corn-fields all on flame,
I triumph'd o'er the setting sun!
And all the while the work was done,
On as I strode with my huge strides,   50
I flung back my head and I held my sides,
It was so rare a piece of fun
To see the sweltered cattle run

22-3   And I have spill'd the blood since then
          Of thrice ten hundred thousand men. *M.P.*

22 drunk] drank *An. Anth., S. L. 1828, 1829.*   24 *Both*] FIRE and FAMINE *M.P.*   25 Four letters form his name. *M.P.*   29 Their wives and children *M.P.*   32 and the carrion crow *M.P., An. Anth.*   39 *Both*] SLAUGHTER and FIRE *M.P.*   42 *Both*] SLAUGHTER and FIRE *M.P.*   43 Four letters form his name. *M.P.*   47 Hedge] Huts *M.P.*   48 om. *An. Anth.*   49 Halloo! halloo! the work was done *An. Anth.* 50 As on I strode with monstrous strides *M.P.*: And on as I strode with my great strides *An. Anth.*   51 and held *M.P., An. Anth.*

FIRE, FAMINE, AND SLAUGHTER

With uncouth gallop through the night,
Scared by the red and noisy light! 55
By the light of his own blazing cot
Was many a naked Rebel shot:
The house-stream met the flame and hissed,
While crash! fell in the roof, I wist,
On some of those old bed-rid nurses, 60
That deal in discontent and curses.

Both. Who bade you do 't?
Fire.   The same! the same!
Letters four do form his name.
He let me loose, and cried Halloo!
To him alone the praise is due. 65

All. He let us loose, and cried Halloo!
How shall we yield him honour due?

Fam. Wisdom comes with lack of food.
I'll gnaw, I'll gnaw the multitude,
Till the cup of rage o'erbrim: 70
They shall seize him and his brood—

Slau. They shall tear him limb from limb!

Fire. O thankless beldames and untrue!
And is this all that you can do
For him, who did so much for you? 75
Ninety months he, by my troth!
Hath richly catered for you both;

---

54 through] all *M. P.*   58 flame] fire *M. F.*, flames *An. Anth.*
59 While crash the roof fell in I wish *M. P.*   62 *Both*] SLAUGHTER and FAMINE *M. P.*   63 Four letters form his name. *M. P.*   65 How shall I give him honour due? *M. P.*   67 we] I *M. P.*   71 and] of *M. P.*
75 foll.   For him that did so much for you.

[*To Slaughter.*
For *you* he turn'd the dust to mud
With his fellow creatures' blood!

[*To Famine.*
And hunger scorch'd as many more,
To make *your* cup of joy run o'er.

[*To Both.*
Full ninety moons, he by my troth!
Hath richly cater'd for you both!
And in an hour would you repay
An eight years' debt? Away! away!
I alone am faithful! I
Cling to him everlastingly.
                              LABERIUS. *M. P.*

240 FIRE, FAMINE, AND SLAUGHTER

And in an hour would you repay
An eight years' work?—Away! away!
I alone am faithful! I 80
Cling to him everlastingly.

1798.

FROST AT MIDNIGHT[1]

THE Frost performs its secret ministry,
Unhelped by any wind. The owlet's cry
Came loud—and hark, again! loud as before.
The inmates of my cottage, all at rest,
Have left me to that solitude, which suits 5
Abstruser musings: save that at my side
My cradled infant slumbers peacefully.
'Tis calm indeed! so calm, that it disturbs
And vexes meditation with its strange
And extreme silentness. Sea, hill, and wood, 10
This populous village! Sea, and hill, and wood,
With all the numberless goings-on of life,
Inaudible as dreams! the thin blue flame
Lies on my low-burnt fire, and quivers not;
Only that film,[2] which fluttered on the grate, 15
Still flutters there, the sole unquiet thing.
Methinks, its motion in this hush of nature
Gives it dim sympathies with me who live,
Making it a companionable form,
Whose puny flaps and freaks the idling Spirit 20

---

[1] First published in a quarto pamphlet 'printed by Johnson in S. Paul's Churchyard, 1798': included in *Poetical Register*, 1808–9 (1812): in *Fears in Solitude*, &c., printed by Law and Gilbert, (?) 1812: in *Sibylline Leaves*, 1817, 1828, 1829, and 1834.

[2] *Only that film*. In all parts of the kingdom these films are called *strangers* and supposed to portend the arrival of some absent friend. 4°, *P. R.*

Below 81 1798] 1796 *S. L.* 1828, 1829, and 1834.
Between 19–25
　　　With which I can hold commune. Idle thought!
　　　But still the living spirit in our frame,
　　　That loves not to behold a lifeless thing,
　　　Transfuses into all its own delights,
　　　Its own volition, sometimes with deep faith
　　　And sometimes with fantastic playfulness.

FROST AT MIDNIGHT 241

By its own moods interprets, every where
Echo or mirror seeking of itself,
And makes a toy of Thought.

                        But O! how oft,
How oft, at school, with most believing mind,
Presageful, have I gazed upon the bars,   25
To watch that fluttering *stranger*! and as oft
With unclosed lids, already had I dreamt
Of my sweet birth-place, and the old church-tower,
Whose bells, the poor man's only music, rang
From morn to evening, all the hot Fair-day,   30
So sweetly, that they stirred and haunted me
With a wild pleasure, falling on mine ear
Most like articulate sounds of things to come!
So gazed I, till the soothing things, I dreamt,
Lulled me to sleep, and sleep prolonged my dreams!   35
And so I brooded all the following morn,
Awed by the stern preceptor's face, mine eye
Fixed with mock study on my swimming book:
Save if the door half opened, and I snatched
A hasty glance, and still my heart leaped up,   40

    Ah me! amus'd by no such curious toys
    Of the self-watching subtilizing mind,
    How often in my early school-boy days
    With most believing superstitious wish. *4º.*

    With which I can hold commune: haply hence,
    That still the living spirit in our frame,
    Which loves not to behold a lifeless thing,
    Transfuses into all things its own Will,
    And its own pleasures; sometimes with deep faith,
    And sometimes with a wilful playfulness
    That stealing pardon from our common sense
    Smiles, as self-scornful, to disarm the scorn
    For these wild reliques of our childish Thought,
    That flit about, oft go, and oft return
    Not uninvited.
              Ah there was a time,
    When oft amused by no such subtle toys
    Of the self-watching mind, a child at school,
    With most believing superstitious wish. *P. R.*

Between 19–23
    To which the living spirit in our frame,
    That loves not to behold a lifeless thing,
    Transfuses its own pleasures, its own will. *S. L. 1828.*

26 To watch the *stranger* there! and oft belike *4º, P. R.*   27 had] have
P. R.   32 wild] sweet *S. L.* (for *sweet* read *wild*. *Errata, S. L.*, p. [xii]).

For still I hoped to see the *stranger's* face,
Townsman, or aunt, or sister more beloved,
My play-mate when we both were clothed alike!

Dear Babe, that sleepest cradled by my side,
Whose gentle breathings, heard in this deep calm, 45
Fill up the interspersèd vacancies
And momentary pauses of the thought!
My babe so beautiful! it thrills my heart
With tender gladness, thus to look at thee,
And think that thou shalt learn far other lore, 50
And in far other scenes! For I was reared
In the great city, pent 'mid cloisters dim,
And saw nought lovely but the sky and stars.
But *thou*, my babe! shalt wander like a breeze
By lakes and sandy shores, beneath the crags 55
Of ancient mountain, and beneath the clouds,
Which image in their bulk both lakes and shores
And mountain crags: so shalt thou see and hear
The lovely shapes and sounds intelligible
Of that eternal language, which thy God 60
Utters, who from eternity doth teach
Himself in all, and all things in himself.
Great universal Teacher! he shall mould
Thy spirit, and by giving make it ask.

Therefore all seasons shall be sweet to thee, 65
Whether the summer clothe the general earth
With greenness, or the redbreast sit and sing
Betwixt the tufts of snow on the bare branch
Of mossy apple-tree, while the nigh thatch
Smokes in the sun-thaw; whether the eave-drops fall 70
Heard only in the trances of the blast,
Or if the secret ministry of frost
Shall hang them up in silent icicles,
Quietly shining to the quiet Moon.

February, 1798.[1]

---

[1] The date is omitted in *1829* and in *1834*.

45 deep] dead *4º, P. R., S. L.* (for *dead* read *deep*. Errata, *S. L.*, p. [xii]).
46 Fill] Fill'd *S. L.* (for *Fill'd* read *Fill*. Errata, *S. L.*, p. [xii]). 48
thrills] fills *4º, P. R., S. L.* (for *fills* read *thrills*. Errata, *S. L.*, p. [xii]).
67 redbreast] redbreasts *4º, P. R.* 69 the nigh] all the *4º*. 71
trances] traces *S. L.* (for *traces* read *trances*. Errata, *S. L.*, p. [xii]).

72–end   Or whether the secret ministery of cold
         Shall hang them up in silent icicles,

FRANCE: AN ODE[1]

I

Ye Clouds! that far above me float and pause,
  Whose pathless march no mortal may controul!
Ye Ocean-Waves! that, wheresoe'er ye roll,
Yield homage only to eternal laws!

[1] First published in the *Morning Post*, April 16, 1798: included in quarto pamphlet published by J. Johnson, 1798: reprinted in *Morning Post*, Oct. 14, 1802: included in *Poetical Register* for 1808-9 (1812); in *Fears in Solitude, &c.*, printed by Law and Gilbert, (?) 1812; in *Sibylline Leaves*, 1817, 1828, 1829, and 1834. Lines 85, 98 are quoted from 'France, a Palinodia', in *Biog. Lit.*, 1817, i. 195. To the first *Morning Post* version (1798) an editorial note was prefixed:—

ORIGINAL POETRY.

The following excellent Ode will be in unison with the feelings of every friend to Liberty and foe to Oppression; of all who, admiring the French Revolution, detest and deplore the conduct of France towards Switzerland. It is very satisfactory to find so zealous and steady an advocate for Freedom as Mr. COLERIDGE concur with us in condemning the conduct of France towards the Swiss Cantons. Indeed his concurrence is not singular; we know of no Friend to Liberty who is not of his opinion. What we most admire is the *avowal* of his sentiments, and public censure of the unprincipled and atrocious conduct of France. The Poem itself is written with great energy. The second, third, and fourth stanzas contain some of the most vigorous lines we have ever read. The lines in the fourth stanza:—

'To scatter rage and trait'rous guilt
  Where Peace her jealous home had built,'

to the end of the stanza are particularly expressive and beautiful.

To the second *Morning Post* version (1802) a note and Argument were prefixed:—

The following ODE was first published in this paper (in the beginning of the year 1798) in a less perfect state. The present state of France and

---

Quietly shining to the quiet moon,
Like those, my babe! which ere tomorrow's warmth
Have capp'd their sharp keen points with pendulous drops,
Will catch thine eye, and with their novelty
Suspend thy little soul; then make thee shout,
And stretch and flutter from thy mother's arms
As thou wouldst fly for very eagerness. *4°.*

France—Title] The Recantation: an Ode. By S. T. Coleridge. *1798.*

1 and] or *1802.*   2 Veering your pathless march without controul *1802.*

Ye Woods! that listen to the night-birds singing,
  Midway the smooth and perilous slope reclined,
Save when your own imperious branches swinging,
  Have made a solemn music of the wind!
Where, like a man beloved of God,
Through glooms, which never woodman trod,
    How oft, pursuing fancies holy,
My moonlight way o'er flowering weeds I wound,
  Inspired, beyond the guess of folly,
By each rude shape and wild unconquerable sound!
O ye loud Waves! and O ye Forests high!
  And O ye Clouds that far above me soared!
Thou rising Sun! thou blue rejoicing Sky!
  Yea, every thing that is and will be free!
  Bear witness for me, wheresoe'er ye be,
  With what deep worship I have still adored
    The spirit of divinest Liberty.

Switzerland give it so peculiar an interest at the present time that we wished to re-publish it and accordingly have procured from the Author a corrected copy.

ARGUMENT.

'*First Stanza*. An invocation to those objects in Nature the contemplation of which had inspired the Poet with a devotional love of Liberty. *Second Stanza*. The exultation of the Poet at the commencement of the French Revolution, and his unqualified abhorrence of the Alliance against the Republic. *Third Stanza*. The blasphemies and horrors during the domination of the Terrorists regarded by the Poet as a transient storm, and as the natural consequence of the former despotism and of the foul superstition of Popery. Reason, indeed, began to suggest many apprehensions; yet still the Poet struggled to retain the hope that France would make conquests by no other means than by presenting to the observation of Europe a people more happy and better instructed than under other forms of Government. *Fourth Stanza*. Switzerland, and the Poet's recantation. *Fifth Stanza*. An address to Liberty, in which the Poet expresses his conviction that those feelings and that grand *ideal* of Freedom which the mind attains by its contemplation of its individual nature, and of the sublime surrounding objects (see Stanza the First) do not belong to men, as a society, nor can possibly be either gratified or realised, under any form of human government; but belong to the individual man, so far as he is pure, and inflamed with the love and adoration of God in Nature.'

---

5 night-birds] night bird's *1798, 4°, 1802*: night-birds' *S. L., 1828, 1829*.
6 slope] steep *1798, 4°, 1802, P. R.*   12 way] path *1802*.

FRANCE: AN ODE

II

When France in wrath her giant-limbs upreared,
   And with that oath, which smote air, earth, and sea,
   Stamped her strong foot and said she would be free,
Bear witness for me, how I hoped and feared!
With what a joy my lofty gratulation
   Unawed I sang, amid a slavish band:
And when to whelm the disenchanted nation,
   Like fiends embattled by a wizard's wand,
     The Monarchs marched in evil day,
     And Britain joined the dire array;
Though dear her shores and circling ocean,
Though many friendships, many youthful loves
   Had swoln the patriot emotion
And flung a magic light o'er all her hills and groves;
Yet still my voice, unaltered, sang defeat
   To all that braved the tyrant-quelling lance,
And shame too long delayed and vain retreat!
For ne'er, O Liberty! with partial aim
I dimmed thy light or damped thy holy flame;
   But blessed the paeans of delivered France,
And hung my head and wept at Britain's name.

III

'And what,' I said, 'though Blasphemy's loud scream
   With that sweet music of deliverance strove!
   Though all the fierce and drunken passions wove
A dance more wild than e'er was maniac's dream!
Ye storms, that round the dawning East assembled,
The Sun was rising, though ye hid his light!'
   And when, to soothe my soul, that hoped and trembled,
The dissonance ceased, and all seemed calm and bright;
   When France her front deep-scarr'd and gory
   Concealed with clustering wreaths of glory;

---

23 smote air, earth, and sea] smote earth, air, and sea *1798, 4°, P. R.*: shook earth, air, and sea *1802*.   24 foot] feet *1798*.   26 lofty] eager *1802*.   27 sang] sung *1798, 4°, P. R.*   30 marched] mov'd *1802*.   34 the] that *1802*.   35 flung] spread *1802*.   41 But] I *1802*.   44 that sweet music] those sweet Pæans *1802*.   46 e'er was] ever *1798, 4°, P. R.*   51 deep-scarr'd] deep-scar'd *1798, 4°, P. R., S. L.*

When, insupportably advancing,
  Her arm made mockery of the warrior's ramp;
    While timid looks of fury glancing,
  Domestic treason, crushed beneath her fatal stamp,
Writhed like a wounded dragon in his gore;
  Then I reproached my fears that would not flee;
'And soon,' I said, 'shall Wisdom teach her lore
In the low huts of them that toil and groan!
And, conquering by her happiness alone,
  Shall France compel the nations to be free,
Till Love and Joy look round, and call the Earth their own.'

IV

Forgive me, Freedom! O forgive those dreams!
  I hear thy voice, I hear thy loud lament,
    From bleak Helvetia's icy caverns sent—
I hear thy groans upon her blood-stained streams!
Heroes, that for your peaceful country perished,
And ye that, fleeing, spot your mountain-snows
  With bleeding wounds; forgive me, that I cherished
One thought that ever blessed your cruel foes!
  To scatter rage, and traitorous guilt,
  Where Peace her jealous home had built;
    A patriot-race to disinherit
Of all that made their stormy wilds so dear;
    And with inexpiable spirit
To taint the bloodless freedom of the mountaineer—
O France, that mockest Heaven, adulterous, blind,
  And patriot only in pernicious toils!
Are these thy boasts, Champion of human kind?
  To mix with Kings in the low lust of sway,
Yell in the hunt, and share the murderous prey;
To insult the shrine of Liberty with spoils
  From freemen torn; to tempt and to betray?

---

53 insupportably] irresistibly *1802*.   54 ramp] tramp *1828, 1829, 1834, 1852*. [Text of *1834* is here corrected.]   58 reproached] rebuk'd *1802*. 59 said] cried *1802*.   62 compel] persuade *1802*.   63 call the Earth] lo! the earth's *1802*.   64 those] these *4º, P. R.*   66 caverns] cavern *1834, 1852*. [Text of *1834* is here corrected.]   69 And ye that flying spot the [your *1802*] mountain-snows *1798* : And ye that fleeing spot the mountain-snows *4º, P. R.*   75 stormy] native *1802*.   77 taint] stain *1802*.   79 patriot] patient *1798, 1802*.   80 Was this thy boast *1802*. 81 Kings in the low lust] monarchs in the lust *1802*.

FRANCE: AN ODE

V

The Sensual and the Dark rebel in vain, 85
 Slaves by their own compulsion! In mad game
 They burst their manacles and wear the name
  Of Freedom, graven on a heavier chain!
O Liberty! with profitless endeavour
Have I pursued thee, many a weary hour; 90
 But thou nor swell'st the victor's strain, nor ever
Didst breathe thy soul in forms of human power.
 Alike from all, howe'er they praise thee,
 (Nor prayer, nor boastful name delays thee)
  Alike from Priestcraft's harpy minions, 95
 And factious Blasphemy's obscener slaves,
  Thou speedest on thy subtle pinions,
The guide of homeless winds, and playmate of the waves!
And there I felt thee!—on that sea-cliff's verge,
 Whose pines, scarce travelled by the breeze above, 100
Had made one murmur with the distant surge!
Yes, while I stood and gazed, my temples bare,
And shot my being through earth, sea, and air,
 Possessing all things with intensest love,
  O Liberty! my spirit felt thee there. 105

February, 1798.

85–9. The fifth stanza, which alluded to the African Slave Trade as conducted by this Country, and to the present Ministry and their supporters, has been omitted, and would have been omitted without remark if the commencing lines of the sixth stanza had not referred to it.

VI

Shall I with *these* my patriot zeal combine?
No, Afric, no! they stand before my ken
Loath'd as th' Hyaenas, that in murky den
Whine o'er their prey and mangle while they whine,
Divinest Liberty! with vain endeavour 1798.

87 burst] break *1802*. and] to *B. L., i. 194*. name] *name B. L.*
91 strain] pomp *B. L.* 92 in] on *1802*. 95 Priestcraft's] priesthood's *4°, P. R.*: superstition's *B. L.* 97 subtle] cherub *B. L.*
 98 To live amid the winds and move upon the waves *1798, 4°, P. R.*
  To live among the winds and brood upon the waves *1802*.
 99 there] *there 1798* : then *4°, P. R.* that] yon *1802*. 100 scarce] just *1802*.
102 Yes, as I stood and gazed my forehead bare *1802*. 104 with] by *1802*.

THE OLD MAN OF THE ALPS[1]

STRANGER! whose eyes a look of pity shew,
Say, will you listen to a tale of woe?
A tale in no unwonted horrors drest;
But sweet is pity to an agéd breast.
This voice did falter with old age before;   5
Sad recollections make it falter more.
Beside the torrent and beneath a wood,
High in these Alps my summer cottage stood;
One daughter still remain'd to cheer my way,
The evening-star of life's declining day: 10
Duly she hied to fill her milking-pail,
Ere shout of herdsmen rang from cliff or vale;
When she return'd, before the summer shiel,
On the fresh grass she spread the dairy meal;
Just as the snowy peaks began to lose   15
In glittering silver lights their rosy hues.
Singing in woods or bounding o'er the lawn,
No blither creature hail'd the early dawn;
And if I spoke of hearts by pain oppress'd,
When every friend is gone to them that rest;   20
Or of old men that leave, when they expire,
Daughters, that should have perish'd with their sire—
Leave them to toil all day through paths unknown,
And house at night behind some sheltering stone;
Impatient of the thought, with lively cheer   25
She broke half-closed the tasteless tale severe.
She play'd with fancies of a gayer hue,
Enamour'd of the scenes her *wishes* drew;
And oft she prattled with an eager tongue
Of promised joys that would not loiter long,   30

---

[1] First published in the *Morning Post*, March 8, 1798: first collected *P. and D. W.*, 1877-80: not included in *P. W.*, 1893. Coleridge affixed the signature Nicias Erythraeus to these lines and to *Lewti*, which was published in the *Morning Post* five weeks later, April 13, 1798. For a biographical notice of Janus Nicius Erythraeus (Giovanni Vittorio d'Rossi, 1577-1647) by the late Richard Garnett, see *Literature*, October 22, 1898.

THE OLD MAN OF THE ALPS

Till with her tearless eyes so bright and fair,
She seem'd to see them realis'd in air!
In fancy oft, within some sunny dell,
Where never wolf should howl or tempest yell,
She built a little home of joy and rest, 35
And fill'd it with the friends whom she lov'd best:
She named the inmates of her fancied cot,
And gave to each his own peculiar lot;
Which with our little herd abroad should roam,
And which should tend the dairy's toil at home, 40
And now the hour approach'd which should restore
Her lover from the wars, to part no more.
Her whole frame flutter'd with uneasy joy;
I long'd myself to clasp the valiant boy;
And though I strove to calm *her* eager mood, 45
It was my own sole thought in solitude.
I told it to the Saints amid my hymns—
For O! you know not, on an old man's limbs
How thrillingly the pleasant sun-beams play,
That shine upon his daughter's wedding-day. 50
I hoped, that those fierce tempests, soon to rave
Unheard, unfelt, around *my* mountain grave,
Not undelightfully would break *her* rest,
While she lay pillow'd on her lover's breast;
Or join'd his pious prayer for pilgrims driven 55
Out to the mercy of the winds of heaven.
Yes! now the hour approach'd that should restore
Her lover from the wars to part no more.
Her thoughts were wild, her soul was in her eye,
She wept and laugh'd as if she knew not why; 60
And she had made a song about the wars,
And sang it to the sun and to the stars!
But while she look'd and listen'd, stood and ran,
And saw him plain in every distant man,
By treachery stabbed, on NANSY's murderous day, 65
A senseless corse th' expected husband lay.
A wounded man, who met us in the wood,
Heavily ask'd her where *my* cottage stood,
And told us all: she cast her eyes around
As if his words had been but empty sound. 70
Then look'd to Heav'n, like one that would deny
That such a thing *could be* beneath the sky.
Again he ask'd her if she knew my name,
And instantly an anguish wrench'd her frame,
And left her mind imperfect. No delight 75

Thenceforth she found in any cheerful sight,
Not ev'n in those time-haunted wells and groves,
Scenes of past joy, and birth-place of her loves.
If to her spirit any sound was dear,
'Twas the deep moan that spoke the tempest near; 80
Or sighs which chasms of icy vales outbreathe,
Sent from the dark, imprison'd floods beneath.
She wander'd up the crag and down the slope,
But not, as in her happy days of hope,
To seek the churning-plant of sovereign power, 85
That grew in clefts and bore a scarlet flower!
She roam'd, without a purpose, all alone,
Thro' high grey vales unknowing and unknown.

Kind-hearted stranger! patiently you hear
A tedious tale: I thank you for that tear. 90
May never other tears o'ercloud your eye,
Than those which gentle Pity can supply!
Did you not mark a towering convent hang,
Where the huge rocks with sounds of torrents rang?
Ev'n yet, methinks, its spiry turrets swim 95
Amid yon purple gloom ascending dim!
For thither oft would my poor child repair,
To ease her soul by penitence and prayer.
I knew that peace at good men's prayers returns
Home to the contrite heart of him that mourns, 100
And check'd her not; and often there she found
A timely pallet when the evening frown'd.
And there I trusted that my child would light
On shelter and on food, one dreadful night,
When there was uproar in the element, 105
And she was absent. To my rest I went:
I thought her safe, yet often did I wake
And felt my very heart within me ache.
No daughter near me, at this very door,
Next morn I listen'd to the dying roar. 110
Above, below, the prowling vulture wail'd,
And down the cliffs the heavy vapour sail'd.
Up by the wide-spread waves in fury torn,
Homestalls and pines along the vale were borne.
The Dalesmen in thick crowds appear'd below 115
Clearing the road, o'erwhelm'd with hills of snow.
At times to the proud gust's ascending swell,
A pack of blood-hounds flung their doleful yell:

For after nights of storm, that dismal train
The pious convent sends, with hope humane, 120
To find some out-stretch'd man—perchance to save,
Or give, at least, that last good gift, a grave!
But now a gathering crowd did I survey,
That slowly up the pasture bent their way;
Nor could I doubt but that their care had found 125
Some pilgrim in th' unchannel'd torrent drown'd.
And down the lawn I hasten'd to implore
That they would bring the body to my door;
But soon exclaim'd a boy, who ran before,
'Thrown by the last night's waters from their bed, 130
Your daughter has been found, and she is dead!'

The old man paused—May he who, sternly just,
Lays at his will his creatures in the dust;
Some ere the earliest buds of hope be blown,
And some, when every bloom of joy is flown; 135
May he the parent to his child restore
In that unchanging realm, where Love reigns evermore!

March 8, 1798.

NICIAS ERYTHRAEUS.

TO A YOUNG LADY[1]

[MISS LAVINIA POOLE]

ON HER RECOVERY FROM A FEVER

WHY need I say, Louisa dear!
How glad I am to see you here,
  A lovely convalescent;
Risen from the bed of pain and fear,
  And feverish heat incessant.   5

The sunny showers, the dappled sky,
The little birds that warble high,
  Their vernal loves commencing,
Will better welcome you than I
  With their sweet influencing.   10

Believe me, while in bed you lay,
Your danger taught us all to pray:
  You made us grow devouter!
Each eye looked up and seemed to say,
  How can we do without her?   15

Besides, what vexed us worse, we knew,
They have no need of such as you
  In the place where you were going:
This World has angels all too few,
  And Heaven is overflowing!   20

March 31, 1798.

---

[1] First published in the *Morning Post*, Dec. 9, 1799, included in the *Annual Anthology*, 1800, in *Sibylline Leaves*, 1828, 1829, and 1834.

To a Young Lady, &c.—Title] To a Young Lady, on Her First Appearance After A Dangerous Illness. Written in the Spring of 1799 [1799 must be a slip for 1798]. *M. P., An. Anth.*
1 Louisa] Ophelia *M. P., An. Anth.*
6–7   The breezy air, the sun, the sky,
    The little birds that sing on high *M. P., An. Anth.*

12 all] how *M. P., An. Anth.*   13 grow] all *M. P., An. Anth.*   16 what] which *M. P., An. Anth.*   17 have] had *M. P., An. Anth.*   19 This] The *M. P.*   *Below* 20 Laberius *M. P., An. Anth.*

LEWTI[1]

OR THE CIRCASSIAN LOVE-CHAUNT

At midnight by the stream I roved,
To forget the form I loved.
Image of Lewti! from my mind
Depart; for Lewti is not kind.
The Moon was high, the moonlight gleam   5
  And the shadow of a star
Heaved upon Tamaha's stream;
  But the rock shone brighter far,
The rock half sheltered from my view
By pendent boughs of tressy yew.—   10
So shines my Lewti's forehead fair,
Gleaming through her sable hair.
Image of Lewti! from my mind
Depart; for Lewti is not kind.

---

[1] First published in the *Morning Post* (under the signature *Nicias Erythraeus*), April 13, 1798: included in the *Annual Anthology*, 1800; *Sibylline Leaves*, 1817, 1828, 1829, and 1834. For MS. versions vide Appendices. '*Lewti* was to have been included in the *Lyrical Ballads* of 1798, but at the last moment the sheets containing it were cancelled and *The Nightingale* substituted.' (Note to reprint of *L. B.* (1898), edited by T. Hutchinson.) A copy which belonged to Southey, with the new *Table of Contents* and *The Nightingale* bound up with the text as at first printed, is in the British Museum. Another copy is extant which contains the first *Table of Contents* only, and *Lewti* without the addition of *The Nightingale*. In the *M. P.* the following note accompanies the poem:—
'It is not amongst the least pleasing of our recollections, that we have been the means of gratifying the public taste with some exquisite pieces of Original Poetry. For many of them we have been indebted to the author of the Circassian's Love Chant. Amidst images of war and woe, amidst scenes of carnage and horror of devastation and dismay, it may afford the mind a temporary relief to wander to the magic haunts of the Muses, to bowers and fountains which the despoiling powers of war have never visited, and where the lover pours forth his complaint, or receives the recompense of his constancy. The whole of the subsequent Love Chant is in a warm and impassioned strain. The fifth and last stanzas are, we think, the best.'

Lewti, &c.—Title] Lewti; or the Circassian's Love Chant *M. P.*
Between lines 14–15
    I saw the white waves, o'er and o'er,
    Break against the distant shore.

I saw a cloud of palest hue,
  Onward to the moon it passed;
Still brighter and more bright it grew,
With floating colours not a few,
  Till it reached the moon at last:
Then the cloud was wholly bright,
With a rich and amber light!
And so with many a hope I seek,
  And with such joy I find my Lewti;
And even so my pale wan cheek
  Drinks in as deep a flush of beauty!
Nay, treacherous image! leave my mind,
If Lewti never will be kind.

The little cloud—it floats away,
  Away it goes; away so soon!
Alas! it has no power to stay:
Its hues are dim, its hues are grey—
  Away it passes from the moon!
How mournfully it seems to fly,
  Ever fading more and more,
To joyless regions of the sky—
  And now 'tis whiter than before!
As white as my poor cheek will be,
  When, Lewti! on my couch I lie,
A dying man for love of thee.
Nay, treacherous image! leave my mind—
And yet, thou didst not look unkind.

I saw a vapour in the sky,
Thin, and white, and very high;

  All at once upon the sight,
  All at once they broke in light;
  I heard no murmur of their roar,
  Nor ever I beheld them flowing,
  Neither coming, neither going;
  But only saw them o'er and o'er,
  Break against the curved shore:
  Now disappearing from the sight,
  Now twinkling regular and white,
  And Lewti's smiling mouth can shew
  As white and regular a row.
  Nay, treach'rous image from my mind
  Depart; for Lewti is not kind. *M. P.*

LEWTI

I ne'er beheld so thin a cloud:
  Perhaps the breezes that can fly   45
  Now below and now above,
Have snatched aloft the lawny shroud [1]
  Of Lady fair—that died for love.
For maids, as well as youths, have perished
From fruitless love too fondly cherished.   50
Nay, treacherous image! leave my mind—
For Lewti never will be kind.

Hush! my heedless feet from under
  Slip the crumbling banks for ever:
Like echoes to a distant thunder,   55
  They plunge into the gentle river.
The river-swans have heard my tread,
And startle from their reedy bed.
O beauteous birds! methinks ye measure
  Your movements to some heavenly tune!   60
O beauteous birds! 'tis such a pleasure
  To see you move beneath the moon,
I would it were your true delight
To sleep by day and wake all night.

---

[1] This image was borrowed by Miss Bailey (*sic*) in her Basil as the dates of the poems prove. *MS. Note by S. T. C.*

---

52 For] Tho' *M. P.*

Between lines 52-3

    This hand should make his life-blood flow
      That ever scorn'd my Lewti so.

I cannot chuse but fix my sight
  On that small vapour, thin and white!
So thin it scarcely, I protest,
  Bedims the star that shines behind it!
And pity dwells in Lewti's breast
  Alas! if I knew how to find it.
And O! how sweet it were, I wist,
  To see my Lewti's eyes to-morrow
Shine brightly thro' as thin a mist
  Of pity and repentant sorrow!
Nay treach'rous image! leave my mind—
Ah, Lewti! why art thou unkind?

53 Hush!] Slush! *Sibylline Leaves* (*Errata, S. L.*, p. [xi], for *Slush* r. *Hush*).

I know the place where Lewti lies,
    When silent night has closed her eyes:
    It is a breezy jasmine-bower,
The nightingale sings o'er her head:
    Voice of the Night! had I the power
That leafy labyrinth to thread,
And creep, like thee, with soundless tread,
I then might view her bosom white
Heaving lovely to my sight,
As these two swans together heave
On the gently-swelling wave.

Oh! that she saw me in a dream,
    And dreamt that I had died for care;
All pale and wasted I would seem,
    Yet fair withal, as spirits are!
I'd die indeed, if I might see
Her bosom heave, and heave for me!
Soothe, gentle image! soothe my mind!
To-morrow Lewti may be kind.

1798.

FEARS IN SOLITUDE [1]

WRITTEN IN APRIL 1798, DURING THE ALARM
OF AN INVASION

A GREEN and silent spot, amid the hills,
A small and silent dell! O'er stiller place

[1] First published in a quarto pamphlet 'printed by J. Johnson in S. Paul's Churchyard, 1798': included in *Poetical Register*, 1808–9 (1812), and, with the same text, in an octavo pamphlet printed by Law and Gilbert in (?) 1812: in *Sibylline Leaves*, 1817, 1828, 1829, and 1834. Lines 129–97 were

---

69–71   Had I the enviable power
        To creep unseen with noiseless tread
        Then should I view *M. P., An. Anth.*
        O beating heart had I the power.
                    MS. Corr. An. Anth. by S. T. C.
73 my] the *M. P., An. Anth.*
Below 83 Signed Nicias Erythraeus. *M. P.*
Fears in Solitude—Title] Fears &c. Written, April 1798, during the Alarms of an Invasion *MS., W., 4°*: Fears &c. Written April 1798, &c. *P. R.*

No singing sky-lark ever poised himself.
The hills are heathy, save that swelling slope,
Which hath a gay and gorgeous covering on,
All golden with the never-bloomless furze,
Which now blooms most profusely: but the dell,
Bathed by the mist, is fresh and delicate
As vernal corn-field, or the unripe flax,
When, through its half-transparent stalks, at eve,
The level sunshine glimmers with green light.
Oh! 'tis a quiet spirit-healing nook!
Which all, methinks, would love; but chiefly he,
The humble man, who, in his youthful years,
Knew just so much of folly, as had made
His early manhood more securely wise!
Here he might lie on fern or withered heath,
While from the singing lark (that sings unseen
The minstrelsy that solitude loves best),
And from the sun, and from the breezy air,
Sweet influences trembled o'er his frame;
And he, with many feelings, many thoughts,
Made up a meditative joy, and found
Religious meanings in the forms of Nature!
And so, his senses gradually wrapt
In a half sleep, he dreams of better worlds,
And dreaming hears thee still, O singing lark,
That singest like an angel in the clouds!

My God! it is a melancholy thing
For such a man, who would full fain preserve
His soul in calmness, yet perforce must feel
For all his human brethren—O my God!
It weighs upon the heart, that he must think

reprinted in the *Morning Post*, Oct. 14, 1802. They follow the reprint of
France : an Ode, and are thus prefaced :—'The following extracts are made
from a Poem by the same author, written in April 1798 during the alarm
respecting the threatened invasion.' They were included in *The Friend*,
No. II (June 8, 1809), as *Fears of Solitude.*' An autograph MS. (in the
possession of Professor Dowden), undated but initialled S. T. C., is subscribed
as follows :—' N. B. The above is perhaps not Poetry,—but rather a sort of
middle thing between Poetry and Oratory—sermoni propriora.—Some
parts are, I am conscious, too tame even for animated prose.' An autograph
MS. dated (as below 232) is in the possession of Mr. Gordon Wordsworth.

19 that] which *4°, P. R.*
33   It is indeed a melancholy thing
            And weighs upon the heart *4°, P. R., S. L.*

258 FEARS IN SOLITUDE

What uproar and what strife may now be stirring
This way or that way o'er these silent hills— 35
Invasion, and the thunder and the shout,
And all the crash of onset; fear and rage,
And undetermined conflict—even now,
Even now, perchance, and in his native isle:
Carnage and groans beneath this blessed sun! 40
We have offended, Oh! my countrymen!
We have offended very grievously,
And been most tyrannous. From east to west
A groan of accusation pierces Heaven!
The wretched plead against us; multitudes 45
Countless and vehement, the sons of God,
Our brethren! Like a cloud that travels on,
Steamed up from Cairo's swamps of pestilence,
Even so, my countrymen! have we gone forth
And borne to distant tribes slavery and pangs, 50
And, deadlier far, our vices, whose deep taint
With slow perdition murders the whole man,
His body and his soul! Meanwhile, at home,
All individual dignity and power
Engulfed in Courts, Committees, Institutions, 55
Associations and Societies,
A vain, speech-mouthing, speech-reporting Guild,
One Benefit-Club for mutual flattery,
We have drunk up, demure as at a grace,
Pollutions from the brimming cup of wealth; 60
Contemptuous of all honourable rule,
Yet bartering freedom and the poor man's life
For gold, as at a market! The sweet words
Of Christian promise, words that even yet
Might stem destruction, were they wisely preached, 65

---

40 groans] screams 4°, *P. R.*   43 And have been tyrannous 4°, *P. R.*
44–60   The groan of accusation pleads against us.
* * * * *

Desunt aliqua
. . . Meanwhile at home
We have been drinking with a riotous thirst
Pollutions, &c. *MS. D.*

53–9   Meanwhile at home
We have been drinking with a riotous thirst.
Pollutions from the brimming cup of wealth
A selfish, lewd, effeminated race. *MS. W.*, 4°, *P. R.*

[Lines 54–8 of the text were added in *Sibylline Leaves, 1817.*]

Are muttered o'er by men, whose tones proclaim
How flat and wearisome they feel their trade:
Rank scoffers some, but most too indolent
To deem them falsehoods or to know their truth.
Oh! blasphemous! the Book of Life is made 70
A superstitious instrument, on which
We gabble o'er the oaths we mean to break;
For all must swear—all and in every place,
College and wharf, council and justice-court;
All, all must swear, the briber and the bribed, 75
Merchant and lawyer, senator and priest,
The rich, the poor, the old man and the young;
All, all make up one scheme of perjury,
That faith doth reel; the very name of God
Sounds like a juggler's charm; and, bold with joy, 80
Forth from his dark and lonely hiding-place,
(Portentous sight!) the owlet Atheism,
Sailing on obscene wings athwart the noon,
Drops his blue-fringéd lids, and holds them close,
And hooting at the glorious sun in Heaven, 85
Cries out, 'Where is it?'

                      Thankless too for peace,
(Peace long preserved by fleets and perilous seas)
Secure from actual warfare, we have loved
To swell the war-whoop, passionate for war!
Alas! for ages ignorant of all 90
Its ghastlier workings, (famine or blue plague,
Battle, or siege, or flight through wintry snows,)
We, this whole people, have been clamorous
For war and bloodshed; animating sports,
The which we pay for as a thing to talk of, 95
Spectators and not combatants! No guess
Anticipative of a wrong unfelt,
No speculation on contingency,
However dim and vague, too vague and dim
To yield a justifying cause; and forth, 100
(Stuffed out with big preamble, holy names,
And adjurations of the God in Heaven,)
We send our mandates for the certain death
Of thousands and ten thousands! Boys and girls,
And women, that would groan to see a child 105
Pull off an insect's leg, all read of war,

69 know] *know MS. W., 4°, P. R.*

The best amusement for our morning meal!
The poor wretch, who has learnt his only prayers
From curses, who knows scarcely words enough
To ask a blessing from his Heavenly Father, 110
Becomes a fluent phraseman, absolute
And technical in victories and defeats,
And all our dainty terms for fratricide;
Terms which we trundle smoothly o'er our tongues
Like mere abstractions, empty sounds to which 115
We join no feeling and attach no form!
As if the soldier died without a wound;
As if the fibres of this godlike frame
Were gored without a pang; as if the wretch,
Who fell in battle, doing bloody deeds, 120
Passed off to Heaven, translated and not killed;
As though he had no wife to pine for him,
No God to judge him! Therefore, evil days
Are coming on us, O my countrymen!
And what if all-avenging Providence, 125
Strong and retributive, should make us know
The meaning of our words, force us to feel
The desolation and the agony
Of our fierce doings?

     Spare us yet awhile,
Father and God! O! spare us yet awhile! 130
Oh! let not English women drag their flight
Fainting beneath the burthen of their babes,
Of the sweet infants, that but yesterday
Laughed at the breast! Sons, brothers, husbands, all
Who ever gazed with fondness on the forms 135
Which grew up with you round the same fire-side,
And all who ever heard the sabbath-bells
Without the infidel's scorn, make yourselves pure!
Stand forth! be men! repel an impious foe,
Impious and false, a light yet cruel race, 140

 110 from] of *4°, P. R.* 112 defeats] deceit *S. L.* [*Probably a misprint*].
121 translated] *translated 4°, P. R.* 131 drag] speed *1809.* 133
that] who *1802, 1809.* 134 Laugh'd at the bosom! Husbands,
fathers, all *1802* : Smil'd at the bosom! Husbands, Brothers, all *The
Friend, 1809.* 136 Which] That *1802.* 138 pure] strong *1809.*
139 foe] race *1809.*
 138-9 Without the Infidel's scorn, stand forth, be men,
   Make yourselves strong, repel an impious foe *1802.*
 140 yet] and *MS. W.*

FEARS IN SOLITUDE

Who laugh away all virtue, mingling mirth
With deeds of murder; and still promising
Freedom, themselves too sensual to be free,
Poison life's amities, and cheat the heart
Of faith and quiet hope, and all that soothes,   145
And all that lifts the spirit! Stand we forth;
Render them back upon the insulted ocean,
And let them toss as idly on its waves
As the vile sea-weed, which some mountain-blast
Swept from our shores! And oh! may we return   150
Not with a drunken triumph, but with fear,
Repenting of the wrongs with which we stung
So fierce a foe to frenzy!

                 I have told,
O Britons! O my brethren! I have told
Most bitter truth, but without bitterness.   155
Nor deem my zeal or factious or mistimed;
For never can true courage dwell with them,
Who, playing tricks with conscience, dare not look
At their own vices. We have been too long
Dupes of a deep delusion! Some, belike,   160
Groaning with restless enmity, expect
All change from change of constituted power;
As if a Government had been a robe,

---

141 Who] That *4º, P. R., 1802, 1809.*   146 we] ye *1809.*   148 toss] float *1809.*   149 sea-weed] sea-weeds *MS. W., 4º, 1802.* some] the *1809.*
150 Swept] Sweeps *1809.*   151 fear] awe *1802.*

    151-3   Not in a drunken triumph, but with awe
          Repentant of the wrongs, with which we stung
          So fierce a race to Frenzy. *1809.*

154 O men of England! Brothers! I have told *1809.*   155 truth] truths *1802, 1809.*   156 factious] factitious *1809.*   157 courage] freedom *1802.*   159-61 At their own vices. Fondly some expect [We have been . . . enmity *om.*] *1802.*   162 constituted] delegated *1802.*

    161-4   Restless in enmity have thought all change
          Involv'd in change of constituted power.
          As if a Government were but a robe
          On which our vice and wretchedness were sewn. *1809.*

163 had been] were but *1809.*

    163-75   As if a government were but a robe
           To which our crimes and miseries were affix'd,
           Like fringe, or epaulet, and with the robe
           Pull'd off at pleasure. Others, the meantime,
           Doat with a mad idolatry, and all
           Who will not bow their heads, and close their eyes,
           And worship blindly—these are enemies
           Even of their country. Such have they deemed *me. 1802.*

On which our vice and wretchedness were tagged
Like fancy-points and fringes, with the robe 165
Pulled off at pleasure. Fondly these attach
A radical causation to a few
Poor drudges of chastising Providence,
Who borrow all their hues and qualities
From our own folly and rank wickedness, 170
Which gave them birth and nursed them. Others, meanwhile,
Dote with a mad idolatry; and all
Who will not fall before their images,
And yield them worship, they are enemies
Even of their country!

                Such have I been deemed.— 175
But, O dear Britain! O my Mother Isle!
Needs must thou prove a name most dear and holy
To me, a son, a brother, and a friend,
A husband, and a father! who revere
All bonds of natural love, and find them all 180
Within the limits of thy rocky shores.
O native Britain! O my Mother Isle!
How shouldst thou prove aught else but dear and holy
To me, who from thy lakes and mountain-hills,
Thy clouds, thy quiet dales, thy rocks and seas, 185
Have drunk in all my intellectual life,
All sweet sensations, all ennobling thoughts,
All adoration of the God in nature,
All lovely and all honourable things,
Whatever makes this mortal spirit feel 190
The joy and greatness of its future being?
There lives nor form nor feeling in my soul
Unborrowed from my country! O divine
And beauteous island! thou hast been my sole
And most magnificent temple, in the which 195

166-71 Fondly ... nursed them *om. 1809.*   171 nursed] nurse *4°, S. L.*   meanwhile] meantime *1809.*   175 *Such have I been deemed 1809.*   177 prove] be *1802, 1809.*   179 father] parent *1809.*   180 All natural bonds of *1802.*   181 limits] circle *1802, 1809.*   183 couldst thou be *1802*: shouldst thou be *1809.*

  184-5   To me who from thy brooks and mountain-hills,
             Thy quiet fields, thy clouds, thy rocks, thy seas *1802.*
           To me who from thy seas and rocky shores
             Thy quiet fields thy streams and wooded hills *1809.*

FEARS IN SOLITUDE

I walk with awe, and sing my stately songs,
Loving the God that made me!—

                          May my fears,
My filial fears, be vain! and may the vaunts
And menace of the vengeful enemy
Pass like the gust, that roared and died away   200
In the distant tree: which heard, and only heard
In this low dell, bowed not the delicate grass.

But now the gentle dew-fall sends abroad
The fruit-like perfume of the golden furze:
The light has left the summit of the hill,   205
Though still a sunny gleam lies beautiful,
Aslant the ivied beacon. Now farewell,
Farewell, awhile, O soft and silent spot!
On the green sheep-track, up the heathy hill,
Homeward I wind my way; and lo! recalled   210
From bodings that have well-nigh wearied me,
I find myself upon the brow, and pause
Startled! And after lonely sojourning
In such a quiet and surrounded nook,
This burst of prospect, here the shadowy main,   215
Dim-tinted, there the mighty majesty
Of that huge amphitheatre of rich
And elmy fields, seems like society—
Conversing with the mind, and giving it
A livelier impulse and a dance of thought!   220
And now, belovéd Stowey! I behold
Thy church-tower, and, methinks, the four huge elms
Clustering, which mark the mansion of my friend;
And close behind them, hidden from my view,
Is my own lowly cottage, where my babe   225
And my babe's mother dwell in peace! With light
And quickened footsteps thitherward I tend,
Remembering thee, O green and silent dell!
And grateful, that by nature's quietness
And solitary musings, all my heart   230
Is softened, and made worthy to indulge
Love, and the thoughts that yearn for human kind.

    NETHER STOWEY, *April* 20, 1798.

  207 Aslant the ivied] On the long-ivied *MS. W.*, *4º*.   214 nook] scene *MS. W.*, *4º*, *P. R.*

THE NIGHTINGALE[1]

A CONVERSATION POEM, APRIL, 1798

No cloud, no relique of the sunken day
Distinguishes the West, no long thin slip
Of sullen light, no obscure trembling hues.
Come, we will rest on this old mossy bridge!
You see the glimmer of the stream beneath,   5
But hear no murmuring: it flows silently,
O'er its soft bed of verdure. All is still,
A balmy night! and though the stars be dim,
Yet let us think upon the vernal showers
That gladden the green earth, and we shall find   10
A pleasure in the dimness of the stars.
And hark! the Nightingale begins its song,
'Most musical, most melancholy' bird![2]
A melancholy bird? Oh! idle thought!
In Nature there is nothing melancholy.   15
But some night-wandering man whose heart was pierced
With the remembrance of a grievous wrong,
Or slow distemper, or neglected love,
(And so, poor wretch! filled all things with himself,
And made all gentle sounds tell back the tale   20
Of his own sorrow) he, and such as he,
First named these notes a melancholy strain.
And many a poet echoes the conceit;
Poet who hath been building up the rhyme

---

[1] First published in *Lyrical Ballads*, 1798, reprinted in *Lyrical Ballads*, 1800, 1802, and 1805: included in *Sibylline Leaves*, 1817, 1828, 1829, and 1834.

[2] '*Most musical, most melancholy.*' This passage in Milton possesses an excellence far superior to that of mere description; it is spoken in the character of the melancholy Man, and has therefore a *dramatic* propriety. The Author makes this remark, to rescue himself from the charge of having alluded with levity to a line in Milton; a charge than which none could be more painful to him, except perhaps that of having ridiculed his Bible. *Footnote* to l. 13 *L. B.* 1798, *L. B.* 1800, *S. L.* 1817, 1828, 1829. In 1834 the footnote ends with the word 'Milton', the last sentence being omitted.

Note. In the Table of Contents of *1828* and *1829* 'The Nightingale' is omitted.

The Nightingale—Title] The Nightingale; a Conversational Poem, written in April, 1798 *L. B. 1798*: The Nightingale, written in April, 1798 *L. B. 1800*: The Nightingale A Conversation Poem, written in April, 1798 *S. L.*, 1828, 1829.

21 sorrow] sorrows *L. B. 1798, 1800*.

And he beheld the moon, and, hushed at once,
Suspends his sobs, and laughs most silently,
While his fair eyes, that swam with undropped tears,
Did glitter in the yellow moon-beam! Well!—   105
It is a father's tale: But if that Heaven
Should give me life, his childhood shall grow up
Familiar with these songs, that with the night
He may associate joy.—Once more, farewell,
Sweet Nightingale! once more, my friends! farewell.   110
1798.

THE THREE GRAVES[1]

A FRAGMENT OF A SEXTON'S TALE

'THE Author has published the following humble fragment, encouraged by the decisive recommendation of more than one of our most celebrated living Poets. The language was intended to be dramatic; that is, suited to the narrator; and the metre corresponds to the homeliness of the diction. It is therefore presented as the fragment, not of a Poem, but of a common Ballad-tale.[2] Whether this is sufficient to justify the adoption of such a style, in any metrical composition not professedly ludicrous, the Author is himself in some doubt. At all events, it is not presented as poetry, and it is in no way connected with the Author's judgment concerning poetic diction. Its merits, if any, are exclusively psychological. The

[1] Parts III and IV of the *Three Graves* were first published in *The Friend*, No. VI, September 21, 1809. They were included in *Sibylline Leaves*, 1817, 1828, 1829, and 1834. Parts I and II, which were probably written in the spring of 1798, at the same time as Parts III and IV, were first published, from an autograph MS. copy, in *Poems*, 1893. [For evidence of date compare ll. 255-8 with Dorothy Wordsworth's *Alfoxden Journal* for March 20, 24, and April 6, 8.] The original MS. of Parts III and IV is not forthcoming. The MS. of the poem as published in *The Friend* is in the handwriting of Miss Sarah Stoddart (afterwards Mrs. Hazlitt), and is preserved with other 'copy' of *The Friend* (of which the greater part is in the handwriting of Miss Sarah Hutchinson) in the Forster Collection which forms part of the Victoria and Albert Museum, South Kensington. The preface and emendations are in the handwriting of S. T. C. The poem was reprinted in the *British Minstrel*, Glasgow, 1821 as 'a modern ballad of the very first rank'. In a marginal note in Mr. Samuel's copy of *Sibylline Leaves* Coleridge writes:—'This very poem was selected, notwithstanding the preface, as a proof of my judgment and poetic diction, and a fair specimen of the style of my poems generally (see the *Mirror*): nay! the very words of the preface were used, omitting the *not*,' &c. See for this and other critical matter, *Lyrical Ballads*, 1798, edited by Thomas Hutchinson, 1898. *Notes*, p. 257.

[2] in the common ballad metre *MS*.

102 beheld] beholds *L. B. 1798, 1800*.

story which must be supposed to have been narrated in the first and second parts is as follows:—

'Edward, a young farmer, meets at the house of Ellen her bosom-friend Mary, and commences an acquaintance, which ends in a mutual attachment. With her consent, and by the advice of their common friend Ellen, he announces his hopes and intentions to Mary's mother, a widow-woman bordering on her fortieth year, and from constant health, the possession of a competent property, and from having had no other children but Mary and another daughter (the father died in their infancy), retaining for the greater part her personal attractions and comeliness of appearance; but a woman of low education and violent temper. The answer which she at once returned to Edward's application was remarkable—"Well, Edward! you are a handsome young fellow, and you shall have my daughter." From this time all their wooing passed under the mother's eye; and, in fine, she became herself enamoured of her future son-in-law, and practised every art, both of endearment and of calumny, to transfer his affections from her daughter to herself. (The outlines of the Tale are positive facts, and of no very distant date, though the author has purposely altered the names and the scene of action, as well as invented the characters of the parties and the detail of the incidents.) Edward, however, though perplexed by her strange detractions from her daughter's good qualities, yet in the innocence of his own heart still mistook[1] her increasing fondness for motherly affection; she at length, overcome by her miserable passion, after much abuse of Mary's temper and moral tendencies, exclaimed with violent emotion—"O Edward! indeed, indeed, she is not fit for you—she has not a heart to love you as you deserve. It is I that love you! Marry me, Edward! and I will this very day settle all my property on you." The Lover's eyes were now opened; and thus taken by surprise, whether from the effect of the horror which he felt, acting as it were hysterically on his nervous system, or that at the first moment he lost the sense of the guilt of the proposal in the feeling of its strangeness and absurdity, he flung her from him and burst into a fit of laughter. Irritated by this almost to frenzy, the woman fell on her knees, and in a loud voice that approached to a scream, she prayed for a curse both on him and on her own child. Mary happened to be in the room directly above them, heard Edward's laugh, and her mother's blasphemous prayer, and fainted away. He, hearing the fall, ran upstairs, and taking her in his arms, carried her

[1] mistaking *The Friend*.

off to Ellen's home; and after some fruitless attempts on her part toward a reconciliation with her mother, she was married to him.—And here the third part of the Tale begins.

'I was not led to choose this story from any partiality to tragic, much less to monstrous events (though at the time that I composed the verses, somewhat more than twelve years ago, I was less averse to such subjects than at present), but from finding in it a striking proof of the possible effect on the imagination, from an idea violently and suddenly impressed on it. I had been reading Bryan Edwards's account of the effects of the *Oby* witchcraft on the Negroes in the West Indies, and Hearne's deeply interesting anecdotes of similar workings on the imagination of the Copper Indians (those of my readers who have it in their power will be well repaid for the trouble of referring to those works for the passages alluded to); and I conceived the design of shewing that instances of this kind are not peculiar to savage or barbarous tribes, and of illustrating the mode in which the mind is affected in these cases, and the progress and symptoms of the morbid action on the fancy from the beginning.

'The Tale is supposed to be narrated by an old Sexton, in a country church-yard, to a traveller whose curiosity had been awakened by the appearance of three graves, close by each other, to two only of which there were grave-stones. On the first of these was the name, and dates, as usual: on the second, no name, but only a date, and the words, "The Mercy of God is infinite."[1]' *S. L. 1817, 1828, 1829.*

[PART I—FROM MS.]

BENEATH this thorn when I was young,
   This thorn that blooms so sweet,
We loved to stretch our lazy limbs
   In summer's noon-tide heat.

---

[1] In the first issue of *The Friend*, No. VI, September 21, 1809, the poem was thus introduced:—'As I wish to commence the important Subject of—*The Principles* of political Justice with a separate number of THE FRIEND, and shall at the same time comply with the wishes communicated to me by one of my female Readers, who writes as the representative of many others, I shall conclude this Number with the following Fragment, or the third and fourth [second and third *MS. S.T.C.*] parts of a Tale consisting of six. The two last parts may be given hereafter, if the present should appear to have afforded pleasure, and to have answered the purpose of a relief and amusement to my Readers. The story as it is contained in the first and second parts is as follows: *Edward a young farmer*, etc.'

4 In the silent summer heat *MS. alternative reading.*

And hither too the old man came, 5
  The maiden and her feer,
'Then tell me, Sexton, tell me why
  The toad has harbour here.

'The Thorn is neither dry nor dead,
  But still it blossoms sweet; 10
Then tell me why all round its roots
  The dock and nettle meet.

'Why here the hemlock, &c. [*sic in MS.*]

'Why these three graves all side by side,
  Beneath the flow'ry thorn, 15
Stretch out so green and dark a length,
  By any foot unworn.'

There, there a ruthless mother lies
  Beneath the flowery thorn;
And there a barren wife is laid, 20
  And there a maid forlorn.

The barren wife and maid forlorn
  Did love each other dear;
The ruthless mother wrought the woe,
  And cost them many a tear. 25

Fair Ellen was of serious mind,
  Her temper mild and even,
And Mary, graceful as the fir
  That points the spire to heaven.

Young Edward he to Mary said, 30
  'I would you were my bride,'
And she was scarlet as he spoke,
  And turned her face to hide.

'You know my mother she is rich,
  And you have little gear; 35
And go and if she say not Nay,
  Then I will be your fere.'

Young Edward to the mother went,
  To him the mother said:
'In truth you are a comely man; 40
  You shall my daughter wed.'

14 Why these three graves all in a row *MS. alternative reading.*
16 Stretch out their dark and gloomy length *MS. erased.*
33 turned] strove *MS. erased.*

THE THREE GRAVES

[1] [In Mary's joy fair Eleanor
  Did bear a sister's part;
For why, though not akin in blood,
  They sisters were in heart.] 45

Small need to tell to any man
  That ever shed a tear
What passed within the lover's heart
  The happy day so near.

The mother, more than mothers use, 50
  Rejoiced when they were by;
And all the 'course of wooing' passed [2]
  Beneath the mother's eye.

And here within the flowering thorn
  How deep they drank of joy: 55
The mother fed upon the sight,
  Nor . . .   [*sic in MS.*]

[PART II—FROM MS.] [3]

And now the wedding day was fix'd,
  The wedding-ring was bought;
The wedding-cake with her own hand 60
  The ruthless mother brought.

'And when to-morrow's sun shines forth
  The maid shall be a bride';
Thus Edward to the mother spake
  While she sate by his side. 65

Alone they sate within the bower:
  The mother's colour fled,
For Mary's foot was heard above—
  She decked the bridal bed.

And when her foot was on the stairs 70
  To meet her at the door,
With steady step the mother rose,
  And silent left the bower.

---

[1] It is uncertain whether this stanza is erased, or merely blotted in the MS.   [2] *Othello* iii. 3.
[3] The words 'Part II' are not in the MS.

---

49 happy] wedding *MS. variant.*

She stood, her back against the door,
 And when her child drew near—
'Away! away!' the mother cried,
 'Ye shall not enter here.

'Would ye come here, ye maiden vile.
 And rob me of my mate?'
And on her child the mother scowled
 A deadly leer of hate.

Fast rooted to the spot, you guess,
 The wretched maiden stood,
As pale as any ghost of night
 That wanteth flesh and blood.

She did not groan, she did not fall,
 She did not shed a tear,
Nor did she cry, 'Oh! mother, why
 May I not enter here?'

But wildly up the stairs she ran,
 As if her sense was fled,
And then her trembling limbs she threw
 Upon the bridal bed.

The mother she to Edward went
 Where he sate in the bower,
And said, 'That woman is not fit
 To be your paramour.

'She is my child—it makes my heart
 With grief and trouble swell;
I rue the hour that gave her birth,
 For never worse befel.

'For she is fierce and she is proud,
 And of an envious mind;
A wily hypocrite she is,
 And giddy as the wind.

'And if you go to church with her,
 You'll rue the bitter smart;
For she will wrong your marriage-bed,
 And she will break your heart.

81 A deadly] The ghastly *MS. erased.*

THE THREE GRAVES

'Oh God, to think that I have shared
  Her deadly sin so long;
She is my child, and therefore I
  As mother held my tongue.

'She is my child, I've risked for her
  My living soul's estate:
I cannot say my daily prayers,
  The burthen is so great.

'And she would scatter gold about
  Until her back was bare;
And should you swing for lust of hers
  In truth she'd little care.'

Then in a softer tone she said,
  And took him by the hand:
'Sweet Edward, for one kiss of your's
  I'd give my house and land.

'And if you'll go to church with me,
  And take me for your bride,
I'll make you heir of all I have—
  Nothing shall be denied.'

Then Edward started from his seat,
  And he laughed loud and long—
'In truth, good mother, you are mad,
  Or drunk with liquor strong.'

To him no word the mother said,
  But on her knees she fell,
And fetched her breath while thrice your hand
  Might toll the passing-bell.

'Thou daughter now above my head,
  Whom in my womb I bore,
May every drop of thy heart's blood
  Be curst for ever more.

'And curséd be the hour when first
  I heard thee wawl and cry;
And in the Church-yard curséd be
  The grave where thou shalt lie!'

And Mary on the bridal-bed
  Her mother's curse had heard;
And while the cruel mother spake
  The bed beneath her stirred.

In wrath young Edward left the hall,   150
  And turning round he sees
The mother looking up to God
  And still upon her knees.

Young Edward he to Mary went
  When on the bed she lay: 155
'Sweet love, this is a wicked house—
  Sweet love, we must away.'

He raised her from the bridal-bed,
  All pale and wan with fear;
'No Dog,' quoth he, 'if he were mine,   160
  No Dog would kennel here.'

He led her from the bridal-bed,
  He led her from the stairs.
[Had sense been hers she had not dar'd
  To venture on her prayers. *MS. erased.*]

The mother still was in the bower,
  And with a greedy heart   165
She *drank perdition* on her knees,
  Which never may depart.

But when their steps were heard below
  On God she did not call;
She did forget the God of Heaven,   170
  For they were in the hall.

She started up—the servant maid
  Did see her when she rose;
And she has oft declared to me
  The blood within her froze.   175

As Edward led his bride away
  And hurried to the door,
The ruthless mother springing forth
  Stopped midway on the floor.

What did she mean? What did she mean?   180
  For with a smile she cried:
'Unblest ye shall not pass my door,
  The bride-groom and his bride.

THE THREE GRAVES

Be blithe as lambs in April are,
  As flies when fruits are red;
May God forbid that thought of me
  Should haunt your marriage-bed.

'And let the night be given to bliss,
  The day be given to glee:
I am a woman weak and old,
  Why turn a thought on me?

'What can an agéd mother do,
  And what have ye to dread?
A curse is wind, it hath no shape
  To haunt your marriage-bed.'

When they were gone and out of sight
  She rent her hoary hair,
And foamed like any Dog of June
  When sultry sun-beams glare.

* * * * * *

Now ask you why the barren wife,
  And why the maid forlorn,
And why the ruthless mother lies
  Beneath the flowery thorn?

Three times, three times this spade of mine,
  In spite of bolt or bar,
Did from beneath the belfry come,
  When spirits wandering are.

And when the mother's soul to Hell
  By howling fiends was borne,
This spade was seen to mark her grave
  Beneath the flowery thorn.

And when the death-knock at the door
  Called home the maid forlorn,
This spade was seen to mark her grave
  Beneath the flowery thorn.

And 'tis a fearful, fearful tree;
  The ghosts that round it meet,
'Tis they that cut the rind at night,
  Yet still it blossoms sweet.

* * * * * *

[*End of MS.*]

Part III[1]

The grapes upon the Vicar's wall
  Were ripe as ripe could be;
And yellow leaves in sun and wind
  Were falling from the tree.

On the hedge-elms in the narrow lane
  Still swung the spikes of corn:
Dear Lord! it seems but yesterday—
  Young Edward's marriage-morn.

Up through that wood behind the church,
  There leads from Edward's door
A mossy track, all over boughed,
  For half a mile or more.

And from their house-door by that track
  The bride and bridegroom went;
Sweet Mary, though she was not gay,
  Seemed cheerful and content.

But when they to the church-yard came,
  I've heard poor Mary say,
As soon as she stepped into the sun,
  Her heart it died away.

And when the Vicar join'd their hands,
  Her limbs did creep and freeze:
But when they prayed, she thought she saw
  Her mother on her knees.

---

[1] In the MS. of *The Friend*, Part III is headed:—'The Three Graves. A Sexton's Tale. A Fragment.' A MS. note *erased* in the handwriting of S. T. C. is attached:—'N.B. Written for me by Sarah Stoddart before her brother was an entire Blank. I have not *voluntarily* been guilty of any desecration of holy *Names*.' In *The Friend*, in *Sibylline Leaves*, in 1828, 1829, and 1834, the poem is headed 'The Three Graves, &c.' The heading 'Part III' first appeared in 1893.

Part III] III *MS. erased*.
220 foll. In *The Friend* the lines were printed continuously. The division into stanzas (as in the MS.) dates from the republication of the poem in *Sibylline Leaves*, 1817. 221 as ripe] as they *MS*. 224 High on the hedge-elms in the lane *MS. erased*. 225 spikes] strikes *Sibylline Leaves, 1817*. [*Note*. It is possible that 'strikes'—a Somersetshire word—(compare 'strikes of flax') was deliberately substituted for 'spikes'. It does not appear in the long list of *Errata* prefixed to *Sibylline Leaves*. Wagons passing through narrow lanes leave on the hedge-rows not single 'spikes', but little swathes or fillets of corn.] 230 over boughed] over-bough'd *MS*. 242 they] he *MS. The Friend, 1809*.

THE THREE GRAVES

And o'er the church-path they returned—
  I saw poor Mary's back,   245
Just as she stepped beneath the boughs
  Into the mossy track.

Her feet upon the mossy track
  The married maiden set:
That moment—I have heard her say—   250
  She wished she could forget.

The shade o'er-flushed her limbs with heat—
  Then came a chill like death:
And when the merry bells rang out,
  They seemed to stop her breath.   255

Beneath the foulest mother's curse
  No child could ever thrive:
A mother is a mother still,
  The holiest thing alive.

So five months passed: the mother still   260
  Would never heal the strife;
But Edward was a loving man
  And Mary a fond wife.

'My sister may not visit us,
  My mother says her nay: 265
O Edward! you are all to me,
I wish for your sake I could be
  More lifesome and more gay.

'I'm dull and sad! indeed, indeed
  I know I have no reason!   270
Perhaps I am not well in health,
  And 'tis a gloomy season.'

'Twas a drizzly time—no ice, no snow!
  And on the few fine days
She stirred not out, lest she might meet   275
  Her mother in the ways.

But Ellen, spite of miry ways
  And weather dark and dreary,
Trudged every day to Edward's house,
  And made them all more cheery.   280

---

260 So five months passed: this mother foul *MS erased*.   278 dark]
dank *MS. The Friend, 1809.*

Oh! Ellen was a faithful friend,
  More dear than any sister!
As cheerful too as singing lark;
And she ne'er left them till 'twas dark,
  And then they always missed her.   285

And now Ash-Wednesday came—that day
  But few to church repair:
For on that day you know we read
  The Commination prayer.

Our late old Vicar, a kind man,   290
  Once, Sir, he said to me,
He wished that service was clean out
  Of our good Liturgy.

The mother walked into the church—
  To Ellen's seat she went: 295
Though Ellen always kept her church
  All church-days during Lent.

And gentle Ellen welcomed her
  With courteous looks and mild:
Thought she, 'What if her heart should melt, 300
  And all be reconciled!'

The day was scarcely like a day—
  The clouds were black outright:
And many a night, with half a moon,
  I've seen the church more light.   305

The wind was wild; against the glass
  The rain did beat and bicker;
The church-tower swinging over head,
  You scarce could hear the Vicar!

And then and there the mother knelt,   310
  And audibly she cried—
'Oh! may a clinging curse consume
  This woman by my side!

'O hear me, hear me, Lord in Heaven,
  Although you take my life—   315
O curse this woman, at whose house
  Young Edward woo'd his wife.

---

308 swinging] singing *MS. The Friend, 1809*: swaying *S. L.*   309 You **could not** hear the Vicar. *MS. The Friend, 1809.*   315 you] thou *The Friend, 1809*

THE THREE GRAVES

'By night and day, in bed and bower,
  O let her cursèd be!!!'
So having prayed, steady and slow,　　　　　320
  She rose up from her knee!
And left the church, nor e'er again
  The church-door entered she.

I saw poor Ellen kneeling still,
  So pale! I guessed not why:　　　　　325
When she stood up, there plainly was
  A trouble in her eye.

And when the prayers were done, we all
  Came round and asked her why:
Giddy she seemed, and sure, there was　　　　　330
  A trouble in her eye.

But ere she from the church-door stepped
  She smiled and told us why:
'It was a wicked woman's curse,'
  Quoth she, 'and what care I?'　　　　　335

She smiled, and smiled, and passed it off
  Ere from the door she stept—
But all agree it would have been
  Much better had she wept.

And if her heart was not at ease,　　　　　340
  This was her constant cry—
'It was a wicked woman's curse—
  God's good, and what care I?'

There was a hurry in her looks,
  Her struggles she redoubled:　　　　　345
'It was a wicked woman's curse,
  And why should I be troubled?'

These tears will come—I dandled her
  When 'twas the merest fairy—
Good creature! and she hid it all:　　　　　350
  She told it not to Mary.

But Mary heard the tale: her arms
  Round Ellen's neck she threw;
'O Ellen, Ellen, she cursed me,
  And now she hath cursed you!'　　　　　355

I saw young Edward by himself
  Stalk fast adown the lee,
He snatched a stick from every fence,
  A twig from every tree.

He snapped them still with hand or knee,   360
  And then away they flew!
As if with his uneasy limbs
  He knew not what to do!

You see, good sir! that single hill?
  His farm lies underneath: 365
He heard it there, he heard it all,
  And only gnashed his teeth.

Now Ellen was a darling love
  In all his joys and cares:
And Ellen's name and Mary's name   370
Fast-linked they both together came,
  Whene'er he said his prayers.

And in the moment of his prayers
  He loved them both alike:
Yea, both sweet names with one sweet joy   375
  Upon his heart did strike!

He reach'd his home, and by his looks
  They saw his inward strife:
And they clung round him with their arms,
  Both Ellen and his wife.   380

And Mary could not check her tears,
  So on his breast she bowed;
Then frenzy melted into grief,
  And Edward wept aloud.

Dear Ellen did not weep at all,   385
  But closelier did she cling,
And turned her face and looked as if
  She saw some frightful thing.

Part IV

To see a man tread over graves
  I hold it no good mark;   390
'Tis wicked in the sun and moon,
  And bad luck in the dark!

Part IV] The Three Graves, a Sexton's Tale, Part the IVth *MS.*

THE THREE GRAVES

You see that grave? The Lord he gives,
   The Lord, he takes away:
O Sir! the child of my old age
   Lies there as cold as clay.   395

Except that grave, you scarce see one
   That was not dug by me;
I'd rather dance upon 'em all
   Than tread upon these three!   400

'Aye, Sexton! 'tis a touching tale.'
   You, Sir! are but a lad;
This month I'm in my seventieth year,
   And still it makes me sad.

And Mary's sister told it me,   405
   For three good hours and more;
Though I had heard it, in the main,
   From Edward's self, before.

Well! it passed off! the gentle Ellen
   Did well nigh dote on Mary;   410
And she went oftener than before,
And Mary loved her more and more:
   She managed all the dairy.

To market she on market-days,
   To church on Sundays came;   415
All seemed the same: all seemed so, Sir!
   But all was not the same!

Had Ellen lost her mirth? Oh! no!
   But she was seldom cheerful;
And Edward looked as if he thought   420
   That Ellen's mirth was fearful.

When by herself, she to herself
   Must sing some merry rhyme;
She could not now be glad for hours,
   Yet silent all the time.   425

And when she soothed her friend, through all
   Her soothing words 'twas plain
She had a sore grief of her own,
   A haunting in her brain.

---

395 O Sir!] Oh! 'tis *S. L.*

And oft she said, I'm not grown thin! 430
　And then her wrist she spanned;
And once when Mary was down-cast,
　She took her by the hand,
And gazed upon her, and at first
　She gently pressed her hand; 435

Then harder, till her grasp at length
　Did gripe like a convulsion!
Alas!' said she, 'we ne'er can be
　Made happy by compulsion!'

And once her both arms suddenly 440
　Round Mary's neck she flung,
And her heart panted, and she felt
　The words upon her tongue.

She felt them coming, but no power
　Had she the words to smother; 445
And with a kind of shriek she cried,
　'Oh Christ! you're like your mother!'

So gentle Ellen now no more
　Could make this sad house cheery;
And Mary's melancholy ways 450
　Drove Edward wild and weary.

Lingering he raised his latch at eve,
　Though tired in heart and limb:
He loved no other place, and yet
　Home was no home to him. 455

One evening he took up a book,
　And nothing in it read;
Then flung it down, and groaning cried,
　'O! Heaven! that I were dead.'

Mary looked up into his face, 460
　And nothing to him said;
She tried to smile, and on his arm
　Mournfully leaned her head.

And he burst into tears, and fell
　Upon his knees in prayer: 465
'Her heart is broke! O God! my grief,
　It is too great to bear!'

447 you're] how MS.

THE THREE GRAVES

'Twas such a foggy time as makes
  Old sextons, Sir! like me,
Rest on their spades to cough; the spring   470
  Was late uncommonly.

And then the hot days, all at once,
  They came, we knew not how:
You looked about for shade, when scarce
  A leaf was on a bough.   475

It happened then ('twas in the bower,
  A furlong up the wood:
Perhaps you know the place, and yet
  I scarce know how you should,)

No path leads thither, 'tis not nigh   480
  To any pasture-plot;
But clustered near the chattering brook,
  Lone hollies marked the spot.

Those hollies of themselves a shape
  As of an arbour took,   485
A close, round arbour; and it stands
  Not three strides from a brook.

Within this arbour, which was still
  With scarlet berries hung,
Were these three friends, one Sunday morn,   490
  Just as the first bell rung.

'Tis sweet to hear a brook, 'tis sweet
  To hear the Sabbath-bell,
'Tis sweet to hear them both at once,
  Deep in a woody dell.   495

His limbs along the moss, his head
  Upon a mossy heap,
With shut-up senses, Edward lay:
That brook e'en on a working day
  Might chatter one to sleep.   500

And he had passed a restless night,
  And was not well in health;
The women sat down by his side,
  And talked as 'twere by stealth.

---

473 we] one *MS. The Friend, 1809.*   483 Lone] Some *MS. The Friend, 1809.*   487 a] the *MS. The Friend, 1809.*   490 friends] dears *MS. erased.*

'The Sun peeps through the close thick leaves, 505
　See, dearest Ellen! see!
'Tis in the leaves, a little sun,
　No bigger than your ee;

'A tiny sun, and it has got
　A perfect glory too; 510
Ten thousand threads and hairs of light,
Make up a glory gay and bright
　Round that small orb, so blue.'

And then they argued of those rays,
　What colour they might be; 515
Says this, 'They're mostly green'; says that,
　'They're amber-like to me.'

So they sat chatting, while bad thoughts
　Were troubling Edward's rest;
But soon they heard his hard quick pants, 520
　And the thumping in his breast.

'A mother too!' these self-same words
　Did Edward mutter plain;
His face was drawn back on itself,
　With horror and huge pain. 525

Both groaned at once, for both knew well
　What thoughts were in his mind;
When he waked up, and stared like one
　That hath been just struck blind.

He sat upright; and ere the dream 530
　Had had time to depart,
'O God, forgive me!' (he exclaimed)
　'I have torn out her heart.'

Then Ellen shrieked, and forthwith burst
　Into ungentle laughter; 535
And Mary shivered, where she sat,
　And never she smiled after.

1797–1809.

Carmen reliquum in futurum tempus relegatum. To-morrow! and To-morrow! and To-morrow!

507 in] *in MS. The Friend*, 1809.　　511 *inserted by S. T. C. MS.*

530-1　　　He sat upright; and with quick voice
　　　　　While his eyes seem'd to start *MS. erased.*

THE WANDERINGS OF CAIN[1]

PREFATORY NOTE

A PROSE composition, one not in metre at least, seems *primâ facie* to require explanation or apology. It was written in the year 1798, near Nether Stowey, in Somersetshire, at which place (*sanctum et amabile nomen!* rich by so many associations and recollections) the author had taken up his residence in order to enjoy the society and close neighbourhood of a dear and honoured friend, T. Poole, Esq. The work was to

---

[1] *The Wanderings of Cain* in its present shape was first published in 1828: included in 1829, and (with the omission of that part of the Prefatory Note which follows the verses) in 1834. The verses ('Encinctured', &c.) were first published in the 'Conclusion' of *Aids to Reflection*, 1825, p. 383, with the following apologetic note:—'Will the Reader forgive me if I attempt at once to illustrate and relieve the subject ["the enthusiastic Mystics"] by annexing the first stanza of the Poem, composed in the same year in which I wrote the Ancient Mariner and the first Book of Christabel.' The *prose* was first published without the verses or 'Prefatory Note' in the *Bijou* for 1828. [See *Poems*, 1893, *Notes*, p. 600.]

A rough draft of a continuation or alternative version of the *Wanderings of Cain* was found among Coleridge's papers. The greater portion of these fragmentary sheets was printed by the Editor, in the *Athenaeum* of January 27, 1894, p. 114. The introduction of 'alligators' and an 'immense meadow' help to fix the date of *The Wanderings of Cain*. The imagery is derived from William Bartram's *Travels in Florida and Carolina*, which Coleridge and Wordsworth studied in 1798. Mr. Hutchinson, who reprints (*Lyrical Ballads of 1798*, Notes, pp. 259-60) a selected passage from the MS. fragment, points out 'that Coleridge had for a time thought of shaping the poem as a narrative addressed by Cain to his wife'.

'He falls down in a trance—when he awakes he sees a luminous body coming before him. It stands before him an orb of fire. It goes on, he moves not. It returns to him again, again retires as if wishing him to follow it. It then goes on and he follows: they are led to near the bottom of the wild woods, brooks, forests etc. etc. The Fire gradually shapes itself, retaining its luminous appearance, into the lineaments of a man. A dialogue between the fiery shape and Cain, in which the being presses upon him the enormity of his guilt and that he must make some expiation to the true deity, who is a severe God, and persuades him to burn out his eyes. Cain opposes this idea, and says that God himself who had inflicted this punishment upon him, had done it because he neglected to make a proper use of his senses, etc. The evil spirit answers him that God is indeed a God of mercy, and that an example must be given to mankind, that this end will be answered by his terrible appearance, at the same time he will be gratified with the most delicious sights and feelings. Cain, over-persuaded, consents to do it, but wishes to go to the top of the rocks to take a farewell of the earth. His farewell speech concluding with an abrupt address to the promised redeemer, and he abandons the idea on which the being had accompanied him, and turning round to declare this to the being

have been written in concert with another [Wordsworth], whose name is too venerable within the precincts of genius to be unnecessarily brought into connection with such a trifle, and who was then residing at a small distance from Nether Stowey. The title and subject were suggested by myself, who likewise drew up the scheme and the contents for each of the three books or cantos, of which the work was to consist, and which, the reader is to be informed, was to have been finished in one night! My partner undertook the first canto: I the second: and which ever had *done first*, was to set about the third. Almost thirty years have passed by; yet at this moment I cannot without something more than a smile moot the question which of the two things was the more impracticable, for a mind so eminently original to compose another man's thoughts and fancies, or for a taste so austerely pure and simple to imitate the Death of Abel? Methinks I see his grand and noble countenance as at the moment when having despatched my own portion of the task at full finger-speed, I hastened to him with my manuscript—

---

he sees him dancing from rock to rock in his former shape down those interminable precipices.

'Child affeared by his father's ravings, goes out to pluck the fruits in the moonlight wildness. Cain's soliloquy. Child returns with a pitcher of water and a cake. Cain wonders what kind of beings dwell in that place—whether any created since man or whether this world had any beings rescued from the Chaos, wandering like shipwrecked beings from another world etc.

'Midnight on the Euphrates. Cedars, palms, pines. Cain discovered sitting on the upper part of the ragged rock, where is cavern overlooking the Euphrates, the moon rising on the horizon. His soliloquy. The Beasts are out on the ramp—he hears the screams of a woman and children surrounded by tigers. Cain makes a soliloquy debating whether he shall save the woman. Cain advances, wishing death, and the tigers rush off. It proves to be Cain's wife with her two children, determined to follow her husband. She prevails upon him at last to tell his story. Cain's wife tells him that her son Enoch was placed suddenly by her side. Cain addresses all the elements to cease for a while to persecute him, while he tells his story. He begins with telling her that he had first after his leaving her found out a dwelling in the desart under a juniper tree etc., etc., how he meets in the desart a young man whom upon a nearer approach he perceives to be Abel, on whose countenance appears marks of the greatest misery ... of another being who had power after this life, greater than Jehovah. He is going to offer sacrifices to this being, and persuades Cain to follow him—he comes to an immense gulph filled with water, whither they descend followed by alligators etc. They go till they come to an immense meadow so surrounded as to be inaccessible, and from its depth so vast that you could not see it from above. Abel offers sacrifice from the blood of his arm. A gleam of light illumines the meadow—the countenance of Abel becomes more beautiful, and his arms glistering—he then persuades Cain to offer sacrifice, for himself and his son Enoch by cutting his child's arm and letting the blood fall from it. Cain is about to do it when Abel himself in his angelic appearance, attended by Michael, is seen in the heavens, whence they sail slowly down. Abel addresses Cain with terror, warning him not to offer up his innocent child. The evil spirit throws off the countenance of Abel, assumes its own shape, flies off pursuing a flying battle with Michael. Abel carries off the child.'

that look of humourous despondency fixed on his almost blank sheet of paper, and then its silent mock-piteous admission of failure struggling with the sense of the exceeding ridiculousness of the whole scheme—which broke up in a laugh: and the Ancient Mariner was written instead.

Years afterward, however, the draft of the plan and proposed incidents, and the portion executed, obtained favour in the eyes of more than one person, whose judgment on a poetic work could not but have weighed with me, even though no parental partiality had been thrown into the same scale, as a make-weight: and I determined on commencing anew, and composing the whole in stanzas, and made some progress in realising this intention, when adverse gales drove my bark off the 'Fortunate Isles' of the Muses: and then other and more momentous interests prompted a different voyage, to firmer anchorage and a securer port. I have in vain tried to recover the lines from the palimpsest tablet of my memory: and I can only offer the introductory stanza, which had been committed to writing for the purpose of procuring a friend's judgment on the metre, as a specimen:—

> Encinctured with a twine of leaves,
> That leafy twine his only dress!
> A lovely Boy was plucking fruits,
> By moonlight, in a wilderness.
> (In a moonlight wilderness *Aids to Reflection, 1825*.)
> The moon was bright, the air was free,
> And fruits and flowers together grew
> On many a shrub and many a tree:
> And all put on a gentle hue,
> Hanging in the shadowy air
> Like a picture rich and rare.
> It was a climate where, they say,
> The night is more belov'd than day.
> But who that beauteous Boy beguil'd,
> That beauteous Boy to linger here?
> Alone, by night, a little child,
> In place so silent and so wild—
> Has he no friend, no loving mother near?

I have here given the birth, parentage, and premature decease of the 'Wanderings of Cain, a poem',—intreating, however, my Readers, not to think so meanly of my judgment as to suppose that I either regard or offer it as any excuse for the publication of the following fragment (and I may add, of one or two others in its neighbourhood) in its primitive crudity. But I should find still greater difficulty in forgiving myself were I to record pro *taedio publico* a set of petty mishaps and annoyances which I myself wish to forget. I must be content therefore with assuring the friendly Reader, that the less he attributes its appearance to the Author's will, choice, or judgment, the nearer to the truth he will be.

S. T. COLERIDGE (1828).

THE WANDERINGS OF CAIN

CANTO II

'A LITTLE further, O my father, yet a little further, and we shall come into the open moonlight.' Their road was through a forest of fir-trees; at its entrance the trees stood at distances from each other, and the path was broad, and the moonlight and the moonlight shadows reposed upon it, and appeared quietly to inhabit that solitude. But soon the path winded and became narrow; the sun at high noon sometimes speckled, but never illumined it, and now it was dark as a cavern.

'It is dark, O my father!' said Enos, 'but the path under our feet is smooth and soft, and we shall soon come out into the open moonlight.'

'Lead on, my child!' said Cain; 'guide me, little child!' And the innocent little child clasped a finger of the hand which had murdered the righteous Abel, and he guided his father. 'The fir branches drip upon thee, my son.' 'Yea, pleasantly, father, for I ran fast and eagerly to bring thee the pitcher and the cake, and my body is not yet cool. How happy the squirrels are that feed on these fir-trees! they leap from bough to bough, and the old squirrels play round their young ones in the nest. I clomb a tree yesterday at noon, O my father, that I might play with them, but they leaped away from the branches, even to the slender twigs did they leap, and in a moment I beheld them on another tree. Why, O my father, would they not play with me? I would be good to them as thou art good to me: and I groaned to them even as thou groanest when thou givest me to eat, and when thou coverest me at evening, and as often as I stand at thy knee and thine eyes look at me?' Then Cain stopped, and stifling his groans he sank to the earth, and the child Enos stood in the darkness beside him.

And Cain lifted up his voice and cried bitterly, and said, 'The Mighty One that persecuteth me is on this side and on that; he pursueth my soul like the wind, like the sand-blast he passeth through me; he is around me even as the air! O that I might be utterly no more! I desire to die—yea,

---

12 *moonlight.* Ah, why dost thou groan so deeply? *MS. Bijou, 1828.* 25 *with me?* Is it because we are not so happy, as they? Is it because I groan sometimes even as thou groanest? *Then Cain stopped,* &c. *MS. Bijou, 1828.*

the things that never had life, neither move they upon the earth—behold! they seem precious to mine eyes. O that a man might live without the breath of his nostrils. So I might abide in darkness, and blackness, and an empty space! Yea, I would lie down, I would not rise, neither would I stir my limbs till I became as the rock in the den of the lion, on which the young lion resteth his head whilst he sleepeth. For the torrent that roareth far off hath a voice: and the clouds in heaven look terribly on me; the Mighty One who is against me speaketh in the wind of the cedar grove; and in silence am I dried up.' Then Enos spake to his father, 'Arise, my father, arise, we are but a little way from the place where I found the cake and the pitcher.' And Cain said, 'How knowest thou!' and the child answered—'Behold the bare rocks are a few of thy strides distant from the forest; and while even now thou wert lifting up thy voice, I heard the echo.' Then the child took hold of his father, as if he would raise him: and Cain being faint and feeble rose slowly on his knees and pressed himself against the trunk of a fir, and stood upright and followed the child.

The path was dark till within three strides' length of its termination, when it turned suddenly; the thick black trees formed a low arch, and the moonlight appeared for a moment like a dazzling portal. Enos ran before and stood in the open air; and when Cain, his father, emerged from the darkness, the child was affrighted. For the mighty limbs of Cain were wasted as by fire; his hair was as the matted curls on the bison's forehead, and so glared his fierce and sullen eye beneath: and the black abundant locks on either side, a rank and tangled mass, were stained and scorched, as though the grasp of a burning iron hand had striven to rend them; and his countenance told in a strange and terrible language of agonies that had been, and were, and were still to continue to be.

The scene around was desolate; as far as the eye could reach it was desolate: the bare rocks faced each other, and left a long and wide interval of thin white sand. You might wander on and look round and round, and peep into the crevices of the rocks and discover nothing that acknowledged the influence of the seasons. There was no spring, no summer, no autumn: and the winter's snow, that would have been lovely, fell not on these hot rocks and scorching sands. Never morning lark had poised himself over this desert; but the huge

63-8 *by fire*: his hair was black, and matted into loathly curls, and his countenance was dark and wild, and *told*, &c. *MS. Bijou, 1828.*

serpent often hissed there beneath the talons of the vulture, and the vulture screamed, his wings imprisoned within the coils of the serpent. The pointed and shattered summits of the ridges of the rocks made a rude mimicry of human concerns, and seemed to prophecy mutely of things that then were not; steeples, and battlements, and ships with naked masts. As far from the wood as a boy might sling a pebble of the brook, there was one rock by itself at a small distance from the main ridge. It had been precipitated there perhaps by the groan which the Earth uttered when our first father fell. Before you approached, it appeared to lie flat on the ground, but its base slanted from its point, and between its point and the sands a tall man might stand upright. It was here that Enos had found the pitcher and cake, and to this place he led his father. But ere they had reached the rock they beheld a human shape: his back was towards them, and they were advancing unperceived, when they heard him smite his breast and cry aloud, 'Woe is me! woe is me! I must never die again, and yet I am perishing with thirst and hunger.'

Pallid, as the reflection of the sheeted lightning on the heavy-sailing night-cloud, became the face of Cain; but the child Enos took hold of the shaggy skin, his father's robe, and raised his eyes to his father, and listening whispered, 'Ere yet I could speak, I am sure, O my father, that I heard that voice. Have not I often said that I remembered a sweet voice? O my father! this is it': and Cain trembled exceedingly. The voice was sweet indeed, but it was thin and querulous, like that of a feeble slave in misery, who despairs altogether, yet can not refrain himself from weeping and lamentation. And, behold! Enos glided forward, and creeping softly round the base of the rock, stood before the stranger, and looked up into his face. And the Shape shrieked, and turned round, and Cain beheld him, that his limbs and his face were those of his brother Abel whom he had killed! And Cain stood like one who struggles in his sleep because of the exceeding terribleness of a dream.

Thus as he stood in silence and darkness of soul, the Shape fell at his feet, and embraced his knees, and cried out with a bitter outcry, 'Thou eldest born of Adam, whom

87 *by the* terrible groan the Earth gave *when*, &c. MS. *Bijou*, 1828. 92-3 *But ere they* arrived there *they beheld*, MS. *Bijou*, 1828. 94 advancing] coming up MS. *Bijou*, 1828. 98-101 The face of Cain turned pale, but Enos said, '*Ere yet*, &c. MS. *Bijou*, 1828. 108-9 *Enos* crept softly round the base of the rock and *stood before* MS. *Bijou*, 1828. 114-16 *of a dream* ; and ere he had recovered himself from the tumult of his agitation, *the Shape*, &c. MS. *Bijou*, 1828.

Eve, my mother, brought forth, cease to torment me! I was feeding my flocks in green pastures by the side of quiet rivers, and thou killedst me; and now I am in misery.' Then Cain closed his eyes, and hid them with his hands; and again he opened his eyes, and looked around him, and said to Enos, 'What beholdest thou? Didst thou hear a voice, my son?' 'Yes, my father, I beheld a man in unclean garments, and he uttered a sweet voice, full of lamentation.' Then Cain raised up the Shape that was like Abel, and said:—'The Creator of our father, who had respect unto thee, and unto thy offering, wherefore hath he forsaken thee?' Then the Shape shrieked a second time, and rent his garment, and his naked skin was like the white sands beneath their feet; and he shrieked yet a third time, and threw himself on his face upon the sand that was black with the shadow of the rock, and Cain and Enos sate beside him; the child by his right hand, and Cain by his left. They were all three under the rock, and within the shadow. The Shape that was like Abel raised himself up, and spake to the child, 'I know where the cold waters are, but I may not drink, wherefore didst thou then take away my pitcher?' But Cain said, 'Didst thou not find favour in the sight of the Lord thy God?' The Shape answered, 'The Lord is God of the living only, the dead have another God.' Then the child Enos lifted up his eyes and prayed; but Cain rejoiced secretly in his heart. 'Wretched shall they be all the days of their mortal life,' exclaimed the Shape, 'who sacrifice worthy and acceptable sacrifices to the God of the dead; but after death their toil ceaseth. Woe is me, for I was well beloved by the God of the living, and cruel wert thou, O my brother, who didst snatch me away from his power and his dominion.' Having uttered these words, he rose suddenly, and fled over the sands: and Cain said in his heart, 'The curse of the Lord is on me; but who is the God of the dead?' and he ran after the Shape, and the Shape fled shrieking over the sands, and the sands rose like white mists behind the steps of Cain, but the feet of him that was like Abel disturbed not the sands. He greatly outrun Cain, and turning short, he wheeled round, and came again to the rock where they had been sitting, and where Enos still stood; and the child caught hold of his garment as he passed by, and he fell upon the ground. And Cain stopped, and beholding him not, said, 'he has passed into the dark woods,' and he walked slowly back to the rocks; and when he

160 and walked *Bijou, 1828*.   rocks] rock *MS.*

292 THE WANDERINGS OF CAIN

reached it the child told him that he had caught hold of his garment as he passed by, and that the man had fallen upon the ground: and Cain once more sate beside him, and said, 'Abel, my brother, I would lament for thee, but that the spirit
165 within me is withered, and burnt up with extreme agony. Now, I pray thee, by thy flocks, and by thy pastures, and by the quiet rivers which thou lovedst, that thou tell me all that thou knowest. Who is the God of the dead? where doth he make his dwelling? what sacrifices are acceptable unto him?
170 for I have offered, but have not been received; I have prayed, and have not been heard; and how can I be afflicted more than I already am?' The Shape arose and answered, 'O that thou hadst had pity on me as I will have pity on thee. Follow me, Son of Adam! and bring thy child with thee!'
175 And they three passed over the white sands between the rocks, silent as the shadows.

1798.

TO ——[1]

I MIX in life, and labour to seem free,
  With common persons pleas'd and common things,
While every thought and action tends to thee,
  And every impulse from thy influence springs.

?1798.

---

[1] First published without title in *Literary Remains*, 1836, i. 280 (among other short pieces and fragments 'communicated by Mr. Gutch'). First collected, again without title, in *P. and D. W.*, 1877-80.

---

170 but] and *MS.*   176 the] their *MS.*
To —— Title] To —— *1893*. The heading *Ubi Thesaurus Ibi Cor* was prefixed to the illustrated edition of *The Poems of Coleridge*, 1907.

THE BALLAD OF THE DARK LADIÉ[1]

A FRAGMENT

BENEATH yon birch with silver bark,
And boughs so pendulous and fair,
The brook falls scatter'd down the rock:
    And all is mossy there!

And there upon the moss she sits, 5
The Dark Ladié in silent pain;
The heavy tear is in her eye,
    And drops and swells again.

Three times she sends her little page
Up the castled mountain's breast, 10
If he might find the Knight that wears
    The Griffin for his crest.

The sun was sloping down the sky,
And she had linger'd there all day,
Counting moments, dreaming fears— 15
    Oh wherefore can he stay?

---

[1] First published in 1834. 'In a manuscript list (undated) of the poems drawn up by Coleridge appear these items together: *Love* 96 lines ... *The Black Ladié* 190 lines.' *Note* to *P. W.*, 1893, p. 614. A MS. of the three last stanzas is extant. In Chapter XIV of the *Biographia Literaria*, 1817, ii. 3 Coleridge synchronizes the *Dark Ladié* (a poem which he was 'preparing') with the *Christabel*. It would seem probable that it belongs to the spring or early summer of 1798, and that it was anterior to *Love*, which was first published in the *Morning Post*, December 21, 1799, under the heading 'Introduction to the Tale of the Dark Ladié'. If the MS. List of Poems is the record of poems actually written, two-thirds of the *Dark Ladié* must have perished long before 1817, when *Sibylline Leaves* was passing through the press, and it was found necessary to swell the Contents with 'two School-boy Poems' and 'with a song modernized with some additions from one of our elder poets'.

She hears a rustling o'er the brook,
She sees far off a swinging bough!
'Tis He! 'Tis my betrothéd Knight!
    Lord Falkland, it is Thou!'   20

She springs, she clasps him round the neck,
She sobs a thousand hopes and fears,
Her kisses glowing on his cheeks
    She quenches with her tears.

    *   *   *   *

'My friends with rude ungentle words   25
They scoff and bid me fly to thee!
O give me shelter in thy breast!
    O shield and shelter me!

'My Henry, I have given thee much,
I gave what I can ne'er recall,   30
I gave my heart, I gave my peace,
    O Heaven! I gave thee all.'

The Knight made answer to the Maid,
While to his heart he held her hand,
'Nine castles hath my noble sire,   35
    None statelier in the land.

'The fairest one shall be my love's,
The fairest castle of the nine!
Wait only till the stars peep out,
    The fairest shall be thine: 40

'Wait only till the hand of eve
Hath wholly closed yon western bars,
And through the dark we two will steal
    Beneath the twinkling stars!'—

'The dark? the dark? No! not the dark?   45
The twinkling stars? How, Henry? How?'
O God! 'twas in the eye of noon
    He pledged his sacred vow!

And in the eye of noon my love
Shall lead me from my mother's door,   50
Sweet boys and girls all clothed in white
    Strewing flowers before:

> But first the nodding minstrels go
> With music meet for lordly bowers,
> The children next in snow-white vests,   55
>   Strewing buds and flowers!
>
> And then my love and I shall pace,
> My jet black hair in pearly braids,
> Between our comely bachelors
>   And blushing bridal maids.

        *   *   *   *

1798.

KUBLA KHAN[1]:

Or, A Vision in a Dream. A Fragment.

The following fragment is here published at the request of a poet of great and deserved celebrity [Lord Byron], and, as far as the Author's own opinions are concerned, rather as a psychological curiosity, than on the ground of any supposed *poetic* merits.   5

In the summer of the year 1797[2], the Author, then in ill

---

[1] First published together with *Christabel* and *The Pains of Sleep*, 1816: included in 1828, 1829, and 1834.

[2] There can be little doubt that Coleridge should have written 'the summer of 1798'. In an unpublished MS. note dated November 3, 1810, he connects the retirement between 'Linton and Porlock' and a recourse to opium with his quarrel with Charles Lloyd, and consequent distress of mind. That quarrel was at its height in May 1798. He alludes to distress of mind arising from 'calumny and ingratitude from men who have been fostered in the bosom of my confidence' in a letter to J. P. Estlin, dated May 14, 1798; and, in a letter to Charles Lamb, dated [Spring] 1798, he enlarges on his quarrel with Lloyd and quotes from Lloyd's novel of *Edmund Oliver* which was published in 1798. See *Letters of Samuel Taylor Coleridge*, 1895, i. 245, note 1. I discovered and read for the first time the unpublished note of November 3, 1810, whilst the edition of 1893 was in the press, and in a footnote to p. xlii of his *Introduction* the editor, J. D. Campbell, explains that it is too late to alter the position and date of *Kubla Khan*, but accepts the later date (May, 1798) on the evidence of the MS. note.

53–6   And first the nodding Minstrels go
                With music fit for lovely Bowers,
                The children then in snowy robes,
                      Strewing Buds and Flowers. *MS. S. T. C.*

57 pace] go *MS. S. T. C.*

Kubla Khan, &c. Title of Introduction :—Of the Fragment of Kubla Khan *1816*, *1828*, *1829*.

1–5 *om.* 1834.

health, had retired to a lonely farm-house between Porlock and Linton, on the Exmoor confines of Somerset and Devonshire. In consequence of a slight indisposition, an anodyne had been prescribed, from the effects of which he fell asleep in his chair at the moment that he was reading the following sentence, or words of the same substance, in 'Purchas's Pilgrimage': 'Here the Khan Kubla commanded a palace to be built, and a stately garden thereunto. And thus ten miles of fertile ground were inclosed with a wall.'[1] The Author continued for about three hours in a profound sleep, at least of the external senses, during which time he has the most vivid confidence, that he could not have composed less than from two to three hundred lines; if that indeed can be called composition in which all the images rose up before him as *things*, with a parallel production of the correspondent expressions, without any sensation or consciousness of effort. On awaking he appeared to himself to have a distinct recollection of the whole, and taking his pen, ink, and paper, instantly and eagerly wrote down the lines that are here preserved. At this moment he was unfortunately called out by a person on business from Porlock, and detained by him above an hour, and on his return to his room, found, to his no small surprise and mortification, that though he still retained some vague and dim recollection of the general purport of the vision, yet, with the exception of some eight or ten scattered lines and images, all the rest had passed away like the images on the surface of a stream into which a stone has been cast, but, alas! without the after restoration of the latter!

> Then all the charm
> Is broken—all that phantom-world so fair
> Vanishes, and a thousand circlets spread,
> And each mis-shape['s] the other. Stay awhile,
> Poor youth! who scarcely dar'st lift up thine eyes—
> The stream will soon renew its smoothness, soon
> The visions will return! And lo, he stays,
> And soon the fragments dim of lovely forms
> Come trembling back, unite, and now once more
> The pool becomes a mirror.
> [From *The Picture; or, the Lover's Resolution*, ll. 91-100.]

[1] 'In Xamdu did Cublai Can build a stately Palace, encompassing sixteene miles of plaine ground with a wall, wherein are fertile Meddowes, pleasant Springs, delightfull Streames, and all sorts of beasts of chase and game, and in the middest thereof a sumptuous house of pleasure.'—*Purchas his Pilgrimage*: Lond. fol. 1626, Bk. IV, chap. xiii, p. 418.

Yet from the still surviving recollections in his mind, the Author has frequently purposed to finish for himself what had been originally, as it were, given to him. Σαμερον αδιον ασω[1] [Αὔριον ἅδιον ᾄσω 1834]: but the to-morrow is yet to come.

As a contrast to this vision, I have annexed a fragment of a very different character, describing with equal fidelity the dream of pain and disease.[2]

KUBLA KHAN

In Xanadu did Kubla Khan
A stately pleasure-dome decree:
Where Alph, the sacred river, ran
Through caverns measureless to man
  Down to a sunless sea. 5
So twice five miles of fertile ground
With walls and towers were girdled round:
And there were gardens bright with sinuous rills,
Where blossomed many an incense-bearing tree;
And here were forests ancient as the hills, 10
Enfolding sunny spots of greenery.

But oh! that deep romantic chasm which slanted
Down the green hill athwart a cedarn cover!
A savage place! as holy and enchanted
As e'er beneath a waning moon was haunted 15
By woman wailing for her demon-lover![3]
[4]And from this chasm, with ceaseless turmoil seething,
As if this earth in fast thick pants were breathing,
A mighty fountain momently was forced:
Amid whose swift half-intermitted burst 20
Huge fragments vaulted like rebounding hail,
Or chaffy grain beneath the thresher's flail:
And 'mid these dancing rocks at once and ever
It flung up momently the sacred river.
Five miles meandering with a mazy motion 25

[1] The quotation is from Theocritus, i. 145:—ἐς ὕστερον ἅδιον ᾄσῶ.
[2] *The Pains of Sleep.*
[3] And woman wailing for her Demon Lover. Motto to Byron's *Heaven and Earth*, published in *The Liberal*, No. II, January 1, 1823.
[4] With lines 17-24 compare William Bartram's description of the 'Alligator-Hole'. *Travels in North and South Carolina*, 1794, pp. 236-8.

---

8 there] here *S. L.* 1828, 1829.   11 Enfolding] And folding *1816*. The word 'Enfolding' is a pencil emendation in David Hinves's copy of Christabel. ? by S. T. C.   19 In the early copies of *1893* this line was accidentally omitted.

Through wood and dale the sacred river ran,
Then reached the caverns measureless to man,
And sank in tumult to a lifeless ocean:
And 'mid this tumult Kubla heard from far
Ancestral voices prophesying war! 30
　　The shadow of the dome of pleasure
　　Floated midway on the waves;
　　Where was heard the mingled measure
　　From the fountain and the caves.
It was a miracle of rare device, 35
A sunny pleasure-dome with caves of ice![1]

　　A damsel with a dulcimer
　　In a vision once I saw:
　　It was an Abyssinian maid,
　　And on her dulcimer she played, 40
　　Singing of Mount Abora.
　　Could I revive within me
　　Her symphony and song,
　　To such a deep delight 'twould win me,
That with music loud and long, 45
I would build that dome in air,
That sunny dome! those caves of ice![2]
And all who heard should see them there,
And all should cry, Beware! Beware!
His flashing eyes, his floating hair! 50
Weave a circle round him thrice,
And close your eyes with holy dread,
For he on honey-dew hath fed,
And drunk the milk of Paradise.
　　1798.

[1] Compare Thomas Maurice's *History of Hindostan*, 1795, i. 107. The reference is supplied by Coleridge in the *Gutch Memorandum Note Book* (B. M. Add. MSS., No. 27,901), p. 47: 'In a cave in the mountains of Cashmere an Image of Ice,' &c.

[2] In her 'Lines to S. T. Coleridge, Esq.,' Mrs. Robinson (Perdita) writes:—

　　　'I'll mark thy "sunny domes" and view
　　　　Thy "caves of ice", and "fields of dew".'

It is possible that she had seen a MS. copy of *Kubla Khan* containing these variants from the text.

---

54 drunk] drank *1816, 1828, 1829.*

RECANTATION[1]

ILLUSTRATED IN THE STORY OF THE MAD OX

I

An Ox, long fed with musty hay,
  And work'd with yoke and chain,
Was turn'd out on an April day,
When fields are in their best array,
And growing grasses sparkle gay 5
  At once with Sun and rain.

II

The grass was fine, the Sun was bright—
  With truth I may aver it;
The ox was glad, as well he might,
Thought a green meadow no bad sight, 10
And frisk'd,—to shew his huge delight,
  Much like a beast of spirit.

III

'Stop, neighbours, stop, why these alarms?
  The ox is only glad!'
But still they pour from cots and farms— 15
'Halloo!' the parish is up in arms,
(A *hoaxing*-hunt has always charms)
  'Halloo! the ox is mad.'

---

[1] First published in the *Morning Post* for July 30, 1798, with the following title and introduction:—'ORIGINAL POETRY. A TALE. The following amusing Tale gives a very humourous description of the French Revolution, which is represented as an Ox': included in *Annual Anthology*, 1800, and *Sibylline Leaves*, 1817; reprinted in *Essays on His Own Times*, 1850, iii. 963-9. First collected in *P. and D.W.*, 1877-80. In a copy of the *Annual Anthology* of 1800 Coleridge writes over against the heading of this poem, 'Written when fears were entertained of an invasion, and Mr. Sheridan and Mr. Tierney were absurdly represented as having *recanted* because to [The French Revolution (?)] in its origin they, [having been favourable, changed their opinion when the Revolutionists became unfaithful to their principles (?)].' See *Note to P. W.*, 1893.

The text is that of *Sibylline Leaves* and *Essays on his Own Times*.

---

3 turn'd out] loosen'd *M. P.*   9 ox] beast *M. P.*

IV

> The frighted beast scamper'd about—
>   Plunge! through the hedge he drove:
> The mob pursue with hideous rout,
> A bull-dog fastens on his snout;
>   'He gores the dog! his tongue hangs out!
>   He's mad, he's mad, by Jove!'

V

> 'STOP, NEIGHBOURS, STOP!' aloud did call
>   A sage of sober hue.
> But all at once, on him they fall,
> And women squeak and children squall,
>   'What? would you have him toss us all?
>   And dam'me, who are you?'

VI

> Oh! hapless sage! his ears they stun,
>   And curse him o'er and o'er!
> 'You bloody-minded dog! (cries one,)
> To slit your windpipe were good fun,
>   'Od blast you for an *impious* son[1]
>   Of a Presbyterian wh——re!'

VII

> 'You'd have him gore the Parish-priest,
>   And run against the altar!
> You fiend!' the sage his warnings ceas'd,
> And north and south, and west and east,
>   Halloo! they follow the poor beast,
>   Mat, Dick, Tom, Bob and Walter.

VIII

> Old Lewis ('twas his evil day),
>   Stood trembling in his shoes;

---

[1] One of the many fine words which the most uneducated had about this time a constant opportunity of acquiring, from the sermons in the pulpit and the proclamations on [in *S. L.*] the —— corners. AN. *Anth.*, *S. L.*

---

19 beast] ox *M. P.*   22 fastens] fasten'd *M. P.*   27 'You cruel dog!' at once they bawl. *M. P.*   31 Oh] Ah! *M. P., An. Anth.*   35-6 *om. Essays, &c.*   38 run] drive *M. P.*   39 fiend] rogue *M. P.*   42 Mat, Tom, Bob, Dick *M. P.*

RECANTATION

The ox was his—what cou'd he say? 45
His legs were stiffen'd with dismay,
The ox ran o'er him mid the fray,
And gave him his death's bruise.

IX

The frighted beast ran on—(but here,
No tale, (tho' in print, more true is) 50
My Muse stops short in mid career—
Nay, gentle Reader, do not sneer!
I cannot chuse but drop a tear,
A tear for good old Lewis!)

X

The frighted beast ran through the town, 55
All follow'd, boy and dad,
Bull-dog, parson, shopman, clown:
The publicans rush'd from the Crown,
'Halloo! hamstring him! cut him down!'
THEY DROVE THE POOR OX MAD. 60

XI

Should you a Rat to madness tease
Why ev'n a Rat may plague you:
There's no Philosopher but sees
That Rage and Fear are one disease—
Though that may burn, and this may freeze, 65
They're both alike the Ague.

XII

And so this Ox, in frantic mood,
Fac'd round like any Bull!
The mob turn'd tail, and he pursued,
Till they with heat and fright were stew'd, 70
And not a chick of all this brood
But had his belly full!

---

49 The baited ox drove on *M. P., An. Anth.*   50 No . . . print] The Gospel scarce *M. P., An. Anth.*   53 cannot] could *M. P.*   55 The ox drove on, right through the town *M. P.*   62 may] might *M. P., An. Anth.*   68 any] a mad *M. P.*   70 heat and fright] flight and fear *M. P., An. Anth.*   71 this] the *M. P.*

XIII

Old Nick 's astride the beast, 'tis clear!
  Old Nicholas, to a tittle!
But all agree he'd disappear,
Would but the Parson venture near,
And through his teeth,[1] right o'er the steer,
  Squirt out some fasting-spittle.

XIV

Achilles was a warrior fleet,
  The Trojans he could worry:
Our Parson too was swift of feet,
But shew'd it chiefly in retreat:
The victor Ox scour'd down the street,
  The mob fled hurry-scurry.

XV

Through gardens, lanes and fields new-plough'd,
  Through *his* hedge, and through *her* hedge,
He plung'd and toss'd and bellow'd loud—
Till in his madness he grew proud
To see this helter-skelter crowd
  That had more wrath than courage!

XVI

Alas! to mend the breaches wide
  He made for these poor ninnies,
They all must work, whate'er betide,
Both days and months, and pay beside
(Sad news for Av'rice and for Pride),
  A *sight* of golden guineas!

---

[1] According to the common superstition there are two ways of fighting with the Devil. You may cut him in half with a straw, or he will vanish if you spit over his horns with a fasting spittle. *Note by S. T. C. in M. P.* According to the superstition of the West-Countries, if you meet the Devil, you may either cut him in half with a straw, or force him to disappear by spitting over his horns. *An. Anth., S. L.*

---

73 beast] ox *M. P.*   75 agree] agreed *M. P.*   83 scour'd] drove *M. P.*
91 Alas] Alack *M. P.*

XVII

But here once more to view did pop
    The man that kept his senses—
And now he cried,—'Stop, neighbours, stop!
The Ox is mad! I would not swop,
No! not a school-boy's farthing top
    For all the parish-fences.'

XVIII

'The Ox is mad! Ho! Dick, Bob, Mat!
    'What means this coward fuss?
Ho! stretch this rope across the plat—
'Twill trip him up—or if not that,
Why, dam'me! we must lay him flat—
    See! here's my blunderbuss.'

XIX

'*A lying dog! just now he said*
    The Ox was only glad—
Let's break his Presbyterian head!'
'Hush!' quoth the sage, 'you've been misled;
No quarrels now! let's all make head,
    YOU DROVE THE POOR OX MAD.'

XX

As thus I sat, in careless chat,
    With the morning's wet newspaper,
In eager haste, without his hat,
As blind and blund'ring as a bat,
In came that fierce Aristocrat,
    Our pursy woollen-draper.

XXI

And so my Muse per force drew bit;
    And in he rush'd and panted!
'Well, have you heard?' No, not a whit.
'What, *ha'nt* you heard?' Come, out with it!
'That Tierney votes for Mister PITT,
    And Sheridan's *recanted*!'
1798.

---

99 cried] bawl'd *M. P.*   103 Tom! Walter! Mat! *M. P.*   109 *lying*] *bare-faced M. P.*   115 But lo! to interrupt my chat *M. P.*   119 In came] In rush'd *M. P.*   122 And he rush'd in *M. P.*
    125-6   That Tierney's wounded Mister PITT,
            And his fine tongue enchanted! *M. P.*

HEXAMETERS[1]

William, my teacher, my friend! dear William and dear Dorothea!
Smooth out the folds of my letter, and place it on desk or on table;
Place it on table or desk; and your right hands loosely half-closing,[2]
Gently sustain them in air, and extending the digit didactic,
Rest it a moment on each of the forks of the five-forked left hand,   5
Twice on the breadth of the thumb, and once on the tip of each finger;
Read with a nod of the head in a humouring recitativo;
And, as I live, you will see my hexameters hopping before you.
This is a galloping measure; a hop, and a trot, and a gallop!

All my hexameters fly, like stags pursued by the staghounds,   10
Breathless and panting, and ready to drop, yet flying still onwards,[3]
I would full fain pull in my hard-mouthed runaway hunter;
But our English Spondeans are clumsy yet impotent curb-reins;
And so to make him go slowly, no way left have I but to lame him.

William, my head and my heart! dear Poet that feelest and thinkest!   15
Dorothy, eager of soul, my most affectionate sister!
Many a mile, O! many a wearisome mile are ye distant,
Long, long comfortless roads, with no one eye that doth know us.

---

[1] First published in *Memoirs of W. Wordsworth*, 1851, i. 139-41: reprinted in *Life* by Prof. Knight, 1889, i. 185. First collected as a whole in *P. W.* [ed. T. Ashe], 1885. Lines 30-6, 'O what a life is the eye', &c., were first published in *Friendship's Offering*, and are included in *P. W.*, 1834. They were reprinted by Cottle in *E. R.*, 1837, i. 226. The 'Hexameters' were sent in a letter, written in the winter of 1798-9 from Ratzeburg to the Wordsworths at Goslar.

[2] False metre. *S. T. C.*

[3] '*Still* flying onwards' were perhaps better. *S. T. C.*

O! it is all too far to send you mockeries idle:
Yea, and I feel it not right! But O! my friends, my belovéd! 20
Feverish and wakeful I lie,—I am weary of feeling and thinking.
Every thought is worn *down*, I am weary yet cannot be vacant.
Five long hours have I tossed, rheumatic heats, dry and flushing,
Gnawing behind in my head, and wandering and throbbing about me,
Busy and tiresome, my friends, as the beat of the boding night-spider.[1] 25

I forget the beginning of the line:

. . . my eyes are a burthen,
Now unwillingly closed, now open and aching with darkness.
O! what a life is the eye! what a strange and inscrutable essence!
Him that is utterly blind, nor glimpses the fire that warms him;
Him that never beheld the swelling breast of his mother; 30
Him that smiled in his gladness as a babe that smiles in its slumber;
Even for him it exists, it moves and stirs in its prison;
Lives with a separate life, and 'Is it a Spirit?' he murmurs:
'Sure it has thoughts of its own, and to see is only a language.'

There was a great deal more, which I have forgotten. . . . The last line which I wrote, I remember, and write it for the truth of the sentiment, scarcely less true in company than in pain and solitude:—

William, my head and my heart! dear William and dear Dorothea! 35
You have all in each other; but I am lonely, and want you!

1798–9.

[1] False metre. S. T. C.

---

28 strange] fine *Letter*, 1798–9, *Cottle*, 1837.   29 Him] He *Cottle*, 1837.
30 Him] He *Cottle*, 1837.   31 Him that ne'er smiled at the bosom as babe *Letter*, 1798–9: He that smiled at the bosom, the babe *Cottle*, 1837.
32 Even to him it exists, it stirs and moves *Letter*, 1798–9: Even to him it exists, it moves and stirs *Cottle*, 1837.   33 a Spirit] the Spirit *Letter*, 1798–9.   34 a] its *Letter*, 1798–9.

TRANSLATION OF A PASSAGE IN OTTFRIED'S METRICAL PARAPHRASE OF THE GOSPEL

[This paraphrase, written about the time of Charlemagne, is by no means deficient in occasional passages of considerable poetic merit. There is a flow and a tender enthusiasm in the following lines which even in the translation will not, I flatter myself, fail to interest the reader. Ottfried is describing the circumstances immediately following the birth of our Lord. Most interesting is it to consider the effect when the feelings are wrought above the natural pitch by the belief of something mysterious, while all the images are purely natural. Then it is that religion and poetry strike deepest. *Biog. Lit.*, 1817, i, 203-4.[1]]

> She gave with joy her virgin breast;
> She hid it not, she bared the breast
> Which suckled that divinest babe!
> Blessed, blessed were the breasts
> Which the Saviour infant kiss'd;   5
> And blessed, blessed was the mother
> Who wrapp'd his limbs in swaddling clothes,
> Singing placed him on her lap,
> Hung o'er him with her looks of love,
> And soothed him with a lulling motion.   10
> Blessed! for she shelter'd him
> From the damp and chilling air;
> Blessed, blessed! for she lay
> With such a babe in one blest bed,
> Close as babes and mothers lie!   15
> Blessed, blessed evermore,
> With her virgin lips she kiss'd,
> With her arms, and to her breast,
> She embraced the babe divine,
> Her babe divine the virgin mother!   20
> There lives not on this ring of earth
> A mortal that can sing her praise.
> Mighty mother, virgin pure,
> In the darkness and the night
> For us she *bore* the heavenly Lord!   25

? 1799.

---

[1] First published as a footnote to Chapter X of the *Biographia Literaria* (ed. 1817, i. 203-4). First collected in 1863 (Appendix, pp. 401-2). The translation is from *Otfridi Evang.*, lib. i, cap. xi, ll. 73-108 (included in Schilter's *Thesaurus Antiquitatum Teutonicarum*, pp. 50-1, *Biog. Lit.*, 1847, i. 213). Otfrid, 'a monk at Weissenburg in Elsass', composed his *Evangelienbuch* about 870 A.D. (Note by J. Shawcross, *Biog. Lit.*, 1907, ii. 259). As Coleridge says that 'he read through Ottfried's metrical paraphrase of the Gospel' when he was at Göttingen, it may be assumed that the translation was made in 1799.

---

5 Saviour infant] infant Saviour *1863*.

CATULLIAN HENDECASYLLABLES[1]

HEAR, my belovéd, an old Milesian story!—
High, and embosom'd in congregated laurels,
Glimmer'd a temple upon a breezy headland;
In the dim distance amid the skiey billows
Rose a fair island; the god of flocks had blest it.   5
From the far shores of the bleat-resounding island
Oft by the moonlight a little boat came floating,
Came to the sea-cave beneath the breezy headland,
Where amid myrtles a pathway stole in mazes
Up to the groves of the high embosom'd temple.   10
There in a thicket of dedicated roses,
Oft did a priestess, as lovely as a vision,
Pouring her soul to the son of Cytherea,
Pray him to hover around the slight canoe-boat,
And with invisible pilotage to guide it   15
Over the dusk wave, until the nightly sailor
Shivering with ecstasy sank upon her bosom.
?1799.

THE HOMERIC HEXAMETER[2]

DESCRIBED AND EXEMPLIFIED

STRONGLY it bears us along in swelling and limitless billows,
Nothing before and nothing behind but the sky and the ocean,
?1799.

---

[1] First published in 1834. These lines, which are not 'Hendecasyllables', are a translation of part of Friedrich von Matthisson's *Milesisches Mährchen*. For the original see Note to *Poems*, 1852. There is no evidence as to the date of composition. The emendations in lines 5 and 6 were first printed in *P. W.*, 1893.

[2] First published (together with the 'Ovidian Elegiac Metre', &c.) in *Friendship's Offering*, 1834: included in *P. W.*, 1834. An acknowledgement that these 'experiments in metre' are translations from Schiller was first made in a Note to *Poems*, 1844, p. 371. The originals were given on p. 372. There is no evidence as to the date of composition.

---

5 blest] plac'd *1834, 1844, 1852*.   6 bleat-resounding] bleak-resounding *1834, 1852*.   16 nightly] mighty *1834, 1844*.

THE OVIDIAN ELEGIAC METRE

DESCRIBED AND EXEMPLIFIED

In the hexameter rises the fountain's silvery column;
In the pentameter aye falling in melody back.
1799.

ON A CATARACT [1]

FROM A CAVERN NEAR THE SUMMIT OF A MOUNTAIN PRECIPICE

STROPHE

Unperishing youth!
Thou leapest from forth
The cell of thy hidden nativity;
Never mortal saw
The cradle of the strong one; 5
Never mortal heard
The gathering of his voices;
The deep-murmured charm of the son of the rock,
That is lisp'd evermore at his slumberless fountain.
There's a cloud at the portal, a spray-woven veil 10
At the shrine of his ceaseless renewing;
It embosoms the roses of dawn,
It entangles the shafts of the noon,
And into the bed of its stillness
The moonshine sinks down as in slumber, 15
That the son of the rock, that the nursling of heaven
May be born in a holy twilight!

[1] First published in 1834. For the original (*Unsterblicher Jüngling*) by Count F. L. Stolberg see Note to *Poems*, 1844, pp. 371-2.

On a Cataract—Title] Improved from Stolberg. On a Cataract, &c. 1844, 1852.

2-3   Thou streamest from forth
        The cleft of thy ceaseless Nativity *MS. S. T. C.*

Between 7 *and* 13.
    The murmuring songs of the Son of the Rock,
    When he feeds evermore at the slumberless Fountain.
    There abideth a Cloud,
    At the Portal a Veil,
    At the shrine of thy self-renewing;
    It embodies the Visions of Dawn,
    It entangles, &c. *MS. S. T. C.*

ANTISTROPHE

The wild goat in awe
Looks up and beholds
Above thee the cliff inaccessible;— 20
Thou at once full-born
Madd'nest in thy joyance,
Whirlest, shatter'st, splitt'st,
Life invulnerable.

?1799.

TELL'S BIRTH-PLACE[1]

IMITATED FROM STOLBERG

I

Mark this holy chapel well!
The birth-place, this, of William Tell.
Here, where stands God's altar dread,
Stood his parents' marriage-bed.

II

Here, first, an infant to her breast, 5
Him his loving mother prest;
And kissed the babe, and blessed the day,
And prayed as mothers use to pray.

III

'Vouchsafe him health, O God! and give
The child thy servant still to live!' 10
But God had destined to do more
Through him, than through an arméd power.

IV

God gave him reverence of laws,
Yet stirring blood in Freedom's cause—
A spirit to his rocks akin, 15
The eye of the hawk, and the fire therein!

---

[1] First published in *Sibylline Leaves*, 1817: included in 1828, 1829, and 1834. There is no evidence as to the date of composition.

---

20 Below thee the cliff inaccessible *MS. S. T. C.*
22-3   Flockest in thy Joyance,
          Wheelest, shatter'st, start'st. *MS. S. T. C.*

V

To Nature and to Holy Writ
Alone did God the boy commit:
Where flashed and roared the torrent, oft
His soul found wings, and soared aloft!   20

VI

The straining oar and chamois chase
Had formed his limbs to strength and grace:
On wave and wind the boy would toss,
Was great, nor knew how great he was!

VII

He knew not that his chosen hand,   25
Made strong by God, his native land
Would rescue from the shameful yoke
Of Slavery——the which he broke!

? 1799.

THE VISIT OF THE GODS[1]

IMITATED FROM SCHILLER

NEVER, believe me,
Appear the Immortals,
Never alone:
Scarce had I welcomed the Sorrow-beguiler,
Iacchus! but in came Boy Cupid the Smiler;   5
Lo! Phoebus the Glorious descends from his throne!
They advance, they float in, the Olympians all!
With Divinities fills my
Terrestrial hall!

How shall I yield you   10
Due entertainment,
Celestial quire?
Me rather, bright guests! with your wings of upbuoyance
Bear aloft to your homes, to your banquets of joyance,

---

[1] First published in *Sibylline Leaves*, 1817: included in 1828, 1829 ('Vision of the Gods', Contents, vol. i, pp. 322-3 of both editions), and in 1834.

---

28 Slavery] *Slavery, all editions to 1834.*

That the roofs of Olympus may echo my lyre! 15
Hah! we mount! on their pinions they waft up my soul!
    O give me the nectar!
    O fill me the bowl!

    Give him the nectar!
    Pour out for the poet, 20
    Hebe! pour free!
Quicken his eyes with celestial dew,
That Styx the detested no more he may view,
And like one of us Gods may conceit him to be!
Thanks, Hebe! I quaff it! Io Paean, I cry! 25
    The wine of the Immortals
    Forbids me to die!

?1799.

FROM THE GERMAN [1]

Know'st thou the land where the pale citrons grow,
The golden fruits in darker foliage glow?
Soft blows the wind that breathes from that blue sky!
Still stands the myrtle and the laurel high!
Know'st thou it well, that land, belovéd Friend? 5
Thither with thee, O, thither would I wend!
?1799.

WATER BALLAD [2]

[FROM THE FRENCH]

'Come hither, gently rowing,
  Come, bear me quickly o'er
This stream so brightly flowing
  To yonder woodland shore.
But vain were my endeavour 5
  To pay thee, courteous guide;
Row on, row on, for ever
  I'd have thee by my side.

---

[1] First published in 1834. The original is 'Mignon's Song' in Goethe's *Wilhelm Meister*.

[2] First published in *The Athenaeum*, October 29, 1831. First collected in *P. and D. W.*, 1877–80. The original is the 'Barcarolle de Marie' of François Antoine Eugène de Planard.

'Good boatman, prithee haste thee,
  I seek my father-land.'— 10
'Say, when I there have placed thee,
  Dare I demand thy hand?'
'A maiden's head can never
  So hard a point decide;
Row on, row on, for ever 15
  I'd have thee by my side.'

The happy bridal over
  The wanderer ceased to roam,
For, seated by her lover,
  The boat became her home. 20
And still they sang together
  As steering o'er the tide:
'Row on through wind and weather
  For ever by my side.'

?1799.

ON AN INFANT[1]

WHICH DIED BEFORE BAPTISM

'BE, rather than be called, a child of God,'
Death whispered! With assenting nod,
  Its head upon its mother's breast,
The Baby bowed, without demur—
  Of the kingdom of the Blest
    Possessor, not Inheritor.

April 8, 1799.

---

[1] First published in *P. W.*, 1834. These lines were sent in a letter from Coleridge to his wife, dated Göttingen, April 6, 1799:—'Ah, my poor Berkeley!' [b. May 15, 1798, d. Feb. 10, 1799] he writes, 'A few weeks ago an Englishman desired me to write an epitaph on an infant who had died before its Christening. While I wrote it, my heart with a deep misgiving turned my thoughts homeward. "On an Infant", &c. It refers to the second question in the Church Catechism.' *Letters of S. T. C.*, 1895, i. 287.

---

1 called] *call'd MS. Letter, 1799*.   3 its] the *MS. Letter, 1799*.   4 bow'd and went without demur *MS. Letter, 1799*.

SOMETHING CHILDISH, BUT VERY NATURAL[1]

WRITTEN IN GERMANY

If I had but two little wings
  And were a little feathery bird,
    To you I'd fly, my dear!
But thoughts like these are idle things,
    And I stay here.   5

But in my sleep to you I fly:
  I'm always with you in my sleep!
    The world is all one's own.
But then one wakes, and where am I?
    All, all alone.   10

Sleep stays not, though a monarch bids:
  So I love to wake ere break of day:
    For though my sleep be gone,
Yet while 'tis dark, one shuts one's lids,
    And still dreams on.   15
April 23, 1799.

---

[1] First published in the *Annual Anthology* (1800), with the signature 'Cordomi': included in *Sibylline Leaves*, 1817, 1828, 1829, and 1834. The lines, without title or heading, were sent in a letter from Coleridge to his wife, dated Göttingen, April 23, 1799 (*Letters of S. T. C.*, 1895, i. 294–5). They are an imitation (see F. Freiligrath's *Biographical Memoir* to the Tauchnitz edition of 1852) of the German Folk-song *Wenn ich ein Vöglein wär'*. The title 'Something Childish', &c., was prefixed in the *Annual Anthology*, 1800.

---

3 you] *you MS. Letter, 1799.*   6 you] *you MS. Letter, 1799.*

HOME-SICK[1]

WRITTEN IN GERMANY

'Tis sweet to him who all the week
    Through city-crowds must push his way,
To stroll alone through fields and woods,
    And hallow thus the Sabbath-day.

And sweet it is, in summer bower,   5
    Sincere, affectionate and gay,
One's own dear children feasting round,
    To celebrate one's marriage-day.

But what is all to his delight,
    Who having long been doomed to roam,   10
Throws off the bundle from his back,
    Before the door of his own home?

Home-sickness is a wasting pang;
    This feel I hourly more and more:
There's healing only in thy wings,   15
    Thou breeze that play'st on Albion's shore!

May 6, 1799.

---

[1] First published in the *Annual Anthology* (1800), with the signature 'Cordomi': included in *Sibylline Leaves*, 1817, 1828, 1829, 1834. The lines, without title or heading, were sent in a letter from Coleridge to Poole, dated May 6, 1799 (*Letters of S. T. C.*, 1895, i. 298). Dr. Carlyon in his *Early Years*, &c. (1856, i. 66), prints stanzas 1, 3, and 4. He says that they were written from Coleridge's dictation, in the Brockenstammbuch at the little inn on the Brocken. The title 'Home-Sick', &c., was prefixed in the *Annual Anthology*, 1800.

---

13 a wasting pang] no baby-pang *MS. Letter, 1799, An. Anth.*
15 There's only music in thy wings *MS. Letter, 1799.*

LINES[1]

WRITTEN IN THE ALBUM AT ELBINGERODE,
IN THE HARTZ FOREST

I STOOD on Brocken's[2] sovran height, and saw
Woods crowding upon woods, hills over hills,
A surging scene, and only limited
By the blue distance. Heavily my way
Downward I dragged through fir groves evermore,   5
Where bright green moss heaves in sepulchral forms
Speckled with sunshine; and, but seldom heard,
The sweet bird's song became a hollow sound;
And the breeze, murmuring indivisibly,
Preserved its solemn murmur most distinct   10
From many a note of many a waterfall,
And the brook's chatter; 'mid whose islet-stones
The dingy kidling with its tinkling bell
Leaped frolicsome, or old romantic goat
Sat, his white beard slow waving. I moved on   15
In low and languid mood:[3] for I had found

---

[1] First published in the *Morning Post*, September 17, 1799: included in the *Annual Anthology* (1800) [signed C.], in *Sibylline Leaves*, 1817, 1828, 1829, and 1834. The lines were sent in a letter from Coleridge to his wife, dated May 17, 1799. Part of the letter was printed in the *Amulet*, 1829, and the whole in the *Monthly Magazine* for October, 1835. A long extract is given in Gillman's *Life of S. T. C.*, 1838, pp. 125-38.

[2] The highest Mountain in the Harz, and indeed in North Germany.

[3]
            ———————— When I have gaz'd
From some high eminence on goodly vales,
And cots and villages embower'd below,
The thought would rise that all to me was strange
Amid the scenes so fair, nor one small spot
Where my tired mind might rest and call it home.
                      SOUTHEY'S *Hymn to the Penates.*

---

3 surging] surging *M. P.*   4 Heavily] Wearily *MS. Letter.*   6 heaves] mov'd *MS. Letter.*   8 a] an *all editions to 1834.*   9 breeze] gale *MS. Letter.*   11 waterfall] waterbreak *MS. Letter.*   12 'mid] on *MS. Letter*
16 With low and languid thought, for I had found *MS. Letter.*

That outward forms, the loftiest, still receive
Their finer influence from the Life within;—
Fair cyphers else: fair, but of import vague
Or unconcerning, where the heart not finds   20
History or prophecy of friend, or child,
Or gentle maid, our first and early love,
Or father, or the venerable name
Of our adoréd country! O thou Queen,
Thou delegated Deity of Earth,   25
O dear, dear England! how my longing eye
Turned westward, shaping in the steady clouds
Thy sands and high white cliffs!

                            My native Land!
Filled with the thought of thee this heart was proud,
Yea, mine eye swam with tears: that all the view   30
From sovran Brocken, woods and woody hills,
Floated away, like a departing dream,
Feeble and dim! Stranger, these impulses
Blame thou not lightly; nor will I profane,
With hasty judgment or injurious doubt,   35
That man's sublimer spirit, who can feel
That God is everywhere! the God who framed
Mankind to be one mighty family,
Himself our Father, and the World our Home.
  May 17, 1799.

17 That grandest scenes have but imperfect charms *MS. Letter*, *M. P.*, *An. Anth.*
  18 Where the eye vainly wanders nor beholds *MS. Letter*.
    Where the sight, &c. *M. P.*, *An. Anth.*
  19 One spot with which the heart associates *MS. Letter*, *M. P.*, *An. Anth.*
  19-21   Fair cyphers of vague import, where the Eye
          Traces no spot, in which the Heart may read
          History or Prophecy *S. L. 1817, 1828*.
  20 Holy Remembrances of Child or Friend *MS. Letter*.
    Holy Remembrances of Friend or Child *M. P.*, *An. Anth.*
  26 eye] eyes *MS. Letter*.
  28-30   Sweet native Isle
    This heart was proud, yea mine eyes swam with tears
    To think of thee: and all the goodly view *MS. Letter*.

28 O native land *M. P.*, *An. Anth.*   34 I] *I MS. Letter.*   38 family] brother-hood *MS. Letter.*

THE BRITISH STRIPLING'S WAR-SONG[1]

IMITATED FROM STOLBERG

YES, noble old Warrior! this heart has beat high,
  Since you told of the deeds which our countrymen wrought;
O lend me the sabre that hung by thy thigh,
  And I too will fight as my forefathers fought.

Despise not my youth, for my spirit is steel'd,   5
  And I know there is strength in the grasp of my hand;
Yea, as firm as thyself would I march to the field,
  And as proudly would die for my dear native land.

In the sports of my childhood I mimick'd the fight,
  The sound of a trumpet suspended my breath;   10
And my fancy still wander'd by day and by night,
  Amid battle and tumult, 'mid conquest and death.

My own shout of onset, when the Armies advance,
  How oft it awakes me from visions of glory;
When I meant to have leapt on the Hero of France,   15
  And have dash'd him to earth, pale and breathless and gory.

---

[1] First published in the *Morning Post*, August 24, 1799: included in the *Annual Anthology* for 1800: reprinted in *Literary Remains*, 1836, i. 276, in the *Gentleman's Magazine*, 1848. ('Communicated to the *Bath Herald* during the Volunteer Frenzy of 1803') (*N. S.* xxix, p. 60), and in *Essays on His Own Times*, iii. 988-9. First collected in *P. W.*, 1877-80, ii. 200-1. The MS. is preserved in the British Museum. The text follows that of the *Annual Anthology*, 1800, pp. 173-4.

The British Stripling's, &c.—Title] The Stripling's War-Song. Imitated from the German of Stolberg *MS*. The Stripling's, &c. Imitated from Stolberg *L. R.* The British Stripling's War Song *M. P., An. Anth., Essays, &c.* The Volunteer Stripling. A Song *G. M.*
1 Yes] My *MS., L. R.*   2 Since] When *G. M.* which] that *MS., L. R.* our] your *M. P., Essays, &c.*   3 Ah! give me the sabre [~~Falchion~~] that [which *L. R.*] *MS., Essays, &c.*   5 O despise *MS., L. R., Essays, &c.*   7 march] move *MS., L. R.*   8 would] could *Essays, &c.*   native land] fatherland *L. R.*
9 fight] sight *G. M.*   10 sound] shrill [~~sound~~] *MS., L. R.* a] the *M. P., Essays, &c.*   12 Amid tumults [tumult *L. R.*] and perils *MS.*   'mid] and *Essays, &c.*   Mid battle and bloodshed *G. M.*
13 My own eager shout in the heat of my trance *MS., MS. correction in An. Anth., L. R.*
My own shout of onset, { in the heat of my trance *G. M., 1893.*
                               { ~~when the armies advance~~ *MS.*
14 visions] dreams full *MS., L. R.*   How oft it has wak'd *G. M.*   15 When I dreamt that I rush'd *G. M.*   16 breathless] deathless *L. R.* pale, breathless *G. M.*

318   THE BRITISH STRIPLING'S WAR-SONG

As late thro' the city with banners all streaming
  To the music of trumpets the Warriors flew by,
With helmet and scimitars naked and gleaming,
  On their proud-trampling, thunder-hoof'd steeds did they
    fly;   20

I sped to yon heath that is lonely and bare,
  For each nerve was unquiet, each pulse in alarm;
And I hurl'd the mock-lance thro' the objectless air,
  And in open-eyed dream proved the strength of my arm.

Yes, noble old Warrior! this heart has beat high,   25
  Since you told of the deeds that our countrymen wrought;
O lend me the sabre that hung by thy thigh,
  And I too will fight as my forefathers fought!

    ?1799.

NAMES[1]

[FROM LESSING]

I ASK'D my fair one happy day,
  What I should call her in my lay;
  By what sweet name from Rome or Greece;

---

[1] First published in the *Morning Post*: reprinted in the *Poetical Register* for 1803 (1805) with the signature HARLEY. PHILADELPHIA, in the *Keepsake* for 1829, in Cottle's *Early Recollections* (two versions) 1837, ii. 67, and in *Essays on His Own Times*, iii. 990, 'As it first appeared' in the *Morning Post*. First collected in 1834.

---

17 city] town *G. M.*
17–18   { with bannerets streaming
         { ~~with a terrible beauty~~
    To [And *L. R.*] the music *MS.*
19 scimitars] scymetar *MS., L. R., Essays, &c., G. M.*: scymeter *M. P.*
Between 20–1
  And the Host pacing after in gorgeous parade
  All mov'd to one measure in front and in rear;
  And the Pipe, Drum and Trumpet, such harmony made
  As the souls of the Slaughter'd would loiter to hear. *MS. erased.*
21 that] which *L. R.*   22 For my soul *MS. erased.*   23 I hurl'd my *MS., L. R., Essays, &c.* objectless] mind-peopled *G. M.*   26 Since] When *G. M.*   27 Ah! give me the falchion *MS., L. R.*

Names—Title] Song from Lessing *M. P., Essays, &c.*: From the German of Lessing *P. R.*: Epigram *Keepsake, 1829, Cottle's Early Recollections.*
1 fair] love *Cottle, E. R.*

Lalage, Neaera, Chloris,
Sappho, Lesbia, or Doris 5
    Arethusa or Lucrece.

'Ah!' replied my gentle fair,
'Belovéd, what are names but air?
    Choose thou whatever suits the line;
Call me Sappho, call me Chloris, 10
Call me Lalage or Doris,
    Only, only call me Thine.'

1799.

THE DEVIL'S THOUGHTS[1]

I

From his brimstone bed at break of day
A walking the Devil is gone,
To visit his snug little farm the earth,
And see how his stock goes on.

---

[1] First published in the *Morning Post*, September 6, 1799: included in 1828, 1829, and 1834. It is printed separately as the *Devil's Walk*, a Poem, By Professor Porson, London, Marsh and Miller, &c., 1830. In 1827, by way of repudiating Porson's alleged authorship of *The Devil's Thoughts*, Southey expanded the *Devil's Thoughts* of 1799 into a poem of fifty-seven

---

4 Iphigenia, Clelia, Chloris, *M. P., Cottle, E. R., P. R.*
   Neaera, Laura, Daphne, Chloris, *Keepsake.*
5 Laura, Lesbia, or Doris, *MS. 1799, M. P., Cottle, E. R.*
   Carina, Lalage, or Doris, *Keepsake.*
6 Dorimene, or Lucrece, *MS. 1799, M. P., Cottle, E. R., P. R., Keepsake.*
8 Belovéd.] Dear one *Keepsake.*
9 Choose thou] Take thou *M. P., P. R.* : Take *Cottle, E. R.*   10 Call me Laura, call me Chloris *MS. 1799, Keepsake.*
10-11 Call me Clelia, call me Chloris,
       Laura, Lesbia or Doris *M.P., Cottle, E. R.*
10-12 Clelia, Iphigenia, Chloris,
       Laura, Lesbia, Delia, Doris,
       But don't forget to call me *thine. P. R.*

The Devil's Thoughts.
3-4 {To look at his little snug farm of the Earth
     {To visit, &c. *1828, 1829.*
     And see how his stock went on. *M. P., 1828, 1829.*

THE DEVIL'S THOUGHTS

II

Over the hill and over the dale,
And he went over the plain,
And backward and forward he switched his long tail
As a gentleman switches his cane.

III

And how then was the Devil drest?
Oh! he was in his Sunday's best:
His jacket was red and his breeches were blue,
And there was a hole where the tail came through.

IV

He saw a Lawyer killing a Viper
On a dunghill hard by his own stable;
And the Devil smiled, for it put him in mind
Of Cain and his brother, Abel.

V

He saw an Apothecary on a white horse
Ride by on his vocations,
And the Devil thought of his old Friend
Death in the Revelations.[1]

stanzas entitled *The Devil's Walk*. See *P. W.*, 1838, iii. pp. 87–100. In the *Morning Post* the poem numbered fourteen stanzas; in 1828, 1829 it is reduced to ten, and in 1834 enlarged to seventeen stanzas. Stanzas iii and xiv–xvi of the text are not in the *M. P.* Stanzas iv and v appeared as iii, iv; stanza vi as ix; stanza vii as v; stanza viii as x; stanza ix as viii; stanza x as vi; stanza xi as vii; stanza xvii as xiv. In 1828, 1829, the poem consists of stanzas i–ix of the text, and of the concluding stanzas stanza xi ('Old Nicholas', &c.) of the *M. P.* version was not reprinted. Stanzas xiv–xvi of the text were first acknowledged by Coleridge in 1834.

[1] And I looked, and behold a pale horse, and his name that sat on him was Death, Rev. vi. 8. *M. P.*

---

7 switched] swish'd *M.P.*, *1828, 1829*.   8 switches] swishes *M. P.*, *1828, 1829*.   9–12 *Not in M. P.*   14 On the dunghill beside his stable *M. P.*: On a dung-heap beside his stable *1828, 1829*.

15–16   Oh! oh; quoth he, for it put him in mind
            Of the story of Cain and Abel *M.P.*

16 his] *his* 1828, 1829.   17 He ... on] An Apothecary on *M. P.*: A Pothecary on *1828, 1829*.   18 Ride] Rode *M. P.*, *1828, 1829*.   vocations] vocation *M. P.*   20 Revelations] Revelation *M. P.*

VI

He saw a cottage with a double coach-house,
    A cottage of gentility;
And the Devil did grin, for his darling sin
    Is pride that apes humility.

VII

He peep'd into a rich bookseller's shop,
    Quoth he! we are both of one college!
For I sate myself, like a cormorant, once
    Hard by the tree of knowledge.[1]

---

[1] This anecdote is related by that most interesting of the Devil's Biographers, Mr. John Milton, in his *Paradise Lost*, and we have here the Devil's own testimony to the truth and accuracy of it. *M. P.*

> 'And all amid them stood the TREE OF LIFE
> High, eminent, blooming ambrosial fruit
> Of vegetable gold (query *paper-money*), and next to Life
> *Our* Death, the TREE OF KNOWLEDGE, grew fast by.—
>   *   *   *   *   *
>   *   *   *   *   *
> So clomb this first grand thief—
> Thence up he flew, and on the tree of life
> Sat like a cormorant.'—*Par. Lost*, iv.

The allegory here is so apt, that in a catalogue of *various readings* obtained from collating the MSS. one might expect to find it noted, that for 'LIFE' *Cod. quid. habent*, 'TRADE.' Though indeed THE TRADE, *i.e.* the bibliopolic, so called κατ' ἐξοχήν, may be regarded as LIFE sensu *eminentiori*; a suggestion, which I owe to a young retailer in the hosiery line, who on hearing a description of the net profits, dinner parties, country houses, etc., of the trade, exclaimed, 'Ay! that's what I call LIFE now!'—This 'Life, *our* Death,' is thus happily contrasted with the fruits of Authorship.—Sic nos non nobis mellificamus Apes.

Of this poem, which with the 'Fire, Famine, and Slaughter' first appeared in the *Morning Post* [6th Sept. 1799], the 1st, 2nd, 3rd, 9th, and 16th stanzas* were dictated by Mr. Southey. See Apologetic Preface [to *Fire, Famine and Slaughter*]. [Between the ninth and the concluding stanza, two or three are omitted, as grounded on subjects which have lost their interest—and for better reasons. *1828, 1829.*]

If any one should ask who General —— meant, the Author begs leave to inform him, that he did once see a red-faced person in a dream whom by the dress he took for a General; but he might have been mistaken, and most certainly he did not hear any names mentioned. In simple verity, the author never meant any one, or indeed any thing but to put a concluding stanza to his doggerel.

* The three first stanzas, which are worth all the rest, and the ninth *1828, 1829.*

---

21 saw] past *M. P.*   23 And he grinn'd at the sight, for his favourite vice *M. P.*   25 peep'd] went *M. P., 1828, 1829.*   27 sate myself] **myself** sate *1828, 1829.*   28 Hard by] Upon *M. P.*: Fast by *1828, 1829.*

VIII

Down the river did glide, with wind and tide,
  A pig with vast celerity;
And the Devil look'd wise as he saw how the while,
It cut its own throat. 'There!' quoth he with a smile,
  'Goes "England's commercial prosperity."'

IX

As he went through Cold-Bath Fields he saw
  A solitary cell;
And the Devil was pleased, for it gave him a hint
  For improving his prisons in Hell.

X

He saw a Turnkey in a trice
  Fetter a troublesome blade;
'Nimbly,' quoth he, 'do the fingers move
  If a man be but used to his trade.'

XI

He saw the same Turnkey unfetter a man,
  With but little expedition,
Which put him in mind of the long debate
  On the Slave-trade abolition.

XII

He saw an old acquaintance
  As he passed by a Methodist meeting;—

29-33   He saw a pig right rapidly
            Adown the river float,
        The pig swam well, but every stroke
           Was cutting his own throat. *M. P.*
29 did glide] there plied *1828, 1829.*
Between 33-4   Old Nicholas grinn'd and swish'd his tail
           For joy and admiration;
       And he thought of his daughter, Victory,
           And his darling babe, Taxation. *M. P.*
34-5   As he went through —— —— fields he look'd
       At a *M. P.*
37 his] the *M. P.*   in] of *M. P.*   39 Fetter] Hand-cuff *M. P.*
Unfetter *1834.*
  40-1   'Nimbly', quoth he, 'the fingers move
        If a man is but us'd to his trade.' *M. P.*
42 unfetter] unfettering *M. P.*   44 And he laugh'd for he thought
of the long debates *M. P.*   46 saw] met *M. P.*   47 Just by the
Methodist meeting. *M. P.*

She holds a consecrated key,
　And the devil nods her a greeting.

XIII

She turned up her nose, and said, 50
　'Avaunt! my name's Religion,'
And she looked to Mr. ——
　And leered like a love-sick pigeon.

XIV

He saw a certain minister
　(A minister to his mind) 55
Go up into a certain House,
　With a majority behind.

XV

The Devil quoted Genesis
　Like a very learnéd clerk,
How 'Noah and his creeping things 60
　Went up into the Ark.'

XVI

He took from the poor,
　And he gave to the rich,
And he shook hands with a Scotchman,
　For he was not afraid of the —— 65

XVII

General ——————[1] burning face
　He saw with consternation,
And back to hell his way did he take,
For the Devil thought by a slight mistake
　It was general conflagration. 70

1799.

[1] In a MS. copy in the B. M. and in some pirated versions the blank is filled up by the word 'Gascoigne's'; but in a MS. copy taken at Highgate, in June, 1820, by Derwent Coleridge the line runs 'General Tarleton's', &c.

---

48 holds] held *M.P.*　　key] flag* *M.P.*　　49 And the Devil nods a greeting. *M.P.*

50-2　　She tip'd him the wink, then frown'd and cri'd
　　　'Avaunt! my name's ——
　　And turn'd to Mr. W—— *M.P.*

66 General ——] General ——'s *M.P.*　　68 way did take *M.P.*
70 general] General *M.P.*

* The allusion is to Archbishop Randolph consecrating the Duke of York's banners. See S. T. Coleridge's *Notizbuch aus den Jahren 1795-8* ... von A. Brandl, 1896, p. 354 (p. 25 a, l. 18 of *Gutch Memorandum Book*, B. M. Add. MSS. 27,901).

LINES COMPOSED IN A CONCERT-ROOM[1]

Nor cold, nor stern, my soul! yet I detest
    These scented Rooms, where, to a gaudy throng,
Heaves the proud Harlot her distended breast,
    In intricacies of laborious song.

These feel not Music's genuine power, nor deign 5
    To melt at Nature's passion-warbled plaint;
But when the long-breathed singer's uptrilled strain
    Bursts in a squall—they gape for wonderment.

Hark! the deep buzz of Vanity and Hate!
    Scornful, yet envious, with self-torturing sneer 10
My lady eyes some maid of humbler state,
    While the pert Captain, or the primmer Priest,
Prattles accordant scandal in her ear.

O give me, from this heartless scene released,
    To hear our old Musician, blind and grey, 15
(Whom stretching from my nurse's arms I kissed,)
    His Scottish tunes and warlike marches play,
By moonshine, on the balmy summer-night,
    The while I dance amid the tedded hay
With merry maids, whose ringlets toss in light. 20

[1] First published in the *Morning Post*, September 24, 1799: included in *Sibylline Leaves*, 1817, 1828, 1829, and 1834. There is no evidence as to the date of composition. In a letter to Coleridge, dated July 5, 1796, Lamb writes 'Have a care, good Master Poet, of the Statute *de Contumeliá*. What do you mean by calling Madame Mara harlots and naughty things? The goodness of the verse would not save you in a Court of Justice'—but it is by no means certain that Lamb is referring to the *Lines Composed in a Concert-Room*, or that there is any allusion in line 3 to Madame Mara. If, as J. D. Campbell suggested, the poem as it appeared in the *Morning Post* is a recast of some earlier verses, it is possible that the scene is Ottery, and that 'Edmund' is the 'Friend who died dead of' a 'Frenzy Fever' (vide *ante*, p. 76). In this case a probable date would be the summer of 1793. But the poem as a whole suggests a later date. Coleridge and Southey spent some weeks at Exeter in September 1799. They visited Ottery St. Mary, and walked through Newton Abbot to Ashburton and Dartmouth. It is possible that the 'Concert-Room,' the 'pert Captain,' and 'primmer Priest' are reminiscences of Exeter, the 'heath-plant,' and the 'ocean caves' of Dartmoor and Torbay. If so, the 'shame and absolute rout' (l. 49 of variant, p. 325) would refer to the victory of Suwaroff over Joubert at Novi, which took place August 15, 1799. See *Letters of S. T. C.*, 1895, i. 307.

---

14 heartless] loathsome *M. P.*

LINES COMPOSED IN A CONCERT-ROOM

> Or lies the purple evening on the bay
> Of the calm glossy lake, O let me hide
>   Unheard, unseen, behind the alder-trees,
> For round their roots the fisher's boat is tied,
>   On whose trim seat doth Edmund stretch at ease,
> And while the lazy boat sways to and fro,
>   Breathes in his flute sad airs, so wild and slow,
> That his own cheek is wet with quiet tears.
>
> But O, dear Anne! when midnight wind careers,
> And the gust pelting on the out-house shed
>   Makes the cock shrilly in the rainstorm crow,
>   To hear thee sing some ballad full of woe,
> Ballad of ship-wreck'd sailor floating dead,
>   Whom his own true-love buried in the sands!
> Thee, gentle woman, for thy voice remeasures
> Whatever tones and melancholy pleasures
>   The things of Nature utter; birds or trees,
> Or moan of ocean-gale in weedy caves,
> Or where the stiff grass mid the heath-plant waves,
>   Murmur and music thin of sudden breeze.

1799.

24 Around whose roots *M. P.*, *S. L.*   40 thin] then *M. P.*

After line 40

> Dear Maid! whose form in solitude I seek,
> Such songs in such a mood to hear thee sing,
> It were a deep delight!—But thou shalt fling
> Thy white arm round my neck, and kiss my cheek,
>   And love the brightness of my gladder eye
> The while I tell thee what a holier joy
>
> It were in proud and stately step to go,
>   With trump and timbrel clang, and popular shout,
>   To celebrate the shame and absolute rout
> Unhealable of Freedom's latest foe,
>   Whose tower'd might shall to its centre nod.
>
> When human feelings, sudden, deep and vast,
> As all good spirits of all ages past
>   Were armied in the hearts of living men,
> Shall purge the earth, and violently sweep
> These vile and painted locusts to the deep,
>   Leaving un——— ——— undebas'd
> A ——— world made worthy of its God.   *M. P.*

[The words in lines 57, 58 were left as blanks in the *Morning Post*, from what cause or with what object must remain a matter of doubt.]

WESTPHALIAN SONG[1]

[The following is an almost literal translation of a very old and very favourite song among the Westphalian Boors. The turn at the end is the same with one of Mr. Dibdin's excellent songs, and the air to which it is sung by the Boors is remarkably sweet and lively.]

> When thou to my true-love com'st
> Greet her from me kindly;
> When she asks thee how I fare?
> Say, folks in Heaven fare finely.
>
> When she asks, 'What! Is he sick?' 5
> Say, dead!—and when for sorrow
> She begins to sob and cry,
> Say, I come to-morrow.

? 1799.

HEXAMETERS[2]

PARAPHRASE OF PSALM XLVI

Gōd ĭs oŭr Strēngth ănd oŭr Rēfŭge: thĕrefōre wĭll wĕ nŏt trĕmblĕ,
Thō' thĕ Eārth bĕ rĕmōvĕd ănd thō' thĕ pĕrpētŭăl Moūntaīns
Sink in the Swell of the Ocean! God is our Strength and our Refuge.
There is a River the Flowing whereof shall gladden the City,
Hallelujah! the City of God! Jehova shall help her. 5
The Idōlātĕrs rāgĕd, the kingdoms were moving in fury;
But he uttered his Voice: Earth melted away from beneath them.
Halleluja! th' Eternal is with us, Almighty Jehova!
Fearful the works of the Lord, yea fearful his Desolations;
But He maketh the Battle to cease, he burneth the Spear and the Chariot. 10
Halleluja! th' Eternal is with us, the God of our Fathers!

1799.

---

[1] First published in the *Morning Post*, Sept. 27, 1802: reprinted in *Essays on His Own Times*, 1850, iii. 992. First collected in *P. W.*, 1877–80, ii. 170.

[2] Now published for the first time. The lines were sent in a letter to George Coleridge dated September 29, 1799. They were prefaced as follows:—'We were talking of Hexameters with you. I will, for want of something better, fill up the paper with a translation of one of my favourite Psalms into that metre which allowing trochees for spondees, as the nature of our Language demands, you will find pretty accurate a scansion.' *Mahomet* and, no doubt, the *Hymn to the Earth* may be assigned to the end of September or the beginning of October, 1799.

HYMN TO THE EARTH[1]

[IMITATED FROM STOLBERG'S *HYMNE AN DIE ERDE*]

HEXAMETERS

EARTH! thou mother of numberless children, the nurse and
 the mother,
Hail! O Goddess, thrice hail! Blest be thou! and, blessing,
 I hymn thee!

[1] First published in *Friendship's Offering*, 1834, pp. 165-7, with other pieces, under the general heading:—*Fragments from the Wreck of Memory: or Portions of Poems composed in Early Manhood: by S. T. Coleridge*. A Note was prefixed:—'It may not be without use or interest to youthful, and especially to intelligent female readers of poetry, to observe that in the attempt to adapt the Greek metres to the English language, we must begin by substituting *quality* of sound for *quantity*—that is, accentuated or comparatively emphasized syllables, for what in the Greek and Latin Verse, are named long, and of which the prosodial mark is — ; and *vice versâ*, unaccented syllables for short marked ◡. Now the Hexameter verse consists of two sorts of *feet*, the spondee composed of two long syllables, and the dactyl, composed of one long syllable followed by two short. The following verse from the Psalms is a rare instance of a *perfect* hexameter (i. e. line of six feet) in the English language:—

Gōd cāme | ūp wĭth ă | shōut : oūr | Lōrd wĭth thĕ | sōund ŏf ă | trūmpĕt.

But so few are the truly *spondaic* words in our language, such as Ēgȳpt, ūprōar, tūrmoīl, &c., that we are compelled to substitute, in most instances, the trochee; or — ◡, i. e. in such words as mērrȳ, līghtlȳ, &c., for the proper spondee. It need only be added, that in the hexameter the fifth foot must be a dactyl, and the sixth a spondee, or trochee. I will end this note with two hexameter lines, likewise from the Psalms :—

Thēre ĭs ă | rīvĕr thĕ | flōwĭng whĕre|ŏf shāll | glāddĕn thĕ | cītȳ,
Hāllĕ|lūjäh thĕ | cītȳ ŏf | Gōd Jĕ|hōväh hăth | blĕst hĕr. S. T. C.'

On some proof-sheets, or loose pages of a copy of *The Hymn* as published in *Friendship's Offering* for 1834, which Coleridge annotated, no doubt with a view to his corrections being adopted in the forthcoming edition of his poems (1834), he adds in MS. the following supplementary note:—'To make any considerable number of Hexameters feasible in our monosyllabic trocheeo-iambic language, there must, I fear, be other licenses granted—in the *first* foot, at least—*ex. gr.* a superfluous ◡ prefixed in cases of particles such as 'of', 'and', and the like: likewise — ◡ — where the stronger accent is on the first syllable.—S. T. C.'

The *Hymn to the Earth* is a free translation of F. L. Stolberg's *Hymne an die Erde*. (See F. Freiligrath's *Biographical Memoirs* prefixed to the Tauchnitz edition of the *Poems* published in 1852.) The translation exceeds the German original by two lines. The Hexameters 'from the Psalms' are taken from a metrical experiment which Coleridge sent to his brother George, in a letter dated September 29, 1799 (vide *ante*). First collected in 1834. The acknowledgement that the *Hymn to the Earth* is imitated from Stolberg's *Hymne an die Erde* was first prefixed by J. D. Campbell in 1893.

HYMN TO THE EARTH

Forth, ye sweet sounds! from my harp, and my voice shall float on your surges—
Soar thou aloft, O my soul! and bear up my song on thy pinions.

Travelling the vale with mine eyes—green meadows and lake with green island,
Dark in its basin of rock, and the bare stream flowing in brightness,
Thrilled with thy beauty and love in the wooded slope of the mountain,
Here, great mother, I lie, thy child, with his head on thy bosom!
Playful the spirits of noon, that rushing soft through thy tresses,
Green-haired goddess! refresh me; and hark! as they hurry or linger,
Fill the pause of my harp, or sustain it with musical murmurs.
Into my being thou murmurest joy, and tenderest sadness
Shedd'st thou, like dew, on my heart, till the joy and the heavenly sadness
Pour themselves forth from my heart in tears, and the hymn of thanksgiving.

Earth! thou mother of numberless children, the nurse and the mother,
Sister thou of the stars, and beloved by the Sun, the rejoicer!
Guardian and friend of the moon, O Earth, whom the comets forget not,
Yea, in the measureless distance wheel round and again they behold thee!
Fadeless and young (and what if the latest birth of creation?)
Bride and consort of Heaven, that looks down upon thee enamoured!
Say, mysterious Earth! O say, great mother and goddess,
Was it not well with thee then, when first thy lap was ungirdled,
Thy lap to the genial Heaven, the day that he wooed thee and won thee!
Fair was thy blush, the fairest and first of the blushes of morning!
Deep was the shudder, O Earth! the throe of thy self-retention:

---

8 his] its *F. O. 1834.*   9 that creep or rush through thy tresses *F. O. 1834.*

Inly thou strovest to flee, and didst seek thyself at thy centre!
Mightier far was the joy of thy sudden resilience; and forthwith
Myriad myriads of lives teemed forth from the mighty embracement.
Thousand-fold tribes of dwellers, impelled by thousand-fold instincts,
Filled, as a dream, the wide waters; the rivers sang on their channels;   30
Laughed on their shores the hoarse seas; the yearning ocean swelled upward;
Young life lowed through the meadows, the woods, and the echoing mountains,
Wandered bleating in valleys, and warbled on blossoming branches.

1799.

MAHOMET[1]

UTTER the song, O my soul! the flight and return of Mohammed,
Prophet and priest, who scatter'd abroad both evil and blessing,
Huge wasteful empires founded and hallow'd slow persecution,
Soul-withering, but crush'd the blasphemous rites of the Pagan   4
And idolatrous Christians.—For veiling the Gospel of Jesus,
They, the best corrupting, had made it worse than the vilest.
Wherefore Heaven decreed th' enthusiast warrior of Mecca,
Choosing good from iniquity rather than evil from goodness.
  Loud the tumult in Mecca surrounding the fane of the idol;—

---

[1] First published in 1834. In an unpublished letter to Southey, dated Sept. 25, 1799, Coleridge writes, 'I shall go on with the Mohammed'. There can be no doubt that these fourteen lines, which represent Coleridge's contribution to a poem on 'Mahomet' which he had planned in conjunction with Southey, were at that time already in existence. For Southey's portion, which numbered 109 lines, see *Oliver Newman*. By Robert Southey, 1845, pp. 113–15.

---

33 on] in *F. O. 1834.*   *After* 33 * * * * * * *F. O. 1834.*

320 MAHOMET

Naked and prostrate the priesthood were laid — the people **with
 mad shouts**   10
Thundering now, and now with saddest ululation
Flew, as over the channel of rock-stone the ruinous river
Shatters its waters abreast, and in mazy uproar bewilder'd,
Rushes dividuous all—all rushing impetuous onward.

? 1799.

LOVE[1]

ALL thoughts, all passions, all delights,
Whatever stirs this mortal frame,
All are but ministers of Love,
 And feed his sacred flame.

---

[1] First published (with four preliminary and three concluding **stanzas**) as the *Introduction to the Tale of the Dark Ladie*, in the *Morning Post*, Dec. 21, 1799 (for complete text with introductory letter vide Appendices): included (as *Love*) in the *Lyrical Ballads* of 1800, 1802, 1805: reprinted with the text of the *Morning Post* in *English Minstrelsy*, 1810 (ii. 131–9) with the following prefatory note:—'These exquisite stanzas appeared some years ago in

---

Love—Title] Introduction to the Tale of the Dark Ladie *M. P.*: Fragment, S. T. Coleridge *English Minstrelsy, 1810*.

Opening stanzas

    O leave the Lilly on its stem;
      O leave the Rose upon the spray;
    O leave the Elder-bloom, fair Maids!
      And listen to my lay.

    A Cypress and a Myrtle bough,
      This morn around my harp you twin'd,
    Because it fashion'd mournfully
      Its murmurs in the wind.

    And now a Tale of Love and Woe,
      A woeful Tale of Love I sing:
    Hark, gentle Maidens, hark! it sighs
      And trembles on the string.

    But most, my own dear Genevieve!
      It sighs and trembles most for thee!
    O come and hear what cruel wrongs
      Befel the dark Ladie.

The fifth stanza of the *Introduction* finds its place as the fifth stanza **of the text, and the sixth stanza as the first.

3 All are] Are all *S. L.* (For *Are all* r. *All are.* Errata, p. [xi]).

> Oft in my waking dreams do I
> Live o'er again that happy hour,
> When midway on the mount I lay,
> Beside the ruined tower.

5

a London Newspaper, and have since that time been republished in Mr. Wordsworth's Lyrical Ballads, but with some alterations; the Poet having apparently relinquished his intention of writing the Fate of the Dark Ladye': included (as *Love*) in *Sibylline Leaves*, 1828, 1829, and 1834. The four opening and three concluding stanzas with prefatory note were republished in *Literary Remains*, 1836, pp. 50-2, and were first collected in 1844. For a facsimile of the MS. of *Love* as printed in the *Lyrical Ballads*, 1800 (i. 138-44), see *Wordsworth and Coleridge MSS.*, edited by W. Hale White, 1897 (between pp. 34-5). For a collation of the *Introduction to the Tale of the Dark Ladie* with two MSS. in the British Museum [Add. MSS., No. 27,902] see *Coleridge's Poems*. A Facsimile Reproduction, &c. Ed. by James Dykes Campbell, 1899, and Appendices of this edition.

It is probable that the greater part of the *Introduction to the Tale of the Dark Ladie* was written either during or shortly after a visit which Coleridge paid to the Wordsworths's friends, George and Mary, and Sarah Hutchinson, at Sockburn, a farm-house on the banks of the Tees, in November, 1799. In the first draft, ll. 13-16, 'She leaned, &c.' runs thus :—

> She lean'd against a grey stone rudely carv'd,
> The statue of an arméd Knight:
> She lean'd in melancholy mood
> Amid the lingering light.

In the church at Sockburn there is a recumbent statue of an 'armed knight' (of the Conyers family), and in a field near the farm-house there is a 'Grey-Stone' which is said to commemorate the slaying of a monstrous wyverne or 'worme' by the knight who is buried in the church. It is difficult to believe that the 'arméd knight' and the 'grey stone' of the first draft were not suggested by the statue in Sockburn Church, and the 'Grey-Stone' in the adjoining field. It has been argued that the *Ballad of the Dark Ladié*, of which only a fragment remains, was written after Coleridge returned from Germany, and that the *Introduction to the Tale of the Dark Ladie*, which embodies *Love*, was written at Stowey in 1797 or 1798. But in referring to 'the plan' of the *Lyrical Ballads* of 1798 (*Biog. Lit.*, 1817, Cap. XIV, ii. 3) Coleridge says that he had written the *Ancient Mariner*, and was preparing the *Dark Ladie* and the *Christabel* (both unpublished poems when this Chapter was written), but says nothing of so typical a poem as *Love*. By the *Dark Ladié* he must have meant the unfinished *Ballad of the Dark Ladié*, which, at one time, numbered 190 lines, not the *Introduction to the Tale of the Dark Ladie*, which later on he refers to as the 'poem entitled Love' (*Biog. Lit.*, 1817, Cap. XXIV, ii. 298), and which had appeared under that title in the *Lyrical Ballads* of 1800, 1802, and 1805.

In *Sibylline Leaves*, 1828, 1829, and 1834, *Love*, which was the first

---

5-6   O ever in my waking dreams
             I dwell upon *M. P., MS. erased.*
7 lay] sate *M. P.*

The moonshine, stealing o'er the scene
Had blended with the lights of eve;   10
And she was there, my hope, my joy,
    My own dear Genevieve!

She leant against the armèd man,
The statue of the armèd knight;
She stood and listened to my lay,   15
    Amid the lingering light.

Few sorrows hath she of her own,
My hope! my joy! my Genevieve!
She loves me best, whene'er I sing
    The songs that make her grieve.   20

I played a soft and doleful air,
I sang an old and moving story—
An old rude song, that suited well
    That ruin wild and hoary.

She listened with a flitting blush,   25
With downcast eyes and modest grace;
For well she knew, I could not choose
    But gaze upon her face.

I told her of the Knight that wore
Upon his shield a burning brand;   30
And that for ten long years he wooed
    The Lady of the Land.

in order of a group of poems with the sub-title 'Love Poems', was prefaced by the following motto :—

> Quas humilis tenero stylus olim effudit in aevo,
> Perlegis hic lacrymas, et quod pharetratus acuta
> Ille puer puero fecit mihi cuspide vulnus.
> Omnia paulatim consumit longior aetas,
> Vivendoque simul morimur, rapimurque manendo.
> Ipse mihi collatus enim non ille videbor:
> Frons alia est, moresque alii, nova mentis imago,
> Voxque aliud sonat—
> Pectore nunc gelido calidos miseremur amantes,
> Jamque arsisse pudet. Veteres tranquilla tumultus
> Mens horret, relegensque alium putat ista locutum.
>   PETRARCH.

---

15 lay] harp *M. P., MS., L. B.*   21 soft] sad *M. P., MS. erased.*   23 suited] fitted *M. P., MS., L. B.*   22 sang] sung *E. M.*   24 That ruin] The Ruin *M. P., MS., L. B.* : The ruins *E. M.*   29 that] who *M. P.*   31 that] how *M. P.*

LOVE

I told her how he pined: and ah!
The deep, the low, the pleading tone
With which I sang another's love,
    Interpreted my own.   35

She listened with a flitting blush,
With downcast eyes, and modest grace;
And she forgave me, that I gazed
    Too fondly on her face!   40

But when I told the cruel scorn
That crazed that bold and lovely Knight,
And that he crossed the mountain-woods,
    Nor rested day nor night;

That sometimes from the savage den,   45
And sometimes from the darksome shade,
And sometimes starting up at once
    In green and sunny glade,—

There came and looked him in the face
An angel beautiful and bright;   50
And that he knew it was a Fiend,
    This miserable Knight!

And that unknowing what he did,
He leaped amid a murderous band,
And saved from outrage worse than death   55
    The Lady of the Land!

And how she wept, and clasped his knees;
And how she tended him in vain—
And ever strove to expiate
    The scorn that crazed his brain;—   60

---

34 The low, the deep *MS., L. B.*   35 In which I told *E. M.*   42 That] Which *MS., L. B.*   that] this *M. P., MS., L. B.*   43 And how he roam'd *M. P.*   that] how *MS. erased.*

Between 44–5
    And how he cross'd the Woodman's paths [path *E. M.*]
      Tho' briars and swampy mosses beat,
    How boughs rebounding scourg'd his limbs,
    And low stubs gor'd his feet. *M. P.*

45 That] How *M. P., MS. erased.*   51 that] how *M. P., MS. erased.*
53 that] how *M. P., MS. erased.*   54 murderous] lawless *M. P.*
59 ever] meekly *M. P.* For still she *MS. erased.*

And that she nursed him in a cave;
And how his madness went away,
When on the yellow forest-leaves
    A dying man he lay;—

His dying words—but when I reached   65
That tenderest strain of all the ditty,
My faultering voice and pausing harp
    Disturbed her soul with pity!

All impulses of soul and sense
Had thrilled my guileless Genevieve;   70
The music and the doleful tale,
    The rich and balmy eve;

And hopes, and fears that kindle hope,
An undistinguishable throng,
And gentle wishes long subdued,   75
    Subdued and cherished long!

She wept with pity and delight,
She blushed with love, and virgin-shame;
And like the murmur of a dream,
    I heard her breathe my name.   80

Her bosom heaved—she stepped aside,
As conscious of my look she stepped—
Then suddenly, with timorous eye
    She fled to me and wept.

She half enclosed me with her arms,   85
She pressed me with a meek embrace;
And bending back her head, looked up,
    And gazed upon my face.

'Twas partly love, and partly fear,
And partly 'twas a bashful art,   90
That I might rather feel, than see,
    The swelling of her heart.

---

61 that] how *M. P., MS. erased.*   78 virgin-] maiden- *M. P., MS., L. B.*
79 murmur] murmurs *M. P.*
Between 80–1 I saw her bosom { heave / ~~rise~~ and swell,
      Heave and swell with inward sighs—
   I could not choose but love to see
     Her gentle bosom rise. *M. P., MS. erased.*
81 Her wet cheek glowed *M. P., MS. erased.*   84 fled] flew *M. P.*

I calmed her fears, and she was calm,
And told her love with virgin pride;
And so I won my Genevieve,
    My bright and beauteous Bride. 95

1799.

ODE TO GEORGIANA, DUCHESS OF DEVONSHIRE[1]

ON THE TWENTY-FOURTH STANZA IN HER 'PASSAGE OVER MOUNT GOTHARD'

And hail the Chapel! hail the Platform wild!
  Where Tell directed the avenging dart,
With well-strung arm, that first preservst his child,
  Then aim'd the arrow at the tyrant's heart.

SPLENDOUR's fondly-fostered child!
And did you hail the platform wild,
  Where once the Austrian fell
  Beneath the shaft of Tell!
O Lady, nursed in pomp and pleasure! 5
Whence learn'd you that heroic measure?

---

[1] First published in the *Morning Post*, December 24, 1799 (in four numbered stanzas): included in the *Annual Anthology*, 1800, in *Sibylline Leaves*, 1817, 1828, 1829, and 1834. The Duchess's poem entitled 'Passage over Mount Gothard' was published in the *Morning Chronicle* on Dec. 20 and in the *Morning Post*, Dec. 21, 1799.

---

94 virgin] maiden *MS. erased.*   95 so] thus *M. P.*

After 96 And now once more a tale of woe,
    A woeful tale of love I sing;
  For thee, my Genevieve! it sighs,
    And trembles on the string.

    When last I sang [sung *E. M.*] the cruel scorn
      That craz'd this bold and lonely [lovely *E. M.*] knight,
    And how he roam'd the mountain woods,
        Nor rested day or night;

  I promis'd thee a sister tale
    Of Man's perfidious Cruelty;
  Come, then, and hear what cruel wrong
    Befel the Dark Ladie.
                End of the Introduction M. P.

Ode to Georgiana, &c.—Motto 4 Then wing'd the arrow to *M. P., An. Anth.* Sub-title] On the 24th stanza in her Poem, entitled 'The Passage of the Mountain of St. Gothard.' *M. P.*

1-2   Lady, Splendor's foster'd child
           And did *you M. P.*

2 you] *you An. Anth.*

336 ODE TO THE DUCHESS OF DEVONSHIRE

    Light as a dream your days their circlets ran,
From all that teaches brotherhood to Man
Far, far removed! from want, from hope, from fear!
Enchanting music lulled your infant ear,   10
Obeisance, praises soothed your infant heart:
Emblazonments and old ancestral crests,
With many a bright obtrusive form of art,
Detained your eye from Nature: stately vests,
That veiling strove to deck your charms divine,   15
Rich viands, and the pleasurable wine,
Were yours unearned by toil; nor could you see
The unenjoying toiler's misery.
And yet, free Nature's uncorrupted child,
You hailed the Chapel and the Platform wild,   20
    Where once the Austrian fell
    Beneath the shaft of Tell!
  O Lady, nursed in pomp and pleasure!
Whence learn'd you that heroic measure?

There crowd your finely-fibred frame   25
    All living faculties of bliss;
And Genius to your cradle came,
His forehead wreathed with lambent flame,
    And bending low, with godlike kiss
    Breath'd in a more celestial life;   30
But boasts not many a fair compeer
    A heart as sensitive to joy and fear?
And some, perchance, might wage an equal strife,
Some few, to nobler being wrought,
Corrivals in the nobler gift of thought.   35
    Yet these delight to celebrate
    Laurelled War and plumy State;
    Or in verse and music dress
    Tales of rustic happiness—

---

7 your years their courses *M. P.*   9 Ah! far remov'd from want and hope and fear *M. P.*   11 Obeisant praises *M. P.*   14 stately] gorgeous *M. P.*   15 om. *An. Anth.*

    31 foll.   But many of your many fair compeers
                    [But many of thy many fair compeers *M. P.*]
                    Have frames as sensible of joys and fears;
                    And some might wage an equal strife *An. Anth.*
    34–5   (Some few perchance to nobler being wrought),
                    Corrivals in the plastic powers of thought. *M. P.*

  35 Corrivals] co-rivals *An. Anth., S. L. 1828.*   36 these] *these S. L. 1828, 1829.*

Pernicious tales! insidious strains! 40
   That steel the rich man's breast,
   And mock the lot unblest,
The sordid vices and the abject pains,
Which evermore must be
   The doom of ignorance and penury! 45
But you, free Nature's uncorrupted child,
You hailed the Chapel and the Platform wild,
   Where once the Austrian fell
   Beneath the shaft of Tell!
   O Lady, nursed in pomp and pleasure! 50
   Whence learn'd you that heroic measure?

You were a Mother! That most holy name,
   Which Heaven and Nature bless,
I may not vilely prostitute to those
   Whose infants owe them less 55
Than the poor caterpillar owes
   Its gaudy parent fly.
You were a mother! at your bosom fed
The babes that loved you. You, with laughing eye,
Each twilight-thought, each nascent feeling read, 60
Which you yourself created. Oh! delight!
   A second time to be a mother,
   Without the mother's bitter groans:
   Another thought, and yet another,
   By touch, or taste, by looks or tones, 65
   O'er the growing sense to roll,
   The mother of your infant's soul!
The Angel of the Earth, who, while he guides[1]
His chariot-planet round the goal of day,
All trembling gazes on the eye of God 70
A moment turned his awful face away;
And as he viewed you, from his aspect sweet
   New influences in your being rose,
Blest intuitions and communions fleet
   With living Nature, in her joys and woes! 75

---

[1] In a copy of the *Annual Anthology* Coleridge drew his pen through ll. 68-77, but the lines appeared in *Sibylline Leaves*, 1817, and in all later editions (see *P. W.*, 1893, p. 624).

---

40 insidious] insulting *M. P.*   45 penury] poverty *M. P., An. Anth.*
47 Hail'd the low Chapel *M. P., An. Anth.*   51 Whence] Where *An. Anth., S. L. 1828, 1829.*   56 caterpillar] Reptile *M. P., An. Anth.*   60 each] and *M. P.*   72 you] thee *M. P.*   73 your] thy *M. P.*

338 ODE TO THE DUCHESS OF DEVONSHIRE

> Thenceforth your soul rejoiced to see
> The shrine of social Liberty!
> O beautiful! O Nature's child!
> 'Twas thence you hailed the Platform wild,
>   Where once the Austrian fell
>   Beneath the shaft of Tell!
> O Lady, nursed in pomp and pleasure!
> Thence learn'd you that heroic measure.

1799.

A CHRISTMAS CAROL[1]

I

> The shepherds went their hasty way,
>   And found the lowly stable-shed
> Where the Virgin-Mother lay:
>   And now they checked their eager tread,
> For to the Babe, that at her bosom clung,
> A Mother's song the Virgin-Mother sung.

II

> They told her how a glorious light,
>   Streaming from a heavenly throng,
> Around them shone, suspending night!
>   While sweeter than a mother's song,
> Blest Angels heralded the Saviour's birth,
> Glory to God on high! and Peace on Earth.

III

> She listened to the tale divine,
>   And closer still the Babe she pressed;
> And while she cried, the Babe is mine!
>   The milk rushed faster to her breast:
> Joy rose within her, like a summer's morn;
> Peace, Peace on Earth! the Prince of Peace is born.

[1] First published in the *Morning Post*, December 25, 1799: included in the *Annual Anthology*, 1800, in *Sibylline Leaves*, 1817, 1828, 1829, and 1834.

---

76 O Lady thence ye joy'd to see *M. P.*
A Christmas Carol—8 a] an *M. P., An. Anth.*   10 While] And *M. P.*

IV

Thou Mother of the Prince of Peace,
    Poor, simple, and of low estate!   20
That strife should vanish, battle cease,
    O why should this thy soul elate?
Sweet Music's loudest note, the Poet's story,——
Didst thou ne'er love to hear of fame and glory?

V

And is not War a youthful king,   25
    A stately Hero clad in mail?
Beneath his footsteps laurels spring;
    Him Earth's majestic monarchs hail
Their friend, their playmate! and his bold bright eye
Compels the maiden's love-confessing sigh.   30

VI

'Tell this in some more courtly scene,
    To maids and youths in robes of state!
I am a woman poor and mean,
    And therefore is my soul elate.
War is a ruffian, all with guilt defiled,   35
That from the agéd father tears his child!

VII

'A murderous fiend, by fiends adored,
    He kills the sire and starves the son;
The husband kills, and from her board
    Steals all his widow's toil had won;   40
Plunders God's world of beauty; rends away
All safety from the night, all comfort from the day.

VIII

'Then wisely is my soul elate,
    That strife should vanish, battle cease:

---

35 War is a ruffian Thief, with gore defil'd *M.P., An. Anth.*   37 fiend] Thief *M.P., An. Anth.*   41 rends] tears *M.P.*

  I'm poor and of a low estate,   45
   The Mother of the Prince of Peace.
 Joy rises in me, like a summer's morn:
   Peace, Peace on Earth! the Prince of Peace is born.'
1799.

TALLEYRAND TO LORD GRENVILLE[1]

A METRICAL EPISTLE

[As printed in *Morning Post* for January 10, 1800.]

To the Editor of *The Morning Post*.

MR. EDITOR,—An unmetrical letter from Talleyrand to Lord Grenville has already appeared, and from an authority too high to be questioned: otherwise I could adduce some arguments for the exclusive authenticity of the following metrical epistle. The very epithet which the wise ancients used, '*aurea carmina*,' might have been supposed likely to have determined the choice of the French minister in favour of verse; and the rather when we recollect that this phrase of '*golden verses*' is applied emphatically to the works of that philosopher who imposed *silence* on all with whom he had to deal. Besides is it not somewhat improbable that Talleyrand should have preferred prose to rhyme, when the latter alone *has got the chink*? Is it not likewise curious that in our official answer no notice whatever is taken of the Chief Consul, Bonaparte, as if there had been no such person [man *Essays, &c., 1850*] existing; notwithstanding that his existence is pretty generally admitted, nay that some have been so rash as to believe that he has created as great a sensation in the world as Lord Grenville, or even the Duke of Portland? But the Minister of Foreign Affairs, Talleyrand, *is* acknowledged, which, in our opinion, could not have happened had he written only that insignificant prose-letter, which seems to precede Bonaparte's, as in old romances a dwarf always ran before to proclaim the advent or arrival of knight or giant. That Talleyrand's character and practices more resemble those of some *regular*

---

[1] First published in the *Morning Post*, January 10, 1800: reprinted in *Essays on His Own Times*, 1850, i. 233-7. First collected *P. and D. W.*, 1877, 1880.

After 49 Strange prophecy! Could half the screams
   Of half the men that since have died
  To realise War's kingly dreams,
   Have risen at once in one vast tide,
  The choral music of Heav'n's multitude
  Had been o'erpower'd, and lost amid the uproar rude!
            ESTEESI.
             M. P., An. Anth.

Governments than Bonaparte's I admit; but this of itself does not appear a satisfactory explanation. However, let the letter speak for itself. The second line is supererogative in syllables, whether from the oscitancy of the transcriber, or from the trepidation which might have overpowered the modest Frenchman, on finding himself in the act of writing to so *great* a man, I shall not dare to determine. A few Notes are added by

Your servant,
GNOME.

P.S.—As mottoes are now fashionable, especially if taken from out of the way books, you may prefix, if you please, the following lines from Sidonius Apollinaris:

> 'Saxa, et robora, corneasque fibras
> Mollit dulciloquâ canorus arte!'

TALLEYRAND, MINISTER OF FOREIGN AFFAIRS AT PARIS, TO LORD GRENVILLE, SECRETARY OF STATE IN GREAT BRITAIN FOR FOREIGN AFFAIRS, AUDITOR OF THE EXCHEQUER, A LORD OF TRADE, AN ELDER BROTHER OF TRINITY HOUSE, ETC.

My Lord! though your Lordship repel deviation
From forms long establish'd, yet with high consideration,
I plead for the honour to hope that no blame
Will attach, should this letter *begin* with my name.
I dar'd not presume on your Lordship to bounce,   5
But thought it more *exquisite* first to *announce*!

My Lord! I've the honour to be Talleyrand,
And the letter's from *me*! you'll not draw back your hand
Nor yet take it up by the rim in dismay,
As boys pick up ha'pence on April fool-day.   10
I'm no Jacobin foul, or red-hot Cordelier
That your Lordship's *un*gauntleted fingers need fear
An infection or burn! Believe me, 'tis true,
With a scorn like another I look down on the crew
That bawl and hold up to the mob's detestation   15
The most delicate wish for a *silent persuasion*.
A form long-establish'd these Terrorists call
Bribes, perjury, theft, and the devil and all!
And yet spite of all that the Moralist[1] prates,
'Tis the keystone and cement of *civilized States*.   20

---

[1] This sarcasm on the writings of moralists is, in general, extremely just; but had Talleyrand continued long enough in England, he might have found an honourable exception in the second volume of Dr. Paley's *Moral Philosophy*; in which both Secret Influence, and all the other *Established Forms*, are justified and placed in their true light.

---

14 With a scorn, like your own *Essay, &c., 1850.*

Those American *Reps*![1] And i' faith, they were serious!
It shock'd us at Paris, like something mysterious,
That men who've a Congress—But no more of 't! I'm proud
To have stood so distinct from the Jacobin crowd.

My Lord! though the vulgar in wonder be lost at 25
My transfigurations, and name me *Apostate*,
Such a meaningless nickname, which never incens'd me,
Cannot prejudice you or your Cousin against me:
I'm Ex-bishop. What then? Burke himself would agree
That I left not the Church—'twas the Church that left me.
My titles prelatic I lov'd and retain'd, 31
As long as what *I* meant by Prelate remain'd:
And tho' Mitres no longer will *pass* in our mart,
I'm *episcopal* still to the core of my heart.
No time from my name this my motto shall sever: 35
'Twill be *Non sine pulvere palma*[2] for ever!

Your goodness, my Lord, I conceive as excessive,
Or I dar'd not present you a scroll so digressive;
And in truth with my pen thro' and thro' I should strike it;
But I hear that your Lordship's own style is just like it. 40
Dear my Lord, we are right: for what charms can be shew'd
In a thing that goes straight like an old Roman road?
The tortoise crawls straight, the hare doubles about;
And the true line of beauty still winds in and out.
It argues, my Lord! of fine thoughts such a brood in us 45
To split and divide into heads multitudinous,
While charms that surprise (it can ne'er be denied us)
Sprout forth from each head, like the ears from King Midas.
Were a genius of rank, like a commonplace dunce,
Compell'd to drive on to the main point at once, 50
What a plentiful vintage of initiations[3]

---

[1] A fashionable abbreviation in the higher circles for Republicans. Thus *Mob* was originally the Mobility.

[2] *Palma non sine pulvere.* In plain English, an itching palm, not without the yellow dust.

[3] The word *Initiations* is borrowed from the new Constitution, and can only mean, in plain English, introductory matter. If the manuscript would bear us out, we should propose to read the line thus—'What a plentiful *Verbage*, what Initiations!' inasmuch as Vintage must necessarily refer to wine, really or figuratively; and we cannot guess what species Lord Grenville's eloquence may be supposed to resemble, unless, indeed, it be *Cowslip* wine. A slashing critic to whom we read the manuscript, proposed to read, 'What a plenty of Flowers—what initiations!' and supposes it may allude indiscriminately to Poppy Flowers, or Flour of Brimstone. The most modest emendation, perhaps, would be this—for Vintage read Ventage.

TALLEYRAND TO LORD GRENVILLE

Would Noble Lords lose in your Lordship's orations.
My fancy transports me! As mute as a mouse,
And as fleet as a pigeon, I'm borne to the house
Where all those who *are* Lords, from father to son,   55
Discuss the affairs of all those who are none.
I behold you, my Lord! of your feelings quite full,
'Fore the woolsack arise, like a sack full of wool!
You rise on each Anti-Grenvillian Member,
Short, thick and blustrous, like a day in November![1]   60
Short in person, I mean: for the length of your speeches
Fame herself, that most famous reporter, ne'er reaches.
Lo! Patience beholds you contemn her brief reign,
And Time, that all-panting toil'd after in vain,
(Like the Beldam who raced for a smock with her grand-child)   65
Drops and cries: 'Were such lungs e'er assign'd to a man-child?'
Your strokes at her vitals pale Truth has confess'd,
And Zeal unresisted entempests your breast![2]
Though some noble Lords may be wishing to sup,
Your merit self-conscious, my Lord, *keeps you up*,   70
Unextinguish'd and swoln, as a balloon of paper
Keeps aloft by the smoke of its own farthing taper.
Ye SIXTEENS[3] of Scotland, your snuffs ye must trim;
Your Geminies, fix'd stars of England! grow dim,

---

[1] We cannot sufficiently admire the accuracy of this simile. For as Lord Grenville, though short, is certainly not the shortest man in the House, even so is it with the days in November.

[2] An evident plagiarism of the Ex-Bishop's from Dr. Johnson:—

'Existence saw him spurn her bounded reign,
And panting Time toil'd after him in vain:
His pow'rful strokes presiding Truth confess'd,
And unresisting Passion storm'd the breast.'

[3] This line and the following are involved in an almost Lycophrontic tenebricosity. On repeating them, however, to an *Illuminant*, whose confidence I possess, he informed me (and he ought to know, for he is a Tallow-chandler by trade) that certain candles go by the name of *sixteens*. This explains the whole, the Scotch Peers are destined to burn out—and so are candles! The English are perpetual, and are therefore styled Fixed Stars! The word *Geminies* is, we confess, still obscure to us; though we venture to suggest that it may perhaps be a metaphor (daringly sublime) for the two eyes which noble Lords do in general possess. It is certainly used by the poet Fletcher in this sense, in the 31st stanza of his *Purple Island*:—

'What! shall I then need seek a patron out,
  Or beg a favour from a mistress' eyes,
To fence my song against the vulgar rout,
  And shine upon me with her *geminies*?'

And but for *a form long-establish'd*, no doubt
Twinkling faster and faster, ye all would *go out*. 75

Apropos, my dear Lord! a ridiculous blunder
Of some of our Journalists caused us some wonder:
It was said that in aspect malignant and sinister
In the Isle of Great Britain a great Foreign Minister 80
Turn'd as pale as a journeyman miller's frock coat is
On observing a star that appear'd in BOOTES!
When the whole truth was this (O those ignorant brutes!)
Your Lordship had made his appearance in boots.
You, my Lord, with your star, sat in boots, and the Spanish
Ambassador thereupon thought fit to vanish. 86

But perhaps, dear my Lord, among other worse crimes,
The whole was no more than a lie of *The Times*.
It is monstrous, my Lord! in a civilis'd state
That such Newspaper rogues should have license to prate. 90
Indeed printing in general—but for the taxes,
Is in theory false and pernicious in praxis!
You and I, and your Cousin, and Abbé Sieyes,
And all the great Statesmen that live in these days,
Are agreed that no nation secure is from vi'lence 95
Unless all who must think are maintain'd all in silence.
This printing, my Lord—but 'tis useless to mention
What we both of us think—'twas a cursèd invention,
And Germany might have been honestly prouder
Had she left it alone, and found out only powder. 100
My Lord! when I think of our labours and cares
Who rule the Department of foreign affairs,
And how with their libels these journalists bore us,
Though Rage I acknowledge than Scorn less decorous;
Yet their presses and types I could shiver in splinters, 105
Those Printers' black Devils! those Devils of Printers!
In case of a peace—but perhaps it were better
To proceed to the absolute point of my letter:
For the deep wounds of France, Bonaparte, my master,
Has found out a new sort of *basilicon* plaister. 110
But your time, my dear Lord! is your nation's best treasure,
I've intruded already too long on your leisure;
If so, I entreat you with penitent sorrow
To pause, and resume the remainder to-morrow.
    1800.

APOLOGIA PRO VITA SUA[1]

The poet in his lone yet genial hour
Gives to his eyes a magnifying power:
Or rather he emancipates his eyes
From the black shapeless accidents of size—
In unctuous cones of kindling coal,   5
Or smoke upwreathing from the pipe's trim bole,
 His gifted ken can see
  Phantoms of sublimity.

1800.

THE KEEPSAKE[2]

The tedded hay, the first fruits of the soil,
The tedded hay and corn-sheaves in one field,
Show summer gone, ere come. The foxglove tall
Sheds its loose purple bells, or in the gust,
Or when it bends beneath the up-springing lark,   5
Or mountain-finch alighting. And the rose
(In vain the darling of successful love)
Stands, like some boasted beauty of past years,
The thorns remaining, and the flowers all gone.
Nor can I find, amid my lonely walk   10
By rivulet, or spring, or wet roadside,
That blue and bright-eyed floweret of the brook,

---

[1] Included in the text of *The Historie and Gests of Maxilian*: first published in *Blackwood's Edinburgh Magazine*, January, 1822, vol. xi, p. 12. The lines were taken from a MS. note-book, dated August 28, 1800. First collected *P. and D. W.*, 1877–80.

[2] First published in the *Morning Post*, September 17, 1802 (signed, ΕΣΤΗΣΕ): included in *Sibylline Leaves*, 1817, 1828, 1829, 1834. 'It had been composed two years before' (1802), *Note*, 1893, p. 624. Mr. Campbell may have seen a dated MS. Internal evidence would point to the autumn of 1802, when it was published in the *Morning Post*.

Apologia, &c.—Title] The Poet's ken *P. W.*, *1885*: Apologia, &c. *1907*.
1–4   The poet's eye in his tipsy hour
    Hath a magnifying power
  Or rather emancipates his eyes
  Of the accidents of size *MS*.

5 cones] cone *MS*.   6 Or smoke from his pipe's bole *MS*.   7 His eye can see *MS*.

The Keepsake—1 om. *M. P.*   2 one] *one M. P.*   12 *Line 13 precedes line 12 M. P.*

    Hope's gentle gem, the sweet Forget-me-not![1]
So will not fade the flowers which Emmeline
With delicate fingers on the snow-white silk   15
Has worked (the flowers which most she knew I loved),
And, more beloved than they, her auburn hair.

    In the cool morning twilight, early waked
By her full bosom's joyous restlessness,
Softly she rose, and lightly stole along,   20
Down the slope coppice to the woodbine bower,
Whose rich flowers, swinging in the morning breeze,
Over their dim fast-moving shadows hung,
Making a quiet image of disquiet
In the smooth, scarcely moving river-pool.   25
There, in that bower where first she owned her love,
And let me kiss my own warm tear of joy
From off her glowing cheek, she sate and stretched
The silk upon the frame, and worked her name
Between the Moss-Rose and Forget-me-not—   30
Her own dear name, with her own auburn hair!
That forced to wander till sweet spring return,
I yet might ne'er forget her smile, her look,
Her voice, (that even in her mirthful mood
Has made me wish to steal away and weep,)   35
Nor yet the entrancement of that maiden kiss
With which she promised, that when spring returned,
She would resign one half of that dear name,
And own thenceforth no other name but mine!
?1800.

---

[1] One of the names (and meriting to be the only one) of the *Myosotis Scorpioides Palustris*, a flower from six to twelve inches high, with blue blossom and bright yellow eye. It has the same name over the whole Empire of Germany (*Vergissmeinnicht*) and, we believe, in Denmark and Sweden.

---

  17 they] all *M. P.*   19 joyous] joyless *S. L. 1828.*
  19–21   joyous restlessness,
          Leaving the soft bed to her sister,
          Softly she rose, and lightly stole along,
          Her fair face flushing in the purple dawn,
          Adown the meadow to the woodbine bower *M. P.*
  Between 19–20 Leaving the soft bed to her sleeping sister *S. L. 1817.*
  25 scarcely moving] scarcely-flowing *M. P.*   39 thenceforth] henceforth *M. P.*

A THOUGHT SUGGESTED BY A VIEW[1]

OF SADDLEBACK IN CUMBERLAND

On stern Blencartha's perilous height
  The winds are tyrannous and strong;
And flashing forth unsteady light
From stern Blencartha's skiey height,
  As loud the torrents throng!   5
Beneath the moon, in gentle weather,
  They bind the earth and sky together.
But oh! the sky and all its forms, how quiet!
The things that seek the earth, how full of noise and riot!

1800.

THE MAD MONK[2]

I heard a voice from Etna's side;
  Where o'er a cavern's mouth
  That fronted to the south
A chesnut spread its umbrage wide:

---

[1] First published in the *Amulet*, 1833, reprinted in *Friendship's Offering*, 1834: included in *Essays on His Own Times*, 1850, iii. 997. First collected in *P. and D. W.*, 1877–80. These lines are inserted in one of the Malta Notebooks, and appear from the context to have been written at Olevano in 1806; but it is almost certain that they belong to the autumn of 1800 when Coleridge made a first acquaintance of 'Blencathara's rugged coves'. The first line is an adaptation of a line in a poem of Isaac Ritson, quoted in Hutchinson's *History of Cumberland*, a work which supplied him with some of the place-names in the Second Part of *Christabel*. Compare, too, a sentence in a letter to Sir H. Davy of Oct. 18, 1800:—'At the bottom of the Carrock Man . . . the wind became so fearful and *tyrannous*, etc.'

[2] First published in the *Morning Post*, October 13, 1800 (signed *Cassiani junior*): reprinted in *Wild Wreath* (By M. E. Robinson), 1804, pp. 141–4. First collected in *P. W.*, 1880 (ii, Supplement, p. 362).

A Thought Suggested, &c.—Title] A Versified Reflection *F. O. 1834*. In *F. O. 1834*, the lines were prefaced by a note:—[A Force is the provincial term in Cumberland for any narrow fall of water from the summit of a mountain precipice. The following stanza (it may not arrogate the name of poem) or versified reflection was composed while the author was gazing on three parallel *Forces* on a moonlight night, at the foot of the Saddleback Fell. *S. T. C.*] A —— by the view of Saddleback, near Threlkeld in Cumberland. *Essays, &c.*

1 Blencartha's] Blenkarthur's *MS.*: Blencarthur's *F. O.*: Blenharthur's *Essays, &c., 1850.*   2 The wind is *F. O.*   4 Blencartha's] Blenkarthur's *MS.*: Blencarthur's *F. O.*: Blenharthur's *Essays, &c., 1850.*   8 oh!] ah! *Essays, &c.*

The Mad Monk—Title] The Voice from the Side of Etna; or the Mad Monk: An Ode in Mrs. Ratcliff's Manner *M. P.*

THE MAD MONK

A hermit or a monk the man might be;
  But him I could not see:
And thus the music flow'd along,
In melody most like to old Sicilian song:

'There was a time when earth, and sea, and skies,
  The bright green vale, and forest's dark recess,
With all things, lay before mine eyes
  In steady loveliness:
But now I feel, on earth's uneasy scene,
  Such sorrows as will never cease;—
    I only ask for peace;
If I must live to know that such a time has been!'
A silence then ensued:
    Till from the cavern came
    A voice;—it was the same!
And thus, in mournful tone, its dreary plaint renew'd:

'Last night, as o'er the sloping turf I trod,
  The smooth green turf, to me a vision gave
Beneath mine eyes, the sod—
  The roof of Rosa's grave!

My heart has need with dreams like these to strive,
  For, when I woke, beneath mine eyes I found
  The plot of mossy ground,
On which we oft have sat when Rosa was alive.—
Why must the rock, and margin of the flood,
  Why must the hills so many flow'rets bear,
Whose colours to a *murder'd* maiden's blood,
  Such sad resemblance wear?—

'*I struck the wound*,—this hand of mine!
For Oh, thou maid divine,
  I lov'd to agony!
The youth whom thou call'd'st thine
  Did never love like me!

'Is it the stormy clouds above
  That flash'd so red a gleam?

---

8 to] an *M. P.*   14 sorrows] motions *M. P.*   16 Then wherefore must I know *M. P.*   23 I saw the sod *M. P.*   26 woke] wak'd *M. P.*
27 The] That *M. P.*   28 On which so oft we sat *M. P.*   31 a wounded woman's blood *M. P.*

38-9   It is the stormy clouds above
        That flash *M. P.*

THE MAD MONK

    On yonder downward trickling stream?—   40
'Tis not the blood of her I love.—
The sun torments me from his western bed,
  Oh, let him cease for ever to diffuse
    Those crimson spectre hues!
Oh, let me lie in peace, and be for ever dead!'   45

Here ceas'd the voice. In deep dismay,
Down thro' the forest I pursu'd my way.

1800.

INSCRIPTION FOR A SEAT BY THE ROAD SIDE HALF-WAY UP A STEEP HILL FACING SOUTH[1]

THOU who in youthful vigour rich, and light
With youthful thoughts dost need no rest! O thou,
To whom alike the valley and the hill
Present a path of ease! Should e'er thine eye
Glance on this sod, and this rude tablet, stop!   5
'Tis a rude spot, yet here, with thankful hearts,
The foot-worn soldier and his family
Have rested, wife and babe, and boy, perchance
Some eight years old or less, and scantly fed,
Garbed like his father, and already bound   10
To his poor father's trade. Or think of him

---

[1] First published in the *Morning Post*, October 21, 1800 (Coleridge's birthday) under the signature VENTIFRONS: reprinted in the *Lake Herald*, November 2, 1906. Now first included in Coleridge's *Poetical Works*. Venti Frons is dog-Latin for Windy Brow, a point of view immediately above the River Greta, on the lower slope of Latrigg. Here it was that on Wednesday, August 13, 1800, Wordsworth, his sister Dorothy, and Coleridge 'made the Windy Brow seat'—a 'seat of sods'. In a letter to his printers, Biggs and Cottle, of October 10, 1800, Wordsworth says that 'a friend [the author of the *Ancient Mariner*, &c.] has also furnished me with a few of these Poems in the second volume [of the *Lyrical Ballads*] which are classed under the title of "Poems on the Naming of Places"' (*Wordsworth and Coleridge MSS.*, Ed. W. Hale White, 1897, pp. 27, 28). No such poems or poem appeared, and it has been taken for granted that none were ever written. At any rate *one* 'Inscription', now at last forthcoming, was something more than a 'story from the land of dreams'!

After 47   The twilight fays came forth in dewy shoon
            Ere I within the Cabin had withdrawn
            The goatherd's tent upon the open lawn—
            That night there was no moon. *M. P.*

Who, laden with his implements of toil,
Returns at night to some far distant home,
And having plodded on through rain and mire
With limbs o'erlaboured, weak from feverish heat, 15
And chafed and fretted by December blasts,
Here pauses, thankful he hath reached so far,
And 'mid the sheltering warmth of these bleak trees
Finds restoration—or reflect on those
Who in the spring to meet the warmer sun 20
Crawl up this steep hill-side, that needlessly
Bends double their weak frames, already bowed
By age or malady, and when, at last,
They gain this wished-for turf, this seat of sods,
Repose—and, well-admonished, ponder here 25
On final rest. And if a serious thought
Should come uncalled—how soon *thy* motions high,
Thy balmy spirits and thy fervid blood
Must change to feeble, withered, cold and dry,
Cherish the wholesome sadness! And where'er 30
The tide of Life impel thee, O be prompt
To make thy present strength the staff of all,
Their staff and resting-place—so shalt thou give
To Youth the sweetest joy that Youth can know;
And for thy future self thou shalt provide 35
Through every change of various life, a seat,
Not built by hands, on which thy inner part,
Imperishable, many a grievous hour,
Or bleak or sultry may repose—yea, sleep
The sleep of Death, and dream of blissful worlds, 40
Then wake in Heaven, and find the dream all true.
1800.

A STRANGER MINSTREL[1]

WRITTEN [TO MRS. ROBINSON,] A FEW WEEKS BEFORE HER DEATH

As late on Skiddaw's mount I lay supine,
Midway th' ascent, in that repose divine

[1] First published in *Memoirs of the late Mrs. Robinson*, Written by herself. With some Posthumous Pieces, 1801, iv. 141: reprinted in *Poetical Works of the late Mrs. Mary Robinson*, 1806, i. xlviii, li. First collected in *P. W.*, 1877-80.

1 Skiddaw's] Skiddaw *1801*.

A STRANGER MINSTREL

When the soul centred in the heart's recess
Hath quaff'd its fill of Nature's loveliness,
Yet still beside the fountain's marge will stay
   And fain would thirst again, again to quaff;
Then when the tear, slow travelling on its way,
   Fills up the wrinkles of a silent laugh—
In that sweet mood of sad and humorous thought
A form within me rose, within me wrought
With such strong magic, that I cried aloud,
'Thou ancient Skiddaw by thy helm of cloud,
And by thy many-colour'd chasms deep,
And by their shadows that for ever sleep,
By yon small flaky mists that love to creep
Along the edges of those spots of light,
Those sunny islands on thy smooth green height,
   And by yon shepherds with their sheep,
   And dogs and boys, a gladsome crowd,
   That rush e'en now with clamour loud
   Sudden from forth thy topmost cloud,
   And by this laugh, and by this tear,
   I would, old Skiddaw, she were here!
   A lady of sweet song is she,
   Her soft blue eye was made for thee!
   O ancient Skiddaw, by this tear,
   I would, I would that she were here!'

Then ancient Skiddaw, stern and proud,
   In sullen majesty replying,
Thus spake from out his helm of cloud
   (His voice was like an echo dying!):—
'She dwells belike in scenes more fair,
And scorns a mount so bleak and bare.'

I only sigh'd when this I heard,
Such mournful thoughts within me stirr'd
That all my heart was faint and weak,
   So sorely was I troubled!
No laughter wrinkled on my cheek,
   But O the tears were doubled!
But ancient Skiddaw green and high
Heard and understood my sigh;

---

8 wrinkles] wrinkle *1801*.   13 chasms so deep *1801*.   17 sunny] sunshine *1801*.   32 in] by *1801*.   38 on] now *1801*.

And now, in tones less stern and rude,
As if he wish'd to end the feud,
Spake he, the proud response renewing
(His voice was like a monarch wooing):— 45
'Nay, but thou dost not know her might,
  The pinions of her soul how strong!
But many a stranger in my height
  Hath sung to me her magic song,
    Sending forth his ecstasy 50
    In her divinest melody,
And hence I know her soul is free,
She is where'er she wills to be,
  Unfetter'd by mortality!
Now to the "haunted beach" can fly,[1] 55
  Beside the threshold scourged with waves,
  Now where the maniac wildly raves,
"*Pale moon, thou spectre of the sky!*"[2]
  No wind that hurries o'er my height
  Can travel with so swift a flight. 60
    I too, methinks, might merit
    The presence of her spirit!
    To me too might belong
The honour of her song and witching melody,
    Which most resembles me, 65
    Soft, various, and sublime,
    Exempt from wrongs of Time!'

Thus spake the mighty Mount, and I
Made answer, with a deep-drawn sigh:—
'Thou ancient Skiddaw, by this tear, 70
I would, I would that she were here!'

November, 1800.

---

[1] 'The Haunted Beach,' by Mrs. Robinson, was included in the *Annual Anthology* for 1800.

[2] From 'Jasper', a ballad by Mrs. Robinson, included in the *Annual Anthology* for 1800.

---

57 Now to the maniac while he raves *1801*.

ALCAEUS TO SAPPHO[1]

How sweet, when crimson colours dart
  Across a breast of snow,
To see that you are in the heart
  That beats and throbs below.

All Heaven is in a maiden's blush,   5
  In which the soul doth speak,
That it was you who sent the flush
  Into the maiden's cheek.

Large steadfast eyes! eyes gently rolled
  In shades of changing blue,   10
How sweet are they, if they behold
  No dearer sight than you.

And, can a lip more richly glow,
  Or be more fair than this?
The world will surely answer, No!   15
  I, SAPPHO, answer, Yes!

Then grant one smile, tho' it should mean
  A thing of doubtful birth;
That I may say these eyes have seen
  The fairest face on earth!   20

1800.

THE TWO ROUND SPACES ON THE TOMBSTONE[2]

THE Devil believes that the Lord will come,
  Stealing a march without beat of drum,

---

[1] First published in the *Morning Post*, November 24, 1800: reprinted in *Letters from the Lake Poets*, 1889, p. 16. It is probable that these lines, sent in a letter to Daniel Stuart (Editor of the *Morning Post*), dated October 7, 1800, were addressed to Mrs. Robinson, who was a frequent contributor of verses signed 'Sappho'. A sequence of Sonnets entitled 'Sappho to Phaon' is included in the collected edition of her *Poems*, 1806, iii. 63-107.

[2] First published in the *Morning Post*, December 4, 1800: reprinted in *Fraser's Magazine* both in February and in May, 1833, and in Payne Collier's *Old Man's Diary*, i. 35. First collected in *P. W.*, 1834, with the

---

Two Round Spaces, &c.—Title] Skeltoniad (To be read in the Recitative Lilt) *MS. Letter*: The Two Round Spaces; A Skeltoniad *M. P.*
1 The Devil believes the *Fraser (1)*.

354 TWO ROUND SPACES ON THE TOMBSTONE

About the same time that he came last,
On an Old Christmas-day in a snowy blast:
Till he bids the trump sound neither body nor soul stirs,   5
For the dead men's heads have slipt under their bolsters.

    Oh! ho! brother Bard, in our churchyard,
    Both beds and bolsters are soft and green;
    Save one alone, and that's of stone,
    And under it lies a Counsellor keen.   10
'Twould be a square tomb, if it were not too long;
And 'tis fenced round with irons sharp, spear-like, and strong.

This fellow from Aberdeen hither did skip
With a waxy face and a blubber lip,

following Prefatory Note :—'See the apology for the "Fire, Famine, and Slaughter", in first volume. This is the first time the author ever published these lines. He would have been glad, had they perished ; but they have now been printed repeatedly in magazines, and he is told that the verses will not perish. Here, therefore, they are owned, with a hope that they will be taken—as assuredly they were composed—in mere sport.' These lines, which were directed against Sir James Mackintosh, were included in a letter to [Sir] Humphry Davy, dated October 9, 1800. There is a MS. version in the British Museum in the handwriting of R. Heber, presented by him to J. Mitford. Mr. Campbell questions the accuracy of Coleridge's statement with regard to his never having published the poem on his own account. But it is possible that Davy may have sent the lines to the Press without Coleridge's authority. Daniel Stuart, the Editor of the *Morning Post*, in the *Gentleman's Magazine* for May, 1838, says that 'Coleridge sent one [poem] attacking Mackintosh, too obviously for me not to understand, and of course it was not published. Mackintosh had had one of his front teeth broken and the stump was black'. Stuart remembered that the lines attacking his brother-in-law had been suppressed, but forgot that he had inserted the rest of the poem. The poem as printed in 1893, despite the heading, does not follow the text of the *Morning Post*.

---

   3 time] hour *MS. Letter*, *M. P.*, *Fraser* (1), *Collier*.   At the same hour *MS. H.*   4 an Old] a cold *Fraser* (1) : On Old *MS. H.*   5 neither] nor *MS. Letter*, *M. P.* Till he bids the trump blow nor *Fraser* (2) : Till the trump then shall sound no *Collier* : Until that time not a body or *MS. H.*   6 their] the *Collier*.   7 Oh! ho!] Ho! Ho! *M. P.*, *MS. H.* : Oho *Fraser* (1). Brother *Collier*.   our] our *MS. Letter*.   8 Both bed and bolster *Fraser* (2). The graves and bolsters *MS. H.*   9 Except one alone *MS. H.*   10 under] in *Fraser* (2).   11 This tomb would be square *M. P.* : 'Twould be a square stone if it were not so long *Fraser* (1).   It would be square *MS. H.*   tomb] grave *Collier*.   12 And 'tis railed round with iron tall *M. P.* : And 'tis edg'd round with iron *Fraser* (1) : 'Tis fenc'd round with irons tall *Fraser* (2) : And 'tis fenc'd round with iron tall *Collier*.   'tis] its *MS. H.*   13–20 *om.* *M. P.*   13 From Aberdeen hither this fellow *MS. Letter*   hither] here *Fraser* (2).   14 blubber] blabber *MS. Letter*, *Fraser* (1), (2), *MS. H.*

TWO ROUND SPACES ON THE TOMBSTONE 355

  And a black tooth in front, to show in part   15
And a black tooth in front, to show in part
What was the colour of his whole heart.
   This Counsellor sweet,
   This Scotchman complete,
  (The Devil scotch him for a snake!)
I trust he lies in his grave awake.   20
   On the sixth of January,
  When all around is white with snow,
   As a Cheshire yeoman's dairy,
    Brother Bard, ho! ho! believe it, or no,
  On that stone tomb to you I'll show   25
  Two round spaces void of snow.
I swear by our Knight, and his forefathers' souls,
That in size and shape they are just like the holes
   In the house of privity
   Of that ancient family.   30
On those two places void of snow,
There have sat in the night for an hour or so,
Before sunrise, and after cock-crow,
He kicking his heels, she cursing her corns,
All to the tune of the wind in their horns,   35
   The Devil and his Grannam,
  With a snow-blast to fan 'em ;
Expecting and hoping the trumpet to blow,
For they are cock-sure of the fellow below!
1800.

15 in front] before *MS. H.*   17 Counsellor] lawyer so *MS. H.*   19 The Devil] Apollyon *MS. Letter.*   scotch] *scotch Collier.*   20 trust] hope *Collier.* (A humane wish) *Note in MS. Letter.*   21 sixth] seventh *M.P., Collier*: fifth *MS. H.*   22 When all is white both high and low *MS. Letter, M.P., Fraser* (2), *Collier, MS. H.*: When the ground All around Is as white as snow *Fraser* (1). 23 As] Or *Fraser* (1) : Like *MS. H.*   24 ho! ho!] oho! *Fraser* (1).   it] me *M. P.*   25 stone] tall *MS. Letter, M.P., Fraser* (2), *Collier.*   On the stone to you *MS. H.*   25-6 om. *Fraser* (1).   *Between* 25-6 After sunset and before cockcrow *M. P.*   Before sunrise and after cockcrow *Fraser* (2).   26 void] clear *M. P.*   27 I swear by the might Of the darkness of night, I swear by the sleep of our forefathers' souls *Fraser* (1).   souls] soul *MS. H.*   26-8 *om. Fraser* (2).   28 Both in shape and size *MS. Letter*: Both in shape and in size *M.P.*: That in shape and size they resembled *Fraser* (1), *Collier*: That in shape and size they are just like the Hole *MS.H.*   29 In the large house *M.P.*

29-30   In mansions not seen by the general eye
    Of that right ancient family. *Fraser* (1).

31 two] round *MS. Letter.*   places] spaces *Collier, MS. H.*   void] clear *M.P.* 32 Have sat *Fraser* (1), (2) : There have sat for an hour *MS. H.*   33 *om. MS. Letter, M.P.*   36 Devil] De'il *M.P.*   37 With the snow-drift *M.P.*: With a snow-blast to fan *MS. Letter.*   38 Expecting and wishing the trumpet would blow *Collier.*

THE SNOW-DROP[1]

1

Fear no more, thou timid Flower!
Fear thou no more the winter's might,
The whelming thaw, the ponderous shower,
The silence of the freezing night!
Since Laura murmur'd o'er thy leaves   5
The potent sorceries of song,
To thee, meek Flowret! gentler gales
   And cloudless skies belong.

2

Her eye with tearful meanings fraught,
She gaz'd till all the body mov'd   10
Interpreting the Spirit's thought—
The Spirit's eager sympathy

---

[1] First published in *P. W.*, 1893. The two last stanzas [*] were omitted as 'too imperfect to print'. The MS. bears the following heading: LINES WRITTEN IMMEDIATELY AFTER THE PERUSAL OF MRS. ROBINSON'S SNOW DROP.

To the Editor of the Morning Post.

Sir,
I am one of your many readers who have been highly gratified by some extracts from Mrs. Robinson's 'Walsingham': you will oblige me by inserting the following lines [*sic*] immediately on the perusal of her beautiful poem 'The Snow Drop'.—ZAGRI.

The 'Lines' were never sent or never appeared in the *Morning Post*.

To the Snow Drop.

1

Fear thou no more the wintry storm,
Sweet Flowret, blest by LAURA'S song:
She gaz'd upon thy slender form,
The mild Enchantress gaz'd so long;
That trembling as she saw thee droop,
Poor Trembler! o'er thy snowy bed,
With imitation's sympathy
   She too inclin'd her head.

2

She droop'd her head, she stretch'd her arm,
She whisper'd low her witching rhymes:
A gentle Sylphid heard the charm,
And bore thee to Pierian climes!
Fear thou no more the sparkling Frost,
The Tempest's Howl, the Fog-damp's gloom:
For thus mid laurels evergreen
   Immortal thou shalt bloom!

THE SNOW-DROP

Now trembled with thy trembling stem,
And while thou droopedst o'er thy bed,
With sweet unconscious sympathy
    Inclin'd the drooping head.[1]

3

She droop'd her head, she stretch'd her arm,
She whisper'd low her witching rhymes,
Fame unreluctant heard the charm,
And bore thee to Pierian climes!
Fear thou no more the Matin Frost
That sparkled on thy bed of snow;
For there, mid laurels ever green,
    Immortal thou shalt blow.

4

Thy petals boast a white more soft,
The spell hath so perfuméd thee,
That careless Love shall deem thee oft
A blossom from his Myrtle tree.
Then, laughing at the fair deceit,
Shall race with some Etesian wind

---

[1] The second stanza of Mrs. Robinson's ('Perdita') 'Ode to the Snow-drop' runs thus:

> All weak and wan, with head inclin'd,
>   Its parent-breast the drifted snow,
> It trembles, while the ruthless wind
> Bends its slim form; the tempest lowers,
> Its em'rald eye drops crystal show'rs
>   On its cold bed below.

The Poetical Works of the late Mrs. Mary Robinson, 1806, i. 123.

---

    3 [Stanza 2]
With eager ~~feelings~~ unreprov'd
With ~~steady eye and brooding thought~~
Her eye with tearful meanings fraught,
~~My Fancy saw her gaze at thee~~
She gaz'd till all the body mov'd
~~Till all the moving body caught,~~
Interpreting, the Spirit's sympathy—
The Spirit's eager sympathy
Now trembled with thy trembling stem,
And while thou drooped'st o'er thy bed,
With sweet unconscious sympathy
    Inclin'd { her ~~portraiture~~
            { the drooping head.
          First draft of Stanzas 1-3. *MS. S. T. C.*

THE SNOW-DROP

To seek the woven arboret
    Where Laura lies reclin'd.

5

All them whom Love and Fancy grace,
When grosser eyes are clos'd in sleep,
The gentle spirits of the place
Waft up the insuperable steep,   35
On whose vast summit broad and smooth
Her nest the Phœnix Bird conceals,
And where by cypresses o'erhung
    The heavenly Lethe steals.   40

6

A sea-like sound the branches breathe,
Stirr'd by the Breeze that loiters there;
And all that stretch their limbs beneath,
Forget the coil of mortal care.
Strange mists along the margins rise,   45
To heal the guests who thither come,
And fit the soul to re-endure
    Its earthly martyrdom.

7*

The margin dear to moonlight elves
Where Zephyr-trembling Lilies grow,   50
And bend to kiss their softer selves
That tremble in the stream below:—
There nightly borne does Laura lie
A magic Slumber heaves her breast:
Her arm, white wanderer of the Harp,   55
    Beneath her cheek is prest.

8*

The Harp uphung by golden chains
Of that low wind which whispers round,
With coy reproachfulness complains,
In snatches of reluctant sound: 60
The music hovers half-perceiv'd,
And only moulds the slumberer's dreams;
Remember'd Loves relume her cheek
    With Youth's returning gleams.

1800.

---

36   insuperable] unvoyageable *MS. erased.*
53-4   Along that marge does Laura lie
          Full oft where Slumber heaves her breast *MS. erased.*
64   With Beauty's morning gleams *MS. erased.*

ON REVISITING THE SEA-SHORE[1]

AFTER LONG ABSENCE, UNDER STRONG MEDICAL RECOMMENDATION NOT TO BATHE

God be with thee, gladsome Ocean!
  How gladly greet I thee once more!
Ships and waves, and ceaseless motion,
  And men rejoicing on thy shore.

Dissuading spake the mild Physician, 5
  'Those briny waves for thee are Death!'
But my soul fulfilled her mission,
  And lo! I breathe untroubled breath!

Fashion's pining sons and daughters,
  That seek the crowd they seem to fly, 10
Trembling they approach thy waters;
  And what cares Nature, if they die?

Me a thousand hopes and pleasures,
  A thousand recollections bland,
Thoughts sublime, and stately measures, 15
  Revisit on thy echoing strand:

Dreams (the Soul herself forsaking),
  Tearful raptures, boyish mirth;
Silent adorations, making
  A blessed shadow of this Earth! 20

---

[1] First published in the *Morning Post* (signed Εστησε), September 15, 1801: included in the *Sibylline Leaves*, 1817, 1828, 1829, and 1834. The lines were sent in an unpublished letter to Southey dated August 15, 1801. An autograph MS. is in the possession of Miss Arnold of Foxhow.

On Revisiting, &c.—Title] A flowering weed on the sweet Hill of Poesy *MS. Letter, 1801*: Ode After Bathing in the Sea, Contrary to Medical Advice *M. P.* After bathing in the Sea at Scarborough in company with T. Hutchinson. Aug. 1801 *MS. A.*

3 ceaseless] endless *MS. Letter, M. P., MS. A.*   4 men] life *MS. Letter, M. P., MS. A.*   5 Gravely said the { sage Physician *MS. Letter* : Mildly said the mild Physician *M. P.* { mild *MS. A.*   6 To bathe me on thy shores were death *MS. Letter, M. P., MS. A.*   10 That love the city's gilded sty *MS. Letter, M. P., MS. A.*   13 hopes] loves *MS. Letter, MS. A.*   16 echoing] sounding *MS. Letter, M. P., MS. A.*   18 Grief-like transports *MS. Letter, M. P., MS. A.*

O ye hopes, that stir within me,
  Health comes with you from above!
God is with me, God is in me!
  I cannot die, if Life be Love.

August, 1801.

ODE TO TRANQUILLITY[1]

Tranquillity! thou better name
Than all the family of Fame!
Thou ne'er wilt leave my riper age
To low intrigue, or factious rage;
  For oh! dear child of thoughtful Truth,   5
  To thee I gave my early youth,
And left the bark, and blest the steadfast shore,
Ere yet the tempest rose and scared me with its roar.

Who late and lingering seeks thy shrine,
On him but seldom, Power divine,   10
  Thy spirit rests! Satiety
  And Sloth, poor counterfeits of thee,

---

[1] First published in the *Morning Post* (with two additional stanzas at the commencement of the poem), December 4, 1801: reprinted in *The Friend* (without heading or title), No. 1, Thursday, June 1, 1809: included in *Sibylline Leaves*, 1817, 1828, 1829, and 1834. The stanzas were not indented in the *Morning Post* or *The Friend*.

Ode to Tranquillity—Title] *Vix ea nostra voco M. P.*

Before 1
  What Statesmen scheme and Soldiers work,
  Whether the Pontiff or the Turk,
  Will e'er renew th' expiring lease
  Of Empire; whether War or Peace
  Will best play off the Consul's game;
  What fancy-figures, and what name
  Half-thinking, sensual France, a natural Slave,
  On those ne'er-broken Chains, her self-forg'd Chains, will grave;

  Disturb not me! Some tears I shed
  When bow'd the Swiss his noble head;
  Since then, with quiet heart have view'd
  Both distant Fights and Treaties crude,
  Whose heap'd up terms, which Fear compels,
  (Live Discord's green Combustibles,
  And future Fuel of the funeral Pyre)
  Now hide, and soon, alas! will feed the low-burnt Fire. *M. P.*

8 tempest] storm-wind *M. P.*

ODE TO TRANQUILLITY

    Mock the tired worldling. Idle Hope
    And dire Remembrance interlope,
To vex the feverish slumbers of the mind: 15
The bubble floats before, the spectre stalks behind.

    But me thy gentle hand will lead
    At morning through the accustomed mead;
    And in the sultry summer's heat
    Will build me up a mossy seat;   20
    And when the gust of Autumn crowds,
    And breaks the busy moonlight clouds,
Thou best the thought canst raise, the heart attune,
Light as the busy clouds, calm as the gliding moon.

    The feeling heart, the searching soul,   25
    To thee I dedicate the whole!
    And while within myself I trace
    The greatness of some future race,
    Aloof with hermit-eye I scan
    The present works of present man—   30
A wild and dream-like trade of blood and guile,
Too foolish for a tear, too wicked for a smile!

1801.

TO ASRA[1]

Are there two things, of all which men possess,
That are so like each other and so near,
As mutual Love seems like to Happiness?
Dear Asra, woman beyond utterance dear!
This Love which ever welling at my heart,   5
Now in its living fount doth heave and fall,
Now overflowing pours thro' every part
Of all my frame, and fills and changes all,
Like vernal waters springing up through snow,

---

[1] First published in 1893. The Sonnet to 'Asra' was prefixed to the MS. of *Christabel* which Coleridge presented to Miss Sarah Hutchinson in 1804.

---

15 To] And *The Friend*, 1809.   slumbers] slumber *M. P.*, *The Friend*.
17 thy gentle hand] the power Divine *M. P.*   21 Autumn] Summer *M. P.*   23 The best the thoughts will lift *M. P.*   26 thee] her *M. P.*
28 some] a *M. P.*   29 hermit] hermit's *M. P.*

This Love that seeming great beyond the power 10
Of growth, yet seemeth ever more to grow,
Could I transmute the whole to one rich Dower
Of Happy Life, and give it all to Thee,
Thy lot, methinks, were Heaven, thy age, Eternity!

1801.

LOVE'S SANCTUARY[1]

This yearning heart (Love! witness what I say)
Enshrines thy form as purely as it may,
Round which, as to some spirit uttering bliss,
My thoughts all stand ministrant night and day
Like saintly Priests, that dare not think amiss. 5

? 1801.

DEJECTION: AN ODE[2]

[WRITTEN APRIL 4, 1802]

> Late, late yestreen I saw the new Moon,
> With the old Moon in her arms;
> And I fear, I fear, my Master dear!
> We shall have a deadly storm.
>
> *Ballad of Sir Patrick Spence.*

I

Well! If the Bard was weather-wise, who made
The grand old ballad of Sir Patrick Spence,
This night, so tranquil now, will not go hence
Unroused by winds, that ply a busier trade

---

[1] First published from a MS. in 1893.
[2] First published in the *Morning Post*, October 4, 1802. Included in

---

Dejection: An Ode—Title] Dejection, &c., written April 4, 1802 *M. P.*
2 grand] dear *Letter to Sotheby, July 19, 1802.*

DEJECTION: AN ODE

Than those which mould yon cloud in lazy flakes, 5
Or the dull sobbing draft, that moans and rakes
Upon the strings of this Æolian lute,
    Which better far were mute.
For lo! the New-moon winter-bright!
And overspread with phantom light, 10
(With swimming phantom light o'erspread
But rimmed and circled by a silver thread)
I see the old Moon in her lap, foretelling
The coming-on of rain and squally blast.
And oh! that even now the gust were swelling, 15
And the slant night-shower driving loud and fast!
Those sounds which oft have raised me, whilst they awed,
    And sent my soul abroad,
Might now perhaps their wonted impulse give,
Might startle this dull pain, and make it move and live! 20

Sibylline Leaves, 1817, 1828, 1829, and 1834. The Ode was sent in a letter to W. Sotheby, dated Keswick, July 19, 1802 (*Letters of S. T. C.*, 1895, i. 379–84). Two other MS. versions are preserved at Coleorton (*P. W. of W. Wordsworth*, ed. by William Knight, 1896, iii. App., pp. 400, 401). Lines 37, 38 were quoted by Coleridge in the *Historie and Gests of Maxilian* (first published in *Blackwood's Edinburgh Magazine* for January, 1822, and reprinted in *Miscellanies, &c.*, ed. by T. Ashe, 1885, p. 282): l. 38 by Wordsworth in his pamphlet on *The Convention of Cintra*, 1809, p. 135: lines 47–75, followed by lines 29–38, were quoted by Coleridge in *Essays on the Fine Arts*, No. III (which were first published in *Felix Farley's Bristol Journal*, Sept. 10, 1814, and reprinted by Cottle, *E. R.*, 1837, ii. 201–40); and lines 21–28, *ibid.*, in illustration of the following *Scholium*:—'We have sufficiently distinguished the beautiful from the agreeable, by the sure criterion, that when we find an object agreeable, the *sensation* of pleasure always precedes the judgment, and is its determining cause. We *find* it agreeable. But when we declare an object beautiful, the contemplation or intuition of its beauty precedes the *feeling* of complacency, in order of nature at least: nay in great depression of spirits may even exist without sensibly producing it.' Lines 76–93 are quoted in a letter to Southey of July 29, 1802; lines 76–83 are quoted in a letter to Allsop, September 30, 1819, *Letters, &c.*, 1836, i. 17. Lines 80, 81 are quoted in the *Biographia Literaria*, 1817, ii. 182, and lines 87–93 in a letter to Josiah Wedgwood, dated October 20, 1802; see Cottle's *Rem.*, 1848, p. 44, and *Tom Wedgwood* by R. B. Litchfield, 1903, pp. 114, 115

---

5 Than that which moulds yon clouds *Letter, July 19, 1802.* cloud] clouds *M. P., S. L.* 6 moans] drones *Letter, July 19, 1802, M. P.* 12 by] with *Letter, July 19, 1802.* 17–20 *om. Letter, July 19, 1802, M. P.*

II

A grief without a pang, void, dark, and drear,
  A stifled, drowsy, unimpassioned grief,
  Which finds no natural outlet, no relief,
      In word, or sigh, or tear—
O Lady! in this wan and heartless mood,   25
To other thoughts by yonder throstle woo'd,
  All this long eve, so balmy and serene,
Have I been gazing on the western sky,
  And its peculiar tint of yellow green:
And still I gaze—and with how blank an eye!   30
And those thin clouds above, in flakes and bars,
That give away their motion to the stars;
Those stars, that glide behind them or between,
Now sparkling, now bedimmed, but always seen:
Yon crescent Moon, as fixed as if it grew   35
In its own cloudless, starless lake of blue;
I see them all so excellently fair,
I see, not feel, how beautiful they are!

21–8 Quoted as illustrative of a 'Scholium' in *Felix Farley's Journal*, 1814.
22 stifled] stifling *Letter, July 19. 1802.*   23 Which] That *Letter. July 19, 1802, F. F.*

Between 24–7
  This, William, well thou knowst
  Is the sore evil which I dread the most
  And oft'nest suffer. In this heartless mood
  To other thoughts by yonder throstle woo'd
  That pipes within the larch-tree, not unseen,
  The larch, that pushes out in tassels green
  Its bundled leafits, woo'd to mild delights
  By all the tender sounds and gentle sights
  Of this sweet primrose-month and vainly woo'd!
  O dearest Poet in this heartless mood. *Letter, July 19, 1802.*

25 O Edmund *M.P.*: O William *Coleorton MS.*: O dearest Lady in this heartless mood *F. F.*   26 by yon sweet throstle woo'd *F. F.*   28 on] at *F. F.*   29 peculiar] celestial *F. F.*   yellow green] yellow-green *Letter, July 19, 1802, M. P.*   30 blank] black *Cottle, 1837.*

35–6   Yon crescent moon that seems as if it grew
       In its own starless, cloudless *F. F.*

Between 36–7 A boat becalm'd! thy own sweet sky-canoe *Letter, July 19, 1802*: A boat becalm'd! a lovely sky-canoe *M. P.*   38 I see not feel *M. P., Letter, July 19, 1802*: I see .... they are *F. F.*

DEJECTION: AN ODE

III

    My genial spirits fail;
      And what can these avail
To lift the smothering weight from off my breast?
      It were a vain endeavour,
      Though I should gaze for ever
On that green light that lingers in the west:
I may not hope from outward forms to win
The passion and the life, whose fountains are within.

IV

O Lady! we receive but what we give,
And in our life alone does Nature live:
Ours is her wedding garment, ours her shroud!
    And would we aught behold, of higher worth,
Than that inanimate cold world allowed
To the poor loveless ever-anxious crowd,
    Ah! from the soul itself must issue forth
A light, a glory, a fair luminous cloud
      Enveloping the Earth—
And from the soul itself must there be sent
    A sweet and potent voice, of its own birth,
Of all sweet sounds the life and element!

V

O pure of heart! thou need'st not ask of me
What this strong music in the soul may be!
What, and wherein it doth exist,
This light, this glory, this fair luminous mist,
This beautiful and beauty-making power.
    Joy, virtuous Lady! Joy that ne'er was given,
Save to the pure, and in their purest hour,
Life, and Life's effluence, cloud at once and shower,

45-6 Quoted in the *Gests of Maxilian*, Jan. 1822, and *Convention of Cintra*, 1809, p. 135.   47 Lady] Wordsworth *Letter, July 19, 1802*: William *Coleorton MS.*: Edmund *M. P., F. F.*   we *receive* but what we *give Coleorton MS., F. F.*   48 our] *our M. P., F. F.*   51 allowed] allow'd *Letter, July 19, 1802, M. P.*   57 potent] powerful *Letter, July 19, 1802, F. F.*

V] Stanza v is included in stanza iv in *M. P.*

60 What] *What Letter, July 19, 1802.*   61 exist] subsist *F. F.*   64 virtuous Lady] blameless Poet *Letter, July 19, 1802*: virtuous Edmund *M. P.*   Joy, O belovéd, Joy that *F. F.*   66 om. *Letter, July 19, 1802, M. P.*: Life of our life the parent and the birth *F. F.*   effluence] effulgence *S. L.* Corr. in *Errata* p. [xii], and in text by S. T. C. (*MS.*).

366 DEJECTION: AN ODE

Joy, Lady! is the spirit and the power,
Which wedding Nature to us gives in dower
   A new Earth and new Heaven,
Undreamt of by the sensual and the proud—   70
Joy is the sweet voice, Joy the luminous cloud—
    We in ourselves rejoice!
And thence flows all that charms or ear or sight,
   All melodies the echoes of that voice,
All colours a suffusion from that light.   75

VI

There was a time when, though my path was rough,
   This joy within me dallied with distress,
And all misfortunes were but as the stuff
   Whence Fancy made me dreams of happiness:
For hope grew round me, like the twining vine,   80
And fruits, and foliage, not my own, seemed mine.
But now afflictions bow me down to earth:
Nor care I that they rob me of my mirth;
    But oh! each visitation
Suspends what nature gave me at my birth,   85
   My shaping spirit of Imagination.

---

67 Lady] William *Letter, July 19, 1802* : Edmund *M. P.* : om. *F. F.*   68
Which] That *Letter, July 19, 1802.*   69 A new heaven and new
earth *F. F.*   71 om. *Letter, July 19, 1802* : This is the strong voice, this
the luminous cloud *F. F.*   72 We, we ourselves *Letter, July 19, 1802*,
M. P. : Our inmost selves *F. F.*   73 flows] comes *Letter, July 19, 1802*.
charms] glads *F. F.*   74 the echoes] an echo *Letter, July 19, 1802*.

After 75   Calm steadfast Spirit, guided from above,
   O Wordsworth! friend of my devoutest choice,
   Great son of genius! full of light and love
      Thus, thus dost thou rejoice.
   To thee do all things live from pole to pole,
   Their life the eddying of thy living soul
   Brother and friend of my devoutest choice
   Thus may'st thou ever, evermore rejoice! *Letter, July 19, 1802*.

Before 76 Yes, dearest poet, yes *Letter, July 19, 1802* : Yes, dearest
William! Yes! *Coleorton MS.* [Stanza v] Yes, dearest Edmund, yes *M. P.*
76 The time when *Letter, Sept. 30, 1819*.   77 This] The *Letters, July 19, 1802*,
Sept. 30, 1819.   I had a heart that dallied *Letter to Southey, July 29, 1802*.
80 For] When *Biog. Lit., Letter, Sept. 30, 1819.*   twining] climbing *Letters,
July 19, 29, 1802, Biog. Lit.*   80-1 Quoted in *Biog. Lit.,* 1817, ii. 180.   81
fruits] fruit *Letter, July 19, 1802*.   82 But seared thoughts now *Letter,
Sept. 30, 1819*.   83 care] car'd *Letter, July 19, 1802*.   86 In *M. P.* the
words 'The sixth and seventh stanzas omitted' preceded three rows of
four asterisks, lines 87-93 (quoted in *Letter to Josiah Wedgwood*, Oct. 20,
1802) being omitted. The Coleorton MS. ends with line 86.

DEJECTION: AN ODE

For not to think of what I needs must feel,
  But to be still and patient, all I can;
And haply by abstruse research to steal
  From my own nature all the natural man—   90
This was my sole resource, my only plan:
Till that which suits a part infects the whole,
And now is almost grown the habit of my soul.

VII

Hence, viper thoughts, that coil around my mind,
  Reality's dark dream!   95
I turn from you, and listen to the wind,
  Which long has raved unnoticed. What a scream
Of agony by torture lengthened out
That lute sent forth! Thou Wind, that rav'st without,
  Bare crag, or mountain-tairn,[1] or blasted tree,   100
Or pine-grove whither woodman never clomb,
Or lonely house, long held the witches' home,
  Methinks were fitter instruments for thee,
Mad Lutanist! who in this month of showers,
Of dark-brown gardens, and of peeping flowers,   105
Mak'st Devils' yule, with worse than wintry song,
The blossoms, buds, and timorous leaves among.
  Thou Actor, perfect in all tragic sounds!
Thou mighty Poet, e'en to frenzy bold!
    What tell'st thou now about?   110
  'Tis of the rushing of an host in rout,
  With groans, of trampled men, with smarting wounds—

---

[1] Tairn is a small lake, generally if not always applied to the lakes up in the mountains and which are the feeders of those in the valleys. This address to the Storm-wind [wind *S. L.*] will not appear extravagant to those who have heard it at night and in a mountainous country.

---

87 think] *think Letters, July 19, 29, 1802.*   91 was] is *Letter, Sept. 30, 1819.*
only] wisest *Letters, July 19, 29, 1802.*   92 Till] And *Letters, July 19, 29, 1802.*
93 habit] temper *Letters, July 19, 29, Oct. 20, 1802.*

94-5   Nay [O *M. P.*] wherefore did I let it haunt my mind
    This dark distressful dream. *Letter, July 19, 1802.*

96 you] it *Letter, July 19, 1802, M. P.*   99 That lute sent out! O thou wild storm without *Letter, July 19, 1802.*   O Wind *M. P.*   104 who] that *Letter, July 19, 1802.*   112 With many groans from men *Letter, July 19, 1802*: With many groans of men *M. P.*

At once they groan with pain, and shudder with the cold!
But hush! there is a pause of deepest silence!
   And all that noise, as of a rushing crowd,   115
With groans, and tremulous shudderings—all is over—
   It tells another tale, with sounds less deep and loud!
      A tale of less affright,
      And tempered with delight,
As Otway's self had framed the tender lay,—   120
      'Tis of a little child
      Upon a lonesome wild,
Not far from home, but she hath lost her way:
And now moans low in bitter grief and fear,
And now screams loud, and hopes to make her mother hear.

VIII

'Tis midnight, but small thoughts have I of sleep: 126
Full seldom may my friend such vigils keep!
Visit her, gentle Sleep! with wings of healing,
   And may this storm be but a mountain-birth,
May all the stars hang bright above her dwelling,   130
   Silent as though they watched the sleeping Earth!
      With light heart may she rise,
      Gay fancy, cheerful eyes,
Joy lift her spirit, joy attune her voice;
To her may all things live, from pole to pole,   135
Their life the eddying of her living soul!
O simple spirit, guided from above,
Dear Lady! friend devoutest of my choice,
Thus mayest thou ever, evermore rejoice.

1802.

115 Again! but all that noise *Letter, July 19, 1802.*   117 And it has other sounds less fearful and less loud *Letter, July 19, 1802.*   120 Otway's self] thou thyself *Letter, July 19, 1802*: Edmund's self *M. P.* 122 lonesome] heath *Letter, July 19, 1802.*   124 bitter] utter *Letter, July 19, 1802, M. P.*   125 hear] hear *Letter, July 19, 1802, M. P.*

VIII] om. *Letter, July 19, 1802.*   126 but] and *M. P.*   128 her] him *M. P.*   130 her] his *M. P.*   131 watched] *watch'd M. P.*   132 she] he *M. P.*

After 133
        And sing his lofty song and teach me to rejoice!
        O Edmund, friend of my devoutest choice,
        O rais'd from anxious dread and busy care,
        By the immenseness of the good and fair
           Which thou see'st everywhere,   5

THE PICTURE[1]

OR THE LOVER'S RESOLUTION

Through weeds and thorns, and matted underwood
I force my way; now climb, and now descend
O'er rocks, or bare or mossy, with wild foot
Crushing the purple whorts;[2] while oft unseen,
Hurrying along the drifted forest-leaves,   5
The scared snake rustles. Onward still I toil,
I know not, ask not whither! A new joy,
Lovely as light, sudden as summer gust,
And gladsome as the first-born of the spring,
Beckons me on, or follows from behind,   10
Playmate, or guide! The master-passion quelled,
I feel that I am free. With dun-red bark
The fir-trees, and the unfrequent slender oak,
Forth from this tangle wild of bush and brake
Soar up, and form a melancholy vault   15
High o'er me, murmuring like a distant sea.

Here Wisdom might resort, and here Remorse;
Here too the love-lorn man, who, sick in soul,
And of this busy human heart aweary,
Worships the spirit of unconscious life   20

---

[1] First published in the *Morning Post*, September 6, 1802: included in the *Poetical Register* for 1802 (1804), in *Sibylline Leaves*, 1817, 1828, 1829, and 1834.
It has been pointed out to me (by Mr. Arthur Turnbull) that the conception of the 'Resolution' that failed was suggested by Gessner's Idyll *Der feste Vorsatz* ('The Fixed Resolution'):—*S. Gessner's Schriften*, i. 104-7; *Works*, 1802, ii. 219-21.

[2] *Vaccinium Myrtillus*, known by the different names of Whorts, Whortle-berries, Bilberries; and in the North of England, Blea-berries and Bloom-berries. [*Note by S. T. C.* 1802.]

    Joy lifts thy spirit, joy attunes thy voice,
    To thee do all things live from pole to pole,
    Their life the eddying of thy living soul!
    O simple Spirit, guided from above,
    O lofty Poet, full of life and love,   10
    Brother and Friend of my devoutest choice,
    Thus may'st thou ever, evermore rejoice!
                      ΕΣΤΗΣΕ. *M. P.*

[*Note.*—For lines 7, 8, 11, 12 of this variant, vide *ante*, variant of lines 75 foll.]

3 wild] blind *M. P., P. R.*   17-26 *om. M. P., P. R.*   17-25 Quoted in *Letter to Cottle*, May 27, 1814.   18 love-lorn] woe-worn (heart-sick *erased*) *Letter*, 1814.   20 *unconscious life Letter*, 1814.

THE PICTURE

In tree or wild-flower.—Gentle lunatic!
If so he might not wholly cease to be,
He would far rather not be that he is;
But would be something that he knows not of,
In winds or waters, or among the rocks! 25

But hence, fond wretch! breathe not contagion here!
No myrtle-walks are these: these are no groves
Where Love dare loiter! If in sullen mood
He should stray hither, the low stumps shall gore
His dainty feet, the briar and the thorn 30
Make his plumes haggard. Like a wounded bird
Easily caught, ensnare him, O ye Nymphs,
Ye Oreads chaste, ye dusky Dryades!
And you, ye Earth-winds! you that make at morn
The dew-drops quiver on the spiders' webs! 35
You, O ye wingless Airs! that creep between
The rigid stems of heath and bitten furze,
Within whose scanty shade, at summer-noon,
The mother-sheep hath worn a hollow bed—
Ye, that now cool her fleece with dropless damp, 40
Now pant and murmur with her feeding lamb.
Chase, chase him, all ye Fays, and elfin Gnomes!
With prickles sharper than his darts bemock
His little Godship, making him perforce
Creep through a thorn-bush on yon hedgehog's back. 45

This is my hour of triumph! I can now
With my own fancies play the merry fool,
And laugh away worse folly, being free.
Here will I seat myself, beside this old,
Hollow, and weedy oak, which ivy-twine 50
Clothes as with net-work: here will I couch my limbs,
Close by this river, in this silent shade,
As safe and sacred from the step of man
As an invisible world—unheard, unseen,
And listening only to the pebbly brook 55

22 *wholly cease* to BE *Letter, 1814*.   27 these] here *M. P.*   28 For Love to dwell in; the low stumps would gore *M. P., P. R.*
31-3   till, like wounded bird
          Easily caught, the dusky Dryades
          With prickles sharper than his darts would mock.
          His little Godship   *M. P., P. R.*
34-42, 44 *om. M. P., P. R.*   51 here will couch *M. P., P. R., S. L.*   55 brook] stream *M. P., P. R., S. L.* (for *stream* read *brook* Errata, *S. L.*, p. [xi]).

THE PICTURE

That murmurs with a dead, yet tinkling sound;
Or to the bees, that in the neighbouring trunk
Make honey-hoards. The breeze, that visits me,
Was never Love's accomplice, never raised
The tendril ringlets from the maiden's brow,   60
And the blue, delicate veins above her cheek;
Ne'er played the wanton—never half disclosed
The maiden's snowy bosom, scattering thence
Eye-poisons for some love-distempered youth,
Who ne'er henceforth may see an aspen-grove   65
Shiver in sunshine, but his feeble heart
Shall flow away like a dissolving thing.

Sweet breeze! thou only, if I guess aright,
Liftest the feathers of the robin's breast,
That swells its little breast, so full of song,   70
Singing above me, on the mountain-ash.
And thou too, desert stream! no pool of thine,
Though clear as lake in latest summer-eve,
Did e'er reflect the stately virgin's robe,
The face, the form divine, the downcast look   75
Contemplative! Behold! her open palm
Presses her cheek and brow! her elbow rests
On the bare branch of half-uprooted tree,
That leans towards its mirror! Who erewhile
Had from her countenance turned, or looked by stealth,
(For Fear is true-love's cruel nurse), he now   81
With steadfast gaze and unoffending eye,
Worships the watery idol, dreaming hopes
Delicious to the soul, but fleeting, vain,
E'en as that phantom-world on which he gazed,   85
But not unheeded gazed: for see, ah! see,
The sportive tyrant with her left hand plucks

56–7   yet bell-like sound
                 Tinkling, or bees *M. P., P. R., S. L. 1828.*

58 The] This *M. P., P. R., S. L.*   70 That swells its] Who swells his
M. P., P. R., S. L.   75 the] her downcast *M. P., P. R.* Her face, her
form divine, her downcast look *S. L.*
76–7   Contemplative, her cheek upon her palm
          Supported; the white arm and elbow rest *M. P., P. R.*
          Contemplative! Ah see! her open palm
          Presses *S. L.*
79–80   He, meanwhile,
          Who from *M. P., P. R., S. L.*
86 *om. M. P., P. R., S. L.*   87 The] She *M. P., P. R., S. L.*

THE PICTURE

The heads of tall flowers that behind her grow,
Lychnis, and willow-herb, and fox-glove bells:
And suddenly, as one that toys with time, 90
Scatters them on the pool! Then all the charm
Is broken—all that phantom world so fair
Vanishes, and a thousand circlets spread,
And each mis-shape the other. Stay awhile,
Poor youth, who scarcely dar'st lift up thine eyes! 95
The stream will soon renew its smoothness, soon
The visions will return! And lo! he stays:
And soon the fragments dim of lovely forms
Come trembling back, unite, and now once more
The pool becomes a mirror; and behold 100
Each wildflower on the marge inverted there,
And there the half-uprooted tree—but where,
O where the virgin's snowy arm, that leaned
On its bare branch? He turns, and she is gone!
Homeward she steals through many a woodland maze 105
Which he shall seek in vain. Ill-fated youth!
Go, day by day, and waste thy manly prime
In mad love-yearning by the vacant brook,
Till sickly thoughts bewitch thine eyes, and thou
Behold'st her shadow still abiding there, 110
The Naiad of the mirror!

      Not to thee,
O wild and desert stream! belongs this tale:
Gloomy and dark art thou—the crowded firs
Spire from thy shores, and stretch across thy bed,
Making thee doleful as a cavern-well: 115
Save when the shy king-fishers build their nest
On thy steep banks, no loves hast thou, wild stream!

This be my chosen haunt—emancipate
From Passion's dreams, a freeman, and alone,
I rise and trace its devious course. O lead, 120
Lead me to deeper shades and lonelier glooms.
Lo! stealing through the canopy of firs,
How fair the sunshine spots that mossy rock,
Isle of the river, whose disparted waves

91-100 These lines are quoted in the prefatory note to *Kubla Khan*.
94 mis-shape] mis-shapes *M. P.*   108 love-yearning by] love-gazing
on *M. P., P. R.*   114 Spire] Tow'r *M. P., P. R., S. L.*   118 my] thy
S. L. (for *thy* read *my Errata, S. L.*, p. [xi]).   121 and] to *M. P., P. R.*
124 waves] waters *P. R., S. L.*

THE PICTURE

Dart off asunder with an angry sound,   125
How soon to re-unite! And see! they meet,
Each in the other lost and found: and see
Placeless, as spirits, one soft water-sun
Throbbing within them, heart at once and eye!
With its soft neighbourhood of filmy clouds,   130
The stains and shadings of forgotten tears,
Dimness o'erswum with lustre! Such the hour
Of deep enjoyment, following love's brief feuds
And hark, the noise of a near waterfall!
I pass forth into light—I find myself   135
Beneath a weeping birch (most beautiful
Of forest trees, the Lady of the Woods),
Hard by the brink of a tall weedy rock
That overbrows the cataract. How bursts
The landscape on my sight! Two crescent hills   140
Fold in behind each other, and so make
A circular vale, and land-locked, as might seem,
With brook and bridge, and grey stone cottages,
Half hid by rocks and fruit-trees. At my feet,
The whortle-berries are bedewed with spray,   145
Dashed upwards by the furious waterfall.
How solemnly the pendent ivy-mass
Swings in its winnow: All the air is calm.
The smoke from cottage-chimneys, tinged with light,
Rises in columns; from this house alone,   150
Close by the water-fall, the column slants,
And feels its ceaseless breeze. But what is this?
That cottage, with its slanting chimney-smoke,
And close beside its porch a sleeping child,
His dear head pillowed on a sleeping dog—   155
One arm between its fore-legs, and the hand
Holds loosely its small handful of wild-flowers
Unfilletted, and of unequal lengths.
A curious picture, with a master's haste
Sketched on a strip of pinky-silver skin,   160

126–32 *How soon to re-unite!* They meet, they join
        In deep embrace, and open to the sun
        Lie calm and smooth. Such the delicious hour *M.P., P.R., S.L.*

133 Of deep enjoyment, foll'wing Love's brief quarrels *M.P., P.R.* Lines 126–33 are supplied in the *Errata, S. L.* 1817 (p. xi).   134 And] But *Errata, S. L.* (p. xi).   135 I come out into light *M.P., P.R.*: I came out into light *S. L.*   For *came* read *come Errata, S. L.* (p. xi).   144 At] Beneath *M.P., P.R., S.L.* (for *Beneath* read *At Errata, S.L.*, p. [xi]).   152 this] *this M. P., P. R.*: THIS *S. L.* 1828, 1829.

374 THE PICTURE

Peeled from the birchen bark! Divinest maid!
Yon bark her canvas, and those purple berries
Her pencil! See, the juice is scarcely dried
On the fine skin! She has been newly here;
And lo! yon patch of heath has been her couch— 165
The pressure still remains! O blessèd couch!
For this may'st thou flower early, and the sun,
Slanting at eve, rest bright, and linger long
Upon thy purple bells! O Isabel!
Daughter of genius! stateliest of our maids! 170
More beautiful than whom Alcaeus wooed,
The Lesbian woman of immortal song!
O child of genius! stately, beautiful,
And full of love to all, save only me,
And not ungentle e'en to me! My heart, 175
Why beats it thus? Through yonder coppice-wood
Needs must the pathway turn, that leads straightway
On to her father's house. She is alone!
The night draws on—such ways are hard to hit—
And fit it is I should restore this sketch, 180
Dropt unawares, no doubt. Why should I yearn
To keep the relique? 'twill but idly feed
The passion that consumes me. Let me haste!
The picture in my hand which she has left;
She cannot blame me that I followed her: 185
And I may be her guide the long wood through.
1802.

TO MATILDA BETHAM FROM A STRANGER [1]

['ONE of our most celebrated poets, who had, I was told, picked out and praised the little piece 'On a Cloud,' another had quoted (saying it would have been faultless if I had not used the word *Phoebus* in it, which he thought inadmissible in modern poetry), sent me some verses inscribed "To Matilda Betham, from a Stranger"; and dated "Keswick, Sept. 9, 1802, S. T. C." I should have guessed whence they came, but dared not flatter myself so highly as satisfactorily to believe it, before I obtained the avowal of the lady who had transmitted them. *Excerpt from 'Autobiographical Sketch'*.]

MATILDA! I have heard a sweet tune played
On a sweet instrument—thy Poesie—

[1] First printed in a 'privately printed autobiographical sketch of

---

162 those] these *P. R.* 174 me] one *M. P., P. R.* 177 straightway] away *M. P., P. R.* 184 The] This *M. P., P. R.*

TO MATILDA BETHAM FROM A STRANGER

Sent to my soul by Boughton's pleading voice,
Where friendship's zealous wish inspirited,
Deepened and filled the subtle tones of *taste*:
(So have I heard a Nightingale's fine notes
Blend with the murmur of a hidden stream!)
And now the fair, wild offspring of thy genius,
Those wanderers whom thy fancy had sent forth
To seek their fortune in this motley world,
Have found a little home within *my* heart,
And brought me, as the quit-rent of their lodging,
Rose-buds, and fruit-blossoms, and pretty weeds,
And timorous laurel leaflets half-disclosed,
Engarlanded with gadding woodbine tendrils!
A coronal, which, with undoubting hand,
I twine around the brows of patriot HOPE!

The Almighty, having first composed a Man,
Set him to music, framing Woman for him,
And fitted each to each, and made them one!
And 'tis my faith, that there's a natural bond
Between the female mind and measured sounds,
Nor do I know a sweeter Hope than this,
That this sweet Hope, by judgment unreproved,
That our own Britain, our dear mother Isle,
May boast one Maid, a poetess *indeed*,
Great as th' impassioned Lesbian, in sweet song,
And O! of holier mind, and happier fate.

Matilda! I dare twine *thy* vernal wreath
Around the brows of patriot Hope! But thou
Be wise! be bold! fulfil my auspices!
Tho' sweet thy measures, stern must be thy thought,
Patient thy study, watchful thy mild eye!
Poetic feelings, like the stretching boughs
Of mighty oaks, pay homage to the gales,

Miss Matilda Betham', preserved in a volume of tracts arranged and bound up by Southey, now in the Forster Collection in the Victoria and Albert Museum: reprinted (by J. Dykes Campbell) in the *Athenaeum* (March 15, 1890): and, again, in *A House of Letters*, by Ernest Betham [1905], pp. 76-7. First collected in 1893 (see Editor's *Note*, p. 630). Lines 33-41 are quoted in a Letter to Sotheby, September 10, 1802. See *Letters of S. T. C.*, 1895, i. 404.

---

7 murmur] murmurs 1893.   16 coronal] coronel *P. Sketch*.   34 stretching] flexuous *MS. Letter, Sept. 10, 1802*.   35 pay] yield *MS. Letter, 1802*.

376 TO MATILDA BETHAM FROM A STRANGER

Toss in the strong winds, drive before the gust,
Themselves one giddy storm of fluttering leaves;
Yet, all the while self-limited, remain
Equally near the fixed and solid trunk
Of Truth and Nature in the howling storm,　　　　40
As in the calm that stills the aspen grove.
Be bold, meek Woman! but be wisely bold!
Fly, ostrich-like, firm land beneath thy feet,
Yet hurried onward by thy wings of fancy
Swift as the whirlwind, singing in their quills.　　　45
Look round thee! look within thee! think and feel!
What nobler meed, Matilda! canst thou win,
Than tears of gladness in a BOUGHTON'S[1] eyes,
And exultation even in strangers' hearts?

1802.

HYMN BEFORE SUN-RISE, IN THE VALE OF CHAMOUNI[2]

BESIDES the Rivers, Arve and Arveiron, which have their sources in the foot of Mont Blanc, five conspicuous torrents rush down its sides; and within a few paces of the Glaciers, the Gentiana Major grows in immense numbers, with its 'flowers of loveliest [liveliest *Friend, 1809*] blue.'

HAST thou a charm to stay the morning-star
In his steep course? So long he seems to pause
On thy bald awful head, O sovran BLANC,

---

[1] Catherine Rose, wife of Sir Charles William Rouse-Boughton, Bart. Sir Charles and Lady Boughton visited Greta Hall in September, 1802.

[2] First published in the *Morning Post*, Sept. 11, 1802: reprinted in the *Poetical Register* for 1802 (1803), ii. 308, 311, and in *The Friend*, No. XI, Oct. 26, 1809: included in *Sibylline Leaves*, 1817, 1828, 1829, and 1834. Three MSS. are extant: (1) *MS. A*, sent to Sir George Beaumont, Oct. 1803 (see *Coleorton Letters*, 1886, i. 26 ; (2) *MS. B*, the MS. of the version as printed in *The Friend*, Oct. 26, 1809 (now in the Forster Collection in the Victoria and Albert Museum); (3) *MS. C*, presented to Mrs. Brabant in 1815 (now in the British Museum). The *Hymn before Sunrise, &c.*, 'Hymn in the manner of the Psalms,' is an expansion, in part, of a translation of

---

39 solid] parent *MS. Letter, 1802.*　　　40 Of truth in Nature—in the howling blast *MS. Letter, 1802.*

Hymn before, &c.—Title] Chamouny The Hour before Sunrise A Hymn *M. P., P. R.*: Mount Blanc, The Summit of the Vale of Chamouny, An Hour before Sunrise: A Hymn *MS. A.*

3 On thy bald awful head O Chamouny *M. P., P. R.*: On thy bald awful top O Chamouny *MS. A*: On thy bald awful top O Sovran Blanc *Friend, 1809.*

The Arve and Arveiron at thy base
Rave ceaselessly; but thou, most awful Form!   5
Risest from forth thy silent sea of pines,
How silently! Around thee and above
Deep is the air and dark, substantial, black,
An ebon mass: methinks thou piercest it,
As with a wedge! But when I look again,   10
It is thine own calm home, thy crystal shrine,
Thy habitation from eternity!
O dread and silent Mount! I gazed upon thee,
Till thou, still present to the bodily sense,
Didst vanish from my thought: entranced in prayer   15
I worshipped the Invisible alone.

Yet, like some sweet beguiling melody,

Friederika Brun's 'Ode to Chamouny', addressed to Klopstock, which numbers some twenty lines. The German original was first appended to Coleridge's *Poetical Works* in 1844 (p. 372). A translation was given in a footnote, *P. W.* (ed. by T. Ashe), 1885, ii. 86, 87. In the *Morning Post* and *Poetical Register* the following explanatory note preceded the poem:—

'CHAMOUNI, THE HOUR BEFORE SUNRISE.

'[Chamouni is one of the highest mountain valleys of the Barony of Faucigny in the Savoy Alps; and exhibits a kind of fairy world, in which the wildest appearances (I had almost said horrors) of Nature alternate with the softest and most beautiful. The chain of Mont Blanc is its boundary; and besides the Arve it is filled with sounds from the Arveiron, which rushes from the melted glaciers, like a giant, mad with joy, from a dungeon, and forms other torrents of snow-water, having their rise in the glaciers which slope down into the valley. The beautiful *Gentiana major*, or greater gentian, with blossoms of the brightest blue, grows in large companies a few steps from the never-melted ice of the glaciers. I thought it an affecting emblem of the boldness of human hope, venturing near, and, as it were, leaning over the brink of the grave. Indeed, the whole vale, its every light, its every sound, must needs impress every mind not utterly callous with the thought—Who *would* be, who *could* be an Atheist in this valley of wonders! If any of the readers of the MORNING POST [Those who have *P. R.*] have visited this vale in their journeys among the Alps, I am confident that they [that they *om. P. R.*] will not find the sentiments and feelings expressed, or attempted to be expressed, in the following poem, extravagant.]'

---

4 Arve] Arvè *M. P., P. R., MS. (O).* 5 dread mountain form *M. P., P. R., MS. A.* most] dread *Friend, 1809.* 6 forth] out *MS. A.* 8 Deep is the sky, and black: transpicuous, deep *M. P., P. R.*: Deep is the sky, and black-transpicuous, black. *MS. A.* 11 is thine] seems thy *M. P., P. R.* 13 Mount] form *M. P., P. R., MS. A.* 14 the bodily sense] my bodily eye *M. P., P. R.*: my bodily sense *MS. A.* 16 Invisible] INVISIBLE *M. P., P. R., Friend, 1809, MS. A.*

So sweet, we know not we are listening to it,
Thou, the meanwhile, wast blending with my Thought,
Yea, with my Life and Life's own secret joy: 20
Till the dilating Soul, enrapt, transfused,
Into the mighty vision passing—there
As in her natural form, swelled vast to Heaven!

Awake, my soul! not only passive praise
Thou owest! not alone these swelling tears, 25
Mute thanks and secret ecstasy! Awake,
Voice of sweet song! Awake, my heart, awake!
Green vales and icy cliffs, all join my Hymn.

Thou first and chief, sole sovereign of the Vale!
O struggling with the darkness all the night,[1] 30
And visited all night by troops of stars,
Or when they climb the sky or when they sink:
Companion of the morning-star at dawn,
Thyself Earth's rosy star, and of the dawn
Co-herald: wake, O wake, and utter praise! 35
Who sank thy sunless pillars deep in Earth?
Who filled thy countenance with rosy light?
Who made thee parent of perpetual streams?

And you, ye five wild torrents fiercely glad!
Who called you forth from night and utter death, 40
From dark and icy caverns called you forth,

---

[1] I had written a much finer line when Sca' Fell was in my thoughts, viz.:—
    O blacker than the darkness all the night
    And visited *Note to MS. A.*

---

17 Yet thou meantime, wast working on my soul,
    E'en like some deep enchanting melody *M. P., P. R., MS. A.*
19 *foll.* But [Now *MS. A*] I awake, and with a busier mind,
    And active will self-conscious, offer now
    Not as before, involuntary pray'r
    And passive adoration!
                    Hand and voice,
    Awake, awake! and thou, my heart, awake!
    Awake ye rocks! Ye forest pines awake! (*Not in MS. A.*)
    Green fields *M. P., P. R., MS. A.*
29-30 And thou, O silent Mountain, sole and bare *MS. A*
    O blacker than the darkness all the night *M. P., P. R.*
29 And thou, thou silent mountain, lone and bare *MS. A.* The first and chief, stern Monarch of the Vale *Errata to 'Hymn', &c., The Friend, No. XIII, Nov. 16, 1809.* 38 parent] father *M. P., P. R., MS. A.*
41 From darkness let you loose and icy dens *M. P., P. R., MS. A.*

HYMN BEFORE SUNRISE

Down those precipitous, black, jaggéd rocks,
For ever shattered and the same for ever?
Who gave you your invulnerable life,
Your strength, your speed, your fury, and your joy, 45
Unceasing thunder and eternal foam?
And who commanded (and the silence came),
Here let the billows stiffen, and have rest?

Ye Ice-falls! ye that from the mountain's brow
Adown enormous ravines slope amain— 50
Torrents, methinks, that heard a mighty voice,
And stopped at once amid their maddest plunge!
Motionless torrents! silent cataracts!
Who made you glorious as the Gates of Heaven
Beneath the keen full moon? Who bade the sun 55
Clothe you with rainbows? Who, with living flowers[1]
Of loveliest blue, spread garlands at your feet?—
GOD! let the torrents, like a shout of nations,
Answer! and let the ice-plains echo, GOD!
GOD! sing ye meadow-streams with gladsome voice! 60
Ye pine-groves, with your soft and soul-like sounds!
And they too have a voice, yon piles of snow,
And in their perilous fall shall thunder, GOD!

Ye living flowers that skirt the eternal frost!
Ye wild goats sporting round the eagle's nest! 65

---

[1] The *Gentiana major* grows in large companies a stride's distance from the foot of several of the glaciers. Its *blue* flower, the colour of Hope: is it not a pretty emblem of Hope creeping onward even to the edge of the grave, to the very verge of utter desolation? *Note to MS. A.*

---

46 Eternal thunder and unceasing foam *MS. A.*   48 'Here shall the billows...' *M. P., P. R.*: Here shall your billows *MS. A.*   49 the mountain's brow] yon dizzy heights *M. P., P. R.*   50 Adown enormous ravines steeply slope *M. P., P. R., MS. A.* [A *bad* line; but I hope to be able to alter it *Note to MS. A.*].

56   with lovely flowers
         Of living blue *M. P., P. R., MS. A.*

Between 58-64
         GOD! GOD! the torrents like a shout of nations
         Utter! the ice-plain bursts and answers GOD!
         GOD, sing the meadow-streams with gladsome voice,
         And pine-groves with their soft and soul-like sound,
         The silent snow-mass, loos'ning thunders God! *M. P., P. R.*
These lines were omitted in MS. A.

64 Ye dreadless flow'rs that fringe *M. P., P. R.*   living] azure *MS. A.* livery *S. L.* (corrected in *Errata*, p. [xi]).   65 sporting round] bounding by *M. P., P. R., MS. A.*

Ye eagles, play-mates of the mountain-storm!
Ye lightnings, the dread arrows of the clouds!
Ye signs and wonders of the element!
Utter forth God, and fill the hills with praise!

Thou too, hoar Mount! with thy sky-pointing peaks,
Oft from whose feet the avalanche,[1] unheard, 71
Shoots downward, glittering through the pure serene
Into the depth of clouds, that veil thy breast—
Thou too again, stupendous Mountain! thou
That as I raise my head, awhile bowed low 75
In adoration, upward from thy base
Slow travelling with dim eyes suffused with tears,
Solemnly seemest, like a vapoury cloud,
To rise before me—Rise, O ever rise,
Rise like a cloud of incense from the Earth! 80
Thou kingly Spirit throned among the hills,
Thou dread ambassador from Earth to Heaven,
Great Hierarch! tell thou the silent sky,
And tell the stars, and tell yon rising sun
Earth, with her thousand voices, praises GOD. 85
1802.

[1] The fall of vast masses of snow, so called. *Note MS. (C).*

---

66 mountain-storm] mountain blast *M. P., P. R.*   69 God] GOD. *M. P., P. R.*

Between 70-80

    And thou, O silent Form, alone and bare
    Whom, as I lift again my head bow'd low
    In adoration, I again behold,
    And to thy summit upward from thy base
    Sweep slowly with dim eyes suffus'd by tears,
    Awake thou mountain form! rise, like a cloud *M. P., P. R.*
    And thou thou silent mountain, lone and bare
    Whom as I lift again my head bow'd low
    In adoration, I again behold!
    And from thy summit upward to the base
    Sweep slowly, with dim eyes suffus'd with tears
    Rise, mighty form! even as thou *seem'st* to rise. *MS. A.*

70 Thou too] And thou, *Errata, Friend, No. XIII.* Once more, hoar Mount *MS. (C), S. L.* (For *once more*, read *Thou too Errata, S. L.*, p. [xi]). 72 through] in *Friend, 1809.* In the blue serene *MS. (C).*   74 again] once more *MS. (C).*   75 That as once more I raise my Head bow'd low *Friend, No. XI, 1809* (see the *Errata, No. XIII*).

83-4   tell thou the silent stars,
      Tell the blue sky *MS. A.*

84 yon] the *M. P., P. R., MS. A.*   85 praises] calls on *M. P., P. R., MS. A.*

THE GOOD, GREAT MAN [1]

'How seldom, friend! a good great man inherits
  Honour or wealth with all his worth and pains!
It sounds like stories from the land of spirits
If any man obtain that which he merits
  Or any merit that which he obtains.'   5

REPLY TO THE ABOVE

For shame, dear friend, renounce this canting strain!
What would'st thou have a good great man obtain?
Place? titles? salary? a gilded chain?
Or throne of corses which his sword had slain?   10
Greatness and goodness are not *means*, but *ends*!
Hath he not always treasures, always friends,
The good great man? *three* treasures, Love, and Light,
  And Calm Thoughts, regular as infant's breath:
And three firm friends, more sure than day and night,   15
  Himself, his Maker, and the Angel Death!

1802.

INSCRIPTION FOR A FOUNTAIN ON A HEATH [2]

This Sycamore, oft musical with bees,—
Such tents the Patriarchs loved! O long unharmed
May all its agéd boughs o'er-canopy
The small round basin, which this jutting stone
Keeps pure from falling leaves! Long may the Spring,   5

---

[1] First published in the *Morning Post* (as an 'Epigram', signed ΕΣΤΗΣΕ), September 23, 1802: reprinted in the *Poetical Register* for 1802 (1803, p. 246): included in *The Friend*, No. XIX, December 28, 1809, and in *Literary Remains*, 1836, i. 53. First collected in 1844.

[2] First published in the *Morning Post*, September 24, 1802: reprinted in the *Poetical Register* for 1802 (1803, p. 338): included in *Sibylline Leaves*, 1828, 1829, and 1834.

The Good, Great Man—Title] Epigram *M. P.*: Epigrams *P. R.*: Complaint *Lit. Rem.*, *1844, 1852*: The Good, &c. *1893*.   6 Reply to the above *M. P.*: Reply *The Friend, 1809*: Reproof *Lit. Rem., 1844*.

Inscription, &c.—Title] Inscription on a Jutting Stone, over a Spring *M. P.*, *P. R.*

3 agéd] darksome *M. P., P. R.*   5 Still may this spring *M. P., P. R.*

382 INSCRIPTION FOR A FOUNTAIN ON A HEATH

> Quietly as a sleeping infant's breath,
> Send up cold waters to the traveller
> With soft and even pulse! Nor ever cease
> Yon tiny cone of sand its soundless dance,[1]
> Which at the bottom, like a Fairy's Page,   10
> As merry and no taller, dances still,
> Nor wrinkles the smooth surface of the Fount.
> Here Twilight is and Coolness: here is moss,
> A soft seat, and a deep and ample shade.
> Thou may'st toil far and find no second tree.   15
> Drink, Pilgrim, here; Here rest! and if thy heart
> Be innocent, here too shalt thou refresh
> Thy spirit, listening to some gentle sound,
> Or passing gale or hum of murmuring bees!

1802.

AN ODE TO THE RAIN [2]

COMPOSED BEFORE DAYLIGHT, ON THE MORNING APPOINTED FOR THE DEPARTURE OF A VERY WORTHY, BUT NOT VERY PLEASANT VISITOR, WHOM IT WAS FEARED THE RAIN MIGHT DETAIN

I

> I know it is dark; and though I have lain,
> Awake, as I guess, an hour or twain,

---

[1] Compare *Anima Poetae*, 1895, p. 17 : 'The spring with the little tiny cone of loose sand ever rising and sinking to the bottom, but its surface without a wrinkle.'

[2] First published in the *Morning Post* (?), Oct. 7, 1802 : included in *Sibylline Leaves*, 1817: in *Literary Remains*, 1836, i. 54–6. First collected in 1844. In *Literary Remains* the poem is dated 1809, but in a letter to J. Wedgwood, Oct. 20, 1802, Coleridge seems to imply that the *Ode to the Rain* had appeared recently in the *Morning Post*. A MS. note of Mrs. H. N. Coleridge, included in other memoranda intended for publication in *Essays on His Own Times*, gives the date, 'Ode to Rain, October 7'. The issue for October 7 is missing in the volume for 1802 preserved

---

7 waters] water *P. R.*   to] for *M. P., P. R.*   9 soundless] noiseless *M. P., P. R.*   10 Which] That *M. P., P. R.*   13 Here coolness dwell, and twilight *M. P., P. R.*

16 *foll.* Here, stranger, drink! Here rest! And if thy heart
            Be innocent, here too may'st thou renew
            Thy spirits, listening to these gentle sounds,
            The passing gale, or ever-murm'ring bees.   *M. P., P. R.*

AN ODE TO THE RAIN

I have not once opened the lids of my eyes,
But I lie in the dark, as a blind man lies.
O Rain! that I lie listening to,
You're but a doleful sound at best:
I owe you little thanks, 'tis true,
For breaking thus my needful rest!
Yet if, as soon as it is light,
O Rain! you will but take your flight,
I'll neither rail, nor malice keep,
Though sick and sore for want of sleep.
But only now, for this one day,
Do go, dear Rain! do go away!

II

O Rain! with your dull two-fold sound,
The clash hard by, and the murmur all round!
You know, if you know aught, that we,
Both night and day, but ill agree:
For days and months, and almost years,
Have limped on through this vale of tears,
Since body of mine, and rainy weather,
Have lived on easy terms together.
Yet if, as soon as it is light,
O Rain! you will but take your flight,
Though you should come again to-morrow,
And bring with you both pain and sorrow;
Though stomach should sicken and knees should swell—
I'll nothing speak of you but well.
But only now for this one day,
Do go, dear Rain! do go away!

III

Dear Rain! I ne'er refused to say
You're a good creature in your way;
Nay, I could write a book myself,
Would fit a parson's lower shelf,
Showing how very good you are.—

---

in the British Museum, and it may be presumed that it was in that number the *Ode to the Rain* first appeared. It is possible that the 'Ode' was written on the morning after the unexpected arrival of Charles and Mary Lamb at Greta Hall in August, 1802.

What then? sometimes it must be fair
And if sometimes, why not to-day?
Do go, dear Rain! do go away!

IV

Dear Rain! if I've been cold and shy,
Take no offence! I'll tell you why.
A dear old Friend e'en now is here,
And with him came my sister dear;
After long absence now first met,
Long months by pain and grief beset—
We three dear friends! in truth, we groan
Impatiently to be alone.
We three, you mark! and not one more!
The strong wish makes my spirit sore.
We have so much to talk about,
So many sad things to let out;
So many tears in our eye-corners,
Sitting like little Jacky Horners—
In short, as soon as it is day,
Do go, dear Rain! do go away.

V

And this I'll swear to you, dear Rain!
Whenever you shall come again,
Be you as dull as e'er you could
(And by the bye 'tis understood,
You're not so pleasant as you're good),
Yet, knowing well your worth and place,
I'll welcome you with cheerful face;
And though you stayed a week or more,
Were ten times duller than before;
Yet with kind heart, and right good will,
I'll sit and listen to you still;
Nor should you go away, dear Rain!
Uninvited to remain.
But only now, for this one day,
Do go, dear Rain! do go away.

1802.

45 We] With *L. R. 1844, 1852.* [The text was amended in *P. W.,* 1877-80.]

A DAY-DREAM[1]

My eyes make pictures, when they are shut:
   I see a fountain, large and fair,
A willow and a ruined hut,
   And thee, and me and Mary there.
O Mary! make thy gentle lap our pillow!   5
Bend o'er us, like a bower, my beautiful green willow!

A wild-rose roofs the ruined shed,
   And that and summer well agree:
And lo! where Mary leans her head,
   Two dear names carved upon the tree!   10
And Mary's tears, they are not tears of sorrow:
Our sister and our friend will both be here to-morrow.

'Twas day! but now few, large, and bright,
   The stars are round the crescent moon!
And now it is a dark warm night,
   The balmiest of the month of June!   15
A glow-worm fall'n, and on the marge remounting
Shines, and its shadow shines, fit stars for our sweet fountain.

O ever—ever be thou blest!
   For dearly, Asra! love I thee!   20
This brooding warmth across my breast,
   This depth of tranquil bliss—ah, me!
Fount, tree and shed are gone, I know not whither,
But in one quiet room we three are still together.

The shadows dance upon the wall,   25
   By the still dancing fire-flames made;
And now they slumber, moveless all!
   And now they melt to one deep shade!
But not from me shall this mild darkness steal thee:
I dream thee with mine eyes, and at my heart I feel thee!   30

---

[1] First published in the *Bijou* for 1828: included in 1828, 1829, and 1834. Asra is Miss Sarah Hutchinson; 'Our Sister and our Friend,' William and Dorothy Wordsworth. There can be little doubt that these lines were written in 1801 or 1802.

---

8 well] will *Bijou, 1828*.   17 on] in *Bijou, 1828*.   20 For Asra, dearly *Bijou, 1828*.   28 one] me *Bijou, 1828*.

Thine eyelash on my cheek doth play—
'Tis Mary's hand upon my brow!
But let me check this tender lay
 Which none may hear but she and thou!
Like the still hive at quiet midnight humming, 35
Murmur it to yourselves, ye two beloved women!
1802.

ANSWER TO A CHILD'S QUESTION[1]

Do you ask what the birds say? The Sparrow, the Dove,
The Linnet and Thrush say, 'I love and I love!'
In the winter they're silent—the wind is so strong;
What it says, I don't know, but it sings a loud song.
But green leaves, and blossoms, and sunny warm weather, 5
And singing, and loving—all come back together.
But the Lark is so brimful of gladness and love,
The green fields below him, the blue sky above,
That he sings, and he sings; and for ever sings he—
'I love my Love, and my Love loves me!' 10
1802.

THE DAY-DREAM[2]

FROM AN EMIGRANT TO HIS ABSENT WIFE

If thou wert here, these tears were tears of light!
But from as sweet a vision did I start

[1] First published in the *Morning Post*, October 16, 1802: included in *Sibylline Leaves*, in 1828, 1829, and 1834.
[2] First published in the *Morning Post*, October 19, 1802. First collected in *Poems*, 1852. A note (p. 384), was affixed:—'This little poem first appeared

---

Answer to a Child's Question—Title] The Language of Birds : Lines spoken extempore, to a little child, in early spring *M. P.*
Between 6-7 'I love, and I love,' almost all the birds say
 From sunrise to star-rise, so gladsome are they. *M. P.*
After 10 'Tis no wonder that he's full of joy to the brim,
 When He loves his Love, and his Love loves him. *M. P.*

Line 10 is adapted from the refrain of Prior's *Song* ('One morning very early, one morning in the spring'):—'I love my love, because I know my love loves me.'

THE DAY-DREAM

As ever made these eyes grow idly bright!
And though I weep, yet still around my heart
A sweet and playful tenderness doth linger,   5
Touching my heart as with an infant's finger.

My mouth half open, like a witless man,
  I saw our couch, I saw our quiet room,
  Its shadows heaving by the fire-light gloom;
And o'er my lips a subtle feeling ran,   10
All o'er my lips a soft and breeze-like feeling—
I know not what—but had the same been stealing

Upon a sleeping mother's lips, I guess
It would have made the loving mother dream
That she was softly bending down to kiss   15
  Her babe, that something more than babe did seem,
A floating presence of its darling father,
And yet its own dear baby self far rather!

Across my chest there lay a weight, so warm!
  As if some bird had taken shelter there;   20
And lo! I seemed to see a woman's form—
  Thine, Sara, thine? O joy, if thine it were!
I gazed with stifled breath, and feared to stir it,
No deeper trance e'er wrapt a yearning spirit!

And now, when I seemed sure thy face to see,   25
  Thy own dear self in our own quiet home;
There came an elfish laugh, and wakened me:
  'Twas Frederic, who behind my chair had clomb,
And with his bright eyes at my face was peeping.
I blessed him, tried to laugh, and fell a-weeping!   30
1801-2.

---

in the *Morning Post* in 1802, but was doubtless composed in Germany. It seems to have been forgotten by its author, for this was the only occasion on which it saw the light through him. The Editors think that it will plead against parental neglect in the mind of most readers.' Internal evidence seems to point to 1801 or 1802 as the most probable date of composition.

Below line 30 ΕΣΤΗΣΕ.

THE HAPPY HUSBAND[1]

A FRAGMENT

OFT, oft methinks, the while with thee,
  I breathe, as from the heart, thy dear
  And dedicated name, I hear
A promise and a mystery,
  A pledge of more than passing life, 5
  Yea, in that very name of Wife!

A pulse of love, that ne'er can sleep!
  A feeling that upbraids the heart
  With happiness beyond desert,
That gladness half requests to weep! 10
  Nor bless I not the keener sense
  And unalarming turbulence

Of transient joys, that ask no sting
  From jealous fears, or coy denying;
  But born beneath Love's brooding wing, 15
And into tenderness soon dying,
  Wheel out their giddy moment, then
  Resign the soul to love again;—

A more precipitated vein
  Of notes, that eddy in the flow 20
  Of smoothest song, they come, they go,
And leave their sweeter understrain,
  Its own sweet self—a love of Thee
  That seems, yet cannot greater be!

? 1802.

---

[1] First published in *Sibylline Leaves*, 1817: included in 1828, 1829, 1834. There is no evidence as to the date of composition.

---

13 ask] fear *S. L.* (for *fear* no sting read *ask* no sting *Errata*, p. [xi]).

THE PAINS OF SLEEP[1]

Ere on my bed my limbs I lay,
It hath not been my use to pray
With moving lips or bended knees;
But silently, by slow degrees,
My spirit I to Love compose, 5
In humble trust mine eye-lids close,
With reverential resignation,
No wish conceived, no thought exprest,
Only a sense of supplication;
A sense o'er all my soul imprest 10
That I am weak, yet not unblest,
Since in me, round me, every where
Eternal Strength and Wisdom are.

But yester-night I prayed aloud
In anguish and in agony, 15
Up-starting from the fiendish crowd
Of shapes and thoughts that tortured me:
A lurid light, a trampling throng,
Sense of intolerable wrong,
And whom I scorned, those only strong! 20

[1] First published, together with *Christabel*, in 1816: included in 1828, 1829, i. 334-6 (but not in *Contents*), and 1834. A first draft of these lines was sent in a Letter to Southey, Sept. 11, 1803 (*Letters of S. T. C.*, 1895, i. 435-7). An amended version of lines 18-32 was included in an unpublished Letter to Poole, dated Oct. 3, 1803.

---

1 Ere] When *MS. Letter to Southey, Sept. 11, 1803*. 9 sense] *sense MS. Letter to Southey, 1816, 1828, 1829.* 10 sense] *sense MS. Letter to Southey.* 12 Since round me, in me, everywhere *MS. Letter to Southey.* 13 Wisdom] Goodness *MS. Letter to Southey.* 16 Up-starting] Awaking *MS. Letter to Southey.*

Between 18-26   Desire with loathing strangely mixt,
On wild or hateful objects fixt.
Sense of revenge, the powerless will,
Still baffled and consuming still;
Sense of intolerable wrong,
And men whom I despis'd made strong!
Vain-glorious threats, unmanly vaunting,
Bad men my boasts and fury taunting:
Rage, sensual passion, mad'ning Brawl,
MS. Letter to Southey.

18 trampling] ghastly *MS. Letter to Poole, Oct. 3, 1803.* 19 intolerable] insufferable *MS. Letter to Poole.* 20 those] they *MS. Letter to Poole.*

Thirst of revenge, the powerless will
Still baffled, and yet burning still!
Desire with loathing strangely mixed
On wild or hateful objects fixed.
Fantastic passions! maddening brawl! 25
And shame and terror over all!
Deeds to be hid which were not hid,
Which all confused I could not know
Whether I suffered, or I did:
For all seemed guilt, remorse or woe, 30
My own or others still the same
Life-stifling fear, soul-stifling shame.

So two nights passed: the night's dismay
Saddened and stunned the coming day.
Sleep, the wide blessing, seemed to me 35
Distemper's worst calamity.
The third night, when my own loud scream
Had waked me from the fiendish dream,
O'ercome with sufferings strange and wild,
I wept as I had been a child; 40
And having thus by tears subdued
My anguish to a milder mood,
Such punishments, I said, were due
To natures deepliest stained with sin,—
For aye entempesting anew 45
The unfathomable hell within,
The horror of their deeds to view,
To know and loathe, yet wish and do!

Between 22-4
    Tempestuous pride, vain-glorious vaunting
    Base men my vices justly taunting *MS. Letter to Poole.*

27 which] that *MS. Letters to Southey and Poole.*   28 could] might *MS. Letters to Southey and Poole.*   30 For all was Horror, Guilt, and Woe *MS. Letter to Southey* : For all was Guilt, and Shame, and Woe *MS. Letter to Poole.*   33 So] Thus *MS. Letter to Southey.*   34 coming] boding *MS. Letter to Southey.*

35-6   I fear'd to sleep: sleep seem'd to be
        Disease's worst malignity *MS. Letter to Southey.*

38 **waked**] freed *MS. Letter to Southey.*   39 O'ercome by sufferings dark and wild *MS. Letter to Southey.*   42 anguish] Trouble *MS. Letter to Southey.*   43 said] thought *MS. Letter to Southey.*

45-6   Still to be stirring up anew
        The self-created Hell within *MS. Letter to Southey.*

47 their deeds] the crimes *MS. Letter to Southey.*   48 and] to *MS Letter to Southey.*

Such griefs with such men well agree,
But wherefore, wherefore fall on me? 50
To be beloved is all I need,
And whom I love, I love indeed.

1803.

THE EXCHANGE[1]

WE pledged our hearts, my love and I,—
  I in my arms the maiden clasping;
I could not guess the reason why,
  But, oh! I trembled like an aspen.

Her father's love she bade me gain; 5
  I went, but shook like any reed!
I strove to act the man—in vain!
  We had exchanged our hearts indeed.

1804.

AD VILMUM AXIOLOGUM[2]
[TO WILLIAM WORDSWORTH]

THIS be the meed, that thy song creates a thousand-fold echo!
Sweet as the warble of woods, that awakes at the gale of the morning!

---

[1] First published in the *Courier*, April 16, 1804: included in the *Poetica Register* for 1804 (1805); reprinted in *Literary Souvenir* for 1826, p. 408, and in *Literary Remains*, 1836, i. 59. First collected in 1844.

[2] First published in *P. W.*, 1893. These lines were found in one of Coleridge's Notebooks (No. 24). The first draft immediately follows the

---

Between 48–51
    With such let fiends make mockery—
    But I—Oh, wherefore this *on me*?
    Frail is my soul, yea, strengthless wholly,
    Unequal, restless, melancholy.
    But free from Hate and sensual Folly. *MS. Letter to Southey.*

51 be] live *MS. Letter to Southey.*   *After* 52 And etc., etc., etc., etc. *MS. Letter to Southey.*

The Exchange—Title] The Exchange of Hearts *Courier, 1804.*   2 Me in her arms *Courier, 1804.*   3 guess] tell *Lit. Souvenir, Lit. Rem., 1844.*
5 Her father's leave *Courier, 1804, P. R. 1804, 1893.*   6 but] and *Lit. Souvenir, Lit. Rem., 1844.*

Ad Vilmum, &c.—1 *foll.*
What is the meed of thy song? 'Tis the ceaseless the thousandfold echo,
Which from the welcoming Hearts of the Pure repeats and prolongs it—
Each with a different Tone, compleat or in musical fragments.
                  Or
This be the meed, that thy Song awakes to a thousandfold echo
  Welcoming Hearts; is it their voice or is it thy own?

List! the Hearts of the Pure, like caves in the ancient mountains
Deep, deep *in* the Bosom, and *from* the Bosom resound it,
Each with a different tone, complete or in musical fragments— 5
All have welcomed thy Voice, and receive and retain and prolong it!

This is the word of the Lord! it is spoken, and Beings Eternal
Live and are borne as an Infant; the Eternal begets the Immortal:
Love is the Spirit of Life, and Music the Life of the Spirit!
? 1805.

AN EXILE[1]

Friend, Lover, Husband, Sister, Brother!
Dear names close in upon each other!
Alas! poor Fancy's bitter-sweet—
Our names, and but our names can meet.
1805.

SONNET[2]

[translated from marini]

Lady, to Death we're doom'd, our crime the same!
Thou, that in me thou kindled'st such fierce heat;
I, that my heart did of a Sun so sweet
The rays concentre to so hot a flame.

transcription of a series of **Dante's** *Canzoni* begun at Malta in 1805. If the Hexameters were composed at the same time, it is possible that they were inspired by a perusal or re-perusal of a MS. copy of Wordsworth's unpublished poems which had been made for his use whilst he was abroad. As Mr. Campbell points out (*P. W.*, p. 614), Wordsworth himself was responsible for the Latinization of his name. A *Sonnet on seeing Miss Helen Maria Williams weeping at a tale of distress*, which was published in the *European Magazine* for March, 1787, is signed ' Axiologus '.

[1] First published, with title 'An Exile', in 1893. These lines, without title or heading, are inserted in one of Coleridge's Malta Notebooks.
[2] First published in 1893.

Lost! the Hearts of the Pure, like caves in the ancient mountains
Deep, deep in the bosom, and *from* the bosom resound it,
Each with a different tone, compleat or in musical fragments.
Meet the song they receive, and retain and resound and prolong it!
Welcoming Souls! is it their voice, sweet Poet, or is it thy own voice?
Drafts in Notebook.

I, fascinated by an Adder's eye—
Deaf as an Adder thou to all my pain;
Thou obstinate in Scorn, in Passion I—
I lov'd too much, too much didst thou disdain.
Hear then our doom in Hell as just as stern,
Our sentence equal as our crimes conspire—
Who living bask'd at Beauty's earthly fire,
In living flames eternal these must burn—
Hell for us both fit places too supplies—
In my heart *thou* wilt burn, I *roast* before thine eyes.

? 1805.

PHANTOM[1]

ALL look and likeness caught from earth
All accident of kin and birth,
Had pass'd away. There was no trace
Of aught on that illumined face,
Uprais'd beneath the rifted stone
But of one spirit all her own;—
She, she herself, and only she,
Shone through her body visibly.

1805.

A SUNSET[2]

UPON the mountain's edge with light touch resting,
There a brief while the globe of splendour sits

---

[1] These lines, without title or heading, are quoted ('vide... my lines') in an entry in one of Coleridge's Malta Notebooks, dated Feb. 8, 1805, to illustrate the idea that the love-sense can be abstracted from the accidents of form or person (see *Anima Poetae*, 1895, p. 120). It follows that they were written before that date. *Phantom* was first published in 1834, immediately following (ii. 71) *Phantom or Fact. A dialogue in Verse*, which was first published in 1828, and was probably written about that time. Both poems are 'fragments from the life of dreams'; but it was the reality which lay behind both 'phantom' and 'fact' of which the poet dreamt, having his eyes open. With lines 4, 5 compare the following stanza of one of the MS. versions of the *Dark Ladié*:—

> Against a grey stone rudely carv'd
> The statue of an armed knight,
> She lean'd in melancholy mood
> To watch ['d] the lingering Light.

[2] First published in 1893. The title 'A Sunset' was prefixed by the Editor. These lines are inscribed in one of Coleridge's Malta Note-

---

A Sunset—1 with light touch] all lightly *MS.*

And seems a creature of the earth; but soon
    More changeful than the Moon,
To wane fantastic his great orb submits,
Or cone or mow of fire: till sinking slowly
Even to a star at length he lessens wholly.

Abrupt, as Spirits vanish, he is sunk!
A soul-like breeze possesses all the wood.
    The boughs, the sprays have stood
As motionless as stands the ancient trunk!
But every leaf through all the forest flutters,
And deep the cavern of the fountain mutters.

1805.

WHAT IS LIFE?[1]

RESEMBLES life what once was deem'd of light,
Too ample in itself for human sight?
An absolute self—an element ungrounded—
All that we see, all colours of all shade
    By encroach of darkness made?—
Is very life by consciousness unbounded?
And all the thoughts, pains, joys of mortal breath,
A war-embrace of wrestling life and death?

1805.

books. The following note or comment is attached:—'These lines I wrote as nonsense verses merely to try a metre; but they are by no means contemptible; at least in reading them I am surprised at finding them so good. 16 Aug., 1805, Malta.

'Now will it be a more English music if the first and fourth are double rhymes and the 5th and 6th single? or all single, or the 2nd and 3rd double? Try.' They were afterwards sent to William Worship, Esq., Yarmouth, in a letter dated April 22, 1819, as an unpublished autograph.

[1] First published in *Literary Souvenir*, 1829: included in *Literary Remains*, 1836, i. 60. First collected in 1844. These lines, 'written in the same manner, and for the same purpose, but of course with more conscious effort than the two stanzas on the preceding leaf,' are dated '16 August, 1805, the day of the Valetta Horse-racing—bells jangling, and stupefying music playing all day'. Afterwards, in 1819, Coleridge maintained that they were written 'between the age of 15 and 16'.

---

4 the] this *MS*.   6 A distant Hiss of fire *MS. alternative reading*.
7 lessens] lessened *MS*.   12 flutters] fluttered *MS*.   13 mutters] muttered *MS*.

What is Life?—1 deem'd] held *Lit. Souvenir, 1829*.   2 ample] simple *MS*.
6 { ~~per se~~ (in its own Nature)
   { Is Life itself *MS*.

THE BLOSSOMING OF THE SOLITARY DATE-TREE[1]

A LAMENT

I seem to have an indistinct recollection of having read either in one of the ponderous tomes of George of Venice, or in some other compilation from the uninspired Hebrew writers, an apologue or Rabbinical tradition to the following purpose:

While our first parents stood before their offended Maker, and the last words of the sentence were yet sounding in Adam's ear, the guileful false serpent, a counterfeit and a usurper from the beginning, presumptuously took on himself the character of advocate or mediator, and pretending to intercede for Adam, exclaimed: 'Nay, Lord, in thy justice, not so! for the man was the least in fault. Rather let the Woman return at once to the dust, and let Adam remain in this thy Paradise.' And the word of the Most High answered Satan: '*The tender mercies of the wicked are cruel.* Treacherous Fiend! if with guilt like thine, it had been possible for thee to have the heart of a Man, and to feel the yearning of a human soul for its counterpart, the sentence, which thou now counsellest, should have been inflicted on thyself.'

The title of the following poem was suggested by a fact mentioned by Linnaeus, of a date-tree in a nobleman's garden which year after year had put forth a full show of blossoms, but never produced fruit, till a branch from another date-tree had been conveyed from a distance of some hundred leagues. The first leaf of the MS. from which the poem has been transcribed, and which contained the two or three introductory stanzas, is wanting: and the author has in vain taxed his memory to repair the loss. But a rude draught of the poem contains the substance of the stanzas, and the reader is requested to receive it as the substitute. It is not impossible, that some congenial spirit, whose years do not exceed those of the Author at the time the poem was written, may find a pleasure in restoring the Lament to its original integrity by a reduction of the thoughts to the requisite metre.   S. T. C.

[1] First published in 1828: included in 1829 and 1834.

---

5 stood] were yet standing *1828*.   8 mediator] moderator *1828*.
9 The words 'not so' are omitted in *1828*.   11 *remain* here all the days of his now mortal life, and enjoy the respite thou mayest grant him, in this thy Paradise which thou gavest to him, and hast planted with every tree pleasant to the sight of man and of delicious fruitage. *1828*.   13 foll. *Treacherous Fiend!* guilt deep as thine could not be, yet the love of kind not extinguished. But if having done what thou hast done, thou hadst yet the heart of man within thee, and the yearning of the soul for its answering image and completing counterpart, O spirit, desperately wicked! the sentence thou counsellest had been thy own! *1828*
20 from a Date tree *1828, 1829*.

1

Beneath the blaze of a tropical sun the mountain peaks are the Thrones of Frost, through the absence of objects to reflect the rays. 'What no one with us shares, seems scarce our own.' The presence of a ONE,

> The best belov'd, who loveth me the best,

is for the heart, what the supporting air from within is for the hollow globe with its suspended car. Deprive it of this, and all without, that would have buoyed it aloft even to the seat of the gods, becomes a burthen and crushes it into flatness.

2

The finer the sense for the beautiful and the lovely, and the fairer and lovelier the object presented to the sense; the more exquisite the individual's capacity of joy, and the more ample his means and opportunities of enjoyment, the more heavily will he feel the ache of solitariness, the more unsubstantial becomes the feast spread around him. What matters it, whether in fact the viands and the ministering graces are shadowy or real, to him who has not hand to grasp nor arms to embrace them?

3

Imagination; honourable aims;
Free commune with the choir that cannot die;
Science and song; delight in little things,
The buoyant child surviving in the man;
Fields, forests, ancient mountains, ocean, sky,
With all their voices—O dare I accuse
My earthly lot as guilty of my spleen,
Or call my destiny niggard! O no! no!
It is her largeness, and her overflow,
Which being incomplete, disquieteth me so!

4

For never touch of gladness stirs my heart,
But tim'rously beginning to rejoice
Like a blind Arab, that from sleep doth start
In lonesome tent, I listen for thy voice.

48 Hope, Imagination, &c. *1828.* 53 With all their voices mute—
O dare I accuse *1828.* 55 Or call my niggard destiny! No! No! *1828.*
61 thy] *thy 1828, 1829.*

Belovéd! 'tis not thine; thou art not there!
Then melts the bubble into idle air,
And wishing without hope I restlessly despair.

5

The mother with anticipated glee 65
Smiles o'er the child, that, standing by her chair
And flatt'ning its round cheek upon her knee,
Looks up, and doth its rosy lips prepare
To mock the coming sounds. At that sweet sight
She hears her own voice with a new delight; 70
And if the babe perchance should lisp the notes aright,

6

Then is she tenfold gladder than before!
But should disease or chance the darling take,
What then avail those songs, which sweet of yore
Were only sweet for their sweet echo's sake? 75
Dear maid! no prattler at a mother's knee
Was e'er so dearly prized as I prize thee:
Why was I made for Love and Love denied to me?

1805.

SEPARATION [1]

A sworded man whose trade is blood,
   In grief, in anger, and in fear,
Thro' jungle, swamp, and torrent flood,
   I seek the wealth you hold so dear!

---

[1] First published in 1834. In Pickering's one-volume edition of the issue of 1848 the following note is printed on p. 372:—

'The fourth and last stanzas are adapted from the twelfth and last of Cotton's *Chlorinda* [Ode]:—

    'O my Chlorinda! could'st thou see
    Into the bottom of my heart,
    There's such a Mine of Love for thee,
    The Treasure would supply desert.

    Meanwhile my Exit now draws nigh,
    When, sweet Chlorinda, thou shalt see
    That I have heart enough to die,
    Not half enough to part with thee.

'The fifth stanza is the eleventh of Cotton's poem.'

In 1852 (p. 385) the note reads: 'The fourth and last stanzas are from Cotton's *Chlorinda*, with very slight alteration.'

---

77 thee] *thee* 1828, 1829.

> The dazzling charm of outward form, 5
> The power of gold, the pride of birth,
> Have taken Woman's heart by storm—
> Usurp'd the place of inward worth.
>
> Is not true Love of higher price
> Than outward Form, though fair to see, 10
> Wealth's glittering fairy-dome of ice,
> Or echo of proud ancestry?—
>
> O! Asra, Asra! couldst thou see
> Into the bottom of my heart,
> There's such a mine of Love for thee, 15
> As almost might supply desert!
>
> (This separation is, alas!
> Too great a punishment to bear;
> O! take my life, or let me pass
> That life, that happy life, with her!) 20

A first draft of this adaptation is contained in one of Coleridge's Malta Notebooks:—

[I]

Made worthy by excess of Love
A wretch thro' power of Happiness,
And poor from wealth I dare not use.

[II]

This separation etc.

[III]

~~The Pomp of Wealth~~
~~Stores of Gold, the pomp of Wealth~~
~~Nor less the Pride of Noble Birth~~
The dazzling charm etc.
(l. 4) Supplied the place etc.

[IV]

Is not true Love etc.

[V]

O AΣPA! AΣPA could'st thou see
Into the bottom of my Heart!
There's such a Mine of Love for Thee—
The Treasure would supply desert.

[VI]

Death erst contemn'd—O AΣPA! why
Now terror-stricken do I see—
Oh! I have etc.

SEPARATION 399

> The perils, erst with steadfast eye
>   Encounter'd, now I shrink to see—
> Oh! I have heart enough to die—
>   Not half enough to part from Thee!

? 1805.

THE RASH CONJURER[1]

> Strong spirit-bidding sounds!
>   With deep and hollow voice,
>   Twixt Hope and Dread,
>   Seven Times I said
>   Iohva Mitzoveh
>   Vohoeen![2]
> And up came an imp in the shape of a
>   Pea-hen!
> I saw, I doubted,
> And seven times spouted
>   Johva Mitzoveh
>   Yahóevohāen!
> When Anti-Christ starting up, butting
>   and bāing,
> In the shape of a mischievous curly
>   black Lamb—
> With a vast flock of Devils behind
>   and beside,
> And before 'em their Shepherdess
>   Lucifer's Dam,
>   Riding astride
>   On an old black Ram,

[1] Now first printed from one of Coleridge's Notebooks. The last stanza—the Epilogue—was first published by H. N. Coleridge as part of an 'Uncomposed Poem', in *Literary Remains*, 1836, i. 52: first collected in Appendix to *P. and D. W.*, 1877-80, ii. 366. There is no conclusive evidence as to the date of composition. The handwriting, and the contents of the Notebook might suggest a date between 1813 and 1816. The verses are almost immediately preceded by a detached note printed at the close of an essay entitled 'Self-love in Religion' which is included among the '*Omniana* of 1809', *Literary Remains*, 1834, i. 354–6 : 'O magical, sympathetic, *anima!* [Archeus, *MS.*] *principium hylarchichum! rationes spermaticæ! λόγοι ποιητικοί!* O formidable words! And O Man! thou marvellous beast-angel! thou ambitious beggar! How pompously dost thou trick out thy very ignorance with such glorious disguises, that thou mayest seem to hide in order to worship it.'
With this piece as a whole compare Southey's 'Ballad of a Young Man that would read unlawful Books, and how he was punished'.

[2] A cabbalistic invocation of Jehovah, obscure in the original Hebrew. I am informed that the second word Mitzoveh may stand for 'from Sabaoth'.

With Tartary stirrups, knees up to her chin,
And a sleek chrysom imp to her Dugs muzzled in,—
  'Gee-up, my old Belzy! (she cried,
 As she sung to her suckling cub)
Trit-a-trot, trot! we'll go far and wide
Trot, Ram-Devil! Trot! Belzebub!'
Her petticoat fine was of scarlet Brocade,
And soft in her lap her Baby she lay'd
With his pretty Nubs of Horns a-
     sprouting,
And his pretty little Tail all curly-twirly—
St. Dunstan! and this comes of spouting—
 Of Devils what a Hurly-Burly!
'Behold we are up! what want'st thou then?'
'Sirs! only that'—'Say when and what'—
'You'd be so good'—'Say what and when'
'This moment to get down again!'
'We do it! we do it! we all get down!
But we take you with us to swim
     or drown!
Down a down to the grim Engulpher!'
'O me! I am floundering in Fire and Sulphur!
That the Dragon had scrounched you, squeal
     and squall—
Cabbalists! Conjurers! great and small,
Johva Mitzoveh Evohäen and all!
Had *I* never uttered your jaw-breaking words,
I might now have been sloshing down Junket and Curds,
 Like a Devonshire Christian:
 But now a Philistine!

Ye Earthmen! be warned by a judgement so tragic,
And wipe yourselves cleanly with all books of magic—
Hark! hark! it is Dives! 'Hold your Bother, you Booby!
I am burnt ashy white, and you yet are but ruby.'

Epilogue.

 We ask and urge (here ends the story)
  All Christian Papishes to pray
  That this unhappy Conjurer may
 Instead of Hell, be but in Purgatory—
   For then there's Hope,—
    Long live the Pope!
? 1805, ? 1814.   Catholicus.

A CHILD'S EVENING PRAYER[1]

Ere on my bed my limbs I lay,
God grant me grace my prayers to say:
O God! preserve my mother dear
In strength and health for many a year;
And, O! preserve my father too, 5
And may I pay him reverence due;
And may I my best thoughts employ
To be my parents' hope and joy;
And O! preserve my brothers both
From evil doings and from sloth, 10
And may we always love each other
Our friends, our father, and our mother:
And still, O Lord, to me impart
An innocent and grateful heart,
That after my great sleep I may 15
Awake to thy eternal day! *Amen.*

1806.

METRICAL FEET[2]

LESSON FOR A BOY

Trōchēe trĭps frŏm lōng tŏ shōrt;
From long to long in solemn sort
Slōw Spōndēe stālks; strōng fōot! yet ill able
Ēvĕr tŏ cōme ŭp wĭth Dāctȳl trĭsȳllăblĕ.
Ĭāmbĭcs mārch frŏm shōrt tŏ lōng;— 5
Wĭth ă lēap ănd ă bōund thĕ swĭft Ānăpæsts thrōng;

---

[1] First published in 1852. A transcript in the handwriting of Mrs. S. T. Coleridge is in the possession of the Editor.

[2] First published in 1834. The metrical lesson was begun for Hartley Coleridge in 1806 and, afterwards, finished or adapted for the use of his brother Derwent. The Editor possesses the autograph of a metrical rendering of the Greek alphabet, entitled 'A Greek Song set to Music, and sung by Hartley Coleridge, Esq., Graecologian, philometrist and philomelist'.

---

3 mother] father *MS.* 5 father] mother *MS.* 6 him] her *MS.*
7-8   And may I still my thoughts employ
         To be her comfort and her joy *MS.*
9 O likewise keep *MS.* 13 But chiefly, Lord *MS.* 15 great] last *P. W.* 1877-80, 1893. *After* 16 Our father, &c. *MS.*

Metrical Feet—Title] The chief and most usual Metrical Feet expressed in metre and addressed to Hartley Coleridge *MS. of Lines 1-7.*

One syllable long, with one short at each side,
Ămphībrăchy̆s hāstes wĭth ă stātely̆ stride;—
Fīrst ănd lāst bēing lōng, mĭddlĕ shōrt, Ămphīmācer
Strīkes hĭs thūndĕrĭng hōofs līke ă prōud hĭgh-brĕd Rācer.
If Derwent be innocent, steady, and wise,　　　11
And delight in the things of earth, water, and skies;
Tender warmth at his heart, with these metres to show it,
With sound sense in his brains, may make Derwent a poet,—
May crown him with fame, and must win him the love　15
Of his father on earth and his Father above.

　　　　　My dear, dear child!
Could you stand upon Skiddaw, you would not from its whole ridge
See a man who so loves you as your fond S. T. COLERIDGE.
　1806.

FAREWELL TO LOVE[1]

FAREWELL, sweet Love! yet blame you not my truth;
　More fondly ne'er did mother eye her child
Than I your form: *yours* were my hopes of youth,
　And as *you* shaped my thoughts I sighed or smiled.

---

[1] First published in the *Courier*, September 27, 1806, and reprinted in the *Morning Herald*, October 11, 1806, and in the *Gentleman's Magazine* for November, 1815, vol. lxxxv, p. 448: included in *Literary Remains*, 1836, i. 280, and in *Letters, Conversations, &c.*, [by T. Allsop], 1836, i. 143. First collected, appendix, 1863. This sonnet is modelled upon and in part borrowed from Lord Brooke's (Fulke Greville) Sonnet LXXIV of Coelica: and was inscribed on the margin of Charles Lamb's copy of *Certain Learned and Elegant Works of the Right Honourable Fulke Lord Brooke* . . . 1633, p. 284.

　　　　'*Cœlica*'. Sonnet lxxiv.

FAREWELL sweet Boy, complaine not of my truth;
Thy Mother lov'd thee not with more devotion;
For to thy Boyes play I gave all my youth
Yong Master, I did hope for your promotion.

While some sought Honours, Princes thoughts observing,
Many woo'd *Fame, the child of paine and anguish*,
Others judg'd inward good a chiefe deserving,
I in thy wanton Visions joy'd to languish.

1-2　　Farewell my Love! yet blame ye not my Truth;
　　　　More fondly never mother ey'd her child MS. *1806.*

　　　　Sweet power of Love, farewell! nor blame my truth,
　　　　More fondly never Mother ey'd her Child *Courier, M. H.*

4 And as you wove the dream I sigh'd or smil'd MS. *1806*: And as you wove my thoughts, I sigh'd or smil'd *Courier, M. H.*

FAREWELL TO LOVE 403

While most were wooing wealth, or gaily swerving 5
  To pleasure's secret haunts, and some apart
Stood strong in pride, self-conscious of deserving,
  To you I gave my whole weak wishing heart.

And when I met the maid that realised
  Your fair creations, and had won her kindness, 10
Say, but for her if aught on earth I prized!
  Your dreams alone I dreamt, and caught your blindness.

O grief!—but farewell, Love! I will go play me
With thoughts that please me less, and less betray me.
  1806.

TO WILLIAM WORDSWORTH[1]

COMPOSED ON THE NIGHT AFTER HIS RECITATION OF A POEM ON
THE GROWTH OF AN INDIVIDUAL MIND

FRIEND of the wise! and Teacher of the Good!
Into my heart have I received that Lay

  I bow'd not to thy image for succession,
  Nor bound thy bow to shoot reformed kindnesse,
  The playes of hope and feare were my confession
  The spectacles to my life was thy blindnesse:

  But *Cupid* now farewell, I will goe play me,
  With thoughts that please me lesse, and lesse betray me.

[1] First published in *Sibylline Leaves*, 1817: included in 1828, 1829, 1834.
The poem was sent in a Letter to Sir G. Beaumont dated January, 1807,
and in this shape was first printed by Professor Knight in *Coleorton Letters*,

---

5-7   While some sought Wealth; others to Pleasure swerving,
        Many woo'd Fame: and some stood firm apart
      In joy of pride, self-conscious of deserving *MS. 1806, Courier, M. H.*
6 haunts] haunt *L. R., Letters, &c., 1836, 1863.*   8 weak wishing]
weak-wishing *Courier, M. H.*   9 that] who *Courier, M. H.*   13 will]
must *Courier, M. H.*

To William Wordsworth—Title] To W. Wordsworth. Lines Composed,
for the greater part on the Night, on which he finished the recitation of
his Poem (in thirteen Books) concerning the growth and history of his
own Mind, Jan. 7, 1807, Cole-orton, near Ashby de la Zouch *MS. W.*:
To William Wordsworth. Composed for the greater part on the same
night after the finishing of his recitation of the Poem in thirteen Books,
on the Growth of his own Mind *MS. B*: To a Gentleman, &c. *S. L.
1828, 1829.*
  1   O Friend! O Teacher! God's great gift to me! *MSS. W., B.*

404 TO WILLIAM WORDSWORTH

 More than historic, that prophetic Lay
Wherein (high theme by thee first sung aright)
Of the foundations and the building up
Of a Human Spirit thou hast dared to tell 5
What may be told, to the understanding mind
Revealable; and what within the mind
By vital breathings secret as the soul
Of vernal growth, oft quickens in the heart
Thoughts all too deep for words!— 10

         Theme hard as high!
Of smiles spontaneous, and mysterious fears
(The first-born they of Reason and twin-birth),
Of tides obedient to external force,
And currents self-determined, as might seem, 15
Or by some inner Power; of moments awful,
Now in thy inner life, and now abroad,

1887, i. 213–18; and as Appendix H, pp. 525–6, of *P. W.*, 1893 (MS. B.). An earlier version of about the same date was given to Wordsworth, and is now in the possession of his grandson, Mr. Gordon Wordsworth (*MS. W.*). The text of *Sibylline Leaves* differs widely from that of the original MSS. Lines 11–47 are quoted in a Letter to Wordsworth, dated May 30, 1815 (*Letters of S. T. C.*, 1895, i. 646–7), and lines 65–75 at the end of Chapter X of the *Biographia Literaria*, 1817, i. 220.

Between 5–13 Of thy own Spirit, thou hast lov'd to tell
    What may be told, to th' understanding mind
    Revealable; and what within the mind
    May rise enkindled. Theme as hard as high!
    Of Smiles spontaneous and mysterious Fear. *MS. W.*

    Of thy own spirit thou hast loved to tell
    What *may* be told, by words revealable;
    With heavenly breathings, like the secret soul
    Of vernal growth, oft quickening in the heart,
    Thoughts that obey no mastery of words,
    Pure self-beholdings! theme as hard as high,
    Of *smiles* spontaneous and mysterious *fear*. *MS. B.*

9 By vital breathings like the secret soul *S. L. 1828.*   16 Or by interior power *MS. W*: Or by some central breath *MS. Letter, 1815.* 17 inner] hidden *MSS. W., B.*

Between 17–41 Mid festive crowds, *thy* Brows too garlanded,
    A Brother of the Feast : of Fancies fair,
    Hyblaean murmurs of poetic Thought,
    Industrious in its Joy, by lilied Streams
    Native or outland, Lakes and famous Hills!
    Of more than Fancy, of the Hope of Man
    Amid the tremor of a Realm aglow—

TO WILLIAM WORDSWORTH

When power streamed from thee, and thy soul received
The light reflected, as a light bestowed—
Of fancies fair, and milder hours of youth, 20
Hyblean murmurs of poetic thought
Industrious in its joy, in vales and glens
Native or outland, lakes and famous hills!
Or on the lonely high-road, when the stars
Were rising; or by secret mountain-streams, 25
The guides and the companions of thy way!

Of more than Fancy, of the Social Sense
Distending wide, and man beloved as man,
Where France in all her towns lay vibrating
Like some becalméd bark beneath the burst 30
Of Heaven's immediate thunder, when no cloud
Is visible, or shadow on the main.
For thou wert there, thine own brows garlanded,
Amid the tremor of a realm aglow,
Amid a mighty nation jubilant, 35
When from the general heart of human kind
Hope sprang forth like a full-born Deity!
——Of that dear Hope afflicted and struck down,
So summoned homeward, thenceforth calm and sure
From the dread watch-tower of man's absolute self, 40

> *Where France in all her Towns lay vibrating*
> Ev'n as a Bark becalm'd on sultry seas
> Beneath the voice from Heav'n, the bursting crash
> *Of Heaven's immediate thunder! when no cloud*
> *Is visible, or Shadow on the Main*
> Ah! soon night roll'd on night, and every Cloud
> Open'd its eye of Fire: and Hope aloft
> Now flutter'd, and now toss'd upon the storm
> Floating! Of *Hope afflicted and struck down*
> *Thence summoned homeward*—homeward to thy Heart,
> Oft from the *Watch-tower of Man's absolute self*,
> With light, &c. MS. W.

27 social sense MS. B.   28 Distending, and of man MS. B.

29–30 Even as a bark becalm'd on sultry seas
 Quivers beneath the voice from Heaven, the burst MS. B.

30   Ev'n as a bark becalm'd beneath the burst
                    MS. Letter, 1815, S. L. 1828.

33 thine] thy MS. B., MS. Letter, 1815.   37 a full-born] an arméd
MS. B.   38 Of that dear hope afflicted and amazed MS. Letter, 1815.
39 So homeward summoned MS. Letter, 1815.   40 As from the watch-tower MS. B.

With light unwaning on her eyes, to look
Far on—herself a glory to behold,
The Angel of the vision! Then (last strain)
Of Duty, chosen Laws controlling choice,
Action and joy!—An Orphic song indeed, 45
A song divine of high and passionate thoughts
To their own music chaunted!

                            O great Bard!
Ere yet that last strain dying awed the air,
With stedfast eye I viewed thee in the choir
Of ever-enduring men. The truly great 50
Have all one age, and from one visible space
Shed influence! They, both in power and act,
Are permanent, and Time is not with them,
Save as it worketh for them, they in it.
Nor less a sacred Roll, than those of old, 55
And to be placed, as they, with gradual fame
Among the archives of mankind, thy work
Makes audible a linkéd lay of Truth,
Of Truth profound a sweet continuous lay,
Not learnt, but native, her own natural notes! 60
Ah! as I listened with a heart forlorn,

44 controlling] ? impelling, ? directing *MS. W.*
45-6   Virtue and Love—an Orphic Tale indeed
       A Tale divine *MS. W.*

45 song] tale *MS. B.*   46 song] tale *MS. B.*   thoughts] truths *MS. Letter, 1815.*

47-9   Ah! great Bard
    Ere yet that last swell dying aw'd the air
    With stedfast ken I viewed thee in the choir *MS. W.*

48 that] the *MS. B.*   49 With steadfast eyes I saw thee *MS. B.*
52 for they, both power and act *MS. B.*   53 them] *them S. L. 1828, 1829.*
54 *for* them, they *in* it *S. L. 1828, 1829.*   58 lay] song *MSS. W., B.*
59 lay] song *MSS. W., B.*

61 *foll.*   Dear shall it be to every human heart,
        To me how more than dearest! me, on whom
        Comfort from thee, and utterance of thy love,
        Came with such heights and depths of harmony,
        Such sense of wings uplifting, that the storm 5
        Scatter'd and whirl'd me, till my thoughts became
        A bodily tumult; and thy faithful hopes,
        Thy hopes of me, dear Friend! by me unfelt!
        Were troublous to me, almost as a voice,
        Familiar once, and more than musical; 10
        To one cast forth, whose hope had seem'd to die
        A wanderer with a worn-out heart

TO WILLIAM WORDSWORTH

The pulses of my being beat anew:
And even as Life returns upon the drowned,
Life's joy rekindling roused a throng of pains—
Keen pangs of Love, awakening as a babe 65
Turbulent, with an outcry in the heart;
And fears self-willed, that shunned the eye of Hope;
And Hope that scarce would know itself from Fear;
Sense of past Youth, and Manhood come in vain,
And Genius given, and Knowledge won in vain; 70
And all which I had culled in wood-walks wild,
And all which patient toil had reared, and all,
Commune with thee had opened out—but flowers
Strewed on my corse, and borne upon my bier
In the same coffin, for the self-same grave! 75

That way no more! and ill beseems it me,
Who came a welcomer in herald's guise,
Singing of Glory, and Futurity,
To wander back on such unhealthful road,
Plucking the poisons of self-harm! And ill 80
Such intertwine beseems triumphal wreaths
Strew'd before thy advancing!

      Nor do thou,
Sage Bard! impair the memory of that hour
Of thy communion with my nobler mind
By pity or grief, already felt too long! 85
Nor let my words import more blame than needs.
The tumult rose and ceased: for Peace is nigh

  Mid strangers pining with untended wounds.
  O Friend, too well thou know'st, of what sad years
  The long suppression had benumb'd my soul, 15
  That even as life returns upon the drown'd,
  The unusual joy awoke a throng of pains—
  Keen pangs, &c. MSS. B, W *with the following variants:*

ll. 5-6 Such sense of wings uplifting, that its might
   Scatter'd and quell'd me— *MS. B.*

ll. 11, 12 As a dear woman's voice to one cast forth
   A wanderer with a worn-out heart forlorn.

73 thee] *thee S. L. 1828, 1829.*   74 Strewed] Strewn *MS. B., 1828, 1829*
82 thy] *thy S. L. 1828, 1829.*
82-3   Thou too, Friend!
  O injure not the memory of that hour *MS. W.*
     Thou too, Friend!
  Impair thou not the memory of that Hour *MS. B.*

Where Wisdom's voice has found a listening heart.
Amid the howl of more than wintry storms,
The Halcyon hears the voice of vernal hours   90
Already on the wing.

                  Eve following eve,
Dear tranquil time, when the sweet sense of Home
Is sweetest! moments for their own sake hailed
And more desired, more precious, for thy song,
In silence listening, like a devout child,   95
My soul lay passive, by thy various strain
Driven as in surges now beneath the stars,
With momentary stars of my own birth,
Fair constellated foam,[1] still darting off
Into the darkness; now a tranquil sea,   100
Outspread and bright, yet swelling to the moon.

And when—O Friend! my comforter and guide!
Strong in thyself, and powerful to give strength!—
Thy long sustainéd Song finally closed,
And thy deep voice had ceased—yet thou thyself   105
Wert still before my eyes, and round us both
That happy vision of belovéd faces—
Scarce conscious, and yet conscious of its close
I sate, my being blended in one thought
(Thought was it? or aspiration? or resolve?)   110
Absorbed, yet hanging still upon the sound—
And when I rose, I found myself in prayer.

January, 1807.

---

[1] 'A beautiful white cloud of Foam at momentary intervals coursed by the side of the Vessel with a Roar, and little stars of flame danced and sparkled and went out in it : and every now and then light detachments of this white cloud-like foam dashed off from the vessel's side, each with its own small constellation, over the Sea, and scoured out of sight like a Tartar Troop over a wilderness.' *The Friend*, p. 220. [From Satyrane's First Letter, published in *The Friend*, No. 14, Nov. 23, 1809.]

---

93 Becomes most sweet! hours for their own sake hail'd *MS. W.*
96 thy] the *MS. B.*   98 my] her *MS. B.*   102 and] my *MSS. W., B.*
104 Song] lay *MS. W.*   106 my] mine *MSS. W., B.*
Between 107-8
    (All whom I deepliest love—in one room all!) *MSS. W., B.*

AN ANGEL VISITANT[1]

WITHIN these circling hollies woodbine-clad—
Beneath this small blue roof of vernal sky—
How warm, how still! Tho' tears should dim mine eye,
Yet will my heart for days continue glad,
For here, my love, thou art, and here am I!

? 1801.

RECOLLECTIONS OF LOVE[2]

I

How warm this woodland wild Recess!
　Love surely hath been breathing here;
　And this sweet bed of heath, my dear!
Swells up, then sinks with faint caress,
　As if to have you yet more near.   5

II

Eight springs have flown, since last I lay
　On sea-ward Quantock's heathy hills,
　Where quiet sounds from hidden rills
Float here and there, like things astray,
　And high o'er head the sky-lark shrills.   10

---

[1] First published in *Literary Remains*, 1836, i. 280. First collected in P. and D. W., 1877-80. The title was prefixed to the *Poems of Coleridge* (illustrated edition), 1907. This 'exquisite fragment... was probably composed as the opening of *Recollections of Love*, and abandoned on account of a change of metre.'—*Editor's Note*, 1893 (p. 635). It is in no way a translation, but the thought or idea was suggested by one of the German stanzas which Coleridge selected and copied into one of his Notebooks as models or specimens of various metres.

[2] First published in *Sibylline Leaves*, 1817: included in 1828, 1829, and 1834. It is impossible to fix the date of composition, though internal evidence points to July, 1807, when Coleridge revisited Stowey after a long absence. The first stanza, a variant of the preceding fragment, is introduced into a prose fancy, entitled 'Questions and Answers in the Court of Love', of uncertain date, but perhaps written at Malta in 1805. A first draft of stanzas 1-4 (vide supra) is included in the collection of metrical experiments and metrical schemes, modelled on German and Italian originals, which seems to have been begun in 1801, with a view to a projected 'Essay on Metre'. Stanzas 5, 6 are not contemporary with stanzas 1-4, and, perhaps, date from 1814, 1815, when *Sibylline Leaves* were being prepared for the press.

III

No voice as yet had made the air
  Be music with your name; yet why
  That asking look? that yearning sigh?
That sense of promise every where?
  Belovéd! flew your spirit by?   15

IV

As when a mother doth explore
  The rose-mark on her long-lost child,
  I met, I loved you, maiden mild!
As whom I long had loved before—
  So deeply had I been beguiled.   20

V

You stood before me like a thought,
  A dream remembered in a dream.
  But when those meek eyes first did seem
To tell me, Love within you wrought—
  O Greta, dear domestic stream!   25

VI

Has not, since then, Love's prompture deep,
  Has not Love's whisper evermore
  Been ceaseless, as thy gentle roar?
Sole voice, when other voices sleep,
  Dear under-song in clamor's hour.   30
1807.

TO TWO SISTERS[1]

[MARY MORGAN AND CHARLOTTE BRENT]

A WANDERER'S FAREWELL

To know, to esteem, to love,—and then to part—
Makes up life's tale to many a feeling heart;
Alas for some abiding-place of love,
O'er which my spirit, like the mother dove,
Might brood with warming wings!
                      O fair! O kind! 5

---

[1] First published in *The Courier*, December 10, 1807, with the signature SIESTI. First collected in *P. and D. W.*, 1877-80. The following

TO TWO SISTERS

Sisters in blood, yet each with each intwined
More close by sisterhood of heart and mind!
Me disinherited in form and face
By nature, and mishap of outward grace;
Who, soul and body, through one guiltless fault   10
Waste daily with the poison of sad thought,
Me did you soothe, when solace hoped I none!
And as on unthaw'd ice the winter sun,
Though stern the frost, though brief the genial day,
You bless my heart with many a cheerful ray;   15
For gratitude suspends the heart's despair,
Reflecting bright though cold your image there.
Nay more! its music by some sweeter strain
Makes us live o'er our happiest hours again,
Hope re-appearing dim in memory's guise—   20
Even thus did you call up before mine eyes
Two dear, dear Sisters, prized all price above,
Sisters, like you, with more than sisters' love;
So like you *they*, and so in *you* were seen
Their relative statures, tempers, looks, and mien,   25
That oft, dear ladies! you have been to me
At once a vision and reality.
Sight seem'd a sort of memory, and amaze
Mingled a trouble with affection's gaze.

Oft to my eager soul I whisper blame,   30
A Stranger bid it feel the Stranger's shame—
My eager soul, impatient of the name,
No strangeness owns, no Stranger's form descries:
The chidden heart spreads trembling on the eyes.

abbreviated and altered version was included in *P. W.*, 1834, 1844, and 1852, with the heading 'On taking Leave of —— 1817':—

> To know, to esteem, to love—and then to part,
> Makes up life's tale to many a feeling heart!
> O for some dear abiding-place of Love,
> O'er which my spirit, like the mother dove
> Might brood with warming wings!—O fair as kind,
> Were but one sisterhood with you combined,
> (Your very image they in shape and mind)
> Far rather would I sit in solitude,
> The forms of memory all my mental food,
> And dream of you, sweet sisters, (ah, not mine!)
> And only dream of you (ah dream and pine!)
> Than have the presence, and partake the pride,
> And shine in the eye of all the world beside!

First-seen I gazed, as I would look you thro'! 35
My best-beloved regain'd their youth in you,—
And still I ask, though now familiar grown,
Are you for *their* sakes dear, or for your own?
O doubly dear! may Quiet with you dwell!

In Grief I love you, yet I love you well! 40
Hope long is dead to me! an orphan's tear
Love wept despairing o'er his nurse's bier.
Yet still she flutters o'er her grave's green slope:
For Love's despair is but the ghost of Hope!

Sweet Sisters! were you placed around one hearth 45
With those, your other selves in shape and worth,
Far rather would I sit in solitude,
Fond recollections all my fond heart's food,
And dream of *you*, sweet Sisters! (ah! not mine!)
And only *dream* of you (ah! dream and pine!) 50
Than boast the presence and partake the pride,
And shine in the eye, of all the world beside.
1807.

PSYCHE[1]

THE butterfly the ancient Grecians made
The soul's fair emblem, and its only name—[2]
But of the soul, escaped the slavish trade
Of mortal life!—For in this earthly frame
Ours is the reptile's lot, much toil, much blame, 5
Manifold motions making little speed,
And to deform and kill the things whereon we feed.
1808.

---

[1] First published with a prefatory note:—'The fact that in Greek Psyche is the common name for the soul, and the butterfly, is thus alluded to in the following stanzas from an unpublished poem of the Author', in the *Biographia Literaria*, 1817, i. 82, n.: included (as No. II of 'Three Scraps') in *Amulet*, 1833: *Lit. Rem.*, 1836, i. 53. First collected in 1844. In *Lit. Rem.* and 1844 the poem is dated 1808.

[2] Psyche means both Butterfly and Soul. *Amulet*, 1833.
In some instances the Symbolic and Onomastic are united as in Psyche = Anima et papilio. *MS. S. T. C.* (Hence the word 'name' was italicised in the MS.)

Title] The Butterfly *Amulet, 1833, 1877–81, 1893*.

4 Of earthly life. For in this fleshly frame *MS. S. T. C.*: Of earthly life! For, in this mortal frame *Amulet, 1833, 1893*.

A TOMBLESS EPITAPH[1]

'Tis true, Idoloclastes Satyrane!
(So call him, for so mingling blame with praise,
And smiles with anxious looks, his earliest friends,
Masking his birth-name, wont to character
His wild-wood fancy and impetuous zeal,) 5
'Tis true that, passionate for ancient truths,
And honouring with religious love the Great
Of elder times, he hated to excess,
With an unquiet and intolerant scorn,
The hollow Puppets of a hollow Age, 10
Ever idolatrous, and changing ever
Its worthless Idols! Learning, Power, and Time,
(Too much of all) thus wasting in vain war
Of fervid colloquy. Sickness, 'tis true,
Whole years of weary days, besieged him close, 15
Even to the gates and inlets of his life!
But it is true, no less, that strenuous, firm,
And with a natural gladness, he maintained
The citadel unconquered, and in joy
Was strong to follow the delightful Muse. 20
For not a hidden path, that to the shades
Of the beloved Parnassian forest leads,
Lurked undiscovered by him; not a rill
There issues from the fount of Hippocrene,
But he had traced it upward to its source, 25
Through open glade, dark glen, and secret dell,
Knew the gay wild flowers on its banks, and culled
Its med'cinable herbs. Yea, oft alone,
Piercing the long-neglected holy cave,

---

[1] First published in *The Friend*, No. XIV, November 23, 1809. There is no title or heading to the poem, which occupies the first page of the number, but a footnote is appended:—'Imitated, though in the movements rather than the thoughts, from the vii[th], of *Gli Epitafi* of Chiabrera:

> Fu ver, che Ambrosio Salinero a torto
> Si pose in pena d'odiose liti,' &c.

Included in *Sibylline Leaves*, 1817, 1828, 1829, 1834. Sir Satyrane, 'A Satyres son yborne in forrest wylde' (Spenser's *Faery Queene*, Bk. I, C. vi, l. 21) rescues Una from the violence of Sarazin. Coleridge may have regarded Satyrane as the anonymn of Luther. Idoloclast, as he explains in the preface to 'Satyrane's Letters', is a 'breaker of idols'.

10 a] an *Friend, 1809, S. L. 1828, 1829*.   16 inlets] outlets *Friend, 1809*.

> The haunt obscure of old Philosophy, 30
> He bade with lifted torch its starry walls
> Sparkle, as erst they sparkled to the flame
> Of odorous lamps tended by Saint and Sage.
> O framed for calmer times and nobler hearts!
> O studious Poet, eloquent for truth! 35
> Philosopher! contemning wealth and death,
> Yet docile, childlike, full of Life and Love!
> Here, rather than on monumental stone,
> This record of thy worth thy Friend inscribes,
> Thoughtful, with quiet tears upon his cheek. 40

? 1809.

FOR A MARKET-CLOCK[1]

(IMPROMPTU)

What now, O Man! thou dost or mean'st to do
Will help to give thee peace, or make thee rue,
When hovering o'er the Dot this hand shall tell
The moment that secures thee Heaven or Hell!

1809.

THE MADMAN AND THE LETHARGIST[2]

AN EXAMPLE

Quoth Dick to me, as once at College
We argued on the use of knowledge;—

---

[1] Sent in a letter to T. Poole, October 9, 1809, and transferred to one of Coleridge's Notebooks with the heading 'Inscription proposed on a Clock in a market place': included in 'Omniana' of 1809-16 (*Literary Remains*, 1836, i. 347) with the erroneous title 'Inscription on a Clock in Cheapside'. First collected in 1893.

> What now thou do'st, or art about to do,
> Will help to give thee peace, or make thee rue;
> When hov'ring o'er the line this hand will tell
> The last dread moment—'twill be heaven or hell.

Read for the last two lines:—

> When wav'ring o'er the dot this hand shall tell
> The moment that secures thee Heaven or Hell.

MS. Lit. Rem.

[2] Now published for the first time from one of Coleridge's Notebooks. The use of the party catchword 'Citizen' and the allusion to 'Folks in France' would suggest 1796-7 as a probable date, but the point

---

37 Life] light *The Friend*, 1809.

THE MADMAN AND THE LETHARGIST

In old King Olim's reign, I've read,
There lay two patients in one bed.
The one in fat lethargic trance,
Lay wan and motionless as lead:
The other, (like the Folks in France),
Possess'd a different disposition—
In short, the plain truth to confess,
The man was madder than Mad Bess!
But both diseases, none disputed,
Were unmedicinably rooted;
Yet, so it chanc'd, by Heaven's permission,
Each prov'd the other's true physician.

'Fighting with a ghostly stare
Troops of Despots in the air,
Obstreperously Jacobinical,
The madman froth'd, and foam'd, and roar'd:
The other, snoring octaves cynical,
Like good John Bull, in posture clinical,
Seem'd living only when he snor'd.
The *Citizen* enraged to see
This fat Insensibility,
Or, tir'd with solitary labour,
Determin'd to convert his neighbour;
So up he sprang and to 't he fell,
Like devil piping hot from hell,
With indefatigable fist
Belabr'ing the poor Lethargist;
Till his own limbs were stiff and sore,
And sweat-drops roll'd from every pore:—
Yet, still, with flying fingers fleet,
Duly accompanied by feet,
With some short intervals of biting,
He executes the self-same strain,
Till the Slumberer woke for pain,
And half-prepared himself for fighting—
That moment that his mad Colleague
Sunk down and slept thro' pure fatigue.

or interpretation of the 'Example' was certainly in Coleridge's mind when he put together the first number of *The Friend*, published June 1, 1809 :—'Though all men are in error, they are not all in the same error, nor at the same time ... each therefore may possibly heal the other ... even as two or more physicians, all diseased in their general health, yet under the immediate action of the disease on different days, may remove or alleviate the complaints of each other.'

> So both were cur'd—and this example 40
> Gives demonstration full and ample—
> That *Chance* may bring a thing to bear,
> Where *Art* sits down in blank despair.'

'That's true enough, Dick,' answer'd I,
'But as for the *Example*, 'tis a lie.' 45

? 1809.

THE VISIONARY HOPE[1]

SAD lot, to have no Hope! Though lowly kneeling
He fain would frame a prayer within his breast,
Would fain entreat for some sweet breath of healing,
That his sick body might have ease and rest;
He strove in vain! the dull sighs from his chest 5
Against his will the stifling load revealing,
Though Nature forced; though like some captive guest,
Some royal prisoner at his conqueror's feast,
An alien's restless mood but half concealing,
The sternness on his gentle brow confessed, 10
Sickness within and miserable feeling:
Though obscure pangs made curses of his dreams,
And dreaded sleep, each night repelled in vain,
Each night was scattered by its own loud screams:
Yet never could his heart command, though fain, 15
One deep full wish to be no more in pain.

That Hope, which was his inward bliss and boast,
Which waned and died, yet ever near him stood,
Though changed in nature, wander where he would—
For Love's Despair is but Hope's pining Ghost! 20
For this one hope he makes his hourly moan,
He wishes and can wish for this alone!
Pierced, as with light from Heaven, before its gleams
(So the love-stricken visionary deems)
Disease would vanish, like a summer shower, 25
Whose dews fling sunshine from the noon-tide bower!
Or let it stay! yet this one Hope should give
Such strength that he would bless his pains and live.

? 1810.

---

[1] First published in *Sibylline Leaves*, 1817: included in 1828, 1829, and 1834.

22 can] *can S. L. 1828, 1829.*

EPITAPH ON AN INFANT[1]

Its balmy lips the infant blest
Relaxing from its Mother's breast,
How sweet it heaves the happy sigh
Of innocent satiety!

And such my Infant's latest sigh!   5
Oh tell, rude stone! the passer by,
That here the pretty babe doth lie,
Death sang to sleep with Lullaby.

1811.

THE VIRGIN'S CRADLE-HYMN[2]

COPIED FROM A PRINT OF THE VIRGIN IN A ROMAN CATHOLIC VILLAGE IN GERMANY

Dormi, Jesu! Mater ridet
Quae tam dulcem somnum videt,
  Dormi, Jesu! blandule!
Si non dormis, Mater plorat,
Inter fila cantans orat,   5
  Blande, veni, somnule.

ENGLISH[3]

Sleep, sweet babe! my cares beguiling:
Mother sits beside thee smiling;
  Sleep, my darling, tenderly!

---

[1] First published, with the signature 'Aphilos', in the *Courier*, Wednesday, March 20, 1811: included in *Sibylline Leaves*, 1817, and in 1828, 1829, and 1834.

[2] First published as from 'A Correspondent in Germany' in the *Morning Post*, December 26, 1801.

[3] First published with the Latin in the *Courier*, August 30, 1811, with the following introduction:—'About thirteen years ago or more, travelling through the middle parts of Germany I saw a little print of the Virgin

---

1 balmy] milky *Courier*, *1811*.   5 Infant's] darling's *Courier*, *1811*.
6 Tell simple stone *Courier*, *1811*.   7 the] a *Courier*, *1811*.
The Virgin's Cradle-Hymn, &c. Title—In a Roman Catholic] In a Catholic S. L., *1828*, *1829*.

If thou sleep not, mother mourneth, 10
Singing as her wheel she turneth:
Come, soft slumber, balmily!

1811.

TO A LADY[1]

OFFENDED BY A SPORTIVE OBSERVATION THAT WOMEN HAVE NO SOULS

Nay, dearest Anna! why so grave?
I said, you had no soul, 'tis true!
For what you are, you cannot have:
'Tis I, that have one since I first had you!

? 1811.

REASON FOR LOVE'S BLINDNESS[2]

I have heard of reasons manifold
 Why Love must needs be blind,
But this the best of all I hold—
 His eyes are in his mind.

What outward form and feature are 5
 He guesseth but in part;
But that within is good and fair
 He seeth with the heart.

? 1811.

---

and Child in the small public house of a Catholic Village, with the following beautiful Latin lines under it, which I transcribed. They may be easily adapted to the air of the famous Sicilian Hymn, *Adeste fideles, laeti triumphantes*, by the omission of a few notes.' First collected in *Sibylline Leaves*, 1817: included in 1828, 1829, and 1834.

[1] First published in *Omniana* (1812), i. 238; 'as a playful illustration of the distinction between *To* have *and to* be.' First collected in 1828: included in 1829 and 1834.

[2] First published in 1828: included in 1829 and 1834

To a Lady, &c.—In line 3 'are', 'have', and in line 4 'have', 'you', are italicized in all editions except *1834*.

Reason for, &c.—Title] In *1828, 1829, 1834* these stanzas are printed without a title, but are divided by a space from *Lines to a Lady*. The title appears first in *1893*.

THE SUICIDE'S ARGUMENT [1]

Ere the birth of my life, if I wished it or no,
No question was asked me—it could not be so!
If the life was the question, a thing sent to try,
And to live on be Yes; what can No be? to die.

NATURE'S ANSWER

Is't returned, as 'twas sent? Is't no worse for the wear?
Think first, what you are! Call to mind what you were!
I gave you innocence, I gave you hope,
Gave health, and genius, and an ample scope.
Return you me guilt, lethargy, despair?
Make out the invent'ry; inspect, compare!
Then die—if die you dare!

1811.

TIME, REAL AND IMAGINARY [2]

AN ALLEGORY

On the wide level of a mountain's head,
(I knew not where, but 'twas some faery place)

---

[1] First published in 1828: included in 1829 and 1834. In a Notebook of (?) 1811 these lines are preceded by the following couplet:—
Complained of, complaining, there shov'd and here shoving,
Every one blaming me, ne'er a one loving.

[2] First published in *Sibylline Leaves*, 1817, in the preliminary matter, p. v: included in 1828, 1829, and 1834. In the 'Preface' to *Sibylline Leaves*, p. iii, an apology is offered for its insertion on the plea that it was a 'school boy poem' added 'at the request of the friends of my youth'. The title is explained as follows:—'By imaginary Time, I meant the state of a school boy's mind when on his return to school he projects his being in his day dreams, and lives in his next holidays, six months hence; and this I contrasted with real Time.' In a Notebook of (?) 1811 there is an attempt to analyse and illustrate the 'sense of Time', which appears to have been written before the lines as published in *Sibylline Leaves* took shape: 'How marked the contrast between troubled manhood and joyously-active youth in the sense of time! To the former, time like the sun in an empty sky is never seen to move, but only to have *moved*. There, there it was, and now 'tis here, now distant! yet all a blank between.

---

4 Yes] Yes *1828, 1829*. 6 are] are *1828, 1829*. were] were *1828, 1829*.

Their pinions, ostrich-like, for sails out-spread,
Two lovely children run an endless race,
   A sister and a brother!
   This far outstripp'd the other;
Yet ever runs she with reverted face,
And looks and listens for the boy behind:
   For he, alas! is blind!
O'er rough and smooth with even step he passed,   10
And knows not whether he be first or last.
? 1812.

AN INVOCATION[1]

From *Remorse*

[Act III, Scene i. ll. 69–82.]

Hear, sweet Spirit, hear the spell,
Lest a blacker charm compel!
So shall the midnight breezes swell
With thy deep long-lingering knell.

And at evening evermore,   5
  In a chapel on the shore,
Shall the chaunter, sad and saintly,
Yellow tapers burning faintly,
Doleful masses chaunt for thee,
   Miserere Domine!   10

Hush! the cadence dies away
  On the quiet moonlight sea:
The boatmen rest their oars and say,
   Miserere Domine!
1812.

To the latter it is as the full moon in a fine breezy October night, driving on amid clouds of all shapes and hues, and kindling shifting colours, like an ostrich in its speed, and yet seems not to have moved at all. This I feel to be a just image of time real and time as felt, in two different states of being. The title of the poem therefore (for poem it ought to be) should be time real and time felt (in the sense of time) in active youth, or activity with hope and fullness of aim in any period, and in despondent, objectless manhood—time objective and subjective.' *Anima Poetae*, 1895. pp. 241-2.

[1] First published in *Remorse*, 1813. First collected, 1844.

An Invocation—7 chaunter] chaunters *1813, 1828, 1829, 1893.*   12 quiet] yellow *1813, 1828, 1829.*

THE NIGHT-SCENE[1]

A DRAMATIC FRAGMENT

Sandoval. You loved the daughter of Don Manrique?
Earl Henry.   Loved?
Sand. Did you not say you wooed her?
Earl H.   Once I loved
Her whom I dared not woo!
Sand.   And wooed, perchance,
One whom you loved not!
Earl H.   Oh! I were most base,
Not loving Oropeza. True, I wooed her,   5
Hoping to heal a deeper wound; but she
Met my advances with impassioned pride,
That kindled love with love. And when her sire,
Who in his dream of hope already grasped
The golden circlet in his hand, rejected   10
My suit with insult, and in memory
Of ancient feuds poured curses on my head,
Her blessings overtook and baffled them!
But thou art stern, and with unkindly countenance
Art inly reasoning whilst thou listenest to me.   15
  Sand. Anxiously, Henry! reasoning anxiously.
But Oropeza—
  Earl H.   Blessings gather round her!
Within this wood there winds a secret passage,
Beneath the walls, which opens out at length
Into the gloomiest covert of the garden.—   20
The night ere my departure to the army,
She, nothing trembling, led me through that gloom,
And to that covert by a silent stream,
Which, with one star reflected near its marge,
Was the sole object visible around me.   25
No leaflet stirred; the air was almost sultry;
So deep, so dark, so close, the umbrage o'er us!

---

[1] First published in its present state in *Sibylline Leaves*, 1817: included in 1828, 1829, and 1834. For an earlier draft, forming part of an 'Historic Drama in Five Acts' (unfinished) entitled *The Triumph of Loyalty*, 1801, vide Appendices of this edition. A prose sketch without title or heading is contained in one of Coleridge's earliest notebooks.

---

14 unkindly] unkindling *1893*.   23 And to the covert by that silent stream *S. L.*, corrected in *Errata*, p. [xi].   24 near] o'er *S. L.*, corrected in *Errata*, p. [xi].

No leaflet stirred ;—yet pleasure hung upon
The gloom and stillness of the balmy night-air.
A little further on an arbour stood, 30
Fragrant with flowering trees—I well remember
What an uncertain glimmer in the darkness
Their snow-white blossoms made—thither she led me,
To that sweet bower! Then Oropeza trembled—
I heard her heart beat—if 'twere not my own. 35

   Sand. A rude and scaring note, my friend!
   Earl H.   Oh! no!
I have small memory of aught but pleasure.
The inquietudes of fear, like lesser streams
Still flowing, still were lost in those of love:
So love grew mightier from the fear, and Nature, 40
Fleeing from Pain, sheltered herself in Joy.
The stars above our heads were dim and steady,
Like eyes suffused with rapture. Life was in us:
We were all life, each atom of our frames
A living soul—I vowed to die for her: 45
With the faint voice of one who, having spoken,
Relapses into blessedness, I vowed it:
That solemn vow, a whisper scarcely heard,
A murmur breathed against a lady's ear.
Oh! there is joy above the name of pleasure, 50
Deep self-possession, an intense repose.

   Sand. (*with a sarcastic smile*). No other than as eastern
       sages paint,
The God, who floats upon a Lotos leaf,
Dreams for a thousand ages; then awaking,
Creates a world, and smiling at the bubble, 55
Relapses into bliss.

   Earl H.   Ah! was that bliss
Feared as an alien, and too vast for man?
For suddenly, impatient of its silence,
Did Oropeza, starting, grasp my forehead.
I caught her arms; the veins were swelling on them. 60
Through the dark bower she sent a hollow voice ;—
'Oh! what if all betray me? what if thou?'
I swore, and with an inward thought that seemed
The purpose and the substance of my being,
I swore to her, that were she red with guilt, 65
I would exchange my unblenched state with hers.—
Friend! by that winding passage, to that bower
I now will go—all objects there will teach me

Unwavering love, and singleness of heart.
Go, Sandoval! I am prepared to meet her— 70
Say nothing of me—I myself will seek her—
Nay, leave me, friend! I cannot bear the torment
And keen inquiry of that scanning eye.—
          [*Earl Henry retires into the wood.*
  Sand. (*alone*). O Henry! always striv'st thou to be great
By thine own act—yet art thou never great 75
But by the inspiration of great passion.
The whirl-blast comes, the desert-sands rise up
And shape themselves; from Earth to Heaven they stand,
As though they were the pillars of a temple,
Built by Omnipotence in its own honour! 80
But the blast pauses, and their shaping spirit
Is fled: the mighty columns were but sand,
And lazy snakes trail o'er the level ruins!
1813.

A HYMN[1]

My Maker! of thy power the trace
In every creature's form and face
    The wond'ring soul surveys:
Thy wisdom, infinite above
Seraphic thought, a Father's love 5
    As infinite displays!

From all that meets or eye or ear,
There falls a genial holy fear
Which, like the heavy dew of morn,
Refreshes while it bows the heart forlorn! 10

Great God! thy works how wondrous fair!
Yet sinful man didst thou declare
    The whole Earth's voice and mind!

---

[1] First published in *Poems*, 1852. The MS. was placed in the hands of the Editors by J. W. Wilkins, Esq., of Trinity Hall, Cambridge. 'The accompanying autograph,' writes Mr. Wilkins, 'dated 1814, and addressed to Mrs. Hood of Brunswick Square, was given not later than the year 1817 to a relative of my own who was then residing at Clifton (and was, at the time at which it passed into his hands, an attendant on Mr. Coleridge's lectures, which were in course of delivery at that place), either by the lady to whom it is addressed, or by some other friend of Mr. Coleridge.' 1852, Notes, p. 385.

Lord, ev'n as Thou all-present art,
O may we still with heedful heart   15
   Thy presence know and find!
Then, come what will, of weal or woe,
Joy's bosom-spring shall steady flow;
For though 'tis Heaven THYSELF to see,
Where but thy *Shadow* falls, Grief cannot be!—   20

1814.

TO A LADY[1]

WITH FALCONER'S *SHIPWRECK*

AH! not by Cam or Isis, famous streams,
   In archéd groves, the youthful poet's choice;
Nor while half-listening, 'mid delicious dreams,
   To harp and song from lady's hand and voice;

Not yet while gazing in sublimer mood   5
   On cliff, or cataract, in Alpine dell;
Nor in dim cave with bladdery sea-weed strewed,
   Framing wild fancies to the ocean's swell;

Our sea-bard sang this song! which still he sings,
   And sings for thee, sweet friend! Hark, Pity, hark!
Now mounts, now totters on the tempest's wings,   11
   Now groans, and shivers, the replunging bark!

'Cling to the shrouds!' In vain! The breakers roar—
   Death shrieks! With two alone of all his clan
Forlorn the poet paced the Grecian shore,   15
   No classic roamer, but a shipwrecked man!

---

[1] First published in *Sibylline Leaves*, 1817: included in 1828, 1829, and 1834. A different or emended version headed 'Written in a Blank Leaf of Faulkner's Shipwreck, presented by a friend to Miss K', was published in *Felix Farley's Bristol Journal* of February 21, 1818. [See Note by G. E. Weare, Weston-super-Mare, January, 1905.]

Title] To a Lady With Falkner's 'Shipwreck' *S. L.*
2 archéd] cloyst'ring *F. F.*   3 'mid] midst *F. F.*   4 lady's] woman's *F. F.*   5 sublimer] diviner *F. F.*   6 On torrent falls, on woody mountain dell *F. F.*   7 sea-weed] sea-weeds *F. F.*   8 Attuning wild tales to the ocean's swell *F. F.*   9 this] *this F. F.*   10 thee] *thee F. F.*   11 It mounts, it totters *F. F.*   12 It groans, it quivers *F. F.*   14 of] and *F. F.*   15 Forlorn the] The toil-worn *F. F.*

TO A LADY

Say then, what muse inspired these genial strains,
  And lit his spirit to so bright a flame?
The elevating thought of suffered pains,
  Which gentle hearts shall mourn; but chief, the name 20

Of gratitude! remembrances of friend,
  Or absent or no more! shades of the Past,
Which Love makes substance! Hence to thee I send,
  O dear as long as life and memory last!

I send with deep regards of heart and head, 25
  Sweet maid, for friendship formed! this work to thee:
And thou, the while thou canst not choose but shed
  A tear for Falconer, wilt remember me.

?1814.

HUMAN LIFE[1]

ON THE DENIAL OF IMMORTALITY

If dead, we cease to be; if total gloom
  Swallow up life's brief flash for aye, we fare
As summer-gusts, of sudden birth and doom,
  Whose sound and motion not alone declare,
But are their whole of being! If the breath[2] 5
  Be Life itself, and not its task and tent,
If even a soul like Milton's can know death;
  O Man! thou vessel purposeless, unmeant,
Yet drone-hive strange of phantom purposes!
  Surplus of Nature's dread activity, 10
Which, as she gazed on some nigh-finished vase,
Retreating slow, with meditative pause,
  She formed with restless hands unconsciously.
Blank accident! nothing's anomaly!

---

[1] First published in *Sibylline Leaves*, 1817: included in 1828, 1829, and 1834.
[2] Halitus = anima animae tabernaculum *MS. Note* (? *S. T. C.*)

17-20 Say then what power evoked such genial strains
            And beckon'd godlike to the trembling Muse?
        The thought not pleasureless of suffer'd pains
            But *chiefly* friendship's voice, her holy dues. *F. F.*
21 Demanding dear remembrances of friend *F. F.*   22 Which love makes real! Thence *F. F.*   24 life] love *F. F.*   26 Sweet Maid for friendship framed this song to thee *F. F.*   28 Falconer] Falkner *S. L.*: Faulkner *F. F.*   me] ME *S. L., 1828, 1829.*
5 are] *are S. L., 1828, 1829*   whole] *whole S. L., 1828, 1829.*

HUMAN LIFE

If rootless thus, thus substanceless thy state, 15
Go, weigh thy dreams, and be thy hopes, thy fears,
The counter-weights!—Thy laughter and thy tears
  Mean but themselves, each fittest to create
And to repay the other! Why rejoices
  Thy heart with hollow joy for hollow good? 20
  Why cowl thy face beneath the mourner's hood?
Why waste thy sighs, and thy lamenting voices,
  Image of Image, Ghost of Ghostly Elf,
That such a thing as thou feel'st warm or cold?
Yet what and whence thy gain, if thou withhold 25
  These costless shadows of thy shadowy self?
Be sad! be glad! be neither! seek, or shun!
Thou hast no reason why! Thou canst have none;
Thy being's being is contradiction.

?1815.

SONG[1]

FROM *ZAPOLYA*

A sunny shaft did I behold,
  From sky to earth it slanted:
And poised therein a bird so bold—
  Sweet bird, thou wert enchanted!

He sank, he rose, he twinkled, he trolled 5
  Within that shaft of sunny mist;
His eyes of fire, his beak of gold,
  All else of amethyst!

And thus he sang: 'Adieu! adieu!
Love's dreams prove seldom true. 10

---

[1] First published in *Zapolya*, 1817 (Act II, Scene i, ll. 65-80). First collected in 1844. Two MSS. are extant, one in the possession of Mr. John Murray (*MS. M.*), and a second in the possession of the Editor (*MS. S. T. C.*).

---

19 the] each *1887-80, 1893.*
Song—Title] Sung by Glycine in *Zapolya* 1893 : Glycine's Song *MS. M.*
1 A pillar grey did I behold *MS. S. T. C.* 4 A faery Bird that chanted *MS. S. T. C.*   6 sunny] shiny *MS. S. T. C.*

The blossoms they make no delay:
The sparkling dew-drops will not stay.
　　Sweet month of May,
　　　We must away;
　　　　Far, far away!
1815.　　　　To-day! to-day!'

HUNTING SONG[1]

FROM *ZAPOLYA*

Up, up! ye dames, and lasses gay!
To the meadows trip away.
'Tis you must tend the flocks this morn,
And scare the small birds from the corn.
　　Not a soul at home may stay:
　　　For the shepherds must go
　　　　With lance and bow
　　To hunt the wolf in the woods to-day.

Leave the hearth and leave the house
To the cricket and the mouse:
Find grannam out a sunny seat,
With babe and lambkin at her feet.
　　Not a soul at home may stay:
　　　For the shepherds must go
　　　　With lance and bow
1815.　To hunt the wolf in the woods to-day.

FAITH, HOPE, AND CHARITY[2]

FROM THE ITALIAN OF GUARINI

FAITH

Let those whose low delights to Earth are given
　Chaunt forth their earthly Loves! but we
　　Must make an holier minstrelsy,
And, heavenly-born, will sing the Things of Heaven.

---

[1] First published in *Zapolya* (Act IV, Scene ii, ll. 56-71). First collected, 1844.

[2] From a hitherto unpublished MS. For the original *Dialogo: Fide, Speranza, Fide*, included in the 'Madrigali..' del Signor Cavalier Battista Guarini, 1663, vide Appendices of this edition. The translation in Coleridge's handwriting is preceded by another version transcribed and, possibly, composed by Hartley Coleridge.

11, 12 om. MS *S. T. C.*, MS. M.
Hunting Song—Title] Choral Song 1893.

CHARITY

But who for us the listening Heart shall gain? 5
   Inaudible as of the sphere
   Our music dies upon the ear,
Enchanted with the mortal Syren's strain.

HOPE

Yet let our choral songs abound!
   Th' inspiring Power, its living Source, 10
   May flow with them and give them force,
If, elsewhere all unheard, in Heaven they sound.

ALL

Aid thou our voice, Great Spirit! thou whose flame
   Kindled the Songster sweet of Israel,
   Who made so high to swell 15
Beyond a mortal strain thy glorious Name.

CHARITY AND FAITH

Though rapt to Heaven, our mission and our care
   Is still to sojourn on the Earth,
   To shape, to soothe, Man's second Birth,
And re-ascend to Heaven, Heaven's prodigal Heir! 20

CHARITY

What is Man's soul of Love deprived?

HOPE. FAITH

   It like a Harp untunéd is,
   That sounds, indeed, but sounds amiss.

CHARITY. HOPE

From holy Love all good gifts are derived.

FAITH

   But 'tis time that every nation 25
   Should hear how loftily we sing.

FAITH. HOPE. CHARITY

   See, O World, see thy salvation!
   Let the Heavens with praises ring.
   Who would have a Throne above,
   Let him hope, believe and love; 30
   And whoso loves no earthly song,
   But does for heavenly music long,
   Faith, Hope, and Charity for him,
   Shall sing like wingéd Cherubim.

1815.

TO NATURE[1]

It may indeed be phantasy, when I
  Essay to draw from all created things
  Deep, heartfelt, inward joy that closely clings;
And trace in leaves and flowers that round me lie
Lessons of love and earnest piety.   5
  So let it be; and if the wide world rings
  In mock of this belief, it brings
Nor fear, nor grief, nor vain perplexity.
So will I build my altar in the fields,
  And the blue sky my fretted dome shall be,   10
And the sweet fragrance that the wild flower yields
  Shall be the incense I will yield to Thee,
Thee only God! and thou shalt not despise
Even me, the priest of this poor sacrifice.

? 1820.

LIMBO[2]

*   *   *   *   *

The sole true Something—This! In Limbo's Den
It frightens Ghosts, as here Ghosts frighten men.
Thence cross'd unseiz'd—and shall some fated hour
Be pulveris'd by Demogorgon's power,

---

[1] First published in *Letters, Conversations and Recollections* by S. T. Coleridge, 1836, i. 144. First collected in *Poems*, 1863, Appendix, p. 391.

[2] First published, in its present shape, from an original MS. in 1893 (inscribed in a notebook). Lines 6–10 ('they shrink ... negative eye') were first printed in *The Friend* (1818, iii. 215), and included as a separate fragment with the title 'Moles' in *P. W.*, 1834, i. 259. Lines 11–38 were first printed with the title 'Limbo' in *P. W.*, 1834, i. 272-3. The lines as quoted in *The Friend* were directed against 'the partisans of a crass and sensual materialism, the advocates of the *Nihil nisi ab extra*'. The following variants, now first printed, are from a second MS. (*MS. S. T. C.*) in the possession of Miss Edith Coleridge. In the notebook *Limbo* is followed by the lines entitled *Ne Plus Ultra*, vide *post*, p. 431.

Limbo—Title] Another Fragment, but in a very different style, from a Dream of Purgatory, alias Limbus *MS. S. T. C.* [*Note.*—In this MS. *Phantom*, 'All Look and Likeness,' &c. precedes *Limbo*.]

Between 2–3
    For skimming in the wake it mock'd the care
    Of the old Boat-God for his farthing fare;
    Tho' Irus' Ghost itself he ne'er frown'd blacker on
    The skin and skin-pent Druggist cross'd the Acheron,

And given as poison to annihilate souls— 5
Even now it shrinks them—they shrink in as Moles
(Nature's mute monks, live mandrakes of the ground)
Creep back from Light—then listen for its sound;—
See but to dread, and dread they know not why—
The natural alien of their negative eye. 10

'Tis a strange place, this Limbo!—not a Place,
Yet name it so;—where Time and weary Space
Fettered from flight, with night-mare sense of fleeing,
Strive for their last crepuscular half-being;—
Lank Space, and scytheless Time with branny hands 15
Barren and soundless as the measuring sands,
Not mark'd by flit of Shades,—unmeaning they
As moonlight on the dial of the day!
But that is lovely—looks like Human Time,—
An Old Man with a steady look sublime, 20
That stops his earthly task to watch the skies;
But he is blind—a Statue hath such eyes;—
Yet having moonward turn'd his face by chance,
Gazes the orb with moon-like countenance,
With scant white hairs, with foretop bald and high, 25
He gazes still,—his eyeless face all eye;—
As 'twere an organ full of silent sight,
His whole face seemeth to rejoice in light!
Lip touching lip, all moveless, bust and limb—
He seems to gaze at that which seems to gaze on him! 30
  No such sweet sights doth Limbo den immure,
Wall'd round, and made a spirit-jail secure,

       Styx, and with Periphlegeton Cocytus,—
       (The very names, methinks, might frighten us)
       Unchang'd it cross'd—*and shall some fated hour MS. Notebook.*

[Coleridge marks these lines as 'a specimen of the Sublime dashed to pieces by cutting too close with the fiery Four-in-Hand round the corner of Nonsense.']

6 They, like moles *Friend, 1818*.   8 Shrink from the light, then listen for a sound *Friend, 1818*.   12 so] such *MS. S. T. C.*   16 the] his *MS. S. T. C.*   17 Mark'd but by Flit *MS. S. T. C.*   30 at] on *MS. S. T. C.*

31 *foll.* In one sole Outlet yawns the Phantom Wall,
       And through this grim road to [a] worser thrall
       Oft homeward scouring from a sick Child's dream
       Old Mother Brownrigg shoots upon a scream;

By the mere horror of blank Naught-at-all,
Whose circumambience doth these ghosts enthral.
A lurid thought is growthless, dull Privation,
Yet that is but a Purgatory curse;
Hell knows a fear far worse,
A fear—a future state;—'tis positive Negation!

1817.

NE PLUS ULTRA[1]

Sole Positive of Night!
Antipathist of Light!
Fate's only essence! primal scorpion rod—
The one permitted opposite of God!—
Condensèd blackness and abysmal storm
    Compacted to one sceptre
    Arms the Grasp enorm—
    The Intercepter—
The Substance that still casts the shadow Death!—
    The Dragon foul and fell—
    The unrevealable,
And hidden one, whose breath
Gives wind and fuel to the fires of Hell!
    Ah! sole despair
    Of both th' eternities in Heaven!
Sole interdict of all-bedewing prayer,
    The all-compassionate!
    Save to the Lampads Seven
Reveal'd to none of all th' Angelic State,
    Save to the Lampads Seven,
    That watch the throne of Heaven!

?1826.

---

[1] First published in 1834. The MS., which is inscribed in a notebook, is immediately preceded by that of the first draft of *Limbo* (*ante*, p. 429). The so-called 'Ne Plus Ultra' may have been intended to illustrate a similar paradox—the 'positivity of negation'. No date can be assigned to either of these metaphysical conceits, but there can be little doubt that they were 'written in later life'.

And turning back her Face with hideous Leer,
Leaves Sentry there *Intolerable Fear!*
  A horrid thought is growthless dull Negation:
  Yet that is but a Purgatory Curse,
    She knows a fear far worse
Flee, lest thou hear its Name! Flee, rash Imagination!

   *   *   *   *   *   *   *   *

S. T. Coleridge, 1st Oct. 1827, Grove, Highgate.

THE KNIGHT'S TOMB[1]

Where is the grave of Sir Arthur O'Kellyn?
Where may the grave of that good man be?—
By the side of a spring, on the breast of Helvellyn,
Under the twigs of a young birch tree!
The oak that in summer was sweet to hear,   5
And rustled its leaves in the fall of the year,
And whistled and roared in the winter alone,
Is gone,—and the birch in its stead is grown.—
The Knight's bones are dust,
And his good sword rust;—   10
His soul is with the saints, I trust.

? 1817.

---

[1] First published in *P. W.*, 1834. Gillman (*Life*, p. 276) says that the lines were composed 'as an experiment for a metre', and repeated by the author to 'a mutual friend', who 'spoke of his visit to Highgate' and repeated them to Scott on the following day. The last three lines, 'somewhat altered', are quoted in *Ivanhoe*, chapter viii, and again in *Castle Dangerous*, chapter ix. They run thus:—

> The knights are dust,
> And their good swords are rust;—
> Their souls are with the saints, we trust.

Gillman says that the Ivanhoe quotation convinced Coleridge that Scott was the author of the Waverley Novels. In the Appendix to the 'Notes' to *Castle Dangerous* (1834), which was edited and partly drawn up by Lockhart, the poem is quoted in full, with a prefatory note ('The author has somewhat altered part of a beautiful unpublished fragment of Coleridge').

> Where is the grave of Sir Arthur Orellan,—
> Where may the grave of that good knight be?
> By the marge of a brook, on the slope of Helvellyn,
> Under the boughs of a young birch-tree.
> The Oak that in summer was pleasant to hear,
> That rustled in autumn all wither'd and sear,
> That whistled and groan'd thro' the winter alone,
> He hath gone, and a birch in his place is grown.
>   The knight's bones are dust,
>   His good sword is rust;
> His spirit is with the saints, we trust.

This version must have been transcribed from a MS. in Lockhart's possession, and represents a first draft of the lines as published in 1834. These lines are, no doubt, an 'experiment for a metre'. The upward movement (ll. 1-7) is dactylic: the fall (ll. 8-11) is almost, if not altogether, spondaic. The whole forms a complete stanza, or metrical scheme, which may be compared with ll. 264-78 of the First Part of *Christabel*. Mrs. H. N. Coleridge, who must have been familiar with Gillman's story, dates the *Knight's Tomb* 1802.

ON DONNE'S POETRY[1]

With Donne, whose muse on dromedary trots,
Wreathe iron pokers into true-love knots;
Rhyme's sturdy cripple, fancy's maze and clue,
Wit's forge and fire-blast, meaning's press and screw.
? 1818.

ISRAEL'S LAMENT[2]

'A Hebrew Dirge, chaunted in the Great Synagogue, St. James's Place, Aldgate, on the day of the Funeral of her Royal Highness the Princess Charlotte. By Hyman Hurwitz, Master of the Hebrew Academy, Highgate: with a Translation in English Verse, by S. T. Coleridge, Esq., 1817.'

Mourn, Israel! Sons of Israel, mourn!
  Give utterance to the inward throe!
As wails, of her first love forlorn,
  The Virgin clad in robes of woe.

Mourn the young Mother, snatch'd away 5
  From Light and Life's ascending Sun!
Mourn for the Babe, Death's voiceless prey,
  Earn'd by long pangs and lost ere won.

Mourn the bright Rose that bloom'd and went,
  Ere half disclosed its vernal hue! 10
Mourn the green Bud, so rudely rent,
  It brake the stem on which it grew.

Mourn for the universal woe
  With solemn dirge and fault'ring tongue:
For England's Lady is laid low, 15
  So dear, so lovely, and so young!

---

[1] First published in *Literary Remains*, 1836, i. 148, from 'notes written by Mr. Coleridge in a volume of " Chalmers's Poets "'. Line 2 finds a place in Hartley Coleridge's couplets on Donne which are written on the fly-leaves and covers of his copy of Anderson's *British Poets*. In the original MS. it is enclosed in quotation marks. First collected in P. W., 1885, ii. 409.

[2] First published, together with the Hebrew, as an octavo pamphlet (pp. 13) in 1817. An abbreviated version was included in *Literary Remains*, 1836, i. 57-8 and in the Appendix to *Poems*, 1863. The Lament as a whole was first collected in P. and D. W., 1877-80, ii. 282-5.

Israel's Lament—*Title*] Israel's Lament on the death of the Princess Charlotte of Wales. From the Hebrew of Hyman Hurwitz *L. R.*

The blossoms on her Tree of Life
  Shone with the dews of recent bliss:
Transplanted in that deadly strife,
  She plucks its fruits in Paradise.   20

Mourn for the widow'd Lord in chief,
  Who wails and will not solaced be!
Mourn for the childless Father's grief,
  The wedded Lover's agony!

Mourn for the Prince, who rose at morn   25
  To seek and bless the firstling bud
Of his own Rose, and found the thorn,
  Its point bedew'd with tears of blood.

O press again that murmuring string!
  Again bewail that princely Sire!   30
A destined Queen, a future King,
  He mourns on one funereal pyre.

Mourn for Britannia's hopes decay'd,
  Her daughters wail their dear defence;
Their fair example, prostrate laid,   35
  Chaste Love and fervid Innocence.

While Grief in song shall seek repose,
  We will take up a Mourning yearly:
To wail the blow that crush'd the Rose,
  So dearly priz'd and lov'd so dearly.   40

Long as the fount of Song o'erflows
  Will I the yearly dirge renew:
Mourn for the firstling of the Rose,
  That snapt the stem on which it grew.

The proud shall pass, forgot; the chill, 45
  Damp, trickling Vault their only mourner!
Not so the regal Rose, that still
  Clung to the breast which first had worn her!

O thou, who mark'st the Mourner's path
  To sad Jeshurun's Sons attend!   50
Amid the Light'nings of thy Wrath
  The showers of Consolation send!

19 Transplanted] Translated *L. R., 1863.*   21-4 *om. L. R., 1863.*
29-32 *om. L. R., 1863.*   49-56 *om. L. R., 1863.*   49 Mourner's] Mourners'
L. R., 1863.

Jehovah frowns! the Islands bow!
  And Prince and People kiss the Rod!—
Their dread chastising Judge wert thou!   55
  Be thou their Comforter, O God!
1817.

FANCY IN NUBIBUS[1]

OR THE POET IN THE CLOUDS

O! it is pleasant, with a heart at ease,
  Just after sunset, or by moonlight skies,
To make the shifting clouds be what you please,
  Or let the easily persuaded eyes
Own each quaint likeness issuing from the mould   5
  Of a friend's fancy; or with head bent low
And cheek aslant see rivers flow of gold
  'Twixt crimson banks; and then, a traveller, go
From mount to mount through Cloudland, gorgeous land!
  Or list'ning to the tide, with closéd sight,   10
Be that blind bard, who on the Chian strand
  By those deep sounds possessed with inward light,
Beheld the Iliad and the Odyssee
  Rise to the swelling of the voiceful sea.
1817.

[1] First published in *Felix Farley's Bristol Journal* for February 7, 1818: and afterwards in *Blackwood's Magazine* for November, 1819. First collected in 1828: included in 1829 and 1834. A MS. in the possession of Major Butterworth of Carlisle is signed 'S. T. Coleridge, Little Hampton, Oct. 1818'. In a letter to Coleridge dated Jan. 10, 1820, Lamb asks, 'Who put your marine sonnet [i. e. A Sonnet written on the Sea Coast, vide *Title*] . . . in *Blackwood*?' F. Freiligrath in his Introduction to the Tauchnitz edition says that the last five lines are borrowed from Stolberg's *An das Meer*.

Fancy, &c.—Title] Fancy, &c. A Sonnet Composed by the Seaside, October 1817. *F. F.*: Fancy in Nubibus. A Sonnet, composed on the Sea Coast *1819*.

4 let] bid *1819*.   5 Own] Owe *F. F. 1818*.   quaint] strange *1819*.
6 head] heart *MS*.: head bow'd low *1819*.   9 through] o'er *1819*.

THE TEARS OF A GRATEFUL PEOPLE [1]

A Hebrew Dirge and Hymn, chaunted in the Great Synagogue, St. James' pl. Aldgate, on the Day of the Funeral of King George III. of blessed memory. By Hyman Hurwitz of Highgate, Translated by a Friend.

Dirge

OPPRESS'D, confused, with grief and pain,
   And inly shrinking from the blow,
In vain I seek the dirgeful strain,
   The wonted words refuse to flow.

A fear in every face I find,
   Each voice is that of one who grieves;
And all my Soul, to grief resigned,
   Reflects the sorrow it receives.

The Day-Star of our glory sets!
   Our King has breathed his latest breath!
Each heart its wonted pulse forgets,
   As if it own'd the pow'r of death.

Our Crown, our heart's Desire is fled!
   Britannia's glory moults its wing!
Let us with ashes on our head,
   Raise up a mourning for our King.

Lo! of his beams the Day-Star shorn,[2]
   Sad gleams the Moon through cloudy veil!
The Stars are dim! Our Nobles mourn;
   The Matrons weep, their Children wail.

No age records a King so just,
   His virtues numerous as his days;
The Lord Jehovah was his trust,
   And truth with mercy ruled his ways.

His Love was bounded by no Clime;
   Each diverse Race, each distant Clan
He govern'd by this truth sublime,
   'God only knows the heart—not man.'

---

[1] First published with the Hebrew in pamphlet form in 1820. First collected in 1893.

[2] The author, in the spirit of Hebrew Poetry, here represents the Crown, the Peerage, and the Commonalty, by the figurative expression of the Sun, Moon, and Stars.

His word appall'd the sons of pride,
  Iniquity far wing'd her way; 30
Deceit and fraud were scatter'd wide,
  And truth resum'd her sacred sway.

He sooth'd the wretched, and the prey
  From impious tyranny he tore;
He stay'd th' Usurper's iron sway, 35
  And bade the Spoiler waste no more.

Thou too, Jeshurun's Daughter! thou,
  Th' oppress'd of nations and the scorn!
Didst hail on his benignant brow
  A safety dawning like the morn. 40

The scoff of each unfeeling mind,
  Thy doom was hard, and keen thy grief;
Beneath his throne, peace thou didst find,
  And blest the hand that gave relief.

E'en when a fatal cloud o'erspread 45
  The moonlight splendour of his sway,
Yet still the light remain'd, and shed
  Mild radiance on the traveller's way.

But he is gone—the Just! the Good!
  Nor could a Nation's pray'r delay 50
The heavenly meed, that long had stood
  His portion in the realms of day.

Beyond the mighty Isle's extent
  The mightier Nation mourns her Chief:
Him Judah's Daughter shall lament, 55
  In tears of fervour, love and grief.

Britannia mourns in silent grief;
  Her heart a prey to inward woe.
In vain she strives to find relief,
  Her pang so great, so great the blow. 60

Britannia! Sister! woe is me!
  Full fain would I console thy woe.
But, ah! how shall I comfort thee,
  Who need the balm I would bestow?

United then let us repair, 65
  As round our common Parent's grave;
And pouring out our heart in prayer,
  Our heav'nly Father's mercy crave.

Until Jehovah from his throne
  Shall heed his suffering people's fears;
Shall turn to song the Mourner's groan,
  To smiles of joy the Nation's tears.

Praise to the Lord! Loud praises sing!
  And bless Jehovah's righteous hand!
Again he bids a George, our King,
  Dispense his blessings to the Land.

Hymn

O thron'd in Heav'n! Sole King of kings,
Jehovah! hear thy Children's prayers and sighs!
Thou Binder of the broken heart! with wings
  Of healing on thy people rise!
    Thy mercies, Lord, are sweet;
    And Peace and Mercy meet,
    Before thy Judgment seat:
    Lord, hear us! we entreat!

When angry clouds thy throne surround,
E'en from the cloud thou bid'st thy mercy shine:
And ere thy righteous vengeance strikes the wound,
  Thy grace prepares the balm divine!
    Thy mercies, Lord, are sweet;
      etc.

The Parent tree thy hand did spare—
It fell not till the ripen'd fruit was won:
Beneath its shade the Scion flourish'd fair,
  And for the Sire thou gav'st the Son.
    etc.

This thy own Vine, which thou didst rear,
And train up for us from the royal root,
Protect, O Lord! and to the Nations near
  Long let it shelter yield, and fruit.
    etc.

Lord, comfort thou the royal line:
Let Peace and Joy watch round us hand and hand.
Our Nobles visit with thy grace divine,
  And banish sorrow from the land!
    Thy mercies, Lord, are sweet;
    And Peace and Mercy meet
    Before thy Judgment seat;
    Lord, hear us! we entreat!

1820.

YOUTH AND AGE[1]

Verse, a breeze mid blossoms straying,
Where Hope clung feeding, like a bee—
Both were mine! Life went a-maying
    With Nature, Hope, and Poesy,
        When I was young!   5

When I was young?—Ah, woful When!
Ah! for the change 'twixt Now and Then!
This breathing house not built with hands,
This body that does me grievous wrong,
O'er aery cliffs and glittering sands,   10
How lightly then it flashed along:—
Like those trim skiffs, unknown of yore,
On winding lakes and rivers wide,
That ask no aid of sail or oar,
That fear no spite of wind or tide!   15

---

[1] First published in its present shape in 1834. Lines 1-38, with the heading 'Youth and Age', were first published in the *Literary Souvenir*, 1828, and also in the *Bijou*, 1828: included in 1828, 1829. Lines 39-49 were first published in *Blackwood's Magazine* for June 1832, entitled 'An Old Man's Sigh : a Sonnet', as 'an out-slough or hypertrophic stanza of a certain poem called "Youth and Age".' Of lines 1-43 three MSS. are extant. (1) A fair copy (*MS. 1*) presented to Derwent Coleridge, and now in the Editor's possession. In *MS. 1* the poem is divided into three stanzas : (i) lines 1-17; (ii) lines 18-38; (iii) lines 39-43. The watermark of this MS. on a quarto sheet of Bath Post letter-paper is 1822. (2) A rough draft, in a notebook dated Sept. 10, 1823 ; and (3) a corrected draft of forty-three lines (vide for *MSS. 2, 3* Appendices of this edition). A MS. version of *An Old Man's Sigh*, dated 'Grove, Highgate, April 1832', was contributed to Miss Rotha Quillinan's Album ; and another version numbering only eight lines was inscribed in an album in 1828 when Coleridge was on his Rhine tour with Wordsworth. After line 42 this version continues:—

    As we creep feebly down life's slope,
      Yet courteous dame, accept this truth,
    Hope leaves us not, but we leave hope,
    And quench the inward light of youth.
        T. Colley Grattan's *Beaten Paths*, 1862, ii. 139.

There can be little doubt that lines 1-43 were composed in 1823, and that the last six lines of the text which form part of *An Old Man's Sigh* were composed, as an afterthought, in 1832.

---

1 Verse, a] Verse is a *with the alternative* ? Verse ă breeze *MS. 1*.   2 clung] clings *MS. 1, Bijou*.   6 When I] *When* I *1828, 1829*.   8 This house of clay *MS. 1, Bijou*.   10 O'er hill and dale and sounding sands *MS. 1, Bijou*.   11 then] *then 1828, 1829*.   12 skiffs] boats *MS. 1, Bijou*.

Nought cared this body for wind or weather
When Youth and I lived in't together.

Flowers are lovely; Love is flower-like;
Friendship is a sheltering tree;
O! the joys, that came down shower-like,   20
Of Friendship, Love, and Liberty,
    Ere I was old!

Ere I was old? Ah woful Ere,
Which tells me, Youth's no longer here!
O Youth! for years so many and sweet,   25
'Tis known, that Thou and I were one,
I'll think it but a fond conceit—
It cannot be that Thou art gone!
Thy vesper-bell hath not yet toll'd:—
And thou wert aye a masker bold!   30
What strange disguise hast now put on,
To make believe, that thou art gone?
I see these locks in silvery slips,
This drooping gait, this altered size:
But Spring-tide blossoms on thy lips,   35
And tears take sunshine from thine eyes!
Life is but thought: so think I will
That Youth and I are house-mates still.

Dew-drops are the gems of morning,
But the tears of mournful eve!   40
Where no hope is, life's a warning
That only serves to make us grieve,
    When we are old:

That only serves to make us grieve
With oft and tedious taking-leave,   45

---

20 came] come *Bijou*.   21 Of Beauty, Truth, and Liberty *MS.1, Bijou*.
23 Ere I] *Ere I 1828, 1829*. woful] mournful *Literary Souvenir*.   25 many] merry *Bijou*.   27 fond] false *MS. 1, Bijou*.   32 make believe] make believe *1828, 1829*.   34 drooping] dragging *MS. 1, Bijou*.

42–4   That only serves to make me grieve
     Now I am old!
   Now I am old,—ah woful Now *MS. 1*.

44–5   In our old age
Whose bruised wings quarrel with the bars of the still narrowing cage. *Inserted in 1832*.

YOUTH AND AGE

>   Like some poor nigh-related guest,
>   That may not rudely be dismist;
>   Yet hath outstay'd his welcome while,
>   And tells the jest without the smile.

1823-1832.

THE REPROOF AND REPLY[1]

Or, The Flower-Thief's Apology, for a robbery committed in Mr. and Mrs. ——'s garden, on Sunday morning, 25th of May, 1823, between the hours of eleven and twelve.

>   "Fie, Mr. Coleridge!—and can this be you?
>   Break two commandments? and in church-time too!
>   Have you not heard, or have you heard in vain,
>   The birth-and-parentage-recording strain?—
>   Confessions shrill, that out-shrill'd mack'rel drown   5
>   Fresh from the drop—the youth not yet cut down—
>   Letter to sweet-heart—the last dying speech—
>   And didn't all this begin in Sabbath-breach?
>   You, that knew better! In broad open day,
>   Steal in, steal out, and steal our flowers away?   10
>   What could possess you? Ah! sweet youth, I fear
>   The chap with horns and tail was at your ear!"
>
>   Such sounds of late, accusing fancy brought
>   From fair Chisholm to the Poet's thought.
>   Now hear the meek Parnassian youth's reply:—   15
>   A bow—a pleading look—a downcast eye,—
>   And then:

---

[1] First published in *Friendship's Offering* for 1834, as the first of four 'Lightheartednesses in Rhyme'. A motto was prefixed:—'I expect no sense, worth listening to, from the man who never does talk nonsense.'—*Anon.* In *F. O.*, 1834, Chisholm was printed C—— in line 14, C——m in lines 35, 56, and 60, C——m's in line 43. In 1834, 1844 the name was omitted altogether. The text of the present edition follows the MS. First collected in *P. W.*, 1834. A MS. version is in the possession of Miss Edith Coleridge. These lines were included in 1844, but omitted from 1852, 1863, and 1870.

---

49 *Two lines were added in 1832*:—

>   O might Life cease! and Selfless Mind,
>   Whose total Being is Act, alone remain behind.

The Reproof, &c.—Title] The Reproof and Reply (*the alternative title is omitted*) 1834.

442 THE REPROOF AND REPLY

"Fair dame! a visionary wight,
Hard by your hill-side mansion sparkling white,
His thoughts all hovering round the Muses' home,
Long hath it been your Poet's wont to roam,
And many a morn, on his becharmèd sense 20
So rich a stream of music issued thence,
He deem'd himself, as it flowed warbling on,
Beside the vocal fount of Helicon!
But when, as if to settle the concern,
A Nymph too he beheld, in many a turn, 25
Guiding the sweet rill from its fontal urn,—
Say, can you blame?—No! none that saw and heard
Could blame a bard, that he thus inly stirr'd;
A muse beholding in each fervent trait,
Took Mary H—— for Polly Hymnia! 30
Or haply as there stood beside the maid
One loftier form in sable stole array'd,
If with regretful thought he hail'd in *thee*
Chisholm, his long-lost friend, Mol Pomene!
But most of *you*, soft warblings, I complain! 35
'Twas ye that from the bee-hive of my brain
Did lure the fancies forth, a freakish rout,
And witch'd the air with dreams turn'd inside out.

"Thus all conspir'd—each power of eye and ear, 40
And this gay month, th' enchantress of the year,
To cheat poor me (no conjuror, God wot!)
And Chisholm's self accomplice in the plot.
Can you then wonder if I went astray?
Not bards alone, nor lovers mad as they;— 45
All Nature *day-dreams* in the month of May.
And if I pluck'd 'each flower that *sweetest* blows,'—
Who walks in sleep, needs follow must his *nose*.

Thus, long accustom'd on the twy-fork'd hill,[1]
To pluck both flower and floweret at my will; 50
The garden's maze, like No-man's-land, I tread,
Nor common law, nor statute in my head;
For my own proper smell, sight, fancy, feeling,

---

[1] The English Parnassus is remarkable for its two summits of unequal height, the lower denominated Hampstead, the higher Highgate.

---

31 Mary H——] Mary —— *1834, 1844.*   38 Did lure the] Lured the wild *F. O. 1834.*

With autocratic hand at once repealing
Five Acts of Parliament 'gainst private stealing! 55
But yet from Chisholm who despairs of grace?
There's no spring-gun or man-trap in *that* face!
Let Moses then look black, and Aaron blue,
That look as if they had little else to do:
For Chisholm speaks, 'Poor youth! he's but a waif! 60
The spoons all right? the hen and chickens safe?
Well, well, he shall not forfeit our regards—
The Eighth Commandment was not made for Bards!'"[1]
1823.

FIRST ADVENT OF LOVE [2]

O FAIR is Love's first hope to gentle mind!
As Eve's first star thro' fleecy cloudlet peeping;
And sweeter than the gentle south-west wind,
O'er willowy meads, and shadow'd waters creeping,
And Ceres' golden fields;—the sultry hind 5
Meets it with brow uplift, and stays his reaping.
? 1824.

THE DELINQUENT TRAVELLERS [3]

SOME are home-sick—some two or three,
Their third year on the Arctic Sea—

---

[1] Compare '*The Eighth Commandment* was not made for Love', l. 16 of Elegy I of *The Love Elegies of Abel Shufflebottom*, by R. Southey.

[2] First published in 1834. In a MS. note, dated September 1827, it is included in 'Relics of my School-boy Muse: i.e. fragments of poems composed before my fifteenth year', *P. W.*, 1852, Notes, p. 379; but in an entry in a notebook dated 1824, Coleridge writes: 'A pretty unintended couplet in the prose of Sidney's *Arcadia*:—

'And, sweeter than a gentle south-west wind
O'er flowery fields and shadowed waters creeping
In summer's extreme heat.'

The passage which Coleridge versified is to be found in the *Arcadia*:—
'Her breath is more sweet than a gentle south-west wind, which comes creeping over flowing fields and shadowed waters in the heat of summer.'

[3] From an hitherto unpublished MS., formerly in the possession of Coleridge's friend and amanuensis Joseph Henry Green.

First Advent of Love—Title] Love's First Hope *1893*.

THE DELINQUENT TRAVELLERS

Brave Captain Lyon tells us so [1]—
Spite of those charming Esquimaux.
But O, what scores are sick of Home,
Agog for Paris or for Rome!
Nay! tho' contented to abide,
You should prefer your own fireside;
Yet since grim War has ceas'd its madding,
And Peace has set John Bull agadding,
'Twould such a vulgar taste betray,
For very shame you must away!
'What? not yet seen the coast of France!
The folks will swear, for lack of bail,
You've spent your last five years in jail!'

Keep moving! Steam, or Gas, or Stage,
Hold, cabin, steerage, hencoop's cage—
Tour, Journey, Voyage, Lounge, Ride, Walk,
Skim, Sketch, Excursion, Travel-talk—
For move you must! 'Tis now the rage,
The law and fashion of the Age.
If you but perch, where Dover tallies,
So strangely with the coast of Calais,
With a good glass and knowing look,
You'll soon get matter for a book!
Or else, in Gas-car, take your chance
Like that adventurous king of France,
Who, once, with twenty thousand men
Went up—and then came down again;
At least, he moved if nothing more:
And if there's nought left to explore,
Yet while your well-greased wheels keep spinning,
The traveller's honoured name you're winning,
And, snug as Jonas in the Whale,
You may loll back and dream a tale.
Move, or be moved—there's no protection,
Our Mother Earth has ta'en the infection—
(That rogue Copernicus, 'tis said
First put the whirring in her head,)

---

[1] *The Private Journal of Captain G. F. Lyon of the Mt. Hecla, during the recent voyage of discovery under Captain Parry*, was published by John Murray in 1824. In a letter dated May, 1823, Lucy Caroline Lamb writes to Murray:—'If there is yet time, do tell Captain Lyon, that I, and others far better than I am, are enchanted with his book.' *Memoirs . . . of John Murray*, 1891, i. 145.

THE DELINQUENT TRAVELLERS

A planet She, and can't endure
T'exist without her annual Tour:
The *name* were else a mere misnomer,
Since Planet is but Greek for *Roamer*.
The atmosphere, too, can do no less
Than ventilate her emptiness,
Bilks turn-pike gates, for no one cares,
And gives herself a thousand airs—
While streams and shopkeepers, we see,
Will have their run toward the sea—
And if, meantime, like old King Log,
Or ass with tether and a clog,
Must graze at home! to yawn and bray
'I guess we shall have rain to-day!
Nor clog nor tether can be worse
Than the dead palsy of the purse.
Money, I've heard a wise man say,
Makes herself wings and flys away:
Ah! would She take it in her head
To make a pair for me instead!
At all events, the Fancy's free,
No traveller so bold as she.
From Fear and Poverty released
I'll saddle Pegasus, at least,
And when she's seated to her mind,
I within I can mount behind:
And since this outward I, you know,
Must stay because he cannot go,
My fellow-travellers shall be they
Who go because they cannot stay—
Rogues, rascals, sharpers, blanks and prizes,
Delinquents of all sorts and sizes,
Fraudulent bankrupts, Knights burglarious,
And demireps of means precarious—
All whom Law thwarted, Arms or Arts,
Compel to visit foreign parts,
All hail! No compliments, I pray,
I'll follow where you lead the way!
But ere we cross the main once more,
Methinks, along my native shore,
Dismounting from my steed I'll stray
Beneath the cliffs of Dumpton Bay,[1]

---

[1] A coast village near Ramsgate. Coleridge passed some weeks at Ramsgate in the late autumn of 1824.

Where, Ramsgate and Broadstairs between,
Rude caves and grated doors are seen:
And here I'll watch till break of day,
(For Fancy in her magic might
Can turn broad noon to starless night!)
When lo! methinks a sudden band
Of smock-clad smugglers round me stand.
Denials, oaths, in vain I try,
At once they gag me for a spy,
And stow me in the boat hard by.
Suppose us fairly now afloat,
Till Boulogne mouth receives our Boat.
But, bless us! what a numerous band
Of cockneys anglicise the strand!
Delinquent bankrupts, leg-bail'd debtors,
Some for the news, and some for letters—
With hungry look and tarnished dress,
French shrugs and British surliness.
Sick of the country for their sake
Of them and France *French leave* I take—
And lo! a transport comes in view
I hear the merry motley crew,
Well skill'd in pocket to make entry,
Of Dieman's Land the elected Gentry,
And founders of Australian Races.—
The Rogues! I see it in their faces!
Receive me, Lads! I'll go with you,
Hunt the black swan and kangaroo,
And that New Holland we'll presume
Old England with some elbow-room.
Across the mountains we will roam,
And each man make himself a home:
Or, if old habits ne'er forsaking,
Like clock-work of the Devil's making,
Ourselves inveterate rogues should be,
We'll have a virtuous progeny;
And on the dunghill of our vices
Raise human pine-apples and spices.
Of all the children of John Bull
With empty heads and bellies full,
Who ramble East, West, North and South,
With leaky purse and open mouth,
In search of varieties exotic
The usefullest and most patriotic,

And merriest, too, believe me, Sirs!
Are your Delinquent Travellers!

1824.

WORK WITHOUT HOPE [1]

LINES COMPOSED 21ST FEBRUARY 1825

ALL Nature seems at work. Slugs leave their lair—
The bees are stirring—birds are on the wing—[2]
And Winter slumbering in the open air,
Wears on his smiling face a dream of Spring!
And I the while, the sole unbusy thing, 5
Nor honey make, nor pair, nor build, nor sing.

Yet well I ken the banks where amaranths blow,
Have traced the fount whence streams of nectar flow.
Bloom, O ye amaranths! bloom for whom ye may,
For me ye bloom not! Glide, rich streams, away! 10
With lips unbrightened, wreathless brow, I stroll:
And would you learn the spells that drowse my soul?
Work without Hope draws nectar in a sieve,
And Hope without an object cannot live.

1825.

---

[1] First printed in the *Bijou* for 1828: included in 1828, 1829, and 1834. These lines, as published in the *Bijou* for 1828, were an excerpt from an entry in a notebook, dated Feb. 21, 1825. They were preceded by a prose introduction, now for the first time printed, and followed by a metrical interpretation or afterthought which was first published in the Notes to the Edition of 1893.

[2] Compare the last stanza of George Herbert's *Praise*:—

O raise me thus! Poor Bees that work all day,
  Sting my delay,
Who have a work as well as they,
  And much, much more.

Work Without Hope—Title] Lines composed on a day in February. By S. T. Coleridge, Esq. *Bijou*: Lines composed on the 21st of February, 1827 *1828, 1829, 1834.*
1 Slugs] Snails *erased MS. S. T. C.*: Stags *1828, 1829, 1885.*
11 { With unmoist lip and wreathless brow I stroll
   { With lips unmoisten'd wreathless brow I stroll *MS. S. T. C.*

SANCTI DOMINICI PALLIUM[1]

A DIALOGUE BETWEEN POET AND FRIEND

FOUND WRITTEN ON THE BLANK LEAF AT THE BEGINNING OF BUTLER'S
'BOOK OF THE CHURCH' (1825)

POET

I NOTE the moods and feelings men betray,
And heed them more than aught they do or say;
The lingering ghosts of many a secret deed
Still-born or haply strangled in its birth;
These best reveal the smooth man's inward creed! 5
These mark the spot where lies the treasure—Worth!

Milner, made up of impudence and trick,[2]
With cloven tongue prepared to hiss and lick,
Rome's Brazen Serpent—boldly dares discuss
The roasting of thy heart, O brave John Huss! 10
And with grim triumph and a truculent glee[3]
Absolves anew the Pope-wrought perfidy,

---

[1] First published in the *Evening Standard*, May 21, 1827. 'The poem signed ΕΣΤΗΣΕ appeared likewise in the *St. James's Chronicle*.' See Letter of S. T. C. to J. Blanco White, dated Nov. 28, 1827. *Life*, 1845, i. 439, 440. First collected in 1834. I have amended the text of 1834 in lines 7, 17, 34, 39 in accordance with a MS. in the possession of the poet's granddaughter, Miss Edith Coleridge. The poem as published in 1834 and every subsequent edition (except 1907) is meaningless. Southey's *Book of the Church*, 1825, was answered by Charles Butler's *Book of the Roman Catholic Church*, 1825, and in an anonymous pamphlet by the Vicar Apostolic, Dr. John Milner, entitled *Merlin's Strictures*. Southey retaliated in his *Vindiciae Ecclesiae Anglicanae*, 1826. In the latter work he addresses Butler as 'an honourable and courteous opponent'—and contrasts his 'habitual urbanity' with the malignant and scurrilous attacks of that 'ill-mannered man', Dr. Milner. In the 'Dialogue' the poet reminds his 'Friend' Southey that Rome is Rome, a 'brazen serpent', charm she never so wisely. In the *Vindiciae* Southey devotes pp. 470-506 to an excursus on 'The Rosary'—the invention of St. Dominic. Hence the title—'Sancti Dominici Pallium'.

[2] These lines were written before this Prelate's decease. *Standard*, 1827.

[3] Trŭcŭlĕnt: a tribrach as the isochronous substitute for the Trochee — ⌣. N.B. If our accent, a *quality* of sound were actually equivalent to the *Quantity* in the Greek — ⌣ —, or dactyl — ⌣ ⌣ at least. But it is not so, accent shortens syllables: thus Spĭrĭt, sprite; Hŏnĕy, mŏnĕy, nŏbŏdy, &c. *MS. S. T. C.*

Sancti Dominici Pallium, &c. Title]—A dialogue written on a Blank Page of Butler's Book of the Roman Catholic Church. *Sd. 1827.*

7 Milner] —— *1834, 1852*: Butler *1893*.

> But through the clefts itself has made 5
> We likewise see Love's flashing blade,
> By rust consumed, or snapt in twain;
> And only hilt and stump remain.

?1825.

A CHARACTER[1]

> A BIRD, who for his other sins
> Had liv'd amongst the Jacobins;
> Though like a kitten amid rats,
> Or callow tit in nest of bats,
> He much abhorr'd all democrats; 5
> Yet nathless stood in ill report
> Of wishing ill to Church and Court,
> Tho' he'd nor claw, nor tooth, nor sting,
> And learnt to pipe God save the King;
> Tho' each day did new feathers bring, 10
> All swore he had a leathern wing;
> Nor polish'd wing, nor feather'd tail,
> Nor down-clad thigh would aught avail;
> And tho'—his tongue devoid of gall—
> He civilly assur'd them all:— 15
> 'A bird am I of Phoebus' breed,
> And on the sunflower cling and feed;
> My name, good Sirs, is Thomas Tit!'
> The bats would hail him Brother Cit,
> Or, at the furthest, cousin-german. 20

[1] First published in 1834. It is probable that the immediate provocation of these lines was the publication of Hazlitt's character-sketch of Coleridge in *The Spirit of the Age*, 1825, pp. 57-75. Lines 1-7, 49, 50, 84, 89 are quoted by J. Payne Collier (*An Old Man's Diary*, Oct. 20, 1833, Pt. IV, p. 56) from a MS. presented by Charles Lamb to Martin Burney. A fragmentary MS. with the lines in different order is in the British Museum.

---

5 clefts] slits *MS.*
6-8   We spy no less, too, that the Blade,
              Is cut away or snapt atwain
          And nought but Hilt or Stump remain. *MS.*

A Character—Title] A Trifle *MS. J. P. C.*

1 for] 'mongst *MS. B. M.*   2 amongst] among *J. P. C.*   3 amid] among *J. P. C.*   5 all] the *J. P. C.*   6 ill] bad *J. P. C.*   7 Of ill to Church as well as Court *J. P. C.*   11 had a] had but a *MS. B. M.*

At length the matter to determine,
He publicly denounced the vermin;
He spared the mouse, he praised the owl;
But bats were neither flesh nor fowl.
Blood-sucker, vampire, harpy, goul,   25
Came in full clatter from his throat,
Till his old nest-mates chang'd their note
To hireling, traitor, and turncoat,—
A base apostate who had sold
His very teeth and claws for gold;—   30
And then his feathers!—sharp the jest—
No doubt he feather'd well his nest!
A Tit indeed! aye, tit for tat—
With place and title, brother Bat,
We soon shall see how well he'll play   35
Count Goldfinch, or Sir Joseph Jay!'
Alas, poor Bird! and ill-bestarr'd—
Or rather let us say, poor Bard!
And henceforth quit the allegoric,
With metaphor and simile,   40
For simple facts and style historic:—
Alas, poor Bard! no gold had he;
Behind another's team he stept,
And plough'd and sow'd, while others reapt;
The work was his, but theirs the glory,   45
Sic vos non vobis, his whole story.
Besides, whate'er he wrote or said
Came from his heart as well as head;
And though he never left in lurch
His king, his country, or his church,   50
'Twas but to humour his own cynical
Contempt of doctrines Jacobinical;
To his own conscience only hearty,
'Twas but by chance he serv'd the party;—
The self-same things had said and writ,   55
Had Pitt been Fox, and Fox been Pitt;
Content his own applause to win,
Would never dash thro' thick and thin,
And he can make, so say the wise,
No claim who makes no sacrifice;—   60
And bard still less:—what claim had he,

22 denounced] disowned *MS. B. M.*   31 sharp] smoke *MS. B. M.*
36 Joseph] Judas *MS. B. M.*

A CHARACTER

Who swore it vex'd his soul to see
So grand a cause, so proud a realm,
With Goose and Goody at the helm;
Who long ago had fall'n asunder 65
But for their rivals' baser blunder,
The coward whine and Frenchified
Slaver and slang of the other side?—

Thus, his own whim his only bribe,
Our Bard pursued his old A. B. C. 70
Contented if he could subscribe
In fullest sense his name Ἔστησε;
('Tis Punic Greek for 'he hath stood!')
Whate'er the men, the cause was good;
And therefore with a right good will, 75
Poor fool, he fights their battles still.
Tush! squeak'd the Bats;—a mere bravado
To whitewash that base renegado;
'Tis plain unless you're blind or mad,
His conscience for the bays he barters;— 80
And true it is—as true as sad—
These circlets of green baize he had—
But then, alas! they were his garters!
Ah! silly Bard, unfed, untended,
His lamp but glimmer'd in its socket; 85
He lived unhonour'd and unfriended
With scarce a penny in his pocket;—
Nay—tho' he hid it from the many—
With scarce a pocket for his penny!

1825.

69-74   Yet still pursu'd thro' scoff and gibe
From A. to Z. his old A.B.C.
Content that he could still subscribe
In symbol just his name ΕΣΤΗΣΕ;
(In punic Greek that's He hath stood:)
Whate'er the men, the cause was good. *MS. B. M.*

84 Ah! silly bird and unregarded *J. P. C.*: Poor witless Bard, unfed, untended *MS. B. M.*   86 He liv'd unpraised, and unfriended *MS. B. M.*: unfriended] discarded *J. P. C.*   87 With scarce] Without *J. P. C.*

THE TWO FOUNTS[1]

STANZAS ADDRESSED TO A LADY ON HER RECOVERY WITH UNBLEMISHED LOOKS, FROM A SEVERE ATTACK OF PAIN

'Twas my last waking thought, how it could be
That thou, sweet friend, such anguish should'st endure;
When straight from Dreamland came a Dwarf, and he
Could tell the cause, forsooth, and knew the cure.

Methought he fronted me with peering look   5
Fix'd on my heart; and read aloud in game
The loves and griefs therein, as from a book:
And uttered praise like one who wished to blame.

In every heart (quoth he) since Adam's sin
Two Founts there are, of Suffering and of Cheer!   10
That to let forth, and this to keep within!
But she, whose aspect I find imaged here,

Of Pleasure only will to all dispense,
That Fount alone unlock, by no distress
Choked or turned inward, but still issue thence   15
Unconquered cheer, persistent loveliness.

As on the driving cloud the shiny bow,
That gracious thing made up of tears and light,
Mid the wild rack and rain that slants below
Stands smiling forth, unmoved and freshly bright;   20

As though the spirits of all lovely flowers,
Inweaving each its wreath and dewy crown,
Or ere they sank to earth in vernal showers,
Had built a bridge to tempt the angels down.

[1] First published in the *Annual Register* for 1827: reprinted in the *Bijou* for 1828: included in 1828, 1829, 1834. 'In Gilchrist's *Life of Blake* (1863, i. 337) it is stated that this poem was addressed to Mrs. Aders, the daughter of the engraver Raphael Smith.' *P. W.*, 1892, p. 642.

Title] Stanzas addressed to a Lady on her Recovery from a Severe attack of Pain *Annual Register*.

11 That—this] *That—this 1828, 1829*.   14 That] *That 1828, 1829*.
16-17 In a MS. dated 1826, the following stanza precedes stanza 5 of the text :—

      Was ne'er on earth seen beauty like to this,
        A concentrated satisfying sight!
      In its deep quiet, ask no further bliss—
        At once the form and substance of delight.

19-20   Looks forth upon the troubled air below
        Unmov'd, entire, inviolably bright. *MS. 1826.*

THE TWO FOUNTS

Even so, Eliza! on that face of thine, 25
On that benignant face, whose look alone
(The soul's translucence thro' her crystal shrine!)
Has power to soothe all anguish but thine own,

A beauty hovers still, and ne'er takes wing,
But with a silent charm compels the stern 30
And tort'ring Genius of the bitter spring,
To shrink aback, and cower upon his urn.

Who then needs wonder, if (no outlet found
In passion, spleen, or strife) the Fount of Pain
O'erflowing beats against its lovely mound, 35
And in wild flashes shoots from heart to brain?

Sleep, and the Dwarf with that unsteady gleam
On his raised lip, that aped a critic smile,
Had passed: yet I, my sad thoughts to beguile,
Lay weaving on the tissue of my dream; 40

Till audibly at length I cried, as though
Thou hadst indeed been present to my eyes,
O sweet, sweet sufferer; if the case be so,
I pray thee, be less good, less sweet, less wise!

In every look a barbéd arrow send, 45
On those soft lips let scorn and anger live!
Do any thing, rather than thus, sweet friend!
Hoard for thyself the pain, thou wilt not give!
1826.

CONSTANCY TO AN IDEAL OBJECT[1]

SINCE all that beat about in Nature's range,
Or veer or vanish; why should'st thou remain
The only constant in a world of change,
O yearning Thought! that liv'st but in the brain?
Call to the Hours, that in the distance play, 5
The faery people of the future day——

---

[1] There is no evidence as to date of composition. J. D. Campbell (1893, p. 635) believed that it ' was written at Malta'. Line 18 seems to imply that the poem was not written in England. On the other hand a comparison of ll. 9, 10 with a passage in the *Allegoric Vision*, which was re-written with large additions, and first published in 1817, suggests a much later date. The editors of 1852 include these lines among 'Poems written in Later Life', but the date (? 1826) now assigned is purely conjectural. First published in 1828: included in 1829 and 1834.

31 tort'ring] fost'ring *Annual Register, Bijou*. 44 less—less—less] *less—less—less 1828, 1829*. 47 any] *any 1828, 1829*.

Fond Thought! not one of all that shining swarm
Will breathe on thee with life-enkindling breath,
Till when, like strangers shelt'ring from a storm,[1]
Hope and Despair meet in the porch of Death!   10
Yet still thou haunt'st me; and though well I see,
She is not thou, and only thou art she,
Still, still as though some dear embodied Good,
Some living Love before my eyes there stood
With answering look a ready ear to lend,   15
I mourn to thee and say—'Ah! loveliest friend!
That this the meed of all my toils might be,
To have a home, an English home, and thee!'
Vain repetition! Home and Thou are one.
The peacefull'st cot, the moon shall shine upon,   20
Lulled by the thrush and wakened by the lark,
Without thee were but a becalmèd bark,
Whose Helmsman on an ocean waste and wide
Sits mute and pale his mouldering helm beside.

And art thou nothing? Such thou art, as when   25
The woodman winding westward up the glen
At wintry dawn, where o'er the sheep-track's maze
The viewless snow-mist weaves a glist'ning haze,
Sees full before him, gliding without tread,
An image[2] with a glory round its head;   30
The enamoured rustic worships its fair hues,
Nor knows he makes the shadow, he pursues!

? 1826.

---

[1] With lines 9, 10 J. D. Campbell compares, 'After a pause of silence: even thus, said he, like two strangers that have fled to the same shelter from the same storm, not seldom do Despair and Hope meet for the first time in the porch of Death.' *Allegoric Vision* (1798–1817); vide Appendices of this edition.

[2] This phenomenon, which the Author has himself experienced, and of which the reader may find a description in one of the earlier volumes of the *Manchester Philosophical Transactions*, is applied figuratively to the following passage in the *Aids to Reflection*:—

'Pindar's fine remark respecting the different effects of Music, on different characters, holds equally true of Genius—as many as are not delighted by it are disturbed, perplexed, irritated. The beholder either recognises it as a projected form of his own Being, that moves before him with a Glory round its head, or recoils from it as a Spectre.'—*Aids to Reflection* [1825], p. 220.

---

8 thee] *thee* 1828, 1829.   13 embodied] *embodied* 1828, 1829.
14 living] *living* 1828, 1829.   32 makes] *makes* 1828, 1829.

THE PANG MORE SHARP THAN ALL[1]

AN ALLEGORY

I

He too has flitted from his secret nest,
Hope's last and dearest child without a name!—
Has flitted from me, like the warmthless flame,
That makes false promise of a place of rest
To the tired Pilgrim's still believing mind;— 5
Or like some Elfin Knight in kingly court,
Who having won all guerdons in his sport,
Glides out of view, and whither none can find!

II

Yes! he hath flitted from me—with what aim,
Or why, I know not! 'Twas a home of bliss, 10
And he was innocent, as the pretty shame
Of babe, that tempts and shuns the menaced kiss,

---

[1] First published in 1834. With lines 36-43, and with the poem as a whole, compare the following fragments of uncertain date, which were first published in a note to the edition of 1893. Both the poem as completed and these fragments of earlier drafts seem to belong to the last decade of the poet's life. The water-mark of the scrap of paper on which these drafts are written is 1819, but the tone and workmanship of the verse suggest a much later date, possibly 1826.

> '—— into my Heart
> The magic Child as in a magic glass
> Transfused, and ah! he *left* within my Heart
> A loving Image and a counterpart.'
> '—— into my Heart
> As 'twere some magic Glass the magic child
> Transfused his Image and full counterpart;
> And then he left it like a Sylph beguiled
> To live and yearn and languish incomplete!
> Day following day, more rugged grows my path,
> There dwells a cloud before my heavy eyes;
> A Blank my Heart, and Hope is dead and buried,
> Yet the deep yearning will not die; but Love
> Clings on and cloathes the marrowless remains,
> Like the fresh moss that grows on dead men's bones,
> Quaint mockery! and fills its scarlet cups
> With the chill dewdamps of the Charnel House.
> O ask not for my Heart! my Heart is but
> The darksome vault where Hope lies dead and buried,
> And Love with Asbest Lamp bewails the Corse.'

From its twy-cluster'd hiding place of snow!
Pure as the babe, I ween, and all aglow
As the dear hopes, that swell the mother's breast—
Her eyes down gazing o'er her claspéd charge;—
Yet gay as that twice happy father's kiss,
That well might glance aside, yet never miss,
Where the sweet mark emboss'd so sweet a targe—
Twice wretched he who hath been doubly blest!

III

Like a loose blossom on a gusty night
He flitted from me—and has left behind
(As if to them his faith he ne'er did plight)
Of either sex and answerable mind
Two playmates, twin-births of his foster-dame:—
The one a steady lad (Esteem he hight)
And Kindness is the gentler sister's name.
Dim likeness now, though fair she be and good,
Of that bright Boy who hath us all forsook;—
But in his full-eyed aspect when she stood,
And while her face reflected every look,
And in reflection kindled—she became
So like Him, that almost she seem'd the same!

IV

Ah! he is gone, and yet will not depart!—
Is with me still, yet I from him exiled!
For still there lives within my secret heart
The magic image of the magic Child,
Which there he made up-grow by his strong art,
As in that crystal[1] orb—wise Merlin's feat,—
The wondrous 'World of Glass,' wherein inisled
All long'd-for things their beings did repeat;—
And there he left it, like a Sylph beguiled,
To live and yearn and languish incomplete!

V

Can wit of man a heavier grief reveal?
Can sharper pang from hate or scorn arise?—
Yes! one more sharp there is that deeper lies,
Which fond Esteem but mocks when he would heal.

---

[1] *Faerie Queene*, b. iii. c. 2, s. 19.

Yet neither scorn nor hate did it devise,
But sad compassion and atoning zeal!
One pang more blighting-keen than hope betray'd! 50
And this it is my woeful hap to feel,
When, at her Brother's hest, the twin-born Maid
With face averted and unsteady eyes,
Her truant playmate's faded robe puts on ;
And inly shrinking from her own disguise 55
Enacts the faery Boy that's lost and gone.
O worse than all ! O pang all pangs above
Is Kindness counterfeiting absent Love!
? 1825-6.

DUTY SURVIVING SELF-LOVE[1]

THE ONLY SURE FRIEND OF DECLINING LIFE

A SOLILOQUY

UNCHANGED within, to see all changed without,
Is a blank lot and hard to bear, no doubt.
Yet why at others' wanings should'st thou fret ?
Then only might'st thou feel a just regret,

---

[1] First published in 1828 : included in 1829 and 1834. The MS. of the first draft, dated Sept. 2, 1826, is preceded by the following introductory note :—

'QUESTION, ANSWER, AND SOLILOQUY.

And are *you* (said Alia to Constantius, on whose head sickness and sorrow had antedated Winter, ere yet the time of Vintage had passed), Are you the happier for your Philosophy ? And the smile of Constantius was as the light from a purple cluster of the vine, gleaming through snowflakes, as he replied, The Boons of Philosophy are of higher worth, than what you, O Alia, mean by Happiness. But I will not seem to evade the question—Am *I* the happier for my Philosophy ? The calmer at least and the less unhappy, answered Constantius, for it has enabled me to find that selfless Reason is the best Comforter, and only sure friend of declining Life. At this moment the sounds of a carriage followed by the usual bravura executed on the brazen knocker announced a morning visit: and Alia hastened to receive the party. Meantime the grey-haired philosopher, left to his own musings, continued playing with the thoughts that Alia and Alia's question had excited, till he murmured them to himself in half audible words, which at first casually, and then for the amusement of his ear, he *punctuated* with rhymes, without however conceiting that he had by these means changed them into poetry.'

---

4 When thy own body first the example set. *MS. S. T. C.*

460   DUTY SURVIVING SELF-LOVE

<pre>
    Hadst thou withheld thy love or hid thy light   5
    In selfish forethought of neglect and slight.
    O wiselier then, from feeble yearnings freed,
    While, and on whom, thou may'st—shine on! nor heed
    Whether the object by reflected light
    Return thy radiance or absorb it quite: 10
    And though thou notest from thy safe recess
    Old Friends burn dim, like lamps in noisome air,
    Love them for what they are; nor love them less,
    Because to thee they are not what they were.
1826.
</pre>

HOMELESS[1]

<pre>
      'O! CHRISTMAS Day, Oh! happy day!
         A foretaste from above,
      To him who hath a happy home
         And love returned from love!'

      O! Christmas Day, O gloomy day,   5
         The barb in Memory's dart,
      To him who walks alone through Life,
         The desolate in heart.
1826
</pre>

LINES[2]

SUGGESTED BY THE LAST WORDS OF BERENGARIUS

OB. ANNO DOM. 1088

No more 'twixt conscience staggering and the Pope
Soon shall I now before my God appear,

---

[1] First published in the *Literary Magnet*, January, 1827, p. 71. First collected in 1893. A transcript, possibly in Mrs. Gillman's handwriting, is inscribed on the fly-leaf of a copy of Bartram's *Travels in South Carolina* which Coleridge purchased in April 1818. J. D. Campbell prefixed the title 'Homeless', and assigned 1810 as a conjectural date. Attention was first called to publication in the *Literary Magnet* by Mr. Bertram Dobell in the *Athenaeum*.

[2] First published in the *Literary Souvenir*, 1827. The *Epitaphium Testamentarium* (vide *post*, p. 462) is printed in a footnote to the word 'Berengarius'. Included in 1828, 1829, and 1834.

5-11 *om. MS. S. T. C.*   8 While—on whom] *While—on whom 1828, 1829.*   9 object] Body *MS. S. T. C.*   13 are] *are 1828, 1829.*   14 thee—were] *thee—were 1828, 1829.*

Homeless—Title] An Impromptu on Christmas Day *L. M. 1827.*
4 from] for *L. M. 1827.*

LINES

By him to be acquitted, as I hope;
By him to be condemnéd, as I fear.—

REFLECTION ON THE ABOVE

Lynx amid moles! had I stood by thy bed,
Be of good cheer, meek soul! I would have said:
I see a hope spring from that humble fear.
All are not strong alike through storms to steer
Right onward. What? though dread of threatened death
And dungeon torture made thy hand and breath
Inconstant to the truth within thy heart!
That truth, from which, through fear, thou twice didst start,
Fear haply told thee, was a learned strife,
Or not so vital as to claim thy life:
And myriads had reached Heaven, who never knew
Where lay the difference 'twixt the false and true!

Ye, who secure 'mid trophies not your own,
Judge him who won them when he stood alone,
And proudly talk of recreant Berengare—
O first the age, and then the man compare!
That age how dark! congenial minds how rare!
No host of friends with kindred zeal did burn!
No throbbing hearts awaited his return!
Prostrate alike when prince and peasant fell,
He only disenchanted from the spell,
Like the weak worm that gems the starless night,
Moved in the scanty circlet of his light:
And was it strange if he withdrew the ray
That did but guide the night-birds to their prey?

The ascending day-star with a bolder eye
Hath lit each dew-drop on our trimmer lawn!
Yet not for this, if wise, shall we decry
The spots and struggles of the timid Dawn;
Lest so we tempt th' approaching Noon to scorn
The mists and painted vapours of our Morn.

?1826.

13 learned] *learned L. S.*   19 recreant] *recreant L. S., 1828, 1829.*
23 his] *his L. S.*   32 shall] *will L. S., 1828, 1829.*   34 th' approaching] *the coming L. S.*

EPITAPHIUM TESTAMENTARIUM[1]

Τὸ τοῦ ἜΣΤΗΣΕ τοῦ ἐπιθανοῦς Epitaphium testamentarium αὐτόγραφον.

Quae linquam, aut nihil, aut nihili, aut vix sunt mea. Sordes
Do Morti: reddo caetera, Christe! tibi.

1826.

Ἔρως ἀεὶ λάληθρος ἑταῖρος[2]

In many ways does the full heart reveal
The presence of the love it would conceal;
But in far more th' estrangéd heart lets know
The absence of the love, which yet it fain would shew.

1826.

THE IMPROVISATORE[3]

OR, 'JOHN ANDERSON, MY JO, JOHN'

Scene—A spacious drawing-room, with music-room adjoining.

Katharine. What are the words?
Eliza. Ask our friend, the Improvisatore; here he comes.

---

[1] First published in *Literary Souvenir* of 1827, as footnote to title of the *Lines Suggested by the Last Words of Berengarius*: included in *Literary Remains*, 1836, i. 60: first collected in 1844.

[2] This quatrain was prefixed as a motto to 'Prose in Rhyme; and Epigrams, Moralities, and Things without a Name', the concluding section of 'Poems' in the edition of 1828, 1829, vol. ii, pp. 75-117. It was prefixed to 'Miscellaneous Poems' in 1834, vol. ii, pp. 55-152, and to 'Poems written in Later Life', 1852, pp. 319-78.

[3] First published in the *Amulet* for 1828 (with a prose introduction entitled 'New Thoughts on Old Subjects; or Conversational Dialogues on Interests and Events of Common Life.' By S. T. Coleridge): included in 1829 and 1834. The text of 1834 is identical with that of the *Amulet*,

---

Title] ΕΠΙΤΑΦΙΟΝ ΑΥΤΟΓΡΑΠΤΟΝ *L. R., 1844*: ἐπιθανοῦς] ἐπιθανοὺς *L. S.*

The emendation ἐπιθανοῦς (i. e. moribund) was suggested by the Reader of Macmillan's edition of 1893. Other alternatives, e.g. ἐπιδευοῦς (the lacking), to the word as misprinted in the *Literary Souvenir* have been suggested, but there can be no doubt that what Coleridge intended to imply was that he was near his end.

Greek motto: Ἔρως ἀεὶ λάλος *MS. S. T. C.*

1-4 In many ways I own do we reveal.
   The Presence of the Love we would conceal,
   But in how many more do we let know
   The absence of the *Love* we found would show. *MS. S. T. C.*

Kate has a favour to ask of you, Sir; it is that you will repeat the ballad[1] that Mr. —— sang so sweetly.

Friend. It is in Moore's Irish Melodies; but I do not recollect the words distinctly. The moral of them, however, I take to be this:—

> Love would remain the same if true,
> When we were neither young nor new;
> Yea, and in all within the will that came,
> By the same proofs would show itself the same.

Eliz. What are the lines you repeated from Beaumont and Fletcher, which my mother admired so much? It begins with something about two vines so close that their tendrils intermingle.

Fri. You mean Charles' speech to Angelina, in *The Elder Brother*[2].

> We'll live together, like two neighbour vines,
> Circling our souls and loves in one another!
> We'll spring together, and we'll bear one fruit;
> One joy shall make us smile, and one grief mourn;
> One age go with us, and one hour of death
> Shall close our eyes, and one grave make us happy.

Kath. A precious boon, that would go far to reconcile one to old age—this love—*if* true! But is there any such true love?

Fri. I hope so.

Kath. But do you believe it?

Eliz. (*eagerly*). I am sure he does.

Fri. From a man turned of fifty, Katharine, I imagine, expects a less confident answer.

Kath. A more sincere one, perhaps.

Fri. Even though he should have obtained the nick-name of Improvisatore, by perpetrating charades and extempore verses at Christmas times?

Eliz. Nay, but be serious.

Fri. Serious! Doubtless. A grave personage of my years giving a Love-lecture to two young ladies, cannot well be otherwise. The difficulty, I suspect, would be for them to

---

1828, but the italics in the prose dialogue were not reproduced. They have been replaced in the text of the present issue. The title may have been suggested by L. E. L.'s *Improvisatrice* published in 1824.

[1] 'Believe me if all those endearing young charms.'

[2] See Beaumont and Fletcher, *The Elder Brother*, Act III, Scene v. In the original the lines are printed as prose. In line 1 of the quotation Coleridge has substituted 'neighbour' for 'wanton', and in line 6, 'close' for 'shut'.

remain so. It will be asked whether I am not the 'elderly gentleman' who sate 'despairing beside a clear stream', with a willow for his wig-block.

Eliz. Say another word, and we will call it downright affectation.

Kath. No! we will be affronted, drop a courtesy, and ask pardon for our presumption in expecting that Mr. —— would waste his sense on two insignificant girls.

Fri. Well, well, I will be serious. Hem! Now then commences the discourse; Mr. Moore's song being the text. Love, as distinguished from Friendship, on the one hand, and from the passion that too often usurps its name, on the other—

Lucius (*Eliza's brother, who had just joined the trio, in a whisper to the Friend*). But is not Love the union of both?

Fri. (*aside to Lucius*). He never loved who thinks so.

Eliz. Brother, we don't want *you*. There! Mrs. H. cannot arrange the flower vase without you. Thank you, Mrs. Hartman.

Luc. I'll have my revenge! I know what I will say!

Eliz. Off! Off! Now, dear Sir,—Love, you were saying—

Fri. Hush! *Preaching*, you mean, Eliza.

Eliz. (*impatiently*). Pshaw!

Fri. Well then, I was *saying* that Love, truly such, is itself not the most common thing in the world: and mutual love still less so. But that enduring personal attachment, so beautifully delineated by Erin's sweet melodist, and still more touchingly, perhaps, in the well-known ballad, 'John Anderson, my Jo, John,' in addition to a depth and constancy of character of no every-day occurrence, supposes a peculiar sensibility and tenderness of nature; a constitutional communicativeness and *utterancy* of heart and soul; a delight in the detail of sympathy, in the outward and visible signs of the sacrament within—to count, as it were, the pulses of the life of love. But above all, it supposes a soul which, even in the pride and summer-tide of life—even in the lustihood of health and strength, had felt oftenest and prized highest that which age cannot take away and which, in all our lovings, is *the* Love;——

Eliz. There is something *here* (*pointing to her heart*) that *seems* to understand you, but wants the *word* that would make it understand itself.

Kath. I, too, seem to *feel* what you mean. Interpret the **feeling** for us.

Fri. —— I mean that *willing* sense of the insufficingness of the *self* for itself, which predisposes a generous nature to see, in the total being of another, the supplement and completion of its own;—that quiet perpetual *seeking* which the presence of the beloved object modulates, not suspends, where the heart momently finds, and, finding, again seeks on;—lastly, when 'life's changeful orb has pass'd the full', a confirmed faith in the nobleness of humanity, thus brought home and pressed, as it were, to the very bosom of hourly experience; it supposes, I say, a heartfelt reverence for worth, not the less deep because divested of its solemnity by habit, by familiarity, by mutual infirmities, and even by a feeling of modesty which will arise in delicate minds, when they are conscious of possessing the same or the correspondent excellence in their own characters. In short, there must be a mind, which, while it feels the beautiful and the excellent in the beloved as its own, and by right of love appropriates it, can call Goodness its Playfellow; and dares make sport of time and infirmity, while, in the person of a thousand-foldly endeared partner, we feel for aged Virtue the caressing fondness that belongs to the Innocence of childhood, and repeat the same attentions and tender courtesies which had been dictated by the same affection to the same object when attired in feminine loveliness or in manly beauty.

Eliz. What a soothing—what an elevating idea!

Kath. If it be not only an *idea*.

Fri. At all events, these qualities which I have enumerated, are rarely found united in a single individual. How much more rare must it be, that two such individuals should meet together in this wide world under circumstances that admit of their union as Husband and Wife. A person may be highly estimable on the whole, nay, amiable as neighbour, friend, housemate—in short, in all the concentric circles of attachment save only the last and inmost; and yet from how many causes be estranged from the highest perfection in this! Pride, coldness, or fastidiousness of nature, worldly cares, an anxious or ambitious disposition, a passion for display, a sullen temper,— one or the other—too often proves 'the dead fly in the compost of spices', and any one is enough to unfit it for the precious balm of unction. For some mighty good sort of people, too, there is not seldom a sort of solemn saturnine, or, if you will, *ursine* vanity, that keeps itself alive by sucking the paws of its own self-importance. And as this high sense, or rather sensation of their own value is, for the most part, grounded on negative qualities, so they have no better means of preserving the same but by *negatives*—that is, by *not* doing or saying any thing, that might be put down for fond, silly, or nonsensical;—or (to use their own phrase) by *never forgetting themselves*, which some of their acquaintance are uncharitable enough to think the most worthless object they could be employed in remembering.

Eliz. (*in answer to a whisper from Katharine*). To a hair! He must have sate for it himself. Save me from such folks! But they are out of the question.

Fri. True! but the same effect is produced in thousands by the too general insensibility to a very important truth; this, namely, that the MISERY of human life is made up of large masses, each separated from the other by certain intervals. One year, the death of a child; years after, a failure in trade; after another longer or shorter interval, a daughter may have married unhappily;—in all but the singularly unfortunate, the integral parts that compose the sum total of the unhappiness of a man's life, are easily counted, and distinctly remembered. The HAPPINESS of life, on the contrary, is made up of minute fractions—the little, soon-forgotten charities of a kiss, a smile, a kind look, a heartfelt compliment in the disguise of playful raillery, and the countless other infinitesimals of pleasurable thought and genial feeling.

Kath. Well, Sir; you have said quite enough to make me despair of finding a 'John Anderson, my Jo, John', with whom to totter down the hill of life.

Fri. Not so! Good men are not, I trust, so much scarcer than good women, but that what another would find in you, you may hope to find in another. But well, however, may that boon be rare, the possession of which would be more than an adequate reward for the rarest virtue.

Eliz. Surely, he, who has described it so well, must have possessed it?

Fri. If he were worthy to have possessed it, and had believingly anticipated and not found it, how bitter the disappointment!

(*Then, after a pause of a few minutes*),

ANSWER, *ex improviso*

Yes, yes! that boon, life's richest treat
He had, or fancied that he had;
Say, 'twas but in his own conceit—
　　The fancy made him glad!

Crown of his cup, and garnish of his dish! 5
The boon, prefigured in his earliest wish,
The fair fulfilment of his poesy,
When his young heart first yearn'd for sympathy!
But e'en the meteor offspring of the brain
        Unnourished wane; 10
Faith asks her daily bread,
And Fancy must be fed!
Now so it chanced—from wet or dry,
It boots not how—I know not why—
She missed her wonted food; and quickly 15
Poor Fancy stagger'd and grew sickly.
Then came a restless state, 'twixt yea and nay,
His faith was fix'd, his heart all ebb and flow;
Or like a bark, in some half-shelter'd bay,
Above its anchor driving to and fro. 20

That boon, which but to have possess'd
In a *belief*, gave life a zest—
Uncertain both what it *had* been,
And if by error lost, or luck;
And what it *was*;—an evergreen 25
Which some insidious blight had struck,
Or annual flower, which, past its blow,
No vernal spell shall e'er revive;
Uncertain, and afraid to know,
  Doubts toss'd him to and fro: 30
Hope keeping Love, Love Hope alive,
Like babes bewildered in a snow,
That cling and huddle from the cold
In hollow tree or ruin'd fold.

Those sparkling colours, once his boast 35
    Fading, one by one away,
Thin and hueless as a ghost,
    Poor Fancy on her sick bed lay;
Ill at distance, worse when near,
Telling her dreams to jealous Fear! 40
Where was it then, the sociable sprite
That crown'd the Poet's cup and deck'd his dish!
Poor shadow cast from an unsteady wish,
Itself a substance by no other right
But that it intercepted Reason's light: 45

It dimm'd his eye, it darken'd on his brow,
A peevish mood, a tedious time, I trow!
   Thank Heaven! 'tis not so now.

O bliss of blissful hours!
The boon of Heaven's decreeing,
While yet in Eden's bowers
Dwelt the first husband and his sinless mate!
The one sweet plant, which, piteous Heaven agreeing,
They bore with them thro' Eden's closing gate!
Of life's gay summer tide the sovran Rose!
Late autumn's Amaranth, that more fragrant blows
When Passion's flowers all fall or fade;
If this were ever his, in outward being,
Or but his own true love's projected shade,
Now that at length by certain proof he knows,
That whether real or a magic show,
Whate'er it *was*, it *is* no longer so;
Though heart be lonesome, Hope laid low,
Yet, Lady! deem him not unblest:
The certainty that struck Hope dead,
Hath left Contentment in her stead:
   And that is next to Best!
1827.

TO MARY PRIDHAM[1]

[AFTERWARDS MRS. DERWENT COLERIDGE]

DEAR tho' unseen! tho' I have left behind
Life's gayer views and all that stirs the mind,
Now I revive, Hope making a new start,
Since I have heard with most believing heart,
That all my glad eyes would grow bright to see,
My Derwent hath found realiz'd in thee,

---

[1] First published in 1893. Lines 7-10 are borrowed from lines 5-8 of the 'Answer *ex improviso*', which forms part of the *Improvisatore* (ll. 7, 8 are transposed). An original MS. is inscribed on the first page of an album presented to Mrs. Derwent Coleridge on her marriage, by her husband's friend, the Reverend John Moultrie. The editor of *P. W.*, 1893, printed from another MS. dated Grove, Highgate, 15th October, 1827.

Title] To Mary S. Pridham *MS. S. T. C.*
1-3 Dear tho' unseen! tho' hard has been my lot
    And rough my path thro' life, I murmur not—
    Rather rejoice— *MS. S. T. C.*
5 That all this shaping heart has yearned to see *MS. S. T. C.*

TO MARY PRIDHAM

The boon prefigur'd in his earliest wish
Crown of his cup and garnish of his dish!
The fair fulfilment of his poesy,
When his young heart first yearn'd for sympathy! 10
Dear tho' unseen! unseen, yet long portray'd!
A Father's blessing on thee, gentle Maid!

S. T. COLERIDGE.

16*th October* 1827.

ALICE DU CLOS[1]

OR THE FORKED TONGUE

A BALLAD

'One word with two meanings is the traitor's shield and shaft: and a slit tongue be his blazon!'—*Caucasian Proverb*.

'THE Sun is not yet risen,
But the dawn lies red on the dew:
Lord Julian has stolen from the hunters away,
Is seeking, Lady! for you.
Put on your dress of green, 5
Your buskins and your quiver;
Lord Julian is a hasty man,
Long waiting brook'd he never.
I dare not doubt him, that he means
To wed you on a day, 10
Your lord and master for to be,
And you his lady gay.
O Lady! throw your book aside!
I would not that my Lord should chide.'

Thus spake Sir Hugh the vassal knight 15
To Alice, child of old Du Clos,

---

[1] First published in 1834. The date of composition cannot be ascertained. The MS., an early if not a first draft, is certainly of late date. The water-marks of the paper (Bath Post) are 1822 and 1828. There is a second draft (*MS. b*) of lines 97–112. Line 37, 'Dan Ovid's mazy tale of loves,' may be compared with line 100 of *The Garden of Boccaccio*, 'Peers Ovid's Holy Book of Love's sweet smart,' and it is probable that *Alice Du Clos* was written about the same time, 1828–9. In line 91 'Ellen' is no doubt a slip of the pen for 'Alice'.

---

8 his] the *MS. S. T. C.*   his] the *MS. S. T. C.*
Title] Alice Du Clós: or &c. *MS.*

ALICE DU CLOS

As spotless fair, as airy light
  As that moon-shiny doe,
The gold star on its brow, her sire's ancestral crest
For ere the lark had left his nest,
  She in the garden bower below
Sate loosely wrapt in maiden white,
Her face half drooping from the sight,
  A snow-drop on a tuft of snow!

O close your eyes, and strive to see
The studious maid, with book on knee,—
  Ah! earliest-open'd flower;
While yet with keen unblunted light
The morning star shone opposite
  The lattice of her bower—
Alone of all the starry host,
  As if in prideful scorn
Of flight and fear he stay'd behind,
  To brave th' advancing morn.

O! Alice could read passing well,
  And she was conning then
Dan Ovid's mazy tale of loves,
  And gods, and beasts, and men.

The vassal's speech, his taunting vein,
It thrill'd like venom thro' her brain;
  Yet never from the book
She rais'd her head, nor did she deign
  The knight a single look.

'Off, traitor friend! how dar'st thou fix
  Thy wanton gaze on me?
And why, against my earnest suit,
  Does Julian send by thee?

19-25   Her sires had chosen for their Crest
      A star atwixt its brow,
   For she, already up and drest
    Sate in the garden bower below.
    For she enwrapt in } Maiden white
    Enwrapt in robe of }
     { face half drooping
  Her { ~~visage drooping~~   from the sight
    A snow-drop in a tuft of snow
  Ere the first lark had left the nest
    Sate in the garden bower below. *MS. erased.*

ALICE DU CLOS

He bit his lip, he wrung his glove,
He look'd around, he look'd above,
  But pretext none could find or frame.
Alas! alas! and well-a-day!
It grieves me sore to think, to say,   110
That names so seldom meet with Love,
  Yet Love wants courage without a name!

Straight from the forest's skirt the trees
  O'er-branching, made an aisle,
Where hermit old might pace and chaunt   115
  As in a minster's pile.

From underneath its leafy screen,
  And from the twilight shade,
You pass at once into a green,
  A green and lightsome glade.   120

And there Lord Julian sate on steed;
  Behind him, in a round,
Stood knight and squire, and menial train;
Against the leash the greyhounds strain;
  The horses paw'd the ground.   125

When up the alley green, Sir Hugh
  Spurr'd in upon the sward,
And mute, without a word, did he
  Fall in behind his lord.

Lord Julian turn'd his steed half round,—   130
  'What! doth not Alice deign
To accept your loving convoy, knight?
Or doth she fear our woodland sleight,
  And join us on the plain?'

With stifled tones the knight replied,   135
And look'd askance on either side,—
  'Nay, let the hunt proceed!—
The Lady's message that I bear,
I guess would scantly please your ear,
  And less deserves your heed.   140

---

107 He look'd far round *MS. b*.   110 sore] sair *MS. b, MS. erased*.
111 Tho' names too seldom *MS. b*.   122 With all his gay hunt round *MS*.
126 When] And *MS*.   128 And dark of Brow, without a word *MS*.
135 stifled] muttering *MS. erased*.   136 And Look askance *MS*.: Yet not unheard *MS. erased*.

ALICE DU CLOS

'You sent betimes. Not yet unbarr'd
    I found the middle door;—
Two stirrers only met my eyes,
    Fair Alice, and one more.

'I came unlook'd for; and, it seem'd,   145
    In an unwelcome hour;
And found the daughter of Du Clos
    Within the lattic'd bower.

'But hush! the rest may wait. If lost,
    No great loss, I divine;   150
And idle words will better suit
    A fair maid's lips than mine.'

'God's wrath! speak out, man,' Julian cried,
    O'ermaster'd by the sudden smart;—
And feigning wrath, sharp, blunt, and rude,   155
The knight his subtle shift pursued.—
'Scowl not at me; command my skill,
To lure your hawk back, if you will,
    But not a woman's heart.

'"Go! (said she) tell him,—slow is sure;   160
    Fair speed his shafts to-day!
I follow here a stronger lure,
    And chase a gentler prey."

'The game, pardie, was full in sight,
That then did, if I saw aright,   165
    The fair dame's eyes engage;
For turning, as I took my ways,
I saw them fix'd with steadfast gaze
    Full on her wanton page.'

The last word of the traitor knight   170
    It had but entered Julian's ear,—

153-7
    God's wrath! speak out! { Lord Julian cry'd
                                          { What mean'st thou man?
    { Recoiling with a start
    { Cried Julian with a start.
           { well-feign'd anger
    With { feign'd resentment blunt and rude
    Sir Hugh his deep revenge pursued
    Why scowl at me? Command my skill. *MS. erased (first draft).*
159 She bade me tell you *MS. erased.*   167 For as she clos'd her scoffing phrase *MS. erased.*

From two o'erarching oaks between,
With glist'ning helm-like cap is seen,
  Borne on in giddy cheer,

A youth, that ill his steed can guide· 175
Yet with reverted face doth ride,
  As answering to a voice,
That seems at once to laugh and chide—
'Not mine, dear mistress,' still he cried,
  ''Tis this mad filly's choice.' 180

With sudden bound, beyond the boy,
See! see! that face of hope and joy,
  That regal front! those cheeks aglow!
Thou needed'st but the crescent sheen,
A quiver'd Dian to have been, 185
  Thou lovely child of old Du Clos!

Dark as a dream Lord Julian stood,
Swift as a dream, from forth the wood,
  Sprang on the plighted Maid!
With fatal aim, and frantic force, 190
The shaft was hurl'd!—a lifeless corse,
Fair Alice from her vaulting horse,
  Lies bleeding on the glade.

?1828.

LOVE'S BURIAL-PLACE[1]

Lady. If Love be dead—
  Poet. And I aver it!
Lady. Tell me, Bard! where Love lies buried?
  Poet. Love lies buried where 'twas born:
Oh, gentle dame! think it no scorn 5
If, in my fancy, I presume
To call thy bosom poor Love's Tomb.

---

[1] First published in 1828: included in the *Amulet*, 1833, as the first of 'Three Scraps', and in 1852. The present text is that of the *Amulet*, 1833.

173-4   And who from twixt those opening Trees
           Pricks on with laughing cheer *MS. erased (first draft).*

Love's Burial-Place—Title] The Alienated Mistress: A Madrigal (From an unfinished Melodrama) *1828, 1852.*

1-3 *Lady.* If Love be dead (and you aver it!)
       Tell me Bard! where Love lies buried. *1828, 1852.*

5 Ah faithless nymph *1828, 1852.*   7 call] name *1828, 1852.*

476   LOVE'S BURIAL-PLACE

    And on that tomb to read the line:—
    ' Here lies a Love that once seem'd mine,
    But caught a chill, as I divine,   10
    And died at length of a Decline.'
1828.

LINES[1]

TO A COMIC AUTHOR, ON AN ABUSIVE REVIEW

WHAT though the chilly wide-mouth'd quacking chorus
From the rank swamps of murk Review-land croak:
So was it, neighbour, in the times before us,
When Momus, throwing on his Attic cloak,
Romp'd with the Graces; and each tickled Muse   5
(That Turk, Dan Phœbus, whom bards call divine,
Was married to—at least, he kept—all nine)
Fled, but still with reverted faces ran;
Yet, somewhat the broad freedoms to excuse,
They had allured the audacious Greek to use,   10
Swore they mistook him for their own good man.
This Momus—Aristophanes on earth
Men call'd him—maugre all his wit and worth,

---

[1] First published in *Friendship's Offering*, 1834, as No. III of 'Light-heartednesses in Rhyme': included in 1834.

---

9 seem'd] was *1828, 1852*.   10 caught] took *1828, 1852*.

Lines to a Comic Author, &c.—Title] To a Comic Author on an abusive review of his Aristophanes *MS*.

1 *foll.*   They fled;—
    Friend yet unknown! What tho' a brainless rout
    Usurp the sacred title of the Bard—
    What tho' the chilly wide-mouth'd chorus
    From Styx or Lethe's oozy Channel croak:
    So was it, Peter, in the times before us
    When Momus throwing on his Attic cloak
    Romp'd with the Graces and each tickled Muse
    The plighted coterie of Phœbus he bespoke
    And laughing with reverted faces ran,
    And somewhat the broad freedom to excuse
    They had allow'd the audacious Greek to use
    Swore they mistook him for their own good man!
    If the good dulness be the home of worth
    Duller than Frogs co-ax'd, or Jeffrey writ
    We, too, will Aristoff (*sic*) and welcome it—   *First draft MS. B. M.*

7 kept] kept *F.O. 1834*.

Was croak'd and gabbled at. How, then, should you,
Or I, friend, hope to 'scape the skulking crew?
No! laugh, and say aloud, in tones of glee,
'I hate the quacking tribe, and they hate me!'
? 1825.

COLOGNE[1]

In Köhln[2], a town of monks and bones[3],
And pavements fang'd with murderous stones
And rags, and hags, and hideous wenches;
I counted two and seventy stenches,
All well defined, and several stinks!
Ye Nymphs that reign o'er sewers and sinks,
The river Rhine, it is well known,
Doth wash your city of Cologne;
But tell me, Nymphs, what power divine
Shall henceforth wash the river Rhine[4]?
1828.

ON MY JOYFUL DEPARTURE[5]

FROM THE SAME CITY

As I am a Rhymer[6],
And now at least a merry one,
Mr. Mum's Rudesheimer[7]
And the church of St. Geryon
Are the two things alone
That deserve to be known
In the body-and-soul-stinking town of Cologne.
1828.

---

[1] First published in *Friendship's Offering*, 1834, as No. IV of 'Light-heartednesses in Rhyme'. It follows the lines 'On my joyful Departure', &c., and is headed 'Expectoration the Second'. First collected in 1834.

[2] Köhln] Coln *F.O.* The German Name of Cologne. *F.O.*

[3] Of the eleven thousand virgin Martyrs. *F.O.*

[4] As Necessity is the mother of Invention, and extremes beget each other, the facts above recorded may explain how this *ancient* town (which, alas! as sometimes happens with venison, *has been kept too long*), came to be *the birthplace of the most fragrant of spirituous fluids*, the EAU DE COLOGNE. *F.O.*

[5] First published in *Friendship's Offering*, 1834, with the heading 'An Expectoration, or Splenetic Extempore, on my joyful departure from the City of Cologne'. First collected in 1834.

[6] As I am Rhymer, *F.O.*, *P.W.*, 1834, 1893. The 'a' is inserted by Coleridge on a page of *F.O.*, 1834; the correction was not adopted in *P.W.*, 1834.

[7] The *apotheosis* of Rhenish wine.

THE GARDEN OF BOCCACCIO [1]

Of late, in one of those most weary hours,
When life seems emptied of all genial powers,
A dreary mood, which he who ne'er has known
May bless his happy lot, I sate alone;
And, from the numbing spell to win relief,   5
Call'd on the Past for thought of glee or grief.
In vain! bereft alike of grief and glee,
I sate and cow'r'd o'er my own vacancy!
And as I watch'd the dull continuous ache,
Which, all else slumb'ring, seem'd alone to wake;   10
O Friend [2]! long wont to notice yet conceal,
And soothe by silence what words cannot heal,
I but half saw that quiet hand of thine
Place on my desk this exquisite design.
Boccaccio's Garden and its faery,   15
The love, the joyaunce, and the gallantry!
An Idyll, with Boccaccio's spirit warm,
Framed in the silent poesy of form.

Like flocks adown a newly-bathéd steep
  Emerging from a mist: or like a stream   20
Of music soft that not dispels the sleep,
  But casts in happier moulds the slumberer's dream,
Gazed by an idle eye with silent might
The picture stole upon my inward sight.
A tremulous warmth crept gradual o'er my chest,   25
As though an infant's finger touch'd my breast.
And one by one (I know not whence) were brought
All spirits of power that most had stirr'd my thought
In selfless boyhood, on a new world tost
Of wonder, and in its own fancies lost;   30
Or charm'd my youth, that, kindled from above,
Loved ere it loved, and sought a form for love;
Or lent a lustre to the earnest scan
Of manhood, musing what and whence is man!
Wild strain of Scalds, that in the sea-worn caves   35
Rehearsed their war-spell to the winds and waves;
Or fateful hymn of those prophetic maids,

---

[1] First published in *The Keepsake* for 1829, to accompany a plate by Stothard: included in 1829 and 1834. The variant of lines 49-56, probably a fragment of some earlier unprinted poem, is inserted in one of Coleridge's Notebooks.   [2] Mrs. Gillman.

That call'd on Hertha in deep forest glades;
Or minstrel lay, that cheer'd the baron's feast;
Or rhyme of city pomp, of monk and priest, 40
Judge, mayor, and many a guild in long array,
To high-church pacing on the great saint's day:
And many a verse which to myself I sang,
That woke the tear, yet stole away the pang
Of hopes, which in lamenting I renew'd: 45
And last, a matron now, of sober mien,
Yet radiant still and with no earthly sheen,
Whom as a faery child my childhood woo'd
Even in my dawn of thought—Philosophy;
Though then unconscious of herself, pardie, 50
She bore no other name than Poesy;
And, like a gift from heaven, in lifeful glee,
That had but newly left a mother's knee,
Prattled and play'd with bird and flower, and stone,
As if with elfin playfellows well known, 55
And life reveal'd to innocence alone.

Thanks, gentle artist! now I can descry
Thy fair creation with a mastering eye,
And all awake! And now in fix'd gaze stand,
Now wander through the Eden of thy hand; 60
Praise the green arches, on the fountain clear
See fragment shadows of the crossing deer;
And with that serviceable nymph I stoop,
The crystal, from its restless pool, to scoop.
I see no longer! I myself am there, 65
Sit on the ground-sward, and the banquet share.
'Tis I, that sweep that lute's love-echoing strings,
And gaze upon the maid who gazing sings:
Or pause and listen to the tinkling bells
From the high tower, and think that there she dwells.
With old Boccaccio's soul I stand possest, 71
And breathe an air like life, that swells my chest.
The brightness of the world, O thou once free,

49-56   And there was young Philosophy
        Unconscious of herself, pardie;
        And now she hight poesy,
        And like a child in playful glee
        Prattles and plays with flower and stone,
        As youth's fairy playfellows
        Revealed to Innocence alone. *MS. S. T. C.*

59 all] *all Keepsake, 1829.*

And always fair, rare land of courtesy!
O Florence! with the Tuscan fields and hills 75
And famous Arno, fed with all their rills;
Thou brightest star of star-bright Italy!
Rich, ornate, populous,—all treasures thine,
The golden corn, the olive, and the vine.
Fair cities, gallant mansions, castles old, 80
And forests, where beside his leafy hold
The sullen boar hath heard the distant horn,
And whets his tusks against the gnarléd thorn;
Palladian palace with its storied halls;
Fountains, where Love lies listening to their falls; 85
Gardens, where flings the bridge its airy span,
And Nature makes her happy home with man;
Where many a gorgeous flower is duly fed
With its own rill, on its own spangled bed,
And wreathes the marble urn, or leans its head, 90
A mimic mourner, that with veil withdrawn
Weeps liquid gems, the presents of the dawn;—
Thine all delights, and every muse is thine;
And more than all, the embrace and intertwine
Of all with all in gay and twinkling dance! 95
Mid gods of Greece and warriors of romance,
See! Boccace sits, unfolding on his knees
The new-found roll of old Maeonides;[1]
But from his mantle's fold, and near the heart,
Peers Ovid's Holy Book of Love's sweet smart![2] 100

---

[1] Boccaccio claimed for himself the glory of having first introduced the works of Homer to his countrymen.

[2] I know few more striking or more interesting proofs of the overwhelming influence which the study of the Greek and Roman classics exercised on the judgments, feelings, and imaginations of the literati ot Europe at the commencement of the restoration of literature, than the passage in the *Filocopo* of Boccaccio, where the sage instructor, Racheo, as soon as the young prince and the beautiful girl Biancofiore had learned their letters, sets them to study the Holy Book, Ovid's Art of Love. 'Incominciò Racheo a mettere il suo [officio] in esecuzione con intera sollecitudine. E loro, in breve tempo, insegnato a conoscer le lettere, fece leggere il santo libro d'Ovvidio, [! ! *S. T. C.*] nel quale il sommo poeta mostra, come i santi fuochi di Venere si debbano ne' freddi cuori con sollecitudine accendere.' ['Deeply interesting—but observe, p. 63, ll. 33–5 [*loc. cit.*], The *holy Book*—Ovid's Art of Love!! This is not the result of mere Immorality :—

Multum, Multum
Hic jacet sepultum.'

MS. note on the fly-leaf of S. T. C.'s copy of vol. i of Boccaccio's *Opere*, 1723.]

O all-enjoying and all-blending sage,
Long be it mine to con thy mazy page,
Where, half conceal'd, the eye of fancy views
Fauns, nymphs, and wingéd saints, all gracious to thy muse!

Still in thy garden let me watch their pranks, 105
And see in Dian's vest between the ranks
Of the trim vines, some maid that half believes
The vestal fires, of which her lover grieves,
With that sly satyr peeping through the leaves!
1828.

LOVE, HOPE, AND PATIENCE IN EDUCATION [1]

O'er wayward childhood would'st thou hold firm rule,
And sun thee in the light of happy faces;
Love, Hope, and Patience, these must be thy graces,
And in thine own heart let them first keep school.
For as old Atlas on his broad neck places 5
Heaven's starry globe, and there sustains it;—so
Do these upbear the little world below
Of Education,—Patience, Love, and Hope.

[1] First published in *The Keepsake* for 1830: included in *P. W.*, 1834, iii. 331. An MS. version was forwarded to W. Sotheby in an unpublished letter of July 12, 1829. A second MS., dated July 1, 1829, is inscribed in an album now in the Editor's possession, which belonged to Miss Emily Trevenen (the author of *Little Derwent's Breakfast*, 1839). With regard to the variant of ll. 24–6, vide *infra*, Coleridge writes (Letter of July 12, 1829):—'They were struck out by the author, not because he thought them bad lines in themselves (quamvis Della Cruscam fortasse nimis redolere videantur), but because they diverted and retarded the stream of the thought, and injured the organic unity of the composition. *Più nel uno* is Francesco de Sallez' brief and happy definition of the beautiful, and the shorter the poem the more indispensable is it that the *Più* should not overlay the *Uno*, that the unity should be evident. But to sacrifice the *gratification*, the sting of *pleasure*, from a fine *passage* to the *satisfaction*, the sense of *complacency* arising from the contemplation of a symmetrical *Whole* is among the last conquests achieved by men of genial powers.'

---

108 vestal] *vestal Keepsake, 1829*.

Title] Lines in a Lady's Album in answer to her question respecting the accomplishments most desirable in the Mistress or Governess of a Preparatory School *Letter, July 1829* : The Poet's Answer, To a Lady's Question respecting the accomplishments most desirable in an instructress of Children *Keepsake, 1830*.

2 And] Yet *Letter, 1829*.   3 thy] *thy Keepsake*.   4 keep school] *keep school Keepsake*.

Methinks, I see them group'd in seemly show,
The straiten'd arms upraised, the palms aslope,   10
And robes that touching as adown they flow,
Distinctly blend, like snow emboss'd in snow.

O part them never! If Hope prostrate lie,
   Love too will sink and die.
But Love is subtle, and doth proof derive   15
From her own life that Hope is yet alive;
And bending o'er, with soul-transfusing eyes,
And the soft murmurs of the mother dove,
Woos back the fleeting spirit, and half supplies;—
Thus Love repays to Hope what Hope first gave to Love.

Yet haply there will come a weary day,   21
   When overtask'd at length
Both Love and Hope beneath the load give way.
Then with a statue's smile, a statue's strength,
Stands the mute sister, Patience, nothing loth,   25
And both supporting does the work of both.

1829.

TO MISS A. T.[1]

Verse, pictures, music, thoughts both grave and gay,
Remembrances of dear-loved friends away,
On spotless page of virgin white displayed,
Such should thine Album be, for such art thou, sweet maid!

1829.

First published in *Essays on His Own Times*, 1850, iii. 998 with the title 'To Miss A. T.' First collected in 1893, with the title 'In Miss E. Trevenen's Album'. 'Miss A. T.' may have been a misprint for Miss E. T., but there is no MS. authority for the title prefixed in 1893.

9-11   Methinks I see them now, the triune group,
   With straiten'd arms uprais'd, the Palms aslope
   Robe touching Robe beneath, and blending as they flow.
   Letter, July 1829.

15 doth] will *Keepsake, 1833.*

24-6   Then like a Statue with a Statue's strength,
   And with a Smile, the Sister Fay of those
      Who at meek Evening's Close
      To teach our Grief repose,
   Their freshly-gathered store of Moonbeams wreath
   On Marble Lips, a Chantrey has made breathe.
   Letter, July 1829.

REASON [1]

['Finally, what is Reason? You have often asked me : and this is my answer':—]

WHENE'ER the mist, that stands 'twixt God and thee,
Defecates to a pure transparency,
That intercepts no light and adds no stain—
There Reason is, and then begins her reign!

But alas! 5
—— 'tu stesso, ti fai grosso
Col falso immaginar, sì che non vedi
Ciò che vedresti, se l'avessi scosso.'

      Dante, *Paradiso*, Canto i.
1830.

SELF-KNOWLEDGE [2]

—E coelo descendit γνῶθι σεαυτόν.—JUVENAL, xi. 27.

Γνῶθι σεαυτόν!—and is this the prime
And heaven-sprung adage of the olden time!—
Say, canst thou make thyself?—Learn first that trade;—
Haply thou mayst know what thyself had made.
What hast thou, Man, that thou dar'st call thine own?— 5
What is there in thee, Man, that can be known?—
Dark fluxion, all unfixable by thought,
A phantom dim of past and future wrought,
Vain sister of the worm,—life, death, soul, clod—
Ignore thyself, and strive to know thy God! 10

1832.

---

[1] First published as the conclusion of *On the Constitution of the Church and State*, 1830, p. 227. First collected, *P. and D. W.*, 1877–80, ii. 374.
[2] First published in 1834.

Self-knowledge—Title] The heading 'Self-knowledge' appears first in 1893.

FORBEARANCE[1]

Beareth all things.—1 Cor. xiii. 7.

Gently I took that which ungently came,[2]
And without scorn forgave:—Do thou the same.
A wrong done to thee think a cat's-eye spark
Thou wouldst not see, were not thine own heart dark.
Thine own keen sense of wrong that thirsts for sin,　　5
Fear that—the spark self-kindled from within,
Which blown upon will blind thee with its glare,
Or smother'd stifle thee with noisome air.
Clap on the extinguisher, pull up the blinds,
And soon the ventilated spirit finds　　10
Its natural daylight. If a foe have kenn'd,
Or worse than foe, an alienated friend,
A rib of dry rot in thy ship's stout side,
Think it God's message, and in humble pride
With heart of oak replace it;—thine the gains—　　15
Give him the rotten timber for his pains!

? 1832.

LOVE'S APPARITION AND EVANISHMENT[3]

AN ALLEGORIC ROMANCE

Like a lone Arab, old and blind,
Some caravan had left behind,

---

[1] First published in 1834.
[2] Compare Spenser's *Shepherd's Calendar* (Februarie):—

'Ne ever was to Fortune foeman,
But gently took that ungently came.'

[3] Lines 1–28 were first published in *Friendship's Offering* for 1834, signed and dated 'S. T. Coleridge, August 1833': included in *P. W.*, 1834. Lines 29–32 were first added as 'L'Envoy' in 1852. J. D. Campbell in a note to this poem (1893, p. 644) prints an expanded version of these lines, which were composed on April 24, 1824, 'as Coleridge says, "without taking my pen off the paper"'. The same lines were sent in a letter to Allsop, April 27, 1824 (*Letters, &c.*, 1836, ii. 174–5) with a single variant (line 3) 'uneclips'd' for 'unperturb'd'. In the draft of April 24, four lines were added, and of these an alternative version was published in *P. W.*, 1834, with the heading 'Desire' (vide *ante*, p. 485). For an earlier draft in S. T. C.'s handwriting vide Appendices of this edition.

Forbearance—Title] The heading 'Forbearance' appears first in 1893.

LOVE'S APPARITION AND EVANISHMENT

Who sits beside a ruin'd well,
Where the shy sand-asps bask and swell;
And now he hangs his agéd head aslant,
And listens for a human sound—in vain!
And now the aid, which Heaven alone can grant,
Upturns his eyeless face from Heaven to gain;—
Even thus, in vacant mood, one sultry hour,
Resting my eye upon a drooping plant,
With brow low-bent, within my garden-bower,
I sate upon the couch of camomile;
And—whether 'twas a transient sleep, perchance,
Flitted across the idle brain, the while
I watch'd the sickly calm with aimless scope,
In my own heart; or that, indeed a trance,
Turn'd my eye inward—thee, O genial Hope,
Love's elder sister! thee did I behold,
Drest as a bridesmaid, but all pale and cold,
With roseless cheek, all pale and cold and dim,
  Lie lifeless at my feet!
And then came Love, a sylph in bridal trim,
  And stood beside my seat;
She bent, and kiss'd her sister's lips,
  As she was wont to do;—
Alas! 'twas but a chilling breath
Woke just enough of life in death
  To make Hope die anew.

L'ENVOY

In vain we supplicate the Powers above;
There is no resurrection for the Love
That, nursed in tenderest care, yet fades away
In the chill'd heart by gradual self-decay.
  1833.

4 Where basking Dipsads* hiss and swell *F. O. 1834.*

  * The Asps of the sand-desert, anciently named Dipsads.

7 And now] Anon *F. O. 1834.*   14 Flitting across the idle sense the while *F. O. 1834.*   27 That woke enough *F. O. 1834.*

29-32   Idly we supplicate the Powers above:
        There is no resurrection for a Love
        That uneclips'd, unshadow'd, wanes away
        In the chill'd heart by inward self-decay.
        Poor mimic of the Past! the love is o'er
        That must *resolve* to do what did itself of yore.
                      Letter, April 27, 1824.

TO THE YOUNG ARTIST[1]

KAYSER OF KASERWERTH

KAYSER! to whom, as to a second self,
Nature, or Nature's next-of-kin, the Elf,
Hight Genius, hath dispensed the happy skill
To cheer or soothe the parting friend's 'Alas!'
Turning the blank scroll to a magic glass, 5
That makes the absent present at our will;
And to the shadowing of thy pencil gives
Such seeming substance, that it almost lives.

Well hast thou given the thoughtful Poet's face!
Yet hast thou on the tablet of his mind 10
A more delightful portrait left behind—
Even thy own youthful beauty, and artless grace,
Thy natural gladness and eyes bright with glee!
      Kayser! farewell!
Be wise! be happy! and forget not me.
  1833.

MY BAPTISMAL BIRTH-DAY[2]

GOD's child in Christ adopted,—Christ my all,—
What that earth boasts were not lost cheaply, rather
Than forfeit that blest name, by which I call
The Holy One, the Almighty God, my Father?—
Father! in Christ we live, and Christ in Thee— 5
Eternal Thou, and everlasting we.
The heir of heaven, henceforth I fear not death:
In Christ I live! in Christ I draw the breath

---

[1] First published in 1834. The original of Kayser's portrait of S. T. C., a pencil-sketch, is in the possession of the Editor. In 1852 Kaserwerth is printed Kayserwerth. The modern spelling is Kaiserswerth.
[2] First published in *Friendship's Offering* for 1834: included in P. W., 1834. Emerson heard Coleridge repeat an earlier version of these lines on Aug. 5, 1833.

My Baptismal Birth-day—Title] Lines composed on a sick-bed, under severe bodily suffering, on my spiritual birthday, October 28th. *F. O.*
1 Born unto God in Christ—in Christ, my All! *F. O.*   3 I] we *F. O.*
4 my] our *F. O.*   7 fear] dread *F. O.*

FRAGMENTS[1]

1

O'er the raised earth the gales of evening sigh;
And, see, a daisy peeps upon its slope!
I wipe the dimming waters from mine eye;
Even on the cold grave lights the Cherub Hope.[2]

? 1787. First published in *Poems*, 1852 (p. 379, Note 1). First collected 1893.

---

[1] The following 'Fragments', numbered 1–63, consist of a few translations and versicles inserted by Coleridge in his various prose works, and a larger number of fragments, properly so called, which were published from MS. sources in 1893, or are now published for the first time. These fragments are taken exclusively from Coleridge's Notebooks (the source of *Anima Poetæ*, 1895), and were collected, transcribed, and dated by the present Editor for publication in 1893. The fragments now published for the first time were either not used by J. D. Campbell in 1893, or had not been discovered or transcribed. The very slight emendations of the text are due to the fact that Mr. Campbell printed from copies, and that the collection as a whole has now for the second time been collated with the original MSS. Fragments numbered 64, 96, 98, 111, 113, in *P. W.*, 1893, are quotations from the plays and poems of William Cartwright (1611–1643). They are not included in the present issue. Fragments 56, 58, 59, 61, 63, 67, 80, 81, 83, 88, 91, 93, 94, 117–120, are inserted in the text or among ' Jeux d'Esprit ', or under other headings. The chronological order is for the most part conjectural, and differs from that suggested in 1893. It must be borne in mind that the entries in Coleridge's Notebooks are not continuous, and that the additional matter in prose or verse was inserted from time to time, wherever a page or half a page was not filled up. It follows that the context is an uncertain guide to the date of any given entry. Pains have been taken to exclude quotations from older writers, which Coleridge neither claimed nor intended to claim for his own, but it is possible that two or three of these fragments of verse are not original.

[2] This quatrain, described as 'The concluding stanza of an Elegy on a Lady who died in Early Youth', is from part of a memorandum in S. T. C.'s handwriting headed 'Relics of my School-boy Muse; i.e. fragments of poems composed before my fifteenth year'. It follows *First Advent of Love*, 'O fair is Love's first hope,' &c. (vide *ante*, p. 443), and is compared with Age—a stanza written forty years later than the preceding—'Dew-drops are the gems of morning,' &c. (p. 440).

ANOTHER VERSION.
O'er her piled grave the gale of evening sighs,
And flowers will grow upon its grassy slope,
I wipe the dimming waters from mine eye
Even on the cold grave dwells the Cherub Hope.

Unpublished Letter to Thomas Poole, Feb. 1, 1801, on the death of Mrs. Robinson ('Perdita').

2

Sea-ward, white gleaming thro' the busy scud
With arching Wings, the sea-mew o'er my head
Posts on, as bent on speed, now passaging
Edges the stiffer Breeze, now, yielding, drifts,
Now floats upon the air, and sends from far
A wildly-wailing Note.

Now first published from an MS. Compare Fragment No. 29 of Fragments from a Notebook.

3

OVER MY COTTAGE

The Pleasures sport beneath the thatch;
But Prudence sits upon the watch;
Nor Dun nor Doctor lifts the latch!

1799. First published from an MS. in 1893. Suggested by Lessing's *Sinngedicht* No. 104.

4

In the lame and limping metre of a barbarous Latin poet—
Est meum et est tuum, amice! at si amborum nequit esse,
Sit meum, amice, precor: quia certe sum mage pauper.

'Tis mine and it is likewise yours;
But and if this will not do,
Let it be mine, because that I
Am the poorer of the Two!

Nov. 1, 1801. First published in the Preface to *Christabel*, 1816. First collected 1893.

5

Names do not always meet with Love,
And Love wants courage without a *name*.[1]

Dec. 1801. Now first published from an MS.

6

The Moon, how definite its orb!
Yet gaze again, and with a steady gaze—
'Tis there indeed,—but where is it not?—
It is suffused o'er all the sapphire Heaven,
Trees, herbage, snake-like stream, unwrinkled Lake,
Whose very murmur does of it partake!

---

[1] These two lines, slightly altered, were afterwards included in *Alice du Clos* (ll. 111, 112), *ante*, p. 473.

FRAGMENTS

19

[DE PROFUNDIS CLAMAVI]

Come, come thou bleak December wind,
And blow the dry leaves from the tree!
Flash, like a love-thought, thro' me, Death!
And take a life that wearies me.

Leghorn, June 7, 1806. First published in *Letters of S. T. C.*, 1895, ii. 499, n. 1. Now collected for the first time. Adapted from Percy's version of 'Waly, Waly, Love be bonny', st. 8.

Martinmas wind when wilt thou blaw,
And shake the green leaves aff the tree?
O gentle death, when wilt thou cum?
For of my life I am wearie.

20

As some vast Tropic tree, itself a wood,
That crests its head with clouds, beneath the flood
Feeds its deep roots, and with the bulging flank
Of its wide base contröls the fronting bank—
(By the slant current's pressure scoop'd away
The fronting bank becomes a foam-piled bay)
High in the Fork the uncouth Idol knits
His channel'd brow; low murmurs stir by fits
And dark below the horrid Faquir sits—
An Horror from its broad Head's branching wreath
Broods o'er the rude Idolatry beneath—

1806-7. Now first published from an MS.

21

Let Eagle bid the Tortoise sunward soar—
As vainly Strength speaks to a broken Mind.[1]

1807. First published in *Thomas Poole and His Friends*, 1888, ii. 195.

22

The body,
Eternal Shadow of the finite Soul,
The Soul's self-symbol, its image of itself.
Its own yet not itself.

Now first published from an MS.

[1] These lines, 'slip torn from some old letter,' are endorsed by Poole, 'Reply of Coleridge on my urging him to exert himself.' First collected in 1893.

FRAGMENTS

15

O th' Oppressive, irksome weight
Felt in an uncertain state:
Comfort, peace, and rest adieu
Should I prove at last untrue!
Self-confiding wretch, I thought
I could love thee as I ought,
Win thee and deserve to feel
All the Love thou canst reveal,
And still I chuse thee, follow still.

1805. First published from an MS. in 1893.

16

'Twas not a mist, nor was it quite a cloud,
But it pass'd smoothly on towards the sea—
Smoothly and lightly between Earth and Heaven:
So, thin a cloud,
It scarce bedimm'd the star that shone behind it:
And Hesper now
Paus'd on the welkin blue, and cloudless brink,
A golden circlet! while the Star of Jove—
That other lovely star—high o'er my head
Shone whitely in the centre of his Haze
. . . one black-blue cloud
Stretch'd, like the heaven, o'er all the cope of Heaven.

Dec. 1797. First published from an MS. in 1893.

17

[NOT A CRITIC—BUT A JUDGE]

Whom should I choose for my Judge? the earnest, impersonal reader,
Who, in the work, forgets me and the world and himself!
You who have eyes to detect, and Gall to Chastise the imperfect,
Have you the heart, too, that loves,—feels and rewards the Compleat?

1805. Now first published from an MS.

18

A sumptuous and magnificent Revenge.

March 1806. First published from an MS. in 1893.

FRAGMENTS

Sent out, like fingers, five projecting trunks—
The shortest twice 6 (?) of a tall man's strides,—
One curving upward in its middle growth
Rose straight with grove of twigs—a pollard tree:—
The rest more backward, gradual in descent—
One in the brook and one befoamed its waters:
One ran along the bank in the elk-like head
And pomp of antlers—

Jan. 1804. Now first published from MS. (pencil).

11

I from the influence of thy Looks receive,
Access in every virtue, in thy Sight
More wise, more wakeful, stronger, if need were
Of outward strength.—

1804. Now first published from an MS.

12

WHAT never is, but only is to be
This is not Life:—
O hopeless Hope, and Death's Hypocrisy!
And with perpetual promise breaks its promises.

1804–5. Now first published from an MS.

13

THE silence of a City, how awful at Midnight!
Mute as the battlements and crags and towers
That Fancy makes in the clouds, yea, as mute
As the moonlight that sleeps on the steady vanes.

The cell of a departed anchoret,
His skeleton and flitting ghost are there,
Sole tenants—
And all the City silent as the Moon
That sleeps in quiet light the steady vanes
Of her huge temples.

1804–5. Now first published from an MS.

14

O BEAUTY in a beauteous body dight!
Body that veiling brightness, beamest bright;
Fair cloud which less we see, than by thee see the light.

1805. First published from an MS. in 1893.

FRAGMENTS

And low and close the broad smooth mountain is more
a thing of Heaven than when distinct by one dim shade, and
yet undivided from the universal cloud in which it towers
infinite in height.

?1801. First published in MS. in 1893.

7

Such love as mourning Husbands have
To her whose Spirit has been newly given
To her guardian Saint in Heaven—
Whose Beauty lieth in the grave—
(Unconquered, as if the Soul could find no purer Tabernacle,
nor place of sojourn than the virgin Body it had before dwelt
in, and wished to stay there till the Resurrection)—
Far liker to a Flower now than when alive,
Cold to the Touch and blooming to the eye.

Sept. 1803. Now first published from MS.

8

[THE NIGHT-MARE DEATH IN LIFE]

I know 'tis but a dream, yet feel more anguish
Than if 'twere truth. It has been often so :
Must I die under it? Is no one near?
Will no one hear these stifled groans and wake me?

? 1803. Now first published from MS.

9

Bright clouds of reverence, sufferably bright,
That intercept the dazzle, not the Light ;
That veil the finite form, the boundless power reveal,
Itself an earthly sun of pure intensest white.

1803. First published from an MS. in 1893.

10

A BECK IN WINTER[1]

Over the broad, the shallow, rapid stream,
The Alder, a vast hollow Trunk, and ribb'd—
All mossy green with mosses manifold,
And ferns still waving in the river-breeze

[1] The lines are an attempt to reduce to blank verse one of many minute descriptions of natural objects and scenic effects. The concluding lines are illegible.

495

23

Or Wren or Linnet,
In Bush and Bushet;
No tree, but in it
A cooing Cushat.

May 1807. Now first published from an MS.

24

The reed roof'd village still bepatch'd with snow
Smok'd in the sun-thaw.

1798. Now first published from an MS. Compare *Frost at Midnight*, ll. 69-70, *ante*, p. 242.

25

And in Life's noisiest hour
There whispers still the ceaseless love of thee,
The heart's self-solace } and soliloquy.
   commune }

1807. Now first published from an MS.

26

You mould my Hopes you fashion me within:
And to the leading love-throb in the heart,
Through all my being, through my pulses beat;
You lie in all my many thoughts like Light,
Like the fair light of Dawn, or summer Eve,
On rippling stream, or cloud-reflecting lake;
And looking to the Heaven that bends above you,
How oft! I bless the lot that made me love you.

1807. Now first published from an MS.

27

And my heart mantles in its own delight.

Now first published from an MS.

28

The spruce and limber yellow-hammer
In the dawn of spring and sultry summer,
In hedge or tree the hours beguiling
With notes as of one who brass is filing.

1807. Now first published from an MS.

29

FRAGMENT OF AN ODE ON NAPOLEON

O'erhung with yew, midway the Muses mount
  From thy sweet murmurs far, O Hippocrene!
Turbid and black upboils an angry fount
  Tossing its shatter'd foam in vengeful spleen—
Phlegethon's rage Cocytus' wailings hoarse
Alternate now, now mixt, made known its headlong course:
  Thither with terror stricken and surprise,
(For sure such haunts were ne'er to Muse's choice)
  Euterpe led me. Mute with asking eyes
I stood expectant of her heavenly voice.
Her voice entranc'd my terror and made flow
In a rude understrain the maniac fount below.
'Whene'er (the Goddess said) abhorr'd of Jove
Usurping Power his hands in blood imbrues—

? 1808. Now first published from an MS.

30

The singing Kettle and the purring Cat,
The gentle breathing of the cradled Babe,
The silence of the Mother's love-bright eye,
And tender smile answering its smile of Sleep.

1803. First published from an MS. in 1893.

31

Two wedded hearts, if ere were such,
Imprison'd in adjoining cells,
Across whose thin partition-wall
The builder left one narrow rent,
And where, most content in discontent,
A joy with itself at strife—
Die into an intenser life.

1808. First published from an MS. in 1893.

Another Version

The builder left one narrow rent,
  Two wedded hearts, if ere were such,
Contented most in discontent,
  Still there cling, and try in vain to touch!

FRAGMENTS 501

O Joy! with thy own joy at strife,
  That yearning for the Realm above
Wouldst die into intenser Life,
  And Union absolute of Love!

1808. First published from an MS. in 1893.

32

Sole Maid, associate sole, to me beyond
Compare all living creatures dear—
Thoughts, which have found their harbour in thy heart
Dearest! *me* thought of *him* to thee so dear!

1809. First published from an MS. in 1893.

33

EPIGRAM ON KEPLER

FROM THE GERMAN

No mortal spirit yet had clomb so high
As Kepler—yet his Country saw him die
For very want! the *Minds* alone he fed,
And so the *Bodies* left him without bread.

1799. First published in *The Friend*, Nov. 30, 1809 (1818, ii. 95; 1850, ii. 69). First collected *P. and D. W.*, 1877, ii. 374.

---

1 spirit] Genius *MS.*   2 yet] and *MS.*   3 *Minds*] Souls *MS. erased*.

34

When Hope but made Tranquillity be felt:
A flight of Hope for ever on the wing
But made Tranquillity a conscious thing;
And wheeling round and round in sportive coil,
Fann'd the calm air upon the brow of Toil.

1810. First published from an MS. in 1893.

35

                I have experienced
The worst the world can wreak on me—the worst
That can make Life indifferent, yet disturb
With whisper'd discontent the dying prayer—
I have beheld the whole of all, wherein
My heart had any interest in this life
To be disrent and torn from off my Hopes

That nothing now is left. Why then live on?
That hostage that the world had in its keeping
Given by me as a pledge that I would live—
That hope of Her, say rather that pure Faith
In her fix'd Love, which held me to keep truce
With the tyranny of Life—is gone, ah! whither?
What boots it to reply? 'tis gone! and now
Well may I break this Pact, this league of Blood
That ties me to myself—and break I shall.

1810. First published from an MS. in 1893.

36

As when the new or full Moon urges
The high, large, long, unbreaking surges
Of the Pacific main.

1811. First published from an MS. in 1893.

37

O MERCY, O me, miserable man!
Slowly my wisdom, and how slowly comes
My Virtue! and how rapidly pass off
My Joys! *my Hopes*! my Friendships, and my Love!

1811. Now first published from an MS.

38

A LOW dead Thunder mutter'd thro' the night,
As 'twere a giant angry in his sleep—
Nature! sweet nurse, O take me in thy lap
And tell me of my Father yet unseen,
Sweet tales, and true, that lull me into sleep
And leave me dreaming.

1811. First published from an MS. in 1893.

39

HIS own fair countenance, his kingly forehead,
His tender smiles, Love's day-dawn on his lips.
Put on such heavenly, spiritual light,
At the same moment in his steadfast eye
Were Virtue's native crest, th' innocent soul's
Unconscious meek self-heraldry,—to man
Genial, and pleasant to his guardian angel.
He suffer'd nor complain'd;—though oft with tears

He mourn'd th' oppression of his helpless brethren,—
And sometimes with a deeper holier grief
Mourn'd for the oppressor—but this in sabbath hours—
A solemn grief, that like a cloud at sunset,
Was but the veil of inward meditation
Pierced thro' and saturate with the intellectual rays
It soften'd.

1812. First published (with many alterations of the MS.) in *Lit. Rem.*, i. 277. First collected *P. and D. W.*, 1887, ii. 364. Compare Teresa's speech to Valdez, *Remorse*, Act IV, Scene II, lines 52-63 (*ante*, p. 866).

40

[ARS POETICA]

In the two following lines, for instance, there is nothing objectionable, nothing which would preclude them from forming, in their proper place, part of a descriptive poem:—

'Behold yon row of pines, that shorn and bow'd
Bend from the sea-blast, seen at twilight eve.'

But with a small alteration of rhythm, the same words would be equally in their place in a book of topography, or in a descriptive tour. The same image will rise into a semblance of poetry if thus conveyed:—

'Yon row of bleak and visionary pines,
By twilight-glimpse discerned, mark! how they flee
From the fierce sea-blast, all their tresses wild
Streaming before them.'

1815. First published in *Biog. Lit.*, 1817, ii. 18; 1847, ii. 20. First collected 1893.

41

TRANSLATION OF THE FIRST STROPHE OF PINDAR'S SECOND OLYMPIC

'*As nearly as possible word for word.*'

Ye harp-controlling hymns!
(or)
Ye hymns the sovereigns of harps!
What God? what Hero?
What Man shall we celebrate?
Truly Pisa indeed is of Jove,
But the Olympiad (or the Olympic games) did Hercules establish,
The first-fruits of the spoils of war.
But Theron for the four-horsed car

That bore victory to him.
It behoves us now to voice aloud
The Just, the Hospitable,
The Bulwark of Agrigentum,
Of renowned fathers
The Flower, even him
Who preserves his native city erect and safe.

1815. First published in *Biog. Lit.*, 1817, ii. 90 ; 1847, ii. 93. First collected 1893.

42

O! SUPERSTITION is the giant shadow
Which the solicitude of weak mortality,
Its back toward Religion's rising sun,
Casts on the thin mist of th' uncertain future.

1816. First published from an MS. in 1893.

43

TRANSLATION OF A FRAGMENT OF HERACLITUS[1]

Not hers
To win the sense by words of rhetoric,
Lip-blossoms breathing perishable sweets ;
But by the power of the informing Word
Roll sounding onward through a thousand years
Her deep prophetic bodements.

1816. First published in *Lit. Rem.*, iii. 418, 419. First collected *P. and D. W.*, 1877, ii. 367.

---

[1] The translation is embodied in a marginal note on the following quotation from *The Select Discourses* by John Smith, 1660 :—

'So the Sibyl was noted by Heraclitus as μαινομένῳ στόματι γελαστὰ καὶ ἀκαλλώπιστα φθεγγομένη, as one speaking ridiculous and unseemly speeches with her furious mouth.' The fragment is misquoted and misunderstood : for γελαστά, etc., should be ἀμύριστα unperfumed, inornate lays, not redolent of art.—Render it thus :

Not her's, etc.

Στόματι μαινομένῳ is 'with ecstatic mouth'.

J. D. Campbell in a note to this Fragment (*P. W.*, 1893, pp. 464-5) quotes the 'following prose translation of the same passage', from Coleridge's *Statesman's Manual* (1816, p. 132) : 'Multiscience (or a variety and quantity of acquired knowledge) does not test intelligence. But the Sibyll with wild enthusiastic mirth shrilling forth unmirthful, inornate and unperfumed truths, reaches to a thousand years with her voice through the power of God.'

The prose translation is an amalgam of two fragments. The first sentence is quoted by Diogenes Laertius, ix. 1 : the second by Plutarch, de Pyth. orac. 6, p. 377.

44

Truth I pursued, as Fancy sketch'd the way,
And wiser men than I went worse astray.

First published as Motto to Essay II, *The Friend*, 1818, ii. 37; 1850, ii. 27. First collected 1893.

45

IMITATED FROM ARISTOPHANES

(*Nubes* 315, 317.)

μεγάλαι θεαὶ ἀνδράσιν ἀργοῖς,
αἵπερ γνώμην καὶ διάλεξιν καὶ νοῦν ἡμῖν παρέχουσι
καὶ τερατείαν καὶ περίλεξιν καὶ κροῦσιν καὶ κατάληψιν.

For the ancients . . . had their glittering vapors which (as the comic poet tells us) fed a host of sophists.

Great goddesses are they to lazy folks,
Who pour down on us gifts of fluent speech,
Sense most sententious, wonderful fine *effect*,
And how to talk about it and about it,
Thoughts brisk as bees, and pathos soft and thawy.

1817. First published in *The Friend*, 1818, iii. 179; 1850, iii. 138. First collected 1893.

46

Let clumps of earth, however glorified,
Roll round and round and still renew their cycle—
Man rushes like a winged Cherub through
The infinite space, and that which has been
Can therefore never be again——

1820. First published from an MS. in 1893.

47

TO EDWARD IRVING

But *you*, honored Irving, are as little disposed as myself to favor *such* doctrine! [as that of Mant and D'Oyly on Infant Baptism].

Friend pure of heart and fervent! we have learnt
A different lore! We may not thus profane
The Idea and Name of Him whose Absolute Will
Is Reason—Truth Supreme!—Essential Order!

1824. First published in *Aids to Reflection*, 1825, p. 373. First collected 1893.

48

[LUTHER—DE DÆMONIBUS]

The devils are in woods, in waters, in wildernesses, and in dark pooly places, ready to hurt and prejudice people, etc.—Doctoris Martini Lutheri Colloquia Mensalia—(Translated by Captain Henry Bell. London, 1652, p. 370).

> 'The angel's like a flea,
> The devil is a bore ;—'
> No matter for that! quoth S. T. C.,
> I love him the better therefore.

Yes! heroic Swan, I love thee even when thou gabblest like a goose ; for thy geese helped to save the Capitol.

1826. First published in *Lit. Rem.*, 1839, iv. 52. First collected *P. and D. W.*, 1877, ii. 367.

49

THE NETHERLANDS

WATER and windmills, greenness, Islets green ;—
Willows whose Trunks beside the shadows stood
Of their own higher half, and willowy swamp:—
Farmhouses that at anchor seem'd—in the inland sky
The fog-transfixing Spires—
Water, wide water, greenness and green banks,
And water seen—

June 1828. Now first published from an MS.

50

ELISA[1]

TRANSLATED FROM CLAUDIAN

DULCIA dona mihi tu mittis semper Elisa.
Et quicquid mittis Thura putare decet.

The above adapted from an Epigram of Claudian [No. lxxxii, Ad Maximum Qui mel misit], by substituting *Thura* for *Mella*: the original Distich being in return for a present of Honey.

Imitation

Sweet Gift! and always doth Elisa send
Sweet Gifts and full of fragrance to her Friend
Enough for Him to know they come from HER:
Whate'er she sends is Frankincense and Myrrh.

[1] These rhymes were addressed to a Miss Eliza Nixon, who supplied S. T. C. with books from a lending library.

FRAGMENTS

ANOTHER ON THE SAME SUBJECT BY S. T. C. HIMSELF

Semper Elisa! mihi tu suaveolentia donas:
Nam quicquid donas, te redolere puto.

Translation

Whate'er thou giv'st, it still is sweet to me,
For *still* I find it redolent of thee.

1833, 4. Now first published from an MS.

51

PROFUSE KINDNESS

Νήπιοι οὐδὲ ἴσασιν ὅσῳ πλέον ἥμισυ πάντος.
HESIOD. [*Works and Days*, 1. 40.]

WHAT a spring-tide of Love to dear friends in a shoal!
Half of it to one were worth double the whole!

Undated. First published in *P. W.*, 1834.

52

I STAND alone, nor tho' my heart should break,
Have I, to whom I may complain or speak.
Here I stand, a hopeless man and sad,
Who hoped to have seen my Love, my Life.
And strange it were indeed, could I be glad
Remembering her, my soul's betrothéd wife.
For in this world no creature that has life
Was e'er to me so gracious and so good.
Her loss is to my Heart, like the Heart's blood.

? S. T. C. Undated. First published from an MS. in 1893. These lines are inscribed on a fly-leaf of Tom. II of Benedetto Menzini's *Poesie*, 1782.

53

NAPOLEON

THE Sun with gentle beams his rage disguises,
And, like aspiring Tyrants, temporises—
Never to be endured but when he falls or rises.

? S. T. C. Undated. Now first published from an MS.

54

THICKER than rain-drops on November thorn.

Undated. Now first published from an MS.

55

His native accents to her stranger's ear,
Skill'd in the tongues of France and Italy—
Or while she warbles with bright eyes upraised,
Her fingers shoot like streams of silver light
Amid the golden haze of thrilling strings.

Undated. First published from an MS. in 1893.

56

Each crime that once estranges from the virtues
Doth make the memory of their features daily
More dim and vague, till each coarse counterfeit
Can have the passport to our confidence
Sign'd by ourselves. And fitly are they punish'd
Who prize and seek the honest man but as
A safer lock to guard dishonest treasures.

? S. T. C. Undated. First published in *Lit. Rem.*, i. 281. First collected *P. and D. W.*, 1877, ii. 365.

57

Where'er I find the Good, the True, the Fair,
I ask no names—God's spirit dwelleth there!
The unconfounded, undivided Three,
Each for itself, and all in each, to see
In man and Nature, is Philosophy.

Undated. First published from an MS. in 1893.

58

A wind that with Aurora hath abiding
Among the Arabian and the Persian Hills.

Undated. First published from an MS. in 1893.

59

I [S. T. C.] find the following lines among my papers, in my own writing, but whether an unfinished fragment, or a contribution to some friend's production, I know not:—

What boots to tell how o'er his grave
She wept, that would have died to save;
Little they know the heart, who deem
Her sorrow but an infant's dream
  Of transient love begotten;
A passing gale, that as it blows
Just shakes the ripe drop from the rose—
  That dies and is forgotten.

O Woman! nurse of hopes and fears,
All lovely in thy spring of years,
  Thy soul in blameless mirth possessing,
Most lovely in affliction's tears,
  More lovely still than tears suppressing.

Undated. First published in Allsop's *Letters, Conversations*, &c. First collected *P. and D. W.*, 1877, ii. 373.

60
THE THREE SORTS OF FRIENDS

Though friendships differ endless *in degree*,
The *sorts*, methinks, may be reduced to three.
*A*cquaintance many, and *Con*quaintance few;
But for *In*quaintance I know only two—
The friend I've mourned with, and the maid I woo!

My dear Gillman—The ground and *matériel* of this division of one's friends into *ac*, *con* and *in*quaintance, was given by Hartley Coleridge when he was scarcely five years old [1801]. On some one asking him if Anny Sealy (a little girl he went to school with) was an acquaintance of his, he replied, very fervently pressing his right hand on his heart, 'No, she is an *in*quaintance!' 'Well! 'tis a father's tale'; and the recollection soothes your old friend and *in*quaintance, S. T. Coleridge.

Undated. First published in *Fraser's Magazine* for Jan. 1835, Art. *Coleridgeiana*, p. 54. First collected 1893.

61

        If fair by Nature
She honours the fair Boon with fair adorning,
And graces that bespeak a gracious breeding,
Can gracious Nature lessen Nature's Graces?
If taught by both she betters both and honours
Fair gifts with fair adorning, know you not
There is a beauty that resides within;—
A fine and delicate spirit of womanhood
Of inward birth?—

Now first published from an MS.

62
BO-PEEP AND I SPY—

  In the corner *one*—
    I spy Love!
  In the corner *None*,
    I spy Love.

1826. Now first published from an MS.

63
A SIMILE

As the shy hind, the soft-eyed gentle Brute
Now moves, now stops, approaches by degrees—
At length emerges from the shelt'ring Trees,
Lur'd by her Hunter with the Shepherd's flute,
Whose music travelling on the twilight breeze,
  When all besides was mute—
She oft had heard, and ever lov'd to hear;
She fearful Beast! but that no sound of Fear——

Undated. Now first published from an MS.

64
BARON GUELPH OF ADELSTAN. A FRAGMENT

For ever in the world of Fame
We live and yet abide the same:
  Clouds may intercept our rays,
  Or desert Lands reflect our blaze.

The beauteous Month of May began,
  And all was Mirth and Sport,
When Baron Guelph of Adelstan
  Took leave and left the Court.

From Fête and Rout and Opera far
  The full town he forsook,
And changed his wand and golden star
  For Shepherd's Crown and Crook.

The knotted net of light and shade
  Beneath the budding tree,
A sweeter day-bed for him made
  Than Couch and Canopy.

In copse or lane, as Choice or Chance
  Might lead him was he seen;
And join'd at eve the village dance
  Upon the village green.

Nor endless—

Undated. Now first published from an MS.

METRICAL EXPERIMENTS[1]

1

AN EXPERIMENT FOR A METRE

I HEARD a voice pealing loud triumph to-day:
The voice of the Triumph, O Freedom, was thine!
Sumptuous Tyranny challeng'd the fray,[2]
'Drunk with Idolatry, drunk with wine.'
Whose could the Triumph be Freedom but thine?
   Stars of the Heaven shine to feed thee;
   Hush'd are the Whirl-blasts and heed thee;—
By her depth, by her height, Nature swears thou art mine!

---

[1] 'He attributed in part, his writing so little, to the extreme care and labour which he applied in elaborating his metres. He said that when he was intent on a new experiment in metre, the time and labour he bestowed were inconceivable; that he was quite an epicure in sound.' —Wordsworth on Coleridge (as reported by Mr. Justice Coleridge), *Memoirs of W. Wordsworth*, 1851, ii. 306.

In a letter to Poole dated March 16, 1801, Coleridge writes: 'I shall ... immediately publish my *Christabel*, with the Essays on the "Preternatural", and on Metre' (*Letters of S. T. C.*, 1895, i. 349). Something had been done towards the collection of materials for the first 'Essay', a great deal for the second. In a notebook (No. 22) which contains dated entries of 1805, 1815, &c., but of which the greater portion, as the context and various handwritings indicate, belongs to a much earlier date, there are some forty-eight numbered specimens of various metres derived from German and Italian sources. To some of these stanzas or strophes a metrical scheme with original variants is attached, whilst other schemes are exemplified by metrical experiments in English, headed 'Nonsense Verses'. Two specimens of these experiments, headed 'A Sunset' and 'What is Life', are included in the text of *P. W.*, 1893 (pp. 172, 173), and in that of the present issue, pp. 393, 394. They are dated 1805 in accordance with the dates of Coleridge's own comments or afterthoughts, but it is almost certain that both sets of verses were composed in 1801. The stanza entitled 'An Angel Visitant' belongs to the same period. Ten other sets of 'Nonsense Verses' of uncertain but early date are now printed for the first time.

[2] Sumptuous Tyranny floating this way. [MS.] On p. 17 of Notebook 22 Coleridge writes:—

$$- \cup \cup, - \cup \cup, - \cup, -$$
    Drunk with I—dolatry—drunk with, Wine.

A noble metre if I can find a metre to precede or follow.

    Sŭmptŭŏus Dālĭlă flōatĭng thĭs wāy
    Drunk with Idolatry, drunk with wine.

Both lines are from Milton's *Samson Agonistes*.

1. Amphibrach tetrameter catalectic ∪ – ∪ | ∪ – – ∪ | ∪ – ∪ | ∪ –
2. Ditto.
3. Three pseudo amphimacers, and one long syllable.
4. Two dactyls, and one perfect Amphimacer.
5. = 1 and 2.
6. – ∪ – | – ∪ – ∪ |
7. – ∪ – | – ∪ – ∪ |
8. – ∪ – | – ∪ –, – ∪ –, – ∪ –

1801.   Now first published from an MS.

2

TROCHAICS

Thus she said, and, all around,
  Her diviner spirit, gan to borrow;
Earthly Hearings hear unearthly sound,
Hearts heroic faint, and sink aswound.
  Welcome, welcome, spite of pain and sorrow,
    Love to-day, and Thought to-morrow.

1801.   Now first published from an MS.

3

THE PROPER UNMODIFIED DOCHMIUS

(*i.e.* antispastic Catalectic)

Bĕnīgn shōōtĭng stārs, ĕcstātĭc dĕlīght.
or The Lord's throne in Heaven ămīd āngĕl troops
Amid troops of Angels God throned on high.

1801.   Now first published from an MS.

4

IAMBICS

No cold shall thee benumb,
Nor darkness stain thy sight;
To thee new Heat, new Light
Shall from this object come,
Whose Praises if thou now wilt sound aright,
My Pen shall give thee leave hereafter to be dumb.

1801.   Now first published from an MS.

5
NONSENSE

Sing impassionate Soul! of Mohammed the complicate story:
  Sing, unfearful of Man, groaning and ending in care.
Short the Command and the Toil, but endlessly mighty the Glory!
  Standing aloof if it chance, vainly our enemy's scare:
What tho' we wretchedly fare, wearily drawing the Breath—,
  Malice in wonder may stare; merrily move we to Death.

Now first published from an MS.

6
A PLAINTIVE MOVEMENT
[11′ 4ˋ 11′ 4ˋ | 10′ 6ˋ 4′ 10ˋ]

Go little Pipe! for ever I must leave thee,
  Ah, vainly true!
Never, ah never! must I more receive thee?
  Adieu! adieu!
Well, thou art gone! and what remains behind,
  Soothing the soul to Hope?
    The moaning Wind—
Hide with sere leaves my Grave's undaisied Slope.

(?) October, 1814.

[It would be better to alter this metre—
  10′ 6ˋ 6′ 10ˋ | 11′ 4ˋ 11′ 4ˋ: and still more plaintive if the 1st and 4th were 11′ 11′ as well as the 5th and 7th.]

Now first published from an MS.

7
NONSENSE VERSES

[AN EXPERIMENT FOR A METRE]

Ye fowls of ill presage,
  Go vanish into Night!
Let all things sweet and fair
Yield homage to the pair:
  From Infancy to Age
Each Brow be smooth and bright,
As Lake in evening light.
To-day be Joy! and Sorrow
  Devoid of Blame
  (The widow'd Dame)
Shall welcome be to-morrow.
Thou, too, dull Night! may'st come unchid:

> This wall of Flame the Dark hath hid
> With turrets each a Pyramid;—
> For the Tears that we shed, are Gladness,
>   A mockery of Sadness!

Now first published from an MS.

8

NONSENSE

[AN EXPERIMENT FOR A METRE]

> I wish on earth to sing
> Of Jove the bounteous store,
> That all the Earth may ring
> With Tale of Wrong no more.
> I fear no foe in field or tent,
> Tho' weak our cause yet strong his Grace:
> As Polar roamers clad in Fur,
> Unweeting whither we were bent
> We found as 'twere a native place,
>   Where not a Blast could stir:
> { For Jove had his Almighty Presence lent:
> { Each eye beheld, in each transfigured Face,
> { The radiant light of Joy, and Hope's forgotten Trace.
> or { O then I sing Jove's bounteous store—
> { On rushing wing while sea-mews roar,
> { And raking Tides roll Thunder on the shore.

Now first published from an MS.

9

EXPERIMENTS IN METRE

> There in some darksome shade
>   Methinks I'd weep
>   Myself asleep,
> And there forgotten fade.

First published from an MS. in 1893.

10

> Once again, sweet Willow, wave thee!
>   Why stays my Love?
> Bend, and in yon streamlet—lave thee!
>   Why stays my Love?
> Oft have I at evening straying,

METRICAL EXPERIMENTS

  Stood, thy branches long surveying,
   Graceful in the light breeze playing,—
    Why stays my Love?

1. Four Trochees ∕.
2. One spondee, Iambic ∖.
3. Four Trochees 1.
4. Repeated from 2.
5, 6, 7. A triplet of 4 Trochees—8 repeated.

First published from an MS. in 1893.

11

$$-\cup, -\cup\cup, -\cup\cup, -\cup\cup$$
$$-\cup, -\cup\cup, -\cup\cup, -$$
$$-\cup, -\cup\cup, -\cup\cup, -\cup\cup$$
$$\cup-\cup, -\cup\cup, -\cup\cup, -$$
$$-\cup\cup, -\cup$$
$$\cup-\cup\cup, -\cup \text{ etc.}$$

  Songs of Shepherds and rustical Roundelays,
  Forms of Fancies and whistled on Reeds,
  Songs to solace young Nymphs upon Holidays
  Are too unworthy for wonderful deeds—
    Round about, hornéd
    Lucinda they swarméd,
    And her they informéd,
    How minded they were,
    Each God and Goddess,
    To take human Bodies
  As Lords and Ladies to follow the Hare.

Now first published from an MS.

12

A METRICAL ACCIDENT

Curious instance of casual metre and rhyme in a prose narrative (*The Life of Jerome of Prague*). The metre is Amphibrach dimeter Catalectic $\cup - \cup \mid \cup -$, and the rhymes antistrophic.

Then Jerome did call *a*
From his flame-pointed Fence; *b*
Which under he trod, *c*
As upward to mount *d*
From the fiery flood,—*e*

'I summon you all, *a*
A hundred years hence, *b*
To appear before God, *c*
To give an account *d*
Of my innocent blood!' *e*

July 7, 1826. Now first published from an MS.

NOTES BY GEORGE SAINTSBURY

1. I think most ears would take these as anapaestic throughout. But the introduction of Milton's

   Drunk with Idolatry, drunk with wine

as a *leit-motiv* is of the first interest.

Description of it, l. 4, very curious. I should have thought no one could have run 'drunk with wine' together as one foot.

2. Admirable! I hardly know better trochaics.

3. Very interesting: but the terminology odd. The dochmius, a five-syllabled foot, is (in *one* form—there are about thirty!) an antispast ∪ − − ∪ *plus* a syllable. Catalectic means (*properly*) *minus* a syllable. But the verses as quantified are really dochmiac, and the only attempts I have seen. Shall I own I can't get any *English* Rhythm on them?

4. More ordinary: but a good arrangement and wonderful for the date.

5. Not nonsense at all: but, metrically, really his usual elegiac.

6. This, *if early*, is almost priceless. It is not only lovely in itself, but an obvious attempt to recover the zig-zag outline and varied cadence of seventeenth century born—the things that Shelley to some extent, Beddoes and Darley more, and Tennyson and Browning most were to master. I subscribe (most humbly) to his suggestions, especially his second.

7. Like 6, and charming.

8. A sort of recurrence to *Pindaric*—again pioneer, as the soul of S. T. C. *had* to be always.

9 and 10. Ditto.

12. Again, *I* should say, anapaestic—but this anapaest and amphibrach quarrel is ἄσπονδος.

APPENDIXES

FIRST DRAFTS, EARLY VERSIONS ETC.

Mechaniz'd matter as th' organic harps 45
And each one's Tunes be that, which each calls I.

But thy more serious Look a mild Reproof
Darts, O beloved Woman, and thy words
Pious and calm check these unhallow'd Thoughts,
These Shapings of the unregen'rate Soul, 50
Bubbles, that glitter as they rise and break
On vain Philosophy's aye-babbling Spring:
Thou biddest me walk humbly with my God!
Meek Daughter in the family of Christ.
Wisely thou sayest, and holy are thy words! 55
Nor may I unblam'd or speak or think of Him,
Th' INCOMPREHENSIBLE! save when with Awe
I praise him, and with Faith that inly feels,
Who with his saving Mercies healèd me,
A sinful and most miserable man 60
Wilder'd and dark, and gave me to possess
PEACE and this COT, and THEE, my best-belov'd!

[*MS. R.*]

B

RECOLLECTION[1]

[Vide *ante*, pp. 53, 48]

As the tir'd savage, who his drowsy frame
Had bask'd beneath the sun's unclouded flame
Awakes amid the troubles of the air,
The skiey deluge and white lightning's glare,
Aghast he scours before the tempest's sweep, 5
And sad recalls the sunny hour of sleep!
So tost by storms along life's wild'ring way
Mine eye reverted views that cloudless day,
When by my native brook I wont to rove,
While HOPE with kisses nurs'd the infant LOVE! 10

Dear native brook! like peace so placidly
Smoothing thro' fertile fields thy current meek—
Dear native brook! where first young POESY
Star'd wildly eager in her noon-tide dream;

---

[1] First published in *The Watchman*, No. V, April 2, 1796: reprinted in Note 39 (p. 566) of *P. W.*, 1892. The Editor (J. D. Campbell) points out that this poem as printed in *The Watchman* is made up of lines 71–86 of *Lines on an Autumnal Evening* (vide *ante*, p. 53), of lines 2–11 of *Sonnet to the River Otter*, and of lines 13, 14 of *The Gentle Look*, and *Anna and Harland*.

Where blameless Pleasures dimpled Quiet's cheek, 15
As water-lilies *ripple* thy slow stream!
How many various-fated years have past,
What blissful and what anguish'd hours, since last
I skimm'd the smooth thin stone along thy breast
Numb'ring its light leaps! Yet so deep imprest 20
Sink the sweet scenes of childhood, that mine eyes
I never shut amid the sunny blaze,
But strait, with all their tints, thy waters rise,
The crossing plank, and margin's willowy maze,
And bedded sand, that, vein'd with various dyes, 25
Gleam'd thro' thy bright transparence to the gaze—
Ah! fair tho' faint those forms of memory seem
Like Heaven's bright bow on thy smooth evening stream.

C

THE DESTINY OF NATIONS

[Add. MSS. 34,225. f. 5. Vide *ante*, p. 131.]

[DRAFT I]

AUSPICIOUS Reverence! Hush all meaner song,
Till we the deep prelusive strain have pour'd
To the Great Father, only Rightful King,
Eternal Father! king omnipotent;
Beneath whose shadowing banners wide-unfurl'd 5
Justice leads forth her tyrant-quelling Hosts.
Such Symphony demands best Instrument.

Seize, then, my Soul, from Freedom's trophied dome
The harp which hanging high between the shields
Of Brutus and Leonidas, oft gives 10
A fitful music, when with breeze-like Touch
Great Spirits passing thrill its wings: the Bard
Listens and knows, thy will to work by Fame.
For what is Freedom, but the unfetter'd use
Of all the powers which God for use had given? 15
But chiefly this, him first to view, him last,
Thro' shapes, and sounds, and all the world of sense,
The change of empires, and the deeds of Man
Translucent, as thro' clouds that veil the Light.
But most, O Man! in thine in wasted Sense 20
And the still growth of Immortality

Image of God, and his Eternity.
But some there are who deem themselves most wise
When they within this gross and visible sphere
Chain down the winged thought, scoffing ascent   25
Proud in their meanness—and themselves they mock
With noisy emptiness of learned phrase
Their subtle fluids, impacts, essences,
Self-working tools, uncaused effects, and all
Those blind Omniscients, those Almighty Slaves,   30
Untenanting Creation of its God!

But properties are God: the Naked Mass
(If Mass there be, at best a guess obscure,)
Acts only by its inactivity.
Here we pause humbly. Others boldlier dream,   35
That as one body is the Aggregate
Of Atoms numberless, each organiz'd,
So by a strange and dim similitude
Infinite myriads of self-conscious minds
Form one all-conscious Spirit, who controls   40
With absolute ubiquity of Thought
All his component Monads: linked Minds,
Each in his own sphere evermore evolving
Its own entrusted powers—Howe'er this be,
Whether a dream presumptious, caught from earth   45
And earthly form, or vision veiling Truth,
Yet the Omnific Father of all Worlds
God in God immanent, the eternal Word,
That gives forth, yet remains—Sun, that at once
Dawns, rises, sets and crowns the Height of Heaven,   50
Great general Agent in all finite souls,
Doth in that action put on finiteness,
For all his Thoughts are acts, and every act
A Being of Substance ; God impersonal,
Yet in all worlds impersonate in all,   55
Absolute Infinite, whose dazzling robe
Flows in rich folds, and darts in shooting Hues
Of infinite Finiteness! he rolls each orb
Matures each planet, and Tree, and spread thro' all
Wields all the Universe of Life and Thought,   60
[Yet leaves to all the Creatures meanest, highest,
Angelic Right, self-conscious Agency—]

[*Note.* The last two lines of Draft I are erased.]

APPENDIX I

[Draft II]

Auspicious Reverence ! Hush all meaner song,
Ere we the deep prelusive strain have pour'd
To the Great Father, only Rightful king
All-gracious Father, king Omnipotent!
Mind ! co-eternal Word ! forth-breathing Sound !　　5
Aye unconfounded : undivided Trine—
Birth and Procession ; ever re-incircling Act!
God in God immanent, distinct yet one !
Omnific, Omniform. The Immoveable,
That goes forth and remains, eke—— and at once　　10
Dawns, rises, and sets and crowns the height of Heaven!

[Cf. *Anima Poetæ*, 1895, p. 162.]

Such Symphony demands best Instrument.
Seize then, my soul! from Freedom's trophied dome.
The harp which hanging high between the shields
Of Brutus and Leonidas, gives oft　　15
A fateful Music, when with breeze-like Touch
Pure spirits thrill its strings : the Poet's heart
Listens, and smiling knows that Poets demand
Once more to live for Man and work by Fame :
For what is Freedom, but th' unfetter'd use　　20
Of all the Powers, which God for use had given !
Thro' the sweet Influence of harmonious Word——

. . . . . .

The zephyr-travell'd Harp, that flashes forth
Jets and low wooings of wild melody
That sally forth and seek the meeting Ear,　　25
Then start away, half-wanton, half-afraid
Like the red-breast forced by wintry snows,
In the first visits by the genial Hearth,
From the fair Hand, that tempts it to—
Or like a course of flame, from the deep sigh　　30
Of the idly-musing Lover dreaming of his Love
With thoughts and hopes and fears, {sinking, snatching, as warily, upward
Bending, recoiling, fluttering as itself

. . . . . .

And cheats us with false prophecies of sound

---

9 i. e. jure suo, by any inherent Right.

FIRST DRAFTS, EARLY VERSIONS, ETC. 525

[DRAFT III]

Auspicious Reverence! Hush all meaner song,
Till we the deep prelusive strain have pour'd
To the Great Father, only Rightful king,
All Gracious Father, king Omnipotent!
To Him, the inseparate, unconfounded Trine,   5
Mind! Co-eternal Word! Forth-breathing Sound!
Birth! and Procession! Ever-circling Act!
GOD in GOD immanent, distinct yet one!
Sole Rest, true Substance of all finite Being!
Omnific! Omniform! The Immoveable,   10
That goes forth and remaineth: and at once
Dawns, rises, sets and crowns the height of Heaven!

. . . . . .

Such Symphony demands best Instrument.
Seize then, my Soul! from Freedom's trophied dome
The Harp, that hanging high between the Shields   15
Of Brutus and Leonidas, flashes forth
Starts of shrill-music, when with breeze-like Touch
Departed Patriots thrill the——

D

Passages in Southey's *Joan of Arc* (First Edition, 1796)
contributed by S. T. Coleridge[1].

[Vide *ante*, p. 131]

Book I, ll. 33–51.

"*O France,*" *he cried,* "*my country*"!
When soft as breeze that curls the summer clouds
At close of day, stole on his ear a voice   35
Seraphic.
      "Son of Orleans! grieve no more.
"His eye not slept, tho' long the All-just endured

37 not slept] slept not *MS. corr. by Southey.*

---

[1] Over and above the contributions to the Second Book of the *Joan of Arc*, which Southey acknowledged, and which were afterwards embodied in the *Destiny of Nations*, Coleridge claimed a number of passages in Books I, III, and IV. The passages are marked by S. T. C. in an annotated copy of the First Edition 4°, at one time the property of Coleridge's friend W. Hood of Bristol, and afterwards of John Taylor Brown. See *North British Review*, January, 1864.

"The woes of France; at length his bar'd right arm
"Volleys red thunder. From his veiling clouds
"Rushes the storm, Ruin and Fear and Death. 40
"Take Son of Orleans the relief of Heaven:
"Nor thou the wintry hours of adverse fate
"Dream useless: tho' unhous'd thou roam awhile,
"The keen and icy wind that shivers *thee*
"Shall brace thine arm, and with stern discipline 45
"Firm thy strong heart for fearless enterprise
"As who, through many a summer night serene
"Had hover'd round the fold with coward wish;
"Horrid with brumal ice, the fiercer wolf
"From his bleak mountain and his den of snows 50
"Leaps terrible and mocks the shepherd's spears."

ll. 57–59.

nor those ingredients dire
Erictho mingled on Pharsalia's field,
Making the soul retenant its cold corse.

ll. 220–222.

the groves of Paradise
Gave their mild echoes to the choral songs
Of new-born beings.—

ll. 267–280.

And oft the tear from his averted eye
He dried; mindful of fertile fields laid waste,
Dispeopled hamlets, the lorn widow's groan,
And the pale orphan's feeble cry for bread. 270
But when he told of those fierce sons of guilt
That o'er this earth which God had fram'd so fair
Spread desolation, and its wood-crown'd hills
Make echo to the merciless war-dog's howl;
And how himself from such foul savagery 275
Had scarce escap'd with life, then his stretch'd arm
Seem'd, as it wielded the resistless sword
Of Vengeance: in his eager eye the soul
Was eloquent; warm glow'd his manly cheek;
And beat against his side the indignant heart. 280

39 red] S. T. C. notes this word as Southey's. 46 Firm] S. T. C. writes against this word *Not English*.

FIRST DRAFTS, EARLY VERSIONS, ETC.

ll. 454–460.

then methought
From a dark lowering cloud, the womb of tempests, 455
A giant arm burst forth and dropt a sword
That pierc'd like lightning thro' the midnight air.
Then was there heard a voice, which in mine ear
Shall echo, at that hour of dreadful joy
When the pale foe shall wither in my rage. 460

ll. 484–496.[1]

Last evening lone in thought I wandered forth.
Down in the dingle's depth there is a brook 485
That makes its way between the craggy stones,
Murmuring hoarse murmurs. On an aged oak
Whose root uptorn by tempests overhangs
The stream, I sat, and mark'd the deep red clouds
Gather before the wind, while the rude dash 490
Of waters rock'd my senses, and the mists
Rose round: there as I gazed, a form dim-seen
Descended, like the dark and moving clouds
That in the moonbeam change their shadowy shapes.
His voice was on the breeze; he bade me hail 495
The missioned Maid! for lo! the hour was come.

Book III, ll. 73–82.

Martyr'd patriots—spirits pure
Wept by the good ye fell! Yet still survives
Sow'd by your toil and by your blood manur'd 75
Th' imperishable seed, soon to become
The Tree, beneath whose vast and mighty shade
The sons of men shall pitch their tents in peace,
And in the unity of truth preserve
The bond of love. For by the eye of God 80
Hath Virtue sworn, that never one good act
Was work'd in vain.

Book IV, ll. 328–336.

The murmuring tide
Lull'd her, and many a pensive pleasing dream
Rose in sad shadowy trains at Memory's call. 330
She thought of Arc, and of the dingled brook,

[1] Suggested and in part written by S. T. C.

Whose waves oft leaping on their craggy course
Made dance the low-hung willow's dripping twigs;
And where it spread into a glassy lake,
Of the old oak which on the smooth expanse   335
Imag'd its hoary mossy-mantled boughs.

E

[Vide *ante*, p. 186.]

THE RIME OF THE ANCYENT MARINERE[1],
IN SEVEN PARTS.

ARGUMENT

How a Ship having passed the Line was driven by Storms to the cold Country towards the South Pole; and how from thence she made her course to the Tropical Latitude of the Great Pacific Ocean; and of the strange things that befell; and in what manner the Ancyent Marinere came back to his own Country.

I.

It is an ancyent Marinere,
   And he stoppeth one of three:
"By thy long grey beard and thy glittering eye
   "Now wherefore stoppest me?

"The Bridegroom's doors are open'd wide,   5
   "And I am next of kin;
"The Guests are met, the Feast is set,—
   "May'st hear the merry din.

But still he holds the wedding-guest—
   There was a Ship, quoth he—   10
"Nay, if thou'st got a laughsome tale,
   "Marinere! come with me."

---

[1] First published in *Lyrical Ballads*, 1798, pp. [1]-27; republished in *Lyrical Ballads*, 1800, vol. i; *Lyrical Ballads*, 1802, vol. i; *Lyrical Ballads*, 1805, vol. i; reprinted in *The Poems of Samuel Taylor Coleridge*, Appendix, pp. 404-29, London: E. Moxon, Son, and Company, [1870]; reprinted in *Lyrical Ballads* edition of 1798, edited by Edward Dowden, LL.D., 1890, in *P. W.*, 1893, Appendix E, pp. 512-20, and in *Lyrical Ballads*, . . . 1798, edited by Thomas Hutchinson, 1898. The text of the present issue has been collated with that of an early copy of *Lyrical Ballads*, 1798 (containing *Lewti*, pp. 63-7), presented by Coleridge to his sister-in-law, Miss Martha Fricker. The lines were not numbered in L. B., 1798.

FIRST DRAFTS, EARLY VERSIONS, ETC. 529

He holds him with his skinny hand,
  Quoth he, there was a Ship—
"Now get thee hence, thou grey-beard Loon!   15
  "Or my Staff shall make thee skip.

He holds him with his glittering eye—
  The wedding guest stood still
And listens like a three year's child;
  The Marinere hath his will.   20

The wedding-guest sate on a stone.
  He cannot chuse but hear:
And thus spake on that ancyent man,
  The bright-eyed Marinere.

The Ship was cheer'd, the Harbour clear'd—   25
  Merrily did we drop
Below the Kirk, below the Hill,
  Below the Light-house top.

The Sun came up upon the left,
  Out of the Sea came he: 30
And he shone bright, and on the right
  Went down into the Sea.

Higher and higher every day,
  Till over the mast at noon—
The wedding-guest here beat his breast,   35
  For he heard the loud bassoon.

The Bride hath pac'd into the Hall,
  Red as a rose is she;
Nodding their heads before her goes
  The merry Minstralsy.   40

The wedding-guest he beat his breast,
  Yet he cannot chuse but hear:
And thus spake on that ancyent Man,
  The bright-eyed Marinere.

Listen, Stranger! Storm and Wind,   45
  A Wind and Tempest strong!
For days and weeks it play'd us freaks—
  Like Chaff we drove along.

Listen, Stranger! Mist and Snow,
  And it grew wond'rous cauld: 50
And Ice mast-high came floating by
  As green as Emerauld.

And thro' the drifts the snowy clifts
　Did send a dismal sheen;
Ne shapes of men ne beasts we ken—　　　　55
　The Ice was all between.

The Ice was here, the Ice was there,
　The Ice was all around:
It crack'd and growl'd, and roar'd and howl'd—
　Like noises of a swound.　　　　　　　　60

At length did cross an Albatross,
　Thorough the Fog it came;
And an it were a Christian Soul,
　We hail'd it in God's name.

The Marineres gave it biscuit-worms,　　　65
　And round and round it flew:
The Ice did split with a Thunder-fit,
　The Helmsman steer'd us thro'.

And a good south wind sprung up behind,
　The Albatross did follow;　　　　　　　70
And every day for food or play
　Came to the Marinere's hollo!

In mist or cloud on mast or shroud,
　It perch'd for vespers nine,
Whiles all the night thro' fog smoke-white,　75
　Glimmer'd the white moon-shine.

"God save thee, ancyent Marinere!
　"From the fiends that plague thee thus—
"Why look'st thou so?"—with my cross bow
　I shot the Albatross.　　　　　　　　　80

II.

The Sun came up upon the right,
　Out of the Sea came he;
And broad as a weft upon the left
　Went down into the Sea.

And the good south wind still blew behind,　85
　But no sweet Bird did follow
Ne any day for food or play
　Came to the Marinere's hollo!

---

63 And an] As if *MS. corr. by S. T. C.*　　75 *Corrected in the Errata to* fog-smoke white.　　83 ~~weft~~ [*S. T. C.*]

And I had done an hellish thing
  And it would work 'em woe: 90
For all averr'd, I had kill'd the Bird
  That made the Breeze to blow.

Ne dim ne red, like God's own head,
  The glorious Sun uprist:
Then all averr'd, I had kill'd the Bird 95
  That brought the fog and mist.
'Twas right, said they, such birds to slay
  That bring the fog and mist.

The breezes blew, the white foam flew,
  The furrow follow'd free: 100
We were the first that ever burst
  Into that silent Sea.

Down dropt the breeze, the Sails dropt down,
  'Twas sad as sad could be
And we did speak only to break 105
  The silence of the Sea.

All in a hot and copper sky
  The bloody sun at noon,
Right up above the mast did stand,
  No bigger than the moon. 110

Day after day, day after day,
  We stuck, ne breath ne motion,
As idle as a painted Ship
  Upon a painted Ocean.

Water, water, every where, 115
  And all the boards did shrink;
Water, water, everywhere,
  Ne any drop to drink.

The very deeps did rot: O Christ!
  That ever this should be! 120
Yea, slimy things did crawl with legs
  Upon the slimy Sea.

About, about, in reel and rout,
  The Death-fires danc'd at night;
The water, like a witch's oils, 125
  Burnt green and blue and white.

And some in dreams assured were
  Of the Spirit that plagued us so:
Nine fathom deep he had follow'd us
  From the Land of Mist and Snow.   130

And every tongue thro' utter drouth
  Was wither'd at the root;
We could not speak no more than if
  We had been choked with soot.

Ah wel-a-day! what evil looks   135
  Had I from old and young;
Instead of the Cross the Albatross
  About my neck was hung.

III.

I saw a something in the Sky
  No bigger than my fist;   140
At first it seem'd a little speck
  And then it seem'd a mist:
It mov'd and mov'd, and took at last
  A certain shape, I wist.

A speck, a mist, a shape, I wist!   145
  And still it ner'd and ner'd;
And, an it dodg'd a water-sprite,
  It plung'd and tack'd and veer'd.

With throat unslack'd, with black lips bak'd
  Ne could we laugh, ne wail: 150
Then while thro' drouth all dumb they stood
I bit my arm and suck'd the blood
  And cry'd, A sail! a sail!

With throat unslack'd, with black lips bak'd
  Agape they hear'd me call: 155
Gramercy! they for joy did grin
And all at once their breath drew in
  As they were drinking all.

She doth not tack from side to side—
  Hither to work us weal
Withouten wind, withouten tide   160
  She steddies with upright keel.

The western wave was all a flame,
  The day was well nigh done!
Almost upon the western wave   165
  Rested the broad bright Sun;
When that strange shape drove suddenly
  Betwixt us and the Sun.

And strait the Sun was fleck'd with bars
  (Heaven's mother send us grace)   170
As if thro' a dungeon grate he peer'd
  With broad and burning face.

Alas! (thought I, and my heart beat loud)
  How fast she neres and neres!
Are those *her* Sails that glance in the Sun 175
  Like restless gossameres?

Are those *her* naked ribs, which fleck'd
  The sun that did behind them peer?
And are those two all, all the crew,
  That woman and her fleshless Pheere?   180

His bones were black with many a crack,
  All black and bare, I ween;
Jet-black and bare, save where with rust
Of mouldy damps and charnel crust
  They're patch'd with purple and green. 185

Her lips are red, *her* looks are free,
  Her locks are yellow as gold:
Her skin is as white as leprosy,
And she is far liker Death than he;
  Her flesh makes the still air cold.   190

The naked Hulk alongside came
  And the Twain were playing dice;
"The Game is done! I've won, I've won!"
  Quoth she, and whistled thrice.

A gust of wind sterte up behind   195
  And whistled thro' his bones;
Thro' the holes of his eyes and the hole of his mouth
  Half-whistles and half-groans.

---

179 For "those" read "these" *Errata, p.* [*221*], *L. B. 1798.*

With never a whisper in the Sea
  Off darts the Spectre-ship;
While clombe above the Eastern bar
The horned Moon, with one bright Star
  Almost atween the tips.

One after one by the horned Moon
  (Listen, O Stranger! to me)
Each turn'd his face with a ghastly pang
  And curs'd me with his ee.

Four times fifty living men,
  With never a sigh or groan,
With heavy thump, a lifeless lump
  They dropp'd down one by one.

Their souls did from their bodies fly,—
  They fled to bliss or woe;
And every soul it pass'd me by,
  Like the whiz of my Cross-bow.

IV.

"I fear thee, ancyent Marinere!
  "I fear thy skinny hand;
"And thou art long, and lank, and brown,
  "As is the ribb'd Sea-sand.

"I fear thee and thy glittering eye
  "And thy skinny hand so brown—
Fear not, fear not, thou wedding guest!
  This body dropt not down.

Alone, alone, all all alone
  Alone on the wide wide Sea;
And Christ would take no pity on
  My soul in agony.

The many men so beautiful,
  And they all dead did lie!
And a million million slimy things
  Liv'd on—and so did I.

I look'd upon the rotting Sea,
  And drew my eyes away;
I look'd upon the eldritch deck,
  And there the dead men lay.

I look'd to Heav'n, and try'd to pray;
  But or ever a prayer had gusht,
A wicked whisper came and made
  My heart as dry as dust.

I clos'd my lids and kept them close   240
  Till the balls like pulses beat;
For the sky and the sea, and the sea and the sky
Lay like a load on my weary eye,
  And the dead were at my feet.

The cold sweat melted from their limbs,   245
  Ne rot, ne reek did they;
The look with which they look'd on me,
  Had never pass'd away.

An orphan's curse would drag to Hell
  A spirit from on high: 250
But O! more horrible than that
  Is the curse in a dead man's eye!
Seven days, seven nights I saw that curse,
  And yet I could not die.

The moving Moon went up the sky,   255
  And no where did abide:
Softly she was going up
  And a star or two beside

Her beams bemock'd the sultry main
  Like morning frosts yspread;   260
But where the ship's huge shadow lay,
The charmed water burnt alway
  A still and awful red.

Beyond the shadow of the ship
  I watch'd the water-snakes: 265
They mov'd in tracks of shining white;
And when they rear'd, the elfish light
  Fell off in hoary flakes.

Within the shadow of the ship
  I watch'd their rich attire: 270
Blue, glossy green, and velvet black
They coil'd and swam; and every track
  Was a flash of golden fire.

O happy living things! no tongue
  Their beauty might declare: 275
A spring of love gusht from my heart,
  And I bless'd them unaware!
Sure my kind saint took pity on me,
  And I bless'd them unaware.

The self-same moment I could pray; 280
  And from my neck so free
The Albatross fell off, and sank
  Like lead into the sea.

v.

O sleep, it is a gentle thing,
  Belov'd from pole to pole! 285
To Mary-queen the praise be yeven
She sent the gentle sleep from heaven
  That slid into my soul.

The silly buckets on the deck
  That had so long remain'd, 290
I dreamt that they were fill'd with dew
  And when I awoke it rain'd.

My lips were wet, my throat was cold,
  My garments all were dank;
Sure I had drunken in my dreams 295
  And still my body drank.

I mov'd and could not feel my limbs,
  I was so light, almost
I thought that I had died in sleep,
  And was a blessed Ghost. 300

The roaring wind! it roar'd far off,
  It did not come anear;
But with its sound it shook the sails
  That were so thin and sere.

The upper air bursts into life, 305
  And a hundred fire-flags sheen
To and fro they are hurried about;
And to and fro, and in and out
  The stars dance on between.

FIRST DRAFTS, EARLY VERSIONS, ETC. 537

> The coming wind doth roar more loud; 310
> The sails do sigh, like sedge:
> The rain pours down from one black cloud
> And the Moon is at its edge.
>
> Hark! hark! the thick black cloud is cleft,
> And the Moon is at its side: 315
> Like waters shot from some high crag,
> The lightning falls with never a jag
> A river steep and wide.
>
> The strong wind reach'd the ship: it roar'd
> And dropp'd down, like a stone! 320
> Beneath the lightning and the moon
> The dead men gave a groan.
>
> They groan'd, they stirr'd, they all uprose,
> Ne spake, ne mov'd their eyes:
> It had been strange, even in a dream 325
> To have seen those dead men rise.
>
> The helmsman steer'd, the ship mov'd on;
> Yet never a breeze up-blew;
> The Marineres all 'gan work the ropes,
> Where they were wont to do: 330
> They rais'd their limbs like lifeless tools—
> We were a ghastly crew.
>
> The body of my brother's son
> Stood by me knee to knee:
> The body and I pull'd at one rope, 335
> But he said nought to me—
> And I quak'd to think of my own voice
> How frightful it would be!
>
> The day-light dawn'd—they dropp'd their arms,
> And cluster'd round the mast: 340
> Sweet sounds rose slowly thro' their mouths
> And from their bodies pass'd.
>
> Around, around, flew each sweet sound,
> Then darted to the sun:
> Slowly the sounds came back again 345
> Now mix'd, now one by one.

After 338 * * * * * * *MS., L. B. 1798.*

Sometimes a dropping from the sky
  I heard the Lavrock sing;
Sometimes all little birds that are
How they seem'd to fill the sea and air   350
  With their sweet jargoning.

And now 'twas like all instruments,
  Now like a lonely flute;
And now it is an angel's song
  That makes the heavens be mute.   355

It ceas'd: yet still the sails made on
  A pleasant noise till noon,
A noise like of a hidden brook
  In the leafy month of June,
That to the sleeping woods all night   360
  Singeth a quiet tune.

Listen, O listen, thou Wedding-guest!
  "Marinere! thou hast thy will:
"For that, which comes out of thine eye, doth make
  "My body and soul to be still."   365

Never sadder tale was told
  To a man of woman born:
Sadder and wiser thou wedding-guest!
  Thou'lt rise to-morrow morn.

Never sadder tale was heard   370
  By a man of woman born:
The Marineres all return'd to work
  As silent as beforne.

The Marineres all 'gan pull the ropes,
  But look at me they n'old: 375
Thought I, I am as thin as air—
  They cannot me behold.

Till noon we silently sail'd on
  Yet never a breeze did breathe:
Slowly and smoothly went the ship   380
  Mov'd onward from beneath.

Under the keel nine fathom deep
  From the land of mist and snow
The spirit slid: and it was He
  That made the Ship to go.   385
The sails at noon left off their tune
  And the Ship stood still also.

FIRST DRAFTS, EARLY VERSIONS, ETC.

The sun right up above the mast
  Had fix'd her to the ocean:
But in a minute she 'gan stir   390
  With a short uneasy motion—
Backwards and forwards half her length
  With a short uneasy motion.

Then, like a pawing horse let go,
  She made a sudden bound: 395
It flung the blood into my head,
  And I fell into a swound.

How long in that same fit I lay,
  I have not to declare;
But ere my living life return'd,   400
I heard and in my soul discern'd
  Two voices in the air,

"Is it he?" quoth one, "Is this the man?
  "By him who died on cross,
"With his cruel bow he lay'd full low   405
  "The harmless Albatross.

"The spirit who 'bideth by himself
  "In the land of mist and snow,
"He lov'd the bird that lov'd the man
  "Who shot him with his bow.   410

The other was a softer voice,
  As soft as honey-dew:
Quoth he the man hath penance done,
  And penance more will do.

VI.

First Voice.

"But tell me, tell me! speak again,   415
  "Thy soft response renewing—
"What makes that ship drive on so fast?
  "What is the Ocean doing?

Second Voice.

"Still as a Slave before his Lord,
  "The Ocean hath no blast: 420
"His great bright eye most silently
  "Up to the moon is cast—

"If he may know which way to go,
  "For she guides him smooth or grim.
"See, brother, see! how graciously
  "She looketh down on him.

First Voice.

"But why drives on that ship so fast
  "Withouten wave or wind?

Second Voice.

"The air is cut away before,
  "And closes from behind.

"Fly, brother, fly! more high, more high,
  "Or we shall be belated:
"For slow and slow that ship will go,
  "When the Marinere's trance is abated."

I woke, and we were sailing on
  As in a gentle weather:
'Twas night, calm night, the moon was high;
  The dead men stood together.

All stood together on the deck,
  For a charnel-dungeon fitter:
All fix'd on me their stony eyes
  That in the moon did glitter.

The pang, the curse, with which they died,
  Had never pass'd away:
I could not draw my een from theirs
  Ne turn them up to pray.

And in its time the spell was snapt,
  And I could move my een:
I look'd far-forth, but little saw
  Of what might else be seen.

Like one, that on a lonely road
  Doth walk in fear and dread,
And having once turn'd round, walks on
  And turns no more his head:
Because he knows, a frightful fiend
  Doth close behind him tread.

But soon there breath'd a wind on me,
  Ne sound ne motion made:
Its path was not upon the sea
  In ripple or in shade.

FIRST DRAFTS, EARLY VERSIONS, ETC. 541

It rais'd my hair, it fann'd my cheek,
    Like a meadow-gale of spring—
It mingled strangely with my fears,
    Yet it felt like a welcoming.

Swiftly, swiftly flew the ship, 465
    Yet she sail'd softly too:
Sweetly, sweetly blew the breeze—
    On me alone it blew.

O dream of joy! is this indeed
    The light-house top I see? 470
Is this the Hill? Is this the Kirk?
    Is this mine own countrée?

We drifted o'er the Harbour-bar,
    And I with sobs did pray—
"O let me be awake, my God! 475
    "Or let me sleep alway!"

The harbour-bay was clear as glass,
    So smoothly it was strewn!
And on the bay the moon light lay,
    And the shadow of the moon. 480

The moonlight bay was white all o'er,
    Till rising from the same,
Full many shapes, that shadows were,
    Like as of torches came.

A little distance from the prow 485
    Those dark-red shadows were;
But soon I saw that my own flesh
    Was red as in a glare.

I turn'd my head in fear and dread,
    And by the holy rood, 490
The bodies had advanc'd, and now
    Before the mast they stood.

They lifted up their stiff right arms,
    They held them strait and tight;
And each right-arm burnt like a torch, 495
    A torch that's borne upright.
Their stony eye-balls glitter'd on
    In the red and smoky light.

I pray'd and turn'd my head away
   Forth looking as before.
There was no breeze upon the bay,   500
   No wave against the shore.

The rock shone bright, the kirk no less
   That stands above the rock:
The moonlight steep'd in silentness   505
   The steady weathercock.

And the bay was white with silent light,
   Till rising from the same
Full many shapes, that shadows were,
   In crimson colours came.   510

A little distance from the prow
   Those crimson shadows were:
I turn'd my eyes upon the deck—
   O Christ! what saw I there?

Each corse lay flat, lifeless and flat;   515
   And by the Holy rood
A man all light, a seraph-man,
   On every corse there stood.

This seraph-band, each wav'd his hand:
   It was a heavenly sight: 520
They stood as signals to the land,
   Each one a lovely light:

This seraph-band, each wav'd his hand,
   No voice did they impart—
No voice; but O! the silence sank,   525
   Like music on my heart.

Eftsones I heard the dash of oars,
   I heard the pilot's cheer:
My head was turn'd perforce away
   And I saw a boat appear.   530

Then vanish'd all the lovely lights;
   The bodies rose anew:
With silent pace, each to his place
   Came back the ghastly crew.
The wind, that shade nor motion made,   535
   On me alone it blew.

The pilot, and the pilot's boy
  I heard them coming fast:
Dear Lord in Heaven! it was a joy,
  The dead men could not blast.   540

I saw a third—I heard his voice:
  It is the Hermit good!
He singeth loud his godly hymns
  That he makes in the wood.
He'll shrieve my soul, he'll wash away   545
  The Albatross's blood.

VII.

This Hermit good lives in that wood
  Which slopes down to the Sea.
How loudly his sweet voice he rears!
He loves to talk with Marineres   550
  That come from a far Contrée.

He kneels at morn and noon and eve—
  He hath a cushion plump:
It is the moss, that wholly hides
  The rotted old Oak-stump.   555

The Skiff-boat ne'rd: I heard them talk,
  "Why, this is strange, I trow!
"Where are those lights so many and fair
  "That signal made but now?

"Strange, by my faith! the Hermit said—   560
  "And they answer'd not our cheer.
"The planks look warp'd, and see those sails
  "How thin they are and sere!
"I never saw aught like to them
  "Unless perchance it were   565

"The skeletons of leaves that lag
  "My forest-brook along:
"When the Ivy-tod is heavy with snow,
"And the Owlet whoops to the wolf below
  "That eats the she-wolf's young.   570

"Dear Lord! it has a fiendish look—
  (The Pilot made reply)
"I am afear'd—"Push on, push on!
  "Said the Hermit cheerily.

The Boat came closer to the Ship,
  But I ne spake ne stirr'd!   575
The Boat came close beneath the Ship.
  And strait a sound was heard!

Under the water it rumbled on,
  Still louder and more dread: 580
It reach'd the Ship, it split the bay;
  The Ship went down like lead.

Stunn'd by that loud and dreadful sound,
  Which sky and ocean smote:
Like one that had been seven days drown'd   585
  My body lay afloat:
But, swift as dreams, myself I found
  Within the Pilot's boat.

Upon the whirl, where sank the Ship,
  The boat spun round and round: 590
And all was still, save that the hill
  Was telling of the sound.

I mov'd my lips: the Pilot shriek'd
  And fell down in a fit.
The Holy Hermit rais'd his eyes   595
  And pray'd where he did sit.

I took the oars: the Pilot's boy,
  Who now doth crazy go,
Laugh'd loud and long, and all the while
  His eyes went to and fro,   600
"Ha! ha!" quoth he—"full plain I see,
"The devil knows how to row."

And now all in mine own Countrée
  I stood on the firm land!
The Hermit stepp'd forth from the boat,   605
  And scarcely he could stand.

"O shrieve me, shrieve me, holy Man!
  The Hermit cross'd his brow—
"Say quick," quoth he, "I bid thee say
  "What manner man art thou?"   610

Forthwith this frame of mine was wrench'd
  With a woeful agony,
Which forc'd me to begin my tale
  And then it left me free.

FIRST DRAFTS, EARLY VERSIONS, ETC. 545

Since then at an uncertain hour, 615
  Now oftimes and now fewer,
That anguish comes and makes me tell
  My ghastly aventure.

I pass, like night, from land to land;
  I have strange power of speech; 620
The moment that his face I see
I know the man that must hear me;
  To him my tale I teach.

What loud uproar bursts from that door!
  The Wedding-guests are there; 625
But in the Garden-bower the Bride
  And Bride-maids singing are:
And hark the little Vesper-bell
  Which biddeth me to prayer.

O Wedding-guest! this soul hath been 630
  Alone on a wide wide sea:
So lonely 'twas, that God himself
  Scarce seemed there to be.

O sweeter than the Marriage-feast,
  'Tis sweeter far to me 635
To walk together to the Kirk
  With a goodly company.

To walk together to the Kirk
  And all together pray,
While each to his great Father bends, 640
Old men, and babes, and loving friends,
  And Youths, and Maidens gay.

Farewell, farewell! but this I tell
  To thee, thou wedding-guest!
He prayeth well who loveth well, 645
  Both man and bird and beast.

He prayeth best who loveth best,
  All things both great and small:
For the dear God, who loveth us,
  He made and loveth all. 650

The Marinere, whose eye is bright,
  Whose beard with age is hoar,
Is gone; and now the wedding-guest
  Turn'd from the bridegroom's door.

He went, like one that hath been stunn'd   655
    And is of sense forlorn:
  A sadder and a wiser man
    He rose the morrow morn.

F

THE RAVEN

[As printed in the *Morning Post*, March 10, 1798.]

[Vide *ante*, p. 169.]

UNDER the arms of a goodly oak-tree,
There was of Swine a large company.
They were making a rude repast,
Grunting as they crunch'd the mast.
Then they trotted away: for the wind blew high—   5
One acorn they left, ne more mote you spy.
Next came a Raven, who lik'd not such folly;
He belong'd, I believe, to the witch MELANCHOLY!
Blacker was he than the blackest jet;
Flew low in the rain; his feathers were wet.   10
He pick'd up the acorn and buried it strait,
By the side of a river both deep and great.
  Where then did the Raven go?
  He went high and low—
O'er hill, o'er dale did the black Raven go!   15
  Many Autumns, many Springs;
  Travell'd he with wand'ring wings;
  Many Summers, many Winters—
  I can't tell half his adventures.
At length he return'd, and with him a she;   20
And the acorn was grown a large oak-tree.
They built them a nest in the topmost bough,
And young ones they had, and were jolly enow.
But soon came a Woodman in leathern guise:
His brow like a pent-house hung over his eyes.   25
He'd an axe in his hand, and he nothing spoke,
But with many a hem! and a sturdy stroke,
At last he brought down the poor Raven's own oak.
His young ones were kill'd, for they could not depart,
And his wife she did die of a broken heart!   30

FIRST DRAFTS, EARLY VERSIONS, ETC.

The branches from off it the Woodman did sever!
And they floated it down on the course of the River:
They saw'd it to planks, and it's rind they did strip,
And with this tree and others they built up a ship.
The ship, it was launch'd; but in sight of the land,   35
A tempest arose which no ship could withstand.
It bulg'd on a rock, and the waves rush'd in fast—
The auld Raven flew round and round, and caw'd to the blast.
He heard the sea-shriek of their perishing souls—
They be sunk! O'er the top-mast the mad water rolls.   40
The Raven was glad that such fate they did meet,
They had taken his all, and Revenge was sweet!

G

LEWTI; OR THE CIRCASSIAN'S LOVE-CHANT[1]

[Vide *ante*, p. 253.]

(1)

[Add. MSS. 27,902.]

High o er the silver rocks I roved
To forget the form I loved
In hopes fond fancy would be kind
And steal my Mary from my mind
   T'was twilight and the lunar beam   5
Sailed slowly o'er Tamaha's stream
As down its sides the water strayed
Bright on a rock the moonbeam playe[d]
It shone, half-sheltered from the view
By pendent boughs of tressy yew   10
True, true to love but false to rest,
So fancy whispered to my breast,
So shines her forehead smooth and fair
Gleaming through her sable hair
I turned to heaven—but viewed on high   15
The languid lustre of her eye

---

[1] The first ten lines of MS. version (1) were first published in *Note* 44 of *P. W.*, 1893, p. 518, and the MS. as a whole is included in *Coleridge's Poems*, A Facsimile Reproduction of The Proofs and MSS., &c., 1899, pp. 132-4. MSS. (2) and (3) are now printed for the first time.

The moons mild radiant edge I saw
Peeping a black-arched cloud below
Nor yet its faint and paly beam
Could tinge its skirt with yellow gleam   20
  I saw the white waves o'er and o'er
Break against a curved shore
Now disappearing from the sight
Now twinkling regular and white
Her mouth, her smiling mouth can shew   25
As white and regular a row
Haste Haste, some God indulgent prove
And bear me, bear me to my love
Then might—for yet the sultry hour
Glows from the sun's oppressive power   30
Then might her bosom soft and white
Heave upon my swimming sight
As yon two swans together heave
Upon the gently-swelling wave
Haste—haste some God indulgent prove   35
And bear—oh bear me to my love.

(2)

[Add. MSS. 35,343.]

THE CIRCASSIAN'S LOVE-CHAUNT
~~Wild Indians~~

HIGH o'er the rocks at night I rov'd
To forget the ~~silver~~ form I lov'd.
Image of LEWTI! from my mind
Depart! for LEWTI ~~Cora~~ is not kind!
~~Cora~~

Bright was the Moon: the Moon's bright beam   5
Speckled with many a moving shade,
Danc'd upon Tamaha's stream;
But brightlier on the Rock it play'd,
The Rock, half-shelter'd from my view
By pendent boughs of tressy Yew!   10
True to Love, but false to Rest,
My fancy whisper'd in my breast—
So shines my Lewti's forehead fair
Gleaming thro' her sable hair,

FIRST DRAFTS, EARLY VERSIONS, ETC. 549

  Image of LEWTI! from my mind   15
    ~~Cora~~
  Depart! for LEWTI is not kind.
     ~~Cora~~

  I saw a cloud of whitest hue;
  Onward to the Moon it pass'd!
  Still brighter and more bright it grew
  With floating colours not a few,   20
  Till it reach'd the Moon at last.

LEWTI; OR THE CIRCASSIAN'S LOVE-CHANT

(3)

[Add. MSS. 35,343, f. 3 recto.]

  HIGH o'er the rocks at night I rov'd
  To forget the form I lov'd.
  Image of LEWTI! from my mind
  Depart: for LEWTI is not kind.   25

  Bright was the Moon: the Moon's bright bea[m]
  Speckled with many a moving shade,
  Danc'd upon TAMAHA's stream;
  But brightlier on the Rock it play'd,
  The Rock, half-shelter'd from my view   30
  By pendent boughs of tressy Yew!
  True to Love, but false to Rest,
  My fancy whisper'd in my breast—
  So shines my LEWTI's forehead fair
  Gleaming thro' her sable hair!   35
  Image of LEWTI! from my mind
  Depart—for LEWTI is not kind.

  I saw a Cloud of whitest hue—
  Onward to the Moon it pass'd.
  Still brighter and more bright it grew   40
  With floating colours not a few,
  Till it reach'd the Moon at last:
  Then the Cloud was wholly bright
  With a rich and amber light!
     deep
  And so with many a hope I seek,   45
  And so with joy I find my LEWTI:
  And even so my pale wan cheek
  Drinks in as deep a flush of Beauty

Image of LEWTI! leave my mind
If Lewti never will be kind! 50

Away the little Cloud, away.
Away it goes—away so soon
~~alone~~
Alas! it has no power to stay:
It's hues are dim, it's hues are grey
Away it passes from the Moon. 55
And now tis whiter than before—
As white as my poor cheek will be,
When, LEWTI! on my couch I lie
A dying Man for Love of thee!
~~Thou living Image~~
Image of LEWTI in my mind, 60
Methinks thou lookest not ~~kin~~ unkind!

H

INTRODUCTION TO THE TALE OF THE DARK LADIE[1]

[Vide *ante*, p. 330.]

TO THE EDITOR OF THE MORNING POST.

SIR,

The following Poem is the Introduction to a somewhat longer one, for which I shall solicit insertion on your next open day. The use of the Old Ballad word, *Ladie*, for Lady, is the only piece of obsoleteness in it; and as it is professedly a tale of ancient times, I trust, that 'the affectionate lovers of venerable antiquity' (as Camden says) will grant me their pardon, and perhaps may be induced to admit a force and propriety in it. A heavier objection may be adduced against the Author, that in these times of fear and expectation, when novelties *explode* around us in all directions, he should presume

---

[1] Published in the *Morning Post*, Dec. 21, 1799. Collated with two MSS.—*MS.* (*1*); *MS.* (*2*)—in the British Museum [Add. MSS. 27,902]. See *Coleridge's Poems*, A Facsimile of the Proofs, &c., edited by the late James Dykes Campbell, 1899. *MS. 1* consists of thirty-two stanzas (unnumbered), written on nine pages: *MS. 2* (which begins with stanza 6, and ends with stanza 30) of fourteen stanzas (unnumbered) written on four pages.

Title—The Dark Ladiè. *MS. B.M.* (*1*).

FIRST DRAFTS, EARLY VERSIONS, ETC. 551

to offer to the public a silly tale of old fashioned love; and, five years ago, I own, I should have allowed and felt the force of this objection. But, alas! explosion has succeeded explosion so rapidly, that novelty itself ceases to appear new; and it is possible that now, even a simple story, wholly unspired [? inspired] with politics or personality, may find some attention amid the hubbub of Revolutions, as to those who have resided a long time by the falls of Niagara, the lowest whispering becomes distinctly audible.

S. T. Coleridge.

1

O leave the Lily on its stem;
  O leave the Rose upon the spray;
O leave the Elder-bloom, fair Maids!
  And listen to my lay.

2

A Cypress and a Myrtle bough,   5
  This morn around my harp you twin'd,
Because it fashion'd mournfully
  Its murmurs in the wind.

3

And now a Tale of Love and Woe,
  A woeful Tale of Love I sing: 10
Hark, gentle Maidens, hark! it sighs
  And trembles on the string.

4

But most, my own dear Genevieve!
  It sighs and trembles most for thee!
O come and hear the cruel wrongs   15
  Befel the dark Ladie!

5

Few sorrows hath she of her own,
  My hope, my joy, my Genevieve!
She loves me best whene'er I sing
  The songs that make her grieve.   20

---

2 Rose upon] Rose-bud on *MS. B.M.* (*1*).   3 fair] dear *erased MS.* (*1*).   7 mournfully] sad and sweet *MS.* (*1*).   8 in] to *MS.* (*1*).   16 Ladie] Ladié *MS.* (*2*).   20 The song that makes her grieve. *MS.* (*1*).

APPENDIX I

6

All thoughts, all passions, all delights,
  Whatever stirs this mortal frame,
All are but ministers of Love,
  And feed his sacred flame.

7

O ever in my waking dreams,   25
  I dwell upon that happy hour,
When midway on the Mount I sate
  Beside the ruin'd Tow'r.

8

The moonshine, stealing o'er the scene,
  Had blended with the lights of eve,   30
And she was there, my hope! my joy!
  My own dear Genevieve!

9

She lean'd against the armed Man
The statue of the armed Knight—

21-4   Each thought, each feeling of the Soul,
           All lovely sights, each tender name,
           All, all are ministers of Love,
              That stir our mortal frame. *MS. (1)*.
  22 All, all that stirs this mortal frame *MS. B.M. (2)*.   24 feed] fan *MS. (2)*.

25   O ever in my lonely walk *erased MS. (1)*.
          In lonely walk and noontide dreams *MS. (1)*.
          O ever when I walk alone *erased MS. (1)*.
26   I feed upon that blissful hour *MS. (1)*.
         I feed upon that hour of Bliss *erased MS. (1)*.
         That ruddy eve that blissful hour *erased MS. (1)*.
26 dwell] feed *MS. (2)*.

                      we sate
27   When midway on the mount I stood *MS. (1)*.
        When we too stood upon the Hill *erased MS. (1)*.
29   The Moonshine stole upon the ground *erased MS. (1)*.
      The Moon be blended on the ground *MS. (1)*.
30 Had] And *erased MS. (1)*.   31 was there] stood near (was there *erased*) *MS. (1)*.

33-6   Against a grey stone rudely carv'd,
             The statue of an armed Knight,
                  in
            She lean'd the melancholy mood,
            And To watch'd the lingering Light *MS. (1)*.
33-4   She lean'd against a chissold stone
                       tall
        The statue of a *MS. (1)*.
34 the] an *MS. (1)* [Stanza 10, revised.]

FIRST DRAFTS, EARLY VERSIONS, ETC. 553

> She stood and listen'd to my harp,   35
>   Amid the ling'ring light.

10

> I play'd a sad and doleful air,
>   I sang an old and moving story,
> An old rude song, that fitted well
>   The ruin wild and hoary.   40

11

> She listen'd with a flitting blush,
>   With downcast eyes and modest grace:
> For well she knew, I could not choose
>   But gaze upon her face.

12

> I told her of the Knight that wore   45
>   Upon his shield a burning brand,
> And how for ten long years he woo'd
>   The Ladie of the Land:

13

> I told her, how he pin'd, and ah!
>   The deep, the low, the pleading tone,   50
> With which I sang another's love,
>   Interpreted my own!

14

> She listen'd with a flitting blush,
>   With downcast eyes and modest grace.
> And she forgave me, that I gaz'd   55
>   Too fondly on her face!

37 sad] soft *MSS.* (*1, 2*).   doleful] mournful *erased MS.* (*1*).   39 An] And *MS.* (*2*).   rude] wild *erased MS.* (*1*).
41–4   With flitting Blush and downcast eyes,
       In modest melancholy grace
     The Maiden stood: perchance I gaz'd
       Too fondly on her face. *Erased MS.* (*1*).
45–8 om. *MS.* (*1*).   49 I gaz'd and when I sang of love *MS.* (*1*).
53–6   With flitting Blush and downcast eyes
           and
     With downcast eyes *in* modest grace
           for
     She listen'd; and perchance I gaz'd
       Too fondly on her face. *MS.* (*1*).
55 And] Yet *MS.* (*1*).

COLERIDGE, F.S.   T

15

But when I told the cruel scorn,
  That craz'd this bold and lovely Knight;
And how he roam'd the mountain woods,
  Nor rested day or night;   60

16

And how he cross'd the Woodman's paths,
  Thro' briars and swampy mosses beat;
How boughs rebounding scourg'd his limbs,
  And low stubs gor'd his feet.

17

How sometimes from the savage den,   65
  And sometimes from the darksome shade,
And sometimes starting up at once,
  In green and sunny glade;

18

There came and look'd him in the face
  An Angel beautiful and bright,   70
And how he knew it was a Fiend,
  This mis'rable Knight!

19

And how, unknowing what he did,
  He leapt amid a lawless band,
And sav'd from outrage worse than death   75
  The Ladie of the Land.

20

And how she wept, and clasp'd his knees,
  And how she tended him in vain,
And meekly strove to expiate
  The scorn that craz'd his brain;   80

---

57 told] sang *MS. (1)*.   59 roam'd] cross'd *MS. (1)*.   60 or] nor *MS. (1)*.   61-4 *om. MS. (1)*.   65 How sometimes from the hollow Trees *MS. (1)*.

                              look'd
69-72   There came and star'd him in the face
         An[d] Angel beautiful and bright,
      And how he knew it was a fiend
         And yell'd with strange affright. *MS. (1)*.

74 lawless] murderous *MS. (1)*.   77 clasp'd] kiss'd *MS. (1)*.   79 meekly] how she *MS. (1)*.

FIRST DRAFTS, EARLY VERSIONS, ETC. 555

21

And how she nurs'd him in a cave;
    And how his madness went away,
When on the yellow forest leaves
    A dying man he lay;

22

His dying words—but when I reach'd   85
    That tenderest strain of all the ditty,
My fault'ring voice and pausing harp
    Disturb'd her soul with pity.

23

All impulses of soul and sense
    Had thrill'd my guiltless Genevieve—   90
The music and the doleful tale,
    The rich and balmy eve;

24

And hopes and fears that kindle hope,
    An undistinguishable throng;
And gentle wishes long subdu'd,   95
    Subdu'd and cherish'd long.

25

She wept with pity and delight—
    She blush'd with love and maiden shame,
And like the murmurs of a dream,
    I heard her breathe my name.   100

---

87 fault'ring] trembling *MS. (1) erased.*   90 guiltless] guileless *MS. (1).*
Between 96 *and* 97
    And while   midnight
       While Fancy like the nuptial Torch
       That bends and rises in the wind
       Lit up with wild and broken lights
          The Tumult of her mind. *MS. (1) erased.*
99   And like the murmur of a dream *MSS. (1, 2).*
        And in a murmur faint and sweet *MS. (1) erased.*
        She half-pronounced my name.
100   She breathed her Lover's name. *MS. (1) erased.*

26

I saw her bosom heave and swell,
    Heave and swell with inward sighs—
I could not choose but love to see
    Her gentle bosom rise.

27

Her wet cheek glow'd; she stept aside,   105
    As conscious of my look she stept;
Then suddenly, with tim'rous eye,
    She flew to me, and wept;

28

She half-inclos'd me with her arms—
    She press'd me with a meek embrace;   110
And, bending back her head, look'd up,
    And gaz'd upon my face.

29

'Twas partly love, and partly fear,
    And partly 'twas a bashful art,
That I might rather feel than see,   115
    The swelling of her heart.

101–4   I saw her gentle Bosom heave
        Th' inaudible and frequent sigh;
            modest
        And ah! the ~~bashful~~ Maiden mark'd
          The wanderings of my eye [s]   *MS.* (*1*) *erased.*

105–8 *om. MS.* (*1*).   105 cheek] cheeks *MS.* (*2*).   108 flew] fled *MS.* (*2*).
                side
109–16   And closely to my ~~heart~~ she press'd
        And ask'd me with her swimming eyes
            might
        That I ~~would~~ rather feel than see
          Her gentle Bosom rise.—
            side
    Or   And closely to my ~~heart~~ she press'd
        And closer still with bashful art—
        That I might rather feel than see
          The swelling of her Heart.   *MS.* (*1*) *erased.*

111 And] Then *MS.* (*2*) *erased.*

FIRST DRAFTS, EARLY VERSIONS, ETC. 557

30

I calm'd her fears, and she was calm,
  And told her love with virgin pride;
And so I won my Genevieve,
  My bright and beaut'ous bride.   120

31

And now once more a tale of woe,
  A woeful tale of love, I sing:
For thee, my Genevieve! it sighs,
  And trembles on the string.

32

When last I sang the cruel scorn   125
  That craz'd this bold and lonely Knight,
And how he roam'd the mountain woods,
  Nor rested day or night;

33

I promis'd thee a sister tale
  Of Man's perfidious cruelty: 130
Come, then, and hear what cruel wrong
  Befel the Dark Ladie.

End of the Introduction.

117   And now serene, serene and chaste
  But soon in calm and solemn tone *MS.* (*1*) *erased.*
  118 And] She *MS.* (*1*) *erased.*   virgin] maiden *MSS.* (*1, 2*).   120
bright] dear *MS.* (*1*) *erased.*   beaut'ous] lovely *MS.* (*1*) *erased.*
    125-8   When last I sang of Him whose heart
  Was broken by a woman's scorn—
  And how he cross'd the mountain woods
  All frantic and forlorn *MS.* (*1*).
  129 sister] moving *MS.* (*1*).   131 wrong] wrongs *MS.* (*1*).   132
Ladie] Ladié *MS.* (*1*).   *After* 132 *The Dark Ladiè.* *MS.* (*1*).

I

THE TRIUMPH OF LOYALTY.[1]

[Vide *ante*, p. 421.]

AN HISTORIC DRAMA

IN

FIVE ACTS.

FIRST PERFORMED WITH UNIVERSAL APPLAUSE AT THE THEATRE ROYAL, DRURY LANE, ON SATURDAY, FEBRUARY THE 7TH, 1801.

Apoecides.
  Quis hoc scit factum?

Epidicus.
  Ego ita esse factum dico.

Periphanes.
    Scin' tu istuc?

Epidicus.
  Scio.

Periphanes.
     Qui tu scis?

Epidicus.
  Quia ego vidi.

Periphanes.
[Ipse vidistine [Tragediam?]] Nimis factum bene!

Epidicus.
Sed vestita, aurata, ornata, ut lepide! ut concinne! ut nove! [Proh Dii immortales! tempestatem (plausuum Populus) nobis nocte hac misit!][2]

(Plaut. *Epidicus*. Act 2. Scen. 2, ll. 22 sqq.)

LONDON.

PRINTED FOR T. N. LONGMAN AND REES,
PATERNOSTER-ROW.

1801.

DRAMATIS PERSONÆ.

Earl Henry	Mr. Kemble
Don Curio	Mr. C. Kemble
Sandoval	Mr. Barrymore
Alva, the Chancellor	Mr. Aickin
Barnard, Earl Henry's Groom of the Chamber	Mr. Suett
Don Fernandez	Mr. Bannister, jun.
The Governor of the State Prison	Mr. Davis
Herreras (Oropeza's Uncle) and three Conspirators	Messrs. Packer, Wentworth, Mathew, and Gibbon
Officers and Soldiers of Earl Henry's Regiment.	
The Queen of Navarre	Mrs. Siddons
Donna Oropeza	Mrs. Powell
Mira, her attendant	Miss Decamp
Aspasia, a singer	Mrs. Crouch

Scene, partly at the Country seat of Donna Oropeza, and partly in Pampilona [*sic*], the Capital of Navarre.

---

[1] Now first published from an MS. in the British Museum (Add. MSS. 34,225). *The Triumph of Loyalty*, 'a sort of dramatic romance' (see *Letter to Poole*, December 5, 1800; *Letters of S. T. C.*, 1895, i. 343), was begun and left unfinished in the late autumn of 1800. An excerpt (ll. 277–358) was revised and published as 'A Night Scene. A Dramatic Fragment,' in *Sibylline Leaves* (1817), vide *ante*, pp. 421–3. The revision of the excerpt (ll. 263–349) with respect to the order and arrangement of its component parts is indicated by asterisks, which appear to be contemporary with the MS. I have, therefore, in printing the MS., followed the revised and not the original order of these lines. Again, in the hitherto unpublished portion of the MS. (ll. 1–263) I have omitted rough drafts of passages which were rewritten, either on the same page or on the reverse of the leaf.

[2] The words enclosed in brackets are not to be found in the text. They were either invented or adapted by Coleridge *ad hoc*. The text of the passage as a whole has been reconstructed by modern editors.

THE TRIUMPH OF LOYALTY

ACT I

Scene I. *A cultivated Plain, skirted on the Left by a Wood. The Pyrenees are visible in the distance. Small knots of Soldiers all in the military Dress of the middle Ages are seen passing across the Stage. Then*

Enter Earl Henry *and* Sandoval, *both armed.*

Sandoval. A delightful plain this, and doubly pleasant after so long and wearisome a descent from the Pyranees [*sic*]. Did you not observe how our poor over wearied horses mended their pace as soon as they reached it?

Earl Henry. I must entreat your forgiveness, gallant Castilian! I ought ere this to have bade you welcome to my native Navarre.

Sandoval. Cheerily, General! Navarre has indeed but ill repaid your services, in thus recalling you from the head of an army which you yourself had collected and disciplined. But the wrongs and insults which you have suffered——

Earl Henry. Deserve my thanks, Friend! In the sunshine of Court-favor I could only *believe* that I loved my Queen and my Country: now I *know* it. But why name I my Country or my Sovereign? I owe all my wrongs to the private enmity of the Chancellor.

Sandoval. Heaven be praised, you have atchieved [*sic*] a delicious revenge upon him!—that the same Courier who brought the orders for your recall carried back with him the first tidings of your Victory—it was exquisite good fortune!

Earl Henry. Sandoval! my gallant Friend! Let me not deceive you. To you I have vowed an undisguised openness. The gloom which overcast me, was occasioned by causes of less public import.

Sandoval. Connected, I presume, with that Mansion, the spacious pleasure grounds of which we noticed as we were descending from the mountain. Lawn and Grove, River and Hillock—it looked within these high walls, like a World of itself.

FIRST DRAFTS, EARLY VERSIONS, ETC.   561

Earl Henry. This Wood scarcely conceals these high walls from us. Alas! I know the place too well.... Nay, why too well?—But wherefore spake you, Sandoval, of this Mansion? What know you? 33

Sandoval. Nothing. Therefore I spake of it. On our descent from the mountain I pointed it out to you and asked to whom it belonged—you became suddenly absent, and answered me only by looks of Disturbance and Anxiety.

Earl Henry. That Mansion once belonged to Manric [sic], Lord of Valdez. 39

Sandoval. Alas, poor Man! the same, who had dangerous claims to the Throne of Navarre.

Earl Henry. Claims?—Say rather, pretensions—plausible only to the unreasoning Multitude.

Sandoval. Pretensions then (*with bitterness*). 44

Earl Henry. Bad as these were, the means he employed to give effect to them were still worse. He trafficked with France against the independence of his Country. He was a traitor, my Friend! and died a traitor's death. His two sons suffered with him, and many, (I fear, too many) of his adherents. 49

Sandoval. Earl Henry! (*a pause*) If the sentence were just, why was not the execution of it public.... It is reported, that they were—but no! I will not believe it—the honest soul of my friend would not justify so foul a deed.

Earl Henry. Speak plainly—what is reported? 54

Sandoval. That they were all assassinated by order of the new Queen.

Earl Henry. Accursed be the hearts that framed and the tongues that scattered the Calumny!—The Queen was scarcely seated on her throne; the Chancellor, who had been her Guardian, exerted a pernicious influence over her judgement—she was taught to fear dangerous commotions in the Capital, she was intreated to prevent the bloodshed of the deluded citizens, and thus overawed she reluctantly consented to permit the reinforcement of an obsolete law, and——

Sandoval. They were not assassinated then?—— 65

Earl Henry. Why these bitter tones to me, Sandoval? Can a law assassinate? Don Manrique [sic] and his accomplices drank the sleepy poison adjudged by that law in the State Prison at Pampilona. At that time I was with the army on the frontiers of France. 70

Sandoval. Had *you* been in the Capital——

Earl Henry. I would have pledged my life on the safety of a public Trial and a public Punishment. 73

Sandoval. Poisoned! The Father and his Sons!—And this, Earl Henry, was the first act of that Queen, whom you idolize!

Earl Henry. No, Sandoval, No! This was not *her* act. She roused herself from the stupor of alarm, she suspended *in opposition to the advice of her council*, all proceedings against the inferior partisans of the Conspiracy; she facilitated the escape of Don Manrique's brother, and to Donna Oropeza, his daughter and only surviving child, she restored all her father's possessions, nay became herself her Protectress and Friend. These were the acts, these the first acts of my royal Mistress.

Sandoval. And how did Donna Oropeza receive these favors?

Earl Henry. Why ask you that? Did they not fall on her, like heavenly dews? 86

Sandoval. And will they not rise again, like an earthly mist? What is Gratitude opposed to Ambition, filial revenge, and Woman's rivalry—what is it but a cruel Curb in the mouth of a fiery Horse, maddening the fierce animal whom it cannot restrain? Forgive me, Earl Henry! I meant not to move you so deeply. 92

Earl Henry. Sandoval, you have uttered that in a waking hour which having once dreamt, I feared the return of sleep lest I should dream it over again. My Friend (*his Voice trembling*) I woo'd the daughter of Don Manrique, *but* we are interrupted. 97

Sandoval. It is Fernandez.

Earl Henry (*struggling with his emotions*). A true-hearted old fellow—— 100

Sandoval. As splenetic as he is brave.

Enter FERNANDEZ.

Earl Henry. Well, my ancient! how did you like our tour through the mountains. (EARL HENRY *sits down on the seat by the woodside.*) 104

Fernandez. But little, General! and my faithful charger
Liked it still less.
The field of battle in the level plain
By Fontarabia was more to our taste.

Earl Henry. Where is my brother, Don Curio! Have you Seen him of late?

After 88 in which all her wrongs will appear twofold — (or) in a mist of which her Wrongs will wander, magnified into giant shapes. *MS. erased.*

Fernandez. Scarcely, dear General! 110
For by my troth I have been laughing at him
Even till the merry tears so filled my eyes
That I lost sight of him.
  Sandoval. But wherefore, Captain.
  Fernandez. He hath been studying speeches with fierce gestures;
Speeches brimfull of wrath and indignation, 115
The which he hopes to vent in open council:
And, in the heat and fury of this fancy
He grasp'd your groom of the Chamber by the throat
Who squeaking piteously, Ey! quoth your brother,
I cry you Mercy, Fool! Hadst been indeed 120
The Chancellor, I should have strangled thee.
  Sandoval. Ha, ha! poor Barnard!
  Fernandez. What you know my Gentleman,
My Groom of the Chamber, my Sieur Barnard, hey?
  Sandoval. I know him for a barren-pated coxcomb.
  Fernandez. But very weedy, Sir! in worthless phrases, 125
A sedulous eschewer of the popular
And the colloquial—one who seeketh dignity
I' th' paths of circumlocution! It would have
Surpris'd you tho', to hear how nat'rally
He squeak'd when Curio had him by the throat. 130
  Sandoval. I know him too for an habitual scorner
Of Truth.
  Fernandez. And one that lies more dully than
Old Women dream, without pretence of fancy,
Humour or mirth, a most disinterested,
Gratuitous Liar.
  Earl Henry. Ho! enough, enough! 135
Spare him, I pray you, were't but from respect
To the presence of his Lord.
  Sandoval. I stand reprov'd.
  Fernandez. I too, but that I know our noble General
Maintains him near his person, only that
If he should ever go in jeopardy 140
Of being damn'd (as he's now persecuted)
For his virtue and fair sense, he may be sav'd
By the supererogation of this Fellow's
Folly and Worthlessness.———

110 *After* General! And yet I have not stirred from his side. That is to say— *MS. erased.*

Earl Henry.   Hold, hold, good Ancient!
Do you not know that this Barnard saved my life?   145
Well, but my brother——
   Fernandez.   He will soon be here.
I swear by this, my sword, dear General,
I swear he has a Hero's soul—I only
Wish I could communicate to him
My gift of governing the spleen.—Then he   150
Has had his colors, the drums too of the Regiment
All put in cases—O, that stirs the Soldiery.
   Earl Henry. Impetuous Boy!
   Fernandez.   Nay, Fear not for them, General.
The Chancellor, no doubt, will take good care
To let their blood grow cool on garrison duty.   155
   Sandoval. Earl Henry! Frown not thus upon Fernandez;
'Tis said, and all the Soldiery believe it,
That the five Regiments who return with you
Will be dispers'd in garrisons and castles,
And other Jails of honourable name.   160
So great a crime it is to have been present
In duty and devotion to a Hero!
   Fernandez. What now? What now? The politic Chancellor is
The Soldier's friend, and rather than not give
Snug pensions to brave Men, he'll overlook   165
All small disqualifying circumstances
Of youth and health, keen eye and muscular limb,
He'll count our scars, and set them down for maims.
And gain us thus all privileges and profits
Of Invalids and superannuate veterans.   170
   Earl Henry. 'Tis but an idle rumour—See! they come.

Enter BARNARD *and a number of* Soldiers, *their Colours wound up, and the Drums in Cases, and after them* DON CURIO. *All pay the military Honors to the General. During this time* FERNANDEZ *has hurried up in front of the Stage.*

Enter DON CURIO.

   Don Curio (*advancing to* EARL HENRY). Has Barnard told you?
Insult on insult! by mine honor, Brother!
(BARNARD *goes beside* CURIO) And by our Father's soul they mean to saint you,
Having first prov'd your Patience more than mortal.   175

FIRST DRAFTS, EARLY VERSIONS, ETC. 565

Earl Henry. Take heed, Don Curio! lest with greater right
They scoff my Brother for a choleric boy.
What insult then?

Don Curio. Our Friend, the Chancellor,
Welcomes you home, and shares the common joy
In the most happy tidings of your Victory: 180
But as to your demand of instant audience
From the Queen's Royal Person,—'tis rejected!

Sandoval. Rejected?

Barnard (making a deep obeisance). May it please the Earl!

Earl Henry. Speak, Barnard.

Barnard. The noble Youth, your very valiant brother,
And wise as valiant *(bowing to* DON CURIO *who puffs at him)*
rightly doth insinuate 185
Fortune deals nothing singly—whether Honors
Or Insults, whether it be Joys or Sorrows,
They crowd together on us, or at best
Drop in in quick succession.

Fernandez (mocking him). 'Ne'er rains it, but it pours,' or,
at the best, 190
'More sacks upon the mill.' This fellow's a
Perpetual plagiarist from his Grandmother, and
How slily in the parcel wraps [he] up
The stolen goods!

Earl Henry. Be somewhat briefer, Barnard.

Barnard. But could I dare insinuate to your Brother 195
A fearless Truth, Earl Henry—it were this:
Even Lucifer, Prince of the Air, hath claims
Upon our justice.

Fernandez. Give the Devil his Due!
Why, thou base Lacquerer of worm-eaten proverbs,
[And] wherefore dost thou not tell us at once 200
What the Chancellor said to thee?

Barnard (looking round superciliously at FERNANDEZ*).*
The Queen hath left the Capital affecting
Rural retirement, but 'I will hasten'
(Thus said the Chancellor) 'I myself will hasten
And lay before her Majesty the Tidings 205
Both of Earl Henry's Victory and return.
She will vouchsafe, I doubt not, to re-enter
Her Capital, without delay, and grant
The wish'd for Audience with all public honour.'

Don Curio. A mere Device, I say, to pass a slight on us.

Fernandez (*to himself*). To think on 't. Pshaw! A fellow, that must needs 211
Have been decreed an Ass by acclamation,
Had he not looked so very like an Owl.
And he to—— (*turns suddenly round, and faces* BARNARD *who had even then come close beside him*).
Boo!——Ah! is it you, Sieur Barnard!
   Barnard. No other, Sir!
   Fernandez.   And is it not reported, 215
That you once sav'd the General's life?
   Barnard.   'Tis certain!
   Fernandez. Was he asleep? And were the hunters coming
And did you bite him on the nose?
   Barnard.   What mean you?
   Fernandez. That was the way in which the Flea i' th' Fable
Once sav'd the Lion's life.
   Earl Henry.   'Tis well. 220
The Sun hath almost finish'd his Day's Travels;
We too will finish ours. Go, gallant Comrades,
And at the neighbouring Mansion, for us all,
Claim entertainment in your General's name.

     Exeunt Soldiers, &c. *As they are leaving the Stage.*

   Fernandez (*to* BARNARD). A word with you! You act the Chancellor 225
Incomparably well.
   Barnard.   Most valiant Captain,
Vouchsafe a manual union.
   Fernandez (*griping* [sic] *his hand with affected fervor*). 'Tis no wonder,
Don Curio should mistook [*sic*] you for him.
   Barnard.   Truly,
The Chancellor, and I, it hath been notic'd
Are of one stature.
   Fernandez.   And Don Curio's *Gripe* too 230
Had lent a guttural Music to your voice,

Before 211.
     Fortune! Plague take her for a blind old Baggage!
     That such a patch as Barnard should have had
     The Honour to have sav'd our General's life.
     That Barnard! that mock-man! that clumsy forgery
     Of Heaven's Image. Any other heart
     But mine own would have turn'd splenetic to think of it.
                                             MS. erased.

A sort of bagpipe Buz, that suited well
Your dignity of utterance.
  Barnard (*simpering courteously*). Don Fernandez,
Few are the storms that bring unmingled evil.   234
  Fernandez (*mocking him*). 'Tis an ill wind, that blows no
    good, Sieur Barnard!   [*Exeunt.*

           DON CURIO *lingering behind.*

  Don Curio. I have offended you, my brother.
  Earl H.   Yes!
For you've not learnt the noblest part of valour,
To suffer and obey. Drums put in cases,
Colours wound up—what means this Mummery?
We are sunk low indeed, if wrongs like our's   240
Must seek redress in impotent Freaks of Anger.
(This way, Don Sandoval) of boyish anger——

     (*Walks with* SANDOVAL *to the back of the Stage.*)

  Don Curio (*to himself*). Freaks! freaks! But what if they
    have sav'd from bursting
The swelling heart of one, whose Cup of Hope
Was savagely dash'd down—even from his lips?—   245
Permitted just to see the face of War,
Then like a truant boy, scourgd home again
One Field my whole Campaign! One glorious Battle
To madden one with Hope!—Did he not pause
Twice in the fight, and press me to his breastplate, 250
And cry, that all might hear him, Well done, brother!
No blessed Soul, just naturalized in Heaven,
Pac'd ever by the side of an Immortal
More proudly, Henry! than I fought by thine—   254
Shame on these tears!—this, too, is boyish anger! [*Exit.*

  EARL HENRY *and* SANDOVAL *return to the front of the stage.*

  Earl Henry. I spake more harshly to him, than need was.
  Sandoval. Observ'd you how he pull'd his beaver down—
Doubtless to hide the tears, he could not check.
  Earl Henry. Go, sooth [*sic*] him, Friend!—And having
    reach'd the Castle
Gain Oropeza's private ear, and tell her   260
Where you have left me.

              (*As* SANDOVAL *is going*)
                  Nay, stay awhile with me.
I am too full of dreams to meet her now.

Sandoval. You lov'd the daughter of Don Manrique?
Earl Henry. Loved?
Sandoval. Did you not say, you woo'd her?
Earl Henry. Once I lov'd
Her whom I dar'd not woo!——
   Sandoval. And woo'd perchance 265
One whom you lov'd not!
   Earl Henry. O I were most base
Not loving Oropeza. True, I woo'd her
Hoping to heal a deeper wound: but she
Met my advances with an empassion'd Pride
That kindled Love with Love. And when her Sire 270
Who in his dream of Hope already grasp'd
The golden circlet in his hand, rejected
My suit, with Insult, and in memory
Of ancient Feuds, pour'd Curses on my head,
Her Blessings overtook and baffled them. 275
But thou art stern, and with unkindling Countenance
Art inly reasoning whilst thou listenest to me.
   Sandoval. Anxiously, Henry! reasoning anxiously.
But Oropeza—
   Earl Henry. Blessings gather round her!
Within this wood there winds a secret passage, 280
Beneath the walls, which open out at length
Into the gloomiest covert of the Garden.—
The night ere my departure to the Army,
She, nothing trembling, led me through that gloom,
And to the covert by a silent stream, 285
Which, with one star reflected near its marge,
Was the sole object visible around me.
The night so dark, so close, the umbrage o'er us!
No leaflet stirr'd;—yet pleasure hung upon us,
The gloom and stillness of the balmy night-air. 290
A little further on an arbor stood,
Fragrant with flowering Trees—I well remember
What an uncertain glimmer in the Darkness
Their snow-white Blossoms made—thither she led me,

  269 an empassion'd *S. L.*: empassioned *1834*. 276 unkindling]
unkindly *S. L.*, *1834*. 281 open] opens *S. L.* 285 the] that.
a] that *S. L.* (corr. in Errata, p. [xi]) *S. L.* 288 o'er] near *S. L.*
(corr. in Errata, p. [xi]) *S. L.*
   289–290 No leaflet stirr'd; the air was almost sultry;
      So deep, so dark, so close, the umbrage o'er us!
      No leaflet stirr'd, yet pleasure hung upon *S. L.*

FIRST DRAFTS, EARLY VERSIONS, ETC. 569

To that sweet bower! Then Oropeza trembled—   295
I heard her heart beat—if 'twere not my own.
   Sandoval. A rude and scaring note, my friend!
   Earl Henry.   Oh! no!
I have small memory of aught but pleasure.
The inquietudes of fear, like lesser Streams
Still flowing, still were lost in those of Love: 300
So Love grew mightier from the Fear, and Nature,
Fleeing from Pain, shelter'd herself in Joy.
The stars above our heads were dim and steady,
Like eyes suffus'd with rapture. Life was in us:
We were all life, each atom of our Frames   305
A living soul—I vow'd to die for her:
With the faint voice of one who, having spoken,
Relapses into blessedness, I vow'd it:
That solemn Vow, a whisper scarcely heard,
A murmur breath'd against a lady's Cheek.   310
Oh! there is Joy above the name of Pleasure,
Deep self-possession, an intense Repose.
No other than as Eastern Sages feign,
The God, who floats upon a Lotos Leaf,
Dreams for a thousand ages; then awaking,   315
Creates a world, and smiling at the bubble,
Relapses into bliss. Ah! was that bliss
Fear'd as an alien, and too vast for man?
For suddenly, intolerant of its silence,
Did Oropeza, starting, grasp my forehead.   320
I caught her arms; the veins were swelling on them.
Thro' the dark Bower she sent a hollow voice;—
'Oh! what if all betray me? what if thou?'
I swore, and with an inward thought that seemed

310 Cheek] Ear *S. L.*
After 312.

                           Deep repose of bliss we **lay**
              No other than as Eastern Sages gloss,
              The God who floats upon a Lotos leaf
              Dreams for a thousand ages, then awaking
              Creates a World, then loathing the dull task
              Relapses into blessedness, when an omen
              Screamed from the Watch-tower—'twas the Watchman's cry,
              And Oropeza starting. *MS.* (*alternative reading*).

313 feign] paint *S. L.*   *Before* 314 Sandoval (*with a sarcastic smile*) *S. L.*
314-16 Compare Letter to Thelwall, Oct. 16, 1797, *Letters of S. T. C.*, 1895,
i. 229.   317 bliss.—*Earl Henry.* Ah! was that bliss *S. L.*   319
intolerant] impatient *S. L.*

The unity and substance of my Being,   325
I swore to her, that were she red with guilt,
I would exchange my unblench'd state with hers.—
Friend! by that winding passage, to the Bower
I now will go—all objects there will teach me
Unwavering Love, and singleness of Heart.   330
Go, Sandoval! I am prepar'd to meet her—
Say nothing of me—I myself will seek her—
Nay, leave me, friend! I cannot bear the torment
And Inquisition of that scanning eye.—   334

                    [Earl Henry retires into the wood.

  Sandoval (*alone*). O Henry! always striv'st thou to be great
By thine own act—yet art thou never great
But by the Inspiration of great Passion.
The Whirl-blast comes, the desert-sands rise up
And shape themselves; from Heaven to Earth they stand
As though they were the Pillars of a Temple,
Built by Omnipotence in its own honour!   340
But the Blast pauses, and their shaping spirit
Is fled: the mighty Columns were but sand,
And lazy Snakes trail o'er the level ruins!
I know, he loves the Queen. I know she is   345
His Soul's first love, and this is ever his nature—
To his first purpose, his soul toiling back
Like the poor storm-wreck'd [sailor] to his Boat,
Still swept away, still struggling to regain it.   [*Exit.*

  Herreras. He dies, that stirs! Follow me this instant.   350

(First Conspirator *takes his arrow, snaps it, and throws it on the
        ground. The two others do the same.*)

  Herreras. Accursed cowards! I'll go myself, and make
    sure work (*drawing his Dagger*).

325 unity and] purpose and the *S. L.*
After 327
      Even as a Herdsboy mutely plighting troth
      Gives his true Love a Lily for a Rose. *MS. erased.*
334 Inquisition] keen inquiry *S. L.*
Before 335.
      Earl Henry thou art dear to me—perchance
      For these follies; since the Health of Reason,
      Our would-be Sages teach, engenders not
      The Whelks and Tumours of particular Friendship.
                                        MS. erased.
339 Heaven to Earth] Earth to Heaven *S. L.*

FIRST DRAFTS, EARLY VERSIONS, ETC. 571

(HERRERAS *strides towards the arbor, before he reaches it, stops and listens and then returns hastily to the front of the stage, as he turns his Back to the Arbor,* EARL HENRY *appears, watching the Conspirators, and enters the Arbor unseen.*)

First Conspirator. Has she *seen* us think you?

The Mask. No! she has not *seen* us; but she heard us distinctly. 354

Herreras. There was a rustling in the wood—go, all of you, stand on the watch—towards the passage.

A Voice from the Arbor. Mercy! Mercy! Tell me, why you murder me.

Herreras. I'll do it first. (*Strides towards the Arbor,* EARL HENRY *rushes out of it.*)

The Mask. Jesu Maria. (*They all three fly,* EARL HENRY *attempts to seize* HERRERAS, *who defending himself retreats into the Covert follow'd by the* EARL. THE QUEEN *comes from out the arbor, veiled—stands listening a moment, then lifts up her veil, with folded hands assumes the attitude of Prayer, and after a momentary silence breaks into audible soliloquy.*)

The Queen. I pray'd to thee, All-wonderful! And thou
Didst make my very Prayer the Instrument, 362
By which thy Providence sav'd me. Th' armed Murderer
Who with suspended breath stood listening to me,
Groan'd as I spake thy name. In that same moment, 365
O God! thy Mercy shot the swift Remorse
That pierc'd his Heart. And like an Elephant
Gor'd as he rushes to the first assault,
He turn'd at once and trampled his Employers.
But hark! (*drops her veil*)—O God in Heaven! they come again. 370

(EARL HENRY *returns with the Dagger in his hand.*)

Earl Henry (*as he is entering*). The violent pull with which I seiz'd his Dagger
Unpois'd me and I fell.

[END OF THE FRAGMENT.]

J

CHAMOUNY; THE HOUR BEFORE SUNRISE
A Hymn
[Vide *ante*, p. 376.]
[As published in *The Morning Post*, Sept. 11, 1802]

Hast thou a charm to stay the morning star
In his steep course—so long he seems to pause
On thy bald awful head, O Chamouny!
The Arvè and Arveiron at thy base
Rave ceaselessly; but thou, dread mountain form, 5
Resist from forth thy silent sea of pines
How silently! Around thee, and above,
Deep is the sky, and black: transpicuous, deep,
An ebon mass! Methinks thou piercest it
As with a wedge! But when I look again, 10
It seems thy own calm home, thy crystal shrine,
Thy habitation from eternity.
O dread and silent form! I gaz'd upon thee,
Till thou, still present to my bodily eye,
Did'st vanish from my thought. Entranc'd in pray'r, 15
I worshipp'd the Invisible alone.
Yet thou, meantime, wast working on my soul,
E'en like some deep enchanting melody,
So sweet, we know not, we are list'ning to it.
But I awoke, and with a busier mind, 20
And active will self-conscious, offer now
Not, as before, involuntary pray'r
And passive adoration!—
      Hand and voice,
Awake, awake! and thou, my heart, awake!
Awake ye rocks! Ye forest pines, awake! 25
Green fields, and icy cliffs! All join my hymn!
And thou, O silent mountain, sole and bare,
O blacker, than the darkness, all the night,
And visited, all night, by troops of stars,
Or when they climb the sky, or when they sink— 30
Companion of the morning star at dawn,
Thyself Earth's rosy star, and of the dawn
Co-herald! Wake, O wake, and utter praise!
Who sank thy sunless pillars deep in earth?
Who fill'd thy countenance with rosy light? 35
Who made thee father of perpetual streams?
And you, ye five wild torrents, fiercely glad,

Who call'd you forth from Night and utter Death?
From darkness let you loose, and icy dens,
Down those precipitous, black, jagged rocks   40
For ever shatter'd, and the same for ever!
Who gave you your invulnerable life,
Your strength, your speed, your fury, and your joy,
Unceasing thunder, and eternal foam!
And who commanded, and the silence came—   45
'Here shall the billows stiffen, and have rest?'

Ye ice-falls! ye that from yon dizzy heights
Adown enormous ravines steeply slope,
Torrents, methinks, that heard a mighty voice,
And stopp'd at once amid their maddest plunge!   50
Motionless torrents! silent cataracts!
Who made you glorious, as the gates of Heav'n,
Beneath the keen full moon? Who bade the sun
Clothe you with rainbows? Who with lovely flow'rs
Of living blue spread garlands at your feet?   55
GOD! GOD! The torrents like a shout of nations,
Utter! The ice-plain bursts, and answers GOD!
GOD, sing the meadow-streams with gladsome voice,
And pine groves with their soft, and soul-like sound,
The silent snow-mass, loos'ning, thunders GOD!   60
Ye dreadless flow'rs! that fringe th' eternal frost!
Ye wild goats, bounding by the eagle's nest!
Ye eagles, playmates of the mountain blast!
Ye lightnings, the dread arrows of the clouds!
Ye signs and wonders of the element,   65
Utter forth, GOD! and fill the hills with praise!

And thou, O silent Form, alone and bare,
Whom, as I lift again my head bow'd low
In adoration, I again behold,
And to thy summit upward from thy base   70
Sweep slowly with dim eyes suffus'd by tears,
Awake, thou mountain form! rise, like a cloud!
Rise, like a cloud of incense, from the earth!
Thou kingly spirit thron'd among the hills,
Thou dread ambassador from Earth to Heav'n—   75
Great hierarch, tell thou the silent sky,
And tell the stars, and tell the rising sun,
Earth with her thousand voices calls on God!
             ΕΣΤΗΣΕ.

K

DEJECTION: AN ODE[1]

[Vide *ante*, p. 362.]

[As first printed in the *Morning Post*, October 4, 1802.]

"Late, late yestreen I saw the new Moon
"With the Old Moon in her arms;
"And I fear, I fear, my Master dear,
"We shall have a deadly storm."[2]
　　　　　Ballad of Sir Patrick Spence.

DEJECTION:

AN ODE, WRITTEN APRIL 4, 1802.

I

Well! If the Bard was weather-wise, who made
　The grand Old ballad of Sir Patrick Spence,
　This night, so tranquil now, will not go hence
Unrous'd by winds, that ply a busier trade
Than those, which mould yon cloud, in lazy flakes,　　　　5
Or the dull sobbing draft, that drones and rakes
Upon the strings of this Æolian lute,
Which better far were mute.
For lo! the New Moon, winter-bright!
And overspread with phantom light,　　　　10

---

[1] Collated with the text of the poem as sent to W. Sotheby in a letter dated July 19, 1802 (*Letters of S. T. C.*, 1895, i. 379-84).

[2] In the letter of July 19, 1802, the Ode is broken up and quoted in parts or fragments, illustrative of the mind and feelings of the writer. 'Sickness,' he explains, 'first forced me into *downright metaphysics*. For I believe that by nature I have more of the poet in me. In a poem written during that dejection, to Wordsworth, I thus expressed the thought in language more forcible than harmonious.' Then follow lines 76-87 of the text, followed by lines 87-93 of the text first published in *Sibylline Leaves* ('For not to think of what I needs must feel,' &c.). He then reverts to the 'introduction of the poem':—'The first lines allude to a stanza in the Ballad of Sir Patrick Spence: "Late, late yestreen I saw the new moon with the old one in her arms: and I fear, I fear, my master dear, there will be a deadly Storm."' This serves as a motto to lines 1-75 and 129-39 of the first draft of the text. Finally he 'annexes as a *fragment* a few lines (ll. 88-119) on the "Æolian Lute", it having been introduced in its dronings in the first stanzas.'

Motto—2 Moon] one *Letter to S.*　　4 There will be, &c. *Letter to S.*
　2 grand] dear *Letter to S.*　　5 those] that *Letter to S.*　　cloud] clouds *Letter to S.*

FIRST DRAFTS, EARLY VERSIONS, ETC. 575

(With swimming phantom light o'erspread,
But rimm'd and circled by a silver thread)
I see the Old Moon in her lap, foretelling
    The coming on of rain and squally blast:
And O! that even now the gust were swelling,   15
    And the slant night-show'r driving loud and fast!
Those sounds which oft have rais'd me, while they aw'd,
And sent my soul abroad,
Might now perhaps their wonted impulse give,
Might startle this dull pain, and make it move and live! 20

II

A grief without a pang, void, dark, and drear,
    A stifled, drowsy, unimpassion'd grief,
    Which finds no nat'ral outlet, no relief,
In word, or sigh, or tear—
O EDMUND! in this wan and heartless mood,   25
To other thoughts by yonder throstle woo'd,
All this long eve, so balmy and serene,
    Have I been gazing on the Western sky,
And its peculiar tint of yellow-green:
    And still I gaze—and with how blank an eye!   30
And those thin clouds above, in flakes and bars,
That give away their motion to the stars;
Those stars, that glide behind them, or between,
Now sparkling, now bedimm'd, but always seen;
Yon crescent moon, as fix'd as if it grew,   35
In its own cloudless, starless lake of blue,
A boat becalm'd! a lovely sky-canoe!
I see them all so excellently fair—
I *see*, not *feel* how beautiful they are!

12 by] with *Letter to S.*   17-20 *om. Letter to S.*   22 stifled] stifling *Letter to S.*

Between 24 *and* 25.
        This William, well thou knowest,
        Is that sore evil which I dread the most,
        And oftnest suffer. In this heartless mood,
        To other thoughts by yonder throstle woo'd,
        That pipes within the larch-tree, not unseen,
        The larch, that pushes out in tassels green
        Its bundled leafits, woo'd to mild delights,
        By all the tender sounds and gentle sights,
        Of this sweet primrose-month, and vainly woo'd!
        O dearest Poet, in this heartless mood. *Letter to S.*

37 a lovely sky-canoe] thy own sweet sky-canoe *Letter to S.* [*Note.* The reference is to the Prologue to 'Peter Bell'.]

III

My genial spirits fail;
    And what can these avail,   40
To lift the smoth'ring weight from off my breast?
    It were a vain endeavour,
      Though I should gaze for ever
On that green light that lingers in the west: 45
I may not hope from outward forms to win
The passion and the life, whose fountains are within.

IV

O EDMUND! we receive but what we give,
And in *our* life alone does Nature live:
Ours is her wedding-garment, ours her shroud!   50
And would we aught behold, of higher worth,
Than that inanimate cold world, *allow'd*
To the poor loveless ever-anxious crowd,
Ah! from the soul itself must issue forth,
A light, a glory, a fair luminous cloud   55
Enveloping the earth—
And from the soul itself must there be sent
A sweet and potent voice, of its own birth,
Of all sweet sounds the life and element!
O pure of heart! Thou need'st not ask of me   60
What this strong music in the soul may be?
What, and wherein it doth exist,
This light, this glory, this fair luminous mist,
This beautiful and beauty-making pow'r?
    Joy, virtuous EDMUND! joy that ne'er was given,   65
Save to the pure, and in their purest hour,
Joy, EDMUND! is the spirit and the pow'r,
Which wedding Nature to us gives in dow'r,
    A new Earth and new Heaven,
Undream'd of by the sensual and the proud—   70
Joy is the sweet voice, Joy the luminous cloud—
      We, we ourselves rejoice!
And thence flows all that charms or ear or sight,
All melodies the echoes of that voice,
All colours a suffusion from that light.   75

---

48 Edmund] Wordsworth *Letter to S.*   58 potent] powerful *Letter to S.*
65 virtuous Edmund] blameless poet *Letter to S.*   67 Edmund] William
Letter to S.   71 *om. Letter to S.*   74 the echoes] an echo *Letter to S.*

FIRST DRAFTS, EARLY VERSIONS, ETC. 577

     Yes, dearest EDMUND, yes!
There was a time **that**, tho' my path was rough,
 This joy within me dallied with distress,
And all misfortunes were but as the stuff
 Whence fancy made me dreams of happiness: 80
For hope grew round me, like the twining vine,
And fruits, and foliage, not my own, seem'd mine.
But now afflictions bow me down to earth:
Nor care I, that they rob me of my mirth,
 But oh! each visitation   85
Suspends what nature gave me at my birth,
 My shaping spirit of imagination.

[The Sixth and Seventh Stanzas omitted.]

  * * * * * *
  * * * * * *
  * * * * * *

VIII

O wherefore did I let it haunt my mind
 This dark distressful dream?
I turn from it, and listen to the wind   90
 Which long has rav'd unnotic'd. What a scream
Of agony, by torture, lengthen'd out,
That lute sent forth! O wind, that rav'st without,
Bare crag, or mountain-tairn[1], or blasted tree,
Or pine-grove, whither woodman never clomb,   95
Or lonely house, long held the witches' home,
 Methinks were fitter instruments for thee,
Mad Lutanist! who, in this month of show'rs,
Of dark-brown gardens, and of peeping flow'rs,
Mak'st devil's yule, with worse than wintry song,   100
The blossoms, buds, and tim'rous leaves among.
 Thou Actor, perfect in all tragic sounds!
Thou mighty Poet, ev'n to frenzy bold!

---

[1] Tairn, a small lake, generally, if not always, applied to the lakes up in the mountains, and which are the feeders of those in the vallies. This address to the wind will not appear extravagant to those who have heard it at night, in a mountainous country. [Note in *M. P.*]

---

 76 Edmund] poet *Letter to S.* 77 that] when *Letter to S.* 78 This] The *Letter to S.* 82 fruits] fruit *Letter to S.* After 87 six lines 'For not to think', &c., are inserted after a row of asterisks. The direction as to the omission of the Sixth and Seventh Stanzas is only found in the *M.P.* 88 O] Nay *Letter to S.* 93 That lute sent out! O thou wild storm without *Letter to S.* 98 who] that *Letter to S.*

What tell'st thou now about?
'Tis of the rushing of a host in rout, 105
With many groans of men, with smarting wounds—
At once they groan with pain, and shudder with the cold!
But hush! there is a pause of deepest silence!
And all that noise, as of a rushing crowd,
With groans, and tremulous shudderings—all is over! 110
It tells another tale, with sounds less deep and loud—
A tale of less affright.
And temper'd with delight,
As EDMUND's self had fram'd the tender lay—
'Tis of a little child, 115
Upon a lonesome wild
Not far from home; but she hath lost her way—
And now moans low, in utter grief and fear;
And now screams loud, and hopes to make her mother *hear*!

IX

'Tis midnight, and small thoughts have I of sleep; 120
Full seldom may my friend such vigils keep!
Visit him, gentle Sleep, with wings of healing,
And may this storm be but a mountain-birth,
May all the stars hang bright above his dwelling,
Silent, as though they *watch'd* the sleeping Earth! 125
With light heart may he rise,
Gay fancy, cheerful eyes,
And sing his lofty song, and teach me to rejoice!
O EDMUND, friend of my devoutest choice,
O rais'd from anxious dread and busy care, 130
By the immenseness of the good and fair
Which thou see'st everywhere,
Joy lifts thy spirit, joy attunes thy voice,

---

106 of] from *Letter to S.*   109 Again! but all that noise *Letter to S.*
111 And it has other sounds, less fearful and less loud *Letter to S.*   114
Edmund's self] thou thyself *Letter to S.*   120-8 *om. Letter to S.*
129-39   Calm steadfast spirit, guided from above,
O Wordsworth! friend of my devoutest choice,
Great son of genius! full of light and love,
Thus, thus, dost thou rejoice.
To thee do all things live, from pole to pole,
Their life the eddying of thy living Soul!
Brother and friend of my devoutest choice,
Thus may'st thou ever, evermore rejoice!   *Letter to S.*
[*Note.* In the letter these lines follow line 75 of the text of the *M. P.*]

FIRST DRAFTS, EARLY VERSIONS, ETC. 579

To thee do all things live from pole to pole,
Their life the eddying of thy living soul!   135
O simple spirit, guided from above,
O lofty Poet, full of life and love,
Brother and friend of my devoutest choice,
Thus may'st thou ever, evermore rejoice!

ΕΣΤΗΣΕ.

L

TO W. WORDSWORTH[1]

(*Vide ante*, p. 403.)

LINES COMPOSED, FOR THE GREATER PART ON THE NIGHT,
ON WHICH HE FINISHED THE RECITATION OF HIS POEM
(IN THIRTEEN BOOKS) CONCERNING THE GROWTH
AND HISTORY OF HIS OWN MIND

JAN^{RY}, 1807. COLE-ORTON, NEAR ASHBY DE LA ZOUCH.

O FRIEND! O Teacher! God's great Gift to me!
Into my heart have I receiv'd that Lay,
More than historic, that prophetic Lay,
Wherein (high theme by Thee first sung aright)
Of the Foundations and the Building-up   5
Of thy own Spirit, thou hast lov'd to tell
What may be told, to th' understanding mind
Revealable; and what within the mind
May rise enkindled. Theme as hard as high!
Of Smiles spontaneous, and mysterious Fears;   10
(The First-born they of Reason, and Twin-birth)
Of Tides obedient to external Force,
And *currents* self-determin'd, as might seem,
Or by interior Power: of Moments aweful,
Now in thy hidden Life; and now abroad,   15
Mid festive Crowds, *thy* Brows too garlanded,
A Brother of the Feast: of *Fancies* fair,
Hyblæan Murmurs of poetic Thought,
Industrious in its Joy, by lilied Streams
Native or outland, Lakes and famous Hills!   20

[1] Now first printed from an original MS. in the possession of Mr. Gordon Wordsworth.

Of more than Fancy, of the Hope of Man
Amid the tremor of a Realm aglow—
Where France in all her Towns lay vibrating,
Ev'n as a Bark becalm'd on sultry seas
Beneath the voice from Heaven, the bursting Crash 25
Of Heaven's immediate thunder! when no Cloud
Is visible, or Shadow on the Main!
Ah! soon night roll'd on night, and every Cloud
Open'd its eye of Fire: and Hope aloft
Now flutter'd, and now toss'd upon the Storm 30
Floating! Of Hope afflicted, and struck down,
Thence summon'd homeward—homeward to thy Heart,
Oft from the Watch-tower of Man's absolute Self,
With Light unwaning on her eyes, to look
Far on—herself a Glory to behold, 35
The Angel of the Vision! Then (last strain!)
Of *Duty*, chosen Laws controlling choice,
Virtue and Love! An Orphic Tale indeed,
A Tale divine of high and passionate Thoughts
To their own music chaunted!

                        Ah great Bard! 40
Ere yet that last Swell dying aw'd the Air,
With stedfast ken I view'd thee in the Choir
Of ever-enduring Men. The truly Great
Have all one Age, and from one visible space
Shed influence: for they, both power and act, 45
Are permanent, and Time is not with them,
Save as it worketh for them, they in it.
Nor less a sacred Roll, than those of old,
And to be plac'd, as they, with gradual fame
Among the Archives of mankind, thy Work 50
Makes audible a linked Song of Truth,
Of Truth profound a sweet continuous Song
Not learnt, but native, her own natural Notes!
Dear shall it be to every human Heart,
To me how more than dearest! Me, on whom 55
Comfort from Thee and utterance of thy Love
Came with such heights and depths of Harmony
Such sense of Wings uplifting, that the Storm
Scatter'd and whirl'd me, till my Thoughts became
A bodily Tumult! and thy faithful Hopes, 60
Thy Hopes of me, dear Friend! by me unfelt

37 controlling] ? impelling, ? directing.

Were troublous to me, almost as a Voice
Familiar once and more than musical
To one cast forth, whose hope had seem'd to die,
A Wanderer with a worn-out heart, [*sic*]   65
Mid Strangers pining with untended Wounds!

O Friend! too well thou know'st, of what sad years
The long suppression had benumb'd my soul,
That even as Life returns upon the Drown'd,
Th' unusual Joy awoke a throng of Pains—   70
Keen Pangs of LOVE, awakening, as a Babe,
Turbulent, with an outcry in the Heart:
And Fears self-will'd, that shunn'd the eye of Hope,
And Hope, that would not know itself from Fear:
Sense of pass'd Youth, and Manhood come in vain;   75
And Genius given, and knowledge won in vain;
And all, which I had cull'd in Wood-walks wild,
And all, which patient Toil had rear'd, and all,
Commune with Thee had open'd out, but Flowers
Strew'd on my Corse, and borne upon my Bier,   80
In the same Coffin, for the self-same Grave!

   That way no more! and ill beseems it me,
Who came a Welcomer in Herald's guise
Singing of Glory and Futurity,
To wander back on such unhealthful Road   85
Plucking the Poisons of Self-harm! and ill
Such Intertwine beseems triumphal wreaths
Strew'd before thy Advancing! Thou too, Friend!
O injure not the memory of that Hour
Of thy communion with my nobler mind   90
By pity or grief, already felt too long!
Nor let my words import more blame than needs.
The Tumult rose and ceas'd: for Peace is nigh
Where Wisdom's Voice has found a list'ning Heart.
Amid the howl of more than wintry Storms   95
The Halcyon hears the voice of vernal Hours,
Already on the wing!
                 Eve following eve,
Dear tranquil Time, when the sweet sense of Home
Becomes most sweet! hours for their own sake hail'd,
And more desir'd, more precious, for thy song!   100
In silence list'ning, like a devout Child,
My soul lay passive; by thy various strain

Driven as in surges now, beneath the stars,
With momentary Stars of my own Birth,
Fair constellated Foam still darting off
Into the darkness! now a tranquil Sea
Outspread and bright, yet swelling to the Moon!

And when O Friend! my Comforter! my Guide!
Strong in thyself and powerful to give strength!
Thy long sustained Lay finally clos'd,
And thy deep Voice had ceas'd (yet thou thyself
Wert still before mine eyes, and round us both
That happy Vision of beloved Faces!
All, whom I deepliest love, in one room all!),
Scarce conscious and yet conscious of it's Close,
I sate, my Being blended in one Thought,
(Thought was it? or aspiration? or Resolve?)
Absorb'd, yet hanging still upon the sound:
And when I rose, I found myself in Prayer!

S. T. COLERIDGE.

M

YOUTH AND AGE

[Vide *ante*, p. 439.]

MS. I

10 SEPT. 1823. WEDNESDAY MORNING, 10 O'CLOCK

On the tenth day of September,
Eighteen hundred Twenty Three,
Wednesday morn, and I remember
Ten on the *Clock* the Hour to be
[*The Watch and Clock do both agree*]

An *Air* that whizzed διὰ ἐγκεφάλου (right across the diameter of my Brain) exactly like a Hummel Bee, *alias* Dumbeldore, the gentleman with Rappee Spenser (*sic*), with bands of Red, and Orange Plush Breeches, close by my ear, at once sharp and burry, right over the summit of Quantock [item of Skiddaw (*erased*)] at earliest Dawn just between the Nightingale that I stopt to hear in the Copse at the Foot of Quantock, and the

FIRST DRAFTS, EARLY VERSIONS, ETC.   583

first Sky-Lark that was a Song-Fountain, dashing up and sparkling to the Ear's eye, in full column, or ornamented Shaft of sound in the order of Gothic Extravaganza, out of Sight, over the Cornfields on the Descent of the Mountain on the other side—out of sight, tho' twice I beheld its *mute* shoot downward in the sunshine like a falling star of silver:—

Aria Spontanea

Flowers are lovely, Love is flower-like,
Friendship is a shelt'ring tree—   20
O the Joys, that came down shower-like,
Of Beauty, Truth, and Liberty,
When I was young, ere I was old!
[*O Youth that wert so glad, so bold,*
What quaint disguise hast thou put on?   25
Would'st make-believe that thou art gone?
O Youth! thy Vesper Bell] has not yet toll'd.

Thou always were a Masker bold—
What quaint Disguise hast now put on?
To make believe that thou art gone!   30

O Youth, so true, so fair, so free,
Thy Vesper-bell hath not yet toll'd,
Thou always, &c.

Ah! was it not enough, that Thou
In Thy eternal Glory should outgo me?   35
Would'st thou not Grief's sad Victory allow

*   *   *   *   *   *

Hope's a Breeze that robs the Blossoms
Fancy feeds, and murmurs the Bee——

*   *   *   *   *   *

MS. II

1

Verse, that Breeze mid blossoms straying
Where Hope clings feeding like a Bee.
Both were mine: Life went a Maying
With Nature, Hope, and Poesy,
    When I was young.

APPENDIX I

> *When* I was young! ah woeful When!
> Ah for the Change twixt now and then!
> This House of Life, not built with hands
> Where now I sigh, where once I sung.—

Or [This snail-like House, not built with hands,
This Body that does me grievous wrong.]

> O'er Hill and dale and sounding Sands.
> How lightly then it flash'd along—
> Like those trim Boats, unknown of yore,
> On Winding Lakes and Rivers wide,
> That ask no aid of Sail or Oar,
> That fear no spite of Wind or Tide.

Pencil { Nought car'd this Body for wind or weather,
{ When youth and I liv'd in't together.

2

Flowers are lovely, Love is flower-like;
Friendship is a shelt'ring Tree;
O the joys that came down shower-like
Of Beauty, Truth and Liberty
    When I was young
When I was young, ~~ah woeful when~~
~~Ah for the change twixt now and then~~
In Heat or Frost we car'd not whether
Night and day we lodged together
             woeful when
When I was young—ah ~~words of agony~~
Ah for the change 'twixt now and then
~~O youth my Home-Mate dear so long, so long:~~
I thought that thou and I were one
I scarce believe that thou art gone
Thou always wert a Masker bold
I ~~mark that change,~~ in garb and size
  heave the Breath
Those grisled Locks I well behold
But still thy Heart is in thine eyes
What strange disguise hast now put on
To make believe that thou art gone

Or [O youth for years so many so sweet
It seem'd that Thou and I were one
That still I nurse the fond deceit
And scarce believe that thou art gone]

FIRST DRAFTS, EARLY VERSIONS, ETC. 585

> When I was young—ere I was old
> Ah! happy ere, ah! woeful When 25
> When I was young, ah woeful when
> Which says that Youth and I are twain!
> O Youth! for years so many and sweet
> 'Tis known that Thou and I were one
> I'll think it but a false conceit 30
> ~~'Tis but a gloomy~~
>   It cannot be,
> ~~I'll not believe~~ that thou art gone
> Thy Vesper Bell has not yet toll'd
>   always
> ~~And~~ thou wert ~~still~~ a masker bold
> What   hast
> ~~Some~~ strange disguise ~~thou'st~~ now put on
> To make believe that thou art gone? 35
> I see these Locks in silvery slips,
> This dragging gait, this alter'd size
> But spring-tide blossoms on thy Lips
> And ~~the young Heart~~ is in thy eyes
>   tears take sunshine from
> Life is but Thought so think I will 40
> That Youth and I are Housemates still.
>
> Ere I was old
> Ere I was old! ah woeful ere
> Which tells me youth's no longer here!
> O Youth, &c. 45
> Dewdrops are the Gems of Morning,
> But the Tears of mournful Eve:
> Where no Hope is Life's a Warning
>   me
> That only serves to make ~~us~~ grieve,
>   Now I am old. 50

N

LOVE'S APPARITION AND EVANISHMENT[1]

[Vide *ante*, p. 488.]

[FIRST DRAFT]

IN vain I supplicate the Powers above;
There is no Resurrection for the Love
That, nursed with tenderest care, yet fades away
In the chilled heart by inward self-decay.

[1] Now first published from an MS.

  Like a lorn Arab old and blind 5
  Some caravan had left behind
  That sits beside a ruined Well,
  And hangs his wistful head aslant,
   Some sound he fain would catch—
  Suspended there, as it befell, 10
   O'er my own vacancy,
   And while I seemed to watch
  The sickly calm, as were of heart
   A place where Hope lay dead,
  The spirit of departed Love 15
   Stood close beside my bed.
  She bent methought to kiss my lips
   As she was wont to do.
  Alas! 'twas with a chilling breath
  That awoke just enough of life in death 20
   To make it die anew.

O

TWO VERSIONS OF THE EPITAPH[1]

Inscribed in a copy of Grew's *Cosmologia Sacra* (1701)

[Vide *ante*, p. 491.]

1

Epitaph
in Hornsey Church yard
Hic Jacet S. T. C.

Stop, Christian Passer-by! Stop, Child of God!
And read with gentle heart. Beneath this sod
There lies a Poet: or what once was He.
[*Up*] O lift thy soul in prayer for S. T. C.
That He who many a year with toil of breath 5
Found death in life, may here find life in death.
Mercy for praise, to be forgiven for fame
He ask'd, and hoped thro' Christ. Do thou the same.

2

Etesi's [for Estesi's] Epitaph.

Stop, Christian Visitor! Stop, Child of God,
Here lies a Poet: or what once was He!
[*O*] Pause, Traveller, pause and pray for S. T. C.

---

[1] First published in *The Athenaeum*, April 7, 1888: included in the *Notes* to 1893 (p. 645).

FIRST DRAFTS, EARLY VERSIONS, ETC.

That He who many a year with toil of Breath
Found Death in Life, may here find Life in Death. 5

And read with gentle heart! Beneath this sod
There lies a Poet, etc.

'Inscription on the Tomb-stone of one not unknown; yet more commonly known by the Initials of his Name than by the Name itself.'

ESTEESE'S αυτοεπιταφιον [1]

(From a copy of the *Todten-Tanz* which belonged to Thomas Poole.)

Here lies a Poet; or what once was he:
Pray, gentle Reader, pray for S. T. C.
That he who threescore years, with toilsome breath,
Found Death in Life, may now find Life in Death.

P

[HABENT SUA FATA—POETAE] [2]

The Fox, and Statesman subtile wiles ensure,
The Cit, and Polecat stink and are secure;
Toads with their venom, doctors with their drug,
The Priest, and Hedgehog, in their robes are snug!
Oh, Nature! cruel step-mother, and hard, 5
To thy poor, naked, fenceless child the Bard!
No Horns but those by luckless Hymen worn,
And those (alas! alas!) not Plenty's Horn!
With naked feelings, and with aching pride,
He hears th' unbroken blast on every side! 10
Vampire Booksellers drain him to the heart,
And Scorpion Critics cureless venom dart!

---

[1] First published in the *Notes* to 1893 (p. 646).

[2] First published in Cottle's *Early Recollections*, 1839, i. 172. Now collected for the first time. These lines, according to Cottle, were included in a letter written from Lichfield in January, 1796. They illustrate the following sentence: 'The present hour I seem in a quickset hedge of embarrassments! For shame! I ought not to mistrust God! but, indeed, to hope is far more difficult than to fear. Bulls have horns, Lions have talons.'—They are signed 'S. T. C.' and are presumably his composition.

Q

TO JOHN THELWALL[1]

Some, Thelwall! to the Patriot's meed aspire,
Who, in safe rage, without or rent or scar,
Round pictur'd strongholds sketching mimic war
Closet their valour—Thou mid thickest fire
Leapst on the wall: therefore shall Freedom choose 5
Ungaudy flowers that chastest odours breathe,
And weave for thy young locks a Mural wreath;
Nor there my song of grateful praise refuse.
My ill-adventur'd youth by Cam's slow stream
Pin'd for a woman's love in slothful ease: 10
First by thy fair example [taught] to glow
With patriot zeal; from Passion's feverish dream
Starting I tore disdainful from my brow
A Myrtle Crown inwove with Cyprian bough—
Blest if to me in manhood's years belong 15
Thy stern simplicity and vigorous Song.

R[2]

'Relative to a Friend remarkable for Georgoepiscopal Meanderings, and the combination of the *utile dulci* during his walks to and from any given place, composed, together with a book and a half of an Epic Poem, during one of the *Halts*:—

'Lest after this life it should prove my sad story
That my soul must needs go to the Pope's Purgatory,
Many prayers have I sighed, May T. P. * * * * be my guide,
For so often he'll halt, and so lead me about,
That e'er we get there, thro' earth, sea, or air,
The last Day will have come, and the Fires have burnt out.

'Job Junior.
'*circumbendiborum patientissimus.*'

---

[1] Now first published from Cottle's MSS. in the Library of Rugby School.

[2] Endorsed by T. P.: 'On my Walks. Written by Coleridge, September, 1807.' First published *Thomas Poole and His Friends*, by Mrs. Henry Sandford, 1888, ii. 196.

APPENDIX II

ALLEGORIC VISION [1]

A FEELING of sadness, a peculiar melancholy, is wont to take possession of me alike in Spring and in Autumn. But in Spring it is the melancholy of Hope: in Autumn it is the melancholy of Resignation. As I was journeying on foot through the Appennine, I fell in with a pilgrim in whom the Spring and the Autumn and the Melancholy of both seemed to have combined. In his discourse there were the freshness and the colours of April:

> Qual ramicel a ramo,
> Tal da pensier pensiero
> In lui germogliava.

[1] First published in *The Courier*, Saturday, August 31, 1811 : included in 1829, 1834–5, &c. (3 vols.), and in 1844 (1 vol.). Lines 1-56 were first published as part of the 'Introduction' to *A Lay Sermon, &c.*, 1817, pp. xix-xxxi.

The 'Allegoric Vision' dates from August, 1795. It served as a kind of preface or prologue to Coleridge's first Theological Lecture on 'The Origin of Evil. The Necessity of Revelation deduced from the Nature of Man. An Examination and Defence of the Mosaic Dispensation' (see Cottle's *Early Recollections*, 1837, i. 27). The purport of these Lectures was to uphold the golden mean of Unitarian orthodoxy as opposed to the Church on the one hand, and infidelity or materialism on the other. 'Superstition' stood for and symbolized the Church of England. Sixteen years later this opening portion of an unpublished Lecture was rewritten and printed in *The Courier* (Aug. 31, 1811), with the heading 'An Allegoric Vision : Superstition, Religion, Atheism'. The attack was now diverted from the Church of England to the Church of Rome. 'Men clad in black robes,' intent on gathering in their Tenths, become 'men clothed in ceremonial robes, who with menacing countenances drag some reluctant victim to a vast idol, framed of iron bars intercrossed which formed at the same time an immense cage, and yet represented the form of a human Colossus. At the base of the Statue I saw engraved the words "To Dominic holy and merciful, the preventer and avenger of soul-murder".' The vision was turned into a political *jeu d'esprit* levelled at the aiders and abettors of Catholic Emancipation, a measure to which Coleridge was more or less opposed as long as he lived. See *Constitution of Church and State*, 1830, *passim*. A third adaptation of the 'Allegorical Vision' was affixed to the Introduction to *A Lay Sermon : Addressed to the Higher and Middle Classes*, which was published in 1817. The first fifty-six lines, which contain a description of Italian mountain scenery, were entirely new, but the rest of the 'Vision' is an amended and softened reproduction of the preface to the Lecture of 1795. The moral he desires to point is the 'falsehood of extremes'. As Religion is the golden mean between Superstition and Atheism, so the righteous government of a righteous people is the mean between a selfish and oppressive aristocracy, and seditious and unbridled

But as I gazed on his whole form and figure, I bethought me of the not unlovely decays, both of age and of the late season, in the stately elm, after the clusters have been plucked from its entwining vines, and the vines are as bands of dried withies around its trunk and branches. Even so there was a memory on his smooth and ample forehead, which blended with the dedication of his steady eyes, that still looked—I know not, whether upward, or far onward, or rather to the line of meeting where the sky rests upon the distance. But how may I express that dimness of abstraction which lay on the lustre of the pilgrim's eyes like the flitting tarnish from the breath of a sigh on a silver mirror! and which accorded with their slow and reluctant movement, whenever he turned them to any object on the right hand or on the left? It seemed, methought, as if there lay upon the brightness a shadowy presence of disappointments now unfelt, but never forgotten. It was at once the melancholy of hope and of resignation.

We had not long been fellow-travellers, ere a sudden tempest of wind and rain forced us to seek protection in the vaulted door-way of a lone chapelry; and we sate face to face each on the stone bench alongside the low, weather-stained wall, and as close as possible to the massy door.

After a pause of silence: even thus, said he, like two strangers that have fled to the same shelter from the same storm, not seldom do Despair and Hope meet for the first time in the porch of Death! All extremes meet, I answered; but yours was a strange and visionary thought. The better then doth it beseem both the place and me, he replied. From a Visionary wilt thou hear a Vision? Mark that vivid flash through this torrent of rain! Fire and water. Even here thy adage holds true, and its truth is the moral of my Vision. I entreated him to proceed. Sloping his face toward the arch and yet averting his eye from it, he seemed to seek and prepare his words: till listening to the wind that echoed within the hollow edifice, and to the rain without,

mob-rule. A probable 'Source' of the first draft of the 'Vision' is John Aikin's *Hill of Science, A Vision*, which was included in *Elegant Extracts*, 1794, ii. 801. In the present issue the text of 1834 has been collated with that of 1817 and 1829, but not (exhaustively) with the MS. (1795), or at all with the *Courier* version of 1811.

21-3 —the breathed tarnish, shall I name it?—on the lustre of the pilgrim's eyes? Yet had it not a sort of strange accordance with *1817*.
37 Compare: like strangers shelt'ring from a storm,
       Hope and Despair meet in the porch of Death!
Constancy to an Ideal Object, p. 456.
39 VISIONARY *1817, 1829*.   40 VISION *1817, 1829*.

> Which stole on his thoughts with its two-fold sound,
> The clash hard by and the murmur all round,[1]

he gradually sank away, alike from me and from his own purpose, and amid the gloom of the storm and in the duskiness of that place, he sate like an emblem on a rich man's sepulchre, or like a mourner on the sodded grave of an only one—an aged mourner, who is watching the waned moon and sorroweth not. Starting at length from his brief trance of abstraction, with courtesy and an atoning smile he renewed his discourse, and commenced his parable.

During one of those short furloughs from the service of the body, which the soul may sometimes obtain even in this its militant state, I found myself in a vast plain, which I immediately knew to be the Valley of Life. It possessed an astonishing diversity of soils: here was a sunny spot, and there a dark one, forming just such a mixture of sunshine and shade, as we may have observed on the mountains' side in an April day, when the thin broken clouds are scattered over heaven. Almost in the very entrance of the valley stood a large and gloomy pile, into which I seemed constrained to enter. Every part of the building was crowded with tawdry ornaments and fantastic deformity. On every window was portrayed, in glaring and inelegant colours, some horrible tale, or preternatural incident, so that not a ray of light could enter, untinged by the medium through which it passed. The body of the building was full of people, some of them dancing, in and out, in unintelligible figures, with strange ceremonies and antic merriment, while others seemed convulsed with horror, or pining in mad melancholy. Intermingled with these, I observed a number of men, clothed in ceremonial robes, who appeared now to marshal the various groups, and to direct their move-

[1] From the *Ode to the Rain*, 1802, ll. 15-16:—
> O Rain! with your dull two-fold sound,
> The clash hard by, and the murmur all round!

---

49 sank] sunk *1817*.   51-2 *or like* an aged mourner on the sodden grave of an only one—a mourner, *who 1817*.   57-9 It was towards morning when the Brain begins to reassume its waking state, and our dreams approach to the regular trains of Reality, that I found *MS. 1795*.   60 VALLEY OF LIFE *1817, 1829*.   61 and here was *1817, 1829*.   63 mountains' side] Hills *MS. 1795*.   75-86 intermingled with all these I observed a great number of men in Black Robes who appeared now marshalling the various Groups and now collecting with scrupulous care the Tenths of everything that grew within their reach. I stood wondering a while what these Things might be when one of these men approached me and with a reproachful Look bade me uncover my Head for the Place into which I had entered was the Temple of *Religion*. *MS. 1795*.

ments; and now with menacing countenances, to drag some reluctant victim to a vast idol, framed of iron bars intercrossed, which formed at the same time an immense cage, and the shape of a human Colossus.

I stood for a while lost in wonder what these things might mean; when lo! one of the directors came up to me, and with a stern and reproachful look bade me uncover my head, for that the place into which I had entered was the temple of the only true Religion, in the holier recesses of which the great Goddess personally resided. Himself too he bade me reverence, as the consecrated minister of her rites. Awestruck by the name of Religion, I bowed before the priest, and humbly and earnestly intreated him to conduct me into her presence. He assented. Offerings he took from me, with mystic sprinklings of water and with salt he purified, and with strange sufflations he exorcised me; and then led me through many a dark and winding alley, the dew-damps of which chilled my flesh, and the hollow echoes under my feet, mingled, methought, with moanings, affrighted me. At length we entered a large hall, without window, or spiracle, or lamp. The asylum and dormitory it seemed of perennial night—only that the walls were brought to the eye by a number of self-luminous inscriptions in letters of a pale sepulchral light, which held strange neutrality with the darkness, on the verge of which it kept its rayless vigil. I could read them, methought; but though each of the words taken separately I seemed to understand, yet when I took them in sentences, they were riddles and incomprehensible. As I stood meditating on these hard sayings, my guide thus addressed me—'Read and believe: these are mysteries!'—At the extremity of the vast hall the Goddess was placed. Her features, blended with darkness, rose out to my view, terrible, yet vacant. I prostrated myself before her, and then retired with my guide, soul-withered, and wondering, and dissatisfied.

As I re-entered the body of the temple I heard a deep buzz as of discontent. A few whose eyes were bright, and either

80 shape] form *1817*.   92-3 of water he purified me, and then led *MS. 1795*.   94-9 chilled and its hollow echoes beneath my feet affrighted me, till at last we entered a large Hall where not even a Lamp glimmered. Around its walls I observed a number of phosphoric Inscriptions *MS. 1795*. 96-102 *large hall* where not even a single lamp glimmered. It was made half visible by the wan phosphoric rays which proceeded from inscriptions on the walls, in letters of the same pale and sepulchral light. I could read them, methought; but though each one of the *words 1817*.   106 *me*. The fallible becomes infallible, and the infallible remains fallible. Read and believe: these are MYSTERIES! In the middle of *the vast 1817*.   106 MYSTERIES *1829*.   108 *vacant*. No definite thought, no distinct image was afforded me: all was uneasy and obscure feeling. I *prostrated 1817*.

ALLEGORIC VISION

piercing or steady, and whose ample foreheads, with the weighty bar, ridge-like, above the eyebrows, bespoke observation followed by meditative thought; and a much larger number, who were enraged by the severity and insolence of the priests in exacting their offerings, had collected in one tumultuous group, and with a confused outcry of 'This is the Temple of Superstition!' after much contumely, and turmoil, and cruel mal-treatment on all sides, rushed out of the pile: and I, methought, joined them.

We speeded from the Temple with hasty steps, and had now nearly gone round half the valley, when we were addressed by a woman, tall beyond the stature of mortals, and with a something more than human in her countenance and mien, which yet could by mortals be only felt, not conveyed by words or intelligibly distinguished. Deep reflection, animated by ardent feelings, was displayed in them: and hope, without its uncertainty, and a something more than all these, which I understood not, but which yet seemed to blend all these into a divine unity of expression. Her garments were white and matronly, and of the simplest texture. We inquired her name. 'My name,' she replied, 'is Religion.'

The more numerous part of our company, affrighted by the very sound, and sore from recent impostures or sorceries, hurried onwards and examined no farther. A few of us, struck by the manifest opposition of her form and manners to those of the living Idol, whom we had so recently abjured, agreed to follow her, though with cautious circumspection. She led us to an eminence in the midst of the valley, from the top of which we could command the whole plain, and observe the relation of the different parts to each other, and of each to the whole, and of all to each. She then gave us an optic glass which assisted without contradicting our natural vision, and enabled us to see far beyond the limits of the Valley of Life; though our eye even thus assisted permitted us only to behold a light and a glory, but what we could not descry, save only that it was, and that it was most glorious.

And now with the rapid transition of a dream, I had overtaken and rejoined the more numerous party, who had abruptly left us, indignant at the very name of religion. They journied on, goading each other with remembrances of past oppressions, and never looking back, till in the eagerness to recede from the Temple of Superstition they had rounded the whole circle of the valley. And lo! there faced us the mouth of a vast cavern, at the base of a lofty and almost perpendicular rock, the interior side of which, unknown to them and unsuspected, formed the

---

118 Superstition *1817.* 132 Religion *1817, 1829.* 141 *parts* of each to the other. *and of 1817, 1829.* 146 *was 1817, 1829.*

extreme and backward wall of the Temple. An impatient crowd, we entered the vast and dusky cave, which was the only perforation of the precipice. At the mouth of the cave sate
160 two figures ; the first, by her dress and gestures, I knew to be Sensuality ; the second form, from the fierceness of his demeanour, and the brutal scornfulness of his looks, declared himself to be the monster Blasphemy. He uttered big words, and yet ever and anon I observed that he turned pale at his own
165 courage. We entered. Some remained in the opening of the cave, with the one or the other of its guardians. The rest, and I among them, pressed on, till we reached an ample chamber, that seemed the centre of the rock. The climate of the place was unnaturally cold.

170 In the furthest distance of the chamber sate an old dim-eyed man, poring with a microscope over the torso of a statue which had neither basis, nor feet, nor head ; but on its breast was carved Nature! To this he continually applied his glass, and seemed enraptured with the various inequalities which it
175 rendered visible on the seemingly polished surface of the marble.—Yet evermore was this delight and triumph followed by expressions of hatred, and vehement railing against a Being, who yet, he assured us, had no existence. This mystery suddenly recalled to me what I had read in the holiest recess
180 of the temple of Superstition. The old man spake in divers tongues, and continued to utter other and most strange mysteries. Among the rest he talked much and vehemently concerning an infinite series of causes and effects, which he explained to be—a string of blind men, the last of whom
185 caught hold of the skirt of the one before him, he of the next, and so on till they were all out of sight ; and that they all walked infallibly straight, without making one false step though all were alike blind. Methought I borrowed courage from surprise, and asked him—Who then is at the head to
190 guide them ? He looked at me with ineffable contempt, not unmixed with an angry suspicion, and then replied, 'No one.' The string of blind men went on for ever without any beginning ; for although one blind man could not move without stumbling, yet infinite blindness supplied the want of sight. I burst into
195 laughter, which instantly turned to terror—for as he started forward in rage, I caught a glimpse of him from behind ; and lo ! I beheld a monster bi-form and Janus-headed, in the hinder face and shape of which I instantly recognised the dread countenance of Superstition—and in the terror I awoke.

161 SENSUALITY *1817, 1829.*   163 BLASPHEMY *1817, 1829.*   173 NATURE *1817, 1829.*   180 *Superstition 1817, 1829.*   spake] spoke *1817, 1829.*   196 glimpse] glance *1817, 1829.*   199 SUPERSTITION *1817, 1829.*

APPENDIX III

[Vide *ante* p. 237.]

APOLOGETIC PREFACE TO 'FIRE, FAMINE, AND SLAUGHTER'[1]

At the house of a gentleman[2] who by the principles and corresponding virtues of a sincere Christian consecrates a cultivated genius and the favourable accidents of birth, opulence, and splendid connexions, it was my good fortune to meet, in a dinner-party, with more men of celebrity in science or polite literature than are commonly found collected round the same table. In the course of conversation, one of the party reminded an illustrious poet [Scott], then present, of some verses which he had recited that morning, and which had appeared in a newspaper under the name of a War-Eclogue, in which Fire, Famine, and Slaughter were introduced as the speakers. The gentleman so addressed replied, that he was rather surprised that none of us should have noticed or heard of the poem, as it had been, at the time, a good deal talked of in Scotland. It may be easily supposed that my feelings were at this moment not of the most comfortable kind. Of all present, one only [Sir H. Davy] knew, or suspected me to be the author; a man who would have established himself in the first rank of England's living poets[3], if the Genius of our country had not decreed that

---

[1] First published in *Sibylline Leaves* in 1817: included in 1828, 1829, and 1834. The 'Apologetic Preface' must have been put together in 1815, with a view to publication in the volume afterwards named *Sibylline Leaves*, but the incident on which it turns most probably took place in the spring of 1803, when both Scott and Coleridge were in London. Davy writing to Poole, May 1, 1803, says that he generally met Coleridge during his stay in town, 'in the midst of large companies, where he was the image of power and activity,' and Davy, as we know, was one of Sotheby's guests. In a letter to Mrs. Fletcher dated Dec. 18, 1830 (?), Scott tells the story in his own words, but throws no light on date or period. The implied date (1809) in Morritt's report of Dr. Howley's conversation (Lockhart's *Life of Scott*, 1837, ii. 245) is out of the question, as Coleridge did not leave the Lake Country between Sept. 1808 and October 1810. 'Coleridge set great store by "his own stately account of this lion-show"' (ibid.). In a note in a MS. copy of *Sibylline Leaves* presented to his son Derwent he writes:—'With the exception of this slovenly sentence (ll. 109-19) I hold this preface to be my happiest effort in prose composition.'

[2] William Sotheby (1756-1833), translator of Wieland's *Oberon* and the *Georgics* of Virgil. Coleridge met him for the first time at Keswick in July, 1802.

[3] 'The compliment I can witness to be as just as it is handsomely recorded,' Sir W. Scott to Mrs. Fletcher, *Fragmentary Remains* of Sir H. Davy, 1858, p. 113.

he should rather be the first in the first rank of its philosophers and scientific benefactors. It appeared the general wish to hear the lines. As my friend chose to remain silent, I chose to follow his example, and Mr. . . . . . [Scott] recited the poem. This he could do with the better grace, being known to have ever been not only a firm and active Anti-Jacobin and Anti-Gallican, but likewise a zealous admirer of Mr. Pitt, both as a good man and a great statesman. As a poet exclusively, he had been amused with the Eclogue; as a poet he recited it; and in a spirit which made it evident that he would have read and repeated it with the same pleasure had his own name been attached to the imaginary object or agent.

After the recitation our amiable host observed that in his opinion Mr. . . . . . had over-rated the merits of the poetry; but had they been tenfold greater, they could not have compensated for that malignity of heart which could alone have prompted sentiments so atrocious. I perceived that my illustrious friend became greatly distressed on my account; but fortunately I was able to preserve fortitude and presence of mind enough to take up the subject without exciting even a suspicion how nearly and painfully it interested me.

What follows is the substance of what I then replied, but dilated and in language less colloquial. It was not my intention, I said, to justify the publication, whatever its author's feelings might have been at the time of composing it. That they are calculated to call forth so severe a reprobation from a good man, is not the worst feature of such poems. Their moral deformity is aggravated in proportion to the pleasure which they are capable of affording to vindictive, turbulent, and unprincipled readers. Could it be supposed, though for a moment, that the author seriously wished what he had thus wildly imagined, even the attempt to palliate an inhumanity so monstrous would be an insult to the hearers. But it seemed to me worthy of consideration, whether the mood of mind and the general state of sensations in which a poet produces such vivid and fantastic images, is likely to co-exist, or is even compatible with, that gloomy and deliberate ferocity which a serious wish to realize them would pre-suppose. It had been often observed, and all my experience tended to confirm the observation, that prospects of pain and evil to others, and in general all deep feelings of revenge, are commonly expressed in a few words, ironically tame, and mild. The mind under so direful and fiend-like an influence seems to take a morbid pleasure in contrasting the intensity of its wishes and feelings with the slightness or levity of the

24 *he 1817, 1829.*   41 What follows is substantially the same as *I then 1817, 1829.*   56 *realize 1817, 1829.*

PREFACE TO 'FIRE, FAMINE, ETC.'

expressions by which they are hinted; and indeed feelings so intense and solitary, if they were not precluded (as in almost all cases they would be) by a constitutional activity of fancy and association, and by the specific joyousness combined with it, would assuredly themselves preclude such activity. Passion, in its own quality, is the antagonist of action; though in an ordinary and natural degree the former alternates with the latter, and thereby revives and strengthens it. But the more intense and insane the passion is, the fewer and the more fixed are the correspondent forms and notions. A rooted hatred, an inveterate thirst of revenge, is a sort of madness, and still eddies round its favourite object, and exercises as it were a perpetual tautology of mind in thoughts and words which admit of no adequate substitutes. Like a fish in a globe of glass, it moves restlessly round and round the scanty circumference, which it cannot leave without losing its vital element.

There is a second character of such imaginary representations as spring from a real and earnest desire of evil to another, which we often see in real life, and might even anticipate from the nature of the mind. The images, I mean, that a vindictive man places before his imagination, will most often be taken from the realities of life: they will be images of pain and suffering which he has himself seen inflicted on other men, and which he can fancy himself as inflicting on the object of his hatred. I will suppose that we had heard at different times two common sailors, each speaking of some one who had wronged or offended him: that the first with apparent violence had devoted every part of his adversary's body and soul to all the horrid phantoms and fantastic places that ever Quevedo dreamt of, and this in a rapid flow of those outrageous and wildly combined execrations, which too often with our lower classes serve for escape-valves to carry off the excess of their passions, as so much superfluous steam that would endanger the vessel if it were retained. The other, on the contrary, with that sort of calmness of tone which is to the ear what the paleness of anger is to the eye, shall simply say, 'If I chance to be made boatswain, as I hope I soon shall, and can but once get that fellow under my hand (and I shall be upon the watch for him), I'll tickle his pretty skin! I won't hurt him! oh no! I'll only cut the —— to the liver!' I dare appeal to all present, which of the two they would regard as the least deceptive symptom of deliberate malignity? nay, whether it would surprise them to see the first fellow, an hour or two afterwards, cordially shaking hands with the very man the fractional parts of whose

93 outrageous] outrè, *1817, 1829*.   95 *escape-valves 1817, 1829*.
liver *1817, 1829*.   106 afterwards] afterward *1817, 1829*.

598   APPENDIX III

body and soul he had been so charitably disposing of; or even perhaps risking his life for him? What language Shakespeare considered characteristic of malignant disposition we see in the speech of the good-natured Gratiano, who spoke 'an infinite deal of nothing more than any man in all Venice';

—— Too wild, too rude and bold of voice!

the skipping spirit, whose thoughts and words reciprocally ran away with each other;

——— O be thou damn'd, inexorable dog!
And for thy life let justice be accused!

and the wild fancies that follow, contrasted with Shylock's tranquil 'I stand here for Law'.

Or, to take a case more analogous to the present subject, should we hold it either fair or charitable to believe it to have been Dante's serious wish that all the persons mentioned by him (many recently departed, and some even alive at the time,) should actually suffer the fantastic and horrible punishments to which he has sentenced them in his Hell and Purgatory? Or what shall we say of the passages in which Bishop Jeremy Taylor anticipates the state of those who, vicious themselves, have been the cause of vice and misery to their fellow-creatures? Could we endure for a moment to think that a spirit, like Bishop Taylor's, burning with Christian love; that a man constitutionally overflowing with pleasurable kindliness; who scarcely even in a casual illustration introduces the image of woman, child, or bird, but he embalms the thought with so rich a tenderness, as makes the very words seem beauties and fragments of poetry from Euripides or Simonides;—can we endure to think, that a man so natured and so disciplined, did at the time of composing this horrible picture, attach a sober feeling of reality to the phrases? or that he would have described in the same tone of justification, in the same luxuriant flow of phrases, the tortures about to be inflicted on a living individual by a verdict of the Star-Chamber? or the still more atrocious sentences executed on the Scotch anti-prelatists and schismatics, at the command, and in some instances under the very eye of the Duke of Lauderdale, and of that wretched bigot who afterwards dishonoured and forfeited the throne of Great Britain? Or do we not rather feel and understand, that these violent words were mere bubbles, flashes and electrical apparitions, from the magic cauldron of a fervid and ebullient fancy, constantly fuelled by an unexampled opulence of language?

Were I now to have read by myself for the first time the poem

119 'I. ... Law' 1817, 1829.   125 Hell and Purgatory 1817, 1829.   135 a Euripides 1817: an Euripides 1829.   136 so natured 1817, 1829.

PREFACE TO 'FIRE, FAMINE, ETC.'

in question, my conclusion, I fully believe, would be, that the writer must have been some man of warm feelings and active fancy; that he had painted to himself the circumstances that accompany war in so many vivid and yet fantastic forms, as proved that neither the images nor the feelings were the result of observation, or in any way derived from realities. I should judge that they were the product of his own seething imagination, and therefore impregnated with that pleasurable exultation which is experienced in all energetic exertion of intellectual power; that in the same mood he had generalized the causes of the war, and then personified the abstract and christened it by the name which he had been accustomed to hear most often associated with its management and measures. I should guess that the minister was in the author's mind at the moment of composition as completely ἀπαθής, ἀναιμόσαρκος, as Anacreon's grasshopper, and that he had as little notion of a real person of flesh and blood,

> Distinguishable in member, joint, or limb,
>
> [*Paradise Lost*, II. 668.]

as Milton had in the grim and terrible phantom (half person, half allegory) which he has placed at the gates of Hell. I concluded by observing, that the poem was not calculated to excite passion in any mind, or to make any impression except on poetic readers; and that from the culpable levity betrayed at the close of the eclogue by the grotesque union of epigrammatic wit with allegoric personification, in the allusion to the most fearful of thoughts, I should conjecture that the 'rantin' Bardie', instead of really believing, much less wishing, the fate spoken of in the last line, in application to any human individual, would shrink from passing the verdict even on the Devil himself, and exclaim with poor Burns,

> But fare ye weel, auld Nickie-ben!
> Oh! wad ye tak a thought an' men!
> Ye aiblins might—I dinna ken—
>   Still hae a stake—
> I'm wae to think upon yon den,
>   Ev'n for your sake!

I need not say that these thoughts, which are here dilated, were in such a company only rapidly suggested. Our kind host smiled, and with a courteous compliment observed, that the defence was too good for the cause. My voice faltered a little, for I was somewhat agitated; though not so much on my own account as for the uneasiness that so kind and friendly a man would feel from the thought that he had been the occasion of distressing me. At length I brought out these words:

---

172 *passion . . . any* 1817, 1829.   173 *poetic* 1817, 1829. For *betrayed in* r. *betrayed by*, Errata, 1817, p. [xi].   174 *in the grotesque* 1817.

'I must now confess, sir! that I am author of that poem. It was written some years ago. I do not attempt to justify my past self, young as I then was; but as little as I would now write a similar poem, so far was I even then from imagining that the lines would be taken as more or less than a sport of fancy. At all events, if I know my own heart, there was never a moment in my existence in which I should have been more ready, had Mr. Pitt's person been in hazard, to interpose my own body, and defend his life at the risk of my own.'

I have prefaced the poem with this anecdote, because to have printed it without any remark might well have been understood as implying an unconditional approbation on my part, and this after many years' consideration. But if it be asked why I republished it at all, I answer, that the poem had been attributed at different times to different other persons; and what I had dared beget, I thought it neither manly nor honourable not to dare father. From the same motives I should have published perfect copies of two poems, the one entitled The Devil's Thoughts, and the other, The Two Round Spaces on the Tombstone, but that the three first stanzas of the former, which were worth all the rest of the poem, and the best stanza of the remainder, were written by a friend [Southey] of deserved celebrity; and because there are passages in both which might have given offence to the religious feelings of certain readers. I myself indeed see no reason why vulgar superstitions and absurd conceptions that deform the pure faith of a Christian should possess a greater immunity from ridicule than stories of witches, or the fables of Greece and Rome. But there are those who deem it profaneness and irreverence to call an ape an ape, if it but wear a monk's cowl on its head; and I would rather reason with this weakness than offend it.

The passage from Jeremy Taylor to which I referred is found in his second Sermon on Christ's Advent to Judgment; which is likewise the second in his year's course of sermons. Among many remarkable passages of the same character in those discourses, I have selected this as the most so. 'But when this Lion of the tribe of Judah shall appear, then Justice shall strike, and Mercy shall not hold her hands; she shall strike sore strokes, and Pity shall not break the blow. As there are treasures of good things, so hath God a treasure of wrath and fury, and scourges and scorpions; and then shall be produced the shame of Lust and the malice of Envy, and the groans of the oppressed and the persecutions of the saints, and the cares of Covetousness

---

195 am author] am the author *1817*.   203 my body *MS. corr. 1817.*
212-13 The . . . Thoughts *1817, 1829.*   213-14 The . . . Tombstone *1817, 1829.*

and feasting his party-hatred, and with those individuals before the eyes of his imagination enjoying, trait by trait, horror after horror, the picture of their intolerable agonies? Yet this bigot would have an equal right thus to criminate the one good and great man, as these men have to criminate the other. Milton has said, and I doubt not but that Taylor with equal truth could have said it, 'that in his whole life he never spake against a man even that his skin should be grazed.' He asserted this when one of his opponents (either Bishop Hall or his nephew) had called upon the women and children in the streets to take up stones and stone him (Milton). It is known that Milton repeatedly used his interest to protect the royalists; but even at a time when all lies would have been meritorious against him, no charge was made, no story pretended, that he had ever directly or indirectly engaged or assisted in their persecution. Oh! methinks there are other and far better feelings which should be acquired by the perusal of our great elder writers. When I have before me, on the same table, the works of Hammond and Baxter; when I reflect with what joy and dearness their blessed spirits are now loving each other; it seems a mournful thing that their names should be perverted to an occasion of bitterness among us, who are enjoying that happy mean which the human too-much on both sides was perhaps necessary to produce. 'The tangle of delusions which stifled and distorted the growing tree of our well-being has been torn away; the parasite-weeds that fed on its very roots have been plucked up with a salutary violence. To us there remain only quiet duties, the constant care, the gradual improvement, the cautious unhazardous labours of the industrious though contented gardener—to prune, to strengthen, to engraft, and one by one to remove from its leaves and fresh shoots the slug and the caterpillar. But far be it from us to undervalue with light and senseless detraction the conscientious hardihood of our predecessors, or even to condemn in them that vehemence, to which the blessings it won for us leave us now neither temptation nor pretext. We antedate the feelings, in order to criminate the authors, of our present liberty, light and toleration.' (*The Friend*, No. IV. Sept. 7, 1809.) [1818, i. 105.]

If ever two great men might seem, during their whole lives, to have moved in direct opposition, though neither of them has at any time introduced the name of the other, Milton and Jeremy Taylor were they. The former commenced his career by attacking the Church-Liturgy and all set forms of prayer. The latter, but far more successfully, by defending both. Milton's next work was against the Prelacy and the then

335 *him 1817, 1829.*   346 *us 1817, 1829.*   347 *human* TOO-MUCH *1817, 1829.*
349 has] have *1817.*   360 *feelings 1817, 1829.*   361 *authors 1817, 1829.*

existing Church-Government—Taylor's in vindication and support of them. Milton became more and more a stern republican, or rather an advocate for that religious and moral aristocracy which, in his day, was called republicanism, and which, even more than royalism itself, is the direct antipode of modern jacobinism. Taylor, as more and more sceptical concerning the fitness of men in general for power, became more and more attached to the prerogatives of monarchy. From Calvinism, with a still decreasing respect for Fathers, Councils, and for Church-antiquity in general, Milton seems to have ended in an indifference, if not a dislike, to all forms of ecclesiastic government, and to have retreated wholly into the inward and spiritual church-communion of his own spirit with the Light that lighteth every man that cometh into the world. Taylor, with a growing reverence for authority, an increasing sense of the insufficiency of the Scriptures without the aids of tradition and the consent of authorized interpreters, advanced as far in his approaches (not indeed to Popery, but) to Roman-Catholicism, as a conscientious minister of the English Church could well venture. Milton would be and would utter the same to all on all occasions: he would tell the truth, the whole truth, and nothing but the truth. Taylor would become all things to all men, if by any means he might benefit any; hence he availed himself, in his popular writings, of opinions and representations which stand often in striking contrast with the doubts and convictions expressed in his more philosophical works. He appears, indeed, not too severely to have blamed that management of truth (istam falsitatem dispensativam) authorized and exemplified by almost all the fathers: Integrum omnino doctoribus et coetus Christiani antistitibus esse, ut dolos versent, falsa veris intermisceant et imprimis religionis hostes fallant, dummodo veritatis commodis et utilitati inserviant.

The same antithesis might be carried on with the elements of their several intellectual powers. Milton, austere, condensed, imaginative, supporting his truth by direct enunciation of lofty moral sentiment and by distinct visual representations, and in the same spirit overwhelming what he deemed falsehood by moral denunciation and a succession of pictures appalling or repulsive. In his prose, so many metaphors, so many allegorical miniatures. Taylor, eminently discursive, accumulative, and (to use one of his own words) agglomerative; still more rich in images than Milton himself, but images of fancy, and presented to the common and passive eye, rather than to the

---

373 *called 1817, 1829.*   380 *all 1817, 1829.*   387 Roman-Catholicism]
Catholicism *1817, 1829.*   393 *popular 1817, 1829.*   396 *too severely* . . .
management 1817, 1829.   397 *istam . . . dispensativam 1817, 1829.*
agglomerative 1817, 1829.

eye of the imagination. Whether supporting or assailing, he makes his way either by argument or by appeals to the affections, unsurpassed even by the schoolmen in subtlety, agility, and logic wit, and unrivalled by the most rhetorical of the fathers in the copiousness and vividness of his expressions and illustrations. Here words that convey feelings, and words that flash images, and words of abstract notion, flow together, and whirl and rush onward like a stream, at once rapid and full of eddies; and yet still interfused here and there we see a tongue or islet of smooth water, with some picture in it of earth or sky, landscape or living group of quiet beauty.

Differing then so widely and almost contrariantly, wherein did these great men agree? wherein did they resemble each other? In genius, in learning, in unfeigned piety, in blameless purity of life, and in benevolent aspirations and purposes for the moral and temporal improvement of their fellow-creatures! Both of them wrote a Latin Accidence, to render education more easy and less painful to children; both of them composed hymns and psalms proportioned to the capacity of common congregations; both, nearly at the same time, set the glorious example of publicly recommending and supporting general toleration, and the liberty both of the Pulpit and the press! In the writings of neither shall we find a single sentence, like those meek deliverances to God's mercy, with which Laud accompanied his votes for the mutilations and loathsome dungeoning of Leighton and others!—nowhere such a pious prayer as we find in Bishop Hall's memoranda of his own life, concerning the subtle and witty atheist that so grievously perplexed and gravelled him at Sir Robert Drury's till he prayed to the Lord to remove him, and behold! his prayers were heard: for shortly afterward this Philistine-combatant went to London, and there perished of the plague in great misery! In short, nowhere shall we find the least approach, in the lives and writings of John Milton or Jeremy Taylor, to that guarded gentleness, to that sighing reluctance, with which the holy brethren of the Inquisition deliver over a condemned heretic to the civil magistrate, recommending him to mercy, and hoping that the magistrate will treat the erring brother with all possible mildness!—the magistrate who too well knows what would be his own fate if he dared offend them by acting on their recommendation.

416 logic] logical *1817, 1829*.   420 and at once whirl *1817, 1829*.
422 islet | isle *1829*.   Carlyle in the *Life of John Sterling*, cap. viii, quotes the last two words of the Preface. Was it from the same source that he caught up the words 'Balmy sunny islets, islets of the blest and the intelligible' which he uses to illustrate the lucid intervals in Coleridge's monologue?   436 meek . . . mercy *1817, 1829*.   441 he . . . him *1817, 1829*.
450 hoping *1817, 1829*.

The opportunity of diverting the reader from myself to characters more worthy of his attention, has led me far beyond my first intention; but it is not unimportant to expose the false zeal which has occasioned these attacks on our elder patriots. It has been too much the fashion first to personify the Church of England, and then to speak of different individuals, who in different ages have been rulers in that church, as if in some strange way they constituted its personal identity. Why should a clergyman of the present day feel interested in the defence of Laud or Sheldon? Surely it is sufficient for the warmest partisan of our establishment that he can assert with truth,—when our Church persecuted, it was on mistaken principles held in common by all Christendom; and at all events, far less culpable was this intolerance in the Bishops, who were maintaining the existing laws, than the persecuting spirit afterwards shewn by their successful opponents, who had no such excuse, and who should have been taught mercy by their own sufferings, and wisdom by the utter failure of the experiment in their own case. We can say that our Church, apostolical in its faith, primitive in its ceremonies, unequalled in its liturgical forms; that our Church, which has kindled and displayed more bright and burning lights of genius and learning than all other protestant churches since the reformation, was (with the single exception of the times of Laud and Sheldon) least intolerant, when all Christians unhappily deemed a species of intolerance their religious duty; that Bishops of our church were among the first that contended against this error; and finally, that since the reformation, when tolerance became a fashion, the Church of England in a tolerating age, has shewn herself eminently tolerant, and far more so, both in spirit and in fact, than many of her most bitter opponents, who profess to deem toleration itself an insult on the rights of mankind! As to myself, who not only know the Church-Establishment to be tolerant, but who see in it the greatest, if not the sole safe bulwark of toleration, I feel no necessity of defending or palliating oppressions under the two Charleses, in order to exclaim with a full and fervent heart, Esto perpetua!

461 they *1817, 1829*. 467 culpable were the Bishops *1817, 1829*.
481 reformation] Revolution in 1688 *MS. corr. 1817*. 488 bulwark *1817, 1829*. 490 Esto Perpetua *1817, 1829*. *After* 490.
Braving the cry. O the Vanity and self-dotage of Authors! I, yet, after a reperusal of the preceding Apol. Preface, now some 20 years since its first publication, dare deliver it as my own judgement that both in style and thought it is a work creditable to the head and heart of the Author, tho' he happens to have been the same person, only a few stone lighter and with chesnut instead of silver hair, with his Critic and Eulogist.

S. T. Coleridge,
May, 1829.

[*MS. Note in a copy of the edition of 1829, vol. i, p. 353.*]

INDEX OF FIRST LINES

	PAGE
A bird, who for his other sins	451
A blessèd lot hath he, who having passed	173
A green and silent spot, amid the hills	256
A little further, O my father	288
A lovely form there sate beside my bed	484
A low dead Thunder mutter'd thro' the night	502
A mount, not wearisome and bare and steep	155
A sumptuous and magnificent Revenge	497
A sunny shaft did I behold	426
A sworded man whose trade is blood	397
A wind that with Aurora hath abiding	508
Ah! cease thy tears and sobs, my little Life	91
Ah! not by Cam or Isis, famous streams	424
All are not born to soar—and ah! how few	26
All look and likeness caught from earth	393
All Nature seems at work. Slugs leave their lair	447
All thoughts, all passions, all delights	330
Almost awake? Why, what is this, and whence	211
An Ox, long fed with musty hay	299
And in Life's noisiest hour	499
And my heart mantles in its own delight	499
And this place our forefathers made for man	185
And this reft house is that the which he built	211
Are there two things, of all which men possess	361
As I am a Rhymer	477
As late each flower that sweetest blows	45
As late I journey'd o'er the extensive plain	11
As late I lay in Slumber's shadowy vale	80
As late, in wreaths, gay flowers I bound	33
As late on Skiddaw's mount I lay supine	350
As oft mine eye with careless glance	104
As some vast Tropic tree, itself a wood	498
As the shy hind, the soft-eyed gentle Brute	510
As the tir'd savage, who his drowsy frame	521
As when a child on some long Winter's night	85
As when far off the warbled strains are heard	82
As when the new or full Moon urges	502
At midnight by the stream I roved	253
Auspicious Reverence! Hush all meaner song	131, 522
Away, those cloudy looks, that labouring sigh	90
'Be, rather than be called, a child of God'	312
Behold yon row of pines, that shorn and bow'd	503
Beneath the blaze of a tropical sun	396
Beneath this thorn when I was young	269
Beneath yon birch with silver bark	293

INDEX OF FIRST LINES

	PAGE
Benign shooting stars, ecstatic delight	512
Bright cloud of reverence, sufferably bright	495
Britons! when last ye met, with distant streak	150
Charles! my slow heart was only sad, when first	154
Child of my muse! in Barbour's gentle hand	483
Come, come thou bleak December wind	498
Come hither, gently rowing	311
Cupid, if storying Legends tell aright	46
Dear Charles! whilst yet thou wert a babe, I ween	158
Dear native Brook! wild Streamlet of the West	48
Dear tho' unseen! tho' I have left behind	468
Deep in the gulph of Vice and Woe	12
Depart in joy from this world's noise and strife	177
Dim Hour! that sleep'st on pillowing clouds afar	96
Do you ask what the birds say? The Sparrow, the Dove	386
Dormi, Jesu! Mater ridet	417
Each crime that once estranges from the virtues	508
Earth! thou mother of numberless children, the nurse and the mother	327
Edmund! thy grave with aching eye I scan	76
Encinctured with a twine of leaves	287
Ere on my bed my limbs I lay (1803)	389
Ere on my bed my limbs I lay (1806)	401
Ere Sin could blight or Sorrow fade	68
Ere the birth of my life, if I wished it or no	419
Farewell, parental scenes! a sad farewell	29
Farewell, sweet Love! yet blame you not my truth	402
Fear no more, thou timid Flower	356
'Fie, Mr. Coleridge!—and can this be you?	441
Flowers are lovely, Love is flower-like	583, 584
For ever in the world of Fame	510
Frail creatures are we all! To be the best	486
Friend, Lover, Husband, Sister, Brother	392
Friend of the wise! and Teacher of the Good	403
Friend pure of heart and fervent! we have learnt	505
From his brimstone bed at break of day	319
Gently I took that which ungently came	488
Γνῶθι σεαυτόν!—and is this the prime	487
Go little Pipe! for ever I must leave thee	513
God be with thee, gladsome Ocean	359
Gŏd ĭs oŭr Strĕngth ănd oŭr Rĕfŭge	326
God's child in Christ adopted,—Christ my all	490
Good verse most good, and bad verse then seems better	96
Great goddesses are they to lazy folks	505
Hail! festal Easter that dost bring	1
Hast thou a charm to stay the morning-star	376, 572
He too has flitted from his secret nest	457
Hear, my belovéd, an old Milesian story	307

INDEX OF FIRST LINES

	PAGE
Hear, sweet Spirit, hear the spell	420
Heard'st thou yon universal cry	10
Hence, soul-dissolving Harmony	28
Hence that fantastic wantonness of woe	157
Hence! thou fiend of gloomy sway	34
Her attachment may differ from yours in degree	484
Here lies a Poet; or what once was he	587
High o'er the rocks at night I rov'd	548, 549
High o'er the silver rocks I rov'd	547
His native accents to her stranger's ear	508
His own fair countenance, his kingly forehead	502
How long will ye round me be swelling	39
How seldom, friend! a good great man inherits	381
'How sweet, when crimson colours dart	353
How warm this woodland wild Recess	409
Hush! ye clamorous Cares! be mute	92
I ask'd my fair one happy day	318
I from the influence of thy Looks receive	496
I have experienced the worst the world can wreak on me	501
I have heard of reasons manifold	418
I heard a voice from Etna's side	347
I heard a voice pealing loud triumph to-day	511
I know it is dark; and though I have lain	382
I know 'tis but a dream, yet feel more anguish	495
I mix in life, and labour to seem free	292
I never saw the man whom you describe	182
I note the moods and feelings men betray	448
I sigh, fair injur'd stranger! for thy fate	152
I stand alone, nor tho' my heart should break	507
I stood on Brocken's sovran height, and saw	315
I too a sister had! too cruel Death	21
I wish on earth to sing	514
If dead, we cease to be; if total gloom	425
If fair by Nature	509
If I had but two little wings	313
If Love be dead	475
If Pegasus will let *thee* only ride him	21
If thou wert here, these tears were tears of light	386
If while my passion I impart	58
Imagination, honourable aims	396
Imagination, Mistress of my Love	49
In Köhln, a town of monks and bones	477
In many ways does the full heart reveal	462
In the corner *one*	509
In the hexameter rises the fountain's silvery column	308
In vain I supplicate the Powers above	585
In Xanadu did Kubla Khan	297
It is an ancient Mariner	187
It is an ancyent Marinere	528
It may indeed be phantasy, when I	429
It was some Spirit, Sheridan! that breath'd	87
Its balmy lips the infant blest	417
Julia was blest with beauty, wit, and grace	6

INDEX OF FIRST LINES

	PAGE
Kayser! to whom, as to a second self	490
Know'st thou the land where the pale citrons grow	311
Lady, to Death we're doom'd, our crime the same	392
Let clumps of earth, however glorified	505
Let Eagle bid the Tortoise sunward soar	498
Let those whose low delights to Earth are given	427
Like a lone Arab, old and blind	488
Lo! through the dusky silence of the groves	33
Lovely gems of radiance meek	17
Low was our pretty Cot! our tallest Rose	106
Maid of my Love, sweet Genevieve	19
Maid of unboastful charms! whom white-robed Truth	66
Maiden, that with sullen brow	171
Mark this holy chapel well	309
Matilda! I have heard a sweet tune played	374
Mild Splendour of the various-vested Night	5
Mourn, Israel! Sons of Israel, mourn	433
Much on my early youth I love to dwell	64
My eyes make pictures, when they are shut	385
My heart has thanked thee, Bowles! for those soft strains	84, 85
My Lesbia, let us love and live	60
My Lord! though your Lordship repel deviation	341
My Maker! of thy power the trace	423
My pensive Sara! thy soft cheek reclined	100, 519
Myrtle-leaf that, ill besped	172
Names do not always meet with Love	494
Nay, dearest Anna! why so grave?	418
Near the lone pile with ivy overspread	69
Never, believe me	310
No cloud, no relique of the sunken day	264
No cold shall thee benumb	512
No more my visionary soul shall dwell	68
No more 'twixt conscience staggering and the Pope	460
No mortal spirit yet had clomb so high	501
Nor cold, nor stern, my soul! yet I detest	324
Nor travels my meandering eye	97
Not always should the Tear's ambrosial dew	83
Not hers To win the sense by words of rhetoric	504
Not, Stanhope! with the Patriot's doubtful name	89
Now prompts the Muse poetic lays	13
O beauty in a beauteous body dight	496
O! Christmas Day, Oh! happy day!	460
O fair is Love's first hope to gentle mind	443
O form'd t'illume a sunless world forlorn	86
O Friend! O Teacher! God's great Gift to me	579
O! I do love thee, meek *Simplicity*	210
O! it is pleasant, with a heart at ease	435
O leave the Lily on its stem	551
O meek attendant of Sol's setting blaze	16
O mercy, O me, miserable man	502

INDEX OF FIRST LINES

	PAGE
O Muse who sangest late another's pain	18
O Peace, that on a lilied bank dost love	94
O! Superstition is the giant shadow	504
O th' Oppressive, irksome weight	497
O thou wild Fancy, check thy wing! No more	51
O thron'd in Heav'n! Sole King of kings	438
O what a loud and fearful shriek was there	82
O what a wonder seems the fear of death	125
O'er the raised earth the gales of evening sigh	493
O'er wayward childhood would'st thou hold firm rule	481
O'erhung with yew, midway the Muses mount	500
Of late, in one of those most weary hours	478
Oft o'er my brain does that strange fancy roll	153
Oft, oft methinks, the while with thee	388
Oh! might my ill-past hours return again	7
On stern Blencartha's perilous height	347
On the tenth day of September	582
On the wide level of a mountain's head	419
On wide or narrow scale shall Man	30
Once again, sweet Willow, wave thee	514
Once could the Morn's first beams, the healthful breeze	17
Once more! sweet Stream! with slow foot wandering near	58
One kiss, dear Maid! I said and sigh'd	63
Oppress'd, confused, with grief and pain	436
Or Wren or Linnet	499
Over the broad, the shallow, rapid stream	495
Pale Roamer through the night! thou poor Forlorn	71
Pensive at eve on the *hard* world I mus'd	209
Pity! mourn in plaintive tone	61
Poor little Foal of an oppressèd race	74
Promptress of unnumber'd sighs	55
Quae linquam, aut nihil, aut nihili, aut vix sunt mea. Sordes	462
Quoth Dick to me, as once at College	414
Repeating Such verse as Bowles	519
Resembles life what once was deem'd of light	394
Richer than Miser o'er his countless hoards	57
Sad lot, to have no Hope! Though lowly kneeling	416
Schiller! that hour I would have wish'd to die	72
Sea-ward, white gleaming thro' the busy scud	494
Semper Elisa! mihi tu suaveolentia donas	507
Seraphs! around th' Eternal's seat who throng	5
She gave with joy her virgin breast	306
Since all that beat about in Nature's range	455
Sing, impassionate Soul! of Mohammed the complicate story	513
Sister of love-lorn Poets, Philomel	93
Sisters! sisters! who sent you here?	237
Sleep, sweet babe! my cares beguiling	417
Sole maid, associate sole, to me beyond	501
Sole Positive of Night	431
Some are home-sick—some two or three	443
Some, Thelwall! to the Patriot's meed aspire	588

INDEX OF FIRST LINES

	PAGE
Songs of Shepherds and rustical Roundelays	515
Southey! thy melodies steal o'er mine ear	87
Spirit who sweepest the wild Harp of Time	160
Splendour's fondly-fostered child	335
Stanhope! I hail, with ardent Hymn, thy name	89
Stop, Christian passer-by!—Stop, child of God	491, 586
Stranger! whose eyes a look of pity shew	248
Stretch'd on a moulder'd Abbey's broadest wall	73
Strong spirit-bidding sounds	399
Strongly it bears us along in swelling and limitless billows	307
Such love as mourning Husbands have	495
Sweet flower! that peeping from thy russet stem	148
Sweet Gift! and always doth Elisa send	506
Sweet Mercy! how my very heart has bled	93
Sweet Muse! companion of my every hour	16
Tell me, on what holy ground	71
That darling of the Tragic Muse	67
That Jealousy may rule a mind	484
The angel's like a flea	506
The body, Eternal Shadow of the finite Soul	498
The builder left one narrow rent	500
The butterfly the ancient Grecians made	412
The Devil believes that the Lord will come	353
The dubious light sad glimmers o'er the sky	36
The dust flies smothering, as on clatt'ring wheel	56
The early Year's fast-flying vapours stray	148
The fervid Sun had more than halv'd the day	24
The Fox, and Statesman subtile wiles ensure	587
The Frost performs its secret ministry	240
The grapes upon the Vicar's wall	276
The hour-bell sounds, and I must go	61
The indignant Bard composed this furious ode	27
The Moon, how definite its orb	494
The piteous sobs that choke the Virgin's breath	155
The Pleasures sport beneath the thatch	494
The poet in his lone yet genial hour	345
The reed roof'd village still bepatch'd with snow	499
The shepherds went their hasty way	338
The silence of a City, how awful at Midnight	541
The singing Kettle and the purring Cat	500
The sole true Something—This! In Limbo's Den	429
The solemn-breathing air is ended	59
The spruce and limber yellow-hammer	499
The stars that wont to start, as on a chace	486
The stream with languid murmur creeps	38
'The Sun is not yet risen	469
The Sun with gentle beams his rage disguises	507
The tear which mourn'd a brother's fate scarce dry	20
The tedded hay, the first fruits of the soil	345
Then Jerome did call	516
There in some darksome shade	514
Thicker than rain-drops on November thorn	507
This be the meed, that thy song creates a thousand-fold echo	391

INDEX OF FIRST LINES 613

	PAGE
This day among the faithful plac'd	176
This is now—this was erst	22
This is the time, when most divine to hear	108
This Sycamore, oft musical with bees	381
This yearning heart (Love! witness what I say)	362
Thou bleedest, my poor Heart! and thy distress	72
Thou gentle Look, that didst my soul beguile	47
Thou who in youthful vigour rich, and light	349
Though friendships differ endless *in degree*	509
Tho' much averse, dear Jack, to flicker	37
Tho' no bold flights to thee belong	9
Though rous'd by that dark Vizir Riot rude	81
Though veiled in spires of myrtle-wreath	450
Through weeds and thorns, and matted underwood	369
Thus far my scanty brain hath built the rhyme	78
Thus she said, and all around	512
Thy babes ne'er greet thee with the father's name	502
Thy lap-dog, Rufa, is a dainty beast	502
Thy smiles I note, sweet early Flower	149
'Tis hard on Bagshot Heath to try	26
'Tis mine and it is likewise yours	494
'Tis not the lily-brow I prize	483
'Tis sweet to him who all the week	314
'Tis the middle of night by the castle clock	215
'Tis true, Idoloclastes Satyrane	413
To know, to esteem, to love,—and then to part	410
To praise men as good, and to take them for such	486
To tempt the dangerous deep, too venturous youth	2
Tranquillity! thou better name	360
Trŏchĕe trīps frŏm long tŏ shŏrt	401
Truth I pursued, as Fancy sketch'd the way	505
'Twas my last waking thought, how it could be	454
'Twas not a mist, nor was it quite a cloud	542
Two wedded hearts, if ere were such	500
Unboastful Bard! whose verse concise yet clear	102
Unchanged within, to see all changed without	459
Under the arms of a goodly oak-tree	546
Underneath an old oak tree	169
Ungrateful he, who pluck'd thee from thy stalk	70
Unperishing youth	308
Up, up! ye dames, and lasses gay	427
Upon the mountain's edge with light touch resting	393
Utter the song, O my soul! the flight and return of Mohammed	329
Verse, a breeze mid blossoms straying	439
Verse, pictures, music, thoughts both grave and gay	482
Verse, that Breeze mid blossoms straying	583
Virtues and Woes alike too great for man	37
Vivit sed mihi non vivit—nova forte marita	56
Water and windmills, greenness, Islets green	506
We pledged our hearts, my love and I	391
Well! If the Bard was weather-wise, who made	362, 574
Well, they are gone, and here must I remain	178

INDEX OF FIRST LINES

	PAGE
What a spring-tide of Love to dear friends in a shoal	507
What boots to tell how o'er his grave	508
What never is, but only is to be	496
What now, O Man! thou dost or mean'st to do	414
What pleasures shall he ever find	4
What though the chilly wide-mouth'd quacking chorus	476
Whate'er thou giv'st, it still is sweet to me	552
When British Freedom for an happier land	79
When Hope but made Tranquillity be felt	501
When they did greet me father, sudden awe	152
When thou to my true-love com'st	326
When Youth his faery reign began	62
Whene'er the mist, that stands 'twixt God and thee	487
Where deep in mud Cam rolls his slumbrous stream	35
Where graced with many a classic spoil	29
Where is the grave of Sir Arthur O'Kellyn	432
Where true Love burns Desire is Love's pure flame	485
Where'er I find the Good, the True, the Fair	508
While my young cheek retains its healthful hues	236
Whilst pale Anxiety, corrosive Care	69
Whom should I choose for my Judge?	497
Whom the untaught Shepherds call	40
Why need I say, Louisa dear	252
William, my teacher, my friend	304
With Donne, whose muse on dromedary trots	433
With many a pause and oft reverted eye	94
With many a weary step at length I gain	56
Within these circling hollies woodbine-clad	409
Within these wilds was Anna wont to rove	16
Ye Clouds! that far above me float and pause	243
Ye fowls of ill presage	513
Ye Gales, that of the Lark's repose	35
Ye harp-controlling hymns	503
Ye souls unus'd to lofty verse	8
Yes, noble old Warrior! this heart has beat high	317
Yes, yes! that boon, life's richest treat	466
Yet art thou happier far than she	62
Yon row of bleak and visionary pines	503
You loved the daughter of Don Manrique?	421
You mould my Hopes, you fashion me within	499